ARCHIVES OF EMPIRE
EDITED BY BARBARA HARLOW AND MIA CARTER

ARCHIVES OF EMPIRE
VOLUME I · FROM THE EAST
INDIA COMPANY TO
THE SUEZ CANAL

EDITED BY MIA CARTER WITH BARBARA HARLOW

Duke University Press   *Durham and London*   2003

©2003 Duke University Press All rights reserved
Designed by Mary Mendell
Typeset in Caslon by Keystone Typesetting, Inc.
Library of Congress Cataloging-in-Publication Data appear
on the last printed page of this book.

FOR BRIAN, WHO HOLDS

MY HEART IN HIS

HANDS

CONTENTS

Acknowledgments xix

General Introduction: Readings in Imperialism and Orientalism xxi

Volume Introduction: From the Company to the Canal 1

1. COMPANY TO CANAL, 1757–1869

INTRODUCTION: Adventure Capitalism: Mercantilism, Militarism, and the British East India Company 13

Chronology of Events 16

List of the Governors and Governors-General of India 17

List of the Newabs of Bengal 18

India under Cornwallis (1792) [map] 19

India under Wellesley (1799) [map] 19

India under Hastings (1832) [map] 20

India under Dalhousie (1856) [map] 20

G. A. (George Alfred) Henty, Excerpt from *With Clive in India* (n.d.) 21

"Agreement between the Nabob Nudjum-ul-Dowlah and the Company, 12 August 1765" 25

Anonymous, *An Inquiry into the Rights of the East India Company of Making War and Peace* (1772)   27

East India Company Act, 1773   31

James Mill, "The Constitution of the East India Company" (1817)   39

James Mill, Letter to Durmont (1819)   47

John Stuart Mill. Excerpt from *Autobiography* (1873)   48

Government of India Act, 1833   49

Lord Thomas Babington Macaulay, "A Speech, Delivered in the House of Commons on the 10th of July, 1833"   54

Lord Thomas Babington Macaulay, "Lord Clive" (1840)   59

Samuel Lucas, "The Spoliation of Oude" (1857)   72

Sir Arthur Wellesley, "Memorandum on Marquess Wellesley's Government of India" (1806)   81

II. ORIENTAL DESPOTISM

INTRODUCTION: Oriental Despotisms and Political Economies   89

Baron de Montesquieu, "Distinctive Properties of a Despotic Government" (1746)   92

Baron de Montesquieu, Excerpts from *Persian Letters* (1721)   92

Adam Smith, "America and the East Indies" (1776)   95

Robert Orme, "Of the Government and People of Indostan" (1782)   107

John Stuart Mill, Excerpt from *The Principles of Political Economy* (1848)   111

John Stuart Mill, Excerpt from "Considerations on Representative Government" (1861)   113

Karl Marx, "On Imperialism in India" (1853)   117

III. THE IMPEACHMENT OF WARREN HASTINGS

INTRODUCTION: Warren Hastings: Naughty Nabob or National Hero?   131

Warren Hastings, "Warren Hastings to the Court of General Directors, 11 November 1773"   135

Warren Hastings, Excerpt from *Memoirs Relative to the State of India* (1786)   137

Edmund Burke, "Edmund Burke on the Impeachment of Warren Hastings, 15–19 February 1788"   143

Westminster Hall during the trial of Warren Hastings (1788) [illustration]   156

Fanny Burney, Diary Selections (1788)   155

Edmund Burke, "From the Third Day of Edmund Burke's Speech Opening the Impeachment, 18 February 1788"   160

Warren Hastings, "From the Address of Warren Hastings in His Defence, 2 June 1791"   163

Lord Thomas Babington Macaulay, "Warren Hastings" (1841)   166

IV. THE CASE OF TIPU SULTAN

INTRODUCTION: Tipu Sultan: Oriental Despot or National Hero?   171

G. A. Henty, Excerpts from *The Tiger of Mysore* (189?)   173

"Tippoo Sahib at the Lines of Travancore" (1789) [illustration]   174

Major Diram, "Treaties of Peace, and Review of the Consequences of the War" (1793)   175

Selected Letters between Tipu and Company Governors-General, 1798–1799   180

Wilkie Collins, "Prologue: The Storming of Seringapatam, 1799" (1869)   195

V. ORIENTALISM

INTRODUCTION: Orientalism: The East as a Career   203

Mary Shelley, Excerpts from *Frankenstein* (1813/1831)   206

Benjamin Disraeli, Excerpt from *Sibyl, or the Two Nations* (1845)   208

Definitions from the *Hobson-Jobson* Dictionary   209

G. W. F. Hegel, "India" (1822)   219

William Jones, "A Discourse on the Institution of a Society for Inquiring into the History, Civil and Natural, the Antiquities, Arts, Sciences, and Literatures of Asia" (1784)   223

Lord Thomas Babington Macaulay, "Minute on Indian Education" (1835)   227

Max Müller, "The Aryan Section" (1876)   239

VI. LAWS AND ORDERS

INTRODUCTION: Ordering "Chaos": Administering the Law   249

Robert Orme, "Of the Laws and Justice of Indostan" (1782)   251

Sir William Jones, Preface to "Institutes of Hindu Law: Or, the Ordinances of Menu" (1794)   261

Contents xi

Lord Thomas Babington Macaulay, "Introductory Report upon the Indian Penal Code" (1837) 268

VII. THUGGEE/THAGI

INTRODUCTION: Decriminalizing the Landscape: Thugs and Poisoners 285

A thug "family tree" (1836) [illustration] 288

Thug depradations (1836) [map] 288

Thugs giving a demonstration of their method of strangulation (1855) [photo] 289

Captain William H. Sleeman, "The Ramaseeana, or Vocabulary of the Thug Language" (1839) 287

Captain William H. Sleeman, Excerpts from *The Thugs or Phansigars of India: History of the Rise and Progress* (1839) 297

Fanny Parks Parlby, "A Kutcherry or Kachahri" (1850) 307

Philip Meadows Taylor, "Thugs" (1877) 314

Philip Meadows Taylor, Excerpts from *Confessions of a Thug* (1837) 315

Captain William H. Sleeman, "Thug Approvers" (1833–1835?) 322

VIII. SUTTEE/SATI

INTRODUCTION: Sati/Suttee: Observances, Abolition, Observations 337

Colonel Henry Yule and A. C. Burnell, "Suttee" [definition] (1903) 340

Lord William Bentinck, "Bentinck's Minute on Sati, 8 November 1892" 350

Sati Regulation XVII, A.D. 1829 of the Bengal Code,
4 December 1829   361

"The Duties of a Faithful Widow," from *Digest of Hindi Law* (n.d.)   364

Raja Ram Mohan Roy, "Petitions and Addresses on the Practice of Suttee (1818–1831)"   369

G. W. F. Hegel, On Sati (1822)   374

Charles Dickens, Death by Fire of Miss Havisham (1861)   375

Jules Verne, "Fogg Rescues a Sati" (1873)   377

Maspero Jingle [advertisement for Maspero Egyptian cigarettes]   379

Ernest Renan, On Suttee (1893)   380

Flora Annie Steel, "The Reformer's Wife" (1933)   381

IX. THE INDIAN UPRISING/SEPOY MUTINY 1857–1858

INTRODUCTION: The "Asiatic Mystery": The Sepoy Mutiny, Rebellion, or Revolt   391

Chronology of Events   396

Rulers and Rebels: Some Major Figures   397

Excerpts from *The Who's Who of Indian Martyrs* (1969–1973)   400

"Portrait of Nana Sahib" [illustration]   402

"Sepoys, 1757" (1890) [illustration]   406

"Attack of the Mutineers on the Redan Battery at Lucknow, July 30, 1857" (n. d.) [illustration]   406

"The Asiatic Mystery. As Prepared by Sepoy D'Israeli" (1857) [illustration]   407

"Proclamation to the People of Oude on Its Annexation. February 1856"   404

"Sir Henry Lawrence's Essay of 1843, Forecasting the Events of 1857"   409

Rani Lakshmi Bai (The Rani of Jhansi), "Letters of Rani Lakshmi Bai" (1853–1854)   413

Title page from *The Queen's Desire* (1893) [reproduction]   420

Hume Nisbet, Preface and Excerpt from *The Queen's Desire: A Romance of the Indian Mutiny* (1893)   419

"The Ranee's Death" (1893) [illustration]   422

The King of Oude's Manifesto from the *Delhi Gazette*, 29 September 1857   428

Karl Marx, "The Revolt in India," "The Indian Question," "British Incomes in India," and "The Annexation of Oude" (1857–1858)   433

Colonel C. Chester, "Final Orders to the Musketry Schools" (1857)   449

Selected Documents from John William Kaye's *The History of the Sepoy War in India, 1857–1858* (1880), including "The Chupatties" and "The Bone-Dust Story"   451

Act. No. XIV of 1857 (on the punishment of soldiers under Company rule) (1880)   459

Charles Ball, "Summary Justice" (n.d.)   461

"Justice" (1857) [illustration]   479

Selected Correspondence of Queen Victoria (1857)   478

Anonymous, "How to Make an Indian Pickle" (1857)   485

"The British Lion's Vengeance on the Bengal Tiger" (1857) [illustration]   487

Bholanauth-Chunder (attributed to), "The Punishment of Allahabad" (1857)   486

"Pity for the Poor Sepoys!" (1857) [editorial letter]   488

Reverend J. Johnson Walsh, Excerpts from *A Memorial of the Futtehgurh Mission and Her Martyred Missionaries: With Some Remarks on the Mutiny in India* (1859)   489

"The Execution of 'John Company'" (1857) [illustration]   510

Anonymous, "England's Great Mission to India" (1879)   509

Henry Gilbert, "Doubts and Forebodings" (n.d.)   529

Henry Gilbert, "What the Native Thought" (n.d.)   535

Rudyard Kipling, "The Grave of the Hundred Head" (1899)   539

Alfred Tennyson, "The Defence of Lucknow" (1879)   542

Alfred Tennyson, "English War-Song" (n.d.)   546

M. B. Synge, "The Indian Mutiny" (1908)   547

X. THE SUEZ CANAL: THE GALA OPENING

INTRODUCTION: Spectacular Suez: The Opening Gala of the Suez Canal   555

"Opening of the Suez Canal at Port Said: Presence of the Imperial and Royal Visitors" (1869) [illustration]   558

"Opening of the Suez Canal: The Procession of Ships in the Canal" (1869) [illustration]   558

Selected Correspondence of Giuseppe Verdi
(1870)   557

Baron Samuel Selig de Kusel, Excerpt from *An Englishman's Recollections of Egypt 1863 to 1887*
(1915)   566

XI. THE SUEZ CANAL: THE BUILDER, FERDINAND DE LESSEPS

INTRODUCTION: "The Master Builder" and His Designs: Ferdinand De Lesseps   575

"Ferdinand De Lesseps Bestrides His Canal" (n.d.) [illustration]   578

Chronology of Events   579

Ferdinand De Lesseps, "Inquiry into the Opinions of the Commercial Classes of Great Britain on the Suez Ship Canal" (1857) [pamphlet]   580

Ferdinand De Lesseps, Excerpts from *The Suez Canal: Letters and Documents Descriptive of Its Rise and Progress in 1854–56* (1876)   584

Charles Frederic Moberly Bell, Excerpt from *From Pharaoh to Fellah* (1888)   604

XII. THE SUEZ CANAL: THE CANAL AND ITS CONSEQUENCES

INTRODUCTION: The Battlefield of the Future: The Canal and Its Consequences   611

"A Stretch of the Canal Is Hollowed Out / The Men Who Have Hollowed It" (n.d.) [illustration]   614

"From the Great Pyramid. (A Bird's-Eye View of the Canal and Its Consequences.)" (1869) [illustration]   617

Anonymous, "Latest—From the Sphinx" (1869) [editorial poem]   615

Anonymous, "The Sultan's Complaint" (1869) [editorial poem]   617

Ferdinand De Lesseps, "Report to His Highness the Viceroy of Egypt on the Fellah Workmen to be Employed by the International Suez Canal Company" (1856)   619

"The Official Firman of Concession Granted by the Viceroy of Egypt Mohamed Said, to Ferdinand De Lesseps, 1854"   622

"Charter of Concession and Book of Charges for the Construction and Working of the Suez Grand Maritime Canal and Dependencies" (1856)   625

"Agreement of February 22, 1866, Determining the Final Terms as Ratified by the Sublime Porte"   631

Edward Dicey, "Why Not Purchase the Suez Canal?" (1883)   638

Charles Royle, "De Lesseps and the Canal" (1900)   655

D. A. Cameron, "The Suez Canal" (1898)   661

"Mosé in Egitto!!!" (1875) [illustration]   670

Lord Herbert Edward Cecil, "A Day on the Suez Canal (1905)" (1921)   671

"The Lion's Share" (1876) [illustration]   677

XIII. THE ARABI UPRISING

INTRODUCTION: The Arabi Uprising: "Egypt for the Egyptians" or British Egypt   681

Chronology of Events   685

Important Figures   685

"Hold On!" (1882) [illustration]   688

"The Neddy of the Nile" (1882) [illustration]   688

Bob McGee, "De War in Egypt" (1882)   686

W. E. Gladstone, "Aggression on Egypt and Freedom in the East" (1887)   687

Lord Cromer, "The Mutiny of the Egyptian Army" (1908)   696

Arabi's Appeal to Gladstone (1882)   707

"Rioters at Alexandria" (1882) [illustration]   709

"The Crisis in Egypt" (1882) [illustration]   710

E. M. Forster, "The Bombardment of Alexandria (1882)" (with map)   711

Wilfred Scawen Blunt, "The Arabi Trial" (1907)   714

"The Sublime—'Super!'" (1882) [illustration]   737

Lady Gregory, *Arabi and His Household* (1882) [pamphlet]   736

XIV. PILGRIMS, TRAVELERS, AND TOURISTS

INTRODUCTION: Holy Lands and Secular Agendas   747

Lady Duff Gordon, "Cairo Is the Real Arabian Nights" (1865)   749

Richard F. Burton, "Suez" (1855)   752

Stanley Lane-Poole, "The Two Cities" (1902)   769

Charles M. Doughty, Excerpt from *Travels in Arabia Deserta* (1888)   775

Itineraries from *Programme of Arrangements for Visiting Egypt, the Nile, Sudan, Palestine, and Syria* (1929–1930)   779

"Egyptian Native Types" (n.d.) [illustration]   780

ACKNOWLEDGMENTS

MANY PEOPLE AT THE University of Texas at Austin, in other universities across the country, and on at least two additional continents have expressed ongoing interest in and support for *Archives of Empire*. We have spent several years collecting material and sharing presentations of the work-in-progress. The earlier, one-volume edition, *Imperialism and Orientalism: A Documentary Sourcebook,* was published by Blackwell in 1999, having been first envisioned by Blackwell's then-editor Simon Prosser, then produced with the support of Simon Eckley and the talented assistance of our copy editor, Helen Rappaport.

We presently have Ken Wissoker of Duke University Press to thank for supporting and contracting an even larger and more ambitious project than that Blackwell reader. Ken's daring is something to marvel at, and we thank him vociferously for his commitment and support. Some of the materials presented herein were literally disintegrating on the library shelves, but the General Libraries of the University of Texas at Austin and their unfailingly collaborative staff continue to make possible preservation and innovation, all in the interest of the libraries, their resources, and—no less important—their patrons. Their work enables all of us. Thank you, also, to the production staff of Duke University Press. We well know what kind of effort it takes to make a mountain of xeroxed material into an attractive and user-friendly product. Thank you for hanging in there with this one! We would also like to thank Duke's outside reviewers who, somehow, managed to work through and read enthusiastically a very massive package of materials. We thank each of you for the time and energy you contributed to this project; your thoughtful remarks and suggestions were highly appreciated.

Finally, and perhaps most important of all, we would like to thank the students in the University of Texas's ethnic and third-world literatures concentration in the department of English. *Archives of Empire* has been a shared labor. Thank you for being creative and critical historiographers, wonderful cheerleaders, and partners in collecting. Mia would especially like to thank her research assistant and friend, Miriam Murtuza: Miriam, you amaze me. Thank you for constantly replenishing energy, meticulous work, critical acumen, generosity, and good company. It has been, as always, an honor to work with you. And Barbara salutes the unflagging contributions of Eve Dunbar, her research assistant, who saw new ideas in old materials, even as she sorted through the reams and realms of documentary histories and paper trails of race and empire. Bravo! The talented cartographer K. Maria Lane created our maps. Thank you, Maria for sharing your gifts. And thanks to Terry Gregston and Alan Smith of U.T.'s Photographic Services Center (cookies and brownies represent a mere morsel of our gratitude). Mia would also like to thank her family for being zany, life-affirming, unceasingly supportive, and kind. And Mia thanks Barbara too, for being a comrade, a mentor, family member, and true friend. Additionally, Barbara acknowledges gratefully the support of Louann and Larry Temple whose generous endowments to the study of English literature made much of our effort possible. And then there's Mia: what can Barbara say, except that this project—and so much else—couldn't have been done without you. So there! Finally, Mia and Barbara want to thank the talented, patient, and especially generous production team at Duke; they inherited a hulking, unruly leviathan and transformed it into an elegant volume. Thanks to Fiona Morgan, Leigh Anne Couch, Patty Van Norman, the typesetters, designer, Mary Mendell, and special thanks to our amazing copy editor, Patricia Mickelberry.

GENERAL INTRODUCTION
Readings in Imperialism and Orientalism
MIA CARTER AND BARBARA HARLOW

ARCHIVES OF EMPIRE is a four-volume collection of original documents and primary source materials relating to the varied processes and various procedures of the colonial project. Ranging from East India Company charters to Cecil Rhodes's "last will and testament," and including such disparate but historically related artifacts as Salvation Army hymns, missionary tracts, parliamentary debates, adventurers' accounts, administrators' account books, satirical cartoons, popular appeals, and legislative records, the four volumes both provide critical research and teaching resources for students of empire and propose new directions for current inquiries into late-twentieth-century consequences of nineteenth-century imperialism.

Each volume of *Archives of Empire* emphasizes a particular period and its place in the history of British imperialism: *Volume 1: From the Company to the Canal; Volume 2: The Scramble for Africa; Volume 3: The Great Game;* and *Volume 4: Jubilee. From the Company to the Canal* covers the first half of the nineteenth century and British engagements in the Indian subcontinent and in Egypt, from the East India Company's exploits, to its handover to the Crown following the Sepoy Uprising in 1857–1858, to the opening of the Suez Canal in 1869. The opening of the Suez Canal radically altered British relations with its colonial reaches; by shortening the distance—for transportation, commerce, and communication—between England and its representatives in India, the canal significantly transformed British interests along the coast of Africa, in particular in southern Africa. *The Scramble for Africa* concentrates on the European contest over that continent, its peoples, and its resources, particularly following the Berlin Conference of 1885 and the ensuing crises in Khartoum, in the Congo, and during the Anglo-Boer War. India, in its turn, was both the "jewel in the crown" of Victoria and a part of the board on which the "great game"—or the struggle over central Asia—was to be played out. *The Great Game* focuses on that game, its rules, its players, and the larger gameboard from the Crimea to and through the Afghan passes. *Jubilee* examines the beginnings, means, and ends of empire as these conjunctures were staged "at home," in Queen Victoria's England, by schoolboys and scouts, by suffragettes, in the streets, and in the reviews and popular periodicals as well as in parliamentary debates.

Rather than celebrating the riches of empire, however, *Archives of Empire* instead emphasizes, through its sampling of imperialism's documentary history, the richness of the substantial critical resources and the substantive grounds for the critique of imperialism. The volumes thus suggest as well that the imperial project was by no means an uncontested or unargued enterprise, but a much-debated one, even among its putative participants and apparent adherents—between Jonesian orientalists and Macauleyan anglicists, between "patriots" and "pro-Boers." Those sympathetic to the independence-oriented causes of Tipu Sultan in Mysore or Arabi in Egypt argued with strict upholders of imperial law and order. Figures like Florence Nightingale battled against the generals in the Crimea, and Emily Hobhouse passionately called her audience's attention to the dreadful conditions of concentration camps in South Africa. Rescue missions and reforms also highlighted fractures and divisions: Should "Chinese" Gordon be rescued in the Sudan? Could the Indian civil service be revised and reorganized? How to halt atrocities and reform King Leopold's Congo?

In order to draw out such controversies, the four volumes of *Archives of Empire* follow several themes, in particular political economy, parliamentary debate, and popular culture. The issue of political economy, for example, can be traced through the history of charter companies, from the East India Company to the Suez Canal and British South African companies, and through disputes over free trade between jingoists and "little Englanders." Such debates were heard in the houses of Parliament, recorded in Hansard's and in Blue Books, disputed in journals such as the *Pall Mall Gazette* or the *Review of Reviews,* and caricatured in periodicals such as *Punch*. Missionaries supported imperial designs and protested them, explorers traversed and mapped imperial territories and encouraged others to follow in their footsteps, while bureaucrats and businessmen pursued their own interests; such observations, memoirs, and narratives also appear in these volumes. The writers of that time lived in the present moment and observed, by practice, by accident, or, increasingly, by means of graphic and photographic representation, the cultural, political, and social changes that expansionism effected at home and abroad. Literary authors like Charles Dickens and Jules Verne, popular authors like G. A. Henty (writer of boys' adventure novels), and everyday citizens like Flora Annie Steel (wife of a British civil servant stationed in India) recorded the changing times and allowed their imaginations to be inspired or inflamed by travel accounts, news of sensational "discoveries" or spectacular colonial crises. The literatures of that time reflect these firsthand experiences or secondhand representational encounters with "native" peoples and lands. The cultures of imperialism and colonialism were widespread and all encompassing. Sciences, political and governmental theories, and entertainment cultures were equally influenced by colonial trade, imperial exploration, and the material exploitation of foreign lands. Nineteenth-century forms of entertainment included the popular lecture circuit, with travelers like Henry M. Stanley and Mary Kingsley able to fill the house. Architectural innovations were designed to display colonial goods, both human and material; for example, the Crystal Palace was designed to showcase the products, collections, and inventions of both industry and empire. Indian-style bungalows were soon incorporated into the British landscape, and British fashion and cuisine were forever altered by colonial spices and fabrics. Among empire's principal practitioners were men such as Robert Clive, Frederick Lugard, Cecil Rhodes, Benjamin Disraeli, Gladstone, for example, who envisioned the details. What were their shared interests? What were their dramatic differences?

While designed according to the historical specificities and the archival resources of the period, each volume of *Archives of Empire* attempts to address and highlight specific conflicts and crises so as to be useful in its own right but also to complement the other volumes in order to display the continuities, consistencies, and discordances of imperialism. Each individual volume is introduced by an editorial preface that lays out the features of the period, its major personnel, and the debates that accompanied the pursuit of empire there and then. Each volume is then organized into sections that are amply illustrated and preceded by brief introductions, with bibliographies, filmographies, maps, and chronologies included where appropriate, in order to enhance the pedagogical usefulness of the volumes and to offer suggestions for further investigation and research projects.

Archives of Empire builds on the single-volume documentary sourcebook *Imperialism and Orientalism* (Blackwell, 1999) but is significantly different, both in its expansion of the material bases of the archival register of the resources and in its organization into four distinct volumes. While coherent as a series, these volumes are also individually useful for pedagogical and scholarly use according to time and place: the early nineteenth century, the latter half of the nineteenth century, the Indian subcontinent, the African continent, and Great Britain itself. We hope that, as a set and each volume in turn, *Archives of Empire* will be of considerable interest and continuing usefulness to students, teachers, researchers, and readers of the imperial narrative.

ARCHIVES OF EMPIRE

> We sail'd wherever ships could sail;
> We founded many a mighty state;
> Pray God our greatness may not fail
> Through craven fear of being great.
> —Alfred Tennyson, *Hands All Round*

Commerce always sets steadily towards the shortest routes, and under the pressure of the competition from the modern world, Egypt and Mesopotamia will become the chief commercial highways between the East and West. Commercial supremacy, the only sure foundation of political supremacy, is absolutely dependent on the opportunity of roads and markets, or on strategical points and communications as military men call them. Indeed war is another form of commercial antagonism, seeking by violence the same advantages commerce often more surely secures by slower, deadlier sap.
—George Birdwood, Savage Club, December 1892

VOLUME INTRODUCTION
From the Company to the Canal
MIA CARTER

FROM THE SUBCONTINENT TO THE SUEZ

THE EARLY HISTORY of British colonial activity in India began with bold adventure, military conquest, and aggressive and violent international competition. The English East India Company was established at the very end of the sixteenth century, in the year 1599. The Dutch established their own Indian company shortly after the British, in the year 1603, and Great Britain's bitter rivals, the French, set up trade in India with their Compagnie des Indes Orientales in 1664. The French and British battles for control of Indian territories and resources culminated in 1757 with the Battle at Plassey. Led by the inventive and daring military leader Robert Clive, the British finally routed the French and seized firm control of the subcontinent. Clive, who left Great Britain an impoverished, emotionally troubled, and disfavored son, became a national hero, an enormously wealthy merchant (he was reported to be the richest man in England at age thirty-five), a baron, and a model of imperial and mythical masculinity. Clive's exploits and adventures captured domestic imaginations and inspired boys and men to make the East, to quote Benjamin Disraeli, a career. Charlie Marryat, the boy hero of G. A. Henty's novel *With Clive in India, Or, The Beginnings of Empire* (n.d.), goes off to India as the impoverished son of a widowed mother, hears tales of Clive, encounters inspirational men who had served under Clive, follows Clive's lead, and returns home "richer than a Lord." Actual men, like Warren Hastings, would also build their careers alongside and in the footsteps of Clive.

The early Company-inspired romantic tales of danger and economic and military adventure sold the project of empire building at home, although Company administrators and stockholders, both at home and in India, were primarily enamored of Company interests. Before being turned over to the British Crown in 1858, the East India Company was a joint-stock organization, a chartered company owned, managed, and controlled by its shareholders. Company profits were distributed to each investor or subscriber in proportion to the amount the shareholder had contributed. The private and monopolistic nature of the East India Company's organization promoted a high degree of self interest; public and national interests were not the stockholders' primary concerns. The Company aggressively protected its monopoly status and its ability to produce wealth by punishing (by execution, imprisonment, or the imposition of fines) or incorporating its competitors. The interloping privateer and rogue Thomas Pitt, for example, was tried, fined, and then hired by the Company to contain its competitors. (Pitt became the governor of Fort St. George in 1697.) In 1701, the Company executed Captain Kidd for piracy.

The Company's increasingly aggressive military exploits and its enormous profits were protested by those who believed that the British Empire and its numerous citizens should benefit from Indian trade; those who believed the Company's enterprise was destructive and immoral worried about the empire's soul and were concerned about the precarious situation of its "subject races." After the Battle of Plassey, the Company began smuggling opium from India to China to help fund its military operations. Critics of the Company deplored this sinful trade and castigated the Company for destroying Indian cultures, communities, and traditions. The anonymously written pamphlet *An Inquiry into the Rights of the East India Company of Making War and Peace* (1772) and Samuel Lucas's *Dacoitee in Excelsis; or, The Spoliation of Oude by the East India Company* (1857) both accuse the Company's military merchants of fraud, vice, extortion, and crimes against humanity. The critics accused the Company of importing and practicing Western forms of despotism and banditry. Accusations of this nature and the excesses of Company rule led to reforms, like the anti-expansionist and Whig-supported "East India Company Act, 1773," which appointed a supervisory council and governor-general, established a chain of command and a supreme court, limited the Company's ability to seize territories and wage war, and allowed Company employees to be tried in His Majesty's Court for offenses made in India. As controversial governor-general of Bengal, Warren Hastings was prosecuted under the act in 1778. The act also inspired reformers, like statesman, economist, and historian James Mill, to implement further judicial, administrative, military, and constitutional reforms for supervising and controlling the Company and preventing it from governing recklessly. Mill's "Constitution of the East India Company" (1817) instituted a system of checks and balances with its establishment of a primary governing body, the Committee of Correspondence, in addition to a series of subcommittees that oversaw the Company's treasury, accounts, and military, judicial, and mercantile operations.

The adventurers, pirates, and privateers who explored, conquered, and plundered in the seventeenth century were eventually replaced by the merchants, statesmen, scholars, and colonial administrators in the eighteenth and nineteenth centuries. The development of more elaborate, militarily defended, and concentrated trading practices coincided with the emergence of subtle and sophisticated political and economic discourses that frequently exhibited the competing logic and rationales that underwrote the imperialist project. For example, following the lead of antimonopoly economist Adam Smith (*An Inquiry into the Nature and Causes of the Wealth of Nations*, 1776), some administrators, missionaries, scholars, and statesmen argued that free trade would enable the "lower" nations to improve themselves; the lives of the people and their sovereign would thus be enriched. After "opening" India for trade, the subcontinent would be altered by the humanitarian and civilizing influence of British commerce and administration, and despotic modes of Asiatic rule would be replaced with a more equitable economy and more orderly, rational, and advanced modes of government. In other words, British development and administration of free trade would be the crucial component in the campaign to uplift the "backward" nations of the Eastern world. Inventive and ethical statesmen and legislators would combine the energies of commercial industriousness with moral and missionary zeal.

Such administrative and governmental developments were influenced by eighteenth- and nineteenth-century theories of government and political economy. Historians, economists, and philosophers ranging from Baron de Montesquieu, to Adam Smith, Robert Orme, John Stuart Mill (James Mill's son), and Karl Marx examined and imagined the economic and cultural history of India in an attempt to identify India's specific nature and to propose a cure or solution for India's alleged afflictions: despotism, political and economic instability, irrationality, indolence, corruption, and developmental stasis. Proponents of mercantilism (governmentally regulated and protected trade) and supporters of free (unfettered) and unregulated trade were in disagreement over the specific and ideal nature of Indian trade but were equally invested in theorizing and administering governmental policy. British masters and administrators believed India was theirs to manage, and manage they would, for India's good.

Whether moralistic or militaristic in nature, British attempts to administer the subcontinent shared a fundamental assumption that India was out of "civilized," orderly time, hopelessly stuck in the static time of ancients or heathens. The Indian people were allegedly governed by superstition, ruled by hysteria and idolatry, and wholly without functioning economies and markets or life-sustaining communities and traditions. Scholarly, "scientific," religious, artistic, fictional, and administrative representations sustained such widespread and enduring characterizations of this diverse land and its various peoples. Colonial administrators and civil servants, missionaries and travelers arrived well-fed on a diet of broadly disseminated ethnographic and anthropological portraits, geographical theories, and biological and psychological profiles. What was not imagined to exist could not be seen, respected, or understood. As Sudipta Sen argues in *Empire of Free Trade* (1998), "the East India Company's demands for commerce and markets came face to face with a *different* organization of trade, market exchange, and authority. This difference was crucial in determining the nature and outcome of the conflict of economic interests" (3). Many parts of the Indian subcontinent had extant local political economies, mercantile practices, and forms of social and governmental organization and authority—in other words, regionally autonomous and unique traditions. What the British imperialists saw, however, were symptoms in need of cure and golden opportunities to apply, in foreign lands, "enlightened" European administrative, economic, and institutional policies and practices. Sen observes, "One can see then how the squalor and disorder of the Indian bazaars would catch the attention of the English as they tried to bring them into the realm of new commercial respectability" (8). Sen continues,

> Such a neat split between unruly and ideal markets cannot be readily attributed to the marketplaces of India before the officials of the Company came to administer them. Here, riotous crowds at the marketplaces did not threaten an upper-class convention of commoditization and consumption. Rather, the orderly, the disorderly, and the festive shared a more or less even venue of exchange. Market places here carried the invisible imprimatur of ruling authorities. First, there were the imperial designs of the Mughals, expressed through formal architecture marking out avenues of procession, gateways, and walls as well as through elaborate practices of delegation, gift-giving, and appropriation. Second, there were the over-lapping claims of more localized authority, particularly the households of the quasi-autonomous landlords of the countryside: the Zamindars and their dependents. Further, markets were aligned to a landscape dotted with sacred sites, often sharing the same space with established religious edifices: the mosque, the temple, and the saintly tomb. Little wonder, then, that patrons, clients, and frequenters of marketplaces of northern India, as they resisted the new invasions in investment and trade, presented a spectacle of chaos, despotism, and primitivism for the reformers and revenue administrators in the service

of the Company, urging the need for further reordering, reform, and regulation. (8–9)

British attempts at regulation, indoctrination, management, and control went, despite administrators' and Company reformers' good intentions, dreadfully wrong, though not from lack of effort, imagination, or initiative. What the British Company governors and administrators, both at home and in the Indian field, could not understand was that their self-congratulatory superior methods and modern economic and mercantile principles and practices were in fact interruptions, and often devastating and disruptive ones at that. When Indian rulers like the Rani of Jhansi, Tipu Sultan, or the king of Delhi protested against Company practices, they were often declared corrupt rulers or selfish despots. The Rani protested against the Company's practice of declaring rulers' territories "lapsed" (and therefore available for seizure by the Company) if the Company refused to recognize the ruler's designated heir. Company administrators outlawed the Indian rulers' practice of adopting an heir in the absence of a biological one. Ending the "native" practice or tradition, of course, often served Company's interests or broadened its areas and avenues of control. The Rani of Jhansi, after pleading her kingdom's case through legal channels without success, joined other Indian rulers in fighting against the British during the Indian Uprising/Sepoy Mutiny.

Company administrators, scholars, and statesmen developed competing theories of colonial administration and practice. Orientalist scholars, like William "Oriental" Jones, advised colonial administrators to develop "well-mannered" policies that would tolerate Indian beliefs and superstitions. Jones's assessments of Indian legal and religious culture were both appreciative and disparaging; his contradictory discourse reveals the complexities of orientalism and reflects eighteenth- and nineteenth-century Europeans' authorial and interpretive certainty and sense of "superior" cultural authority. Jones could marvel at a Hindu legal text's visionary and noble democratic ideals and simultaneously dismiss an entire subcontinent's population as irrational, incomprehensible, and absurd. Colonial administrators and unapologetic Anglicists like Thomas Babington Macaulay dismissed the orientalist scholars' approach. In Macaulay's view, attempts to understand the Indian mind and Indian culture were pointless; he believed that only systematically introduced English values traditions and institutions would enable successful and effective forms of colonial government. Orientalists and Anglicists alike hoped to develop and implement administrative and legal policies that the natives could easily adapt to and assimilate. The establishment of British law and order in India was considered the most efficient means of encouraging successful and profitable trade. Social and legal reformers like Captain William "Thuggee" Sleeman and William Cavendish Bentinck worked to suppress native traditions (*thuggee* [banditry], *sati* [widow-burning], and polygamy) that were believed to contribute to the subcontinent's immoral, chaotic, and disorderly atmosphere.

Despite ideological and political differences, many—if not most—of the British statesmen, scholars, administrators, and merchants believed that the fate and future of India and its peoples was theirs to determine; despite the variety of agendas and differences of motives and methodologies, British masters and managers considered India the jewel in the crown and the laboratory for the empire's mercantile and governmental inventions. The Indian Uprising/Sepoy Mutiny was the devastating crisis that finally precipitated massive reorganization of Britain's Indian empire. The Company's fluctuating and unpredictable policies of engagement, incorporation, and administration led, increasingly, to more aggressive and direct forms of conquest and rule that were, managerially, largely dependent on sizable portions of the occupied native population. The Indian Uprising/Sepoy Mutiny was characterized by some colonial administrators and military observers as a spontaneous outburst of Indian religious hysteria (arising from Hindu and Muslim reactions to the cow- and pig-fat greased cartridges required to load an Enfield rifle) or as an example of outrageous native treachery and cunning. For many British statesman and leaders, it was easier and far more comforting to believe the uprising was a pathological symptom of the national character rather than an expression of outraged, organized resistance in protest against imperial and colonial disruption of regional culture, tradition, and life. The latter interpretation would have undermined British confidence in the imperial mission. The events of 1857–1858 led to the dismantling of the East India Company and to its takeover by the British Crown. The ending of Company rule initiated the establishment of the Raj and further broadening of Great Britain's colonial and imperial ministrations (the point at which volume 3 of *Archives of Empire*, begins).

ORGANIZATION OF VOLUME I

This volume begins with documents and treaties from the era of the privately owned British East India charter company (1773, 1817, 1833), examines crises that led to the Crown's takeover of the Company (1858), and ends with the opening of the Suez Canal in Egypt (1869) and the expansion of the travel and tourist industries in Egypt. The inauguration of the Suez Canal was a spectacular event that highlighted the drama and increasing sophistication and complexity of international trade and finance. This volume primarily concentrates on Great Britain's eighteenth- and nineteenth-century occupation and colonization of the Indian subcontinent; however, these pages also document a rudimentary model of what is presently known as the global market, that is, the gestation and tumultuous development of international trade. The enterprise that begins in India spreads to Egypt in north Africa and becomes for some—like the English teenager Robert Clive, who went to India a troublesome hooligan and returned a *nabob* (a newly made millionaire)—a capital adventure. For others, like Frenchman Ferdinand De Lesseps, the shortcut to India was itself an international venture. He traveled across Europe and Great Britain, selling the idea of the canal and soliciting stockholders and investors; De Lesseps envisioned the canal as a means of conveyance and an economic conduit, a means of channeling goods and funds. De Lesseps tirelessly marketed his Suez Canal scheme and sold shares for the Universal Suez Maritime Canal Company to British and European shipping magnates and captains of trade. The Indian colony that began with the English East India Company would itself be bolstered and broadened by financial maneuverings and market manipulations; in 1875, British Prime Minister Benjamin Disraeli borrowed four million pounds from the Rothschild's Bank to purchase 44 percent of the market shares in the Suez Company. The prime minister had obtained the "key to India," the shortened route to the empire's subcontinental possessions, as well as a more timely and economical means of managing commercial enterprises and military operations (the need for which the Crimean War and Indian Uprising/Sepoy Mutiny made all too evident). The prime minister later presented India as a "gift" to his sovereign, Queen Victoria, whom Disraeli would additionally bestow with the title Empress of India. The canal's opening also made the colonial possessions available to international consumers; the travel and tourist industries enabled privileged British and European citizens to experience the adventures and see the exotic sights they had heard about on scientific and missionary lecture circuits and had long been reading about in literature, travel narratives, journals, and magazines.

The crises represented in this volume—the trial and impeachment of Warren Hastings (1788–1795), the Indian Uprising/Sepoy Mutiny (1857–1858), and the Arabi Uprising (1881–1882)—additionally exhibit the conflicts that arose with the coincidence of competing national interests, commercial investments, and economic priorities, ignored or unresolved native and local conflicts, and native oppression and abuse. The complexities of colonialism are numerous, and the voices, discourses, and debates contained herein cannot be reduced to a single perspective or simple linear narrative. It might be most useful to understand the history represented here as a series of continental shifts that took place over an extended period of time in which Western peoples attempted to negotiate or balance the mythical and genuine values of the Enlightenment (knowledge, discovery, science, rationalism) with the gross and often brutal realities of commercial competition and material desire.

CONTEMPORARY CRITICAL CONCERNS

The contemporary historian has to establish the value of the study of the past, not as an end in itself, but as a way of providing perspectives on the present that contribute to the solution of problems particular to our own time.—Hayden White, *Tropics of Discourse*

The history of empire is not a finished history; contemporary multinational corporations, international trading blocks, and mercantile treaties (trade agreements) are more elaborate models of yesterday's imperial and colonial enterprises. The North American Free Trade Agreement (NAFTA), General Agreement on Tariffs and Trade (GATT), Free Trade Area of the Americas (FTAA), and Maastricht (European Union) treaties make evident the intersecting interests of government and economy, local and global politics and commerce. Colonialism's "subject nations" are similar to what could be called the resource nations and populations of the late twentieth and twenty-first centuries, the nations and communities in which powerful companies can take advantage of and exploit the availability of cheap labor. And while the opponents of World Trade Conferences (the World Trade Organization protestors in Seattle, for example) have in much of the press been dismissed as mindless hooligans and anarchists, the concerns they and international scholars, political and economic theorists, and activists are articulating with regard to free trade and its alleged benefits for developing nations are serious and legitimate. In other words, there is a relationship between the arguments of today's proponents of free trade, who argue, for example, that "opening" China's markets will reform its repressive government, and the beliefs of yesterday's politicians and statesmen who also held faith in expanded markets and the "democratizing" and uplifting influences of mercantilism. As linguist and social critic Noam Chomsky (1996) has observed in an article on NAFTA, "One consequence of the globalization of the economy is the rise of new governing institutions to serve the interests of private transnational economic power. Another is the spread of the Third World social model, with islands of enormous privilege in a sea of misery and despair." If globalization is, as some argue, an inevitable reality, the economic logic of the future, Adam Smith's model of a moral government—one that could embrace commerce and spread its benefits in an inclusive way—is worth remembering as an imperfect (for it did not recognize the autonomy and full subjecthood of all races and nations) yet valuable idea and a viable ethical imperative. We have much to learn from and about the empires and colonial enterprises of the past; there is also a great deal to learn from the attempts of those who were assumed to be powerless to resist the logic and policies of "progress" and "development" and who, nonetheless, did.

BIBLIOGRAPHY

Alavi, Seema. *The Sepoys and the Company; Tradition and Transition in Northern India, 1770–1830.* Delhi: Oxford University Press, 1995.
Archer, Mildred. *Company Paintings: Indian Paintings of the British Period.* London: The Museum, 1992.
Barber, William J. *British Economic Thought and India, 1600–1858: A Study in the History of Development Economies.* Oxford: Clarendon Press, 1975.
Birdwood, George. Introduction to *The Register of Letters of the Governour and Company of Merchants of London Trading into the East Indies, 1600–1619.* London: B. Quaritch, 1893.
Bowen, H. V. *Elites, Enterprise, and the Making of the British Overseas Empire, 1688–1775.* London: Macmillan, 1996.
Bowen, H. V., Margarette Lincoln, and Nigel Rigby, eds. *The Worlds of the East India Company.* Rochester, N.Y.: D. S. Brewer, 2002.
———. *Revenue and Reform: The Indian Problem in British Politics, 1757–1773.* Cambridge: Cambridge University Press, 1991.
Breckinridge, Carol A., and Peter van der Steer, eds. *Orientalism and the Postcolonial Predicament: Perspectives on South Asia.* Philadelphia: University of Pennsylvania Press, 1993.
Carruthers, Bruce G. *City of Capital: Politics and Markets in the English Financial Revolution.* Princeton, N.J.: Princeton University Press, 1996.
Chomsky, Noam. Notes on NAFTA: The Masters of Mankind. May 1996. In *Documents on Mexican Politics: Issue on NAFTA and Maquiladoras* (May), ed. Alex López-Ortiz. http://www.cs.unb.ca/~alopez-o/politics/chomnafta.html
Dirlik, Arif, and Roxann Prazniak, eds. *Places and Politics in an Age of Globalization.* Lanham, Md.: Rowan and Littlefield, 2001.
Donohue, John D., and Joseph S. Nye Jr., eds. *Governance in a Globalizing World.* Washington, D.C.: Brookings Institution Press, 2000.
Edney, Matthew H. *Mapping an Empire: The Geographical Construction of British India.* Chicago: University of Chicago Press, 1997.
Ekelund, Robert B., Jr., and Robert D. Tollison. *Politicized Economies: Monarchy, Monopoly, and Mercantilism.* College Station, Texas: Texas A and M Press, 1997.
Farrington, Anthony. *Trading Places: The East India Company and Asia, 1600–1834.* London: British Library, 2002.
Gentleman, Tobias. *England's Way to Win Wealth and to Employ Ships and Mariners.* 1614. Reprint. Delmar, N.Y.: Scholars' Facsimiles and Reprints, 1992.

International Third World Legal Studies Association. *Postcolonialism, Globalism, and Law.* Flushing, N.Y.: Valparaiso University School of Law, 2000.

James, Lawrence. *Raj: The Making and Unmaking of British India.* New York: St. Martin's Griffin, 1999.

Lively, Jack, and John Collwyn Rees. *Utilitarian Logic and Politics: James Mill's "Essay on Government," Macaulay's Critique, and the Ensuing Debate.* Oxford: Clarendon Press, 1978.

Magnusson, Lars. *Mercantilism: The Shaping of an Economic Language.* London: Routledge, 1994.

Malleson, G. B. (George Bruce). *The Founders of the Indian Empire.* London: W. H. Allen, 1882; reprint, Delhi: Mayur Publications, 1988.

Metcalf, Thomas R. *Ideologies of the Raj: The New Cambridge History of India.* Cambridge: Cambridge University Press, 1995.

Moir, Martin, ed. *John Stuart Mill: Writings on India.* Toronto: University of Toronto Press, 1990.

Morley, William Hook. *The Administration of Justice in British India, Its Past History and Present State.* London: Williams and Norgate, 1858; reprint New Delhi: Metropolitan Book Co., 1976.

Morris, James. *Pax Britannica: The Climax of an Empire.* London: Faber, 1968.

Muller, Jerry Z. *Adam Smith in His Time and Ours: Designing the Decent Society.* New York: Free Press, 1993.

Parry, Benita. *Delusions and Discoveries: Studies on India in the British Imagination, 1880–1930.* Berkeley: University of California Press, 1972.

Sampson, Gary P., ed. *The Role of the World Trade Organization in Global Governance.* New York: United Nations University Press, 2001.

Schiffler, Samuel. *Boundaries and Allegiances: Problems of Justice and Responsibility in Liberal Thought.* Oxford: Oxford University Press, 2001.

Schweinitz, Karl. *The Rise and Fall of British India: Imperialism as Inequality.* London: Methuen, 1983.

Sen, Sudipta. *Empire of Free Trade: The East India Company and the Making of the Colonial Marketplace.* Philadelphia: University of Pennsylvania Press, 1998.

———. *Distant Sovereignty: National Imperialism and the Origins of British India.* New York: Routledge, 2002.

Spurr, David. *The Rhetoric of Empire: Colonial Discourse, Travel Writing, and Imperial Administration.* Durham, N.C.: Duke University Press, 1993.

Stubbs, Richard, and Geoffrey R. D. Underhill, eds. *Political Economy and the Changing Global Order.* New York: St. Martin's, 2000.

Sykes, Alan. *The Rise and Fall of British Liberalism, 1776–1988.* London: Longman, 1997.

Viswanathan, Gauri. *Masks of Conquest: Literary Study and British Rule in India.* New York: Columbia University Press, 1989.

I
COMPANY TO CANAL, 1757–1869

INTRODUCTION
Adventure Capitalism: Mercantilism, Militarism, and the British East India Company
MIA CARTER

From its inception at the beginning of the seventeenth century, the British East India Company combined military and commercial methods of institutional organization and administration; what began as a corporate enterprise soon evolved into a massively armed colonial empire. The Company's history is characterized by intrigue, national and personal ambition, double-dealing, and even kidnapping and hostage-taking as means of insuring successful treaty negotiations. Great Britain's knowledge of Indian trade was itself acquired by an act of piracy on the high seas when Sir Francis Drake captured five Portuguese vessels containing treasures of the East and detailed documents on trade routes and procedures. The Company also financed itself for a number of years by illegally importing opium to China; Chinese resistance to England's drug trade led to the Opium Wars (1839–1842, 1856–1860) and Britain's seizure of Hong Kong. The East India Company was also used by English families as a disciplinary institution for incorrigible sons. "Naughty" Robert Clive, a delinquent and leader of a protection racket at home, was sent to India to improve himself; he earned a knighthood for his military and administrative services on the Company's behalf. Clive eventually became a British national hero and one of the leading and most-celebrated icons of British imperial masculine identity.

Early on in the Company's history, aggressive protection of its monopoly status was one of the corporation's chief aims. Free trade was discouraged and eventually outlawed. Private competitors were either eliminated, like Captain Kidd, who was executed for piracy in 1701, or incorporated, like Thomas "Diamond" Pitt, an interloper who had individually obtained trading rights from Indian rulers. On his return to England, Pitt was tried, fined, and then hired as a senior administrator by the Company; the former rogue eventually became the governor of Fort St. George. Critics of the Company were not always critics of colonialism per se; often those voicing displeasure were protesting the monopolistic policies and practices and the Company's unchecked and extensive military powers, which, some argued, usurped the powers of the king and Crown. Others objected to the enhancement of the individual fortunes of the nabobs—the Company's newly made millionaires—maintaining that the Company's profits should enrich the kingdom and the state instead. Those who were critical of the Company's policies of annexation, land settlement, and seizure argued that native communities and traditions were being debased; a nation, as Karl Marx and others argued, was being destroyed.

The East India Company Act, 1773 initiated the restructuring of the Company by instituting a supervisory council that provided a system of checks and balances. The act also limited the colonial Administration's ability to wage war and negotiate treaties and allowed Company employees to be tried at home in His Majesty's Court for offenses made in India, a change that would dramatically affect the future of Governor-General Warren Hastings. Despite progressive legal and administrative reforms, disparaging assessments of the native rulers continued and were expansively represented and broadly disseminated. Native rulers were depicted as cruel despots, self-indulgent sex addicts, and spoiled and effeminate children; the Indian people were frequently depicted as people in desperate need of rescue from their own amoral, corrupt, and insensitive leaders. Charges of native misgovernment and mismanagement became the rationale for the ongoing seizure of Indian territories. The reformers' assessments of native rulers' tyrannical despotism and their wide-ranging descriptions of the underdeveloped Indian character or nature supported the representation of the British Administration as a mission of charity, compassion, civilization, and uplift.

Expansionism and increased involvement in the colony's domestic politics engaged the Company in political theory and governmental practice; India was used as a laboratory for imperialistic rule, international economics, and colonial administration. Company improvements included the expansion of the Indian rail, telegraph, and postal systems, all of which served both administrative and military aims. For example, the rail system was used to provide famine relief and to ease and improve the transportation of military staff and supplies; the telegraph system was used to observe famine conditions and to improve military and surveillance operations. Many reformers, like James Mill and Lord Thomas Babington Macaulay, believed the English were destined to rule India; they would develop ideal systems of government with the aim of leading the Indians away from despotism and toward democracy. The Government of India Act, 1833 transferred the Company to the Crown and exemplified the new administrative focus on the direct government of India.

This section on the British East India Company also contains subsections on some of the crises of the Company's rule: the revolt of Tipu Sultan; the cases of alleged forms of Eastern (Tipu Sultan) and Western (Warren Hastings) despotism; and the British campaigns to reform the Indian practices of thuggee and sati/suttee.

BIBLIOGRAPHY

Alavi, Seema. *The Sepoys and the Company: Tradition and Transition in Northern India, 1770–1830*. Delhi: Oxford University Press, 1995.

Chadhuri, K. N. *The Trading World of Asia and the English East India Company, 1600–1760*. Cambridge: Cambridge University Press, 1978.

Clapham, J. H. *Economic History of Modern Britain*, 3 vols. Cambridge: The University Press, 1939.

Clive Museum. *Treasures from India: The Clive Collection at Powis Castle*. New York: Meredith Press, 1987.

Dodwell, H. H. *Dupleix and Clive: The Beginning of Empire*. 1920. Reprint, London: Methuen, 1968.

Gardner, Brian. *The East India Company: A History*. London: McCall Publishing Co., 1971.

Hill, Porter. *The Bombay Marines: An Adam Horne Adventure*. New York: Walter and Co. Souvenir Press, 1985.

Keay, John. *The Honorable Company: A History of the English East India Company*. London: Harper Collins, 1991.

Metcalf, Thomas R. *Ideologies of the Raj*. Cambridge: Cambridge University Press, 1995.

Moir, Martin. *A General Guide to the India Office Records*. London: British Library, 1988.

Philips, C. H. *The East India Company, 1784–1834*. Manchester, England: Manchester University Press, 1961.

Rajan, Balachandra. *Under Western Eyes: India from Milton to Macaulay*. Durham, N.C.: Duke University Press, 1999.

Saha, Sheela. *The European Trading Companies in Bihar*. New Delhi: Wisdom Publications, 1996.

Sen, Sudipta. *Empire of Free Trade: The East India Company and the Making of the Colonial Marketplace*. Philadelphia: University of Pennsylvania Press, 1998.

Sikka, Ram Parkash. *The Civil Service in India: Europeanisation and Indianisation under the East Indian Company, 1765–1857*. New Delhi: Uppal House, 1984.

Sutherland, Lucy. *The East India Company in Eighteenth-Century Politics*. Oxford: Clarendon Press, 1952.

White, David. *Competition and Collaboration: Parsi Merchants and the East India Company in Eighteenth-Century India*. New Delhi: Munshiram Mancharlal Publishers, 1995.

Wild, Antony. *The East India Company: Trade and Conquest from 1600*. London: Harper Collins Illustrated, 1999.

Chronology of Events

1600	Establishment of the East India Company
1757	Battle at Plassey
1769	Foundation of the Royal Academy
1775	Beginning of the American War of Independence
1776	Adam Smith's *The Wealth of Nations* published
1789	Fall of the Bastille
1788–1795	Impeachment proceedings against Warren Hastings
1767–1799	Anglo-Mysore Wars
1792	Treaty of Seringapatam
1798	Battle of Seringapatam
1798	Battle of the Nile
1804	Napoleon made emperor
1813	Emendation of East India Company Charter allowing missionary work in India
1815	Napoleon defeated at Waterloo
1829	Suttee (sati) officially outlawed by Sir William Bentinck
1830	Thuggee outlawed
1832	First Reform Act
1833	Abolition of slavery throughout British Empire
1837	Accession of Queen Victoria
1843	Annexation of Sindh
1849	Annexation of Punjab
1851	Great Exhibition at the Crystal Palace
1853	Annexation of Nagpur
1853	Indian Civil Service opens to competition
1854–1856	Crimean War
1856	Annexation of Oudh (Oude)
1857	Indian Uprising/Sepoy Mutiny
1858	Queen Victoria proclaimed Empress of India

1858	Suez Canal debated in the House of Commons
1858	Universal Company of the Maritime Suez Canal founded
1864	Riots on the isthmus of the Suez Canal
1869	Suez Canal inauguration

Governors and Governors-General of India

Governors of the Presidency of Fort William

1758	Robert Clive
1760	John Holwell
1760	Henry Vansittart
1764	John Spencer
1765	Lord Clive
1767	Henry Verelst
1769	John Cartier
1772	Warren Hastings

Governors-General of Bengal (with authority over Madras and Bombay)

1774–1785	Warren Hastings
1785–1786	Sir John Macpherson
1786–1793	Lord Cornwallis
1793–1798	Lieutenant-General Sir Alured Clarke
1798–1805	Lord Mornington (Lord Richard Wellesley)
1805	Lord Cornwallis
1805–1807	Sir George Barlow
1807–1813	Lord Minto
1813–1823	Lord Moira (Lord Hastings)
1823	John Adam
1823–1828	Lord Amherst
1828–1834	Lord William Bentinck

Viceroys and Governors-General of India

1833–1835   Lord William Bentinck
1835–1836   Sir Charles Metcalfe
1836–1842   Lord Auckland
1842–1844   Lord Ellenborough
1844–1848   Sir Henry Hardinge (Lord Hardinge)
1848–1856   Lord Dalhousie
1856–1868   Lord Canning

Newabs of Bengal

1740–1756   Alivardi Khan
1756–1757   Seraja-daula
1757–1760   Mir Jafar Khan
1760–1763   Mir Kasim Khan
1763–1765   Mir Jafar Khan (restored)
1765–1766   Najm-ud-daula
1766–1770   Saif-ud-daula

India under Cornwallis, 1792
Maps digitally redrawn by K. Maria Lane,
Department of Geography, University
of Texas, Austin

India under Wellesley, 1799

India under Hastings, 1832

Indian under Dalhousie, 1856

Excerpt from *With Clive in India*
G. A. HENTY

[G. A. (George Alfred) Henty (1832–1902) was a prolific author of travel and sensational adventure novels for boys; he also wrote for boys' magazines, including *A Boy's Own* and *The Union Jack*. Henty specialized in fictionalized accounts of imperial wars, including novels on the Battle of Waterloo, the Greek and Italian Wars of Independence, the Afghan and Burmese Wars, and the American Civil War. His significant and related titles include *In Times of Peril: A Tale of India* (1881) and *At the Point of the Bayonet: A Tale of the Mahratta War* (1901).]

CHAPTER I   LEAVING HOME

A lady in deep mourning was sitting crying bitterly by a fire in small lodgings in the town of Yarmouth. Beside her stood a tall lad of sixteen. He was slight in build, but his schoolfellows knew that Charlie Marryat's muscles were as firm and hard as those of any boy in the school. In all sports requiring activity and endurance rather than weight and strength he was always conspicuous. Not one in the school could compete with him in long-distance running, and when he was one of the hares there was but little chance for the hounds. He was a capital swimmer and one of the best boxers in the school. He had a reputation for being a leader in every mischievous prank; but he was honourable and manly, would scorn to shelter himself under the semblance of a lie, and was a prime favourite with his masters as well as his schoolfellows. His mother bewailed the frequency with which he returned home with blackened eyes and bruised face; for between Dr. Willet's school and the fisher lads of Yarmouth there was a standing feud, whose origin dated so far back that none of those now at school could trace it. Consequently fierce fights often took place in the narrow rows, and sometimes the fisher boys would be driven back on to the broad quay shaded by trees, by the river, and there being reinforced from the craft along the side would reassume the offensive and drive their opponents back into the main street.

It was but six months since Charlie had lost his father, who was the officer in command at the coast-guard station, and his scanty pension was now all that remained for the support of his widow and children. His mother had talked his future prospects over many times with Charlie. The latter was willing to do anything, but could suggest nothing. His father had but little naval interest, and had for years been employed on coast-guard service.

Charlie agreed that although he should have liked of all things to go to sea, it was useless to think of it now, for he was past the age at which he could have entered as a midshipman. The matter had been talked over four years before with his father; but the latter had pointed out that a life in the navy without interest is in most cases a very hard one. If a chance of distinguishing himself happened promotion would follow; but if not, he might be for years on shore, starving on half-pay and waiting in vain for an appointment, while officers with more luck and better interest went over his head.

Other professions had been discussed but nothing determined upon, when Lieutenant Marryat suddenly died. Charlie, although an only son, was not an only child, as he had two sisters both younger than himself. After a few months of effort Mrs. Marryat found that the utmost she could hope to do with her scanty income was to maintain herself and daughters and to educate them until they should reach an age when they could earn their own living as governesses, but that Charlie's keep and education were beyond her resources. She had, therefore, very reluctantly written to an uncle whom she had not seen for many years; her family having objected very strongly to her marriage with a penniless lieutenant in the navy. She informed him of the loss of her husband, and that although her income was sufficient to maintain herself and her daughters, she was most anxious to start her son, who was now sixteen, in life, and therefore begged him to use his influence to obtain for him a situation of some sort. The letter which she now held in her hand was the answer to the appeal.

"My dear Niece," it began,—"Since you, by your own foolish conduct and opposition to all our wishes, separated yourself from your family and went your own way in life, I have heard little of you, as the death of your parents so shortly afterwards deprived me of all sources of information. I regret to hear of the loss which you have suffered. I have already taken the necessary steps to carry out your wishes. I yesterday dined with a friend who is one of the directors of the Hon. East India Company, and at my request he has kindly placed a writership in the Company at your son's service. He will have to come up to London to see the board next week, and will probably have to embark for India a fortnight later. I shall be glad if he will take up his abode with me during the intervening time. I shall be glad also if you will favour me with a statement of your income and expenses, with such details as you may think necessary. I inclose four five-pound bank-notes, in order that your son may obtain such garments as may be immediately needful for his appearance before the board of directors and for his journey to London. I remain, my dear niece, yours sincerely "Joshua Tufton."

"It is cruel," Mrs. Marryat sobbed—"cruel to take you away from us and send you to India, where you will most likely die of fever, or be killed by a tiger, or stabbed by one of those horrid natives, in a fortnight."

"Not so bad as that, mother, I hope," Charlie said sympathizingly, although he could not repress a smile; "other people have managed to live out there and have come back safe."

"Yes," Mrs. Marryat said sobbing; "I know how you will come back. A little, yellow, shrivelled up old man with no liver, and a dreadful temper, and a black servant. I know what it will be."

This time Charlie could not help laughing. "That's looking too far ahead altogether, mother. You take the two extremes. If I don't die in a fortnight I am to live to be a shrivelled old man. I'd rather take a happy medium, and look forward to coming back before my liver is all gone, or my temper all destroyed, with lots of money to make you and the girls comfortable. There is only one thing, I wish it had been a cadetship instead of a writership."

"That is my only comfort," Mrs. Marryat said. "If it had been a cadetship I should have written to say that I would not let you go. It is bad enough as it is; but if you had had to fight, I could not have borne it."

Charlie did his best to console his mother by telling her how every one who went to India made fortunes, and how he should be sure to come back with plenty of money, and that when the girls grew up he should be able to find rich husbands for them; and at last he succeeded in getting her to look at matters in a less gloomy light. "And I'm sure, mother," he said, "uncle means most kindly. He sends twenty pounds, you see, and says that that is for immediate necessities; so I have no doubt he means to help to get my outfit, or at any rate to advance money which I can repay him out of my salary. The letter is rather stiff and business-like, of course, but I suppose that's his way; and you see he asks about your income, so perhaps he means to help for the girls' education. I should go away very happy if I knew that you would be able to get on comfortably. Of course it's a long way off, mother, and I should have liked to stay at home to be a help to you and the girls; but one can't have all one wishes. As far as I am concerned myself, I would rather go out as a writer there, where I shall see strange sights and a strange country, than be stuck all my life at a desk in London."

The remainder of Charlie's stay in London passed most pleasantly. They visited all the sights of town, Mr. Tufton performing what he called his duty with an air of protest, but showing a general thoughtfulness and desire to please his visitors, which was very apparent even when he grunted and grumbled the most.

On the evening before he started he called Charlie down into his counting-house.

"To-morrow you are going to sail," he said, "and to start in life on your own account, and I trust that you will, as far as possible, be steady and do your duty to your employers. You will understand that although the pay of a writer is not high there are opportunities for advancement. The Company have the monopoly of the trade of India, and in addition to their great factories at Bombay, Calcutta, and Madras they have many other trading stations. Those who by their good conduct attract the attention of their superiors rise to positions of trust and emolument. There are many who think that the Company will in time enlarge its operations, and as they do so, superior opportunities will offer themselves, and since the subject of India has been prominently brought before my notice I have examined the question and am determined to invest somewhat largely in the stock of the Company, a step which will naturally give me some influence with the board. That influence I shall, always supposing that your conduct warrants it, exercise on your behalf. As we are now at war with France, and it is possible that the vessel in which you are proceeding may be attacked by the way, I have thought it proper that you should be armed. You will, therefore, find in your cabin a brace of pistols, a rifle, and a double-barrel shot-gun, which last, I am informed, is a useful weapon at close quarters. Should your avocations in India permit your doing so, you will find them useful in the pursuit of game. I hope that you will not be extravagant; but as a matter of business I find that it is useful to be able to give entertainments to persons who may be in a position to benefit or advance you. I have, therefore, arranged that you will draw from the factor at Madras the sum of two hundred pounds annually in addition to your pay. It is clearly my duty to see that my nephew has every fair opportunity for making his way. Now, go upstairs at once to your mother. I have letters to write, and am too busy for talking."

So saying, with a peremptory wave of his hand he dismissed his nephew.

SOURCE: Chapter 1 in *With Clive in India, Or, The Beginnings of an Empire* (London: Blackie and Son, n. d.), 10–14, 26–27.

Agreement between the Nabob Nudjum-ul-Dowlah and the Company, 12 August 1765

The King having been graciously pleased to grant to the English Company the Dewanny of Bengal, Behar, and Orissa, with the revenues thereof, as a free gift for ever, on certain conditions, whereof one is that there shall be a sufficient allowance out of the said revenues for supporting the expenses of the Nizamut: be it known to all whom it may concern, that I do agree to accept of the annual sum of Sicca rupees 53,86,131-9, as an adequate allowance for the support of the Nizamut, which is to be regularly paid as follows, *viz.:* the sum of rupees 17,78,854-1, for all my household expenses, servants, &c., and the remaining sum of rupees 36,07,277-8, for the maintenance of such horse, sepoys, peons, bercundauzes, &c., as may be thought necessary for my suwarry and the support of my dignity only, should such an expense hereafter be found necessary to be kept up, but on no account ever to exceed that amount: and having a perfect reliance on ul-Miaeen Dowla, I desire he may have the disbursing of the above sum of rupees 36,07; 277-8, for the purposes before-mentioned. This Agreement (by the blessing of God) I hope will be inviolably observed, as long as the English Company's factories continue in Bengal.

Fort William, 30th September 1765.
(A true copy.)
(Signed) Alexander Campbell, S.S.C.

6. Treaty between the Nawab Shujau-d daula, of Oudh, the Nawab Najmu-d daula, of Bengal, and the East India Company, 16 August, 1765

ARTICLE I

A perpetual and universal peace, sincere friendship, and firm union shall be established between His Highness Shujah-ul-Dowla and his heirs, on the one part, and His Excellency Nudjum-ul-Dowla and the English East India Company on the other; so that the said contracting powers shall give the greatest attention to maintain between themselves, their dominions and their subjects this reciprocal friendship, without permitting, on either side, any kind of hostilities to be committed, from henceforth, for any cause, or under any pretence whatsoever, and everything shall be carefully avoided which might hereafter prejudice the union now happily established.

ARTICLE 2

In case the dominions of His Highness Shujah-ul-Dowla shall at any time hereafter be attacked, His Excellency Nudjum-ul-Dowla and the English Company shall assist him with a part or the whole of their forces, according to the exigency of his affairs, and so far as may be consistent with their own security, and if the dominions of his Excellency Nudjum-ul-Dowla or the English Company, shall be attacked, His Highness shall, in like manner, assist them with a part or the whole of his forces. In the case of the English Company's forces being employed in His Highness's service, the extraordinary expense of the same is to be defrayed by him.

ARTICLE 3

His Highness solemnly engages never to entertain or receive Cossim Ally Khan, the late Soubah-dar of Bengal, &c., Sombre, the assassin of the English, nor any of the European deserters, within his dominions, nor to give the least countenance, support, or protection to them. He likewise solemnly engages to deliver up to the English whatever European may in future desert from them into his country.

ARTICLE 4

The King Shah Aalum shall remain in full possession of Cora, and such part of the Province of Illiabad as he now possesses, which are ceded to His Majesty, as a royal demesne, for the support of his dignity and expenses.

ARTICLE 5

His Highness Shujah-ul-Dowla engages, in a most solemn manner, to continue Bulwant Sing in the zemindarries of Benares, Ghazepore, and all those districts he possessed at the time he came over to the late Nabob Jaffier Ally Khan and the English, on condition of his paying the same revenue as heretofore.

ARTICLE 6

In consideration of the great expense incurred by the English Company in carrying on the late war, His Highness agrees to pay them (50) fifty lakhs of rupees in the following manner; viz. (12) twelve lakhs in money, and a deposit of jewels to the amount of (8) eight lakhs, upon the signing of this Treaty, (5) five lakhs one month after, and the remaining (25) twenty-five lakhs by monthly payments, so as that the whole may be discharged in (13) thirteen months from the date hereof.

ARTICLE 8

His Highness shall allow the English Company to carry on a trade, duty free, throughout the whole of his dominions.

ARTICLE 9

All the relations and subjects of His Highness, who in any manner assisted the English during the course of the late war, shall be forgiven, and no ways molested for the same.

ARTICLE 10

As soon as this Treaty is executed, the English forces shall be withdrawn from the dominions of His Highness, except such as may be necessary for the garrison of Chumar, or for the defence and protection of the King in the city of Illiabad, if His Majesty should require a force for that purpose.

SOURCE: This document can be found in Volume 1 of *Speeches and Documents on India Policy, 1750–1921*, ed. Arthur Berridale Keith (London: Oxford University Press, 1922).

An Inquiry into the Rights of the East India Company of Making War and Peace

[The anonymous author of the "Inquiry" pamphlet is believed to have been an East India Company stockholder or shareholder.]

PREFACE.

It is long fince the nations, which have the misfortune to live near the Eaft-India Company's fettlements, have ftretched out their induftrious and help-lefs hands to our gracious Sovereign, imploring his protection from the op-preffions they were finking under; and it muft give great pleafure to every one who knows how much the interests of Great Britain are connected with those of humanity, to learn, from his Majesty's speech, at the opening of this session, that he had turned his eye to an object so worthy of the royal attention. And, surely, if there is any situation in this life more deplorable than another, it is that of living under the dominion of men, who, wholly intent upon gain, have contrived to establish the most complete system ever known of fraud and violence, by uniting, in the same persons, the several functions of Merchant, Soldier, Financier and Judge; depriving, by that union, all those functions of their mutual checks, by which alone they can be made useful to society.

It is to be hoped that the time is not far off, when those functions, so improperly combined, will be again separated: when his Majesty will resume, from those Merchants, the sword, which, by our happy Constitution, cannot be placed, with energy or safety, in any hand but his own: and when those great territorial revenues in Bengal, which have, of late, been so extravagantly accumulated in the coffers of private men, for trifling or destructive purposes, will be employed in reducing the national debt, as well as in protecting our trade and acquisitions in those distant parts of the world. We might then hope to see an impartial administration of justice in India, without its being subject to the controul of those who are most likely to be the greatest delinquents. We might then hope to see an end to those cruel monopolies, carried on by the Servants of the Company, in the necessaries of life, and to which the wretched natives are obliged to submit, with the bayonet at their throats: and we might then hope to see those Servants once more attentive to the commercial interests of their employers; without attempting to equal, in riches and splendor, the first nobility of the kingdom. But, what is still of greater importance to the free Constitution of this country, we might then hope to see some stop put to the rapid progress of corruption at home; which has been, for some years past, so much promoted by the immense sums lavished by those Servants of the Company, upon their return from India, in order to procure themselves admittance into the House of Commons; where none of them, from the nature of their education, can be supposed to have any thing to say; and where some of them seem to come, as if they were proud of the privilege they had acquired, of mocking the insufficiency of our laws, and of insulting that honourable Assembly, by their presence.

In objection to this salutary change, it has been often urged, "That in a free country like ours, the individuals have their legal rights as well as the state; and that it is always matter of just alarm when the supreme legislative power lays its heavy hand upon those rights, even where there is reason to believe that they have been abused." In this I entirely agree. But when they proceed to tell us, "That the East-India Company have a legal right of making War and

Peace, and of poffeffing their territorial acquifitions, without the participation or infpection of the Britifh Government," I find myfelf obliged to give my diffent. The grounds of that diffent are to be found in the following Letter, written above two years ago, when Sir JOHN LINDSAY was appointed to command his Majefty's fhips in the Eaft-Indies; and though the occafion which produces it now, is fomewhat different from that which at firft gave birth to it; yet I have fuffered it to appear before the public in its original fhape; and the rather, becaufe in that fhape it recalls the memory of a tranfaction, by which the true fpirit of the Gentlemen who have the management of the Company's affairs in Leadenhall-ftreet, had a fair opportunity of difplaying itfelf.

London, Feb. 18, 1772.

A LETTER

You may perceive, my fellow Proprietors, that in this long letter I have faid very little with regard to the expediency or utility of the propofed meafure. This is owing to my having obferved, that the controverfy, at our laft meeting, did not turn upon that point, but barely upon the impropriety of fuffering any encroachment to be made upon the Company's eftablifhed Rights. Were any encroachment intended upon the juft or legal Rights of the Company, there is no one would be feen more forward in their defence than myfelf, both as a friend to the Company, and as a friend to the ftate. The fecurity of private property, and of private rights of every kind, is the root of commerce, of population, of riches, and of ftrength in every ftate; and the ftatefman, who takes any ftep by which thofe private Rights are rendered precarious, difcovers himfelf to be but ill qualified for the place he fills. But here is no fuch invafion attempted; but, on the contrary, an attempt of private perfons to invade the Rights of the public, by challenging to themfelves a prerogative which belongs only to the heads of kingdoms and independent Republics. I have, therefore, endeavoured to fhow you what are in reality the Rights of the Eaft-India Company with regard to making peace and war, by quoting what is to be found in our feveral charters concerning them, and fhall now recapitulate and fum up the whole, by obferving:

That whatever paffages are to be found in thofe charters concerning peace and war, are merely emanations of the royal Willand Pleafure; no fuch being fpecified in the Act of Parliament, which only authorizes King WILLIAM and his fucceffors to grant to the Company, from time to time, by their letters patent, fuch powers and privileges as to him or them fhall feem fitting.

That in none of thefe letters patent, or charters, is it faid, in exprefs terms, that the Company is abfolutely empowered to make war and peace; and that what is mentioned in thofe charters concerning acts of hoftility, is ftrictly confined to fuch acts of hoftility as are for the defence of the Company's property, retaliation of injuries, or other *juft caufe*, the judgment of which cannot, in common fenfe, reft with the Company; but falls to His Majefty, the fupreme Arbiter, by the Britifh conftitution, of all matters of peace and war.

That, although King WILLIAM and the fucceeding Kings of England, had not exprefly referved to themfelves their fovereign Right and Authority over the Eaft-Indian fettlements, and had granted to the Company the moft unlimited power of making war and peace; yet could they not, by any form of words, denude themfelves of that fovereign power, and could only be fuppofed to have delegated it to the Company, as to their Attorney or Plenipotentiary, till fuch time as it fhould be their royal pleafure to refume or limit it.

That, as by the Charters of the 13th of King GEORGE the firft, and of the 27th of King GEORGE the fecond, the Company is authorized *to invade and deftroy upon Juft Caufe* only, and are particularly amenable to His Majesty for any breach of their Charter in this refpect, it is perfectly regular and neceffary that His Majefty fhould have complete knowledge, from his own Officer, of the rife and progrefs of all wars carried on in the Eaft-Indies, in order to know what wars are carried on in compliance with the terms of the Charter, and what not.

And laftly, That when there is the greateft reafon to believe, that the Company's Servants have made a greedy and dangerous ufe of thofe powers, we ought to admire His Majefty's goodnefs, who, inftead of depriving us of them altogether, endeavours to interpofe his fatherly care in preventing any farther abufe of them.

Before I conclude this paper, give me leave, my fellow Proprietors, to add one general Obfervation, which ftruck me on comparing together the feveral Charters of the Eaft-India Company, which is, that in proportion as the *real* power of the Company increafed, its *legal* power and authority have been diminifhed. How far it will be for the advantage of the Proprietors, that Government fhould ftill proceed in narrowing the bounds of the Company's authority, I will not now enquire: but thofe who think farther limitations difadvantageous, will, in my humble opinion, find that the moft effectual method to prevent them, will be by ufing the power they ftill poffefs, with juftice and humanity towards thofe they call their fubjects in India; and with modefty and obedience to thofe whom they ought to confider as their Rulers in Great Britain, I am, with great refpect,

>Gentlemen,
>Your moft obedient,
>and moft humble Servant,
>AN OLD PROPRIETOR.
>London, Auguft 18, 1769.

SOURCE: Anonymous, *An Inquiry into the Rights of the East India Company of Making War and Peace* (London: Walter Shropshire and Samuel Bladon, 1772).

East India Company Act, 1773

VII. And, for the better management of the said United Company's affairs in India, be it further enacted by the authority aforesaid, that, for the government of the Presidency of Fort William in Bengal, there shall be appointed a Governor-General, and four counsellors; and that the whole civil and military government of the said Presidency, and also the ordering, management and government of all the territorial acquisitions and revenues in the kingdoms of Bengal, Behar, and Orissa, shall, during such time as the territorial acquisitions and revenues shall remain in the possession of the said United Company, be, and are hereby vested in the said Governor-General and Council of the said Presidency of Fort William in Bengal, in like manner, to all intents and purposes whatsoever, as the same now are, or at any time heretofore might have been exercised by the President and Council, or Select Committee, in the said kingdoms.

VIII. And be it enacted by the authority aforesaid, that in all cases whatsoever wherein any difference of opinion shall arise upon any question proposed in any consultation, the said Governor-General and Council shall be bound and concluded by the opinion and decision of the major part of those present: And if it shall happen that, by the death or removal, or by the absence, of any of the members of the said Council, such Governor-General and Council shall happen to be equally divided; then, and in every such case, the said Governor-General, or, in his absence, the eldest counsellor present, shall have a casting voice, and his opinion shall be decisive and conclusive.

IX. And be it further enacted by the authority aforesaid, that the said Governor-General and Council, or the major part of them, shall have, and they are hereby authorized to have, power of superintending and controlling the government and management of the Presidencies of Madras, Bombay, and Bencoolen respectively, so far and insomuch as that it shall not be lawful for any President and Council of Madras, Bombay, or Bencoolen, for the time being, to make any orders for commencing hostilities, or declaring or making war, against any Indian princes or powers, or for negotiating or concluding any treaty of peace, or other treaty, with any such Indian princes or powers, without the consent and approbation of the said Governor-General and Council first had and obtained, except in such cases of imminent necessity as would render it dangerous to postpone such hostilities or treaties until the orders from the Governor-General and Council might arrive; and except in such cases where the said Presidents and Councils respectively shall have received special orders from the said United Company; and any President and Council of Madras, Bombay, or Bencoolen, who shall offend in any of the cases aforesaid, shall be liable to be suspended from his or their office by the order of the said Governor-General and Council; and every President and Council of Madras, Bombay, and Bencoolen, for the time being, shall, and they are hereby respectively directed and required, to pay due obedience to such orders as they shall receive, touching the premises from the said Governor-General and Council for the time being, and constantly and diligently to transmit to the said Governor-General and Council advice and intelligence of all transactions and matters whatsoever that shall come to their knowledge, relating to the government, revenues, or interest, of the said United Company; and the said Governor-General and Council for the time being shall, and they are hereby directed and required to pay due obedience to all such orders as they shall receive from the Court of Directors of the said United Company, and to correspond, from time to time, and constantly and diligently transmit to the said Court an exact particular of all advices or intelligence, and of all transactions and matters whatsoever, that shall come to their knowledge, relating to the government, commerce, revenues, or interest, of the said United Company; and the Court of Directors of the said Company, or their successors, shall, and they are hereby directed and required, from time to time, before the expiration of fourteen days after the receiving any such letters or advices, to give in and deliver unto the High Treasurer, or Commissioners of His Majesty's Treasury for the time being, a true and exact copy of such parts of the said letters or advices as shall any way relate to the management of the revenues of the said Company; and in like manner to give in and deliver to one of His Majesty's Principal Secretaries of State for the time being a true and exact copy of all such parts of the said letters or advices as shall any way relate to the civil or military affairs and government of the said Company; all which copies shall be fairly written, and shall be signed by two or more of the Directors of the said Company.

x. And it is hereby further enacted, that Warren Hastings, Esquire, shall be the first Governor-General; and that Lieutenant-General John Clavering, the Honourable George Monson, Richard Barwell, Esquire, and Philip Francis, Esquire, shall be the four first counsellors; and they, and each of them, shall hold and continue in his and their respective offices for and during the term of five years from the time of their arrival at Fort William in Bengal, and taking upon them the government of the said Presidency, and shall not be removable, in the meantime, except by His Majesty, his heirs and successors, upon representation made by the Court of Directors of the said United Company for the time being: and in case of the avoidance of the office of such Governor-General by death, resignation, or removal, his place shall, during the remainder of the term aforesaid, as often as the case shall happen, be supplied by the person of the Council who stands next in rank to such Governor-General; and, in case of the death, removal, resignation, or promotion, of any of the said Council, the Directors of the said United Company are hereby empowered, for and during the remainder of the said term of five years, to nominate and appoint, by and with the consent of His Majesty, his heirs and successors, to be signified under his or their sign manual, a person to succeed to the office so become vacant in the said Council; and until such appointment shall be made, all the powers and authorities vested in the Governor-General and Council shall rest and continue in, and be exercised and executed by, the Governor-General and Council remaining and surviving; and from and after the expiration of the said term of five years, the power of nominating and removing the succeeding Governor-General and Council shall be vested in the Directors of the said United Company.

xiii. And whereas His late Majesty King George the Second did, by his letters patent, bearing date at Westminster the eighth day of January, in the twenty-sixth year of his reign, grant unto the said United Company of Merchants of England trading to the East Indies his royal charter, thereby, amongst other things, constituting and establishing courts of civil, criminal, and ecclesiastical jurisdiction, at the said United Company's respective settlements at Madras-patnam, Bombay on the island of Bombay, and Fort William in Bengal; which said charter does not sufficiently provide for the due administration of justice in such manner as the state and condition of the Company's Presidency of Fort William in Bengal, so long as the said Company shall continue in the possession of the territorial acquisitions before mentioned, do and must require; be it therefore enacted by the authority aforesaid, that it shall and may be lawful for His Majesty, by charter, or letters patent under the great seal of Great Britain, to erect and establish a supreme court of judicature at Fort William aforesaid, to consist of a chief justice and three other judges, being barristers in England or Ireland, of not less than five years standing, to be named from time to time by His Majesty, his heirs and successors; which said Supreme Court of Judicature shall have, and the same Court is hereby declared to have, full power and authority to exercise and perform all civil, criminal, admiralty, and ecclesiastical jurisdiction, and to appoint such clerks, and other ministerial officers of the said Court, with such reasonable salaries, as shall be approved of by the said Governor-General and Council; and to form and establish such rules of practice, and such rules for the process of the said Court, and to do all such other things as shall be found necessary for the administration of justice, and the due execution of all or any of the powers which, by the said charter, shall or may be granted and committed to the said Court; and also shall be, at all times, a court of record, and shall be a court of oyer and terminer, and gaol delivery, in and for the said town of Calcutta, and factory of Fort William, in Bengal aforesaid, and the limits thereof, and the factories subordinate thereto.

XIV. Provided nevertheless, and be it further enacted by the authority aforesaid, that the said new charter which His Majesty is herein-before empowered to grant, and the jurisdiction, powers, and authorities, to be thereby established shall and may extend to all British subjects who shall reside in the kingdoms or provinces of Bengal, Behar, and Orissa, or any of them, under the protection of the said United Company; and the same charter shall be competent and effectual; and the Supreme Court of Judicature therein, and thereby to be established, shall have full power and authority to hear and determine all complaints against any of His Majesty's subjects for any crimes, misdemeanours, or oppressions, committed, or to be committed; and also to entertain, hear, and determine, any suits or actions whatsoever, against any of His Majesty's subjects in Bengal, Behar, and Orissa, and any suit, action or complaint against any person who shall, at the time when such debt, or cause of action, or complaint, shall have arisen, have been employed by, or shall then have been, directly or indirectly, in the service of the said United Company or of any of His Majesty's subjects.

XXIII. And be it further enacted by the authority aforesaid, that no Governor-General, or any of the Council of the said United Company's Presidency of Fort William in Bengal, or any Chief Justice, or any of the Judges of the Supreme Court of Judicature at Fort William aforesaid, shall directly, or indirectly, by themselves, or by any other person or persons for his or their use, or on his or their behalf accept, receive, or take, of or from any person or persons, in any manner, or on any account whatsoever, any present, gift, donation, gratuity, or reward pecuniary or otherwise, or any promise or engagement for any present, gift, donation, gratuity, or reward; and that no Governor-General, or any of the said Council, or any Chief Justice or Judge of the said Court, shall carry on, be concerned in, or have any dealing or transactions, by way of traffick or commerce of any kind whatsoever, either for his or their use or benefit, profit or advantage, or for the benefit or advantage of any other person or persons whatsoever (the trade and commerce of the said United Company only excepted); any usage or custom to the contrary thereof in anywise notwithstanding.

xxiv. And be it further enacted by the authority aforesaid, that from and after the first day of August, one thousand seven hundred and seventy-four, no person holding or exercising any civil or military office under the Crown, or the said United Company in the East Indies, shall accept, receive, or take, direct or indirectly, by himself, or any other person or persons on his behalf, or for his use or benefit, of and from any of the Indian princes or powers, or their ministers or agents (or any of the natives of Asia), any present, gift, donation, gratuity, or reward, pecuniary or otherwise, upon any account or on any pretence whatsoever; or any promise or engagement for any present, gift, donation, gratuity or reward; and if any person, holding or exercising any such civil or military office, shall be guilty of any such offence, and shall be thereof legally convicted in such Supreme Court at Calcutta, or in the Mayor's Court in any other of the said United Company's settlements where such offence shall have been committed; every such person so convicted, shall forfeit double the value of such present, gift, donation, gratuity, or reward, so taken and received; one moiety of which forfeiture shall be to the said United Company, and the other moiety to him or them who shall inform or prosecute for the same; and also shall and may be sent to England, by the order of the Governor and Council of the Presidency or settlement where the offender shall be convicted, unless such person so convicted shall give sufficient security to remove him or themselves within twelve months after such conviction.

xxxvi. And be it further enacted by the authority aforesaid, that it shall and may be lawful for the Governor-General and Council of the said United Company's settlement at Fort William in Bengal, from time to time, to make and issue such rules, ordinances, and regulations, for the good order and civil government of the said United Company's settlement at Fort William aforesaid, and other factories and places subordinate, or to be subordinate thereto, as shall be deemed just and reasonable (such rules, ordinances, and regulations, not being repugnant to the laws of the realm), and to set, impose, inflict, and levy, reasonable fines and forfeitures for the breach or non-observance of such rules, ordinances, and regulations; but nevertheless the same, or any of them, shall not be valid, or of any force or effect, until the same shall be duly registered and published in the said Supreme Court of Judicature, which shall be, by the said new charter, established, with the consent and approbation of the said Court, which registry shall not be made until the expiration of twenty days after the same shall be openly published, and a copy thereof affixed in some conspicuous part of the court-house or place where the said Supreme Court shall be held; and from and immediately after such registry as aforesaid, the same shall be good and valid in law; but, nevertheless, it shall be lawful for any person or persons in India to appeal therefrom to his Majesty, his heirs or successors, in Council, who are hereby empowered, if they think fit, to set aside and repeal any such rules, ordinances, and regulations respectively, so as such appeal, or notice thereof, be lodged in the said new Court of Judicature, within the space of sixty days after the time of the registering and publishing the same; and it shall be lawful for any person or persons in England to appeal therefrom in like manner, within sixty days after the publishing the same in England; and it is hereby directed and required that a copy of such rules, ordinances, and regulations, from time to time, as the same shall be so received, shall be affixed in some conspicuous and public place in the India House, there to remain and be resorted to as occasion shall require; yet nevertheless, such appeal shall not obstruct, impede, or hinder the immediate execution of any rule, ordinance, or regulation, so made and registered as aforesaid, until the same shall appear to have been set aside or repealed, upon the hearing and determination of such appeal.

XXXVII. Provided always, and be it enacted by the authority aforesaid, that the said Governor-General and Council shall, and they are hereby required, from time to time, to transmit copies of all such rules, ordinances, and regulations, as they shall make and issue, to one of His Majesty's principal Secretaries of State for the time being, and that it shall and may be lawful to and for His Majesty, his heirs and successors, from time to time, as they shall think necessary, to signify to the said United Company, under his or their sign manual, his or their disapprobation and disallowance of all such rules, ordinances, and regulations; and that from and immediately after the time that such disapprobation shall be duly registered and published in the said Supreme Court of Judicature at Fort William in Bengal, all such rules, ordinances, and regulations, shall be null and void; but in case His Majesty, his heirs and successors, shall not, within the space of two years from the making of such rules, ordinances, and regulations, signify his or their disapprobation or disallowance thereof, as aforesaid, that then, and in that case, all such rules, ordinances, and regulations, shall be valid and effectual, and have full force.

XXXVIII. And be it further enacted by the authority aforesaid, that the

Governor-General and Council for the time being of the said United Company's settlement at Fort William aforesaid, and the Chief Justice and other Judges of the said Supreme Court of Judicature, shall and may, and they are hereby respectively declared to be, and to have full power and authority to act as justices of the peace for the said settlement, and for the several settlements and factories subordinate thereto; and to do and transact all matters and things which to the office of a justice or justices of the peace do belong and appertain; and for that purpose the said Governor-General and Council are hereby authorized and empowered to hold quarter-sessions within the said settlement of Fort William aforesaid, four times in every year, and the same shall be at all times a court of record.

XXXIX. And be it further enacted by the authority aforesaid, that if any Governor-General, President, or Governor, or Council of any of the said Company's principal or other settlements in India, or the Chief Justice, or any of the Judges of the said Supreme Court of Judicature, to be by the said new charter established, or of any other court in any of the said United Company's settlements, or any other person or persons who now are, or heretofore have been employed by or in the service of the said United Company, in any civil or military station, office, or capacity, or who have or claim, or heretofore have had or claimed, any power or authority, or jurisdiction, by or from the said United Company, or any of His Majesty's subjects residing in India, shall commit any offence against this act, or shall have been, or shall be guilty of, any crime, misdemeanour, or offence, committed against any of His Majesty's subjects, or any of the inhabitants of India within their respective jurisdictions, all such crimes, offences and misdemeanours, may be respectively inquired of, heard, tried, and determined in His Majesty's Court of King's Bench, and all such persons so offending, and not having been before tried for the same offence in India, shall, on conviction, in any such case as is not otherwise specially provided for by this Act, be liable to such fine or corporal punishment as the said Court shall think fit; and moreover shall be liable, at the discretion of the said Court, to be adjudged to be incapable of serving the said United Company in any office, civil or military; and all and every such crimes, offences, and misdemeanours, as aforesaid, may be alleged to be committed, and may be laid, inquired of, and tried in the county of Middlesex.

XL. And whereas the provisions made by former laws for the hearing and determining in England offences committed in India have been found ineffectual, by reason of the difficulty of proving in this kingdom matters done there; be it further enacted by the authority aforesaid, that in all cases of indictments or informations, laid or exhibited in the said Court of King's Bench, for misdemeanours or offences committed in India, it shall and may be lawful for His Majesty's said Court, upon motion to be made on behalf of the prosecutor, or of the defendant or defendants, to award a writ or writs of mandamus, requiring the Chief Justice and Judges of the said Supreme Court of Judicature for the time being, or the Judges of the Mayor's Court at Madras, Bombay, or Bencoolen, as the case may require, who are hereby respectively authorized and required accordingly to hold a court, with all convenient speed, for the examination of witnesses, and receiving other proofs concerning the matters charged in such indictments or informations respectively; and, in the meantime, to cause such public notice to be given of the holding of the said Court, and to issue such summons or other process, as may be requisite for the attendance of witnesses, and of the agents or counsel, of all or any of the parties respectively, and to adjourn, from time to time as occasion may require; and such examination as aforesaid shall be then and there openly and publicly taken viva voce in the said Court, upon the respective oaths of witnesses, and the oaths of skilful interpreters, administered according to the forms of their several religions; and shall, by some sworn officer of such Court, be reduced into one or more writing or writings on parchment in case any duplicate or duplicates should be required by or on behalf of any of the parties interested, and shall be sent to His Majesty, in his Court of King's Bench, closed up, and under the seals of two or more of the judges of the said Court, and one or more of the said judges shall deliver the same to the agent or agents of the party or parties requiring the same; which said agent or agents (or in case of his or their death, the person into whose hands the same shall come) shall deliver the same to one of the clerks in court of His Majesty's Court of King's Bench, in the public office, and make oath that he received the same from the hands of one or more of the judges of such court in India (or if such agent be dead, in what manner the same came into his hands): and that the same has not been opened, or altered, since he so received it (which said oath such clerk in court is hereby authorized and required to administer): and such depositions, being duly taken and returned, according to the true intent and meaning of this Act, shall be allowed and read, and shall be deemed as good and competent evidence as if such witness had been present, and sworn and examined viva voce at any trial for such crimes or misdemeanours, as aforesaid, in His Majesty's said Court of King's Bench, any law or usage to the contrary notwithstanding; and all parties concerned shall be entitled to take copies of such depositions at their own costs and charges.

XLI. And be it further enacted by the authority aforesaid, that in case the said Chief Justice, or Judges of the said Supreme Court of Judicature, or any of them, for the time being, shall commit any offence against this Act, or be guilty of any corrupt practice, or other crime, offence, or misdemeanour, in the execution of their respective offices, it shall and may be lawful for His Majesty's said Court of King's Bench in England, upon an information or indictment laid or exhibited in the said Court for such crime, offence, or misdemeanour, upon motion to be made in the said Court, to award such writ or writs of mandamus, as aforesaid, requiring the Governor-General, and Council of the said United Company's settlement at Fort William aforesaid, who are hereby respectively authorized and required accordingly to assemble themselves in a reasonable time, and to cause all such proceedings to be had and made as are herein-before respectively directed and prescribed concerning the examination of witnesses; and such examination, so taken, shall be returned and proceeded upon in the same manner, in all respects as if the several directions herein-before prescribed and enacted in that behalf were again repeated.

SOURCE: This can be found in volume 1 of *Speeches and Documents on India Policy, 1750–1921*, ed. Arthur Berridale Keith (London: Oxford University Press, 1922).

The Constitution of the East India Company
JAMES MILL

[James Mill (1773–1836) was a prominent philosopher, historian, and economist—the Scottish son of a Presbyterian minister and abolitionist. Mill was also a theorist and practitioner of Utilitarianism, a combined scientific and humanistic approach to politics, economics, and social concerns. Mill and Jeremy Bentham established the *Edinburgh Review*, and Mill helped to found the University of London. James Mill's intellectual and philosophical commitments would highly influence the writing and thinking of his son, John Stuart Mill.]

When the competitors for Indian commerce were united into one corporate body, and the privilege of exclusive trade was founded on legislative authority, the business of the East India Company became regular and uniform. Their capital, composed of the shares of the subscribers, was a fixed and definite sum: Of the modes of dealing, adapted to the nature of the business, little information remained to be acquired: Their proceedings were reduced to an established routine, or a series of operations periodically recurring: A general description, therefore, of the plan upon which the Company conducted themselves, and a statement of its principal results, appear to comprehend every thing which falls within the design of a history of that commercial body, during a period of several years.

When a number of individuals unite themselves in any common interest, reason suggests, that they themselves should manage as much as it is convenient for them to manage; and that they should make choice of persons to execute for them such parts of the business as cannot be conveniently transacted by themselves.

It was upon this principle, that the adventurers in the trade to India originally framed the constitution of their Company. They met in assemblies, which were called Courts of Proprietors, and transacted certain parts of the common business: And they chose a certain number of persons, belonging to their own body, and who were called Committees,[1] to manage for them other parts of the business, which they could not so well perform themselves. The whole of the managing business, therefore, or the whole of the government, was in the hands of,

1st. The Proprietors, assembled in general court;

2dly. The Committees, called afterwards the Directors, assembled in their special courts.

At the time of the award of the Earl of Godolphin, power was distributed between these assemblies according to the following plan:

To have a vote in the Court of Proprietors, that is, any share in its power, it was necessary to be the owner of 500*l.* of the Company's stock: and no additional share, contrary to a more early regulation, gave any advantage, or more to any single proprietor than a single vote.

The Directors were twenty-four in number: No person was competent to be chosen as a Director who possessed less than 2,000*l.* of the Company's stock: And of these Directors, one was Chairman, and another Deputy-Chairman, presiding in the Courts.

The Directors were chosen annually by the Proprietors in their General Court; and no Director could serve for more than a year, except by re-election.

Four Courts of Proprietors, or General Courts, were held regularly in each year, in the month of December, March, June, and September, respectively; the Directors might summon Courts at other times, as often as they saw cause, and were bound to summon Courts within ten days, upon a requisition signed by any nine of the Proprietors, qualified to vote.

The Courts of Directors, of whom thirteen were requisite to constitute a Court, were held by appointment of the Directors themselves, as often, and at

---

1. *Committees;* i.e. Persons to whom something is committed, or entrusted.

such times and places, as they might deem expedient for the dispatch of affairs.[2]

According to this constitution, the supreme power was vested in the Court of Proprietors. In the first place, they held the legislative power entire: All laws and regulations, all determinations of dividend, all grants of money, were made by the Court of Proprietors. To act under their ordinances, and manage the business of routine, was the department reserved for the Court of Directors. In the second place, the supreme power was secured to the Court of Proprietors, by the important power of displacing, annually, the persons whom they chose to act in their behalf.

In this constitution, if the Court of Proprietors be regarded as representing the general body of the people, the Court of Directors as representing an aristocratical senate, and the Chairman as representing the sovereign, we have an image of the British constitution; a system, in which the forms of the different species of government, the monarchical, aristocratical, and democratical, are mixed and combined.

In the constitution, however, of the East India Company, the power allotted to the democratical part was so great, that a small portion may seem to have been reserved to the other two. Not only were the sovereignty, and the aristocracy, both elective, but they were elected from year to year; that is, were in a state of complete dependence upon the democratical part. This was not all: no decrees, but those of the democracy, were binding, at least in the last resort; the aristocracy, therefore, and monarchy, were subordinate, and subject. Under the common impression of democratic ambition, irregularity, and violence, it might be concluded, that the democratic assembly would grasp at the whole of the power; would constrain and disturb the proceedings of the Chairmen, and Directors; would deliberate with violence and animosity; and exhibit all the confusion, precipitation, and imprudence, which are so commonly ascribed to the exercise of popular power.

The actual result is extremely different from what the common modes of reasoning incite common minds to infer. Notwithstanding the power which, by the theory of the constitution, was thus reserved to the popular part of the system, all power has centered in the Court of Directors; and the government of the Company has been an oligarchy, in fact. So far from meddling too much, the Court of Proprietors have not attended to the common affairs even sufficiently for the business of inspection: And the known principles of human nature abundantly secured that unfortunate result. To watch, to scrutinize, to inquire, is labour, and labour is pain. To confide, to take for granted

---

2. Letters Patent. 10 Will. III., Collection of Charters. &c.

that all is well, is easy, is exempt from labour, and, to the great mass of mankind, comparatively delightful. On all ordinary occasions, on all occasions which present not a powerful motive to action, the great mass of mankind are sure to be led by the soft and agreeable feeling. And if they who act have only sufficient prudence to avoid those occurrences which are calculated to rouse the people on account of whom they act, the people will allow them abundant scope to manage the common concerns in a way conformable to their own liking and advantage. It is thus that all constitutions, however democratically formed, have a tendency to become oligarchical in practice. By the numerous body, who constitute the democracy, the objects of ambition are beheld at so great a distance, and the competition for them is shared with so great a number, that in general they make but a feeble impression upon their minds: The small number, on the other hand, entrusted with the management, feel so immediately the advantages, and their affections are so powerfully engaged by the presence, of their object, that they easily concentrate their views, and point their energies with perfect constancy in the selfish direction. The apathy and inattention of the people, on the one hand, and the interested activity of the rulers on the other, are two powers, the action of which may always be counted upon; nor has the art of government as yet exemplified, however the science may or may not have discovered, any certain means by which the unhappy effects of that action may be prevented.[3]

For conducting the affairs of the Company, the Directors divided themselves into parties, called Committees; and the business into as many separate shares.[4]

The first was the Committee of Correspondence, of which the business was more confidential, as well as extensive, than that of any of the rest. Its duties were, To study the advices from India, and to prepare answers for the inspection of the Court of Directors: To report upon the number of ships expedient for the trade of the season, and the stations proper for each: To report upon the number of servants, civil and military, in the different stations abroad; on the demand for alterations, and the applications made for leave of

---

3. Not in the East India Company alone; in the Bank of England also, the constitution of which is similar, oligarchy has always prevailed. Nor will the circumstances be found to differ in any joint stock association in the history of British Commerce. So little does experience countenance the dangerous maxim, of the people's being always eager to grasp at too much power, that the great difficulty, in regard to good government, is, to get them really to exercise that degree of power, their own exercise of which good government absolutely requires.

4. The following account is derived from an official report on the business of the Committees, called for by the Board of Control, and transmitted officially by the Court of Directors, of which the substance is given in Mr. Bruce's Historical View of Plans for the Government of British India, p. 600.

absence, or leave to return: All complaints of grievances, and all pecuniary demands on the Company, were decided upon in the first instance by this Committee, which nominated to all places, in the treasury, and in the secretary's, examiner's, and auditor's offices. It performed, in fact, the prime and governing business of the Company: The rest was secondary and subordinate.

The next Committee was that of Law-suits; of which the business was to deliberate and direct in all cases of litigation; and to examine the bills of law charges. It is not a little remarkable that there should be work of this description sufficient to engross the time of a committee.

The third was the Committee of Treasury. Its business was, to provide, agreeably to the orders of the Court, for the payment of dividends and interest on bonds; to negociate the Company's loans; to purchase gold and silver for exportation: to affix the Company's seal to bonds and other deeds; to examine monthly, or oftener, the balance of cash; and to decide, in the first instance, on applications respecting the loss of bonds, on pecuniary questions in general, and the delivery of unregistered diamonds and bullion.

The Committee of Warehouses was the fourth. The business of importation was the principal part of its charge. It frames the orders for the species of goods of which the investment or importation was intended to consist: It had the superintendance of the servants employed in the inspection of the purchases; determined upon the modes of shipping and conveyance; superintended the landing and warehousing of the goods; arranged the order of sales; and deliberated generally upon the means of promoting and improving the trade.

The fifth was the Committee of Accounts: of whose duties the principal were, to examine bills of exchange, and money certificates; to compare advices with bills; to examine the estimates, and accounts of cash and stock; and to superintend the office of the accountant, and the office of transfer, in which are effected the transfers of the Company's stock and annuities, and in which the foreign letters of attorney for that purpose are examined.

A committee, called the Committee of Buying, was the sixth. Its business was, to superintend the purchase and preparation of the standard articles of export, of which lead and woollens constituted the chief; to contract with the dyers and other tradesmen; to audit their accounts, and keep charge of the goods till deposited in the ships for exportation.

The Committee of the House was the seventh, and its business was mostly of an inferior and ministerial nature. The alterations and repairs of the buildings, regulations for the attendance of the several officers and clerks, the appointment of the inferior servants of the House, and the control of the secretary's accounts for domestic disbursements, were included in its province.

The eighth Committee, that of Shipping, had the charge of purchasing stores, and all other articles of export, except the grand articles appropriated to the Committee of Buying; the business of hiring ships, and of ascertaining the qualifications of their commanders and officers; of distributing the outward cargoes; of fixing seamen's wages; of issuing orders for building, repairing, and fitting out the ships, packets, &c. of which the Company were proprietors; and of regulating and determining the tonage allowed for private trade, to the commanders and officers of the Company's ships.

The ninth was the Committee of Private Trade; and its occupation was to adjust the accounts of freight, and other charges, payable on the goods exported for private account, in the chartered ships of the Company; to regulate the indulgences to private trade homeward; and, by examining the commanders of ships, and other inquiries, to ascertain how far the regulations of the Company had been violated or obeyed.

The tenth Committee was of a characteristic description. It was the Committee for preventing the growth of Private Trade. Its business was to take cognizance of all instances in which the license, granted by the Company for private trade, was exceeded; to decide upon the controversies to which the encroachments of the private traders gave birth; and to make application of the penalties which were provided for transgression. So closely, however, did the provinces of this and the preceding Committee border upon one another; and so little, in truth, were their boundaries defined, that the business of the one was not unfrequently transferred to the other.

The powers exercised by the Governor or President and Council, were, in the first place, those of masters in regard to servants over all the persons who were in the employment of the Company; and as the Company were the sole master, without fellow or competitor, and those under them had adopted their service as the business of their lives, the power of the master, in reality, and in the majority of cases, extended to almost every thing valuable to man. With regard to such of their countrymen, as were not in their service, the Company were armed with powers to seize them, to keep them in confinement, and send them to England, an extent of authority which amounted to confiscation of goods, to imprisonment, and what to a European constitution is the natural effect of any long confinement under an Indian climate, actual death. At an early period of the Company's history, it had been deemed necessary to intrust them with the powers of martial law, for the government of the troops which they maintained in defence of their factories and presidencies; and by a charter of Charles II., granted them in 1661, the Presidents and Councils in their factories were empowered to exercise civil and criminal jurisdiction according to the laws of England. Under this sanction they had exercised judicial powers, during all the changes which their affairs had undergone; but at last it appeared desirable that so important an article of their authority should rest on a better foundation. In the year 1726 a charter was granted, by which the Company were permitted to establish a Mayor's Court at each of their three presidencies, Bombay, Madras, and Calcutta; consisting of a mayor and nine aldermen, empowered to decide in civil cases of all descriptions. From this jurisdiction, the President and Council were erected into a Court of Appeal. They were also vested with the power of holding Courts of Quarter Sessions for the exercise of penal judicature, in all cases, excepting those of high treason. And a Court of Requests, or Court of Conscience, was instituted, for the decision, by summary procedure, of pecuniary questions of inconsiderable amount.

This reform in the judicature of India was not attended with all the beneficial effects which were probably expected from it. Negligence was left to corrupt the business of detail. The charter is said to have been procured by the influence of an individual, for the extension of his own authority; and when his ends were gained, his solicitude expired. The persons appointed to fill the judicial offices were the servants of the Company, bred to commerce, and nursed in its details: while a manuscript book of instructions comprised the whole of the assistance which the wisdom of the King and the Company provided to guide uninstructed men in the administration of justice.

Nor was the obscurity of the English law, and the inexperience of the judges, the only source of the many evils which the new arrangements continued, or produced. Jealousy arose between the Councils, and the Mayor's Courts. The Councils complained that the Courts encroached upon their authority: and the Courts complained that they were oppressed by the Councils. The most violent dissensions often prevailed; and many of the members of the Mayor's Courts quitted the service, and went home with their animosities and complaints.

Besides the above-mentioned tribunals established by the Company for the administration of the British laws to the British people in India, they erected, in the capacity of Zemindar of the district around Calcutta, the usual Zemindary Courts, for the administration of the Indian laws to the Indian people. The Phousdary Court, for the trial of crimes; and the Cutcherry for civil causes; beside the Collector's Court for matters of revenue. The judges, in these tribunals, were servants of the Company, appointed by the Governor and Council, and holding their offices during pleasure; the rule of judgment was the supposed usage of the country, and the discretion of the court; and the mode of procedure was summary. Punishments extended to fine; imprisonment; labour upon the roads in chains for a limited time, or for life; and flagellation, either to a limited degree, or death. The ideas of honour, prevalent among the natives, induced the Mogul government to forbid the European mode of capital punishment, by hanging, in the case of a Mussulman. In compensation, however, it had no objection to his being whipped to death; and the flagellants in India are said to be so dextrous, as to kill a man with a few strokes of the chawbuck.[5]

The executive and judicial functions were combined in the Councils, at the Indian presidencies; the powers even of justices of the peace being granted to the Members of Council, and to them alone. If complaints were not wanting of the oppression by these authorities upon their fellow-servants; it is abundantly evident that the Company were judge in their own cause in all cases in which the dispute existed between them and any other party.

The President was Commander-in-Chief of the Military Force maintained within his presidency. It consisted, partly of the recruits sent out in the ships of the Company; partly of deserters from the other European nations settled in India, French, Dutch, and Portuguese; and partly, at least at Bombay and Surat, of Topasses, or persons whom we may dominate Indo-Portuguese, either the mixed produce of Portuguese and Indian parents, or converts to the Portuguese, from the Indian, faith. These were troops disciplined and uniformed; besides whom, the natives were already, to a small extent, employed by the Company in military service, and called Sepoys, from the Indian term Sipahi, equivalent to soldier. They were made to use the musket, but remained chiefly armed in the fashion of the country, with sword and target; they wore the Indian dress, the turban, *cabay* or vest, and long drawers; and were provided with native officers according to the custom of the country; but ultimately all under English command. It had not as yet been attempted to train them to the European discipline, in which it was possible to render them so expert and steady; but considerable service was derived from them; and under the conduct of European leaders they were found capable of facing danger with great constancy and firmness. What at this time was the average number at each presidency, is not particularly stated. It is mentioned, that at the time when the presidency was established at Calcutta in 1707, an effort was made to augment the garrison to 300 men.

The President was the organ of correspondence, by letter, or otherwise,

---

5. Seventh Report from the Committee of Secrecy on the State of the East India Company, in 1773.

with the country powers. It rested with him to communicate to the Council the account of what he thus transacted, at any time, and in any form, which he deemed expedient; and from this no slight accession to his power was derived.

The several denominations of the Company's servants in India were, writers, factors, junior merchants, and senior merchants: the business of the writers, as the term, in some degree, imports, was that of clerking, with the inferior details of commerce; and when dominion succeeded, of government. In the capacity of writers they remained during five years. The first promotion was to the rank of factor; the next to that of junior merchant; in each of which the period of service was three years. After this extent of service, they became senior merchants. And out of the class of senior merchants were taken by seniority the members of the Council, and, when no particular appointment interfered, even the presidents themselves.

Shortly after the first great era, in the history of the British commerce with India, the nation was delivered from the destructive burthen of the long war with France which preceded the treaty of Utrecht: And though the accession of a new family to the throne, and the resentments which one party of statesmen had to gratify against another, kept the minds of men for a time in a feverish anxiety, not the most favourable to the persevering studies and pursuits on which the triumphs of industry depend, the commerce and wealth of the nation made rapid advances.

SOURCE: In *The History of British India* (Chicago: University of Chicago Press, 1975). This document was originally published in 1817.

Letter to Durmont
JAMES MILL

[In the following letter from 1819, James Mill comments on his service in the executive government of the Company, which he entered in that same year.]

The time of attendance is from 10 till 4, six hours; and the business, though laborious enough, is to me highly interesting. It is the very essence of the internal government of 60 millions of people with whom I have to deal; and as you know that the government of India is carried on by correspondence; and that I am the only man whose business it is, or who has the time to make himself master of the facts scattered in a most voluminous correspondence, on which a just decision must rest, you will conceive to what an extent the real decision on matters belonging to my department rests with the man who is in my situation.

SOURCE: In vol. 3 of *The Works and Correspondence of David Ricardo*, 11 vols., ed. Piero Sraffa (Cambridge: University Press for the Royal Economic Society, 1951–1973), 40, letter 1819021. David Ricardo (1772–1823), an associate of James Mill, was a British economist who was influenced by the works of James Mill, Adam Smith, Jeremy Bentham, and Thomas Malthus.

Excerpt from *Autobiography*
JOHN STUART MILL

[John Stuart Mill (1806–1873) was a philosopher, economist, and lifelong social reformer. He founded the *Westminster Review*, the journal of radical philosophers and reformers. In 1823 he entered the Company's service, where he remained in high administrative office until the Company's abolition in 1858. Mill also served as the head of the Examiner's Office in India House from 1856 to 1858, a period during which he opposed the transfer of the East India Company to the British Crown. His influential works include *Essays on Some Unsettled Questions of Political Economy* (1844) and *Principles of Political Economy* (1848). In the following excerpt, Mill comments on his father's service to the Company.]

In this office [of assistant examiner], and in that of Examiner, which he subsequently attained, the influence which his talents, his reputation, and his decision of character gave him, with superiors who really desired the good government of India, enabled him to a great extent to throw into his drafts of despatches, and to carry through the ordeal of the Court of Directors and Board of Control, without having their force much weakened, his real opinions on Indian subjects. In his History he had set forth, for the first time, many of the true principles of Indian adminstration: and his despatches, following his History, did more than had ever been done before to promote the improvement of India, and teach Indian officials to understand their business. If a selection of them were published, they would, I am convinced, place his character as a practical statesman fully on a level with his eminence as a speculative writer.

SOURCE: Can be found in John Stuart Mill, *Autobiography* (Longmans, Green, Reader, and Dyer, 1873; reprint, London: Oxford University Press, 1924).

Government of India Act, 1833

III. Provided always, and be it enacted, that from and after the said twenty-second day of April one thousand eight hundred and thirty-four the exclusive right of trading with the Dominions of the Emperor of China, and of trading in tea, continued to the said Company by the said Act of the fifty-third year of King George the Third, shall cease.

IV. And be it enacted, that the said Company shall, with all convenient speed after the said twenty-second day of April one thousand eight hundred and thirty-four, close their commercial business, and make sale of all their merchandize and effects at home and abroad, distinguished in their account books as commercial assets, and all their warehouses, lands, tenements, hereditaments, and property whatsoever which may not be retained for the purposes of the Government of the said territories, and get in all debts due to them on account of the commercial branch of their affairs, and reduce their commercial establishments as the same shall become unnecessary, and discontinue and abstain from all commercial business which shall not be incident to the closing of their actual concerns, and to the conversion into money of the property hereinbefore directed to be sold, or which shall not be carried on for the purposes of the said Government.

XXXIX. And be it enacted, that the superintendence, direction, and control of the whole civil and military Government of all the said territories and revenues in India shall be and is hereby invested in a Governor-General and Counsellors, to be styled 'The Governor General of India in Council.'

XL. And be it enacted, that there shall be four ordinary members of the said Council, three of whom shall from time to time be appointed by the said Court of Directors from amongst such persons as shall be or shall have been servants of the said Company; and each of the said three ordinary members of Council shall at the time of his appointment have been in the service of the said Company for at least ten years; and if he shall be in the military service of the said Company, he shall not during his continuance in office as a member of Council hold any military command, or be employed in actual military duties; and that the fourth ordinary member of Council shall from time to time be appointed from amongst persons who shall not be servants of the said Company by the said Court of Directors, subject to the approbation of His Majesty, to be signified in writing by his royal Sign Manual, countersigned by the President of the said Board; provided that such last-mentioned Member of Council shall not be entitled to sit or vote in the said Council except at meetings thereof for making laws and regulations; and it shall be lawful for the said Court of Directors to appoint the Commander-in-Chief of the Company's forces in India, and if there shall be no such Commander-in-Chief, or the offices of such Commander-in-Chief and of Governor-General of India shall be vested in the same person, then the Commander-in-Chief of the forces on the Bengal establishment, to be an extraordinary member of the said Council, and such extraordinary member of Council shall have rank and precedence at the Council Board, next after the Governor-General.

XLI. And be it enacted, that the person who shall be Governor-General of the Presidency of Fort William in Bengal on the twenty-second day of April one thousand eight hundred and thirty four shall be the first Governor-General of India under this act, and such persons as shall be members of Council of the same Presidency on that day shall be respectively members of the Council constituted by this Act.

XLII. And be it enacted, that all vacancies happening in the office of Governor-General of India shall from time to time be filled up by the said Court of Directors, subject to the approbation of His Majesty, to be signified in writing by his royal Sign Manual, countersigned by the President of the said Board.

XLIII. And be it enacted, that the said Governor-General in Council shall have power to make laws and regulations for repealing, amending, or altering any laws or regulations whatever now in force or hereafter to be in force in the said territories or any part thereof, and to make laws and regulations for all persons, whether British or native, foreigners or others, and for all courts of justice, whether established by His Majesty's charters or otherwise, and the jurisdictions thereof, and for all places and things whatsoever within and throughout the whole and every part of the said territories, and for all servants of the said Company within the dominions of princes and states in alliance with the said Company; save and except that the said Governor-General in Council shall not have the power of making any laws or regulations which shall in any way repeal, vary, suspend, or affect any of the provisions of this act, or any of the provisions of the acts for punishing mutiny and desertion of officers and soldiers, whether in the service of His Majesty or the said Company, or any provisions of any act hereafter to be passed in anywise affecting the said Company or the said territories or the inhabitants thereof, or any laws or regulations which shall in any way affect any prerogative of the Crown, or the authority of Parliament, or the constitution or rights of the said Company, or any part of the unwritten laws or constitution of the United Kingdom of Great Britain and Ireland whereon may depend in any degree the allegiance of any person to the Crown of the United Kingdom, or the sovereignty or dominion of the said Crown over any part of the said territories.

LI. Provided always, and be it enacted, that nothing herein contained shall extend to affect in any way the right of Parliament to make laws for the said territories and for all the inhabitants thereof; and it is expressly declared that a full, complete, and constantly existing right and power is intended to be reserved to Parliament to control, supersede, or prevent all proceedings and acts whatsoever of the said Governor-General in Council, and to repeal and alter at any time any law or regulation whatsoever made by the said Governor-General in Council, and in all respects to legislate for the said territories and all the inhabitants thereof in as full and ample a manner as if this Act had not been passed; and the better to enable Parliament to exercise at all times such right and power, all laws and regulations made by the said Governor-General in Council shall be transmitted to England, and laid before both Houses of Parliament, in the same manner as is now by law provided concerning the rules and regulations made by the several governments in India.

LII. And be it enacted, that all enactments, provisions, matters, and things relating to the Governor-General of Fort William in Bengal in Council and the Governor-General of Fort William in Bengal alone, respectively, in any other act or acts contained, so far as the same are now in force, and not repealed by or repugnant to the provisions of this act, shall continue and be in force and be applicable to the Governor-General of India in Council, and to the Governor-General of India alone, respectively.

LIII. And whereas it is expedient that, subject to such special arrangements as local circumstances may require, a general system of judicial establishments and police, to which all persons whatsoever, as well Europeans as natives, may be subject, should be established in the said territories at an early period, and that such laws as may be applicable in common to all classes of the inhabitants of the said territories, due regard being had to the rights, feelings, and peculiar usages of the people, should be enacted, and that all laws and customs having the force of law within the same territories should be ascertained and consolidated, and as occasion may require amended; be it therefore enacted, that the said Governor-General of India in Council shall, as soon as conveniently may be after the passing of this act, issue a commission, and from time to time commissions, to such persons as the said Court of Directors, with the approbation of the said Board of Commissioners, shall recommend for that purpose, and to such other persons, if necessary, as the said Governor-General in Council shall think fit, all such persons, not exceeding in the whole at any one time five in number, and to be styled 'the Indian Law Commissioners', with all such powers as shall be necessary for the purposes hereinafter mentioned; and the said Commissioners shall fully inquire into the jurisdiction, powers, and rules of the existing Courts of Justice and police establishments in the said territories, and all existing forms of judicial procedure, and into the nature and operation of all law, whether civil or criminal, written or customary prevailing and in force in any part of the said territories, and whereto any inhabitants of the said territories, whether Europeans or others, are now subject: and the said Commissioners shall from time to time make reports, in which they shall fully set forth the result of their said inquiries, and shall from time to time suggest such alterations as may in their opinion be beneficially made in the said Courts of Justice and police establishments, forms of judicial procedure and laws, due regard being had to the distinction of castes, difference of religion, and the manners and opinions prevailing among different races and in different parts of the said territories.

LXXXI. And be it enacted, that it shall be lawful for any natural-born subjects of His Majesty to proceed by sea to any port or place having a Custom-house establishment within the said territories, and to reside thereat, or to proceed to and reside in or pass through any part of such of the said territories as were under the Government of the said Company on the first day of January one thousand eight hundred, and in any part of the countries ceded by the Nabob of the Carnatic, of the Province of Cuttack, and of the settlements of Singapore and Malacca, without any licence whatever; provided that all subjects of His Majesty not natives of the said territories shall, on their arrival in any part of the said territories from any port or place not within the said territories, make known in writing their names, places of destination, and objects of pursuit in India, to the chief officer of the Customs or other officer authorized for that purpose at such port or place as aforesaid.

LXXXV. And whereas the removal of restrictions on the intercourse of Europeans with the said territories will render it necessary to provide against any mischief or dangers that may arise therefrom, be it therefore enacted, that the said Governor-General in Council shall and he is hereby required, by law or regulations, to provide with all convenient speed for the protection of the natives of the said territories from insult and outrage in their persons, religions, or opinions.

LXXXVII. And be it enacted, that no native of the said territories, nor any natural-born subject of His Majesty resident therein, shall, by reason only of his religion, place of birth, descent, colour, or any of them, be disabled from holding any place, or employment under the said Company.

CIII. And whereas it is expedient to provide for the due qualifications of persons to be employed in the Civil Service of the said Company in the said territories, be it therefore enacted, that the said Governor-General of India in Council shall as soon as may be after the first day of January in every year, make and transmit to the said Court of Directors a prospective estimate of the number of persons, who in the opinion of the said Governor-General in Council, will be necessary, in addition to those already in India or likely to return from Europe, to supply the expected vacancies in the civil establishments of the respective governments in India in such one of the subsequent years as shall be fixed in the rules and regulations hereinafter mentioned; and it shall be lawful for the said Board of Commissioners to reduce such estimate, so that the reasons for such reduction be given to the said Court of Directors; and in the month of June in every year, if the said estimate shall have been then received by the said Board, and if not, then within one month after such estimate shall have been received, the said Board of Commissioners shall certify to the said Court of Directors what number of persons shall be nominated as candidates for admission, and what number of students shall be admitted to the College of the said Company at Haileybury in the then current year, but so that at least four such candidates, no one of whom shall be under the age of seventeen or above the age of twenty years, be nominated, and no more than one student admitted for every such expected vacancy in the said civil establishments, according to such estimate or reduced estimate as aforesaid; and it shall be lawful for the said Court of Directors to nominate such a number of candidates for admission to the said College as shall be mentioned in the Certificate of the said Board; and if the said Court of Directors shall not within one month after the receipt of such Certificate nominate the whole number mentioned therein, it shall be lawful for the said Board of Commissioners to nominate so many as shall be necessary to supply the deficiency.

cv. And be it enacted, that the said Candidates for admission to the said College shall be subjected to an examination in such branches of knowledge and by such examiners as the said Board shall direct, and shall be classed in a list to be prepared by the examiners, and the Candidates whose names shall stand highest in such list shall be admitted by the said Court as students in the said College until the number to be admitted for that year, according to the Certificate of the said Board, be supplied.

SOURCE: This act can be found in volume 1 of *Speeches and Documents on India Policy, 1750–1921*, ed. Arthur Berridale Keith (London: Oxford University Press, 1922).

A Speech Delivered in the House of Commons on the 10th of July, 1833

LORD THOMAS BABINGTON MACAULAY

[Lord Macaulay, like John Mill, was the son of a Presbyterian minister; he was also a Whig parliamentarian and a social and political reformer. Macaulay served as the secretary for the board of control for the East India Company. In 1834 he was appointed to the Supreme Council of India, where he argued on behalf of the legal equality of Europeans and Indians. During his tenure, Macaulay also established a national system of education in India, advocated for the freedom of the Indian press, and drafted the Indian Penal Code. He later served as secretary of war (1839–1841). On his return to England, Macaulay combined his parliamentary duties with scholarly activities, writing essays, political commentary, and histories. One of his best-known historical works is his multivolume *The History of England from the Accession of James II* (1849–61).]

On Wednesday, the 10th of July, 1833, Mr. Charles Grant, President of the Board of Control, moved that the bill for effecting an arrangement with the India Company, and for the better government of His Majesty's Indian territories, should be read a second time. The motion was carried without a division, but not without a long debate, in the course of which the following Speech was made:

The Company had united in itself two characters, the character of trader and the character of sovereign. Between the trader and the sovereign there was a long and complicated account, almost every item of which furnished matter for litigation. While the monopoly continued, indeed, litigation was averted. The effect of the monopoly was to satisfy the claims both of commerce and of territory at the expense of a third party, the English people; to secure at once funds for the dividend of the stockholder, and funds for the government of the Indian empire, by means of a heavy tax on the tea consumed in this country. But, when the third party would no longer bear this charge, all the great financial questions which had, at the cost of that third party, been kept in abeyance, were opened in an instant. The connection between the Company in its mercantile capacity, and the same Company in its political capacity, was dissolved. Even if the Company were permitted, as has been suggested, to govern India and at the same time to trade with China, no advances would be made from the profits of its Chinese trade for the support of its Indian government. It was in consideration of the exclusive privilege that the Company had hitherto been required to make those advances; it was by the exclusive privilege that the Company had been enabled to make them. When that privilege was taken away, it would be unreasonable in the Legislature to impose such an obligation, and impossible for the Company to fulfil it. The whole system of loans from commerce to territory, and repayments from territory to commerce, must cease. Each party must rest altogether on its own resources. It was, therefore, absolutely necessary to ascertain what resources each party possessed, to bring the long and intricate account between them to a close, and to assign to each a fair portion of assets and liabilities. There was vast property. How much of that property was applicable to purposes of state? How much was applicable to a dividend? There were debts to the amount of many millions. Which of these were the debts of the government that ruled at Calcutta? Which of the great mercantile house that bought tea at Canton? Were the creditors to look to the land revenues of India for their money? Or were they entitled to put executions into the warehouses behind Bishopsgate Street?

We come, then, to the great question. Is it desirable to retain the Company as an organ of government for India? I think that it is desirable. The question is, I acknowledge, beset with difficulties. We have to solve one of the hardest problems in politics. We are trying to make brick without straw, to bring a clean thing out of an unclean, to give a good government to a people to whom we cannot give a free government. In this country, in any neighboring country, it is easy to frame securities against oppression. In Europe you have the materials of good government everywhere ready to your hands. The people are everywhere perfectly competent to hold some share, not in every country an equal share, but some share, of political power. If the question were, What is the best mode of securing good government in Europe? the merest smatterer in politics would answer, representative institutions. In India you cannot have representative institutions. Of all the innumerable speculators who have offered their suggestions on Indian politics, not a single one, as far as I know, however democratical his opinions may be, has ever maintained the possibility of giving, at the present time, such institutions to India. One gentleman, extremely well acquainted with the affairs of our Eastern Empire, a most valuable servant of the Company, and the author of a History of India, which, though certainly not free from faults, is, I think, on the whole, the greatest historical work which has appeared in our language since that of Gibbon—I mean Mr. Mill—was examined on this point. That gentleman is well known to be a very bold and uncompromising politician. He has written strongly, far too strongly, I think, in favor of pure democracy. He has gone so far as to maintain that no nation which has not a representative legislature, chosen by universal suffrage, enjoys security against oppression. But when he was asked before the Committee of last year whether he thought representative government practicable in India, his answer was, "Utterly out of the question." This, then, is the state in which we are. We have to frame a good government for a country into which, by universal acknowledgment, we cannot introduce those institutions which all our habits, which all the reasonings of European philosophers, which all the history of our own part of the world would lead us to consider as the one great security for good government. We have to ingraft on despotism those blessings which are the natural fruits of liberty. In these circumstances, sir, it behooves us to be cautious, even to the verge of timidity. The light of political science and of history are withdrawn: we are walking in darkness: we do not distinctly see whither we are going. It is the wisdom of a man so situated to feel his way, and not to plant his foot till he is well assured that the ground before him is firm.

Some things, however, in the midst of this obscurity, I can see with clearness. I can see, for example, that it is desirable that the authority exercised in this country over the Indian government should be divided between two bodies, between a minister or a board appointed by the Crown, and some other body independent of the Crown. If India is to be a dependency of England, to be at war with our enemies, to be at peace with our allies, to be protected by the English navy from maritime aggression, to have a portion of the English army mixed with its sepoys, it plainly follows that the King, to whom the constitution gives the direction of foreign affairs, and the command of the military and naval forces, ought to have a share in the direction of the Indian government. Yet, on the other hand, that a revenue of twenty millions a year, an army of two hundred thousand men, a civil service abounding with lucrative situations, should be left to the disposal of the Crown, without any check whatever, is what no Minister, I conceive, would venture to propose. This House is indeed the check provided by the constitution on the abuse of the royal prerogative. But that this House is, or is likely ever to be, an efficient check on abuses practised in India, I altogether deny. We have, as I believe we all feel, quite business enough. If we were to undertake the task of looking into Indian affairs as we look into British affairs, if we were to have Indian budgets and Indian estimates, if we were to go into the Indian currency question and the Indian Bank Charter, if to our disputes about Belgium and Holland, Don Pedro and Don Miguel, were to be added disputes about the debts of the Guicowar and the disorders of Mysore, the ex-King of the Afghans and the Maharajah Runjeet Singh; if we were to have one night occupied by the embezzlements of the Benares mint, and another by the panic in the Calcutta money-market; if the questions of Suttee or no Suttee, Pilgrim tax or no Pilgrim tax, Ryotwary or Zemindary, half Batta or whole Batta, were to be debated at the same length at which we have debated Church reform and the assessed taxes, twenty-four hours a day and three hundred and sixty-five days a year would be too short a time for the discharge of our duties. The House, it is plain, has not the necessary time to settle these matters; nor has it the necessary knowledge; nor has it the motives to acquire that knowledge. The late change in its constitution has made it, I believe, a much more faithful representative of the English people. But it is as far as ever from being a representative of the Indian people. A broken head in Cold Bath Fields produces a greater sensation among us than three pitched battles in India. A few weeks ago we had to decide on a claim brought by an individual against the revenues of India. If it had been an English question, the walls would scarcely have held the Members who would have flocked to the division. It was an Indian question; and we could scarcely, by dint of supplication, make a House. Even when my right honorable friend, the President of the Board of Control, gave his able and interesting explanation of the plan which he intended to propose for the government of a hundred millions of human beings, the attendance was not so large as I have often seen it on the turnpike bill or a railroad bill.

That empire is itself the strangest of all political anomalies. That a handful of adventurers from an island in the Atlantic should have subjugated a vast country divided from the place of their birth by half the globe; a country which, at no very distant period, was merely the subject of fable to the nations of Europe; a country never before violated by the most renowned of Western conquerors; a country which Trajan never entered; a country lying beyond the point where the phalanx of Alexander refused to proceed; that we should govern a territory ten thousand miles from us; a territory larger and more populous than France, Spain, Italy, and Germany put together; a territory, the present clear revenue of which exceeds the present clear revenue of any state in the world, France excepted; a territory inhabited by men differing from us in race, color, language, manners, morals, religion; these are prodigies to which the world has seen nothing similar. Reason is confounded. We interrogate the past in vain. General rules are useless where the whole is one vast exception. The Company is an anomaly; but it is part of a system where everything is anomaly. It is the strangest of all governments; but it is designed for the strangest of all Empires.

In what state, then, did we find India? And what have we made India? We found society throughout that vast country in a state to which history scarcely furnishes a parallel. The nearest parallel would, perhaps, be the state of Europe during the fifth century. The Mogul empire in the time of the successors of Aurungzebe, like the Roman empire in the time of the successors of Theodosius, was sinking under the vices of a bad internal administration, and under the assaults of barbarous invaders. At Delhi, as at Ravenna, there was a mock sovereign, immured in a gorgeous state-prison. He was suffered to indulge in every sensual pleasure. He was adored with servile prostrations. He assumed and bestowed the most magnificent titles. But, in fact, he was a mere puppet in the hands of some ambitious subject. While the Honorii and Augustuli of the East, surrounded by their fawning eunuchs, revelled and dozed without knowing or caring what might pass beyond the walls of their palace gardens, the provinces had ceased to respect a government which could neither punish nor protect them. Society was a chaos. Its restless and shifting elements formed themselves every moment into some new combination; which the next moment dissolved. In the course of a single generation a hundred dynasties grew up, flourished, decayed, were extinguished, were forgotten. Every adventurer who could muster a troop of horse might aspire to a throne. Every palace was every year the scene of conspiracies, treasons, revolutions, parricides. Meanwhile a rapid succession of Alarics and Attilas passed over the defenceless empire. A Persian invader penetrated to Delhi, and carried back in triumph the most precious treasures of the House of Tamerlane. The Afghan soon followed, by the same track, to glean whatever the Persian had spared. The Jauts established themselves on the Jumna. The Seiks devasted Lahore. Every part of India, from Tanjore to the Himalayas, was laid under contribution by the Mahrattas. The people were ground down to the dust by the oppressor without and the oppressor within; by the robber from whom the Nabob was unable to protect them, by the Nabob who took whatever the robber had left to them. All the evils of despotism, and all the evils of anarchy, pressed at once on that miserable race. They knew nothing of government but its exactions. Desolation was in their imperial cities, and famine all along the banks of their broad and redundant rivers. It seemed that a few more years would suffice to efface all traces of the opulence and civilization of an earlier age.

SOURCE: In *Macaulay: Miscellaneous Works*, vol. 5., ed. Lady Trevelyan (New York: Harper and Brothers, 1880).

Lord Clive

LORD THOMAS BABINGTON MACAULAY

The great province of Bengal, together with Orissa and Bahar, had long been governed by a viceroy, whom the English called Aliverdy Khan, and who, like the other viceroys of the Mogul, had become virtually independent. He died in 1756, and the sovereignty descended to his grandson, a youth under twenty years of age, who bore the name of Surajah Dowlah. Oriental despots are perhaps the worst class of human beings; and this unhappy boy was one of the worst specimens of his class. His understanding was naturally feeble, and his temper naturally unamiable. His education had been such as would have enervated even a vigorous intellect and perverted even a generous disposition. He was unreasonable, because nobody ever dared to reason with him, and selfish, because he had never been made to feel himself dependent on the good-will of others. Early debauchery had unnerved his body and his mind. He indulged immoderately in the use of ardent spirits, which inflamed his weak brain almost to madness. His chosen companions were flatterers, sprung from the dregs of the people, and recommended by nothing but buffoonery and servility. It is said that he had arrived at that last stage of human depravity, when cruelty becomes pleasing for its own sake, when the sight of pain, as pain, where no advantage is to be gained, no offence punished, no danger averted, is an agreeable excitement. It had early been his amusement to torture beasts and birds; and, when he grew up, he enjoyed with still keener relish the misery of his fellow-creatures.

From a child Surajah Dowlah had hated the English. It was his whim to do so; and his whims were never opposed. He had also formed a very exaggerated notion of the wealth which might be obtained by plundering them; and his feeble and uncultivated mind was incapable of perceiving that the riches of Calcutta, had they been even greater than he imagined, would not compensate him for what he must lose, if the European trade, of which Bengal was a chief seat, should be driven by his violence to some other quarter.

Clive's profession was war; and he felt that there was something discreditable in an accommodation with Surajah Dowlah. But his power was limited. A committee, chiefly composed of servants of the Company who had fled from Calcutta, had the principal direction of affairs; and these persons were eager to be restored to their posts and compensated for their losses. The government of Madras, apprised that war had commenced in Europe, and apprehensive of an attack from the French, became impatient for the return of the armament. The promises of the Nabob were large, the chances of a contest doubtful; and Clive consented to treat, though he expressed his regret that things should not be concluded in so glorious a manner as he could have wished.

With this negotiation commences a new chapter in the life of Clive. Hitherto he had been merely a soldier, carrying into effect, with eminent ability and valour, the plans of others. Henceforth he is to be chiefly regarded as a statesman; and his military movements are to be considered as subordinate to his political designs. That in his new capacity he displayed great talents, and obtained great success, is unquestionable. But it is also unquestionable, that the transactions in which he now began to take a part have left a stain on his moral character.

We can by no means agree with Sir John Malcolm, who is obstinately resolved to see nothing but honour and integrity in the conduct of his hero. But we can as little agree with Mr. Mill, who has gone so far as to say that Clive was a man "to whom deception, when it suited his purpose, never cost a pang." Clive seems to us to have been constitutionally the very opposite of a knave, bold even to temerity, sincere even to indiscretion, hearty in friendship, open in enmity. Neither in his private life, nor in those parts of his public life in which he had to do with his countrymen, do we find any signs of a propensity to cunning. On the contrary, in all the disputes in which he was engaged as an Englishman against Englishmen, from his boxing-matches at school to those stormy altercations at the India House and in Parliament amidst which his later years were passed, his very faults were those of a high and magnanimous spirit. The truth seems to have been that he considered Oriental politics as a game in which nothing was unfair. He knew that the standard of morality among the natives of India differed widely from that established in England. He knew that he had to deal with men destitute of what in Europe is called honour, with men who would give any promise without hesitation, and break any promise without shame, with men who would unscrupulously employ corruption, perjury, forgery, to compass their ends. His letters show that the great difference between Asiatic and European morality was constantly in his thoughts. He seems to have imagined, most erroneously in our opinion, that he could effect nothing against such adversaries, if he was content to be bound by ties from which they were free, if he went on telling truth, and hearing none, if he fulfilled, to his own hurt, all his engagements with confederates who never kept an engagement that was not to their advantage. Accordingly this man, in the other parts of his life an honourable English gentleman and a soldier, was no sooner matched against an Indian intriguer, than he became himself an Indian intriguer, and descended, without scruple, to falsehood, to hypocritical caresses, to the substitution of documents, and to the counterfeiting of hands.

The negotiations between the English and the Nabob were carried on chiefly by two agents, Mr. Watts, a servant of the Company, and a Bengalee of the name of Omichund. This Omichund had been one of the wealthiest native merchants resident at Calcutta, and had sustained great losses in consequence of the Nabob's expedition against that place. In the course of his commercial transactions, he had seen much of the English, and was peculiarly qualified to serve as a medium of communication between them and a native court. He possessed great influence with his own race, and had in large measure the Hindoo talents, quick observations, tact, dexterity, perseverance, and the Hindoo vices, servility, greediness, and treachery.

The Nabob behaved with all the faithlessness of an Indian statesman, and with all the levity of a boy whose mind had been enfeebled by power and self-indulgence. He promised, retracted, hesitated, evaded. At one time he advanced with his army in a threatening manner towards Calcutta; but when he saw the resolute front which the English presented, he fell back in alarm, and consented to make peace with them on their own terms. The treaty was no sooner concluded than he formed new designs against them. He intrigued with the French authorities at Chandernagore. He invited Bussy to march from the Deccan to the Hoogley, and to drive the English out of Bengal. All this was well known to Clive and Watson. They determined accordingly to strike a decisive blow, and to attack Chandernagore, before the force there could be strengthened by new arrivals, either from the south of India or from Europe. Watson directed the expedition by water, Clive by land. The success of the combined movements was rapid and complete. The fort, the garrison, the artillery, the military stores, all fell into the hands of the English. Near five hundred European troops were among the prisoners.

The Nabob had feared and hated the English, even while he was still able to oppose to them their French rivals. The French were now vanquished; and he began to regard the English with still greater fear and still greater hatred. His weak and unprincipled mind oscillated between servility and insolence. One day he sent a large sum to Calcutta, as part of the compensation due for the wrongs which he had committed. The next day he sent a present of jewels to Bussy, exhorting that distinguished officer to hasten to protect Bengal "against Clive, the daring in war, on whom," says his Highness, "may all bad fortune attend." He ordered his army to march against the English. He countermanded his orders. He tore Clive's letters. He then sent answers in the most florid language of compliment. He ordered Watts out of his presence, and threatened to impale him. He again sent for Watts, and begged pardon for the insult. In the meantime, his wretched maladministration, his folly, his dissolute manners, and his love of the lowest company, had disgusted all classes of his subjects, soldiers, traders, civil functionaries, the proud and ostentatious Mahommedans, the timid, supple, and parsimonious Hindoos. A formidable confederacy was formed against him, in which were included Roydullub, the minister of finance, Meer Jaffier, the principal commander of the troops, and Jugget Seit, the richest banker in India. The plot was confided to the English agents, and a communication was opened between the malcontents at Moorshedabad and the committee at Calcutta.

In the committee there was much hesitation; but Clive's voice was given in favour of the conspirators, and his vigour and firmness bore down all opposition. It was determined that the English should lend their powerful assistance to depose Surajah Dowlah, and to place Meer Jaffier on the throne of Bengal. In return, Meer Jaffier promised ample compensation to the Company and its servants, and a liberal donative to the army, the navy, and the committee. The odious vices of Surajah Dowlah, the wrongs which the English had suffered at his hands, the dangers to which our trade must have been exposed had he continued to reign, appear to us fully to justify the resolution of deposing him. But nothing can justify the dissimulation which Clive stooped to practise. He wrote to Surajah Dowlah in terms so affectionate that they for a time lulled that weak prince into perfect security. The same courier who carried this "soothing letter," as Clive calls it, to the Nabob, carried to Mr. Watts a letter in the following terms: "Tell Meer Jaffier to fear nothing. I will join him with five thousand men who never turned their backs. Assure him I will march night and day to his assistance, and stand by him as long as I have a man left."

It was impossible that a plot which had so many ramifications should long remain entirely concealed. Enough reached the ears of the Nabob to arouse his suspicions. But he was soon quieted by the fictions and artifices which the inventive genius of Omichund produced with miraculous readiness. All was going well; the plot was nearly ripe; when Clive learned that Omichund was likely to play false. The artful Bengalee had been promised a liberal compensation for all that he had lost at Calcutta. But this would not satisfy him. His services had been great. He held the thread of the whole intrigue. By one word breathed in the ear of Surajah Dowlah, he could undo all that he had done. The lives of Watts, of Meer Jaffier, of all the conspirators, were at his mercy; and he determined to take advantage of his situation and to make his own terms. He demanded three hundred thousand pounds sterling as the price of his secrecy and his assistance. The committee, incensed by the treachery and appalled by the danger, knew not what course to take. But Clive was more than Omichund's match in Omichund's own arts. The man, he said, was a villain. Any artifice which would defeat such knavery was justifiable. The best course would be to promise what was asked. Omichund would soon be at their mercy; and then they might punish him by withholding from him, not only the bribe which he now demanded, but also the compensation which all the other sufferers of Calcutta were to receive.

His advice was taken. But how was the wary and sagacious Hindoo to be deceived? He had demanded that an article touching his claims should be inserted in the treaty between Meer Jaffier and the English, and he would not be satisfied unless he saw it with his own eyes. Clive had an expedient ready. Two treaties were drawn up, one on white paper, the other on red, the former real, the latter fictitious. In the former Omichund's name was not mentioned; the latter, which was to be shown to him, contained a stipulation in his favour.

But another difficulty arose. Admiral Watson had scruples about signing the red treaty. Omichund's vigilance and acuteness were such that the absence of so important a name would probably awaken his suspicions. But Clive was not a man to do anything by halves. We almost blush to write it. He forged Admiral Watson's name.

All was now ready for action. Mr. Watts fled secretly from Moorshedabad. Clive put his troops in motion, and wrote to the Nabob in a tone very different from that of his previous letters. He set forth all the wrongs which the British had suffered, offered to submit the points in dispute to the arbitration of Meer Jaffier, and concluded by announcing that, as the rains were about to set in, he and his men would do themselves the honour of waiting on his Highness for an answer.

Surajah Dowlah instantly assembled his whole force, and marched to encounter the English. It had been agreed that Meer Jaffier should separate himself from the Nabob, and carry over his division to Clive. But, as the decisive moment approached, the fears of the conspirator overpowered his ambition. Clive had advanced to Cossimbuzar; the Nabob lay with a mighty power a few miles off at Plassey; and still Meer Jaffier delayed to fulfil his engagements, and returned evasive answers to the earnest remonstrances of the English general.

Clive was in a painfully anxious situation. He could place no confidence in the sincerity or in the courage of his confederate: and, whatever confidence he might place in his own military talents, and in the valour and discipline of his troops, it was no light thing to engage an army twenty times as numerous as his own. Before him lay a river over which it was easy to advance, but over which, if things went ill, not one of his little band would ever return. On this occasion, for the first and for the last time, his dauntless spirit, during a few hours, shrank from the fearful responsibility of making a decision. He called a council of war. The majority pronounced against fighting; and Clive declared his concurrence with the majority. Long afterwards, he said that he had never called but one council of war, and that, if he had taken the advice of that council, the British would never have been masters of Bengal. But scarcely had the meeting broken up when he was himself again. He retired alone under the shade of some trees, and passed near an hour there in thought. He came back determined to put everything to the hazard, and gave orders that all should be in readiness for passing the river on the morrow.

The river was passed; and at the close of a toilsome day's march, the army, long after sunset, took up its quarters in a grove of mango-trees near Plassey, within a mile of the enemy. Clive was unable to sleep; he heard, through the whole night, the sound of drums and cymbals from the vast camp of the Nabob. It is not strange that even his stout heart should now and then have sunk, when he reflected against what odds, and for what a prize, he was in a few hours to contend.

Nor was the rest of Surajah Dowlan more peaceful. His mind, at once weak and stormy, was distracted by wild and horrible apprehensions. Appalled by the greatness and nearness of the crisis, distrusting his captains, dreading every one who approached him, dreading to be left alone, he sat gloomily in his tent, haunted, a Greek poet would have said, by the furies of those who had cursed him with their last breath in the Black Hole.

The day broke, the day which was to decide the fate of India. At sunrise the army of the Nabob, pouring through many openings from the camp, began to move towards the grove where the English lay. Forty thousand infantry, armed with firelocks, pikes, swords, bows and arrows, covered the plain. They were accompanied by fifty pieces of ordnance of the largest size, each tugged by a long team of white oxen, and each pushed on from behind by an elephant. Some smaller guns, under the direction of a few French auxiliaries, were perhaps more formidable. The cavalry were fifteen thousand, drawn, not from the effeminate population of Bengal, but from the bolder race which inhabits the northern provinces; and the practised eye of Clive could perceive that both the men and the horses were more powerful than those of the Carnatic. The force which he had to oppose to this great multitude consisted of only three thousand men. But of these nearly a thousand were English; and all were led by English officers, and trained in the English discipline. Conspicuous in the ranks of the little army were the men of the Thirty-Ninth Regiment, which still bears on its colours, amidst many honourable additions won under Wellington in Spain and Gascony, the name of Plassey, and the proud motto, *Primus in Indis*.

The battle commenced with a cannonade in which the artillery of the

Nabob did scarcely any execution, while the few field-pieces of the English produced great effect. Several of the most distinguished officers in Surajah Dowlah's service fell. Disorder began to spread through his ranks. His own terror increased every moment. One of the conspirators urged on him the expediency of retreating. The insidious advice, agreeing as it did with what his own terrors suggested, was readily received. He ordered his army to fall back, and this order decided his fate. Clive snatched the moment, and ordered his troops to advance. The confused and dispirited multitude gave way before the onset of disciplined valour. No mob attacked by regular soldiers was ever more completely routed. The little band of Frenchmen, who alone ventured to confront the English, were swept down the stream of fugitives. In an hour the forces of Surajah Dowlah were dispersed, never to reassemble. Only five hundred of the vanquished were slain. But their camp, their guns, their baggage, innumerable waggons, innumerable cattle, remained in the power of the conquerors. With the loss of twenty-two soldiers killed and fifty wounded, Clive had scattered an army of nearly sixty thousand men, and subdued an empire larger and more populous than Great Britain.

Meer Jaffier had given no assistance to the English during the action. But as soon as he saw that the fate of the day was decided, he drew off his division of the army, and, when the battle was over, sent his congratulations to his ally. The next morning he repaired to the English quarters, not a little uneasy as to the reception which awaited him there. He gave evident signs of alarm when a guard was drawn out to receive him with the honours due to his rank. But his apprehensions were speedily removed. Clive came forward to meet him, embraced him, saluted him as Nabob of the three great provinces of Bengal, Bahar, and Orissa, listened graciously to his apologies, and advised him to march without delay to Moorshedabad.

Surajah Dowlah had fled from the field of battle with all the speed with which a fleet camel could carry him, and arrived at Moorshedabad in little more than twenty-four hours. There he called his councillors round him. The wisest advised him to put himself into the hands of the English, from whom he had nothing worse to fear than deposition and confinement. But he attributed this suggestion to treachery. Others urged him to try the chance of war again. He approved the advice, and issued orders accordingly. But he wanted spirit to adhere even during one day to a manly resolution. He learned that Meer Jaffier had arrived; and his terrors became insupportable. Disguised in a mean dress, with a casket of jewels in his hand, he let himself down at night from a window of his palace, and, accompanied by only two attendants, embarked on the river for Patna.

In a few days Clive arrived at Moorshedabad, escorted by two hundred

English soldiers and three hundred sepoys. For his residence had been assigned a palace, which was surrounded by a garden so spacious that all the troops who accompanied him could conveniently encamp within it. The ceremony of the installation of Meer Jaffier was instantly performed. Clive led the new Nabob to the seat of honour, placed him on it, presented to him, after the immemorial fashion of the East, an offering of gold, and then, turning to the natives who filled the hall, congratulated them on the good fortune which had freed them from a tyrant. He was compelled on this occasion to use the services of an interpreter; for it is remarkable that, long as he resided in India, intimately acquainted as he was with Indian politics and with the Indian character, and adored as he was by his Indian soldiery, he never learned to express himself with facility in any Indian language. He is said indeed to have been sometimes under the necessity of employing, in his intercourse with natives of India, the smattering of Portuguese which he had acquired, when a lad in Brazil.

The new sovereign was now called upon to fulfil the engagements into which he had entered with his allies. A conference was held at the house of Jugget Seit, the great banker, for the purpose of making the necessary arrangements. Omichund came thither, fully believing himself to stand high in the favour of Clive, who, with dissimulation surpassing even the dissimulation of Bengal, had up to that day treated him with undiminished kindness. The white treaty was produced and read. Clive then turned to Mr. Scrafton, one of the servants of the Company, and said in English, "It is now time to undeceive Omichund." "Omichund," said Mr. Scrafton in Hindostanee, "the red treaty is a trick. You are to have nothing." Omichund fell back insensible into the arms of his attendants. He revived; but his mind was irreparably ruined. Clive, who, though little troubled by scruples of conscience in his dealings with Indian politicians, was not inhuman, seems to have been touched. He saw Omichund a few days later, spoke to him kindly, advised him to make a pilgrimage to one of the great temples of India, in the hope that change of scene might restore his health, and was even disposed, notwithstanding all that had passed, again to employ his talents in the public service. But, from the moment of that sudden shock, the unhappy man sank gradually into idiocy. He, who had formerly been distinguished by the strength of his understanding and the simplicity of his habits, now squandered the remains of his fortune on childish trinkets, and loved to exhibit himself dressed in rich garments, and hung with precious stones. In this abject state he languished a few months, and then died.

We should not think it necessary to offer any remarks for the purpose of directing the judgment of our readers with respect to this transaction, had not

Sir John Malcolm undertaken to defend it in all its parts. He regrets, indeed, that it was necessary to employ means so liable to abuse as forgery; but he will not admit that any blame attaches to those who deceived the deceiver. He thinks that the English were not bound to keep faith with one who kept no faith with them, and that, if they had fulfilled their engagements with the wily Bengalee, so signal an example of successful treason would have produced a crowd of imitators. Now, we will not discuss this point on any rigid principles of morality. Indeed, it is quite unnecessary to do so: for, looking at the question as a question of expediency in the lowest sense of the word, and using no arguments but such as Machiavelli might have employed in his conferences with Borgia, we are convinced that Clive was altogether in the wrong, and that he committed, not merely a crime, but a blunder. That honesty is the best policy is a maxim which we firmly believe to be generally correct, even with respect to the temporal interests of individuals; but, with respect to societies, the rule is subject to still fewer exceptions, and that, for this reason, that the life of societies is longer than the life of individuals. It is possible to mention men who have owed great worldly prosperity to breaches of private faith. But we doubt whether it be possible to mention a state which has on the whole been a gainer by a breach of public faith. The entire history of British India is an illustration of the great truth, that it is not prudent to oppose perfidy to perfidy, and that the most efficient weapon with which men can encounter falsehood is truth. During a long course of years, the English rulers of India, surrounded by allies and enemies whom no engagement could bind, have generally acted with sincerity and uprightness; and the event has proved that sincerity and uprightness are wisdom. English valour and English intelligence have done less to extend and to preserve our Oriental empire than English veracity. All that we could have gained by imitating the doublings, the evasions, the fictions, the perjuries which have been employed against us, is as nothing, when compared with what we have gained by being the one power in India on whose word reliance can be placed. No oath which superstition can devise, no hostage however precious, inspires a hundredth part of the confidence which is produced by the "yea, yea," and "nay, nay," of a British envoy. No fastness, however strong by art or nature, gives to its inmates a security like that enjoyed by the chief who, passing through the territories of powerful and deadly enemies, is armed with the British guarantee. The mightiest princes of the East can scarcely, by the offer of enormous usury, draw forth any portion of the wealth which is concealed under the hearths of their subjects. The British Government offers little more than four per cent.; and avarice hastens to bring forth tens of millions of rupees from its most secret repositories. A hostile monarch may promise mountains of gold to our sepoys, on condition that they will desert the standard of the Company. The Company promises only a moderate pension after a long service. But every sepoy knows that the promise of the Company will be kept: he knows that if he lives a hundred years his rice and salt are as secure as the salary of the Governor-General: and he knows that there is not another state in India which would not, in spite of the most solemn vows, leave him to die of hunger in a ditch as soon as he had ceased to be useful. The greatest advantage which a government can possess is to be the one trustworthy government in the midst of governments which nobody can trust. This advantage we enjoy in Asia. Had we acted during the last two generations on the principles which Sir John Malcolm appears to have considered as sound, had we, as often as we had to deal with people like Omichund, retaliated by lying, and forging, and breaking faith, after their fashion, it is our firm belief that no courage or capacity could have upheld our empire.

Sir John Malcolm admits that Clive's breach of faith could be justified only by the strongest necessity. As we think that breach of faith not only unnecessary, but most inexpedient, we need hardly say that we altogether condemn it.

Omichund was not the only victim. Surajah Dowlah was taken a few days after his flight, and was brought before Meer Jaffier. There he flung himself on the ground in convulsions of fear, and with tears and loud cries implored the mercy which he had never shown. Meer Jaffier hesitated; but his son Meeran, a youth of seventeen, who in feebleness of brain and savageness of nature greatly resembled the wretched captive, was implacable. Surajah Dowlah was led into a secret chamber, to which in a short time the ministers of death were sent. In this act the English bore no part; and Meer Jaffier understood so much of their feelings, that he thought it necessary to apologise to them for having avenged them on their most malignant enemy.

The shower of wealth now fell copiously on the Company and its servants. A sum of eight hundred thousand pounds sterling, in coined silver, was sent down the river from Moorshedabad to Fort William. The fleet which conveyed this treasure consisted of more than a hundred boats, and performed its triumphal voyage with flags flying and music playing. Calcutta, which a few months before had been desolate, was now more prosperous than ever. Trade revived; and the signs of affluence appeared in every English house. As to Clive, there was no limit to his acquisitions but his own moderation. The treasury of Bengal was thrown open to him. There were piled up, after the usage of Indian princes, immense masses of coin, among which might not seldom be detected the florins and byzants with which, before any European ship had turned the Cape of Good Hope, the Venetians purchased the stuffs and spices of the East. Clive walked between heaps of gold and silver, crowned with rubies and diamonds, and was at liberty to help himself. He accepted between two and three hundred thousand pounds.

The pecuniary transactions between Meer Jaffier and Clive were sixteen years later condemned by the public voice, and severely criticised in Parliament. They are vehemently defended by Sir John Malcolm. The accusers of the victorious general represented his gains as the wages of corruption, or as plunder extorted at the point of the sword from a helpless ally. The biographer, on the other hand, considers these great acquisitions as free gifts, honourable alike to the donor and to the receiver, and compares them to the rewards bestowed by foreign powers on Marlborough, on Nelson, and on Wellington. It had always, he says, been customary in the East to give and receive presents; and there was, as yet, no Act of Parliament positively prohibiting English functionaries in India from profiting by this Asiatic usage. This reasoning, we own, does not quite satisfy us. We do not suspect Clive of selling the interests of his employers or his country; but we cannot acquit him of having done what, if not in itself evil, was yet of evil example. Nothing is more clear than that a general ought to be the servant of his own government, and of no other. It follows that whatever rewards he receives for his services ought to be given either by his own government, or with the full knowledge and approbation of his own government. This rule ought to be strictly maintained even with respect to the merest bauble, with respect to a cross, a medal, or a yard of coloured riband. But how can any government be well served, if those who command its forces are at liberty, without its permission, without its privity, to accept princely fortunes from its allies? It is idle to say that there was then no Act of Parliament prohibiting the practice of taking presents from Asiatic sovereigns. It is not on the Act which was passed at a later period for the purpose of preventing any such taking of presents, but on grounds which were valid before that Act was passed, on grounds of common law and common sense, that we arraign the conduct of Clive. There is no Act that we know of, prohibiting the Secretary of State for Foreign Affairs from being in the pay of continental powers. But it is not the less true that a Secretary who should receive a secret pension from France would grossly violate his duty, and would deserve severe punishment. Sir John Malcolm compares the conduct of Clive with that of the Duke of Wellington. Suppose—and we beg pardon for putting such a supposition even for the sake of argument—that the Duke of Wellington had, after the campaign of 1815, and while he commanded the army of occupation in France, privately accepted two hundred thousand pounds from Louis the Eighteenth, as a mark of gratitude for the great services which his Grace had rendered to the House of Bourbon; what would be thought of such a transaction? Yet the statute-book no more forbids the taking of presents in Europe now than it forbade the taking of presents in Asia then.

At the same time, it must be admitted that, in Clive's case, there were many extenuating circumstances. He considered himself as the general, not of the Crown, but of the Company. The Company had, by implication at least, authorised its agents to enrich themselves by means of the liberality of the native princes, and by other means still more objectionable. It was hardly to be expected that the servant should entertain stricter notions of his duty than were entertained by his masters. Though Clive did not distinctly acquaint his employers with what had taken place, and request their sanction, he did not, on the other hand, by studied concealment, show that he was conscious of having done wrong. On the contrary, he avowed with the greatest openness that the Nabob's bounty had raised him to affluence. Lastly, though we think that he ought not in such a way to have taken anything, we must admit that he deserves praise for having taken so little. He accepted twenty lacs of rupees. It would have cost him only a word to make the twenty forty. It was a very easy exercise of virtue to declaim in England against Clive's rapacity; but not one in a hundred of his accusers would have shown so much self-command in the treasury of Moorshedabad.

Clive committed great faults; and we have not attempted to disguise them. But his faults, when weighed against his merits, and viewed in connection with his temptations, do not appear to us to deprive him of his right to an honourable place in the estimation of posterity.

From his first visit to India dates the renown of the English arms in the East. Till he appeared, his countrymen were despised as mere pedlars, while the French were revered as a people formed for victory and command. His courage and capacity dissolved the charm. With the defence of Arcot commences that long series of Oriental triumph which closes with the fall of Ghizni. Nor must we forget that he was only twenty-five years old when he approved himself ripe for military command. This is a rare if not a singular distinction. It is true that Alexander, Condé and Charles the Twelfth, won great battles at a still earlier age; but those princes were surrounded by veteran generals of distinguished skill, to whose suggestions must be attributed the victories of the Granicus, of Rocroi, and of Narva. Clive, an inexperienced youth, had yet more experience than any of those who served under him. He had to form himself, to form his officers, and to form his army. The only man, as far as we recollect, who at an equally early age ever gave equal proof of talents for war, was Napoleon Bonaparte.

From Clive's second visit to India dates the political ascendency of the English in that country. His dexterity and resolution realised, in the course of a few months, more than all the gorgeous visions which had floated before the imagination of Dupleix. Such an extent of cultivated territory, such an amount of revenue, such a multitude of subjects, was never added to the dominion of Rome by the most successful proconsul. Nor were such wealthy spoils ever borne under arches of triumph, down the Sacred Way, and through the crowded Forum, to the threshold of Tarpeian Jove. The fame of those who subdued Antiochus and Tigranes grows dim when compared with the splendour of the exploits which the young English adventurer achieved at the head of an army not equal in numbers to one half of a Roman legion.

From Clive's third visit to India dates the purity of the administration of our Eastern empire. When he landed in Calcutta in 1765, Bengal was regarded as a place to which Englishmen were sent only to get rich, by any means, in the shortest possible time. He first made dauntless and unsparing war on that gigantic system of oppression, extortion, and corruption. In that war he manfully put to hazard his ease, his fame, and his splendid fortune. The same sense of justice which forbids us to conceal or extenuate the faults of his earlier days compels us to admit that those faults were nobly repaired. If the reproach of the Company and of its servants has been taken away, if in India the yoke of foreign masters, elsewhere the heaviest of all yokes, has been found lighter than that of any native dynasty, if to that gang of public robbers which formerly spread terror through the whole plain of Bengal has succeeded a body of functionaries not more highly distinguished by ability and diligence than by integrity, disinterestedness, and public spirit, if we now see such men as Munro, Elphinstone, and Metcalfe, after leading victorious armies, after making and deposing kings, return, proud of their honourable poverty, from a land which once held out to every greedy factor the hope of boundless wealth, the praise is in no small measure due to Clive. His name stands high on the roll of conquerors. But it is found in a better list, in the list of those who have done and suffered much for the happiness of mankind. To the warrior, history will assign a place in the same rank with Lucullus and Trajan. Nor will she deny to the reformer a share of that veneration with which France cherishes the memory of Turgot, and with which the latest generations of Hindoos will contemplate the statue of Lord William Bentinck.

SOURCE: In the *Edinburgh Review* 70, no. 142 (January 1840): 295–362.

The Spoliation of Oude

SAMUEL LUCAS

CHAPTER I

Showing how the company made acquaintance with shoojah-ood-dowlah's rupees, and how quickly they improved their intimacy with his treasures and territory.

The kingdom of Oude is situated at the root and in the heart of the Indian peninsula.[1] Interposed between the Ganges and the Himalayas, it comprises about 24,000 square miles, and contains 5,000,000 inhabitants. Its population is bold and warlike, and furnishes the best constituents of our Indian armies. Its fertility is so remarkable among the principalities of this prolific region, that it is commonly spoken of as "the Garden of India"; and its national revenues have been in fitting proportion to its productiveness. The East India Company, with that discernment which has ever distinguished them, turned its capacities of every description to their profit from an early date. Not only have they drawn their best troops from its peasantry, but they have taken a large portion of its revenues for professing to defend its princes with this very soldiery. Oude has been simultaneously their recruiting ground and military chest, their fiscal tributary and bank of advance. By subsidies, loans, exchanges, and other devices, it is computed that they have drawn from it, since their connection with the province, a sum of *not less than fifty millions sterling*. Up to the day when they ruthlessly wrung the neck of the royal goose, this was the rate at which it laid them golden eggs.

The process by which this was managed is highly instructive, and its explanation requires an extended historic statement. Before we knew of its existence, Oude was a country of ancient traditions, and the scene of India's

---

1. "The kingdom of Oude is bounded on the north and north-east by Nepaul; on the east by the British district of Goruckpore; on the south-east by the British districts of Azimgurh and Jounpoor; on the south by the British district of Allahabad; on the south-west by the Doab, including the British districts of Futtehpoor, Gawnpore, and Furrukhabad; and on the north-west by Shahjehanpoor. It lies between N. lat. 29° 6'—25° 34', and 79° 45'—83° 11' E. long.; is 270 miles in length, from south-east to north-west, and 160 in breadth. The area is 23,923 square miles; population, 5,000,000, being 250 5/6 to the square mile."—*M. M. Musseehooddeen.* According to the Post Office authorities, Lucknow, the present capital of Oude, is distant from Calcutta 619 miles. It is a fine city, and reminded Reginald Heber of Dresden. Its architectural and other characteristics are fairly described in the apocryphal narrative, "The Private Life of an Eastern King."

earliest romance. In the first great Sanscrit epic, "the Ramayana," it is the residence of a splendid king and an heroic people, and its capital, Ayodhya or Oude, is filled with gorgeous accessories.² Of its authentic history from this date we know very little, but at the close of the twelfth century, after the conquest of Canouj by the Mahommedans, it was subdued by Kutbuddin Aibuk, Viceroy of India, for Mohummud Ghori, Sultan of Ghuznee. It thenceforward became an integral part of the realm of the sovereigns of Delhi, and on the conquest of the empire by Babar, was easily subjugated. Mr. Macaulay, in a few clear and discriminative sentences, has traced its fortunes in connection with that empire's dissolution.—

"Some of the great viceroys, who held their posts by virtue of commissions from the Mogul, ruled as many subjects as the King of France or the Emperor of Germany. Even the deputies of these deputies might well rank as to extent of territory and amount of revenue with the Grand Duke of Tuscany or the Elector of Saxony. **** Wherever the viceroys of the Mogul retained authority, they became sovereigns. They might still acknowledge, in words, the superiority of the House of Tamerlane, as a Count of Flanders or a Duke of Burgundy might have acknowledged the superiority of the most helpless driveller among the later Carlovingains. They might occasionally send to

---

2. The following is the description from "the Ramayana," taken as nearly as possible from Carey's translation:—

"The streets and alleys of the city were admirably disposed, and the principal streets well watered. It was beautified with gardens, fortified with gates, crowded with charioteers and messengers furnished with arms, adorned with banners, filled with dancing girls and dancing men, crowded with elephants, horses and chariots, merchants and ambassadors from various countries. It resembled a mine of jewels, or the residence of *Sri*. The walls were variegated with diverse sorts of gems like the divisions of a chess board, the houses formed one continued row of equal height, resounding with the music of the tabor, the twang of the bow, and the sacred sound of the Veda. It was perfumed with incense, chaplets of flowers, and articles for sacrifice, by their ordour cheering the heart."

In this city of well fed happy people no one practised a calling not his own, none were without relations, the men loved their wives, the women were faithful and obedient to their husbands, no one was without earrings, no one went unperfumed, no Brahman was without the constant fire, and no man gave less than a thousand rupees to the Brahmans. This city was guarded by warriors as a mountain den by lions, filled with horses from Kamboya and other places, and elephants from the Vindhya and Himalaya mountains, and governed as Indra governs his city, by Dasaratha, chief of the race of Ikshwaku.

This king was perfectly skilled in the Vedas and Vedangas, beloved by his people, a great charioteer, and constant in sacrifice. His courtiers were wise, capable of understanding a nod, and constantly devoted to him. Eight Brahmans are mentioned as chief counsellors, two as chosen priests, and these appear to have been his prime ministers; six others were also in office. "Surrounded by all these counsellors, learned, faithful, eminent, seeking by wise counsels the good of the Kingdom, Dasaratha shone resplendent as the sun, irradiating the world."

their titular sovereign a complimentary present, or solicit from him a title of honour. In truth, however, they were no longer lieutenants, removable at pleasure, but *independent hereditary princes*. In this way originated those great Mussulman houses which formerly ruled Bengal and the Carnatic, and those which still" (written in 1840), "though in a state of vassalage, exercise some of the powers of royalty at Lucknow and Hyderabad."

It was in the position just described, and for which they were certainly not indebted to the Company of English merchants who built Fort William on sufferance in 1699, that the latter princes, thus originally potential, commenced their fatal relations with the East India Company.³

The circumstances under which they were first included in its toils arose out of the Company's dealings with Bengal, from the Subadar of which, in 1698, it had avowedly purchased the ground on which Calcutta now stands, while it had really prepared a fulcrum from which to overturn India. The Company had supported an aspirant to the throne of Bengal, for the consideration which afterwards became so familiar in their various treaties, a large sum of rupees, amounting in this instance to one crore and seventy-seven lacs, when the victory of Clive at Plassey, on the 23rd June, 1757, gave effect to their bargain, by installing their protege and annihilating their antagonist. The protege was removed in 1760, on the plea of incompetency, and a successor set up, who was also deposed, whereupon protege No. 1 was reinstated. The only name among these unfortunate favourites of the Company which is at all

---

3. For the sake of convenience, we list the sovereigns of Oude with the leading dates in the history of the East India Company:

A.D. 1711 Sadat Khan. 1739 Suffder Jung. 1756 Shoojah-ood-Dowlah. 1775 Asoph-ood-Dowlah. 1797 Vizer Allie. (Spurious, and displaced in favour of Saadat Allie.) 1787 Saadat Allie. 1814 Ghazee-ood-Deen Hyder. 1827 Nusseer-ood-deen Hyder. 1837 Mohummud Allie Shah. 1842 Soorye-a-Jah. Amjud Allie Shah. 1847 Wajid Allie Shah.

In A.D. 1601 Queen Elizabeth granted a charter to a company of merchants to trade to the East Indies. In 1634 this company obtained an imperial firman from the Emperor Shah Jehan to trade with Bengal by sea and to establish a factory. In 1652 permission was granted to the company by the same prince to trade throughout the province of Bengal. In 1686 the company of the merchants entertained an armament to maintain their rights. In 1698 leave was obtained from the Subadar of Bengal to purchase the ground on which Calcutta now stands. In 1699 Fort William was completed. In 1717 the company obtained an imperial confirmation of all their former privileges, and continued to conduct their commercial affairs with success until 1756, when Seraj-ood-Dowlah succeeded his grandfather, Ali Verdi, as Subadar of Bengal, and in consequence of Governor Drake having refused to give up a native who had fled with his wealth to Calcutta, he attacked and captured the place. Calcutta was retaken on the 2nd of January, 1757, and Seraj-ood-Dowlah having marched towards Calcutta to oppose the English, was completely routed by Lord Clive, and the first treaty was concluded between the company of merchants trading to the East Indies and Seraj-ood-Dowlah, Subadar of Bengal.

material to our present purpose is that of the preferred and rejected No. 2, Cossim Ali, who, after sustaining a series of defeats in contending against his deposition, fled to Shoojah-ood-Dowlah, Nawaub of Oude, and involved him also in the inconvenience of friendly relations with the Company. Shoojah-ood-Dowlah, in the first instance, espoused the cause of Cossim, and marched his army into Behar; but coming in contact with the forces of the East India Company at Buxar, on the 23rd October, 1764, something less than one hundred years ago, he was there defeated, and was eventually compelled to enter into a treaty for "perpetual" and universal peace, sincere friendship, and firm union, with the East India Company, which by this means inserted its syphon into his treasury, and unsealed the precious fountain of his coveted rupees. This treaty was concluded on the 16th August, 1765. And, in addition to the payment by the Nawaub of £500,000 for the Company's expenses, for which it stipulated, it prepared the Wuzier for a further series of disbursements, as the natural consequence of the "friendship" and "firm union" to which it tied him. Thus, the second article of the treaty provides for mutual offensive and defensive arrangements, and that, "*in the case of the English Company's forces being employed by His Highness, the* EXTRAORDINARY *expense of the same to be defrayed by him.*" The case was, of course, pretty certain to occur; while the expense was fated to become "*extraordinary*" in a very different sense from that professedly contemplated. It was necessary, however, to prepare the victim for the *ordinary* incident of excessive and incessant levies, or to fit the prey for the expectant maw, by a phraseology, which, as it were, *lubricated* it for its gradual but entire absorption.

This was simply the first step; but the process thus begun was never from that moment interrupted, and the syphon then inserted never ceased to flow. By this slender thread the kingdom of Oude was gradually drawn into the meshes of the Company, was taxed and impoverished, cramped, tethered, and tormented, until it was presumed to be ready for final annexation. The process was singularly stealthy and protracted, for it was not assisted by any imprudence or insincerity on the part of the rulers of Oude. Their good faith was never successfully impeached, and at this day their good services are admitted by their worst enemies. Not one letter, it is said, among the many hundreds which were intercepted subsequently, contained aught that could raise the slightest suspicion of their fidelity and attachment.[4] But, three years

---

4. On the contrary, a most signal illustration of their good faith was afforded in this way four years later, in 1772, when two emissaries, bearers of a certain letter from His Excellency to Hyder Naik, the father of Tippoo Sultan, were seized by the English authorities at Lucknow. On

after the above treaty was signed, *rumours*, which were afterwards ascertained by three members of the Council to be without foundation, reached the Indian Government to the effect that the Nawaub of Oude was levying forces in order to oppose them. A correspondence accordingly took place, and explanations were freely given; but the Company improved the occasion by exacting an additional engagement, by which the Wuzier was restricted from entertaining a force exceeding 35,000 men. This restriction, which of course rendered him less independent of British assistance, was the second step in the stealthy process, and it followed in three years on the engagement for "sincere friendship and firm union" with the ally whose power it tended materially to diminish. This restriction, however, was commended to the Nawaub by the accompanying engagement that, so long as it was observed by himself and his successors, the East India Company would not introduce any addition to its provisions. That such apparent securities accompanied most stages of their intercourse was not, however, as practically delusive as might be supposed; for such engagements would soon be estimated at their correct value, if on the part of the Company they were consistently and invariably broken. That such was the case in this instance we shall have many illustrations, and the first of these we shall come upon in the incident next to be mentioned.

The Court of Directors had repeatedly urged upon the Indian Government the importance of acquiring the fortress of Chunar, and had directed that no fit opportunity of obtaining that object should be omitted.[5] Chunar had been retained by the British, under the seventh article of the treaty of

---

ascertaining the contents of this letter, the Resident was satisfied that it was in answer to one sent to His Excellency from Hyder Naik in which that chief had written as follows:—"It surprises me to find that your Excellency, while possessing so large an army and such ample resources, should submit to the yoke of the Christians. It would be more advisable for your Excellency to attach them on your side, while I assail them on mine, and by our united efforts destroy them." The intercepted letter contained this answer—"Fanaticism in religion is for those who have relinquished all interest in worldly affairs; but it would be culpable in persons who, like us, have relative duties to perform towards thousands professing a totally different religion to our own, to show a preference for one sect over another. As for that large army and those ample resources which you have heard that I possess, they are maintained for the purpose of being employed against the enemies of the East India Company. Do not, therefore, expect me to use them otherwise." The Resident, having thus become aware of the contents of the letter, obtained permission from His Excellency the Nawaub to forward it to the Governor-General of India, in order that His Lordship might also be convinced of the sincerity and truth of His Excellency's friendship—*M. M. Musseehood-deen.*

5. "Return to House of Lords of Treaties and Engagements between East India Company and Native Powers in Asia, etc." (1853), p. 55.

1765, as a guarantee for the payment of the half-million sterling payable by its sixth article; but when this sum had been paid, there was no longer any pretext for keeping it in their hands, and it was accordingly again given up to the Nawaub. Still the desire of the Company to possess it had not diminished in consequence of their temporary occupation; but they coveted a permanent retention of the security, in addition to the rupees which they had already pocketed. So a pretext was devised for getting Chunar into their hands, and, simultaneously, for retaining the fort of Allahabad, which, while it was in their occupation, the Emperor of Delhi had made over, in 1771, to the Nawaub of Oude; and the pretext devised was simply "the better to enable the East India Company *to assist His Highness with their forces for the preservation of his dominions.*" It appears that the Mahrattas were then threatening Oude through Rohilcund; that is to say, Oude was threatened to the *north* and *west*, while Allahabad and Chunar were situated to the *south* and *east*. The reason for appropriating these places as a matter of strategy is not, therefore, as obvious as the diplomatic inducements for their transfer. It is not quite so clear that their surrender served the interests of the Nawaub, as that their occupation promoted the ends of the Company. Nevertheless, by a couple of treaties, both dated the 20th of March, 1772, Chunar was taken and Allahabad was kept; and thus, during the lifetime of Shoojah-ood-Dowlah, two steps were taken in advance of the treaty of August, 1765; that is to say, his forces were restricted, his forts were appropriated and he was so far prepared for further exhibitions of the "sincere friendship" and firm "union," the complete fruition of which was reserved for his successors.

Shoojah-ood-Dowlah accordingly was not at his ease, for the firm union was beginning, "to draw" after the manner of an adhesive blister. He therefore sought an interview with Warren Hastings, who had become Governor of Bengal in 1772, and discussed a revision of existing treaties, to which the circumstances of both parties at this time predisposed them. On the one hand, at the period of Hastings' assumption of the Government, the East India Company were in one of those normal crises of their state, in which, having absorbed largely from the substance of India, they had spent all their income, and were struggling with a deficit. The finances of Hastings' government were in an embarrassed state, and to take the history of his acts at this date from Mr. Macaulay, "this embarrassment he was determined to relieve by some means, fair or foul." The language of the eminent historian so admirably describes the conduct of the Governor at this conjuncture, that we adopt it as an indispensable portion of our own narrative. According to Mr. Macaulay, "the principle which directed Hastings' dealings with his neighbours is fully expressed by the old motto of one of the great predatory families of Teviotdale, 'Thou shalt want ere I want.' He seems to have laid it down, as a fundamental proposition which could not be disputed, that when he had not as many lacs of rupees as the public service required, he was to take them from anybody who had. One thing, indeed, is to be said in excuse for him. The pressure applied to him by his employers at home was such as only the highest virtue could have withstood such as left him no choice except to commit great wrongs, or to resign his high post, and with that post all his hopes of fortune and distinction. The directors, it is true, never enjoined or applauded any crime. Far from it. Whoever examines their letters written at that time will find there many just and human sentiments, many excellent precepts—in short, an admirable code of political ethics. But every exhortation is modified or nullified by a demand for money. 'Govern leniently, and send more money;' 'Practise strict justice and moderation towards neighbouring powers, and send more money'—this is in truth the sum of all the instructions that Hastings ever received from home. Now these instructions, being interpreted, mean simply, 'Be the father and oppressor of the people: be just and unjust, moderate and rapacious.' The Directors dealt with India as the Church, in the good old times, dealt with a heretic. They delivered the victim over to the executioners, with an earnest request that all possible tenderness might be shown. We by no means accuse or suspect those who framed these despatches of hypocrisy. It is probable that, writing fifteen thousand miles from the place where their orders were to be carried into effect, they never perceived the gross inconsistency of which they were guilty. But the inconsistency was at once manifest to their Lieutenant at Calcutta, who, with an empty treasury, with an unpaid army, with his own salary often in arrear, with deficient crops, with government tenants daily running away, was called upon to remit home another half-million without fail. Hastings saw that it was absolutely necessary for him to disregard either the moral discourses or the pecuniary requisitions of his employers. Being forced to disobey them in something, he had to consider what kind of disobedience they would most readily pardon; and he correctly judged that the safest course would be to neglect the sermons and to find the rupees."

Now Shoojah-ood-Dowlah possessed rupees, but he was our firm friend and faithful ally. There was no excuse, therefore, for taking them from him against his will, as Hastings did take from the Nabob of Bengal, at this conjuncture, half the income of £320,000 a year, guaranteed by the Company and as he also took from the Mogul, on the plea that he was not independent, the districts of Corah and Allahabad, which had been given to him by the treaty of the 16th of August, 1765. With respect to the latter piece of plunder, the sequestered districts, the difficulty remained that they were so situated that they could be of no present use to the Company. They might, however, be of use to Shoojah-ood-Dowlah, who was thereupon induced to purchase them for about half a million sterling, and the stipulations for this purpose were included in a treaty of the 7th of September, 1773, dated at Benares ("Parliamentary Return of Treaties, &c.," p. 57), by which our favoured Ally was also allowed to assume the title of Wuzier of the monarchy of Hindustan, "just," says Mr. Macaulay, "as, in the last century, the Electors of Saxony and Brandenburgh, though independent of the Emperor, and often in arms against him, were proud to style themselves his 'Grand Chamberlain' and 'Grand Marshal'." There was much economy, if not foresight, in transferring these districts, with title to boot, to the particular purchaser, seeing that in less than thirty years, by the treaty of 1801, the Company were able to exact from Saadat Allie, a successor of Shoojah-ood-Dowlah, the very provinces which the latter now purchased of them, for 50,000,000 rupees, or £500,000 sterling. It is true that for the present they guaranteed "that, in the same manner, as the province of Oude and the other dominions of the Vizier are possessed by him, *so shall he possess Corah and Currah and Allahabad for ever.* He shall by no means," says the emphatic treaty, "and under no pretence, be liable to any obstructions in the aforesaid countries from the Company and the English chiefs; and, exclusive of the money now stipulated, no mention of requisition shall, by any means, be made to him for anything else on this account." Requisition, nevertheless, was made to his heirs and successors to surrender the lands which he had bought and paid for. The money's worth followed the money itself and, like a well-trained pigeon, returned to its former owner, without invalidating the original transfer. It has been said, orientally, in a sort of proverb, that, at least, "curses resemble such fowl, inasmuch as they invariably come home to roost." In this instance, the pretended blessings displayed a power of returning themselves, and, by coming home, left the beatified empty. But at this date they were seemingly a reasonable excuse for a further dip into the treasury of Shoojah-ood-Dowlah; while they were ingeniously and opportunely conferred as a part of that revision of existing treaties which he himself had solicited. As we said, Shoojah-ood-Dowlah was at this time uncomfortable. He had found a sufficient source of anxiety in the "sincere friendship and firm union" with which he was honoured. His army was restricted, his fortresses were occupied; by every fresh arrangement he was brought more directly under the influence and control of the East India Company. If their forces were not indispensable to his support, at all events it was an inevitable consequence of the alliance that they should be quartered upon him, and that he should pay their "expenses." Foreseeing this, with the resolution of an unhappy man who wishes to take a full measure of his calamity, it was his object to ascertain how much he would have to pay henceforth for services thus obtrusively rendered. Therefore, in the treaty which provided for the cession of Corah and Allahabad, he obtained a provision, entitled a security against "disputes," that he should pay for a brigade, at the rate of 2,10,000 Sicca rupees per month,[6] and that, "exclusive of the above-mentioned sum, *no more should, on any account, be demanded of him.*" This treaty, as we stated, was concluded on the 7th of September, 1773, at Benaras, and it was followed by a proceeding, on the part of Shoojah-ood-Dowlah, by which he provided against its infringement in his lifetime,—that is to say, in the year 1775 he died, and so escaped the further demands of his pertinacious Allies.

SOURCE: In *Dacoitee in Excelsis; or, The Spoliation of Oude by the East India Company* (London: J. R. Taylor, 1857).

6. It appears that this was irrespective of the arrangement between Shoojah-ood-Dowlah and the Company for the famous expedition for the subjugation of the Rohillas, which has been so eloquently described by Mr. Macaulay, in his article on Warren Hastings. Before this date, we have seen that Oude was threatened from the direction of Rohilcund by the Mahrattas, and, according to M. M. Musseehood-deen, "after the conclusion of this treaty, the Nawaub Shoojah-ood-Dowlah required the force in question for the conquest of the Rohilla country. After the Rohillas had been subdued but before the troops received orders to return, Nawaub Shoojah-ood-Dowlah died, and the army remained in possession of that principality. The Nawaub had also promised to pay, provided the Rohillas were conquered, *a further sum* of fifty lakhs of rupees, besides the pay of the troops. This is more explicitly set forth in Mr. Hastings' letter to the Nawaub, and the latter's answer thereto." The following is a translation of the letter addressed to H. E. the Nawaub Shoojah-ood-Dowlah by Warren Hastings, and dated 22nd April, 1773:—"In reply to your letter, authorising the Honourable East India Company to annihilate and extirpate the Rohillas, if they refuse to pay the agreed sum of forty lakhs of rupees, I beg leave to inform you that in case of their complying with your request, and placing you in full possession and entire control of their state, will your Excellency promise to pay the amount of fifty lakhs of rupees to the Honourable East India Company, in consideration of this service? As this sum will enable the Company to discharge the tribute they owe to the King of Delhi, and thus relieve themselves from the existing embarrassments upon their finances." The Nawaub writes to Warren Hastings, on the 18th November, 1773, as follows:—"In an interview which took place between us at Benares, it was fixed that I should pay a sum of fifty lakhs of rupees to the East India Company, and by the aid of its troops punish Rohillas, and expel them from the country." Here, then, is evidence of a special bargain for the particular service, and which was independent of the rate per month to be paid for a Brigade, as stipulated by the treaty.

Memorandum on Marquess Wellesley's Government of India
ARTHUR WELLESLEY

[The Irishman Arthur Wellesley (1769–1852), also known as the Duke of Wellington, was posted to India in 1796, where he served under his brother Richard Wellesley (1760–1842), who would later become the governor-general of India (1798–1805). Both brothers were active participants in the wars against Tipu Sultan of Mysore; Arthur Wellesley was appointed governor of Mysore after Tipu's defeat. He later built on his military training in India as commander-in-chief against the Marathas, distinguishing himself at Poona and Assaye (1803). Wellesley was knighted for his military service in 1805, and in 1807 he entered Parliament, where much of his energy was spent defending his brother's government in India. Wellesley's national fame was earned fighting Napoleon during the Peninsula Wars, where he remained undefeated, although the French ruler had allegedly dismissed the British soldier as a trivial "Sepoy General." Wellesley defeated Napoleon at Waterloo in June 1815. After his military service, Wellesley briefly served as George IV's prime minister (1828) and later served as foreign secretary under Peel (1834–1835). Wellesley's funeral was the last heraldic funeral in Great Britain; he was buried at St. Paul's Cathedral.]

The Governor-General having now relieved the peninsula of India from the danger by which it was threatened, and affairs in that quarter having been placed on foundations of strength calculated to afford lasting peace and security, turned his attention to the great and increasing cause of the weakness of the north-west frontier of the Bengal provinces. These provinces were covered in that quarter by the territories of the Nabob Vizier of Oude, who was connected with the Company by a treaty of alliance, by which, in consideration of a subsidy amounting to a sum not exceeding 50 lacs sicca rupees *per annum*, the Company were bound to defend him; and with this view to maintain at all times at least 10,000 men in his territories; and in case this number should for any cause be increased beyond 13,000 men, the Nabob was to pay the actual expense incurred by the Company. This treaty was attended by the usual stipulation of the independence of the Nabob in his internal concerns; which stipulation had been uniformly frustrated by the necessary and uniform interference of the Company in all those concerns for the support of the Nabob's authority, for the preservation of tranquility in the country, and for the security of the funds from which the Company derived so important a portion of the resources applicable to the payment of their military establishments.

For some years previous to 1798 apprehensions had been entertained that Zemaun Shah, the King of Caubul, would carry into execution an old and favourite plan of the Affghan government to invade Hindustan; and these apprehensions had appeared so well founded in 1798 that the Governor-General, Marquess Wellesley, had found it necessary to assemble a large British army in Oude, under the command of Sir J. Craig, for the protection of the Nabob's territories against this expected invasion, notwithstanding the difficulties under which the government laboured at the same period in the peninsula of India.

At the close of the year 1797 the Nabob, Azof ool Dowlah, died, and was succeeded in his government by his supposed son, Vizier Ali. This usurper had been formally deposed by the authority of the British government under Lord Teignmouth, after a full examination of the justice of his claim; and Saadut Ali had been placed in the government of Oude.

This prince was very unpopular with the army, and was not generally agreeable to his subjects. His disposition was parsimonious, and his habits were not of a nature to conciliate the affections of his turbulent subjects.

When the preparations were making to resist the expected invasion of Zemaun Shah, the Nabob, Saadut Ali, although fully convinced of the necessity of collecting the largest force upon the frontier, called for a detachment of the British troops to attend and guard his person against his own turbulent and disaffected troops. He declared repeatedly that these troops were not to be trusted in the day of battle, or on any service; and after viewing their state of discipline and equipment, and obtaining a knowledge of their principles and attachment to the cause of the allied governments, Sir J. Craig considered these troops as worse than useless, as dangerous, and of the nature of an enemy's fortress in his rear; and he actually left a detachment of British troops to watch them, and the turbulent inhabitants of Rohilcund, the frontier province of Oude to the north-west.

The Governor-General, by his negotiations at the court of Persia, had drawn the attention of the King of Caubul to the defence of his own western frontier; and availed himself of the certain tranquillity which he had obtained on the frontiers of Oude to arrange the affairs of that country on a basis better calculated to give it permanent security and tranquillity, and to increase the strength of the British government on its north-west frontier, which was one of its weakest points.

Towards the close of the year 1799 the Governor-General called upon the

Nabob of Oude to dismiss his expensive, useless, and dangerous troops, and to fill their places by increased numbers of the Company's troops. The Nabob had desired the assistance of the Governor-General in the reform of the different establishments of his government; but the British government had a right, under the article of the treaty of 1798, to require that this reform should be made. After some difficulties, arising principally from the defective principle on which the military establishments were formed, paid, and commanded, this great object was effected; and arrangements were made for introducing into the Vizier's territories 3000 additional British troops, at the expense to the Nabob Vizier of 76 lacs of Oude sicca rupees *per annum*.

In order to improve the security of Oude still further, a reform of the civil administration of the government was necessary; and this reform was pressed upon the attention of the Nabob. But while the negotiations for this purpose, and for the final arrangement of the military establishments, were going on, the Nabob plainly declared that he was not able to pay the expense of the troops which had been stationed in his country for its defence at the time of the expected invasion of Zemaun Shah, or the expense of the additional troops which had been necessarily stationed in his country upon the occasion of the reform on his military establishments, although he was bound by treaty to defray the whole of these charges.

A demand was then made upon him to give territorial security, according to the 11th article of the treaty of 1798; and, after a long negotiation, a treaty was concluded on the 10th Nov. 1801, by which, in commutation for subsidy, and for the perpetual defence of his country, the Nabob ceded to the Company the territory of Rohilcund, the Dooab, and Gorruckpoor; the two former being his frontier provinces towards the Mahrattas, the Seiks, and Affghans, and the latter bordering upon the Company; and he engaged, further, to introduce a better system of management into the territories which remained in his hands.

By the whole of this arrangement the Company gained,

1st. The advantage of getting rid of a useless and dangerous body of troops stationed on the very point of their defence, and ready at all times to join an invading enemy:

2ndly. The advantage of acquiring the means of placing upon this weak point additional numbers of the British troops, and thereby increasing its strength, and the general security of the provinces in their rear:

3rdly. Ample territorial security for the regular and perpetual payment of these funds for the support of their military establishments in Bengal:

4thly. By the introduction of their own system of government and management into the countries ceded to them and the employment of their own servants in the administration, they secured the tranquillity of those hitherto disturbed countries, the loyalty and happiness of their hitherto disaffected and turbulent inhabitants; and, above all, they acquired the resources of those rich but hitherto neglected provinces for their armies, in case of the recurrence of the necessity for military operations upon that frontier.

These advantages, the full benefit of which, as will be seen hereafter, was felt in a very few years, were gained without incurring any disadvantage whatever; in particular, that was not incurred which appears most likely to weaken a great continental power, such as the Company is in India, viz. the frontier was not increased. The Company were equally bound to defend, and had actually defended, this same frontier in 1798 and 1799, when the country was governed by the Nabob; so that all was gain and strength, without the smallest degree of disadvantage or weakness.

But the advantages in this arrangement were not gained by the Company only; those of the Nabob were at least equal to those of the Company. Whatever increased the security of the Company manifestly increased his security likewise; and here he acquired a great advantage. But this was not all. It is known that the Nabob of Oude had never collected from the countries ceded, and realised in his treasury, even the sum of 76 lacs of Oude sicca rupees, being the old subsidy paid under the treaty of 1798; much less had he realised the increased sum which he was obliged to pay in consequence of the increase of the number of troops stationed in his country. His pecuniary gain was the difference between the annual sum he realised and that which he was bound to pay. Under the new treaty of Nov. 1801, the Company were bound to defend the territories of the Nabob under all circumstances; and no new demand could be made upon him on any account, whatever might be the extent of the service, or of the expense incurred in their defence. The Nabob has already felt the full advantage of this stipulation.

Besides these advantages of a pecuniary nature, the Nabob derived others from the arrangement. The cession of the provinces had been preceded by the discharge of a large proportion of his troops; and those which remained in his service scattered over the whole surface of his enlarged territories, were unequal to the performance of the duties required from them. These duties could not, with convenience, be performed by the Company's Native troops, commanded as they are by European officers, as the civil government remained in the hands of the Nabob's Native servants. Both the Company's government and the Nabob suffered inconvenience; the former from the frequent calls of the Nabob for the service of their troops in the detail of the collections of the revenue; and the latter from the want of habit of these troops in duties of this description, and the difficulties of performing them through the agency of European officers directed by Native servants. When the provinces were ceded to the Company, the Nabob had the means and advantage of employing in a reduced territory the troops which had been found insufficient for the conduct of the administration of one of greater extent; and these troops, being more immediately under his inspection, and within the reach of his authority, were kept in better order.

Thus then, upon the whole, this arrangement has been advantageous, and has proved satisfactory, to both the parties to it, whatever may have been the difficulties in settling it; and Marquess Wellesley removed by it all the inconveniences and weakness felt upon the north-west frontier of Bengal, and added considerably to the resources of the British government.

SOURCE: Originally published in 1806, this document can be found in *Politics of the British Annexation of India,* ed. Michael Fisher (Delhi: Oxford University Press, 1993).

II
ORIENTAL DESPOTISM

INTRODUCTION
Oriental Despotisms and Political Economies
MIA CARTER AND BARBARA HARLOW

FROM THE GRANTING of its charter by Queen Elizabeth I in 1600 to the transfer of its rule to the British Crown in 1858, the British East India Company traded with and presided over an ever-expanding territory across the British subcontinent. Its practices—at once commercial, political, judicial, cultural, and legislative—provided important, if controversial, examples of the elaboration of inquiries into political economy and philosophies of history during those two-and-a-half centuries. The proponents of mercantilism (or government regulation of trade) argued, for example, with the expounders of laissez-faire and free (unregulated) trade (see Smith, *An Inquiry*). Challengers to Eastern cultures condemned their tendency toward "oriental despotism" and ascribed their susceptibility to conquest to an inherent failure to advance beyond the "Asiatic mode of production" (Marx, *Capital*, 162–63).

The term *despotism* is derived from the Greek *despotes*, meaning both "head of the family" and "master of slaves," but the formula "oriental despotism" during the European Enlightenment also came to suggest the idea of unchecked power of an agrarian emperor, to be found largely in Asia, ruling through an administrative elite and supported by the labor of slaves. The East was represented as being in a state of political, economic, and governmental stasis, allegedly due to the excesses of native rulers. Karl Marx argued in *Capital* (1887) that Indian society appeared to be structured by a rigid "law of nature." It was, therefore, "unchangeable," and its despotic native rulers would either "hoard" India's economic resources or squander its surplus economy on the building of Asiatic culture's characteristically "stupendous monuments." Marx was not alone in his essentialized thinking; other contemporary theorists and orientalists identified a variety of Indian biological and cultural symptoms, ranging from habitual decadence to insanity, as "evidence" of the subcontinent's inability to control its own material and economic resources.

For Robert Orme, one of the causes of India's economic woes was the physical condition of its inhabitants; he described the people as being "born deficient of mechanical strength" and concluded that the men of India were "the most effeminate inhabitants of the globe" (see Robert Orme's *Historical Fragments of the Mogul Empire*, originally published in 1782). The debates over the different forms of proper government and governability between East and West, between Europe and the "Orient," provided grounds for the continuing contest over power and suzerainty and the very question of just how—and, less and less, whether—Britain should rule India.

Nineteenth-century British reformers believed an improved and better-managed Company could cure many of India's ills; an open market and free trade would revive India and restore the subcontinent to a state of democratic health. In this view, free trade was believed to be fundamentally related to Western and humanitarian notions of freedom, progress, and development; the improved modern "science of national wealth," as James Mill described it, would uplift India. The concept of "oriental despotism" figured prominently in considerations of the proper practice of British rule in India—whether in the inquiry into Warren Hastings's activities as the first governor-general of India or in the legends that emerged around the militant resistance of Tipu Sultan to continuing British encroachments on local sovereignties.

BIBLIOGRAPHY

Ahmad, Aijaz. "Marx on India." In *In Theory: Classes, Nations, Literatures*. London: Verso, 1992.

Anderson, Perry. *Lineages of the Absolutist State*. London: N.L.B., 1974.

Brown, Vivienne. *Adam Smith's Discourse: Canonicity, Commerce, and Conscience*. London: Routledge, 1994.

Donner, Wendy. *The Liberal Self: John Stuart Mill's Moral and Political Philosophy*. Ithaca, N.Y.: Cornell University Press, 1991.

Dow, Alexander. *History of Hindostan*. Vol. 3, *Dissertation on Despotism*. London: T. Becket and P. A. De Hondt, 1770–1772.

Duncan, Graeme Campbell. *Marx and Mill: Two Views of Social Conflict and Social Harmony*. Cambridge: Cambridge University Press, 1973.

Embree, Ainslie T. *Imagining India: Essays on Indian History*. Delhi: Oxford University Press, 1989.

Fitzgibbons, Athol. *Adam Smith's System of Liberty, Wealth, and Virtue: The Moral and Political Foundations of the Wealth of Nations*. Oxford: Oxford University Press, 1995.

Korda, Zoltan. *The Drum*. U.S., 1938. Film.

Lipkes, Jeff. *Politics, Religion, and Classical Political Economy in Britain: John Stuart Mill and His Followers*. New York: St. Martin's Press, 1999.

Lux, Kenneth. *Adam Smith's Mistake: How a Moral Philosopher Invented Economics and Ended Morality*. Boston: Shabhala, 1990.

McNamara, Peter. *Political Economy and Statesmanship: Smith, Hamilton, and the Foundation of the Commercial Republic.* DeKalb, Ill.: Northern Illinois University Press, 1998.

Marx, Karl. *Capital.* London: J. M. Dent, 1887.

Minowitz, Peter. *Profits, Priests, and Princes: Adam Smith's Emancipation of Economics from Politics and Religion.* Stanford, Calif.: Stanford University Press, 1993.

Oakley, Allen. *Classical Economic Man: Human Agency and Methodology in the Political Economy of Adam Smith and John Stuart Mill.* Brookfield, Vt.: E. Elgar, 1994.

O'Leary, Brendan. *The Asiatic Mode of Production: Oriental Despotism, Historical Materialism, and Indian History.* Oxford: B. Blackwell, 1989.

Scott, David. "Colonial Governmentality," *Social Text* 13, no. 2 (fall 1995): 191–220.

Smith, Adam. *An Inquiry into the Nature and Causes of the Wealth of Nations.* London: W. Strahan and T. Cadell, 1776. Chapter 7, part 3.

Stephen, Leslie, Sir. *The English Utilitarians.* London: P. Smith, 1900.

Stokes, Eric. *The English Utilitarians and India.* Oxford: Clarendon Press, 1959.

Thapar, Romila. "Ideology and the Interpretation of Early Indian History." In *Interpreting Early India.* Delhi: Oxford University Press, 1993.

Wittfogel, Karl. *Oriental Despotism.* New Haven, Conn.: Yale University Press, 1957.

Zastoupil, Lynn. *John Stuart Mill and India.* Stanford, Calif.: Stanford University Press, 1994.

Distinctive Properties of a Despotic Government
BARON DE MONTESQUIEU

[Baron de Montesquieu (1689–1755) was a French political philosopher. *L'Esprit des lois* (The Spirit of Laws) treated, among other topics, the classification of governments, the separation of powers, and the political influence of climate.]

A large empire supposes a despotic authority in the person who governs. It is necessary that the quickness of the prince's resolutions should supply the distance of the places they are sent to; that fear should prevent the remissness of the distant governor or magistrate; that the law should be derived from a single person, and should shift continually, according to the accidents which incessantly multiply in a state in proportion to its extent.

SOURCE: In *The Spirit of Laws* (1746; English translation [Thomas Nugent], London: J. Nourse and P. Vaillant, 1750), book 8, section 19.

Excerpts from *Persian Letters*
BARON DE MONTESQUIEU

[*Lettres persanes* (or Persian letters) presents a satirical portrait of French and Parisian culture as seen through the eyes of two fictional Persian visitors to the European capital.]

LETTER I

Usbek to his friend Rustan, at Ispahan

We stayed only one day at Com. After we had made our devotions at the tomb of the virgin who gave birth to twelve prophets, we resumed our journey, and yesterday, twenty-five days after our departure from Ispahan, we arrived at Tauris.

Rica and I are perhaps the first Persians who, urged by a thirst for knowledge, have left their country and renounced the delights of a tranquil life in favor of the laborious search for wisdom.

We were born in a flourishing realm, but we did not believe that its boundaries were those of our knowledge, nor that the light of the Orient should alone illuminate us.

Tell me what they are saying about our journey; do not flatter me: I am not counting on many supporters. Address your letter to Erzeroum, where I will stay for some time. Farewell, my dear Rustan. Rest assured that wherever I am in the world, there you have a faithful friend.

Tauris, the 15th of the moon of Saphar, 1711

LETTER II

Usbek to the chief black eunuch, at his seraglio in Ispahan

You are the faithful guardian of the most beautiful women in Persia; to you I have entrusted my dearest worldly possessions; you hold in your hands the keys to those fated doors that are opened only for me. While you guard this precious storehouse of my love, my heart enjoys perfect ease and security. You stand guard in the silence of the night and the tumult of the day. Your untiring care sustains virtue when it falters. If the women you guard should be inclined to stray from their duty, you would destroy their hopes. You are the scourge of vice and the pillar of fidelity.

You command them, and you obey them. You execute blindly their every desire, and you make them execute the laws of the seraglio in the same way. You take pride in providing them with the humblest services; you submit with respect and fear to their legitimate orders; you serve them like the slave of their slaves. But, resuming your power, you command imperiously, even as I, whenever you fear relaxation of the laws of decency and modesty.

Remember always the oblivion from which you, then the meanest of my slaves, were brought when I put you in this employ and entrusted you with the delights of my heart. Abase yourself completely in the company of those who share my love; yet, at the same time, make them feel their entire dependence. Procure every innocent pleasure for them; beguile their anxieties; amuse them with music, dancing, and delicious drink; persuade them to meet together frequently. If they wish to go to the country, you may take them, but have any man who enters their presence put to the sword. Exhort them to cleanliness, the image of the soul's purity; speak to them sometimes of me. Would that I could see them again in that charming place they adorn. Farewell.

Tauris, the 18th of the moon of Sephar, 1711

LETTER XXXVII

Usbek to Ibben, at Smyrna

The king of France is old. We have no examples in our histories of a monarch who has reigned for such a long time. It is said that to a very high degree he possesses the talent for making himself obeyed, and that he governs his family, his court, and his state with equal ability. He has often been heard to say that of all the world's governments, that of the Turks, or that of our august sultan, pleased him most. So highly does he esteem Oriental statecraft!

I have studied his character and found contradictions I cannot resolve. For example: he has a minister of eighteen and a mistress of eighty; he loves his religion but does not suffer those who tell him he must rigorously observe it; he flees from the tumult of the cities and he is personally reticent, yet he is occupied from morning to night with making the world talk about him; he loves trophies and victories, but he fears a good general at the head of his own troops as much as if he were commanding the enemy; he is unique in that he is glutted with riches beyond any princely dreams, and yet at the same time he is afflicted by a poverty that no ordinary person would tolerate.

He enjoys giving favors to those who serve him, but he pays as liberally for the obsequious diligence or, rather, the busy laziness of his courtiers, as for the arduous campaigns of his captains. The man who undresses him, or who hands him his napkin at the table, often receives precedence over someone who captures forts or wins battles for him. He does not believe that his sovereign grandeur ought to be restrictive in the distribution of favors, and he heaps benefits on some men without investigating their real merit, believing that a man is made excellent simply by his decision to honor him. Thus, he has given a small pension to a man who ran two leagues from the enemy, and a handsome governorship to another who ran four.

He is magnificent, especially in his building. There are more statues in his palace gardens than there are citizens in a great city. His personal guard is as powerful as that of the prince before whom all thrones tremble, his armies are as large, his resources as great, and his finances as inexhaustible.

Paris, the 7th of the moon of Maharram, 1713

SOURCE: In *Persian Letters* (1721; English translation [Mr. Ozell], London: J. Tonson, 1722).

America and the East Indies
ADAM SMITH

[Adam Smith (1723–1790) was a professor of logic and, later, moral philosophy at Glasgow University. In 1759 he published his first work, *The Theory of Moral Sentiment*. *The Wealth of Nations* is a massive treatise, considered to be the first major work in political economy. A proponent of free trade, Smith described the market as a self-correcting mechanism, an analysis that would be significant in policy debates in the nineteenth century.]

If too much goes to any employment, profit falls in that employment and the proper distribution is soon restored.

It is thus that the private interests and passions of individuals naturally dispose them to turn their stock towards the employments which in ordinary cases are most advantageous to the society. But if from this natural preference they should turn too much of it towards those employments, the fall of profit in them and the rise of it in all others immediately dispose them to alter this faulty distribution. Without any intervention of law, therefore, the private interests and passions of men naturally lead them to divide and distribute the stock of every society, among all the different employments carried on in it, as nearly as possible in the proportion which is most agreeable to the interest of the whole society.

The mercantile system disturbs this distribution, especially in regard to American and Indian trade.

All the different regulations of the mercantile system, necessarily derange more or less this natural and most advantageous distribution of stock. But those which concern the trade to America and the East Indies derange it perhaps more than any other; because the trade to those two great continents absorbs a greater quantity of stock than any two other branches of trade. The regulations, however, by which this derangement is effected in those two different branches of trade are not altogether the same. Monopoly is the great engine of both; but it is a different sort of monopoly. Monopoly of one kind or another, indeed, seems to be the sole engine of the mercantile system.

The Portuguese attempted at first to exclude all other nations from trading in the Indian Seas, and the Dutch still exclude all other nations from trade with the Spice Islands.

In the trade to America every nation endeavours to engross as much as possible the whole market of its own colonies, by fairly excluding all other nations from any direct trade to them. During the greater part of the sixteenth century, the Portugueze endeavoured to manage the trade to the East Indies in the same manner, by claiming the sole right of sailing in the Indian seas, on account of the merit of having first found out the road to them. The Dutch still continue to exclude all other European nations from any direct trade to their spice islands. Monopolies of this kind are evidently established against all other European nations, who are thereby not only excluded from a trade to which it might be convenient for them to turn some part of their stock, but are obliged to buy the goods which that trade deals in somewhat dearer, than if they could import them themselves directly from the countries which produce them.

Now the principal ports are open, but each country has established an exclusive company.

But since the fall of the power of Portugal, no European nation has claimed the exclusive right of sailing in the Indian seas, of which the principal ports are now open to the ships of all European nations. Except in Portugal, however, and within these few years in France, the trade to the East Indies has in every European country been subjected to an exclusive company. Monopolies of this kind are properly established against the very nation which erects them. The greater part of that nation are thereby not only excluded from a trade to which it might be convenient for them to turn some part of their stock, but are obliged to buy the goods which that trade deals in, somewhat dearer than if it was open and free to all their countrymen. Since the establishment of the English East India company, for example, the other inhabitants of England, over and above being excluded from the trade, must have paid in the price of the East India goods which they have consumed, not only for all the extraordinary profits which the company may have made upon those goods in consequence of their monopoly, but for all the extraordinary waste which the fraud and abuse, inseparable from the management of the affairs of so great a company, must necessarily have occasioned. The absurdity of this second kind of monopoly, therefore, is much more manifest than that of the first.

Both these kinds of monopolies derange more or less the natural distribution of the stock of the society: but they do not always derange it in the same way.

Monopolies of the American kind always attract, but monopolies of exclusive companies sometimes attract, sometimes repel stock.

Monopolies of the first kind always attract to the particular trade in which they are established, a greater proportion of the stock of the society than what would go to that trade of its own accord.

Monopolies of the second kind may sometimes attract stock towards the particular trade in which they are established, and sometimes repel it from that trade according to different circumstances. In poor countries they naturally attract towards that trade more stock than would otherwise go to it. In rich countries they naturally repel from it a good deal of stock which would otherwise go to it.

In poor countries they attract,

Such poor countries as Sweden and Denmark, for example, would probably have never sent a single ship to the East Indies, had not the trade been subjected to an exclusive company. The establishment of such a company necessarily encourages adventurers. Their monopoly secures them against all competitors in the home market, and they have the same chance for foreign markets with the traders of other nations. Their monopoly shows them the certainty of a great profit upon a considerable quantity of goods, and the chance of a considerable profit upon a great quantity. Without such extraordinary encouragement, the poor traders of such poor countries would probably never have thought of hazarding their small capitals in so very distant and uncertain an adventure as the trade to the East Indies must naturally have appeared to them.

in rich they repel.

Such a rich country as Holland, on the contrary, would probably, in the case of a free trade, send many more ships to the East Indies than it actually does. The limited stock of the Dutch East India company probably repels from that trade many great mercantile capitals which would otherwise go to it. The mercantile capital of Holland is so great that it is, as it were, continually overflowing, sometimes into the public funds of foreign countries, sometimes into loans to private traders and adventurers of foreign countries, sometimes into the most roundabout foreign trades of consumption, and sometimes into the carrying trade. All near employments being completely filled up, all the capital which can be placed in them with any tolerable profit being already placed in them, the capital of Holland necessarily flows towards the most distant employments. The trade to the East Indies, if it were altogether free, would probably absorb the greater part of this redundant capital. The East Indies offer a market both for the manufactures of Europe and for the gold and silver as well as for several other productions of America, greater and more extensive than both Europe and America put together.

Both effects are hurtful,

Every derangement of the natural distribution of stock is necessarily hurtful to the society in which it takes place; whether it be by repelling from a particular trade the stock which would otherwise go to it, or by attracting towards a particular trade that which would not otherwise come to it. If, without any exclusive company, the trade of Holland to the East Indies would be greater than it actually is, that country must suffer a considerable loss by part of its capital being excluded from the employment most convenient for that part. And in the same manner, if, without an exclusive company, the trade of Sweden and Denmark to the East Indies would be less than it actually is, or, what perhaps is more probable, would not exist at all, those two countries must likewise suffer a considerable loss by part of their capital being drawn into an employment which must be more or less unsuitable to their present circumstances. Better for them, perhaps, in their present circumstances, to buy East India goods of other nations, even though they should pay somewhat dearer, than to turn so great a part of their small capital to so very distant a trade, in which the returns are so very slow, in which that capital can maintain so small a quantity of productive labour at home, where productive labour is so much wanted, where so little is done, and where so much is to do.

A country which cannot trade to the East Indies without an exclusive company should not trade there.

Though without an exclusive company, therefore, a particular country should not be able to carry on any direct trade to the East Indies, it will not from thence follow that such a company ought to be established there, but only that such a country ought not in these circumstances to trade directly to the East Indies. That such companies are not in general necessary for carrying on the East India trade, is sufficiently demonstrated by the experience of the Portugueze, who enjoyed almost the whole of it for more than a century together without any exclusive company.

The idea that the large capital of a company is necessary is fallacious.

No private merchant, it has been said, could well have capital sufficient to maintain factors and agents in the different ports of the East Indies, in order to provide goods for the ships which he might occasionally send thither; and yet, unless he was able to do this, the difficulty of finding a cargo might frequently make his ships lose the season for returning; and the expence of so long a delay would not only eat up the whole profit of the adventure, but frequently occasion a very considerable loss. This argument, however, if it proved any thing at all, would prove that no one great branch of trade could be carried on without an exclusive company, which is contrary to the experience of all nations. There is no great branch of trade in which the capital of any one private merchant is sufficient, for carrying on all the subordinate branches which must be carried on, in order to carry on the principal one. But when a nation is ripe for any great branch of trade, some merchants naturally turn their capitals towards the principal, and some towards the subordinate branches of it; and though all the different branches of it are in this manner carried on, yet it very seldom happens that they are all carried on by the capital of one private merchant. If a nation, therefore, is ripe for the East India trade, a certain portion of its capital will naturally divide itself among all the different branches of that trade. Some of its merchants will find it for their interest to reside in the East Indies, and to employ their capitals there in providing goods for the ships which are to be sent out by other merchants who reside in Europe. The settlements which different European nations have obtained in the East Indies, if they were taken from the exclusive companies to which they at present belong, and put under the immediate protection of the sovereign, would render this residence both safe and easy, at least to the merchants of the particular nations to whom those settlements belong. If at any particular time that part of the capital of any country which of its own accord tended and inclined, if I may say so, towards the East India trade, was not sufficient for carrying on all those different branches of it, it would be a proof that, at that particular time, that country was not ripe for that trade, and that it would do better to buy for some time, even at a higher price, from other European nations, the East India goods it had occasion for, than to import them itself directly from the East Indies. What it might lose by the high price of those goods could seldom be equal to the loss which it would sustain by the distraction of a large portion of its capital from other employments more necessary, or more useful, or more suitable to its circumstances and situation, than a direct trade to the East Indies.

There are not numerous and thriving colonies in Africa and the East Indies, as in America.

Though the Europeans possess many considerable settlements both upon the coast of Africa and in the East Indies, they have not yet established in either of those countries such numerous and thriving colonies as those in the islands and continent of America. Africa, however, as well as several of the countries comprehended under the general name of the East Indies, are inhabited by barbarous nations. But those nations were by no means so weak and defenceless as the miserable and helpless Americans; and in proportion to the natural fertility of the countries which they inhabited, they were besides much more populous. The most barbarous nations either of Africa or of the East Indies were shepherds; even the Hottentots were so. But the natives of every part of America, except Mexico and Peru, were only hunters; and the difference is very great between the number of shepherds and that of hunters whom the same extent of equally fertile territory can maintain. In Africa and the East Indies, therefore, it was more difficult to displace the natives, and to extend the European plantations over the greater part of the lands of the original inhabitants. The genius of exclusive companies, besides, is unfavourable, it has already been observed, to the growth of new colonies, and has probably been the principal cause of the little progress which they have made in the East Indies. The Portugueze carried on the trade both to Africa and the East Indies without any exclusive companies, and their settlements at Congo, Angola, and Benguela on the coast of Africa, and at Goa in the East Indies, though much depressed by superstition and every sort of bad government, yet bear some faint resemblance to the colonies of America, and are partly inhabited by Portugueze who have been established there for several generations. The Dutch settlements at the Cape of Good Hope and at Batavia, are at present the most considerable colonies which the Europeans have established either in Africa or in the East Indies, and both these settlements are peculiarly fortunate in their situation. The Cape of Good Hope was inhabited by a race of people almost as barbarous and quite as incapable of defending themselves as the natives of America. It is besides the half-way house, if one may say so, between Europe and the East Indies, at which almost every European ship makes some stay both in going and returning. The supplying of those ships with every sort of fresh provisions, with fruit and sometimes with wine, affords alone a very extensive market for the surplus produce of the colonists. What the Cape of Good Hope is between Europe and every part of the East Indies, Batavia is between the principal countries of the East Indies. It lies upon the most frequented road from Indostan to China and Japan, and is nearly about mid-way upon that road. Almost all the ships too that sail between Europe and China touch at Batavia; and it is, over and above all this, the center and principal mart of what is called the country trade of the East Indies; not only of that part of it which is carried on by Europeans, but of that which is carried on by the native Indians; and vessels navigated by the inhabitants of China and Japan, of Tonquin, Malacca, Cochin-China, and the island of Celebes, are frequently to be seen in its port. Such advantageous situations have enabled those two colonies to surmount all the obstacles which the oppressive genius of an exclusive company may have occasionally opposed to their growth. They have enabled Batavia to surmount the additional disadvantage of perhaps the most unwholesome climate in the world.

The Dutch exclusive company destroys spices and nutmeg trees, and has reduced the population of the Moluccas.

The English and Dutch companies, though they have established no considerable colonies, except the two above mentioned, have both made considerable conquests in the East Indies. But in the manner in which they both govern their new subjects, the natural genius of an exclusive company has shown itself most distinctly. In the spice islands the Dutch are said to burn all the spiceries which a fertile season produces beyond what they expect to dispose of in Europe with such a profit as they think sufficient. In the islands where they have no settlements, they give a premium to those who collect the young blossoms and green leaves of the clove and nutmeg trees which naturally grow there, but which this savage policy has now, it is said, almost completely extirpated. Even in the islands where they have settlements they have very much reduced, it is said, the number of those trees. If the produce even of their own islands was much greater than what suited their market, the natives, they suspect, might find means to convey some part of it to other nations; and the best way, they imagine, to secure their own monopoly, is to take care that no more shall grow than what they themselves carry to market. By different arts of oppression they have reduced the population of several of the Moluccas nearly to the number which is sufficient to supply with fresh provisions and other necessaries of life their own insignificant garrisons, and such of their ships as occasionally come there for a cargo of spices. Under the government even of the Portuguese, however, those islands are said to have been tolerably well inhabited.

The English company has the same tendency.

The English company have not yet had time to establish in Bengal so perfectly destructive a system. The plan of their government, however, has had exactly the same tendency. It has not been uncommon, I am well assured, for the chief, that is, the first clerk of a factory, to order a peasant to plough up a rich field of poppies, and sow it with rice or some other grain. The pretence was, to prevent a scarcity of provisions; but the real reason, to give the chief an opportunity of selling at a better price a large quantity of opium, which he happened then to have upon hand. Upon other occasions the order has been reversed; and a rich field of rice or other grain has been ploughed up, in order to make room for a plantation of poppies; when the chief foresaw that extraordinary profit was likely to be made by opium. The servants of the company have upon several occasions attempted to establish in their own favour the monopoly of some of the most important branches, not only of the foreign, but of the inland trade of the country. Had they been allowed to go on, it is impossible that they should not at some time or another have attempted to restrain the production of the particular articles of which they had thus usurped the monopoly, not only to the quantity which they themselves could purchase, but to that which they could expect to sell with such a profit as they might think sufficient. In the course of a century or two, the policy of the English company would in this manner have probably proved as completely destructive as that of the Dutch.

This destructive system is contrary to their interest as sovereigns,

Nothing, however, can be more directly contrary to the real interest of those companies, considered as the sovereigns of the countries which they have conquered, than this destructive plan. In almost all countries the revenue of the sovereign is drawn from that of the people. The greater the revenue of the people, therefore, the greater the annual produce of their land and labour, the more they can afford to the sovereign. It is his interest, therefore, to increase as much as possible that annual produce. But if this is the interest of every sovereign, it is peculiarly so of one whose revenue, like that of the sovereign of Bengal, arises chiefly from a land-rent. That rent must necessarily be in proportion to the quantity and value of the produce, and both the one and the other must depend upon the extent of the market. The quantity will always be suited with more or less exactness to the consumption of those who can afford to pay for it, and the price which they will pay will always be in proportion to the eagerness of their competition. It is the interest of such a sovereign, therefore, to open the most extensive market for the produce of his

Oriental Despotism 103

country, to allow the most perfect freedom of commerce, in order to increase as much as possible the number and the competition of buyers; and upon this account to abolish, not only all monopolies, but all restraints upon the transportation of the home produce from one part of the country to another, upon its exportation to foreign countries, or upon the importation of goods of any kind for which it can be exchanged. He is in this manner most likely to increase both the quantity and value of that produce, and consequently of his own share of it, or of his own revenue.

but they prefer the transitory profits of the monopolist merchant to the permanent revenue of the sovereign.

But a company of merchants are, it seems, incapable of considering themselves as sovereigns, even after they have become such. Trade, or buying in order to sell again, they still consider as their principal business, and by a strange absurdity, regard the character of the sovereign as but an appendix to that of the merchant, as something which ought to be made subservient to it, or by means of which they may be enabled to buy cheaper in India, and thereby to sell with a better profit in Europe. They endeavour for this purpose to keep out as much as possible all competitors from the market of the countries which are subject to their government, and consequently to reduce, at least, some part of the surplus produce of those countries to what is barely sufficient for supplying their own demand, or to what they can expect to sell in Europe with such a profit as they may think reasonable. Their mercantile habits draw them in this manner, almost necessarily, though perhaps insensibly, to prefer upon all ordinary occasions the little and transitory profit of the monopolist to the great and permanent revenue of the sovereign, and would gradually lead them to treat the countries subject to their government nearly as the Dutch treat the Moluccas. It is the interest of the East India company considered as sovereigns, that the European goods which are carried to their Indian dominions, should be sold there as cheap as possible; and that the Indian goods which are brought from thence should bring there as good a price, or should be sold there as dear as possible. But the reverse of this is their interest as merchants. As sovereigns, their interest is exactly the same with that of the country which they govern. As merchants, their interest is directly opposite to that interest.

The administration in India thinks only of buying cheap and selling dear,

But if the genius of such a government, even as to what concerns its direction in Europe, is in this manner essentially and perhaps incurably faulty, that of its administration in India is still more so. That administration is necessarily composed of a council of merchants, a profession no doubt extremely respectable, but which in no country in the world carries along with it that sort of authority which naturally over-awes the people, and without force commands their willing obedience. Such a council can command obedience only by the military force with which they are accompanied, and their government is therefore necessarily military and despotical. Their proper business, however, is that of merchants. It is to sell, upon their masters' account, the European goods consigned to them, and to buy in return Indian goods for the European market. It is to sell the one as dear and to buy the other as cheap as possible, and consequently to exclude as much as possible all rivals from the particular market where they keep their shop. The genius of the administration, therefore, so far as concerns the trade of the company, is the same as that of the direction. It tends to make government subservient to the interest of monopoly, and consequently to stunt the natural growth of some parts at least of the surplus produce of the country to what is barely sufficient for answering the demand of the company.

its members trade on their own account and cannot be prevented from doing so, and this private trade is more extensive and harmful than the public trade of the company.

All the members of the administration, besides, trade more or less upon their own account, and it is in vain to prohibit them from doing so. Nothing can be more completely foolish than to expect that the clerks of a great counting-house at ten thousand miles distance, and consequently almost quite out of sight, should, upon a simple order from their masters, give up at once doing any sort of business upon their own account, abandon for ever all hopes of making a fortune, of which they have the means in their hands, and content themselves with the moderate salaries which those masters allow them, and which, moderate as they are, can seldom be augmented, being commonly as large as the real profits of the company trade can afford. In such circumstances, to prohibit the servants of the company from trading upon their own account, can have scarce any other effect than to enable the superior servants, under pretence of executing their masters order, to oppress such of the inferior ones as have had the misfortune to fall under their displeasure. The servants naturally endeavour to establish the same monopoly in favour of their own private trade as of the public trade of the company. If they are suffered to act as they could wish, they will establish this monopoly openly and directly, by fairly prohibiting all other people from trading in the articles in which they chuse to deal; and this, perhaps, is the best and least oppressive way of establishing it. But if by an order from Europe they are prohibited from doing this, they will, notwithstanding, endeavour to establish a monopoly of the same kind, secretly and indirectly, in a way that is much more destructive to the country. They will employ the whole authority of government, and pervert the administration of justice, in order to harass and ruin those who interfere with them in any branch of commerce which, by means of agents, either concealed, or at least not publicly avowed, they may chuse to carry on. But the private trade of the servants will naturally extend to a much greater variety of articles than the public trade of the company. The public trade of the company extends no further than the trade with Europe, and comprehends a part only of the foreign trade of the country. But the private trade of the servants may extend to all the different branches both of its inland and foreign trade. The monopoly of the company can tend only to stunt the natural growth of that part of the surplus produce which, in the case of a free trade, would be exported to Europe. That of the servants tends to stunt the natural growth of every part of the produce in which they chuse to deal, of what is destined for home consumption, as well as of what is destined for exportation; and consequently to degrade the cultivation of the whole country, and to reduce the number of its inhabitants. It tends to reduce the quantity of every sort of produce, even that of the necessaries of life, whenever the servants of the company chuse to deal in them, to what those servants can both afford to buy and expect to sell with such a profit as pleases them.

The interest of the servants is not, like the real interest of the company, the same as that of the country.

From the nature of their situation too the servants must be more disposed to support with rigorous severity their own interest against that of the country which they govern, than their masters can be to support theirs. The country belongs to their masters, who cannot avoid having some regard for the interest of what belongs to them. But it does not belong to the servants. The real interest of their masters, if they were capable of understanding it, is the same with that of the country, and it is from ignorance chiefly, and the meanness of mercantile prejudice, that they ever oppress it. But the real interest of the servants is by no means the same with that of the country, and the most perfect information would not necessarily put an end to their oppressions. The regulations accordingly which have been sent out from Europe, though they have been frequently weak, have upon most occasions been well-meaning. More intelligence and perhaps less good-meaning has sometimes appeared in those established by the servants in India. It is a very singular government in which every member of the administration wishes to get out of the country, and consequently to have done with the government, as soon as he can, and to whose interest, the day after he has left it and carried his whole fortune with him, it is perfectly indifferent though the whole country was swallowed up by an earthquake.

The evils come from the system, not from the character of the men who administer it.

I mean not, however, by any thing which I have here said, to throw any odious imputation upon the general character of the servants of the East India company, and much less upon that of any particular persons. It is the system of government, the situation in which they are placed, that I mean to censure; not the character of those who have acted in it. They acted as their situation naturally directed, and they who have clamoured the loudest against them would, probably, not have acted better themselves. In war and negociation, the councils of Madras and Calcutta have upon several occasions conducted themselves with a resolution and decisive wisdom which would have done honour to the senate of Rome in the best days of that republic. The members of those councils, however, had been bred to professions very different from war and politics. But their situation alone, without education, experience, or even example, seems to have formed in them all at once the great qualities which it required, and to have inspired them both with abilities and virtues which they themselves could not well know that they possessed. If upon some occasions, therefore, it has animated them to actions of magnanimity which could not well have been expected from them, we should not wonder if upon others it has prompted them to exploits of somewhat a different nature.

Exclusive companies are nuisances.

Such exclusive companies, therefore, are nuisances in every respect; always more or less inconvenient to the countries in which they are established, and destructive to those which have the misfortune to fall under their government.

SOURCE: Chapter 7 in *An Inquiry into the Nature and Causes of the Wealth of Nations* (London: W. Strahan and T. Cadell, 1776), part 3.

Of the Government and People of Indostan
ROBERT ORME

[Robert Orme (1728–1801) was initially employed as a Company writer in 1742; he later became a member of the Madras Council (1754–1758). Orme was also a friend of Robert Clive, and his fortunes rose and fell alongside those of the illustrious warrior-merchant and notorious nabob; Orme would eventually have charges of extortion leveled against him. Years later, in 1769, he was employed as the historiographer for the East India Company.]

NATURE OF THE GOVERNMENT OF INDOSTAN IN GENERAL

Whoever considers the vast extent of the empire of Indostan, will easily conceive, that the influence of the emperor, however despotic, can but faintly reach those parts of his dominion which lay at the greatest distance from his capital.

This extent has occasioned the division of the whole kingdom into distinct provinces, over each of which the Mogul appoints a Viceroy.

These Viceroys are, in their provinces, called Nabobs; and their territories are again subdivided into particular districts, many of which are under the government of Rajahs. These are the descendants of such Gentoo Princes, who, before the conquest of the kingdom, ruled over the same districts.

The Gentoos, having vastly the superiority in numbers throughout the kingdom, have obliged the Moors to submit to this regulation in their government.

The Nabobs ought annually to remit to the throne the revenues of their provinces, which are either ascertained at a fixed sum, or are to be the total produce of the country, authenticated by regular accounts, after deductions made for the expenses of the government.

If the officers of the throne are satisfied, which is oftener effected by intrigue, than by the justice of his administration, the Nabob continues in favour; if not, another is appointed to succeed him.

A new appointed Nabob set out from Delhi, riding with his back turned to the head of his elephant: his attendants asked him the reason of that uncustomary posture; he said that he was looking out for his successor.

On the temper of the Nabob or his favourites, depends, the happiness or misery of the province. On the temper of the King or his ministers, depends the security of the Nabob and his favourites.

The Rajahs who govern in particular districts, are, notwithstanding their hereditary right, subject to the caprice and power of the Nabob, as the army is with him.

Even this appointment of Viceroys was found too weak a representation of the royal power in the extreme parts of the kingdom; to which orders from the court are three months in arriving.

This insurmountable inconvenience occasioned the subjecting several provinces, with their distinct Nabobs, to the authority of one, who is deemed the highest representative of the Mogul.

Princes of this rank are called Subahs. Nizamalmuluck was Subah of the Decan (or southern) provinces. He had under his government all the countries laying to the south of Aurengabad, bordered on the west by the Morattoes and the Malabar coast, to the eastward extending to the sea. The Nabobs of Condanore, Cudapah, Carnatica, Yalore, &c. the Kings of Tritchinopoly, Mysore, Tanjore, are subject to this Subahship. Here is a subject ruling a larger empire than any in Europe, excepting that of the Muscovite.

The consequence of so large a dominion at such a distance from the capital has been, that an active, wily prince, could overwhelm the empire itself, which Nizamalmuluck actually did, by bringing Thamas Kouli Khan into the kingdom.

Allaverdy Khan the Prince of Bengal is a Subah. He too lies at a vast distance from Delhi. He is a great warrior, and has never paid the court any tribute. The Morattoes were sent as freebooters into his country, to divert him from attempting the throne itself. He has, notwithstanding, been able to add to his dominion the whole province of Patna, which before was dependant only on the King. His relations are at this time the Nabobs of that province.

Thus the contumacy of Viceregents resisting their sovereign, or battling amongst themselves, is continually productive of such scenes of bloodshed, and of such deplorable devastations, as no other nation in the universe is subject to.

If the subjects of a despotic power are every where miserable, the miseries of the people of Indostan are multiplied by the incapacity of the power to controul the vast extent of its dominion.

PARTICULAR GOVERNMENT OF THE PROVINCES

Every province is governed by a subordination of officers, who hold from no other power than that of the Nabob.

Nabob (derived from *Naib*, a word signifying deputy) is a title which, at Delhi, none but those who are styled thus in a commission given by the King, dare to assume. In distant provinces Nabobs have governed, who have been registered as dead at Delhi. A Nabob, although appointed by a Subah, ought to have his commission confirmed by the King, or one with an authentic commission appears to supplant him. He then depends upon his own force, or the support of his Subah, and a war between the competitors ensues.

A Nabob is so far despotic in his government, as he can rely upon the protection of his sovereign or his superior. Secure of this, he has nothing to apprehend, but poison or assassination from the treachery or resentment of his subjects.

Nabobs more particularly attach themselves to the command of the army, and leave the civil administration to the Duan.

Duan is properly the judge of the province in civil matters. This office is commonly devolved on a Gentoo, in provinces which by their vicinity or importance to the throne, are more immediately subject to its attention. This officer holds his commission from the King. But by the nature of the government of Indostan, where all look only to one head, he is never more than an assistant; he may be a spy; he cannot be a rival to the power of the Nabob.

He therefore comprehends in his person the offices of Prime Minister, Lord Chancellor, and Secretary of State, without presuming to advise, judge, or issue orders, but according to the will of his master, or to the influence which he has over it. Under the Duan is an officer called the Buggshi, or Buxey, who is the paymaster of the troops, and the disburser of all the public expences of the government. This must be a post of great advantage. The Buxey has under him an Amuldar, who is the overseer and manager of all the occasions of expence.

Revenues, imposts, and taxes, are levied throughout the country, by the appearance, if not by the force of the soldiers. The other officers of the province are therefore more immediately military.

Phousdar signifies the commander of a detached body of the army, and in the military government, is a title next to that of the Nabob. As the governors of particular parts of the province have always some troops under their command, such governors are called Phousdars; although very often the Nabob himself holds no more than this rank at the court of Delhi, from whence all addresses to the rulers of inferior provinces, make use only of this term.

Pollygar, from the word Pollum, which signifies a town situated in a wood, is the governor of such a town and the country about it; and is likewise become the title of all who rule any considerable town, commanding a large district of land. This term is only used on the coast of Coromandel. In other provinces of the empire, all such governors pass under the general title of Zemindars.

A Havildar is the officer placed by the government to superintend a small village.

The Havildar plunders the village, and is himself fleeced by the Zemindar; the Zemindar by the Phousdar; the Phousdar by the Nabob, or his Duan. The Duan is the Nabob's head slave: and the Nabob compounds on the best terms he can make, with his Subah, or the throne. Wherever this gradation is interrupted, bloodshed ensues.

Kellidar is the governor or commander of a fort.

Munsubbar is now a title of honour held from the throne, and exalted according to the number of horsemen which he is permitted in his commission to command. There are Munsubbars of ten thousand, and others of two hundred and fifty. This title originally signified a commissioned officer, who by favour from the throne had obtained a particular district of lands, to be allotted for his maintenance instead of a salary.

Zemindar, derived from Zemin, the word signifying lands, is the proprietor of a tract of land given in inheritance by the King or the Nabob, and who stipulates the revenue which he is to pay for the peaceable possession of it. Such Zemindars are not now to be frequently met with; but the title every where: it is transferred to all the little superintendants or officers under the Phousdar.

Cazee is the Mahomedan judge ecclesiastical, who supports and is supported by the *Alcoran*. He is extremely venerated.

In treating upon the administration of justice in Indostan, farther lights will be thrown upon this subject of the government of the provinces.

SOURCE: In *Historical Fragments of the Mogul Empire* (London: F. Windgrave, 1805, 1782; reprint, New Delhi: Associated Publishing House, 1974).

Excerpt from *The Principles of Political Economy*
JOHN STUART MILL

[John Stuart Mill (1806–1873) was a philosopher, economist, and lifelong social reformer. He founded the *Westminster Review,* the journal of radical philosophers and reformers. Mill was the head of the Examiner's Office in India House (1856–58), a period during which he opposed the transfer of the East India Company to the British Crown. His influential works include *Essays on Some Unsettled Questions of Political Economy* (1844) and *The Principles of Political Economy* (1848).]

The first of these modes of appropriation, by the government, is characteristic of the extensive monarchies which from a time beyond historical record have occupied the plains of Asia. The government, in those countries, though varying in its qualities according to the accidents of personal character, seldom leaves much to the cultivators beyond mere necessaries, and often strips them so bare even of these, that it finds itself obliged, after taking all they have, to lend part of it back to those from whom it has been taken, in order to provide them with seed, and enable them to support life until another harvest. Under the régime in question, though the bulk of the population are ill provided for, the government, by collecting small contributions from great numbers, is enabled, with any tolerable management, to make a show of riches quite out of proportion to the general condition of the society; and hence the inveterate impression, of which Europeans have only at a late period been disabused, concerning the great opulence of Oriental nations. In this wealth, without reckoning the large portion which adheres to the hands employed in collecting it, many persons of course participate, besides the immediate household of the sovereign. A large part is distributed among the various functionaries of government, and among the objects of the sovereign's favour or caprice. A part is occasionally employed in works of public utility. The tanks, wells, and canals for irrigation, without which in many tropical climates cultivation could hardly be carried on; the embankments which confine the rivers, the bazars for dealers, and the seraees for travellers, none of which could have been made by the scanty means in the possession of those using them, owe their existence to the liberality and enlightened self-interest of the better order of princes, or to the benevolence or ostentation of here and there a rich individual, whose fortune, if traced to its source, is always found to have been drawn immediately or remotely from the public revenue, most frequently by a direct grant of a portion of it from the sovereign.

The ruler of a society of this description, after providing largely for his own support, and that of all persons in whom he feels an interest, and after maintaining as many soldiers as he thinks needful for his security or his state, has a disposable residue, which he is glad to exchange for articles of luxury suitable to his disposition: as have also the class of persons who have been enriched by his favour, or by handling the public revenues. A demand thus arises for elaborate and costly manufactured articles, adapted to a narrow but a wealthy market. This demand is often supplied almost exclusively by the merchants of more advanced communities, but often also raises up in the country itself a class of artificers, by whom certain fabrics are carried to as high excellence as can be given by patience, quickness of perception and observation, and manual dexterity, without any considerable knowledge of the properties of objects: such as some of the cotton fabrics of India. These artificers are fed by the surplus food which has been taken by the government and its agents as their share of the produce. So literally is this the case, that in some countries the workman, instead of taking his work home, and being paid for it after it is finished, proceeds with his tools to his customer's house, and is there subsisted until the work is complete. The insecurity, however, of all possessions in this state of society, induces even the richest purchasers to give a preference to such articles as, being of an imperishable nature, and containing great value in small bulk, are adapted for being concealed or carried off. Gold and jewels, therefore, constitute a large proportion of the wealth of these nations, and many a rich Asiatic carries nearly his whole fortune on his person, or on those of the women of his harem. No one, except the monarch, thinks of investing his wealth in a manner not susceptible of removal. He, indeed, if he feels safe on his throne, and reasonably secure of transmitting it to his descendants, sometimes indulges a taste for durable edifices, and produces the Pyramids, or the Taj Mehal and the Mausoleum at Sekundra. The rude manufactures destined for the wants of the cultivators are worked up by village artisans, who are remunerated by land given to them rent-free to cultivate, or by fees paid to them in kind from such share of the crop as is left to the villagers by the government. This state of society, however, is not destitute of a mercantile class; composed of two divisions, grain dealers and money dealers. The grain dealers do not usually buy grain from the producers, but from the agents of government, who, receiving the revenue in kind, are glad to devolve upon others the business of conveying it to the places where the prince, his chief civil and military officers, the bulk of his troops, and the artisans who supply the wants of these various persons, are assembled. The money dealers lend to the unfortunate cultivators, when ruined by bad seasons or fiscal exactions, the means of supporting life and continuing their cultivation, and are repaid with enormous interest at the next harvest; or, on a larger scale, they lend to the government, or to those to whom it has granted a portion of the revenue, and are indemnified by assignments on the revenue collectors, or by having certain districts put into their possession, that they may pay themselves from the revenues; to enable them to do which, a great portion of the powers of government are usually made over simultaneously, to be exercised by them until either the districts are redeemed, or their receipts have liquidated the debt. Thus, the commercial operations of both these classes of dealers take place principally upon that part of the produce of the country which forms the revenue of the government. From that revenue their capital is periodically replaced with a profit, and that is also the source from which their original funds have almost always been derived. Such, in its general features, is the economical condition of most of the countries of Asia, as it has been from beyond the commencement of authentic history, and is still, wherever not disturbed by foreign influences.

SOURCE: John Stuart Mill, *The Principles of Political Economy* (New York: D. Appleton, 1884).

Excerpt from "Considerations on Representative Government"
JOHN STUART MILL

At some period, however, of their history, almost every people, now civilized, have consisted, in majority, of slaves. A people in that condition require to raise them out of it a very different polity from a nation of savages. If they are energetic by nature, and especially if there be associated with them in the same community an industrious class who are neither slaves nor slave-owners (as was the case in Greece), they need, probably, no more to ensure their improvement than to make them free: when freed, they may often be fit, like Roman freedmen, to be admitted at once into the full rights of citizenship. This, however, is not the normal condition of slavery, and is generally a sign that it is becoming obsolete. A slave, properly so called, is a being who has not learnt to help himself. He is, no doubt, one step in advance of a savage. He has not the first lesson of political society still to acquire. He has learnt to obey. But what he obeys is only a direct command. It is the characteristic of *born* slaves to be incapable of conforming their conduct to a rule, or law. They can only do what they are ordered, and only when they are ordered to do it. If a man whom they fear is standing over them and threatening them with punishment, they obey; but when his back is turned, the work remains undone. The motive determining them must appeal not to their interests, but to their instincts; immediate hope or immediate terror. A despotism, which may tame the savage, will, in so far as it is a despotism, only confirm the slaves in their incapacities. Yet a government under their own control would be entirely unmanageable by them. Their improvement cannot come from themselves, but must be superinduced from without. The step which they have to take, and their only path to improvement, is to be raised from a government of will to one of law. They have to be taught self-government, and this, in its initial stage, means the capacity to act on general instructions. What they require is not a government of force, but one of guidance. Being, however, in too low a state to yield to the guidance of any but those to whom they look up as the possessors of force, the sort of government fittest for them is one which possesses force, but seldom uses it: a parental despotism or aristocracy, resembling the St. Simonian form of socialism; maintaining a general superintendence over all the operations of society, so as to keep before each the sense of a present force sufficient to compel his obedience to the rule laid down, but which, owing to the impossibility of descending to regulate all the minutiæ of industry and life, necessarily leaves and induces individuals to do much of themselves. This, which may be termed the government of leading-strings, seems to be the one required to carry such a people the most rapidly through the next necessary step in social progress. Such appears to have been the idea of the government of the Incas of Peru; and such was that of the Jesuits in Paraguay. I need scarcely remark that leading-strings are only admissible as a means of gradually training the people to walk alone.

It would be out of place to carry the illustration further. To attempt to investigate what kind of government is suited to every known state of society, would be to compose a treatise, not on representative government, but on political science at large. For our more limited purpose we borrow from political philosophy only its general principles. To determine the form of government most suited to any particular people, we must be able, among the defects and shortcomings which belong to that people, to distinguish those that are the immediate impediment to progress; to discover what it is which (as it were) stops the way. The best government for them is the one which tends most to give them that for want of which they cannot advance, or advance only in a lame and lopsided manner. We must not, however, forget the reservation necessary in all things which have for their object improvement, or Progress; namely, that in seeking the good which is needed, no damage, or as little as possible, be done to that already possessed. A people of savages should be taught obedience, but not in such a manner as to convert them into a people of slaves. And (to give the observation a higher generality) the form of government which is most effectual for carrying a people through the next stage of progress, was still be very improper for them if it does this in such a manner as to obstruct, or positively unfit them for, the step next beyond. Such cases are frequent, and are among the most melancholy facts in history. The Egyptian hierarchy, the paternal despotism of China, were very fit instruments for carrying those nations up to the point of civilization which they attained. But having reached that point, they were brought to a permanent halt, for want of mental liberty and individuality; requisites of improvement which the institutions that had carried them thus far, entirely incapacitated them from acquiring; and as the institutions did not break down and give place to others, further improvement stopped. In contrast with these nations, let us consider the example of an opposite character afforded by another and a comparatively insignificant Oriental people—the Jews. They, too, had an absolute monarchy and a hierarchy, and their organized institutions were as obviously of sacerdotal origin as those of the Hindoos. These did for them what was done for other Oriental races by their institutions—subdued them to industry and order, and gave them a national life. But neither their kings nor their priests ever obtained, as in those other countries, the exclusive moulding of their character. Their religion, which enabled persons of genius and a high religious tone to be regarded and to regard themselves as inspired from heaven, gave existence to an inestimably precious unorganized institution—the Order (if it may be so termed) of Prophets. Under the protection, generally though not always effectual, of their sacred character, the Prophets were a power in the nation, often more than a match for kings and priests, and kept up, in that little corner of the earth, the antagonism of influences which is the only real security for continued progress. Religion consequently was not there, what it has been in so many other places—a consecration of all that was once established, and a barrier against further improvement. The remark of a distinguished Hebrew, M. Salvador, that the Prophets were, in Church and State, the equivalent of the modern liberty of the press, gives a just but not an adequate conception of the part fulfilled in national and universal history by this great element of Jewish life; by means of which, the canon of inspiration never being complete, the persons most eminent in genius and moral feeling could not only denounce and reprobate, with the direct authority of the Almighty, whatever appeared to them deserving of such treatment, but could give forth better and higher interpretations of the national religion, which thenceforth became part of the religion. Accordingly, whoever can divest himself of the habit of reading the Bible as if it was one book, which until lately was equally inveterate in Christians and in unbelievers, sees with admiration the vast interval between the morality and religion of the Pentateuch, or even of the historical books (the unmistakeable work of Hebrew Conservatives of the sacerdotal order), and the morality and religion of the Prophecies: a distance as wide as between these last and the Gospels. Conditions more favourable to Progress could not easily exist: accordingly, the Jews, instead of being stationary like other Asiatics, were, next to the Greeks, the most progressive people of antiquity, and, jointly with them, have been the starting-point and main propelling agency of modern cultivation.

A good despotism means a government in which, so far as depends on the despot, there is no positive oppression by officers of state, but in which all the collective interests of the people are managed for them, all the thinking that has relation to collective interests done for them, and in which their minds are formed by, and consenting to, this abdication of their own energies. Leaving things to the Government, like leaving them to Providence, is synonymous with caring nothing about them, and accepting their results, when disagreeable, as visitations of Nature. With the exception, therefore, of a few studious men who take an intellectual interest in speculation for its own sake, the intelligence and sentiments of the whole people are given up to the material interests, and when these are provided for, to the amusement and ornamentation, of private life. But to say this is to say, if the whole testimony of history is worth anything, that the era of national decline has arrived: that is, if the nation had ever attained anything to decline from. If it has never risen above the condition of an Oriental people, in that condition it continues to stagnate. But if, like Greece or Rome, it had realized anything higher, through the energy, patriotism, and enlargement of mind, which as national qualities are the fruits solely of freedom, it relapses in a few generations into the Oriental state. And that state does not mean stupid tranquillity, with security against change for the worse; it often means being overrun, conquered, and reduced to domestic slavery, either by a stronger despot, or by the nearest barbarous people who retain along with their savage rudeness the energies of freedom.

In proportion as success in life is seen or believed to be the fruit of fatality or accident and not of exertion, in that same ratio does envy develop itself as a point of national character. The most envious of all mankind are the Orientals. In Oriental moralists, in Oriental tales, the envious man is markedly prominent. In real life, he is the terror of all who possess anything desirable, be it a palace, a handsome child, or even good health and spirits: the supposed effect of his mere look constitutes the all-pervading superstition of the evil eye. Next to Orientals in envy, as in activity, are some of the Southern Europeans. The Spaniards pursued all their great men with it, embittered their lives, and generally succeeded in putting an early stop to their successes.[1] With the French, who are essentially a southern people, the double education of despotism and Catholicism has, in spite of their impulsive temperament, made submission and endurance the common character of the people, and their most received notion of wisdom and excellence: and if envy of one another, and of all superiority, is not more rife among them than it is, the circumstance must be ascribed to the many valuable counteracting elements in the French character, and most of all to the great individual energy which, though less persistent and more intermittent than in the self-helping and struggling Anglo-Saxons, has nevertheless manifested itself among the French in nearly every direction in which the operation of their institutions has been favourable to it.

SOURCE: In *Considerations on Representative Government* (New York: Harper and Brothers, 1862).

On Imperialism in India
KARL MARX

Marx's way of analyzing the problems of an Asian society under European imperial rule is reflected in these two articles which he wrote in English for *The New York Daily Tribune* and which were printed in its issues of June 25 and August 8, 1853. Of special interest in the analysis is the conception he entertained of Oriental despotism as an antique form of class society with a ruling bureaucracy based on large-scale irrigation works. We may note, too, his assumption that it was the fate of non-Western societies like that of India to go the way of bourgeois development as seen in modern Europe.

THE BRITISH RULE IN INDIA

London, Friday, June 10, 1853

Hindostan is an Italy of Asiatic dimensions, the Himalayas for the Alps, the Plains of Bengal for the Plains of Lombardy, the Deccan for the Appenines, and the Isle of Ceylon for the Island of Sicily. The same rich variety

---

1. I limit the expression to past time, because I would say nothing derogatory of a great, and now at last a free, people, who are entering into the general movement of European progress with a vigour which bids fair to make up rapidly the ground they have lost. No one can doubt what Spanish intellect and energy are capable of; and their faults as a people are chiefly those for which freedom and industrial ardour are a real specific.

in the products of the soil, and the same dismemberment in the political configuration. Just as Italy has, from time to time, been compressed by the conqueror's sword into different national masses, so do we find Hindostan, when not under the pressure of the Mohammedan, or the Mogul,[1] or the Briton, dissolved into as many independent and conflicting States as it numbered towns, or even villages. Yet, in a social point of view, Hindostan is not the Italy, but the Ireland of the East. And this strange combination of Italy and of Ireland, of a world of voluptuousness and of a world of woes, is anticipated in the ancient traditions of the religion of Hindostan. That religion is at once a religion of sensualist exuberance, and a religion of self-torturing asceticism; a religion of the Lingam[2] and of the Juggernaut; the religion of the Monk, and of the Bayadere.

I share not the opinion of those who believe in a golden age of Hindostan, without recurring, however, like Sir Charles Wood, for the confirmation of my view, to the authority of Khuli-Khan. But take, for example, the times of Aurung-Zebe;[3] or the epoch, when the Mogul appeared in the North, and the Portuguese in the South; or the age of Mohammedan invasion, and of the Heptarchy[4] in Southern India; or, if you will, go still more back to antiquity, take the mythological chronology of the Brahmin[5] himself, who places the commencement of Indian misery in an epoch even more remote than the Christian creation of the world.

There cannot, however, remain any doubt but that the misery inflicted by the British on Hindostan is of an essentially different and infinitely more intensive kind than all Hindostan had to suffer before. I do not allude to European despotism, planted upon Asiatic despotism, by the British East India Company,[6] forming a more monstrous combination than any of the divine monsters startling us in the temple of Salsette.[7] This is no distinctive

---

1. *Mogul* dynasty: Moslem dynasty founded by Babur in 1526.
2. *Lingam:* Phallic emblem of the Hindu god Shiva. *Juggernaut* (Jaganath): An avatar of the god Vishnu.
3. *Aurung-Zebe:* Mogul emperor (1659–1707) who attempted to suppress Hinduism.
4. The *Heptarchy* (Seven Governments): The conventional designation in English history of the seven Saxon Kingdoms (sixth to eighth century). Marx by analogy uses this term here to denote the feudal dismemberment of the Deccan before its conquest by the Moslems.
5. *Brahmin:* A Hindu of the highest caste.
6. The *British East India Company* was organised in 1600 for the purpose of carrying on a monopoly trade with India. Under cover of the Company's "trading" operations the English capitalists conquered the country and governed it for decades. During the Indian uprising of 1857–1859 the Company was dissolved and the British Government began to rule India directly.
7. *The temple of Salsette:* A cave temple situated on the island of that name near the city of Bombay. It contains a huge number of carvings, chiselled in stone like the entire temple itself.

feature of British colonial rule, but only an imitation of the Dutch, and so much so that in order to characterise the working of the British East India Company, it is sufficient to literally repeat what Sir Stamford Raffles, the *English* Governor of Java, said of the old Dutch East India Company:

"The Dutch Company, actuated solely by the spirit of gain, and viewing their subjects with less regard or consideration than a West India planter formerly viewed a gang upon his estate, because the latter had paid the purchase money of human property, which the other had not, employed all the existing machinery of despotism to squeeze from the people their utmost mite of contribution, the last dregs of their labour, and thus aggravated the evils of a capricious and semi-barbarous Government, by working it with all the practised ingenuity of politicians, and all the monopolising selfishness of traders."

All the civil wars, invasions, revolutions, conquests, famines, strangely complex, rapid and destructive as the successive action in Hindostan may appear, did not go deeper than its surface. England has broken down the entire framework of Indian society, without any symptoms of reconstitution yet appearing. This loss of his old world, with no gain of a new one, imparts a particular kind of melancholy to the present misery of the Hindoo, and separates Hindostan, ruled by Britain, from all its ancient traditions, and from the whole of its past history.

There have been in Asia, generally, from immemorial times, but three departments of Government: that of Finance, or the plunder of the interior; that of War, or the plunder of the exterior; and, finally, the department of Public Works. Climate and territorial conditions, especially the vast tracts of desert, extending from the Sahara, through Arabia, Persia, India and Tartary, to the most elevated Asiatic highlands, constituted artificial irrigation by canals and waterworks the basis of Oriental agriculture. As in Egypt and India, inundations are used for fertilising the soil of Mesopotamia, Persia, etc.; advantage is taken of a high level for feeding irrigative canals. This prime necessity of an economical and common use of water, which, in the Occident, drove private enterprise to voluntary association, as in Flanders and Italy, necessitated, in the Orient where civilisation was too low and the territorial extent too vast to call into life voluntary association, the interference of the centralising power of Government. Hence an economical function devolved upon all Asiatic Governments the function of providing public works. This artificial fertilisation of the soil, dependent on a Central Government, and immediately decaying with the neglect of irrigation and drainage, explains the otherwise strange fact that we now find whole territories barren and desert that were once brilliantly cultivated, as Palmyra, Petra, the ruins in Yemen, and large provinces of Egypt, Persia and Hindostan; it also explains how a single war of devastation has been able to depopulate a country for centuries, and to strip it of all its civilisation.

Now, the British in East India accepted from their predecessors the department of finance and of war, but they have neglected entirely that of public works. Hence the deterioration of an agriculture which is not capable of being conducted on the British principle of free competition, of *laissez-faire* and *laissez-aller*. But in Asiatic empires we are quite accustomed to see agriculture deteriorating under one government and reviving again under some other government. There the harvests correspond to good or bad government, as they change in Europe with good or bad seasons. Thus the oppression and neglect of agriculture, bad as it is, could not be looked upon as the final blow dealt to Indian society by the British intruder, had it not been attended by a circumstance of quite different importance, a novelty in the annals of the whole Asiatic world. However changing the political aspect of India's past must appear, its social condition has remained unaltered since its remotest antiquity, until the first decennium of the 19th century. The hand-loom and the spinning-wheel, producing their regular myriads of spinners and weavers, were the pivots of the structure of that society. From immemorial times, Europe received the admirable textures of Indian labour, sending in return for them her precious metals, and furnishing thereby his material to the goldsmith, that indispensable member of Indian society, whose love of finery is so great that even the lowest class, those who go about nearly naked, have commonly a pair of golden ear-rings and a gold ornament of some kind hung round their necks. Rings on the fingers and toes have also been common. Women as well as children frequently wore massive bracelets and anklets of gold or silver, and statuettes of divinities in gold and silver were met with in the households. It was the British intruder who broke up the Indian hand-loom and destroyed the spinning wheel. England began with driving the Indian cottons from the European market; it then introduced twist into Hindostan and in the end inundated the very mother country of cotton with cottons. From 1818 to 1836 the export of twist from Great Britain to India rose in the proportion of 1 to 5,200. In 1824 the export of British muslins to India hardly amounted to 1,000,000 yards while in 1837 it surpassed 64,000,000 yards. But at the same time the population of Dacca decreased from 150,000 inhabitants to 20,000. This decline of Indian towns celebrated for their fabrics was by no means the worst consequence. British steam and science uprooted, over the whole surface of Hindostan, the union between agricultural and manufacturing industry.

These two circumstances—the Hindoo, on the one hand, leaving, like all

Oriental peoples, to the central government the care of the great public works, the prime condition of his agriculture and commerce, dispersed, on the other hand over the surface of the country, and agglomerated in small centres by the domestic union of agricultural and manufacturing pursuits—these two circumstances had brought about, since the remotest times, a social system of particular features—the so-called *village system*, which gave to each of these small unions their independent organisation and distinct life. The peculiar character of this system may be judged from the following description, contained in an old official report of the British House of Commons on Indian affairs:

"A village, geographically considered, is a tract of country comprising some hundred or thousand acres of arable and waste lands; politically viewed it resembles a corporation or township. Its proper establishment of officers and servants consists of the following description: the *potail*, or head inhabitant, who has generally the superintendence of the affairs of the village, settles the disputes of the inhabitants, attends to the police, and performs the duty of collecting the revenue within his village, a duty which his personal influence and minute acquaintance with the situation and concerns of the people render him the best qualified for this charge. The *kurnum* keeps the accounts of cultivation, and registers everything connected with it. The *Tallier* and the *totie*, the duty of the former of which consists in gaining information of crimes and offences, and in escorting and protecting persons travelling from one village to another; the province of the latter appearing to be more immediately confined to the village, consisting, among other duties, in guarding the crops and assisting in measuring them. The *boundary man*, who preserves the limits of the village, or gives evidence respecting them in cases of dispute. The Superintendent of Tanks and Watercourses distributes the water for the purposes of agriculture. The Brahmin, who performs the village worship. The school-master, who is seen teaching the children in a village to read and write in the sand. The calendar-Brahmin, or astrologer, etc. These officers and servants generally constitute the establishment of a village; but in some parts of the country it is of less extent; some of the duties and functions above described being united in the same person; in others it exceeds the above-named number of individuals. Under this simple form of municipal government, the inhabitants of the country have lived from time immemorial. The boundaries of the villages have been but seldom altered; and though the villages themselves have been sometimes injured, and even desolated by war, famine or disease, the same name, the same limits, the same interests, and even the same families, have continued for ages. The inhabitants gave themselves no trouble about the breaking up and divisions of kingdoms; while the village remains entire, they care not to what power it is transferred, or to what sovereign it devolves; its internal economy remains unchanged. The *potail* is still the head inhabitant, and still acts as the petty judge or magistrate, and collector or rentor of the village."

These small stereotype forms of social organism have been to the greater part dissolved, and are disappearing, not so much through the brutal interference of the British tax-gatherer and the British soldier, as to the working of English steam and English free trade. Those family-communities were based on domestic industry, in that peculiar combination of hand-weaving, hand-spinning and hand-tilling agriculture which gave them self-supporting power. English interference having placed the spinner in Lancashire and the weaver in Bengal, or sweeping away both Hindoo spinner and weaver, dissolved these small semi-barbarian, semi-civilised communities, by blowing up their economical basis, and thus produced the greatest, and, to speak the truth, the only *social* revolution ever heard of in Asia.

Now, sickening as it must be to human feeling to witness those myriads of industrious patriarchal and inoffensive social organisations disorganised and dissolved into their units, thrown into a sea of woes, and their individual members losing at the same time their ancient form of civilisation, and their hereditary means of subsistence, we must not forget that these idyllic village communities, inoffensive though they may appear, had always been the solid foundation of Oriental despotism, that they restrained the human mind within the smallest possible compass, making it the unresisting tool of superstition, enslaving it beneath traditional rules, depriving it of all grandeur and historical energies. We must not forget the barbarian egotism which, concentrating on some miserable patch of land, had quietly witnessed the ruin of empires, the perpetration of unspeakable cruelties, the massacre of the population of large towns, with no other consideration bestowed upon them than on natural events, itself the helpless prey of any aggressor who deigned to notice it at all. We must not forget that this undignified, stagnatory, and vegetative life, that this passive sort of existence evoked on the other part, in contradistinction, wild, aimless, unbounded forces of destruction and rendered murder itself a religious rite in Hindostan. We must not forget that these little communities were contaminated by distinctions of caste and by slavery, that they subjugated man to external circumstances instead of elevating man to be the sovereign of circumstances, that they transformed a self-developing social state into never changing natural destiny, and thus brought about a brutalising worship of nature, exhibiting its degradation in the fact that man, the sovereign of nature, fell down on his knees in adoration of *Hanuman*, the monkey, and *Sabbala*, the cow.

England, it is true, in causing a social revolution in Hindostan, was actuated only by the vilest interests, and was stupid in her manner of enforcing them. But that is not the question. The question is, can mankind fulfill its destiny without a fundamental revolution in the social state of Asia? If not, whatever may have been the crimes of England she was the unconscious tool of history in bringing about that revolution.

Then, whatever bitterness the spectacle of the crumbling of an ancient world may have for our personal feelings, we have the right, in point of history, to exclaim with Goethe:

> "Sollte diese Qual uns quälen,
> Da sie unsre Lust vermehrt,
> Hat nicht Myriaden Seelen
> Timur's Heerschaft aufgezehrt?"[8]

THE FUTURE RESULTS OF BRITISH RULE IN INDIA

London, Friday, July 22, 1853

How came it that English supremacy was established in India? The paramount power of the Great Mogul was broken by the Mogul Viceroys. The power of the Viceroys was broken by the Mahrattas.[9] The power of the Mahrattas was broken by the Afghans, and while all were struggling against all, the Briton rushed in and was enabled to subdue them all. A country not only divided between Mohammedan and Hindoo, but between tribe and tribe, between caste and caste; a society whose framework was based on a sort of equilibrium, resulting from a general repulsion and constitutional exclusiveness between all its members. Such a country and such a society, were they not the predestined prey of conquest? If we knew nothing of the past history of Hindostan, would there not be the one great and incontestable fact, that even at this moment India is held in English thraldom by an Indian army maintained at the cost of India? India, then, could not escape the fate of being conquered, and the whole of her past history, if it be anything, is the history of the successive conquests she has undergone. Indian society has no history at all, at least no known history. What we call its history, is but the history of the successive intruders who founded their empires on the passive

---

8. Should this torture then torment us / Since it brings us greater pleasure? / Were not through the rule of Timur / Souls devoured without measure? (Goethe, *Westöstlicher Diwan. An Suleika*)

9. *Mahrattas:* A group of peoples in Central India which rose against the Mohammedans and in the beginning of the eighteenth century formed a confederation of feudal princedoms.

basis of that unresisting and unchanging society. The question, therefore, is not whether the English had a right to conquer India, but whether we are to prefer India conquered by the Turk, by the Persian, by the Russian, to India conquered by the Briton.

England has to fulfil a double mission in India: one destructive, the other regenerating—the annihilation of old Asiatic society, and the laying of the material foundations of Western society in Asia.

Arabs, Turks, Tartars, Moguls, who had successively overrun India, soon became *Hindooised*, the barbarian conquerors being, by an eternal law of history, conquered themselves by the superior civilisation of their subjects. The British were the first conquerors superior, and therefore, inaccessible to Hindoo civilisation. They destroyed it by breaking up the native communities, by uprooting the native industry, and by levelling all that was great and elevated in the native society. The historic pages of their rule in India report hardly anything beyond that destruction. The work of regeneration hardly transpires through a heap of ruins. Nevertheless it has begun.

The political unity of India, more consolidated, and extending farther than it ever did under the Great Moguls, was the first condition of its regeneration. That unity, imposed by the British sword, will now be strengthened and perpetuated by the electric telegraph. The native army, organised and trained by the British drill-sergeant, was the *sine qua non* of Indian self-emancipation, and of India ceasing to be the prey of the first foreign intruder. The free press, introduced for the first time into Asiatic society, and managed principally by the common offspring of Hindoo and Europeans, is a new and powerful agent of reconstruction. The *Zemindars*[10] and *Ryotwar*[11] themselves, abominable as they are, involve two distinct forms of private property in land—the great *desideratum* of Asiatic society. From the Indian natives, reluctantly and sparingly educated at Calcutta, under English superintendence, a fresh class is springing up, endowed with the requirements for government and imbued with European science. Steam has brought India into regular and rapid communication with Europe, has connected its chief ports with those of the whole south-eastern ocean, and has revindicated it from the isolated position which was the prime law of its stagnation. The day is not far distant when, by a combination of railways and steam vessels, the distance between England

10. *Zemindars:* New big landowners who were established by the British from among former tax collectors and merchant-usurers through the expropriation of the Indian peasantry. The zemindar system was widespread in Northeast India.

11. *Ryotwar:* A system of renting land to peasants for an unlimited period of time. Introduced by the British in the South of India, it permitted the British authorities to let land to peasants on extremely onerous terms.

and India, measured by time, will be shortened to eight days, and when that once fabulous country will thus be actually annexed to the Western world.

The ruling classes of Great Britain have had, till now, but an accidental, transitory and exceptional interest in the progress of India. The aristocracy wanted to conquer it, the moneyocracy to plunder it, and the millocracy to undersell it. But now the tables are turned. The millocracy have discovered that the transformation of India into a reproductive country has become of vital importance to them, and that, to that end, it is necessary, above all, to gift her with means of irrigation and of internal communication. They intend now drawing a net of railways over India. And they will do it. The results must be inappreciable.

It is notorious that the productive powers of India are paralysed by the utter want of means for conveying and exchanging its various produce. Nowhere, more than in India, do we meet with social destitution in the midst of natural plenty, for want of the means of exchange. It was proved before a Committee of the British House of Commons, which sat in 1848, that "when grain was selling from 6s. to 8s. a quarter at Kandeish, it was sold at 64s. to 70s. at Poonah, where the people were dying in the streets of famine, without the possibility of gaining supplies from Kandeish, because the clay-roads were impracticable."

The introduction of railways may be easily made to subserve agricultural purposes by the formation of tanks, where ground is required for embankment, and by the conveyance of water along the different lines. Thus irrigation, the *sine qua non* of farming in the East, might be greatly extended, and the frequently recurring local famines, arising from the want of water, would be averted. The general importance of railways, viewed under this head, must become evident, when we remember that irrigated lands, even in the district near Ghauts, pay three times as much in taxes, afford ten or twelve times as much employment, and yield twelve or fifteen times as much profit, as the same area without irrigation.

Railways will afford the means of diminishing the amount and the cost of the military establishments. Col. Warren, Town Major of the Fort St. William, stated before a Select Committee of the House of Commons:

"The practicability of receiving intelligence from distant parts of the country in as many hours as at present it requires days and even weeks, and of sending instructions with troops and stores, in the more brief period, are considerations which cannot be too highly estimated. Troops could be kept at more distant and healthier stations than at present, and much loss of life from sickness would by this means be spared. Stores could not to the same extent be required at the various dépôts, and the loss by decay, and the destruction incidental to the climate, would also be avoided. The number of troops might be diminished in direct proportion to their effectiveness."

We know that the municipal organisation and the economical basis of the village communities has been broken up, but their worst feature, the dissolution of society into stereotyped and disconnected atoms, has survived their vitality. The village isolation produced the absence of roads in India, and the absence of roads perpetuated the village isolation. On this plan a community existed with a given scale of low conveniences, almost without intercourse with other villages, without the desires and efforts indispensable to social advance. The British having broken up this self-sufficient *inertia* of the villages, railways will provide the new want of communication and intercourse. Besides, "one of the effects of the railway system will be to bring into every village affected by it such knowledge of the contrivances and appliances of other countries, and such means of obtaining them, as will first put the hereditary and stipendiary village artisanship of India to full proof of its capabilities, and then supply its defects." (Chapman, *The Cotton and Commerce of India.*)

I know that the English millocracy intend to endow India with railways with the exclusive view of extracting at diminished expenses the cotton and other raw materials for their manufactures. But when you have once introduced machinery into the locomotion of a country, which possesses iron and coals, you are unable to withhold it from its fabrication. You cannot maintain a net of railways over an immense country without introducing all those industrial processes necessary to meet the immediate and current wants of railway locomotion, and out of which there must grow the application of machinery to those branches of industry not immediately connected with railways. The railway-system will therefore become, in India, truly the forerunner of modern industry. This is the more certain as the Hindoos are allowed by British authorities themselves to possess particular aptitude for accommodating themselves to entirely new labour, and acquiring the requisite knowledge of machinery. Ample proof of this fact is afforded by the capacities and expertness of the native engineers in the Calcutta mint, where they have been for years employed in working the steam machinery, by the natives attached to the several steam engines in the Hurdwar coal districts and by other instances. Mr. Campbell himself, greatly influenced as he is by the prejudices of the East India Company, is obliged to avow "that the great mass of the Indian people possesses a great *industrial energy*, is well fitted to accumulate capital, and remarkable for a mathematical clearness of head, and talent for figures and exact sciences." "Their intellects," he says, "are excellent." Modern industry, resulting from the railway-system, will dissolve the hereditary divisions of labour, upon which rest the Indian castes, those decisive impediments to Indian progress and Indian power.

All the English bourgeoisie may be forced to do will neither emancipate nor materially mend the social condition of the mass of the people, depending not only on the development of the productive powers, but on their appropriation by the people. But what they will not fail to do is to lay down the material premises for both. Has the bourgeoisie ever done more? Has it ever affected a progress without dragging individuals and peoples through blood and dirt, through misery and degradation?

The Indians will not reap the fruits of the new elements of society scattered among them by the British bourgeoisie, till in Great Britain itself the now ruling classes shall have been supplanted by the industrial proletariat, or till the Hindoos themselves shall have grown strong enough to throw off the English yoke altogether. At all events, we may safely expect to see, at a more or less remote period, the regeneration of that great and interesting country, whose gentle natives are, to use the expression of Prince Soltykov, even in the most inferior classes, *"plus fins et plus adroits que les Italiens,"*[12] whose submission even is counterbalanced by a certain calm nobility, who, notwithstanding their natural languor, have astonished the British officers by their bravery, whose country has been the source of our languages, our religions, and who represent the type of the ancient German in the *Jat*[13] and the type of the ancient Greek in the Brahmin.

I cannot part with the subject of India without some concluding remarks.

The profound hypocrisy and inherent barbarism of bourgeois civilisation lies unveiled before our eyes, turning from its home, where it assumes respectable forms, to the colonies, where it goes naked. They are the defenders of property, but did any revolutionary party ever originate agrarian revolutions like those in Bengal, in Madras, and in Bombay? Did they not, in India, to borrow an expression of that great robber, Lord Clive himself, resort to atrocious extortion, when simple corruption could not keep pace with their rapacity? While they prated in Europe about the inviolable sanctity of the national debt, did they not confiscate in India the dividends of the *rajahs*, who had invested their private savings in the Company's own funds? While they combatted the French revolution under the pretext of defending "our holy religion," did they not forbid, at the same time, Christianity to be propagated in India, and did they not, in order to make money out of the pilgrims streaming to the temples of Orissa and Bengal, take up the trade in the

---

12. Marx quotes from A. D. Soltykov's book *Lettres sur l'Inde*, Paris, 1848.
13. *Jats:* A caste in Northwest India.

murder and prostitution perpetrated in the temple of Juggernaut? These are the men of "Property, Order, Family, and Religion."

The devastating effects of English industry, when contemplated with regard to India, a country as vast as Europe, and containing 150 millions of acres, are palpable and confounding. But we must not forget that they are only the organic results of the whole system of production as it is now constituted. That production rests on the supreme rule of capital. The centralisation of capital is essential to the existence of capital as an independent power. The destructive influence of that centralisation upon the markets of the world does but reveal, in the most gigantic dimensions, the inherent organic laws of political economy now at work in every civilised town. The bourgeois period of history has to create the material basis of the new world—on the one hand the universal intercourse founded upon the mutual dependency of mankind, and the means of that intercourse; on the other hand the development of the productive powers of man and the transformation of material production into a scientific domination of natural agencies. Bourgeois industry and commerce create these material conditions of a new world in the same way as geological revolutions have created the surface of the earth. When a great social revolution shall have mastered the results of the bourgeois epoch, the market of the world and the modern powers of production, and subjected them to the common control of the most advanced peoples, then only will human progress cease to resemble that hideous pagan idol, who would not drink the nectar but from the skulls of the slain.

III
THE IMPEACHMENT OF WARREN HASTINGS

INTRODUCTION
Warren Hastings: Naughty Nabob or National Hero?
MIA CARTER

WARREN HASTINGS, like Robert Clive, was central to the early history of the East India Company; both men are considered founding fathers of the British Raj. Hastings's career with the Company spanned the eras of unfettered monopoly trade, aggressive imperial expansionism, and corporate and institutional reform; he is generally described as an effective administrator who was caught up in the shifting tides of policy revision and political change.

Hastings and Clive had similar, impoverished backgrounds, and each first traveled to his respective employment in India as an adolescent; Clive was eighteen years old on his arrival in the colony, Hastings age seventeen. Each man began his career as a humble writer in the junior level of Company appointments; Clive, however, was seven years Hastings's senior and had improved his professional standing in the Company by the time Hastings arrived in India in 1750. In 1749, for example, Clive had been appointed a commissioner of troop provisions and supplies—one of the suspected financial conduits for the fortune he took home with him to England after his first term of service (1743–1753). Clive, the rising national hero, was central to the junior servant's career. After the Battle of Plassey (23 June 1757), when the Company gained control of Mughal viceroy Nawab Siraj-ul-Dowlah's Bengal territories, then Lieutenant Colonel Clive appointed Warren Hastings the Company's representative at the court of Nawabs (1758–1761). Hastings was later appointed to the Company council, the institution's ruling body in Calcutta (1761–1764). Hastings's reign on the council initiated the beginning of his frequently contentious relationship with fellow councilors and Company policymakers; gridlock and obstructionism caused Hastings to resign from the council and return to England in 1765. In 1771 Hastings was appointed governor of the presidency of Fort William. In 1773 he was promoted to governor-general of Bengal, the materially rich region of the Indian subcontinent the English and French had each hoped to gain.

Hastings's career with the Company was assuredly influenced by the spectacular military campaigns of the Clive era. Clive's uninhibited ability to judge situations, make bold and frequently risky decisions involving treaty negotiations, declarations of war, and seizures of native rulers' territories influenced the domestic interpretations of the armed conflicts of the Hastings era. Hastings was far more scholarly, cautious, and conservative than "Naughty Clive"; however, his reputation in England was affected by his association with the financial corruption of the nabobs—the Indian-derived nickname for the Company's newly created millionaires. Hastings's career was also dramatically affected by the parliamentary Whigs' anti-expansionist and free-trade/open-market sympathies. The Whig-supported East India Act of 1773 changed the nature of the governor-general's administrative power; unlike in his governorship of Fort William, Hastings was now subject to the supervision of the Company-appointed council. Some of the council members (Lieutenant-General John Clavering and George Monson) were supported by the anti-nabob members of Parliament and King George III; another, Richard Barwell, was a Hastings loyalist. The fourth member of the council, Philip Francis, was considered a jealous competitor and an anti-expansionist and dogged critic of imperial zealotry; he was suspected to be "Junius," the anonymous and passionate government critic and pamphleteer. Francis, more than any other councilor, was an aggressive and relentless investigator and reformer; his relationship with Hastings was so contentious that the two men eventually engaged in a duel. Francis was wounded and returned to England; once there, he continued to campaign against Hastings.

Hastings's questionable behaviors during his governor-generalship included his extension of the opium trade with China (he used opium profits to finance military campaigns); his requisitioning of treasures from the Begum of Oude; his autonomous decision- and policy-making; his alleged warmongering; and his ambiguous involvement in the trial and eventual execution of Raja Nand Kumar (or Maharaja Nandakumar), who had accused Hastings of bribing him for more than one-third of a million rupees. Nand Kumar claimed to have a letter from Hastings that would support his charges against the governor-general. The case was put before the newly instituted supreme court; the justice serving was a schoolmate and close friend of Hastings. In the course of the proceedings, another Indian suddenly accused Nand Kumar of forgery; the Hastings accuser was tried, found guilty, and executed. Warren Hastings did nothing to prevent or prohibit Nand Kumar's capital punishment.

In Hastings's 1773 "Letter to the Court of Directors," he defended his administrative decisions and declared his commitment to and enjoyment of his professional position ("I have catched the desire of applause in public life"). This line of self-defense continued in his *Memoirs Relative to the State of India*. Hastings also explained that he inherited an institution that was growing and changing before his eyes; his decisions were always made, he argued, with the best interests of the British empire in mind. This argument did not persuade Whig parliamentarian Edmund Burke, who initiated impeachment proceedings against Hastings in 1786. Burke charged Hastings with a series of crimes: abuse of powers, "bribery, oppression, and tyranny; . . . avarice, rapacity, pride, cruelty, ferocity, malignity of temper, haughtiness, insolence," and "blackness" of heart. Burke's high-flown moralistic rhetoric almost suggests that Hastings had become infected by a racial-viral disease, something very closely related to "Oriental despotism." For Burke, one of Hastings's great sins was his alleged abandonment of Western values and ethics. Rather than upholding English constitutional and humanistic values, Hastings had succumbed to "geographical morality."

Thomas Babington Macaulay's 1841 essay on Hastings examined the governor-general across a distance of time and with a cooler heart and mind. Contemporary critics may judge Hastings far more harshly than Macaulay did; many of his actions are clearly deserving of condemnation. However, it is also quite apparent that Warren Hastings was not singularly responsible for the excesses of British imperialism. Hastings's trial lasted from 1788 to 1795; he was eventually acquitted of the charges against him. Contemporary readers might best understand the fantastic legal spectacle as the empire's theater of politics—a proscenium on which the ambivalent feelings about expansionist imperialism and the ethical and financial costs of increasing involvement in colonial governance were pyrotechnically displayed.

BIBLIOGRAPHY

Bernstein, Jeremy. *Dawning of the Raj: The Life and Trials of Warren Hastings*. Chicago: Ivan R. Dee, 2000.
Beveridge, Henry. *Warren Hastings in Bengal*. Calcutta: Sanskrit Pustak Bhondar, 1978.
Broome, Ralph. *A Comparative View of the Administration of Mr. Hastings and Mr. Dundas in War and Peace*. London: John Stockdale, 1791.
Burke, Edmund. *The Complete Works of the Right Honorable Edmund Burke*. Boston: Little Brown, 1866.
Carnall, Geoffrey, and Colin Nicholson, eds. *The Impeachment of Warren Hastings: Papers from a Bicentenary Commemoration*. Edinburgh: Edinburgh University Press, 1989.

Edwardes, Michael. *Warren Hastings: King of the Nabobs*. London: Hart-Davis, MacGibbon, 1976.

Feiling, Keith. *Warren Hastings*. London: Macmillan, 1954.

Feuchtwanger, Lion. *Two Anglo-Saxon Plays: The Oil Islands, Warren Hastings*. London: M. Secker, 1929.

Goldsborne, Sophia. *Hartly House, Calcutta: A Novel of the Days of Warren Hastings*. Calcutta: Stamp Digest, 1789.

Marshall, Peter James. *The Impeachment of Warren Hastings*. London: Oxford University Press, 1965.

Moon, Penderel. *Warren Hastings and British India*. New York: Collier Books, 1947.

Parkash, Ram. *The Foreign Policy of Warren Hastings*. Hoshiarpur: Vishveshvaran and Vedic Research Institute, 1960.

Sen, Sailendra Nath. *Anglo-Maratha Relations during the Administration of Warren Hastings*. Calcutta: Firma K. L. Mukhopadhyay, 1961.

Suleri, Sara. "Edmund Burke and the Indian Sublime." In *The Rhetoric of English India*. Chicago: University Press of Chicago, 1992.

—. "Reading the Trial of Warren Hastings." In *The Rhetoric of English India*. Chicago: University Press of Chicago, 1992.

Warren Hastings to the Court of General Directors, 11 November 1773

Honourable Sirs,

I have been duly honoured with your letter of the 16th April by the *Harcourt* and duplicate of the same by the *Egmont*.

I am at a loss for words to convey the sense which I entertain of the honourable terms in which you have been pleased to express your approbation of my services. While my gratitude is excited by these instances of your kindness, I feel my zeal encouraged by the assurances which you have been pleased to afford me of your continued protection. My best expression of thanks for both must be made by my future conduct, which (if I know my own heart) will never be drawn by any bias, however powerful, from the pursuit of your interests, nor do I wish or aspire to any reward superior to your applause.

While I indulge the pleasure which I receive from the past success of my endeavours, I own I cannot refrain from looking back with a mixture of anxiety on the omissions by which I am sensible I may since have hazarded the diminution of your esteem. All my letters addressed to your honourable Court, and to the Select Committee, repeat the strongest promises of prosecuting the inquiries into the conduct of your servants, which you had been pleased to commit particularly to my charge. You will readily believe that I must have been sincere in those declarations, since it would have argued great indiscretion to have made them, had I foreseen my inability to perform them. I find myself now under the disagreeable necessity of avowing that inability; at the same time that I will boldly take upon me to affirm that on whomsoever you might have delegated that charge, and by whatever powers it might have been accompanied, it would have been sufficient to occupy the entire attention of those who were entrusted with it, and even with all the aids of leisure and authority would have proved ineffectual. I dare appeal to the public records, to the testimony of those who have opportunities of knowing an éclat by innovations, for which the wild scene before him affords ample and justifiable occasion. But innovations of real use require a length of time, and the unremitting application of their original principles to perfect them. Their immediate effects are often hurtful, and their intended benefits remote, or virtually diffused through such concealed channels that their source is not easy to be traced. Of this nature are the late regulations in your revenue customs, and in the commerce of the country, which have been attended with an immediate loss in the collections, and in the price of your investment; and it will require a long and intricate train of reasoning to prove that the future increase of population, of national wealth, of the revenue and trade, should such be the happy effects of these expedients, were really produced by them. But who that looks only for present applause or present credit would hazard both for remote advantages, of which another might arrogate the merit and assume the reward: Or who will labour with equal perseverance for the accomplishment of measures projected by others, as of those of which he was himself the contriver?

Although I disclaim the consideration of my own interest in these speculations, and flatter myself I proceed upon more liberal grounds, yet I am proud to avow the feelings of an honest ambition that stimulates me to aspire at the possession of my present station for years to come. Those who know my natural turn of mind will not ascribe this to sordid views, a very few years possession of the government would undoubtedly enable me to retire with a fortune amply fitted to the measure of my desires, were I to consult only my own ease; but in my present situation I feel my mind expand to something greater. I have catched the desire of applause in public life. The important transactions in which I have been engaged, and my wish to see them take complete effect, the public approbation which you have been pleased to stamp on them, and the estimation which that cannot fail to give me in the general opinion of mankind, lead me to aim at deserving more; and I wish to dedicate all my time, health, and labour to a service which has been so flattering in its commencement.

Such are my views and such my sentiments. I expose them without reserve, because I am conscious you will find nothing unworthy in them, whatever opinion you may form of their expediency.

I shall wait your determination with becoming expectation but without anxiety, nor shall I ever less esteem the favours I have already received, because others are withheld which it may be either not expedient or impracticable to grant.

I have the honour to be, with the greatest respect, honourable Sirs, &c.

SOURCE: In *Speeches and Documents on Indian Policy, 1750–1921*, ed. Arthur Berridale Keith (Delhi: Anmol Publishers, 1985).

Excerpt from *Memoirs Relative to the State of India*

WARREN HASTINGS

I shall add some reflections upon the general subject of the political interests of the Company, or of the British nation in India, which I deem connected with the scope and design of this review, or are connected with the actual state of our affairs: and if in these also I shall appear to speak too much of myself, let it be remembered, that the whole of this composition is in effect a portion of the history of my own life, in those events of it which were blended with the public. Besides, I am not sure that the Company possessed a political character, or can be said to have conducted their intercourse with other nations on any system of established policy, before the period in which I was appointed to the principal administration of their affairs.

I know how readily many will both allow the position, and reprobate the system, and admit me for its author, for the sake of reprobating me also for it. I am not its author. The seed of this wonderful production was sown by the hand of calamity. It was nourished by fortune, and cultivated, and shaped (if I may venture to change the figure) by necessity. Its first existence was commercial: it obtained, in its growth, the sudden accession of military strength and territorial dominion, to which its political adjunct was inevitable. It is useless to inquire whether the Company, or the nation, has derived any substantial benefit from the change, since it is impossible to retrace the perilous and wonderful paths by which they have attained their present elevation, and to redescend to the humble and undreaded character of trading adventurers. Perhaps the term of the national existence in India may have become susceptible of a shorter duration by it; but it is that state which it must henceforth maintain, and it must therefore adopt those principles which are necessary to its preservation in that state. To explain those principles, and to shew the necessity of their construction to the duration of the British dominion in India, is foreign from the present design, as it is perhaps too late to attempt it with any chance of its application to any purpose of utility. Yet so much as I have said, was necessary to obviate the common objection, to which every measure and every maxim are liable, which are built on a different ground from that which exists only in the idea of those who look upon the East India Company still as a body of merchants, and consider commerce as their only object.

I have been represented to the public as a man of ambition, and as too apt to be misled by projects of conquest. Though the only two facts on which this imputation has originated, have been refuted on the clearest conviction, and this in the principal instance is universally acknowledged; the imputation still remains; and I much fear that it has served, with others equally opposite to truth, for the ground of a recent and great national measure, most unfortunate in its construction, if such were the causes of it.

    I can affirm that the charge, so far as it respects myself, and I fear that I stand too conspicuous a mark before my fellow-servants to be missed, or not to have been the aim of its intended direction, is wholly and absolutely false, as it is inconsistent with any motive to which it could be ascribed of pride, avarice or thirst of power; for what profit or advantage could I have acquired, or hoped to acquire, for instance, in a Marattah war; or what reputation in any war, the operations of which must necessarily depend on another, and him either taken in his turn from the roster, or with a choice divided at the most between two or three officers standing at the head of the list of the army? The first acts of the government of Bengal, when I presided over it, were well known at the time to have been of my formation, or formed on principles which I was allowed to dictate. These consisted of a variety of regulations, which included every department of the service, and composed a system as complete as a mind incompetent like my own, though possessed of very superior aids, could form, of military, political, productive, economical, and judicial connection. I found the Treasury empty, the revenue declining, the expenses unchecked, and the whole nation yet languishing under the recent effects of a mortal famine. Neither was this a season for war, nor, occupied as I was in it, would candor impute to me even a possible disposition to war. The land required years of quiet to restore its population and culture; and all my acts were acts of peace. I was busied in raising a great and weighty fabric of which all the parts were yet loose and destitute of the superior weight which was to give them their mutual support; and (if I may so express myself) their collateral strength. A tempest, or an earthquake could not be more fatal to a builder whose walls were uncovered, and his unfinished columns trembling in the breeze, than the ravages or terrors of war would have been to me and to all my hopes.

    I laid my plans before the Court of Directors, and called upon them to give me the powers which were requisite for their accomplishment and duration. These were silently denied me, and those which I before possessed, feeble as they were, were taken from me. Had I been allowed the means which I required, I will inform my readers of the use to which I intended to apply them. I should have sought no accession of territory. I should have rejected the offer of any which would have enlarged our line of defence, without a more than proportionate augmentation of defensive strength and revenue. I should have encouraged, but not solicited, new alliances; and should have rendered that of our government an object of solicitation, by the example of those which already existed. To these I should have observed, as my religion, every principle of good faith; and where they were deficient in the conditions of mutual and equal dependence, I should have endeavoured to render them complete; and this rule I did actually apply to practice in the treaty which I formed with the Nabob Shujah o' Dowlah in the year 1773.

With respect to the provinces of the Company's dominion under my government, I should have studied to augment both their value and strength by an augmentation of their inhabitants and cultivation. This is not a mere phantasy of speculation. The means were most easy, if the power and trust were allowed to use them. Every region of Indostan, even at that time groaned under different degrees of oppression, desolation, and insecurity. The famine which had wasted the provinces of Bengal had raged with equal severity in other parts, and in some with greater, and the remembrance of it yet dwelt on the minds of the inhabitants with every impression of horror and apprehension. I would have afforded an asylum in Bengal, with lands and stock, to all the emigrants of other countries: I would have employed emissaries for their first encouragement; and I would have provided a perpetual and proclaimed incentive to them in the security of the community from foreign molestation, and of the individual members from mutual wrong: to which purpose, the regulations already established were sufficient, with power only competent to enforce them. And for the same purpose and with a professed view to it, I early recommended, even so early as the year 1773, the erection of public granaries on the plan since happily commenced.

Those who have been in the long habits of familiar communication with me, whether by letter or by discourse, will know that the sentiments which I have been describing are of as old a date as that of my late office in the first appointment and state of it: and to every candid reader I appeal for his conviction of their effect, if I had been permitted to follow their direction: for what man is there so immovably attached to his native soil, as to prefer it under the scourge of oppression, the miseries of want, and the desolation of war, embittering or destroying every natural affection, and ultimately invading the source of life itself, to a state of peace, of external tranquillity, and internal protection; of assured plenty, and all the blessings of domestic increase?

Those who have seen, as I did, in a time of profound peace, the wretched inhabitants of the Carnatic, of every age, sex, and condition, tumultuously thronging round the walls of Fort St. George, and lying for many successive days and nights on the burning soil, without covering or food, on a casual rumour, falsely excited, of an approaching enemy, will feelingly attest the truth of the contrast which I have exhibited in one part of it, and will readily draw the conclusion which I have drawn from it even without attending to the rest. That such a state as I have described would have been attained without imperfection or allor. I do not pretend to suppose; but I confidently maintain, that under an equal vigorous, and fixed administration, determined on the execution of such a plan to its accomplishment, it would have been attainable, even with common talents prosecuting it, to a degree as nearly approaching to perfection as human life is capable of receiving. The submissive character of the people; the fewness of their wants; the facility with which the soil and climate, unaided by exertions of labour, can supply them; the abundant resources of subsistence and trafficable wealth which may be drawn from the natural productions, and from the manufactures, both of established usage and of new introduction, to which no men upon earth can bend their minds with a readier accommodation; and above all, the defences with which nature has armed the land, in its mountainous and hilly borders, its bay, its innumerable intersections of rivers, and inoffensive or unpowerful neighbours; are advantages which no united state upon earth possesses in an equal degree; and which leave little to the duty of the magistrate; in effect, nothing but attention, protection, and forbearance.

But though I profess the doctrine of peace, I by no means pretend to have followed it with so implicit a devotion as to make sacrifices to it. I have never yielded a substantial right which I could assert, or submitted to a wrong which I could repel, with a moral assurance of success proportioned to the magnitude of either; and I can allude to instances in which I should have deemed it criminal not to have hazarded both the public safety and my own, in a crisis of uncommon and adequate emergency, or in an occasion of dangerous example.

I have ever deemed it even more unsafe than dishonourable to sue for peace; and more consistent with the love of peace to be the aggressor, in certain cases, than to see preparations of intended hostility; and wait for their maturity, and for their open effect to repel it. The faith of treaties I have ever held inviolate. Of this I have given the most ample and public testimonies in my conduct to the Nabob Shujah o' Dowlah, to the Nabob Assof o' Dowlah, the Nabob Walla Jah, to the Rana of Gohid, to the Nabob Nizam Ally Cawn, Raja Futty Sing, and Mahdajee Sindia; and I have had the satisfaction of seeing the policy, as well as the moral rectitude, of this practice justified by the exemplary sufferings of all who have deviated from it, in acts of perfidy to myself, or to the government over which I presided during the time that I have had charge of it.

If in this display of my own character, I shall appear to have transgressed the bounds of modesty, I shall not decline the charge, nor fear to aggravate it by adding, that I have never yet planned or authorised any military operation, or series of operations, which has not been attended with complete success, in the attainment of its professed objects: and that I have never, in any period of my life, engaged in a negotiation which I did not see terminate as I wished and expected: and let this conclusion be offered as an undeniable proof of the propriety and efficacy of the principles on which I have regulated my conduct in both.

It would not be either an unpleasing or an unprofitable employment to turn from the survey of our neighbours, and from the contemplation of their views, interests, powers, resources and to look back on our own; mixing with the reflections obvious to our habits of thinking, those which would occur to the people with whom we have been engaged in past hostility, or who may expect to be eventually concerned with us, whether as friends or foes, in future operations. Very different would be the observations made by a spectator in such a point of view, from those which pass in the mind of a mere individual, through the clouded medium of his own wants and feelings, and with the terrors and discontents of his fellow-citizens aggravating his own; and such, perhaps, as the following would be his reflections, as the different objects of his contemplation passed in succession before him.

No state can carry on extensive military operations for any length of time, without imposing some burdens upon its subjects, or subjecting them to consequent inconveniencies; and those that suffer will complain, and condemn measures which create partial exigency, without considering their object and tendency. To the complaints of individuals, the adherents of party will superadd their accusations, exaggerate the temporary evil that exists, and darken, by despondency, the bright expectations of a future period. Such particularly has been the case in Bengal; and murmurs, suspicions, and despair, have been transmitted from India to England.

In proportion as our distresses have been, or have appeared to be, pressing, the power, resources, and advantages of our enemies have been supposed to accumulate; and an idea is adopted without reflection, that the cause which diminishes our resources, operates on one side only, without producing a similar effect on the strength of our enemies: as if it were in their power to marshall armies, and undertake military expeditions, without any augmentation of expence or distress to individuals. With as limited a judgement men are apt to draw conclusions from the errors and deficiencies of government, and the mismanagement of military operations, not reflecting that our adversaries have also their difficulties to surmount, which arise out of the imperfection of human policy and the depravations of self-interest; and that the fortune of contending states, as of simple individuals, as often turns on the different effects of their mutual blunders and misconduct, as on the superiority of skill and exertion.

But widely different is the estimate formed by those whom necessity has led us to oppose or attack of our strength and resources. They behold with astonishment the exertions that have been made from the banks of the Ganges; and reasoning as we have done from their own distresses, lament the necessity that has engaged them in wars with a power capable of making such exertions, and whose re-resources, instead of being diminished, must appear to them to augment. Instead of being able to extend their incursions to the capital of our dominions, which at a period little remote from the establishment of the Company's authority they did with success; they find themselves attacked in the center of their own territories, and all their exertions required for the defence of them. They find, notwithstanding the temporary success they have derived from accident or mismanagement, that we have fresh armies ready to take the field, and that whilst our spirit is unabated, our strength is sufficient to give efficacy to its resolutions.

The conclusion I would draw from these premises is, that the vigorous exertions which we have made for the defence and security of our own possessions, have impressed an idea of our strength and resources among the powers of India, which will, more than any other motive, contribute to establish the present peace on firm foundation; to shew that if our resources have suffered a diminution, those of the states with which we have been engaged in war, have felt, in probably a greater degree, the same inconvenience; finally, to evince the propriety of those exertions, notwithstanding the expence with which they have been made, by the event itself, which had evidently proved to all the powers of Hindostan and Deccan, assisted by our great European enemy the French, have not been able to destroy the solid fabric of the English power in the East, nor even to deprive it of any portion of the territories over which its control extends.

SOURCE: Warren Hastings (1732–1818), *Memoirs Relative to the State of India* (London: J. Murray, 1786).

Edmund Burke on the Impeachment of Warren Hastings, 15–19 February 1788

[Edmund Burke (1765–1782) was a prominent Whig parliamentarian. He began his career with a secretarial appointment to the Marquess of Rockingham in 1765, the same year he entered the House of Commons. In 1774 Burke was elected to Parliament. Burke's persuasive arguments were central in convincing Prime Minister William Pitt (the younger) and the House of Commons to initiate impeachment proceedings against William Hastings. In addition to his fiery rhetorical prosecution of the former governor-general of India, Burke was known for his conciliatory attitudes toward the American colonies during the taxation revolt and for advocating on behalf of party politics. Burke also drafted the failed East India Bill of 1783, which proposed an independent board of governance for the Indian colony. Edmund Burke was also a prominent scholar; his best-known scholarly works include his highly influential *A Philosophical Enquiry into the Origin of Our Ideas of the Sublime and the Beautiful* (1757) and his critique of republicanism and revolution, *Reflections on the Revolution in France* (1790).]

My Lords,

The gentlemen who have it in command to support the impeachment against Mr. Hastings, late Governor-General of Bengal, have directed me to open a general view of the grounds upon which the Commons have proceeded in their charge against him; to open a general view of the extent, the magnitude, the nature, the tendency, and effect of the crimes with which they have charged him; and they have also directed me to give such an explanation, as, with their aid, I may be enabled to give, of such circumstances, preceding or concomitant with the crimes with which they charge him, as may tend to explain whatever may be found obscure in the charges as they stand. And they have further commanded me, and enabled me, I hope and trust, to give to your lordships such an explanation of anything in the laws, customs, opinions and manners, of the people concerned, and who are the objects of the crimes with which they charge him, as may tend to remove all doubt and ambiguity from the minds of your lordships upon these subjects. The several articles as they appear before you, will be opened by the other gentlemen with more distinctness, and without doubt with infinitely more particularity, when they come to apply the evidence that they adduce to each charge. This is the plan, my lords, that we mean to pursue on the great charge which is now before your lordships.

My lords, I confess that in this business I come before your lordships with a considerable degree of animation, because I think it is a most auspicious circumstance in a prosecution like this, in which the honour of this kingdom and that of many nations is involved, that from the commencement of our preliminary process to the hour of this solemn trial, not the smallest difference of opinion has arisen between the two houses. My lords, there were persons who, looking rather upon what was to be found in the journals of parliament than what was to be expected from the public justice of parliament, had formed hopes consolatory to them and unfavourable to us. There were persons who entertained hopes that the corruptions of India should have escaped amongst the dissensions of parliament: but they are disappointed. They will be disappointed in all the rest of their expectations which they had formed upon everything except the merits of the cause. The Commons will not have the melancholy and unsocial glory of having acted a right part in an imperfect work. What the greatest inquest of the nation has begun, its highest tribunal will accomplish. Justice will be done to India. It is true your lordships will have your full share in this great and glorious work; but we shall always consider that any honour that is divided with your lordships will be more than doubled to ourselves.

My lords, the powers which Mr. Hastings is charged with having abused are the powers delegated to him by the East India Company. The East India Company itself acts under two sorts of powers, derived from two sources. The first source of its power is under a charter which the Crown was authorized by act of parliament to grant. The next is from several grants and charters indeed, as well as that great fundamental charter which it derived from the Emperor of the Moguls, the person with whose dominions they are chiefly conversant; particularly the great charter by which they acquired the high stewardship of the kingdoms of Bengal, Behar, and Orissa, in 1765. Under those two charters they act. As to the first, it is from that charter that they derive the capacity by which they can be considered as a public body at all, or capable of any public function; it is from thence they acquire the capacity to take any other charter, to acquire any other offices, or to hold any other possessions. This being the root and origin of their power, it makes them responsible to the party from whom that power is derived. As they have emanated from the supreme power of this kingdom, they themselves are responsible—their body as a corporate body, themselves as individuals—and the whole body and train of their servants are responsible, to the high justice of this kingdom. In delegating great power to the India Company, this kingdom has not released its sovereignty. On the contrary, its responsibility is increased by the greatness and sacredness of the power given. For this power they are and must be responsible; and I hope this day your lordships will show that this nation never did give a power without imposing a proportionable degree of responsibility.

As to the other power, which they derived from the Mogul empire by various charters from that crown, and particularly by the charter of 1765, by which they obtained the office of lord high steward, as I said, or diwan, of the kingdoms of Bengal, Behar, and Orissa, by that charter they bound themselves, and bound exclusively all their servants, to perform all the duties belonging to that new office. And by the ties belonging to that new relation they were bound to observe the laws, rights, usages and customs, of the natives, and to pursue their benefit in all things; which was the nature, institution, and purpose, of the office which they received. If the power of the sovereign from whom they derived these powers should be by any misfortune in human affairs annihilated or suspended, the duty of the people below, which they acquired under his charter, is not suspended, is not annihilated, but remains in all its force; and, for the responsibility, they are thrown back upon that country from whence their original power, and along with it their responsibility, both emanated in one and the same act. For when the Company acquired that office in India, an English corporation became an integral part of the Mogul empire. When Great Britain assented to that grant virtually, and afterwards took advantage of it, Great Britain made a virtual act of union with that country, by which they bound themselves as securities for their subjects, to preserve the people in all rights, laws and liberties, which their natural original sovereign was bound to enforce, if he had been in a condition to enforce it. So that the two duties flowing from two different sources are now united in one, and come to have justice called for them at the bar of this House, before the supreme royal justice of this kingdom, from whence originally their powers were derived.

It may be a little necessary, when we are stating the powers they have derived from their charter, and which we state Mr. Hastings to have abused, to state, in as short and as comprehensive words as I can (for the matter is large indeed) what the constitution of the Company is, and particularly what its constitution is in reference to its Indian service; where the great theatre of the abuse was situated, and where those abuses were committed.

Your lordships will recollect that the East India Company—and therefore I shall spare you a long history of that, hoping and trusting that your lordships will think it is not to inform you, but to revive circumstances in your memory, that I enter into this detail—the East India Company had its origin about the latter end of the reign of Elizabeth, a period when all sorts of companies, inventions, and monopolies, were in fashion. And at that time the Company was sent out with large, extensive powers for increasing the commerce and the honour of this country: for to increase its commerce without increasing its honour and reputation would have been thought at that time, and will be thought now, a bad bargain for the country. But their powers were under that charter confined merely to commercial affairs. By degrees, as the theatre of the operation was distant, as its intercourse was with many great, some barbarous, and all of them armed nations, where not only the sovereign but the subjects were also armed in all places, it was found necessary to enlarge their powers. The first power they obtained was a power of naval discipline in their ships—a power which has been since dropped. The next was a power of law martial. The next was a power of civil, and to a degree of criminal, jurisdiction within their own factory, within their own settlements, over their own people and their own servants. The next was—and there was a stretch indeed—the power of peace and war; those great, high prerogatives of sovereignty which never were known before to be parted with to any subjects. But those high sovereign powers were given to the East India Company. So that when it had acquired them all, which it did about the end of the reign of Charles the Second, the East India Company did not seem to be merely a company formed for the extension of the British commerce, but in reality a delegation of the whole power and sovereignty of this kingdom sent into the East. In that light the Company began undoubtedly to be considered, and ought to be considered, as a subordinate sovereign power; that is, sovereign with regard to the objects which it touched, subordinate with regard to the power from whence this great trust was derived.

When the East India Company once appeared in that light, things happened to it totally different from what has happened in all other ordinary affairs, and from what has happened in all the remote mysteries of politicians, or been dreamed of in the world. For, in all other countries, a political body that acts as a commonwealth is first settled, and trade follows as a necessary consequence of the protection obtained by political power. But here the affair was reversed: the constitution of the Company began in commerce and ended in empire; and where powers of peace and war are given, it wants but time and circumstance to make this supersede every other, and the affairs of commerce fall into their proper rank and situation. And accordingly it did happen that, the possession and power of assertion of these great authorities coinciding with the improved state of Europe, with the improved state of arts and the improved state of laws, and (what is much more material) the improved state of military discipline; that coinciding with the general fall of Asia, with the relaxation and dissolution of its government, with the fall of its warlike spirit, and the total disuse almost of all parts of military discipline; those coinciding, the India Company became what it is, a great empire carrying on subordinately under the public authority a great commerce; it became that thing which was supposed by the Roman law so unsuitable—the same power was a trader, the same power was a lord.

In this situation, the India Company, however, still preserved traces of its original mercantile character, and the whole exterior order of its service is still carried on upon a mercantile plan and mercantile principles: in fact, it is a state in the disguise of a merchant, a great public office in the disguise of a counting-house. Accordingly the whole order and series, as I observed, is commercial: while the principal, inward, real part of the Company is entirely political. Accordingly the Company's service—of which the order and discipline is necessary to be explained to your lordships, that you may see in what manner the abuses have affected it—is commercial.

In the first place, all the persons who go abroad in the Company's service enter as clerks in the counting-house, and are called by a name to correspond to it—writers. In that condition they are obliged to serve five years. The next step is that of a factor, in which they are obliged to serve three years. The next step they take is that of a junior merchant, in which they are obliged to serve three years more. Then they become a senior merchant, which is the highest stage of advance in the Company's service, as a rank by which they had pretensions, before the year 1774, to the Council, to the succession of the Presidency, and to whatever other honours the Company has to bestow. Therefore the Company followed this idea in the particulars of their service; having originally established factories in certain places, which factories by degrees grew to the name of Presidencies and Councils, in proportion as the power and influence of the Company increased, and as the political began to dominate over the mercantile. And so it continued till the year 1773, when the legislature broke in, for proper reasons urging them to it, upon that order of the service, and appointed to the superior part persons who were not entitled to it—however some might have been,—by the course and order of service, such as Mr. Hastings was. But, whatever title they had from thence, their legal title was derived from an express act of parliament, nominating them to that Presidency. In all other respects, the whole course of the service denominated by act of parliament does remain upon that footing—that is, a commercial footing.

Your lordships see here a regular system, a regular order, a regular course of gradation, which requires eleven years before persons can arrive at the highest trusts and situations in the Company's service. You will therefore be utterly astonished when you know that, after so long a service and so long a probation was required, things very different have happened, and that in a much shorter time persons have been seen returning to this kingdom with great and affluent fortunes. It will be necessary for you to consider, and it will be a great part of your inquiry, when we come before you to substantiate evidence against Mr. Hastings, to know how that order came to be broken down completely, so that scarce a trace of it, for any good purpose remains. For, though I will not deny that any order in a state may be superseded by the Presidency, when any great parts and talents upon superior exigencies are called forth, yet I must say the order of that service was formed upon wise principles. It gave the persons who were put in that course of probation an opportunity, if circumstances enabled them, of acquiring experience; it gave those who watched them a constant inspection upon them in all their progress; it gave them the necessity of acquiring a character in proportion to their standing, that all they had gained by years should not be lost by misconduct. It was a great, substantial regulation fit to be observed; but scarcely a trace of it remains to be discovered. For Mr. Hastings first broke through that service by making offices which had no reference to gradation, but which were superior in profit to those which the highest gradation might have acquired. He established whole systems of offices, and especially the systems of offices established in 1781, which being new none of the rules of gradation applied to them, and he filled them in such a manner as suited best his own views and purposes; so that in effect the whole of that order, whatever merit was in it, was by him broken down and subverted. The consequence was that persons in the most immature stages of life have been put to conduct affairs which required the greatest maturity of judgment and the greatest possible temper and moderation; and effects consequent have followed upon it. So far with respect to that order of the Company's service.

My lords, I must remark, before I go farther, that there is something peculiar in the service of the East India Company, and different from that of any other nation that has ever transferred its power from one country to another. The East India Company in India is not the British nation. When the Tartars entered into China and into Hindustan—when all the Goths and Vandals entered into Europe—when the Normans came into England—they came as a nation. The Company in India does not exist as a nation. Nobody can go there that does not go in its service. Therefore the English nation in India is nothing but a seminary for the succession of officers. They are a nation of place-men. They are a republic, a commonwealth, without a people. They are a state made up wholly of magistrates. The consequence of which is, that there is no people to control, to watch, to balance against the power of office. The power of office, so far as the English nation is concerned, is the sole power in the country. There is no corrective upon it whatever. The consequence of which is, that, being a kingdom of magistrates, the *esprit de corps* is strong in it—the spirit by the body by which they consider themselves as having a common interest, and a common interest, separated both from the country that sent them out and from the country in which they are, and where there is no control by persons who understand their language, who understand their manners, or can apply their conduct to the laws of the country. Such control does not exist in India. Therefore confederacy is easy, and has been general among them; and therefore your lordships are not to expect that that should happen in such a body which never happened in the world in any body or corporation, namely, that they should ever be a proper check and control upon themselves: it is not in the nature of things. There is a monopoly with an *esprit de corps* at home, called the India Company, and there is an *esprit de corps* abroad; and both those systems are united into one body, animated with the same spirit, that is, with the corporate spirit, which never was a spirit which corrected itself in any time or circumstance in the world, and which is such a thing as has not happened to the Moors, to the Portuguese, to the Romans—to go to any old or new examples. It has not happened in any one time or circumstance in the world, except in this. And out of that has issued a series of abuses, at the head of which Mr. Hastings has put himself, against the authority of the East India Company at home and every authority in this country.

My lords, the next circumstance is—and which is curious too—that the emoluments of office do not in any degree correspond with the trust. For, under the name of junior merchant, and senior merchant, and writer, and those other little names of a counting-house, you have great magistrates; you have the administrators of revenues truly royal; you have judges civil, and in a great degree criminal, who pass judgements upon the greatest properties of the country. You have all these under these names; and the emoluments that belong to them are so weak, so inadequate to the dignity of the character, that it is impossible—I may say of that service that it is absolutely impossible—for the subordinate parts of it to exist, to hope to exist, as Englishmen who look at their home as their ultimate resource—to exist in a state of incorruption. In that service the rule that prevails in many other countries is reversed. In other countries, often the greatest situations are attended with but little emoluments; because glory, fame, reputation, the love, the tears of joy, the honest applause of their country, pay those great and weighty labours which in great situations are sometimes required from the commonwealth; but all other countries pay in money what cannot be paid in fame and reputation. But it is the reverse with the India Company. All the subordinate parts of the gradation are officers, who, notwithstanding the weight and importance of the offices and dignities entrusted to them, are miserably provided for; and the heads, the chiefs, have great emoluments, securing them against every mode of temptation. And this is the thing Mr. Hastings has abused. He was at the head of the service. He has corrupted his hands and sullied his government with bribes. He has used oppression and tyranny in the place of legal government; and, instead of endeavouring to find honest, honourable, and adequate rewards for the persons who served the public, he has left them to prey upon it without the smallest degree of control. He has neither supplied nor taken care to supply, with that unbounded licence which he used over the public revenues, an honest scale of emoluments, suited to the vastness of the power given to the Company's service. He has not employed the public revenue for that purpose; but has left them at large to prey upon the country, and find themselves emoluments as they could. These are the defects of that service. There is no honest emolument, in much the greater part of it, correspondent to the nature and answerable to the expectations of the people who serve. There is an unbounded licence in almost all other respects; and, as one of the honestest and ablest servants of the Company said to me, it resembled the service of the Mahrattas—little pay, but unbounded licence to plunder. This is the pay of the Company's service; a service opened to all dishonest emolument, shut up to all things that are honest and fair. I do not say that the salaries would not sound well here; but when you consider the nature of the trusts, the dignity of the situation whatever the name of it is, the powers that are granted, and the hopes that every man has of establishing himself at home, it is a source of infinite grievance, of infinite abuse; and we charge Mr. Hastings, instead of stopping up, instead of endeavouring to regulate, instead of endeavouring to correct, so grievous and enormous an error, with having increased every part of it.

My lords, the next circumstance which distinguishes the East India Company is the youth of the persons who are employed in the system of that service. They have almost universally been sent out at that period of life, to begin their progress and career in active life and in the use of power, which in all other places has been employed in the course of a rigid education. They have been sent there in fact—to put it in a few words—with a perilous independence, with too inordinate expectations, and with boundless power. They are schoolboys without tutors; they are minors without guardians. The world is let loose upon them with all its temptations; and they are let loose upon the world, with all the powers that despotism can give. This is the situation of the Company's servants.

My lords, you have now heard the principles upon which Mr. Hastings governs the part of Asia subjected to the British empire. You have heard his opinion of 'the mean and depraved state' of those who are subject to it. You have heard his lecture upon arbitrary power, which he states to be the constitution of Asia. You hear the application that he makes of it; and you hear the practices which he employs to justify it, and who the persons were the authority of whose examples he professes to follow. Do your lordships really think that the nation would bear, that any human creature would bear, to hear an English governor defend himself upon such principles? For, if he can defend himself upon such principles, no man has any security for anything but by being totally independent of the British Government. Here he has declared his opinion that he is a despotic prince, that he is to use arbitrary power; and of course all his acts are covered with that shield. 'I know,' says he, 'the constitution of Asia only from its practices.' Will your lordships ever bear the corrupt practices of mankind made the principles of government? It will be your pride and glory to teach men that they are to confirm their practices to principles, and not to draw their principles from the corrupt practices of any man whatever. Was there ever heard, or could it be conceived, that a man would dare to mention the practices of all the villains, all the mad usurpers, all the thieves and robbers, in Asia, that he should gather them all up, and form the whole mass of abuses into one code and call it the duty of a British governor? I believe that till this time so audacious a thing was never attempted by mankind.

He to have arbitrary power! My lords, the East India Company have not arbitrary power to give him; the King has no arbitrary power to give him; your lordships have not; nor the Commons; nor the whole legislature. We have no arbitrary power to give, because arbitrary power is the thing which neither any man can hold nor any man can give away. No man can govern himself by his own will, much less can he be governed by the will of others. We are all born in subjection, all born equally, high and low, governors and governed, in subjection to one great, immutable, pre-existent law, prior to all our devices and prior to all our contrivances, paramount to our very being itself, by which we are knit and connected in the eternal frame of the universe, out of which we cannot stir.

This great law does not arise from our conventions or compacts; on the contrary, it gives to our conventions and compacts all the force and sanction they can have; it does not arise from our vain institutions. Every good gift is of God, all power is of God; and He who has given the power, and from whom it alone originates, will never suffer the exercise of it to be practised upon any less solid foundation than the power itself. Therefore, will it be imagined, if this be true, that He will suffer this great gift of government, the greatest, the best, that was ever given by God to mankind, to be the plaything and the sport of the feeble will of a man, who, by a blasphemous, absurd, and petulant usurpation, would place his own feeble, contemptible, ridiculous will in the place of the Divine wisdom and justice? No, my lords. It is not to be had by conquest; for by conquest, which is a more immediate designation of the hand of God, the conqueror only succeeds to all the painful duties and subordination to the power of God which belonged to the sovereign that held the country before. He cannot have it by succession; for no man can succeed to fraud, rapine, and violence, neither by compact, covenant, or submission, nor by any other means, can arbitrary power be conveyed to any man. Those who give and those who receive arbitrary power are alike criminal, and there is no man but is bound to resist it to the best of his power, wherever it shall show its face to the world. Nothing but absolute impotence can justify men in not resisting it to the best of their power.

Law and arbitrary power are at eternal enmity. Name me a magistrate, and I will name property; name me power, and I will name protection. It is a contradiction in terms, it is blasphemy in religion, it is wickedness in politics, to say that any man can have arbitrary power. Judges are guided and governed by the eternal laws of justice, to which we are all subject. We may bite our chains if we will, but we shall be made to know ourselves, and be taught that man is born to be governed by law; and he that will substitute will in the place of it is an enemy to God. . . .

Therefore I charge Mr. Hastings—and we shall charge him afterwards, when we come to bring the evidence more directly and fully home—with having destroyed, for private purposes, the whole system of government by the six provincial councils which he had no right to destroy.

I charge him with having delegated away from himself that power which the act of parliament had directed him to preserve inalienably in himself.

I charge him with having formed a committee to be mere instruments and tools, at the enormous expense of £62,000 per annum.

I charge him with having appointed a person their diwan, to whom these Englishmen were to be subservient tools, whose name was—to his own knowledge, by the general voice of the Company, by the recorded official transactions, by everything that can make a man known—abhorred and detested, stamped with infamy; and I charge him with the whole power which he had thus separated from the Council General and from the provincial councils.

I charge him with taking bribes of Gunga Govind Sing.

I charge him with not having done that bribe-service which fidelity, even in iniquity, requires at the hands of the worst of men.

I charge him with having robbed those people of whom he took the bribes.

I charge him with having fraudulently alienated the fortunes of widows.

I charge him with having, without right, title, or purchase, taken the lands of orphans and given them to wicked persons under him.

I charge him with having removed the natural guardians of a minor Raja, and given his zemindary to that wicked person, Deby Sing.

I charge him—his wickedness being known to himself and all the world—with having committed to Deby Sing the management of three great provinces; and with having thereby wasted the country, destroyed the landed interest, cruelly harassed the peasants, burnt their houses, seized their crops, tortured and degraded their persons, and destroyed the honour of the whole female race of that country.

In the name of the Commons of England, I charge all this villany upon Warren Hastings in this last moment of my application to you.

My lords, what is it that we want here to a great act of national justice? Do we want a cause, my lords? You have the cause of oppressed princes, of undone women of the first rank, of desolated provinces and of wasted kingdoms.

Do you want a criminal, my lords? When was there so much iniquity ever laid to the charge of any one? No, my lords, you must not look to punish any delinquent in India more. Warren Hastings has not left substance enough in India to nourish such another delinquent.

My lords, is it a prosecutor that you want? You have before you the Commons of Great Britain as prosecutors; and I believe, my lords, that the sun, in his beneficent progress round the world, does not behold a more glorious sight than that of men, separated from a remote people by the material bounds and barriers of nature, united by the bond of a social and moral community;—all the Commons of England resenting as their own the indignities and cruelties that are offered to all the people of India.

Do we want a tribunal? My lords, no example of antiquity, nothing in the modern world, nothing in the range of human imagination, can supply us with a tribunal like this. My lords, here we see virtually, in the mind's eye, that sacred majesty of the Crown, under whose authority you sit and whose power you exercise. We see in that invisible authority, what we all feel in reality and life, the beneficent powers and protecting justice of his Majesty. We have here the heir apparent to the Crown, such as the fond wishes of the people of England wish an heir apparent of the Crown to be. We have here all the branches of the royal family, in a situation between majesty and subjection, between the Crown and the subject, offering a pledge in that situation for the support of the rights of the Crown and the liberties of the people, both which extremities they touch. My lords, we have a great hereditary peerage here; those who have their own honour, the honour of their ancestors and of their posterity, to guard; and who will justify, as they have always justified, that provision in the constitution by which justice is made an hereditary office. My lords, we have here a new nobility, who have risen and exalted themselves by various merits, by great military services, which have extended the fame of this country from the rising to the setting sun. We have those who, by various civil merits and various civil talents, have been exalted to a situation which they well deserve, and in which they will justify the favour of their sovereign and the good opinion of their fellow-subjects, and make them rejoice to see those virtuous characters, that were the other day upon a level with them, now exalted above them in rank, but feeling with them in sympathy what they felt in common before. We have persons exalted from the practice of the law, from the place in which they administered high though subordinate justice, to a seat here, to enlighten with their knowledge and to strengthen with their votes those principles which have distinguished the courts in which they have presided.

My lords, you have before you the lights of our religion—you have the bishops of England. My lords, you have that true image of the primitive church in its ancient form, in its ancient ordinances, purified from the superstitions and the vices which a long succession of ages will bring upon the best institutions. You have the representatives of that religion which says that 'God is love', that the very vital spirit of its institution is charity; a religion which so much hates oppression, that, when the God whom we adore appeared in human form, he did not appear in a form of greatness and majesty, but in sympathy with the lowest of the people; and thereby made it a firm and ruling principle that their welfare was the object of all government, since the person who was the master of nature chose to appear himself in a subordinate situation. These are the considerations which influence them, which animate them and will animate them against all oppression; knowing that he who is called first among them, and first among us all, both of the flock that is fed and of those who feed it, made himself 'the servant of all'.

My lords, these are the securities that we have in all the constituent parts of the body of this house. We know them, we reckon, we rest, upon them; and commit safely the interests of India and of humanity into their hands. Therefore it is with confidence that, ordered by the Commons,

I impeach Warren Hastings, Esquire, of high crimes and misdemeanours.

I impeach him in the name of the Commons of Great Britain in Parliament assembled, whose parliamentary trust he has betrayed.

I impeach him in the name of all the Commons of Great Britain, whose national character he has dishonoured.

I impeach him in the name of the people of India, whose laws, rights, and liberties, he has subverted, whose properties he has destroyed, whose country he has laid waste and desolate.

I impeach him in the name and by virtue of those eternal laws of justice which he has violated.

I impeach him in the name of human nature itself, which he has cruelly outraged, injured, and oppressed, in both sexes, in every age, rank, situation, and condition of life.

SOURCE: In *Speeches and Documents on Indian Policy, 1750–1921*, ed. Arthur Berridale Keith (Delhi: Anmol Publishers, 1985).

Diary Selections
FANNY BURNEY

[Fanny Burney (1754–1840) was the daughter of prominent musician Charles Burney. Dr. Samuel Johnson and Edmund Burke were close friends of the Burney family. The self-educated Burney was widely recognized as a brilliant young woman, renowned for her social commentary and novels of manners. Considered the forerunner of Jane Austen, Burney's best-known fictional works are *Evelina; Or, The History of A Young Lady's Entrance Into the World* (1778) and *Camilla: Or, a Picture of Youth* (1831). Her memoirs can be found under the title *Diary and Letters of Madame d'Arblay, 1842–47.*]

THE IMPEACHMENT PROCEEDINGS:
A SAMPLE

Although the impeachment of Warren Hastings generated some of the most powerful oratory of the time, the records of the proceedings are not readily available, and it has been thought helpful to supply a few extracts taken from *Speeches of the Managers and Counsel in the Trial of Warren Hastings*, ed. E. A. Bond, 4 vols. 1859–1861. These have been supplemented by extracts from the diary of Fanny Burney (*Diary and Letters of Madame d'Arblay*, 7 vols. 1842–1846), and from *The Trial of Warren Hastings, Esquire* (2 vols. 1794): both, it must be said, sources extremely sympathetic to the accused.

From Fanny Burney's Diary, 13 February 1788
(*Diary* IV 56-62)

The Trial, so long impending, of Mr. Hastings, opened to-day. The Queen yesterday asked me if I wished to be present at the beginning, or had rather take another day. I was greatly obliged by her condescension, and preferred the opening. I thought it would give me a general view of the Court, and

Westminster Hall during the trial of Warren Hastings (1788). SOURCE: In Geoffrey Carnall and Colin Nicholson, eds., *The Impeachment of Warren Hastings: Papers from a Bicentenary Commemoration* (Edinburgh: Edinburgh University Press, 1989).

the manner of proceeding, and that I might read hereafter the speeches and evidence.

The business did not begin till near twelve o'clock. The opening to the whole then took place, by the entrance of the *Managers of the Prosecution;* all the company were already long in their boxes or galleries.

I shuddered, and drew involuntarily back, when, as the doors were flung open, I saw Mr. Burke, as Head of the Committee, make his solemn entry. He held a scroll in his hand, and walked alone, his brow knit with corroding care and deep labouring thought,—a brow how different to that which had proved so alluring to my warmest admiration when first I met him! so highly as he had been my favourite, so captivating as I had found his manners and conversation in our first acquaintance, and so much as I had owed to his zeal and kindness to me and my affairs in its progress! How did I grieve to behold him now the cruel Prosecutor (such to me he appeared) of an injured and innocent man!

Mr. Fox followed next, Mr. Sheridan, Mr. Wyndham, Messrs. Anstruther, Grey, Adam, Michael Angelo Taylor, Pelham, Colonel North, Mr. Frederick Montagu, Sir Gilbert Elliot, General Burgoyne, Dudley Long, &c. They were all named over to me by Lady Claremont, or I should not have recollected even those of my acquaintance, from the shortness of my sight.

When the Committee Box was filled the House of Commons at large took their seats on their green benches, which stretched, as I have said, along the whole left side of the Hall, and, taking in a third of the upper end, joined to the Great Chamberlain's Box, from which nothing separated them but a partition of about two feet in height.

Then began the procession, the Clerks entering first, then the Lawyers according to their rank, and the Peers, Bishops, and Officers, all in their coronation robes; concluding with the Princes of the Blood,—Prince William, son to the Duke of Gloucester, coming first, then the Dukes of Cumberland, Gloucester, and York, then the Prince of Wales; and the whole ending by the Chancellor, with his train borne.

They then all took their seats.

A Serjeant-at-Arms arose, and commanded silence in the Court, on pain of imprisonment.

Then some other officer, in a loud voice, called out, as well as I can recollect, words to this purpose:—"Warren Hastings, Esquire, come forth! Answer to the charges brought against you; save your bail, or forfeit your recognizance!"

Indeed I trembled at these words, and hardly could keep my place when I found Mr. Hastings was being brought to the bar. He came forth from some place immediately under the Great Chamberlain's Box, and was preceded by Sir Francis Molyneux, Gentleman-Usher or the Black Rod; and at each side of him walked his bail, Messrs. Sullivan and Sumner.

The moment he came in sight, which was not for full ten minutes after his awful summons, he made a low bow to the Chancellor and Court facing him. I saw not his face, as he was directly under me. He moved on slowly, and, I think, supported between his two Bails, to the opening of his own Box; there, lower still, he bowed again; and then, advancing to the bar, he leant his hands upon it, and dropped on his knees; but a voice in the same moment proclaiming he had leave to rise, he stood up almost instantaneously, and a third time profoundly bowed to the Court.

What an awful moment this for such a man!—a man fallen from such height of power to a situation so humiliating—from the almost unlimited command of so large a part of the Eastern World to be cast at the feet of his enemies, of the great Tribunal of his Country, and of the Nation at large, assembled thus in a body to try and to judge him! Could even his Prosecutors at that moment look on—and not shudder at least, if they did not blush?

The Crier, I think it was, made, in a loud and hollow voice, a public proclamation, "That Warren Hastings, Esquire, late Governor-General of Bengal, was now on his trial for high crimes and misdemeanours, with which he was charged by the Commons of Great Britain; and that all persons whatsoever who had aught to allege against him were now to stand forth."

A general silence followed, and the Chancellor, Lord Thurlow, now made his speech. I will give it you to the best of my power from memory; the newspapers have printed it far less accurately than I have retained it, though I am by no means exact or secure.

"Warren Hastings, you are now brought into this Court to answer to the charges brought against you by the Knights, Esquires, Burgesses, and Commons of Great Britain—charges now standing only as allegations, by them to be legally proved, or by you to be disproved. Bring forth your answers and defence, with that seriousness, respect, and truth, due to accusers so respectable. Time has been allowed you for preparation, proportioned to the intricacies in which the transactions are involved, and to the remote distances whence your documents may have been searched and required. You will still be allowed Bail, for the better forwarding your defence, and whatever you can require will still be yours, of time, witnesses, and all things else you may hold necessary. This is not granted you as any indulgence: it is entirely your due: it is the privilege which every British subject has a right to claim, and which is due to every one who is brought before this high Tribunal."

This speech, uttered in a calm, equal, solemn manner, and in a voice mellow and penetrating, with eyes keen and black, yet softened into some degree of tenderness while fastened full upon the prisoner—this speech, its occasion, its portent, and its object, had an effect upon every hearer of producing the most respectful attention, and, out of the Committee Box at least, the strongest emotions in the cause of Mr. Hastings.

From Fanny Burney's diary, 16 February 1788 (*Diary* IV 95-6)

At length the Peers' procession closed, the Prisoner was brought in, and Mr. Burke began his speech. It was the second day of his harangue; the first I had not been able to attend.

All I had heard of his eloquence, and all I had conceived of his great abilities, was more than answered by his performance. Nervous, clear, and striking was almost all that he uttered: the main business, indeed, of his coming forth was frequently neglected, and not seldom wholly lost; but his excursions were so fanciful, so entertaining, and so ingenious, that no miscellaneous hearer, like myself, could blame them. It is true he was unequal, but his inequality produced an effect which, in so long a speech, was perhaps preferable to greater consistency, since, though it lost attention in its falling off, it recovered it with additional energy by some ascent unexpected and wonderful. When he narrated, he was easy, flowing, and natural; when he declaimed, energetic, warm, and brilliant. The sentiments he interspersed were as nobly conceived as they were highly coloured; his satire had a poignancy of wit that made it as entertaining as it was penetrating; his allusions and quotations, as far as they were English and within my reach, were apt and ingenious; and the wild and sudden flights of his fancy, bursting forth from his creative imagination in language fluent, forcible, and varied, had a charm for my ear and my attention wholly new and perfectly irresistible.

Were talents such as these exercised in the service of truth, unbiassed by party and prejudice, how could we sufficiently applaud their exalted possesser? But though frequently he made me tremble by his strong and horrible representations, his own violence recovered me, by stigmatizing his assertions with personal ill-will and designing illiberality. Yet, at times I confess, with all that I felt, wished, and thought concerning Mr. Hastings, the whirlwind of his eloquence nearly drew me into its vortex.

SOURCE: In *The Impeachment of Warren Hastings: Papers from a Bicentenary Commemoration*, ed. Geoffrey Carnall and Colin Nicholson (Edinburgh: Edinburgh University Press, 1989).

From the Third Day of Edmund Burke's Speech Opening the Impeachment, 18 February 1788
EDMUND BURKE

My Lords, I am obliged to make use of some apology for the horrid scenes that I am now going to open to you. You have had enough, you have had perhaps more than enough, of oppressions upon property and oppressions upon liberty—but here the skin was touched. And, my Lords, permit me to make as my apology to you, that which Commissioner Paterson made—a man with respect to whom I wish that, if ever my name should be mentioned hereafter, it may go down along with his in the same apology, and if possible in second-rate merit as to the same acts. His apology is this, and it is my apology and the apology of us all:

> That the punishments inflicted upon the ryots of both Rungpore and Dinagepore for non-payment were in many instances of such a nature that I would rather wish to draw a veil over them than shock your feelings by the detail. But, however disagreeable the task may be to myself, it is absolutely necessary, for the sake of justice, humanity and the honour of government, that they should be exposed, to be prevented in future.

Let this be my anticipated apology. It is indeed a most disgraceful scene to human nature that I am going to display to you.

My Lords, when the people were stripped of everything, of all that they publicly possessed, it was suspected, and in some cases suspected justly, that the poor, unfortunate, husbandmen had hid in the deserts, disseminated through that country, some share of grain, for subsistence in unproductive months and for seed for future grain. Their bodies were then applied to. The first mode of torture was this:—They began by winding cords about their fingers until they had become incorporated together, and then they hammered wedges of wood and iron between those fingers, until they crushed and maimed those poor, honest, laborious, hands, which never had been lifted to their own mouths but with the scanty supply of the product of their own labour. These are the hands which are so treated, which have for fifteen years furnished the investment for China from which your Lordships, and all this auditory, and all this country, have every day for these fifteen years made that luxurious meal with which we all commence the day. And what was the return of Britain? Cords, hammers, wedges, tortures and maimings, were the return that the British government made to those laborious hands. However, these crippled, undone, hands are in a situation in which they will act with resistless power when they are lifted up to heaven against the authors of their oppression. Then what can withstand such hands? Can the power that crushed and destroyed them? Powerful in prayer, let us at least deprecate and secure ourselves from the vengeance which will follow those who mashed, crippled and disabled, these hands. My Lords, it is a serious thought; for God's sake let us think of it.

They began there, but there they did not stop. The heads of villages, the parochial magistrates, the leading yeomen of the country, respectable for their situation and their age, were taken and tied together by the feet, two and two, thrown over a bar, and there beaten with bamboo canes upon the soles of their feet until their nails started from their toes. And then, falling upon them, while their heads hung down as their feet were above, with sticks and cudgels, their tormentors attacked them with such blind fury that the blood ran out of their mouths, eyes and noses. This was the second step that they took with these unfortunate people.

My Lords, they did not stop there. Bamboos, ratans, canes, common whips and scourges, were not sufficient. I find that there is a tree in that country which bears strong and sharp thorns, which cruelly lacerate the flesh. They were not satisfied with ordinary whips, scourges and torments; but they got branches of this bale tree, as it is called, and scourged these poor people with the thorns, so that mere simple beating and whipping might appear to be mercy in comparison with it. But, refining in their cruelty, searching everything through the devious paths of nature, where she seems to have forgotten her usual plan, and produces things unfavourable to the life of man, they found a poisonous plant called the bechettea plant—a plant which is a deadly caustic, which inflames the parts that are cut, and leaves the body a crust of leprous sores, and often causes death itself. With rods made of this plant they scourged the people whom they had scourged before.

This, one would think, would have satisfied any ordinary cruelty. But we are so made that even the pains of the body fortify it for other pains. The mind strengthens as the body suffers, and rises as it were with an elastic force against those that inflict torments upon it. The mind gets the better of the body. Its pains give it spirit, and it defies the oppressor. These people were dealt with in another manner. There are people who can bear their own torture who cannot bear the sufferings of their families. The innocent children were brought out and scourged before the faces of their parents; young persons were cruelly scourged, both male and female, in the presence of their parents. This was not all. They bound the father and son face to face, arm to arm, body to body; and in that situation they scourged and whipped them, in order, with a refinement of cruelty, that every blow that escaped the father should fall upon the son, that every stroke that escaped the son should strike upon the parent; so that, where they did not lacerate and tear the sense, they should wound the sensibilities and sympathies of nature. This was the common and every-day practice in this country for a long time. But, my Lords, there was more. Virgins, whose fathers kept them from the sight of the sun, were dragged into the public court, that court which was the natural refuge against all wrong, against all oppression, and all iniquity. There, in the presence of day, in the public court, vainly invoking its justice, while their shrieks were mingled with the cries and groans of an indignant people, those virgins were cruelly violated by the basest and wickedest of mankind. It did not end there. The wives of the people of the country only differed in this, that they lost their honour in the bottom of the most cruel dungeons, where all their torments were a little buried from the view of mankind. They were not always left there, though there they suffered those cruel and outrageous wrongs— wrongs to the people, to their manners, to the bodies and feelings of mankind: but they were dragged out, naked and exposed to the public view, and scourged before all the people. Here in my hand is my authority; for otherwise one would think it almost incredible. But it did not end there. In order that nature might be violated in all those circumstances where the sympathies of nature are awakened, where the remembrances of our infancy and all our tender remembrances are combined, they put the nipples of the women into the sharp edges of split bamboos and tore them from their bodies. Grown from ferocity to ferocity, from cruelty to cruelty, they applied burning torches and cruel slow fires—my Lords, I am ashamed to go further—those infernal fiends, in defiance of everything divine and human, planted death in the source of life; and where that modesty, which more distinguishes man even than his rational nature from the base creation, turns from the view and dare not meet the expression, dared those infernal fiends execute their cruel and nefarious tortures—where the modesty of nature and the sanctity of justice dare not follow them or even describe their practices.

These, my Lords, were the horrors that arose from bribery—the cruelties that arose from giving power into the hands of such persons as Deby Sing and such infernal villains as Gunga Govind Sing . . .

My Lords, the people of India are patience itself; their patience is too criminal. But here they burst at once into a wild, universal, uproar and unarmed rebellion. The whole province of Rungpore and a great part of Dinagepore broke out into one general rebellion and revolt.

SOURCE: In *The Impeachment of Warren Hastings: Papers from a Bicentenary Commemoration*, ed. Geoffrey Carnall and Colin Nicholson (Edinburgh: Edinburgh University Press, 1989).

From the Address of Warren Hastings in His Defence, 2 June 1791
WARREN HASTINGS

My Lords, in the course of this trial, my accusers, to excite a popular odium against me, have called me the abettor or usurper of arbitrary power. I certainly did not use the words arbitrary power in the sense which has been imputed to me. The language, it is true, was not my own, for I was indebted for that part of my Defence to the assistance of a friend; but this I can aver, that nothing more was meant by arbitrary power than discretionary power. I considered myself and Council as invested with that discretionary power which commanders-in-chief have over their armies, which the Legislature has lately conferred, in a greater extent, on Lord Cornwallis, singly, and which all Governments have in their legislative capacity over the property of their subjects. I never considered that my will or caprice was to be the guide of my conduct; but that I was responsible for the use of the authority with which I was invested to those who had conferred it on me.

My Lords, let me be tried by this rule:—did I act prudently and consistently with the interest of my superiors and of the people whom I governed? Whatever may be your Lordships' opinion upon this question, I can with a safe conscience declare to all the world that my intentions were perfectly upright, and biassed by no selfish considerations whatever . . .

I must entreat your Lordships to remember that, at the time I formed an intention to levy a fine upon Cheyt Sing, and when I consented to the resumption of the Begum's treasure, our government was in the utmost distress for money. I need not, in this place, enter into a minute detail of the several armies we then had in the field, or of the various demands upon me for immediate supplies of treasure; it is sufficient to say, that the distress was as great as it was possible to be without an actual state of bankruptcy and insolvency. It was very natural, under such circumstances, for me to avail myself of every just means of supply which fortune might throw in my way. It might and, I may say, it actually did incline me to act with greater promptitude and decision than I should otherwise have done.

My Lords, it will depend upon your Lordships to give me what degree of credit you please. Whether I intended, for a moment, to apply any one of the sums received by me to my own use, is a point which can be known only to God and my own conscience. I can solemnly and with a pure conscience affirm that I never did harbour such a thought for an instant. And permit me to add, my Lords, that I was too intent upon the means to be employed for preserving India to Great Britain, from the hour in which I was informed that France meant to strain every nerve to dispute that empire with us, to bestow a thought upon myself or my own private fortune. . . .

My Lords, I will not detain your Lordships by adverting for any length to the story, told by the Manager who opened the general charge, relative to the horrid cruelties practised on the natives of Dhee Jumla by Deby Sing. It will be sufficient to say that the Manager never ventured to introduce this story in the form of a charge, though pressed and urged to do so in the strongest possible terms, both in and out of Parliament.

Mr. Paterson, on whose authority he relied for the truth of his assertions, and with whom he said he wished to go down to posterity, has had the generosity to write to my attorney in Calcutta, for my information, that he felt the sincerest concern to find his reports turned to my disadvantage, as I had acted as might be expected from a man of humanity, throughout all the transactions in which Deby Sing was concerned. Had the cruelties which the Manager stated really been inflicted, it was not possible, as he very well knew at the time, to impute them even by any kind of forced construction to me. My Lords, it is a fact that I was the first person to give Mr. Paterson an ill opinion of Deby Sing, whose conduct upon former occasions had left an unfavourable and, perhaps, an unjust impression upon my mind. In employing Deby Sing, I certainly yielded up my opinion to that of Mr. Anderson and Mr. Shore, who had better opportunities of knowing him than I could have. In the course of the inquiry into his conduct, he received neither favour nor countenance from me, nor from any member of the Board. That inquiry was carried on principally when I was at Lucknow, and was not completed during my government, though it was commenced and continued with every possible solemnity, and with the sincerest desire, on my part and on the part of my colleagues, to do strict and impartial justice. The result I have read in England; and it certainly appears, that, though the man was not entirely innocent, the extent of his guilt bore no sort of proportion to the magnitude of the charges against him. In particular, it proved that the most horrible of those horrible acts, so artfully detailed and with such effect in this place, never were committed at all. Here I leave the subject, convinced that every one of your Lordships must feel for the unparalleled injustice that was done to me by the introduction and propagation of that atrocious calumny.

My Lords, I will not now detain your Lordships by offering many remarks upon the gross injustice that I also sustained, in having been compelled to appear at your Lordships' bar to justify acts which have received the repeated approbation of the King's Ministers and, virtually, of the late House of Commons. My Lords, it is perfectly true that the Articles to which I allude are not insisted upon, or, in other words, that they are abandoned. But I feel the injury most sensibly, and the expense of defending myself against them has been intolerable. . . .

When Great Britain was involved in a complicated war, and her governments in India had, besides European enemies, a confederacy of all the principal powers of India armed against them, I gave the then Minister of this kingdom constant information of all the measures which I had taken, in conjunction with my colleagues in the government, to repel the dangers which pressed us, the motive and objects of those measures, the consequences expected from them, and the measures which I had further in contemplation. And it has since afforded me more than common pleasure to reflect, that every successive letter verified the expectations and the promises of the preceding.

If I had given evidence in my defence, I should have called upon the noble Lord to have produced all my letters in his possession—those, and my letters to the court of Directors. But my letters to Lord North, in a most striking manner, would have shown how careful I was to expose all my actions to their knowledge; and, consequently, how little apprehension I could have felt that there was anything in them that could be deemed reprehensible. In all instances which might have been deemed of a doubtful nature, these communications were virtual references for their sanction or for their future prohibition. If I received neither, their silence was a confirmation, and had more than the effect of an order; since, with their tacit approbation of them, I had imposed upon myself the prior obligation of my own conception of their propriety. Were I therefore for a moment to suppose that the acts with which I am charged and which I so communicated—for I communicated all—to the court of Directors, were intrinsically wrong, yet from such proofs it is evident that I thought them right; and therefore the worst that could be said of them, as they could affect me, is, that they were errors of judgment . . .

Two great sources of revenue, opium and salt, were of my creation. The first, which I am accused for not having made more productive, amounts at this time yearly to the net income of 120,000*l*. The last—and all my colleagues in the Council refused to share with me in the responsibility attendant upon a new system—to the yearly net income of above 800,000*l*.

To sum up all—I maintained the provinces of my immediate administration in a state of peace, plenty and security, when every other member of the British empire was involved in external wars or civil tumult.

In a dreadful season of famine, which visited all the neighbouring states of India during three successive years, I repressed it in its first approach to the countries of the British dominion, and by timely and continued regulations prevented its return . . .

And, lastly, I raised the collective annual income of the Company's possessions under my administration from three to five millions sterling—not of temporary and forced exaction, but of an easy, continued, and still existing production—the surest evidence of a good government, improving agriculture and increased population.

To the Commons of England, in whose name I am arraigned for desolating the provinces of their dominion in India, I dare to reply, that they are—and their representatives annually persist in telling them so—the most flourishing of all the states in India. It was I who made them so. The valour of others acquired—I enlarged and gave shape and consistency to—the dominion which you hold there. I preserved it. I sent forth its armies with an effectual but an economical hand, through unknown and hostile regions, to the support of your other possessions—to the retrieval of one from degradation and dishonour, and of the other from utter loss and subjection.

I maintained the wars which were of your formation, or of that of others—not of mine . . . I gave you all; and you have rewarded me with confiscation, disgrace, and a life of impeachment.

SOURCE: In *The Impeachment of Warren Hastings: Papers from a Bicentenary Commemoration*, ed. Geoffrey Carnall and Colin Nicholson (Edinburgh: Edinburgh University Press, 1989).

Warren Hastings
LORD THOMAS BABINGTON MACAULAY

Whatever we may think of the morality of Hastings, it cannot be denied that the financial results of his policy did honour to his talents. In less than two years after he assumed the government, he had, without imposing any additional burdens on the people subject to his authority, added about four hundred and fifty thousand pounds to the annual income of the Company, besides procuring about a million in ready money. He had also relieved the finances of Bengal from military expenditure, amounting to near a quarter of a million a year, and had thrown that charge on the Nabob of Oude. There can be no doubt that this was a result which, if it had been obtained by honest means, would have entitled him to the warmest gratitude of his country, and which, by whatever means obtained, proved that he possessed great talents for administration.

With all his faults,—and they were neither few nor small,—only one cemetery was worthy to contain his remains. In that temple of silence and reconciliation where the enmities of twenty generations lie buried, in the Great Abbey which has during many ages afforded a quiet resting-place to those whose minds and bodies have been shattered by the contentions of the Great Hall, the dust of the illustrious accused should have mingled with the dust of the illustrious accusers. This was not to be. Yet the place of interment was not ill chosen. Behind the chancel of the parish church of Daylesford, in earth which already held the bones of many chiefs of the house of Hastings, was laid the coffin of the greatest man who has ever borne that ancient and widely extended name. On that very spot probably, fourscore years before, the little Warren, meanly clad and scantily fed, had played with the children of ploughmen. Even then his young mind had revolved plans which might be called romantic. Yet, however romantic, it is not likely that they had been so strange as the truth. Not only had the poor orphan retrieved the fallen fortunes of his line. Not only had he repurchased the old lands, and rebuilt the old dwelling. He had preserved and extended an empire. He had founded a polity. He had administered government and war with more than the capacity of Richelieu. He had patronised learning with the judicious liberality of Cosmo. He had been attacked by the most formidable combination of enemies that ever sought the destruction of a single victim; and over that combination, after a struggle of ten years, he had triumphed. He had at length gone down to his grave in the fulness of age, in peace, after so many troubles, in honour, after so much obloquy.

Those who look on his character without favour or malevolence will pronounce that, in the two great elements of all social virtue, in respect for the rights of others, and in sympathy for the sufferings of others, he was deficient. His principles were somewhat lax. His heart was somewhat hard. But while we cannot with truth describe him either as a righteous or as a merciful ruler, we cannot regard without admiration the amplitude and fertility of his intellect, his rare talents for command, for administration, and for controversy, his dauntless courage, his honourable poverty, his fervent zeal for the interests of the state, his noble equanimity, tried by both extremes of fortune, and never disturbed by either.

SOURCE: In the *Edinburgh Review* 74, no. 149 (October 1841): 160–255.

IV
THE CASE OF TIPU SULTAN

INTRODUCTION
Tipu Sultan: Oriental Despot or National Hero
BARBARA HARLOW

TIPU SULTAN (also known as Tippu Sultan and Tippoo Sultan) was variously acknowledged as at once a ruler loved and respected by his own people and an infamous tyrant and treacherous opponent to Company projects for India. As Lord Cornwallis described him, "Strange, is it not, that [Tipu] should have alienated the high and mighty who are backed by sword and wealth, only to find a place in the hearts of the vast multitude which counts for nothing." Cornwallis, governor-general in India from 1786 to 1793, had himself been involved in wars with Tipu Sultan.

Born in 1750, Tipu Sultan succeeded his father Haidar Ali to rule over Mysore state. Like his father, he assisted in building up the area's military might and in revitalizing the revenue administration, fostering trade and agriculture, and introducing social reforms such as the opposition to bonded labor. The independence of father and son, however, was not appreciated by representatives of the Company, and a series of wars—sometimes referred to as the Anglo-Mysore Wars—from 1767 to 1799 eventually brought about the subjugation of the Mysore state. The third Anglo-Mysore War, from 1790 to 1791, had been concluded with the Treaty of Seringapatam in 1792, in which not only were half of Tipu's dominions ceded to his foes but two of his sons were taken as hostages "for a due performance of the treaty." Subsequently, Tipu Sultan, already impressed by what he knew of the example of the French Revolution, entered into "intercourse" with the French, much to the alarm of the English. Tipu even exchanged letters with Napoleon Bonaparte who in 1798 brought his campaign to Egypt, with the eventual plan of overtaking the British and reaching India itself. As the 1798–1799 correspondence between Tipu and the Company makes clear, issues of territory, political allegiances, and military preparations were paramount to their conflicted relationship. The fourth and final Anglo-Mysore War was concluded on 4 May 1799 with the capture of Seringapatam and Tipu's death in battle. But as pointed out by the Duke of Wellington, the fear remained that "Tipu's memory will live long after the world has ceased to remember you and me."

And indeed, Tipu Sultan was remembered but a few years later in Maria Edgeworth's story "Lame Jervas" (in *Popular Tales*, 1804), in which the young Jervas enters the service of Tipu and discovers the complex significance of the sultan's social reformism and scientific vision. Half a century later, Wilkie Collins's novel *The Moonstone* (1868) reflected on the legacy of Seringapatam for English domestic life. The "moonstone," a brilliantly large diamond stolen from the Seringapatam treasury, is bequeathed to an English family, only to bring unmitigated disaster to its members and friends. Large the jewel might be, but it is also flawed—the narrative weighs whether the precious gem might not finally be all the more valuable if cut into pieces in Amsterdam and sold in parts to interested buyers. Collins's novel, that is, questions perhaps the very pattern of British colonial designs on the Indian subcontinent, a territory that by then was about to become the "jewel in the crown" of Queen Victoria, and the past and present opposition to empire as exemplified and handed down by Tipu Sultan.

BIBLIOGRAPHY

Ali, B. Shaikh. *Tipu Sultan: A Study in Diplomacy and Confrontation*. Mysore: Geetha Book House, 1982.

Anderson, Perry. *Lineages of the Absolutist State*. London: N. L. B., 1974.

East India Company. *The War with Tippoo Sultan*. 1800. Lahore: al-Kitab, 1977.

Edgeworth, Maria. *Popular Tales*. London: C. Mercier & Co., 1804.

Embree, Ainslie T. *Imagining India: Essays on Indian History*. Delhi: Oxford University Press, 1989.

Fernandes, Praxy. *The Tigers of Mysore: A Biography of Hyder Ali and Tipu Sultan*. New Delhi: Viking, 1991.

Gidwani, B. S. *The Sword of Tipu Sultan: A Historical Novel about the Life and Legend of Tipu Sultan of India*. Bombay: Allied Publishers, 1976.

Gopal, M. H. (Mysore Hatti). *Tipu Sultan's Mysore: An Economic Study*. Bombay: Popular Prakashan, 1971.

O'Leary, Brendan. *The Asiatic Mode of Production: Oriental Despotism, Historical Materialism, and Indian History*. Oxford: B. Blackwell, 1989.

Sultan, Tippoo. *Authentic Memoirs of Tippoo Sultan*. London: 1799; reprint, Delhi: Takshila Hardbounds, 1979.

Taylor, Meadows. *Tippoo Sultaun: A Tale of the Mysore War*. London: 188?; reprint, New Delhi: Asian Educational Services, 1986.

Thapar, Romila. "Ideology and the Interpretation of Early Indian History." In *Interpreting Early India*. Delhi: Oxford University Press, 1993.

Wittfogel, Karl. *Oriental Despotism: A Comparative Study of Total Power*. New Haven, Conn.: Yale University Press, 1957.

Excerpts from *The Tiger of Mysore*

G. A. HENTY

[G. A. (George Alfred) Henty (1832–1902) was a prolific and popular author of travel and adventure sensation novels for boys; he also wrote for the boys' magazines *A Boy's Own* and the *Union Jack*. Henty specialized in fictionalized accounts of imperial wars, including novels on the Battle of Waterloo, the Greek and Italian Wars of Independence, the Afghan and Burmese Wars, and the American Civil War. His significant and related titles include *In Times of Peril: A Tale of India* (1881) and *At the Point of the Bayonet: A Tale of the Mahratta War* (1901).]

FROM THE PREFACE

While some of our wars in India are open to the charge that they were undertaken on slight provocation, and were forced on by us in order that we might have an excuse for annexation, our struggle with Tippoo Saib was, on the other hand, marked by a long endurance of wrong, and a toleration of abominable cruelties perpetrated upon Englishmen and our native allies. Hyder Ali was a conqueror of the true Eastern type; he was ambitious in the extreme, he dreamed of becoming the Lord of the whole of Southern India, he was an able leader, and, though ruthless where it was his policy to strike terror, he was not cruel from choice. His son, Tippoo, on the contrary, revelled in acts of the most abominable cruelty. It would seem that he massacred for the very pleasure of massacring, and hundreds of British captives were killed by famine, poison, or torture, simply to gratify his lust for murder. Patience was shown towards this monster until patience became a fault, and our inaction was naturally ascribed by him to fear. Had firmness been shown by Lord Cornwallis, when Seringapatam was practically in his power, the second war would have been avoided and thousands of lives spared. The blunder was a costly one to us, for the work had to be done all over again, and

174   The Case of Tipu Sultan

"Tippoo Sahib at the Lines of Travancore" (1789). In James Grant, ed., *Cassell's Illustrated History of India*, vol. 2, part 1 (New Delhi: Oriental Publishers and Distributors, 1978).

the fault of Lord Cornwallis retrieved by the energy and firmness of the Marquis of Wellesley.

FROM CHAPTER 4, "WAR DECLARED"

Tippoo, on the other hand, is a human tiger; he delights in torturing his victims, and slays his prisoners from pure love of bloodshed. He is proud of the title of 'Tiger'; his footstool is a tiger's head, and the uniforms of his infantry are a sort of imitation of a tiger's stripes. He has military talent, and showed great judgment in command of his division—indeed most of the successes gained during the last war were his work. Since then he had laboured incessantly to improve his army; numbers of regiments have been raised, composed of the captives off from here and from the west coast. They are drilled in European fashion by the English captives he still holds in his hands.

SOURCE: G. A. Henty, *The Tiger of Mysore: A Story of the War with Tippoo Saib* (London: Blackie and Son Limited, 189?).

Treaties of Peace, and Review of the Consequence of the War.
MAJOR DIRAM

CHAPTER I.

Preliminary articles of peace—arrival of the hostages—their reception, and some Account of Tippoo's sons.

"Preliminary articles of a treaty of peace concluded between the allied armies and Tippoo Sultan."

ARTICLE I.

"One half of the dominions of which Tippoo Sultan was in possession before the war, to be ceded to the allies from the countries adjacent, according to their situation."

ARTICLE II.

"Three crores and thirty lacs of rupees, to be paid by Tippoo Sultan, either in gold mohurs, pagodas, or bullion."

"1st. One crore and sixty-five lacs, to be paid immediately."

"2d. One crore and sixty-five lacs, to be paid in three payments, not exceeding four months each."

ARTICLE III.

"All prisoners of the four powers, from the time of Hyder Ally, to be unequivocally restored."

ARTICLE IV.

"Two of Tippoo Sultan's three eldest sons to be given as hostages for a due performance of the treaty."

ARTICLE V.

"When they shall arrive in camp, with the articles of this treaty, under the seal of the Sultan, a counterpart shall be sent from the three powers. Hostilities shall cease, and terms of a treaty of alliance and perpetual friendship shall be agreed upon."

These were the terms, which, after different conferences with the vakeels, were dictated by Earl Cornwallis to Tippoo Sultan, and to which he found it necessary to submit. They were sent to him on the 22d, and returned by him, signed and sealed, the night of the 23d of February.

The allies, Hurry Punt on the part of the Mahrattas, and the Nizam's son, Secunder Jaw, and his minister Azeem-ul-Omrah, on the part of the Nizam, are said to have conducted themselves with the greatest moderation and propriety in the negotiation, and on every occasion on which they had been consulted during the war. And such was the ascendancy gained by a plain and upright conduct in all public transactions, by condescension in all points of form and religious prejudice, and by firmness in all the material operations in the field, that they professed the most perfect confidence in Lord Cornwallis, and declared their willingness to proceed with the siege, or readiness to agree to any terms of peace his Lordship should think fit to conclude with the Sultan.

Tippoo is said to have been prevailed upon with infinite difficulty to subscribe to the terms of peace; and now that all was settled, the uneasiness in the seraglio became extreme in parting with the boys, who were to be sent out as hostages. The Sultan was again entreated to request they might be allowed to remain another day, in order to make suitable preparations for their departure, and Lord Cornwallis, who had dispensed with their coming at the time the treaty was sent, had again the goodness to grant his request.

The vakeels had been instructed to acquaint Tippoo that his Lordship would wait upon the Princes as soon as they came to their tents; and besides the guards and attendants, about 200 allowed to be sent with them, that his Lordship would appoint a careful officer; with a battalion of Sepoys, for their protection. The Sultan sent in answer, "that he was fully sensible of his Lordship's goodness; that he could not agree to his being at the trouble to go first to wait on his sons; and having the most perfect reliance on his honour, it was his own particular desire and request, that he would be pleased to allow them to be brought at once to his tent, and delivered into his own hands."

On the 26th about noon, the Princes left the fort, which appeared to be manned as they went out, and every where crouded with people, who, from curiosity or affection, had come to see them depart. The Sultan himself, was on the rampart above the gateway. They were saluted by the fort on leaving it, and with twenty-one guns from the park as they approached our camp, where the part of the line they passed, was turned out to receive them. The vakeels conducted them to the tents which had been sent from the fort for their accommodation, and pitched near the mosque redoubt, where they were met by Sir John Kennaway, the Mahratta and Nizam's vakeels, and from thence accompanied by them to head quarters.

The Princes were each mounted on an elephant richly caparisoned, and seated in a silver howder, and were attended by their father's vakeels, and the persons already mentioned, also on elephants. The procession was led by several camel harcarras, and seven standard-bearers, carrying small green flags suspended from rockets, followed by one hundred pikemen, with spears inlaid with silver. Their guard of two hundred Sepoys, and a party of horse, brought up the rear. In this order they approached head quarters, where the battalion of Bengal Sepoys, commanded by Captain Welch, appointed for their guard, formed a street to receive them.

Lord Cornwallis, attended by his staff, and some of the principal officers of the army, met the Princes at the door of his large tent as they dismounted from the elephants; and, after embracing them, led them in, one in each hand, to the tent; the eldest, Abdul Kalick, was about ten, the youngest, Mooza-ud-Deen, about eight years of age. When they were seated on each side of Lord Cornwallis, Gullam Ally, the head vakeel, addressed his Lordship as follows. "These children were this morning the sons of the Sultan my master; their situation is now changed, and they must look up to your Lordship as their father."

Lord Cornwallis, who had received the boys as if they had been his own sons, anxiously assured the vakeel and the young Princes themselves, that every attention possible would be shewn to them, and the greatest care taken of their persons. Their little faces brightened up; the scene became highly interesting; and not only their attendants, but all the spectators were delighted to see that any fears they might have harboured were removed, and that they would soon be reconciled to their change of situation, and to their new friends.

The Princes were dressed in long white muslin gowns, and red turbans. They had several rows of large pearls round their necks, from which was suspended an ornament consisting of a ruby and an emerald of considerable size, surrounded by large brilliants; and in their turbans, each had a sprig of rich pearls. Bred up from their infancy with infinite care, and instructed in their manners to imitate the reserve and politeness of age, it astonished all present to see the correctness and propriety of their conduct. The eldest boy, rather dark in his colour, with thick lips, a small flattish nose, and a long thoughtful countenance, was less admired than the youngest, who is remarkably fair, with regular features, a small round face, large full eyes, and a more animated appearance. Placed too, on the right hand of Lord Cornwallis, he was said to be the favourite son, and the Sultan's intended heir. His mother (a sister of Burham-ud-Deen's, who was killed at Sattimungulum), a beautiful delicate, woman, had died of fright and apprehension, a few days after the attack of the lines. This melancholy event made the situation of the youngest boy doubly interesting, and, with the other circumstances, occasioned his attracting by much the most notice. After some conversation, his Lordship presented a handsome gold watch to each of the Princes, with which they seemed much pleased. Beetle-nut and otter of roses, according to the eastern custom, being then distributed, he led them back to their elephants, embraced them again, and they returned, escorted by their suite and the battalion, to their tents.

Next day, the 27th; Lord Cornwallis, attended as yesterday, went to pay the Princes a visit at their tents, pitched near the mosque redoubt, within the green canaut or wall, used by the Sultan in the field, of which we had so often traced the marks during the war.

The canaut of canvas, scollopped at top, was painted of a beautiful sea-green colour, with rich ornamented borders, and formed an elegant inclosure for the tents. It was thrown open to the front, and within it the pikemen, Sepoys, &c. of the Princes' guard formed a street to a tent, whence they came out and met Lord Cornwallis. After embracing them, he led them, one in each hand, into the tent, where chairs were placed for his Lordship, themselves, and his suite. Sir John Kennaway, the Mahratta and the Nizam's vakeels, also attended the conference.

The eldest boy, now seated on his Lordship's right hand, appeared less serious than yesterday; and when he spoke, was not only graceful in his manner, but had a most affable, animated appearance. The youngest, however, appeared to be the favourite with the vakeels; and, at the desire of Gullam Ally, repeated, or rather recited some verses in Arabic, which he had learned by heart from the Koran, and afterwards some verses in Persian, which he did with great ease and confidence, and shewed he had made great progress in his education.

Each of the Princes presented his Lordship with a fine Persian sword, and in return he gave the eldest a fuzee, and the youngest a pair of pistols, of very fine and curious workmanship. Some jewels, shawls, and rich presents were then offered to his Lordship as matter of form; after which, beetle-nut and otter of roses being distributed, the Princes conducted his Lordship without the tent, when he embraced them and took his leave.

The tent in which the Princes received Lord Cornwallis, was lined with fine chintz, and the floor covered with white cloth. The attendants sprinkled rose water during the audience; and there was a degree of state, order, and magnificence in every thing, much superior to what had been seen amongst our allies. The guard of Sepoys drawn up without, was clothed in uniform, and not only regularly and well armed, but, compared to the rabble of infantry in the service of the other native powers, appeared well disciplined and in high order.

From what passed this day, and the lead taken by the eldest son, it seemed uncertain which of them might be intended for Tippoo's heir. Perhaps, and most probably neither; for Hyder Saib, about twenty years of age, has always been said to be Tippoo's eldest son; had been educated accordingly, and had accompanied his father constantly during the war, till lately, when he was sent on a separate command, and distinguished himself very eminently in the relief of Gurramconda. The vakeels, however, asserted that he was not a legitimate son, nor in favour with Tippoo, from being of an unpromising disposition; but there is reason to suspect that they were directed to make this sacrifice of truth to policy, in order to prevent the demand of Hyder Saib as one of the hostages, which, to a prince at his time of life, must have been extremely disagreeable; though the others, from their early age, would feel less in that situation, and would not suffer essentially by removal from their father's care.

Hyder Saib is, from all accounts, a most promising youth, and should he be destined to succeed to the kingdom of Mysore, it may be hoped that the misfortunes which the inordinate ambition of his father has brought upon their family, will lead him to recur to the prudence of his grandfather; and that his reign, as well as the remainder of Tippoo's life, will be employed rather to preserve and improve what remains, than to attempt to recover the half which they have lost of the extensive dominions so lately acquired by the wisdom and valour of old Hyder.

SOURCE: In *A Narrative of the Campaign in India which Terminated the War with Tippoo Sultan in 1792* (London: W. Bulmer and Co., 1793; reprint, New Delhi: Asian Educational Services, 1985).

Selected Letters between Tipu and Company Governor's General, 1798–1799

To Tipu Sultan
Written on the 14th June, 1798

Immediately on my arrival at Bengal, Sir Alured Clarke communicated to me your friendly letter to him, stating that some people of the Coorga country having descended from the woods and mountains, had fixed their residence in the village of Kaunt-mungul and Coloorbaji &c.

(Recapitulate the contents of the letter).

Sir Alured Clarke has also communicated to me your answer to the letter from the late Governor-General Sir John Shore, respecting the claims of the Company and of Your Highness to the District of Wynaad, bordering on Tambercherry.

Being anxious to afford you every proof in my power of my sincere desire to maintain the good understanding which had so long subsisted between Your Highness and the Company, I made it one of the first objects of my attention to examine all the papers existing on the Company's records, as well respecting Wynaad as the District of Souleah, in which it appears that Kaunt-mungul, and Coloorbaji are situated.

From these papers I find that not only the right to the districts of Wynaad and Souleah has remained in doubt, but also the districts of Amerah, and Ersarawaraseemy, and to some other inconsiderable territories on the side of Malabar.

Your Highness is well aware that it is a maxim among States, who are sincerely disposed to maintain the relations of amity and peace to bring all contested points of this nature to a speedy determination.

A reasonable and temperate discussion of those differences of opinion, which must occasionally arise between powers of the most pacific, disposition, tends to prevent quarrels between their subordinate officers, and to obviate the misrepresentations which each party is apt, in such cases to make, to the respective Government. This is the most friendly, as well as the most prudent course, and will always defeat the views of interested and designing persons who may wish to foment jealousy and to disturb the blessing of peace.

For this object Lord Cornwallis, the *Nawwab* Nizam Ali Khan, and the Peshwa *Pandit Pardhan* wisely provided in the treaty of peace concluded with Your Highness at Seringapatam, by establishing a regular mode of bringing to an amicable adjustment with the knowledge and approbation of all parties, any questions which might hereafter arise, between Your Highness and any of the Allies respecting the boundaries of your adjacent territories.

I am persuaded that it is Your Highness's disposition to maintain faithfully your public engagements with the Company. On my part you will always meet with a religious adherence to every article of the Treaties subsisting between us. On this occasion, therefore, it is my intention to depute a respectable and discreet person to meet upon your frontier such of your officers as Your Highness may please to name for the purpose of conferring together, of discussing the grounds of the respective claims, and of satisfying each other on all points respecting which any doubts may be entertained on either side.

It would not be consistent with Your Highness high reputation for justice and good faith, to refuse to enter into this candid investigation, I, therefore, entertain no doubt, that as soon as you shall have fully understood the nature of this representation you will afford every facility to the conduct of the necessary enquiries, and will use your endeavours to bring them to a speedy determination, and for this purpose that you will without delay direct your officers at Korial *Bandar* (i.e. Mangalore) to enter into conference with those deputed by the managers of the Honourable Company's affairs on the coast of Malabar. The result of the conferences will be communicated to me by the Government of Bombay with all practicable despatch; and you may rely upon it, that after a regular discussion shall have taken place according to the established law of nations and to the practice uniformly observed on every occasion of disputed boundary which has arisen between Your Highness and the Allies, since the conclusion of the Treaty of Seringapatam, I will not suspend for one moment the full acknowledgement of whatever shall appear to be your just right.

In the meantime, as the districts of Amerah and Souleah have been in the possession of the Coorgah Raja for several years, Your Highness will no doubt see the propriety and justice of recalling the troops sent into the neighbourhood of Souleah. Your Highness must be sensible that until I have been satisfied of the justice of your claims in a regular and amicable manner, I will never suffer any of the Company's Allies or dependants, whose country and interests I consider to be in every respect the same as those of the Company, to be forcibly deprived of territories, of which they have so long held possession. With the most cordial disposition to maintain the intercourse of friendship with Your Highness, I trust that I shall always meet an equal return on your part, and, therefore, I cannot but lament, that Your Highness did not immediately report to the established channels of peaceable negotiation, in place of stationing a military force upon the frontiers of the territory possessed by an Ally of the Company.

Confident, however that Your Highness upon a full review of all the circumstances of the case, will be equally inclined with myself to conform to the dictates of justice, I am satisfied that after our respective officers shall have conferred together and explained to each other all matters that remain in doubt, we shall have no difficulty in terminating these long depending questions to our mutual satisfaction.

(Signed) Mornington.

From Tipu Sultan to the Governor-General
Received on the 10th July, 1798

Your Lordship's friendly letter containing the agreeable intelligence of your arrival at Calcutta and your taking charge of Company's affairs reached me at the happiest of times and afforded me a degree of pleasure and satisfaction that cannot be adequately expressed upon paper. May the Almighty prosper to Your Lordship this event! By the Divine Grace, the exalted fabric of union and attachment, and the firm foundations of friendship and harmony between the two States are in full strength. To adhere to the obligations of existing treaties is a constant object with me. Your Lordship is from your heart a friend and well-wisher and I am confident will hold in mind the observance of union and concord. I hope you will continue to gratify me by letters notifying your welfare.

To Tipu Sultan
Written on the 4th November, 1798

You have doubtless received information of another excess of that unjustifiable ambition and insatiable rapacity, which have so long marked the conduct of the French Nation. They have invaded Egypt, a country, from which they were in no danger of molestation and from whose government they could not even pretend to have received the slightest provocation. They have committed this act of violence in contempt of the treaties subsisting between France and the Porte, and without any regard to the acknowledged authority of the Grand Seignor, so long established in Egypt. Nothing can more clearly expose their total disregard of every principle of public faith and honour than this unprovoked and unjustifiable aggression; and it will no doubt afford satisfaction to every friend to justice and good faith, and particularly to every friend of the British Nation to hear, that by the success of His Majesty's Arms, that French have already suffered for their injustice, and temerity. Certain intelligence has just been received that thirteen sail of the line, which had been employed in the expedition against Egypt, mounting 1024 guns and carrying about 10,000 men, being at anchor in the port of Baqir, near Rosetta, at the mouth of the Nile, were attacked by an equal number of His Britannic Majesty's fleet; an engagement took place which terminated in the capture of nine ships of the French line; two more were blown up, one of them of 118 guns, the French Admiral's, and only two made their escape from the valour and skill of the British Admiral. All communication being thus cut off between Egypt and Europe, the troops who have landed in Egypt must in all probability perish, either by famine or by the sword.

This very signal victory is to be ascribed to the justice of the British cause, and to the aid of Divine Providence, favouring the gallantry of our forces and punishing the injustice and impiety of our adversary. On the same assistance I rely with confidence for a continuation of similar success and for the final triumph of His Majesty's arms, over a Nation, who have shown themselves the general enemy of mankind. Confident from the union and attachment subsisting between us, that this intelligence will afford you sincere satisfaction, I could not deny myself the pleasure of communicating it.

(Signed) Mornington.

From Tipu Sultan
Received at the Fort St. George on the 25th December, 1798

I have been made happy by the receipt of your Lordship's two friendly letters the contents of which I clearly comprehend (*vide* those written on 4th and 8th November).

The particulars which Your Lordship has communicated to me, relative to the victory obtained by the English fleet over that of the French, near the shores of Egypt; nine of their ships having been captured and two burned, on one of which of the latter was their Admiral, have given me more pleasure than can possibly be conveyed by writing. Indeed I possess the firmest hope that the leaders of the English and the Company *Bahadur*, whoever adhere to the paths of sincerity, friendship and good faith, and are the well-wishers of mankind, will at all times be successful and victorious; and that the French, who are of a crooked disposition, faithless and the enemies of mankind, may be ever depressed and ruined. Your Lordship has written to me with the pen of friendship, "that in no age or country were the baneful and insidious arts of intrigue ever cultivated with such success as they are at present by the French nation". Would to God that no impression had been produced on my mind by that dangerous people, but, that Your Lordship's situation enables you to know, that they have reached my presence, and have endeavoured to pervert the wisdom of my Councils, and to instigate me to war against those who have given me no provocation.

"That it is impossible that I should suppose Your Lordship ignorant of the intercourse which subsists between me and the French, whom I know to be the inveterate enemies of the Company, and to be now engaged in an unjust war with the British Nation, and that I cannot imagine Your Lordship indifference to the transactions, which have passed between me and the enemies of the English."

In this *Sarkar*, (the gift of God) there is a mercantile tribe, who employ themselves in trading by sea and land. Their agents purchased a two masted vessel, and having loaded her with rice, departed with a view to traffic. It happened that she went to the Mauritius, from whence forty persons, French and of a dark colour, of whom ten or twelve were artificers, and the rest servants, paying the hire of the ship, came here in search of employment; those who chose to take service, were entertained, and the remainder departed beyond the confines of this *Sarkar* (the gift of God) and the French who are full of vice and deceit, have perhaps taken advantage of the departure of the ship, to put about reports, with the view to ruffle the minds of both *Sarkars* (of the Company and that of the *Khuda-dad*). This title signifying literally 'God-given' was assigned by the Sultan to his Government in 1792 A.D.

It is the wish of my heart and my constant endeavours to observe and maintain the articles of the agreement of peace, and to perpetuate and strengthen the basis of friendship and union with the *Sarkar* of the Company *Bahadur*, and with the *Sarkar* of the Maharaja *Saheb Streemant*, *Peshwa Bahadur*, and His Highness the *Nawwab Asaf* Jah *Bahadur*, and I am resident at home, at time taking the air, and at others amusing myself with hunting, at a spot, which is used as pleasure ground. In this case, the allusions to "war," in your friendly letter, and the following passage, namely: "prudence required, that both the Company and their Allies should adopt certain measures of precaution and self-defence," have given me the greatest surprise.

It was further written by your friendly pen, that "as Your Lordship is desirous of communicating to me on the behalf of the Company and their Allies, a plan calculated to promote the mutual security and welfare of all parties, Your Lordship proposes to depute to me for this purpose Major Doveton who formerly waited upon me and who will explain to me more fully and particularly, the sole means, which appear to Your Lordship and the Allies to be effectual for the dilutary purpose of removing all existing distrust and suspicions and of establishing peace and good understanding on the most durable foundation; that, therefore, Your Lordship trusts I will let you know at what time and place it will be convenient to me to receive Major Doveton". It has been understood. By the blessing of the Almighty, at the conclusion of the peace, the treaties and engagements entered into among the four *Sarkars* were to firmly established and confirmed as ever to remain fixed and durable, and be an example of the rulers of the age; nor are they ever, be liable to interruption. I cannot imagine, that means more effectual than these can be adopted for giving stability to the foundations of friendship and harmony, promoting the security of States, or the welfare and advantage of all parties.

In the view of those who inspect narrowly into the nature of friendship, peace and amity are the first of all objects, as indeed Your Lordship has yourself written to me, that the Allied *Sarkars* look to no other object than the security and tranquillity of their own dominions, and the ease and comfort of their subjects; praise be to God, that the sum of my views and the wish of my heart are limited to these same points. On such grounds then a just and permanent observance of existing treaties is necessary and these, under the favour of God, daily acquire new strength and improvement, by means of amicable correspondence. Your Lordship is a great *Sardar,* and firm friend, who restores justice and order to the world, and you possess an enlightened judgement. I have the strongest hope that the minds of the wise and intelligent, but particularly of the four States, will not be sullied by doubts and jealousies, but will consider me from my heart desirous of harmony and friendship.

Continue to allow me the pleasure of your correspondence, making me happy by accounts of your health.

What more shall be written?

Dated the 9th of *Rajab*, 1213 *Hijri* (18th December 1798).

To Tipu Sultan
Written on the 16th January, 1799

Your Highness has already been furnished by Lord Clive with a translation of the declaration of War, issued by the *Sublime Porte* against the French, in consequence of their having violated the sacred obligation of Treaty with the *Grand Signior,* and of their having invaded Egypt, in contempt of every principle of good faith, and of the law of Nations. You have also received from me a translation of the Manifesto, published by the *Porte* on the same occasion, exposing in just colours, the overbearing and arrogant spirit, as well as the treachery and falsehood which the French have disclosed in their conduct towards all mankind and especially towards the *Sublime Porte*.

The *Porte,* justly outraged by an aggression so atrocious and unprecedented as the invasion of Egypt, has now united in a common cause with the British Nation, for the purpose of curbing the intemperance of the French, and the *Grand Signior* having learnt the unfortunate alliance, which Your Highness has contracted with his enemies the French, against his friends and Allies the British Nation, His Highness resolved, from motives of friendship towards you, as well as towards the British Nation, to warn you, in an amicable letter, of the dangers of this fatal connection and to exhort you to manifest your zeal for the Mussalman faith, by renouncing all intercourse with the common enemy of every religion, and the aggressor of the Head of the Muhammadans.

Accordingly this letter (the testimony of friendship, and the fruit of wisdom, piety, and faithful zeal) was delivered by the ministers of the *Porte*, under the *Grand Signior's* orders, to Mr. Spencer Smith, the British Minister, resident at Constantinople, by whom it was transmitted to Honourable Mr. Duncan, the Governor of Bombay, who has forwarded it to Lord Clive; the day before yesterday, this letter reached Madras, and a translation accompanied it, by which I learnt the valuable lessons of prudence and truth which it contains. I now forward it to Your Highness; you will read and consider it with the respectful attention, which it demands; there you will find the same friendly admonitions respecting the dangerous views of the French Nation which I have already submitted to your consideration.

When your discerning mind shall have duly examined this respected letter, you will no doubt draw the following conclusions from it:

Firstly: That all the maxims of public law, honour and religion, are despised and profaned by the French Nation, who consider all the thrones of the world, and every system of civil order and religious faith, as the sport and prey of their boundless ambition, insatiable rapine, and indiscriminate sacrilege.

Secondly: That the French have insulted and assaulted the acknowledged Head of the Muhammadan Faith, and that they have wantonly raised an unprovoked and cruel war in the heart of that country, which is revered by every Mussalman, as the repository of the most sacred monuments of the Muhammadan Faith.

Thirdly: That a firm, honourable, and intimate alliance and friendship now subsists between the *Grand Signior* and the British Nation, for the express purpose of opposing a barrier to the excesses of the French.

Fourthly: That the *Grand Signior* is fully apprised of the intercourse and connection, unhappily established between Your Highness and the French, for purposes hostile to the British Nation, that he offers to Your Highness the salutary fruit of that experience which he had already acquired of the ruinous effects of French intrigue, treachery and deceit; and that he admonishes you, not to flatter yourself with the vain hope of friendly aid from those, who (even if they had escaped from the valour and skill of the British Forces) could never have reached you, until they had profaned the Tomb of your Prophet, and overthrown the foundation of your religion.

May the admonition of the Head of your own faith, dispose your mind to the pacific propositions, which I have repeatedly but in vain, submitted to your wisdom ! and may you at length receive the Ambassador, who will be empowered to conclude the definite arrangement of all differences between you and the Allies, and to secure the tranquillity of India against the disturbers of the world !

(Signed) Mornington
(Marquess Wellesley).

Letter from Sultan Salim, to the Indian Sovereign, Tipu Sultan, dated Constantinople, the 20th September, 1798 delivered to Mr. Spencer Smith, His Britannic Majesty's Minister Plenipotentiary etc.

We take this opportunity to acquaint Your Majesty, when the French Republic was engaged in a war with most of the powers of Europe within this latter period, our *Sublime Porte* not only took no part against them, but, regardful of the ancient amity existing with that Nation adopted a system of the strictest neutrality and showed them even such acts of countenance as have given rise to complaints on the part of other Courts.

Thus friendly disposed towards them and reposing a confidence in those sentiments of friendship which they appeared to profess for us, we gave no ear to many propositions and advantageous offers, which had been made to us to side with the belligerent powers, but pursuant to our maxims of moderation and justice, we abstained from breaking with them without direct motive and firmly observed the line of neutrality; all which is well-known to the world.

In this posture of things, when, the French having witnessed the greatest marks of attention from our *Sublime Porte*, a perfect reciprocity was naturally expected on their side, when no cause existed to interrupt the continuance of the peace between the two nations, they all of a sudden have exhibited the unprovoked and treacherous proceedings, of which the following is a sketch:

They began to prepare a Fleet in one of their harbours, called Toulon, with most extraordinary mystery, and when completely fitted out and ready for Sea, embarked a large body of troops, and they put also on board several people, versed in the Arabic Language, and who had been in Egypt before; they gave the command of that armament to one of their Generals, named Buonaparte, who first went to the Island of Malta, of which he took possession and thence proceeded direct for Alexandria, where being arrived on the 17th *Muharram*, all of a sudden landed his troops, and entered the town by open force, publishing soon after menifestoes in Arabics among the different tribes, stating in substance that the object of their enterprise was not to declare war against the *Ottoman Porte*, but to attack the *Beys* of Egypt, for insults and injuries they had committed against the French merchants in the time past; that peace with the Ottoman Empire was permanent, that those of the Arabs, who should join, would meet with the best treatment: but such, as showed opposition would suffer death: with this further insinuation, made in different quarters, but more particularly to certain Courts at amity with us, that the expedition against the *Beys* was with the privity and consent of our *Sublime Porte;* which is a horrible falsity. After this they also took possession of Rosetta, not hesitating to engage in a pitched battle with the Ottoman troops, who had been detached from Cairo to assist the invaded.

It is standing law amongst all Nations, not to encroach upon other's territories, whilst they are supposed to be at peace. When any such events take place as lead to a rupture, the motives, so tending, are previously made known between the parties, nor are any open aggressions attempted against their respective dominions, until a formal declaration of war takes place.

Whilst, therefore, no interruption of the peace, nor the smallest symptom of misunderstanding appeared between our *Sublime Porte* and the French Republic, a conduct, so audacious, so unprovoked, and so deceitfully sudden on their part, is an undeniable trait of the most extreme insult and treachery.

The province of Egypt is considered as a region of general veneration, from the immediate proximity of the noble city of Mecca, the Qiblah of the Mussalmans, (the point of the compass to which all Turks turn their face in performing their prayers) and the sacred town of Medina, where the Tomb of our blessed Prophet is fixed; the inhabitants of both these sacred cities deriving from thence their subsistence.

Independent of this, it has been actually discovered from several letters, which have been intercepted, that the further project of the French is to divide Arabia into various Republics; to attack the whole Mahomedan sect, in its religion and country: and by a gradual progression, to extirpate all Mussalmans from the face of the earth.

It is for these cogent motives and considerations that we have determined to repel this enemy and to adopt every vigorous measure against these persecutors of the faith; we placing all confidence in the Omnipotent God, the source of all succour, and in the intercession of him, who is the glory of Prophets.

Now it being certain, that in addition to the general ties of religion, the bonds of amity and good understanding have ever been firm and permanent with Your Majesty, so justly famed for your zeal and attachment to our faith; and that more than once such public acts of friendly attention have been practised between us, as to have cemented the connection subsisting between the two countries.

We, therefore, sincerely hope from Your Majesty's dignified disposition that you will not refuse entering into concert with us, and giving, our *Sublime*

Porte every possible assistance, by such an exertion of zeal, as your firmness and natural attachment to such a cause cannot fail to excite.

We understand, that in consequence of certain secret intrigues, carried on by the French in India, (after their accustomed system) in order to destroy the settlements and to sow dissensions in the provinces of the English there, a strict connection is expected to take effect between them and Your Majesty for whose service they are to send over a corps of troops by the way of Egypt.

We are persuaded, that the tendency of the French plans cannot in the present days escape Your Majesty's penetration and notice, and that no manner of regard will be given to their deceitful insinuations on your side; and whereas the Court of Great Britain is actually at war with them and our *Sublime Porte* engaged on the other hand in repelling their aggressions, consequently the French are enemies to both; and such a reciprocity of interest must exist between those Courts, as ought to make both parties eager to afford every mutual succour which a common cause requires.

It is well-known that the French bent upon the overthrow of all sects and religions, have invented a new doctrine under the name of Liberty; they themselves professing no other belief but that of *dahris;* (Epicureans, or Pythagoreans) that they have not even spared the territories of the Pope of Rome, a country, since time immemorial held in great reverence by all the European Nations; that they have wrested and shared, with others the whole Venitian State, notwithstanding that fellow Republic and not only abstained from taking part against them, but had rendered them service during the course of the war, thus effacing the name of the Republic of Venice from the annals of history.

There is no doubt that their present attempt against the Ottomans, as well as their ulterior designs, (dictated by their avaricious view towards Oriental riches) tend to make a general conquest of that country (which may God never suffer to take effect!) and to expel every Mussalman from it, under pretence of annoying the English. Their end is to be once admitted in India and then to develope what really lies in their hearts, just as they have done in every place, where they have been able to acquire a footing.

In a word, they are a Nation, whose deceitful intrigues and perfidious pursuits known no bounds. They are intent on nothing, but on depriving people of their lives and properties, and on persecuting religion, wherever their arms can reach.

Upon all this, therefore, coming to Your Majesty's knowledge, it is sincerely hoped, that you will not refuse every needful exertion towards assisting your Brethren Mussalmans, according to the obligations of religion and towards defending Hindustan itself, against the effect of French machinations.

Should it be true, as we hear, that an intimate connection has taken place between your Court and that Nation, we hope, that by weighing present circumstances as well as every future inconvenience, which would result from such a measure, Your Majesty will beware against it, and in the event of your having harboured any idea of joining with them, or of moving against Great Britain, you will lay such resolution aside.

We make it our especial request, that Your Majesty will please to refrain from entering into any measures against the English or lending any complaint ear to the French.

Should there exist any subject of complaint with the English, please do communicate it, certain as you may be, of the employment of every good office on our side to compromise the same; we wish to see the connection above alluded to, exchanged in favour of Great Britain.

We confidently expect that upon consideration of all that is stated in this communication and of the necessity of assisting your Brethren Mussalmans in this general cause of religion, as well as of cooperating towards the above precious Province being delivered from the hands of the enemy, Your Majesty will employ every means, which your natural zeal will point out, to assist the common cause, as to corroborate, by that means, the ancient good understanding so happily existing between our Empires.

Certified translation and copy,
(Signed) Spencer Smith
A true copy.
(Signed) J. A. Grant, Sub-Secretary.

From Tipu Sultan to the Governor-General
Received on the 13th February, 1799

I have been much gratified by the agreeable receipt of your Lordship's two friendly letters, the first brought by a Camelman, the last by a *Harkara*, and understood their contents. The letter of the Prince, in station like Jamshed; with angels as his guards, with troops numerous as the stars; the sun illumining the world of the heaven of empire and dominion; the luminary giving splendour to the universe of the firmament of glory and power; the Sultan of the sea and the land; the King of Rome (i.e. the Grand Signior) be his Empire and his power perpetual; addressed to me, which reached you through the British Envoy and which you transmitted has arrived. Being frequently disposed to make excursions and hunt, I am accordingly proceeding upon a hunting excursion; you will be pleased to despatch Major Doveton (about whose coming your friendly pen has repeatedly written) slightly attended (or unattended).

Always continue to gratify me by friendly letters, notifying your welfare.

DECLARATION OF THE RIGHT HONOURABLE
THE GOVERNOR-GENERAL-IN-COUNCIL

For all the Forces and Affairs of the British Nation in the East India, on behalf of the Honourable the East India Company, and the Allies of the said Company, Their Highnesses the Nizam and the Peshwa.

A solemn Treaty of peace and friendship was concluded at Seringapatam between the Honourable Company and the *Nawwab* Asaf Jah and the Peshwa on the one part, and *Nawwab* Tipu Sultan, on the other part, and from that day all commotion and hostility ceased. Since that day, the three Allied States have invariably manifested a sacred regard for the obligations, contracted under that Treaty with the *Nawwab* Tipu Sultan; of this uniform disposition, abundant proofs have been afforded by each of the Allies: whatever differences have arisen, with regard to the limits of the territory of Mysore, have been amicably adjusted, without difficulty, and with the most exact attention to the principles of equity, and to the stipulations of Treaty; such has been the solicitude of the Allies for the preservation of tranquillity, that they have viewed with forbearance, for some years past, various embassies and military preparations on the part of Tipu Sultan, of a tendency so evidently hostile to the interests of the Allies, as would have justified them, not only in the most serious remonstrances, but even in an appeal to arms. On the part of the British Government, every endeavour has been employed to conciliate the confidence of the Sultan, and to mitigate his vindictive spirit, by the most unequivocal acknowledgement and confirmation of his just rights and by the removal of every cause of jealousy which might tend to interrupt the continuance of peace. These pacific sentiments have been most particularly manifested in the Governor-General's recent decision on Tipu Sultan's claim to the District of Wynaad, and in the negotiation, opened by his Lordship, with regard to the districts of Amerah and Souleah. In every instance the conduct of the British Government in India towards Tipu Sultan has been the natural result of those principles of moderation, justice and good faith, which the legislature of Great Britain, and the Honourable the East India Company have firmly established as the unalterable rule of their intercourse with the Native Princes and States of India.

The exemplary good faith and the pacific disposition of the Allies, since the conclusion of the Treaty of Seringapatam, have never been disputed even by Tipu Sultan. Far from having attempted to allege even the pretext of a complaint against their conduct, he has constantly acknowledged their justice, sincerity and good faith, and has professed, in the most cordial terms, his desire to maintain and strengthen the foundations of harmony and concord with them.

In the midst of these amicable professions, on the part of Tipu Sultan, and at the moment when the British Government had issued orders for the confirmation of his claim to Wynaad, it was with astonishment and indignation that the Allies discovered the engagements, which he had contracted with the French Nation, in direct violation of the Treaty of Seringapatam, as well as of his own most solemn and recent protestations of friendships towards the Allies.

Under the mask of these specious professions, and of a pretended veneration for the obligations of Treaty, Tipu Sultan despatched Ambassadors to the Isle of France, who, in a period of profound peace in India, proposed and concluded, in his name, an offensive alliance with the French, for the avowed purpose of commencing a War of aggression against the Company, and consequently against the Peshwa and the Nizam, the Allies of the Company.

The Ambassadors in the name of Tipu Sultan demanded military succours from the French and actually levied a military force in the Isle of France, with the declared view of prosecuting the intended war.

When the Ambassadors returned in a French ship of war from the Isle of France, Tipu Sultan suffered the military force, which they had levied, for the avowed purpose of making war upon the Allies to land in his country and finally he admitted it into his army; by these personal acts ratifying and confirming the proceedings of his Ambassadors. This military force, however, was not sufficiently powerful to enable him immediately to attempt his declared purpose of attacking the Company's possessions; but in the meanwhile he advanced his hostile preparations, conformably to his engagements with the French, and he was ready to move his army into the Company's territories, whenever he might obtain from France the effectual succours, which he had assiduously solicited from that nation.

But the providence of God, and the victorious arms of the British Nation frustrated his vain hopes, and checked the presumptuous career of the French in Egypt at the moment when he anxiously expected their arrival on the coast of Malabar.

The British Government, the Nizam, and the Peshwa had not omitted the necessary precaution of assembling their forces for the joint protection of their respective dominions. The strict principles of self-defence would have justified the Allies, at that period of time, in making an immediate attack upon the territories of Tipu Sultan; but even the happy intelligence of the glorious success of the British fleet at the mouths of the Nile, did not abate the anxious desire of the Allies to maintain the relations of amity and peace with Tipu Sultan; they attempted by a moderate representation, to recall him to a sense of his obligations, and of the genuine principles of prudence and policy; and they employed every effort to open the channels of negotiation and to facilitate the means of amicable accommodation. With these salutary views, the Governor-General on the 8th November 1798, in the name of the Allies proposed to despatch an Ambassador to Tipu Sultan for the purpose of renewing the bonds of friendship and of concluding such an arrangement as might afford effectual security against any future interruption of the public tranquillity and His Lordship repeated the same proposal on the 10th of December 1798.

Tipu Sultan declined, by various evasions and subterfuges, this friendly and moderate advance on the part of the Allies, and he manifested an evident disposition to reject the means of pacific accommodation, by suddenly breaking up, in the month of December, the conferences, which had commenced with respect to the districts of Amerah and Souleah, and by interrupting the intercourse between his subjects and those of the Company on their respective frontiers. On the 9th of January 1799, the Governor-General, being arrived at Fort St. George (notwithstanding these discouraging circumstances in the conduct of Tipu Sultan) renewed with increased earnestness the expression of His Lordship's anxious desire to despatch an Ambassador to the Sultan.

The Governor-General expressly solicited the Sultan to reply within one day to this letter; and as it involved no proposition either injurious to the rights, dignity, or honour of the Sultan, or in any degree novel or complicated, either in form or substance, it could not require a longer consideration, the Governor, General waited with the utmost solicitude for an answer to the reasonable and distinct proposition contained in his letter of the 9th January, 1799.

Tipu Sultan, however, who must have received the said letter before the 17th of January, remained silent, although the Governor-General had plainly apprised the Prince, that dangerous consequences would result from delay. In the meanwhile the season for military operations had already advanced to so late a period, as to render a speedy decision indispensible to the security of the Allies.

Under these circumstances on the 3rd of February (twelve days having elapsed from the period, when an answer might have been received from Seringapatam to the Governor-General's letter of the 9th of January), His Lordship declared to the Allies, that the necessary measures must now be adopted without delay for securing such advantages, as should place the common safety of the Allies beyond the reach of the insincerity of Tipu

Sultan and the violence of the French. *With this view the Governor-General, on the 3rd of February, issued orders to the British Armies to march and signified to the Commander of His Majesty's squadron that the obstinate silence of the Sultan must be considered as a rejection of the proposed negotiation.*

At length, on the 13th of February a letter from Tipu Sultan reached the Governor-General in which the Sultan signifies to His Lordship "that being frequently disposed to hunt, he was accordingly proceeding upon a hunting excursion," adding "that the Governor-General would be pleased to despatch Major Doveton to him, unattended".

The Allies will not dwell on the peculiar phrases of this letter: but it must be evident in all the States of India that the answer of the Sultan has been deferred to this late period of the Season with no other view than to preclude the Allies by insidious delays from the benefit of those advantages, which their combined military operations would enable them to secure; on those advantages alone (under the recent experience of Tipu Sultan's violation of the Treaty of Seringapatam, and under the peculiar circumstances of that Prince's alliance with the French) can the Allies now venture to rely for the faithful execution of any Treaty of Peace concluded with Tipu Sultan.

The Allies cannot suffer Tipu Sultan to profit by his own studied and systematic delay, nor to impede such a disposition of their military and naval force as shall appear best calculated to give effect to their just views.

Bound by the sacred obligations of public faith professing the most amicable disposition and undisturbed in the possession of those Dominions secured to him by Treaty, Tipu Sultan wantonly violated the relations of amity and peace and compelled the Allies to arm in defence of their rights, their happiness and their honour.

For a period of three months he obstinately rejected every pacific overture, in the hourly expectation of receiving that succour, which he had eagerly solicited for the prosecution of his favourite purposes of ambition and revenge; disappointed in his hopes of immediate vengeance, and conquest, he now resorts to subterfuge and procrastination; and by a tardy, reluctant, and insidious acquiescence in a proposition, which he had so long and repeatedly declined, he endeavours to frustrate the precautions of the Allies, and to protract every effectual operation, until some change of circumstance and of season shall revive his expectations of disturbing the tranquillity of India, by favouring the irruption of a French Army.

The Allies are equally prepared to repel his violence and to counteract his artifices and delays. The Allies are, therefore, resolved to place their army in such a position as shall afford adequate protection against any artifice or insincerity and shall preclude the return of that danger which has so lately menaced their possessions.

The Allies, however, retaining an anxious desire to effect an adjustment with Tipu Sultan, Lieutenant General Harris, Commander-in-Chief of His Majesty's and the Honourable Company's Forces on the Coast of Coromandel and Malabar, is authorized to receive any Embassy which Tipu Sultan may despatch to the Headquarters of the British Army and to concert a treaty on such conditions, as appear to the Allies to be indispensibly necessary for the establishment of a secure and permanent peace.

By order of the Right Honourable the Governor-General.

Fort St. George: February 22, 1799.

SOURCE: In *The Secret Correspondence of Tipu Sultan,* comp. Kabir Kausar (New Delhi: Light and Life Publishers, 1980).

Prologue: The Storming of Seringapatam, 1799
WILKIE COLLINS

[Written by Wilkie Collins (1824–1889), *The Moonstone,* described by T. S. Eliot as the "first, the longest, and the best of modern English detective novels," was originally published in serial form in *All the Year Round,* from 4 January to 8 August 1868. Early in his career, Charles Dickens, editor and publisher of the aforementioned magazine, tutored Collins. Collins's best-known works are *The Moonstone, The Woman in White* (1860), and *No Name* (1862).]

Extracted from a Family Paper

I

I address these lines—written in India—to my relatives in England.

My object is to explain the motive which has induced me to refuse the right hand of friendship to my cousin, John Herncastle. The reserve which I have hitherto maintained in this matter has been misinterpreted by members of my family whose good opinion I cannot consent to forfeit. I request them to suspend their decision until they have read my narrative. And I declare, on my word of honour, that what I am now about to write is, strictly and literally, the truth.

The private difference between my cousin and me took its rise in a great

196   The Case of Tipu Sultan

public event in which we were both concerned—the storming of Seringapatam, under General Baird, on the 4th of May, 1799.

In order that the circumstances may be clearly understood, I must revert for a moment to the period before the assault, and to the stories current in our camp of the treasure in jewels and gold stored up in the Palace of Seringapatam.

II

One of the wildest of these stories related to a Yellow Diamond—a famous gem in the native annals of India.

The earliest known traditions describe the stone as having been set in the forehead of the four-handed Indian god who typifies the Moon. Partly from its peculiar colour, partly from a superstition which represented it as feeling the influence of the deity whom it adorned, and growing and lessening in lustre with the waxing and waning of the moon, it first gained the name by which it continues to be known in India to this day—the name of THE MOONSTONE. A similar superstition was once prevalent, as I have heard, in ancient Greece and Rome; not applying, however (as in India), to a diamond devoted to the service of a god, but to a semitransparent stone of the inferior order of gems, supposed to be affected by the lunar influences—the moon, in this latter case also, giving the name by which the stone is still known to collectors in our own time.

The adventures of the Yellow Diamond begin with the eleventh century of the Christian era.

At that date, the Mohammedan conqueror, Mahmoud of Ghizni, crossed India; seized on the holy city of Somnauth; and stripped of its treasures the famous temple, which had stood for centuries—the shrine of Hindoo pilgrimage, and the wonder of the eastern world.

Of all the deities worshipped in the temple, the moon-god alone escaped the rapacity of the conquering Mohammedans. Preserved by three Brahmins, the inviolate deity, bearing the Yellow Diamond in its forehead, was removed by night, and was transported to the second of the sacred cities of India—the city of Benares.

Here, in a new shrine—in a hall inlaid with precious stones, under a roof supported by pillars of gold—the moon-god was set up and worshipped. Here, on the night when the shrine was completed, Vishnu the Preserver appeared to the three Brahmins in a dream.

The deity breathed the breath of his divinity on the Diamond in the forehead of the god. And the Brahmins knelt and hid their faces in their robes. The deity commanded that the Moonstone should be watched, from that time forth, by three priests in turn, night and day, to the end of the generations of men. And the Brahmins heard, and bowed before his will. The deity predicted certain disaster to the presumptuous mortal who laid hands on the sacred gem, and to all of his house and name who received it after him. And the Brahmins caused the prophecy to be written over the gates of the shrine in letters of gold.

One age followed another—and still, generation after generation, the successors of the three Brahmins watched their priceless Moonstone, night and day. One age followed another, until the first years of the eighteenth Christian century saw the reign of Aurungzebe, Emperor of the Moguls. At his command, havoc and rapine were let loose once more among the temples of the worship of Brahmah. The shrine of the four-handed god was polluted by the slaughter of sacred animals; the images of the deities were broken in pieces; and the Moonstone was seized by an officer of rank in the army of Aurungzebe.

Powerless to recover their lost treasure by open force, the three guardian priests followed and watched it in disguise. The generations succeeded each other; the warrior who had committed the sacrilege perished miserably; the Moonstone passed (carrying its curse with it) from one lawless Mohammedan hand to another; and still, through all chances and changes, the successors of the three guardian priests kept their watch, waiting the day when the will of Vishnu the Preserver should restore to them their sacred gem. Time rolled on from the first to the last years of the eighteenth Christian century. The Diamond fell into the possession of Tippoo, Sultan of Seringapatam, who caused it to be placed as an ornament in the handle of a dagger, and who commanded it to be kept among the choicest treasures of his armoury. Even then—in the palace of the Sultan himself—the three guardian priests still kept their watch in secret. There were three officers of Tippoo's household, strangers to the rest, who had won their master's confidence by conforming, or appearing to conform, to the Mussulman faith; and to those three men report pointed as the three priests in disguise.

III

So, as told in our camp, ran the fanciful story of the Moonstone. It made no serious impression on any of us except my cousin—whose love of the marvellous induced him to believe it. On the night before the assault on Seringapatam, he was absurdly angry with me, and with others, for treating the whole thing as a fable. A foolish wrangle followed; and Herncastle's unlucky temper got the better of him. He declared, in his boastful way, that we should see the Diamond on his finger, if the English army took Seringapatam. The sally was saluted by a roar of laughter, and there, as we all thought that night, the thing ended.

Let me now take you on to the day of the assault.

My cousin and I were separated at the outset. I never saw him when we forded the river; when we planted the English flag in the first breach; when we crossed the ditch beyond; and, fighting every inch of our way, entered the town. It was only at dusk, when the place was ours, and after General Baird himself had found the dead body of Tippoo under a heap of the slain, that Herncastle and I met.

We were each attached to a party sent out by the general's orders to prevent the plunder and confusion which followed our conquest. The camp-followers committed deplorable excesses; and, worse still, the soldiers found their way, by an unguarded door, into the treasury of the Palace, and loaded themselves with gold and jewels. It was in the court outside the treasury that my cousin and I met, to enforce the laws of discipline on our own soldiers. Herncastle's fiery temper had been, as I could plainly see, exasperated to a kind of frenzy by the terrible slaughter through which we had passed. He was very unfit, in my opinion, to perform the duty that had been entrusted to him.

There was riot and confusion enough in the treasury, but no violence that I saw. The men (if I may use such an expression) disgraced themselves good-humouredly. All sorts of rough jests and catchwords were bandied about among them; and the story of the Diamond turned up again unexpectedly, in the form of a mischievous joke. 'Who's got the Moonstone?' was the rallying cry which perpetually caused the plundering, as soon as it was stopped in one place, to break out in another. While I was still vainly trying to establish order, I heard a frightful yelling on the other side of the court-yard, and at once ran towards the cries, in dread of finding some new outbreak of the pillage in that direction.

I got to an open door, and saw the bodies of two Indians (by their dress, as I guessed, officers of the palace) lying across the entrance, dead.

A cry inside hurried me into a room, which appeared to serve as an armoury. A third Indian, mortally wounded, was sinking at the feet of a man whose back was towards me. The man turned at the instant when I came in, and I saw John Herncastle, with a torch in one hand, and a dagger dripping with blood in the other. A stone, set like a pommel, in the end of the dagger's handle, flashed in the torchlight, as he turned on me, like a gleam of fire. The dying Indian sank to his knees, pointed to the dagger in Herncastle's hand, and said, in his native language:—'The Moonstone will have its vengeance yet on you and yours!' He spoke those words, and fell dead on the floor.

Before I could stir in the matter, the men who had followed me across the courtyard crowded in. My cousin rushed to meet them, like a madman. 'Clear the room!' he shouted to me, 'and set a guard on the door!' The men fell back as he threw himself on them with his torch and his dagger. I put two sentinels of my own company, on whom I could rely, to keep the door. Through the remainder of the night, I saw no more of my cousin.

Early in the morning, the plunder still going on, General Baird announced publicly by beat of drum, that any thief detected in the fact, be he whom he might, should be hung. The provost-marshal was in attendance, to prove that the General was in earnest; and in the throng that followed the proclamation, Herncastle and I met again.

He held out his hand, as usual, and said, 'Good morning.'

I waited before I gave him my hand in return.

'Tell me first,' I said, 'how the Indian in the armoury met his death, and what those last words meant, when he pointed to the dagger in your hand.'

'The Indian met his death, as I suppose, by a mortal wound,' said Herncastle. 'What his last words meant I know no more than you do.'

I looked at him narrowly. His frenzy of the previous day had all calmed down. I determined to give him another chance.

'Is that all you have to tell me?' I asked.

He answered, 'That is all.'

I turned my back on him; and we have not spoken since.

IV

I beg it to be understood that what I write here about my cousin (unless some necessity should arise for making it public) is for the information of the family only. Herncastle has said nothing that can justify me in speaking to our commanding officer. He has been taunted more than once about the Diamond, by those who recollect his angry outbreak before the assault; but, as may easily be imagined, his own remembrance of the circumstances under which I surprised him in the armoury has been enough to keep him silent. It is reported that he means to exchange into another regiment, avowedly for the purpose of separating himself from me.

Whether this be true or not, I cannot prevail upon myself to become his accuser—and I think with good reason. If I made the matter public, I have no evidence but moral evidence to bring forward. I have not only no proof that he killed the two men at the door; I cannot even declare that he killed the third man inside—for I cannot say that my own eyes saw the deed committed. It is true that I heard the dying Indian's words; but if those words were pronounced to be the ravings of delirium, how could I contradict the assertion from my own knowledge? Let our relatives, on either side, form their own opinion on what I have written, and decide for themselves whether the aversion I now feel towards this man is well or ill founded.

Although I attach no sort of credit to the fantastic Indian legend of the gem, I must acknowledge, before I conclude, that I am influenced by a certain superstition of my own in this matter. It is my conviction, or my delusion, no matter which, that crime brings its own fatality with it. I am not only persuaded of Herncastle's guilt; I am even fanciful enough to believe that he will live to regret it, if he keeps the Diamond; and that others will live to regret taking it from him, if he gives the Diamond away.

SOURCE: In *The Moonstone* (New York: Harper and Brothers, 1869).

V

ORIENTALISM

INTRODUCTION
Orientalism: The East as a Career
MIA CARTER AND BARBARA HARLOW

The modern East is a corpse. There has been no education for the East. It is as little ripe to-day for liberal institutions as in the first days of history. It has been the lot of Asia to have enjoyed a charming and poetic childhood, and to perish before arriving at manhood. It seems like a dream to think that Hebrew poesy the Moallacat and the admirable literature of India have sprung from a soil, in our own day so dead, so utterly burnt up. The sight of a Levantine excites in me the most painful feelings when I reflect that this pitiful personification of stupidity or cunning hails from the country of Isiah and of Antara, from the country of the mourners for Thammuz, of the worshippers of Jehovah, where Mosaism and Islamism first appeared, where Jesus preached!—Ernest Renan, *The Future of Science*, 1833

EDWARD SAID HAS ARGUED that orientalism was a "Western style for dominating, restructuring, and having authority over the Orient" (*Orientalism*, 3), but orientalism, as Said and others have demonstrated, has had its own disciplinary history in the course of the last two centuries in the Euro-American academy. Sir William Jones (1746–1794), for example, is often credited as the founding father of comparative literature. A scholar—and perhaps a model for Henry Clerval, the orientalist in Mary Shelley's *Frankenstein*—of Eastern languages and cultures, Jones was the first president of the Asiatic Society of Bengal, established in 1784. His translations of literary and legal works from Arabic, Persian, and Sanskrit were decisive in determining the orientalist approach to the question of how the British might rule India. By contrast, Lord Thomas Babington Macaulay argued the imperative of a more Anglicist emphasis: natives should learn the English language and British ways rather than British civil servants and Company officials specializing in orientalist studies. The role of the "scholar" in the imperial project from the beginning was not foregone. As William Jones described it in a letter from Calcutta to Viscount Althorp on 14 October 1783: "Of myself I will only say that, disliking as I did, the politicks and parties of Britain, I am very glad to be out of their way, and to amuse myself a few years in this wonderful country. The substantial good, that I can do, will not, I fear, be very great, as the character of a reformer is too invidious for one to assume; but should I live to return, I may indeed be useful in supplying the legislature with just and accurate intelligence for the reformation of this imperfect judicature" (Cannon, *Letters*, 2:623).

The nature of eighteenth- and nineteenth-century orientalist scholarship was itself strange and mysterious. Linguistic and philological examinations of scripts and texts were mixed with ethnological and biological assessments of the Indian people, both living and dead. For some orientalists, the Indians of ancient and contemporary times were nearly identical, for the land and its people were allegedly fixed in time. Comparative philology, the study of Indo-European languages, was of great interest to orientalists who asserted that "linguistic affinities prove community of descent" (Herbert Risley, *People of India*). Present-day Hindus, for example, could be linked to the ancient Aryans; that linkage would permit scholars to locate and place Indians in the Great Chain of Being and, perhaps, in "appropriate" positions of official or casual service to colonial administrations. Max Müller, for example, argued that Sanskrit provided scientific evidence that the Aryans of India were "our nearest intellectual relatives," describing India as "the missing link in our intellectual ancestry" (Max Müller, *India*, 29). Intellectual relatives might be more valuable than Indians who were considered absolutely different. The same modern scientific practices could, conveniently, prove unrelatedness; members of the dark-skinned "Dravidian" race of Indians were not considered intellectual relations or assimilable subjects. They were more primitive and therefore had less material or professional potential than the Aryan Indians. British colonial and imperial administrators frequently assessed India and Indians in philological terms; while Africans were, due to their primarily orally based cultures, considered by some to be linguistic or preliterary primitives—"living fossils"—Indians were described, comparatively, as mysterious glyphs, puzzling and fantastical aesthetic beings.

In general many orientalists believed that close and careful analysis of Indian texts, scripts, languages, art and architecture, and bodies would provide some of the keys to knowing, understanding, and successfully mastering India. India's literatures and languages also provided scholars with "newly discovered" myths and legends, all sorts of "curious matter" (Jones, "Institutes"), a treasure-trove of cultural materials that rivaled those of the classical Western world. The debate over how to use oriental knowledge and information—disciplinary, commercial, cultural, as well as political—continued throughout the century and functions currently, a century later, even in considerations of "postcolonial" and other "area" studies. Jones's Asiatic Society, however, would go on at that time to propagate not only its own methodologies and ideologies but other societies as well. Max Müller, the German anthropologist whose career developed in England in the latter half of the nineteenth century, spoke eloquently to the point in his address to the 1874 meeting of the second session of the International Congress of Orientalists: "No one likes to be asked, what business he has to exist, and yet, whatever we do, whether singly or in concert with others, the first question which the world never fails to address to us, is . . . Why are you here? . . . What is the good of an International Congress of Orientalists?"

BIBLIOGRAPHY

Arberry, A. J. (Arthur John). *British Orientalists*. London: W. Collins, 1943.
Behdad, Ali. *Belated Travelers: Orientalism in the Age of Colonial Dissolution*. Durham, N.C.: Duke University Press, 1994.
Cannon, Garland Hampton. *The Life and Mind of Oriental Jones: Sir William Jones, the Father of Modern Linguistics*. Cambridge: Cambridge University Press, 1990.
Disraeli, Benjamin. *Sybil, or the Two Nations*. London: H. Colburn, 1845.
Jones, Sir William. *The Letters of Sir William Jones*. Edited by Garland Cannon. Volume 2. Oxford: Clarendon Press, 1970.
——. "Institutes of Hindu Law: Or, the Ordinances of Menu." London: J. Sewell and J. Debret, 1796.
Lowe, Lisa. *Critical Terrains: French and British Orientalisms*. Ithaca, N.Y.: Cornell University, 1991.
Macfie, A. L. (Alec Lawrence), ed. *Orientalism: A Reader*. New York: New York University Press, 2000.
Mojumder, Md. Abu Taher. *Sir William Jones and the East*. Dacca: Zakia Sultana, 1978.
Mukherjee, Soumyendra Nath. *Sir William Jones: A Study in Eighteenth-Century British Attitudes to India*. Bashir Bagh, Hyderabad: Orient Longman, 1987.
Müller, Max. *India: What Can It Teach Us?* London: J. W. Lovell Company, 1833.
Trevelyan, Charles. *On the Education of the People of India* (pamphlet). London: Longman, Orme, Green and Longmans, 1838.
Renan, Ernest. *The Future of Science*. Boston: Roberts Brothers, 1893.
Risley, Sir Herbert. *The People of India*. Calcutta: Thacker Spink and Co., 1915.
Said, Edward. *Orientalism*. New York: Pantheon Books, 1978.
Schwab, Raymond. *The Oriental Renaissance: Europe's Rediscovery of India & the East, 1680–1880*. Translated by Gene Patterson-Black and Victor Reinking. New York: Columbia University Press, 1984.
Singh, Janardan Prasad. *Sir William Jones, His Mind and Art*. New Delhi: S. Chand, 1982.
Suleri, Sara. *The Rhetoric of English India*. Chicago: University of Chicago Press, 1992.
Thapar, Romila. *Interpreting Early India*. Delhi: Oxford University Press, 1993.
Viswanathan, Gauri. *Masks of Conquest: Literary Study and British Rule in India*. New York: Columbia University Press, 1989.

Excerpts from *Frankenstein*
MARY SHELLEY

[Mary Shelley's (1797–1851) novel has become a classic for various schools of contemporary criticism, from generic considerations of the Gothic novel to feminist and colonialist readings. Shelley's dramatis personae, however, might also serve to represent the beginning roster of a later imperial personnel: Robert Walton (whose letters to his sister frame Victor's story) as explorer; Henry Clerval (from the framed story), the budding orientalist; and his friend Victor Frankenstein, the scientist who invents the monster—the colonial/racial other.]

FROM ROBERT WALTON'S LETTERS

I am already far north of London; and as I walk in the streets of Petersburgh, I feel a cold northern breeze play upon my cheeks, which braces my nerves, and fills me with delight. Do you understand this feeling? This breeze, which has travelled from the regions towards which I am advancing, gives me a foretaste of those icy climes. Inspirited by this wind of promise, my day dreams become more fervent and vivid. I try in vain to be persuaded that the pole is the seat of frost and desolation; it ever presents itself to my imagination as the region of beauty and delight. There, Margaret, the sun is for ever visible; its broad disk just skirting the horizon, and diffusing a perpetual splendour. There—for with your leave, my sister, I will put some trust in preceding navigators—there snow and frost are banished; and, sailing over a calm sea, we may be wafted to a land surpassing in wonders and in beauty every region hitherto discovered on the habitable globe. Its productions and features may be without example, as the phenomena of the heavenly bodies undoubtedly are in those undiscovered solitudes. What may not be expected in a country of eternal light? I may there discover the wondrous power which attracts the needle; and may regulate a thousand celestial observations, that require only this voyage to render their seeming eccentricities consistent for ever. I shall satiate my ardent curiosity with the sight of a part of the world never before visited, and may tread a land never before imprinted by the foot of man. These are my enticements, and they are sufficient to conquer all fear of danger or death, and to induce me to commence this laborious voyage with the joy a child feels when he embarks in a little boat, with his holiday mates, on an expedition of discovery up his native river. But, supposing all these conjectures to be false, you cannot contest the inestimable benefit which I shall confer on all mankind to the last generation, by discovering a passage near the pole to those countries, to reach which at present so many months are requisite; or by ascertaining the secret of the magnet, which, if at all possible, can only be effected by an undertaking such as mine.

FROM VICTOR FRANKENSTEIN'S NARRATIVE

Clerval had never sympathized in my tastes for natural science; and his literary pursuits differed wholly from those which had occupied me. He came to the university with the design of making himself complete master of the oriental languages, as thus he should open a field for the plan of life he had marked out for himself. Resolved to pursue no inglorious career, he turned his eyes toward the East, as affording scope for his spirit of enterprise. The Persian, Arabic, and Sanscrit languages engaged his attention, and I was easily induced to enter on the same studies. Idleness had ever been irksome to me, and now that I wished to fly from reflection, and hated my former studies, I felt great relief in being the fellow-pupil with my friend, and found not only instruction but consolation in the works of the orientalists. I did not, like him, attempt a critical knowledge of their dialects, for I did not contemplate making any other use of them than temporary amusement. I read merely to understand their meaning, and they well repaid my labours. Their melancholy is soothing, and their joy elevating, to a degree I never experienced in studying the authors of any other country. When you read their writings, life appears to consist in a warm sun and a garden of roses,—in the smiles and frowns of a fair enemy, and the fire that consumes your own heart. How different from the manly and heroical poetry of Greece and Rome!

SOURCE: Mary Shelley, *Frankenstein* (1818; reprint, London: H. Colburn and R. Bentley, 1831).

Excerpt from *Sibyl, or the Two Nations*
BENJAMIN DISRAELI

[Benjamin Disraeli (1804–1881) was a novelist and, twice, prime minister of England (1869, 1874). His novel, *Sibyl*, anticipated as well a much later (twentieth-century) north/south conflict. The novel itself, set in the early years of Victoria's reign and originally published in 1845, described the class conflict in England of "two nations"—rich/poor and north/south—at once geographically and class determined. The function of England's imperial interests in the construction of these domestic determinations was decisive to Disraeli's narrative analysis. One of the high points of Disraeli's career was his purchase of Isma'il Pasha's Suez Canal Company shares in 1875. The shares gave Great Britain majority ownership and control of the Suez Canal; with the prime minister's bold vision and financial assistance from the Rothschild family, the key to India was obtained. In 1876, Disraeli presented the bill that would declare Queen Victoria Empress of India.]

In a commercial country like England, every half century develops some new and vast source of public wealth, which brings into national notice a new and powerful class. A couple of centuries ago, a Turkish Merchant was the great creator of wealth; the West Indian Planter followed him. In the middle of the last century appeared the Nabob. These characters in their zenith in turn merged in the land, and became English aristocrats; while, the Levant decaying, the West Indies exhausted, and Hindostan plundered, the breeds died away, and now exist only in our English comedies, from Wycherly and Congreve to Cumberland and Morton. The expenditure of the revolutionary war produced the Loanmonger, who succeeded the Nabob; and the application of science to industry developed the Manufacturer, who in turn aspires to be "large-acred," and always will, as long as we have a territorial constitution; a better security for the preponderance of the landed interest than any corn-law, fixed or fluctuating.

Of all these characters, the one that on the whole made the largest fortunes in the most rapid manner—and we do not forget the marvels of the Waterloo loan, or the miracles of Manchester during the continental blockade—was the Anglo-Indian about the time that Hastings was first appointed to the great viceroyalty. It was not unusual for men in positions so obscure that their names had never reached the public in this country, and who yet had not been absent from their native land for a longer period than the siege of Troy, to return with their million.

SOURCE: Benjamin Disraeli, *Sibyl, or the Two Nations* (London: H. Colburn, 1845), bk. 1, chap. 7.

Definitions from the *Hobson-Jobson* Dictionary
COLONEL HENRY YULE AND A. C. BURNELL

[Compiled by participants in the "raj" in the latter half of the nineteenth century, *Hobson-Jobson* has since become a standard reference—and a nomer—for the diction and vocabulary of the English lexical reconstructions of nearly two centuries of British history in India.]

Baboo, s. Beng. and H. *Bābū* [Skt. *vapra*, 'a father']. Properly a term of respect attached to a name, like *Master* or *Mr.*, and formerly in some parts of Hindustan applied to certain persons of distinction. Its application as a term of respect is now almost or altogether confined to Lower Bengal (though C. P. Brown states that it is also used in S. India for 'Sir, My lord, your Honour'). In Bengal and elsewhere, among Anglo-Indians, it is often used with a slight savour of disparagement, as characterizing a superficially cultivated, but too often effeminate, Bengali. And from the extensive employment of the class, to which the term was applied as a title, in the capacity of clerks in English offices, the word has come often to signify 'a native clerk who writes English.'

    1781.—"I said . . . From my youth to this day I am a servant to the English. I have never gone to any Rajahs or Bauboos nor will I go to them."—Depn. of *Dooud Sing*, Commandant. In *Narr. of Insurn. at Banaras* in 1781. Calc. 1782. Reprinted at Roorkee, 1853. App., p. 165.

    1782.—"*Cantoo* Baboo" appears as a subscriber to a famine fund at Madras for 200 Sicca Rupees.—*India Gazette*, Oct. 12.

    1791.—"Here Edmund was making a monstrous ado, About some bloody Letter and Conta Bah-Booh."[1]—*Letters of Sinkin the Second*, 147.

    1803.—" . . . Calling on Mr. Neave I found there Baboo Dheep Narrain, brother to Oodit Narrain; Rajah at Benares."—*Lord Valentia's Travels*, i. 112.

---

1. "Mr. Burke's method of pronouncing it."

1824.—" . . . the immense convent-like mansion of some of the more wealthy Baboos . . . "—*Heber*, i. 31, ed. 1844.

1834.—"The Baboo and other Tales, descriptive of Society in India."—Smith & Elder, London. (By Augustus Prinsep.)

1850.—"If instruction were sought for from them (the Mohammedan historians) we should no longer hear bombastic Baboos, enjoying under our Government the highest degree of personal liberty . . . rave about patriotism, and the degradation of their present position."—*Sir. H. M. Elliot*, Orig. Preface to *Mahom. Historians of India*, in Dowson's ed., I. xxii.

c.1866.—

"But I'd sooner be robbed by a tall man
who showed me a yard of steel,
Than be fleeced by a sneaking Baboo, with
a peon and badge at his heel."
—*Sir A. C. Lyall, The Old Pindaree*

1873.—"The pliable, plastic, receptive Baboo of Bengal eagerly avails himself of this system (of English education) partly from a servile wish to please the *Sahib logue*, and partly from a desire to obtain a Government appointment."—*Fraser's Mag.*, August, 209.

[1880.—"English officers who have become de-Europeanised from long residence among undomesticated natives. . . . Such officials are what Lord Lytton calls White Baboos."—*Aberigh-Mackay, Twenty-one Days*, p. 104.]

N.B.—In Java and the further East *bābū* means a nurse or female servant (Javanese word).

Loot, s. & v. Plunder; Hind, *lūt*, and that from Skt. *lotra*, for *loptra*, root *lup*, 'rob, plunder'; [rather *lunt*, 'to rob']. The word appears in Stockdale's *Vocabulary*, of 1788, as "Loot—plunder, pillage." It has thus long been a familiar item in the Anglo-Indian colloquial. But between the Chinese War of 1841, the Crimean War (1854–5), and the Indian Mutiny (1857–8), it gradually found acceptance in England also, and is now a recognised constituent of the English *Slang Dictionary*. Admiral Smyth has it in his *Nautical Glossary* (1867) thus: "Loot, plunder, or pillage, a term adopted from China."

1545.—St. Francis Xavier in a letter to a friend in Portugal admonishing him from encouraging any friend of his to go to India seems to have the thing *Loot* in his mind, though of course he does not use the word: "Neminem patiaris amicorum tuorum in Indiam cum Praefectura mitti, ad regias pecunias, et negotia tractanda. Nam de illis vere illud scriptum

Orientalism

capere licet: 'Deleantur de libro viventium et cum justis non scribantur.' . . . Invidiam tantum non culpam usus publicus detrahit, dum vix dubitatur tieri non malè quod impunè fit. Ubique, semper, rapitur, congeritur, aufertur. Semel captum nunquam rodditur. Quis enumeret artes et nomina, praedarum? Equidem mirari satis nequeo, quot, praeter usitatos modos, insolitis flexionibus inauspicatum illud rapiendi verbum quaedam avaritiae barbaria conjuget!"—*Epistolae, Prague*, 1667, Lib. V. Ep. vii.

1842.—"I believe I have already told you that I did not take any loot—the Indian word for plunder—so that I have nothing of that kind, to which so many in this expedition helped themselves so bountifully."—*Colin Campbells* to his Sister, in *L. of Ld. Clyde*, i. 120.

1842.—"In the Saugor district the plunderers are beaten whenever they are caught, but there is a good deal of burning and 'looting,' as they call it."—*Indian Administration of Ld. Ellenborough. To the D. of Wellington*, May 17, p. 194.

1847.—"Went to see Marshal Soult's pictures which he looted in Spain. There are many Murillos, all beautiful."—*Ld. Malmesbury, Mem. of an Ex-Minister*, i. 192.

1858.—"There is a word called 'loot,' which gives, unfortunately, a venial character to what would in common English be styled robbery."—*Ld. Elgin, Letters and Journals*, 215.

1860.—"Loot, swag or plunder."—*Slang Dict.* s.v.

1864.—"When I mentioned the 'looting' of villages in 1845, the word was printed in italics as little known. Unhappily it requires no distinction now, custom having rendered it rather common of late."—*Admiral W. H. Sayth, Synopsis*, p. 52.

1875.—"It was the Colonel Sahib who carried off the loot."—*The Dilemma*, ch. xxxvii.

1876.—"Public servants (in Turkey) have vied with one another in a system of universal loot."—*Blackwood's Mag.* No. cxix. p. 115.

1878.—"The city (Hongkong) is now patrolled night and day by strong parties of marines and Sikhs, for both the disposition to loot and the facilities for looting are very great."—*Miss Bird, Golden Chersonese*, 34.

1883.—"'Loot' is a word of Eastern origin, and for a couple of centuries past . . . the looting of Delhi has been the daydream of the most patriotic among the Sikh race."—*Bos. Smith's Life of Ld. Lawrence*, ii. 245.

1883.—"At Ta li fu . . . a year or two ago, a fire, supposed to be an act of incendiarism, broke out among the Tibetan encampments which were then looted by the Chinese."—*Official Memo. on Chinese Trade with Tibet*, 1883.

Looty, Lootiewalla, s.
a. A plunderer. Hind. *lūtī, lūtīyā, lūtīwālā*.

 1757.—"A body of their Louchees (see LOOCHER) or plunderers, who are armed with clubs, passed into the Company's territory."—*Orme*, ed. 1803, ii. 129.

 1782.—"Even the rascally Leoty wallahs, or Mysorean hussars, who had just before been meditating a general desertion to us, now pressed upon our flanks and rear."—*Munro's Narrative*, 295.

 1792.—"The Colonel found him as much dismayed as if he had been surrounded by the whole Austrian army, and busy in placing an ambuscade to catch about six looties."—*Letter of T. Munro*, in *Life*.

 1792.—"This body (horse plunderers round Madras) had been branded generally by the name of Looties, but they had some little title to a better appellation, for they were ... not guilty of those sanguinary and inhuman deeds...."—*Madras Courier*, Jan. 26.

 1793.—"A party was immediately sent, who released 27 half-starved wretches in heavy irons; among them was Mr. Randal Cadman, a midshipman taken 10 years before by Suffrein. The remainder were private soldiers; some of whom had been taken by the Looties; others were deserters...."—*Dirom's Narrative*, p. 157.

b. A different word is the Ar.—Pers. *lūtīy*, bearing a worse meaning, 'one of the people of Lot,' and more generally 'a blackguard.'

 [1824.—"They were singing, dancing, and making the luti all the livelong day."—*Hajji Baba*, ed. 1851, p. 444.

 [1858.—"The Loutis, who wandered from town to town with monkeys and other animals, taught them to cast earth upon their heads (a sign of the deepest grief among Asiatics) when they were asked whether they would be governors of Balkh or Akhcheh."—*Ferrier, H. of the Afghans*, 101.

 [1883.—"Monkeys and baboons are kept and trained by the Lūtis, or professional buffoons."—*Will's Modern Persia*, ed. 1891, p. 306.]

The people of Shiraz are noted for a fondness of jingling phrases, common enough among many Asiatics, including the people of India, where one constantly hears one's servants speak of *chaukī-aukī* (for chairs and tables), *naukar-chākar* (where both are however real words), 'servants,' *lakrīakrī*, 'sticks and staves,' and so forth. Regarding this Mr. Wills tells a story (*Modern*

Persia, p. 239). The late Minister, Kawām-ud-Daulat, a Shirāzi, was asked by the Shāh:

"Why is it, Kawām, that you Shirāzis always talk of *Kabob-mabob* and so on? You always add a nonsense-word; is it for euphony?"

"Oh, Asylum of the Universe, may I be your sacrifice! No respectable person in Shirāz does so, only the lūtī-pūtī says it!"

Nabób, s. Port. *Nabâbo*, and Fr. *Nabab*, from Hind. *Nawāb*, which is the Ar. pl. of sing. *Nāyab* (see NAIB), 'a deputy,' and was applied in a singular sense[2] to a delegate of the supreme chief, viz. to a Viceroy or chief Governor under the Great Mogul *e.g.* the *Nawāb* of Surat, the *Nawāb* of Oudh, the *Nawāb* of Arcot, the *Nawāb Nāzim* of Bengal. From this use it became a title of rank without necessarily having any office attached. It is now a title occasionally conferred, like a peerage, on Mahommedan gentlemen of distinction and good service, as *Rāī* and *Rājā* are upon Hindus.

Nabob is used in two ways: (a) simply as a corruption and representative of *Nawāb*. We get it direct from the Port. *nabâbo*, see quotation from Bluteau below. (b) It began to be applied in the 18th century, when the transactions of Clive made the epithet familiar in England, to Anglo-Indians who returned with fortunes from the East; and Foote's play of 'The Nabob' (*Nábob*) (1768) aided in giving general currency to the word in this sense.

a.—

1604.—" . . . delante del Nauabo quo es justicia mayor."—*Guerrero, Relacion*, 70.

1615.—"There was as Nababo in Surat a certain Persian Mahommedan (*Mouro Parsio*) called Mocarre Bethião, who had come to Goa in the time of the Viceroy Ruy Lourenço de Tavora, and who being treated with much familiarity and kindness by the Portuguese . . . came to confess that it could not but be that truth was with their Law. . . . "—*Bocurro*, p. 354.

1616.—"Catechumeni ergo parentes viros aliquot inducunt honestos et assessores Nauabi, id est, judicis supremi, cui consiliarii erant, uti et Proregi, ut libellum famosum adversus Pinnerum spargerent."—*Jarric, Thesaurus*, iii. 378.

---

2. Dory says (2nd ed. 323) that the plural form has been adopted by mistake. Wilson says 'honorifically.' Possibly in this and other like cases it came from popular misunderstanding of the Arabic plurals. So we have omra, *i.e., umarā*, pl. of *amīr* used singularly and forming a plural *umrāyān*. (See also *Omlah* and *Mehaul*.)

1652.—"The Nahab[3] was sitting, according to the custom of the Country, barefoot, like one of our Taylors, with a great number of Papers sticking between his Toes, and others between the Fingers of his left hand, which Papers he drew sometimes from between his Toes, sometimes from between his Fingers, and order'd what answers should be given to every one."—*Tavernier*, E. T. ii. 99; [ed. *Ball*, i. 291].

1653.—" . . . il prend la qualité de Nabab qui vault autant à dire que monseigneur."—*De la Boullaye-le-Gouz* (ed. 1657), 142.

1666.—"The ill-dealing of the Nahab proceeded from a scurvy trick that was play'd me by three Canary-birds at the Great Mogul's Court. The story whereof was thus in short . . . "—*Tavernier*, E.T. ii. 57; [ed. *Ball*, i. 134].

1673.—"Gaining by these steps a nearer intimacy with the Nabob, he cut the new Business out every day."—*Fryer*, 183.

1675.—"But when we were purposing next day to depart, there came letters out of the Moorish Camp from the Nabab, the field-marshal of the Great Mogul. . . . "—*Heiden Vervaarlijke Schip-Breuk*, 52.

1682.—" . . . Ray Nundelall ye Nábabs *Duan*, who gave me a most courteous reception, rising up and taking of me by ye hands, and ye like at my departure, which I am informed is a greater favour than he has ever shown to any *Franke* . . . "—*Hedges, Diary*, Oct. 27; [Hak. Soc. i. 42]. Hedges writes *Nabob, Nabab, Navab, Narob*.

1716.—"Nabábo. Termo do Mogul. He o Titolo do Ministro que he Cabeça."—*Bluteau*, s.v.

1727.—"A few years ago, the Nabob or Vice-Roy of *Chormondel*, who resides at *Chickakal*, and who superintends that Country for the Mogul, for some Disgust he had received from the Inhabitants of Diu Islands, would have made a Present of them to the Colony of Fort St. George."—*A Hamilton*, i. 374; [ed. 1744].

1742.—"We have had a great man called the Nabob (who is the next person in dignity to the Great Mogul) to visit the Governor. . . . His lady, with all her women attendance, came the night before him. All the guns fired round the fort upon her arrival, as well as upon his; *he* and *she* are Moors, whose women are never seen by any man upon earth except their husbands."—Letter from Madras in *Mrs. Delany's Life*, ii. 169.

1743.—"Every governor of a fort, and every commander of a district had assumed the title of Nabob . . . one day after having received the homage of several of these little lords, Nizam ul muluck said that he had

---

3. The word is so misprinted throughout this part of the English version.

that day seen no less than eighteen Nabobs in the Carnatic."—*Orme*, Reprint, Bk. i. 51.

1752.—"Agreed ... that a present should be made the Nobab that might prove satisfactory."—In *Long*, 33.

1773.—
> "And though my years have passed in this hard duty,
> No Benefit acquired—no Nabob's booty."
> —Epilogue at Fort Marlborough,
>   by W. *Marsden,* in *Mem.* 9.

1787.—
> "Of armaments by flood and field;
> Of Nabobs you have made to yield."
> —*Ritson*, in *Life and Letters*, i. 124.

1807.—"Some say that he is a Tailor who brought out a long bill against some of Lord Wellesley's staff, and was in consequence provided for; others say he was an adventurer, and sold knicknacks to the Nabob of Oude."—*Sir T. Munro*, in *Life*, i. 371.

1809.—"I was surprised that I had heard nothing from the Nawaub of the Carnatic."—*Ld. Valentia*, i. 381.

c. 1858.—"Le vieux Nabab et la Begum d'Arkato."—*Leconte de Lisle*, ed. 1872, p. 156.

b.—

[1764.—"Mogul Pitt and Nabob Bute."—*Horace Walpole, Letters*, ed. 1857, iv. 222 (*Stanf. Dict.*).]

1773.—"I regretted the decay of respect for men of family, and that a Nabob would not carry an election from them.

"JOHNSON: Why, sir the Nabob will carry it by means of his wealth, in a country where money is highly valued, as it must be where nothing can be had without money; but if it comes to personal preference, the man of family will always carry it."—*Boswell, Journal of a Tour to the Hebrides,* under Aug. 25.

1777.—"In such a revolution ... it was impossible but that a number of individuals should have acquired large property. They did acquire it; and with it they seem to have obtained the detestation of their countrymen, and the appellation of nabobs as a term of reproach.—*Price's Tracts*, i. 13.

1780.—"The Intrigues of a Nabob, or Bengal the Fittest Soil for the Growth of Lust, Injustice, and Dishonesty. Dedicated to the Hon. the Court of Directors of the East India Company. By Henry Fred. Thompson. Printed for the Author." (A base book).

1783.—"The office given to a young man going to India is of trifling consequence. But he that goes out an insignificant boy, in a few years returns a great Nabob. Mr. Hastings says he has two hundred and fifty of that kind of raw material, who expect to be speedily manufactured into the merchantlike quality I mention."—*Burke, Speech on Fox's E.I. Bill*, in *Works and Corr.*, ed. 1852, iii. 506.

1787.—"The speakers for him (Hastings) were Burgess, who has completely done for himself in one day; Nichols, a lawyer; Mr. Vansittart, a nabob; Alderman Le Mosurier, a smuggler from Jersey; . . . and Dempster, who is one of the good-natured candid men who connect themselves with every bad man "they can find."—*Ld. Minto*, in *Life*, &c., i. 126.

1848.—"'Isn't he very rich!' said Rebecca.

"'They say all Indian Nabobs are enormously rich.'"—*Vanity Fair*, ed. 1867, i. 17.

1872.—"Ce train de vie facile . . . suffit à me faire décerner . . . le surnom de Nabob par les bourgeois et les visiteurs de la petite ville."—*Rev. des Deux Mondes*, xcviii. 938.

1874.—"At that time (c. 1830) the Royal Society was very differently composed from what it is now. Any wealthy or well-known person, any M.P. . . . or East Indian Nabob, who wished to have F.R.S. added to his name, was sure to obtain admittance."—*Geikie, Life of Murchison*, i. 197.

1878.—" . . . A Tunis?—interrompit le duc. . . . Alors pourquoi ce nom de Nabab?—Bah ? les Parisiens n'y regardent pas de si près. Pour eux tout riche étranger est un Nabab, n'importe d'où il vienne."—*Le* Nabab, par *Alph. Daudet*, ch. i.

It is purism quite erroneously applied when we find Nabob in this sense miswritten *Nawab;* thus:

1878.—"These were days when India, little known still in the land that rules it, was less known than it had been in the previous generation, which had seen Warren Hastings impeached, and burghs* bought and sold by Anglo-India Nawabs."—*Smith's Life of Dr John Wilson*, 30.

But there is no question of purism in the following delicious passage:

1878.—"If . . . the spirited proprietor of the Daily Telegraph had been informed that our aid of their friends the Turks would have taken the form of a tax upon paper, and a concession of the Levis to act as Commanders of Regiments of Bashi-Bozouks, with a request to the Generalissimo to place them in as forward a position as Nabob was given in the host of King David, the harp in Peterborough Court would not have twanged long to the tune of a crusade in behalf of the Sultan of Turkey."—*Truth*, April 11, p. 470. In this passage in which the wit is equalled only by the scriptural knowledge, observe that *Nabob* = Naboth, and *Naboth* = Uriah.

Pundit, s. Skt. *pandita*, 'a learned man.' Properly a man learned in Sanskrit lore. The Pundit of the Supreme Court was a Hindu Law-Officer, whose duty it was to advise the English Judges when needful on questions of Hindu Law. The office became extinct on the constitution of the 'High Court,' superseding the Supreme Court and Sudder Court, under the Queen's Letters Patent of May 14, 1862.

In the Mahratta and Telegu countries, the word *Pandit* is usually pronounced *Pant* (in English colloquial *Punt*); but in this form it has, as with many other Indian words in like case, lost its original significance, and become a mere personal title, familiar in Mahratta history, *e.g.* the *Nānā* Dhundo*pant* of evil fame.

Within the last 30 or 35 years the term has acquired in India a peculiar application to the natives trained in the use of instruments, who have been employed beyond the British Indian frontier in surveying regions inaccessible to Europeans. This application originated in the fact that two of the earliest men to be so employed, the explorations by one of whom acquired great celebrity, were masters of village schools in our Himālayan provinces. And the title *Pundit* is popularly employed there much as *Dominie* used to be in Scotland. The *Pundit* who brought so much fame on the title was the late Nain Singh, C.S.I. [See Markham, *Memoirs of Indian Surveys*, 2nd ed. 148 *seqq.*]

1574.—"I hereby give notice that . . . I hold it good, and it is my pleasure, and therefore I enjoin on all the pandits (*panditos*) and Gentoo physicians (*phisicos gentios*) that they ride not through this City (of Goa) or the suburbs thereof on horseback, nor in andors and palanquins, on pain of paying; on the first offence 10 *cruzados*, and on the second 20, *pera o sapal*,[4] with the forfeiture of such horses, andors, or palanquins, and on

---

4. *Pera o sapal, i.e.* 'for the marsh.' We cannot be certain of the meaning of this; but we may note that in 1548 the King, as a favour to the city of Goa, and for the commodity of its shipping and the landing of goods, &c., makes a grant "of the marsh inundated with sea-water (*do* sapal *alagado dagoa salgada*) which extends along the river-side from the houses of Antonio Correa to the houses of Afonso Piquo, which grant is to be perpetual . . . to serve for a landing-place and quay for the merchants to moor and repair their ships, and to erect their bankshalls (*bangaçaes*), and never to be turned away to any other purpose." Possibly the fines went into a fund for the drainage of this *sapal* and formation of landing-places. See *Archiv. Port. Orient., Fasc.* 2, pp. 130–131.

the third they shall become the galley-slaves of the King my Lord...."
—*Procl.* of the Governor *Antonio Moriz Barreto,* in *Archiv. Port. Orient.* Fascic. 5, p. 899.

1604.—"... llamando tābien on su compania los Pōditos, le presentaron al Nauabo."—*Guerrero, Relaçion,* 70.

1616.—"... Brachmanae una cum Panditis comparentes, simile quid iam inde ab orbis exordio in Indostane visum negant."—*Jarric, Thesaurus,* iii. 81–82.

1663.—"A Pendet Brachman or *Heathen* Doctor whom I had put to serve my Agah ... would needs make his Panegyrick ... and at last concluded seriously with this: *When you put your Foot into the Stirrup, My Lord, and when you march on Horseback in the front of the Cavalry, the Earth trembleth under your Feet, the eight Elephants that hold it up upon their Heads not being able to support it.*"—*Bernier,* E.T., 85; [ed. *Constable,* 264].

1688.—"Je feignis donc d'être malade, et d'avoir la fièvre on fit venir aussitôt un Pandite ou médicin Gentil."—*Dellon, Rel. de l'Inq. de Goa,* 214.

1785.—"I can no longer bear to be at the mercy of your pundits, who deal out Hindu law as they please; and make it at reasonable rates, when they cannot find it ready made."—Letter of *Sir W. Jones,* in Mem. by *Ld. Teignmouth,* 1807, ii. 67.

1791.—"Il était au moment de s'embarquer pour l'Angleterre, plein de perplexité et d'ennui, lorsque les brames de Bénarés lui apprirent que le brame supérieur de la fameuse pagode de Jagrenat ... était seul capable de resoudre toutes les questions de la Société royale de Londres. C'était en effet le plus fameux pandect, ou docteur, dont on eût jamais oui parler."—*B. de St. Pierre, La Chaumière Indienne.* The preceding exquisite passage shows that the blunder which drew forth Macaulay's flaming wrath, in the quotation lower down, was not a new one.

1798.—"... the most learned of the Pundits or Bramin lawyers, were called up from different parts of Bengal."—*Raynal, Hist.* i. 42.

1856.—"Besides ... being a Pundit of learning, he (Sir David Brewster) is a bundle of talents of various kinds."—*Life and Letters of Sydney Dobell,* ii. 14.

1860.—"Mr. Vizetelly next makes me say that the principle of limitation is found 'amongst the Pandects of the Benares....' The Benares he probably supposes to be some Oriental nation. What he supposes their Pandects to be I shall not presume to guess.... If Mr. Vizetelly had consulted the Unitarian Report, he would have seen that I spoke of the

Pundits of Benares, and he might without any very long and costly research have learned where Benares is and what a Pundit is."—*Macaulay,* Preface to his *Speeches.*

1877.—"Colonel Y—. Since Nain Singh's absence from this country precludes my having the pleasure of handing to him in person, this, the Victoria or Patron's Medal, which has been awarded to him, . . . I beg to place it in your charge for transmission to the Pundit."—*Address* by *Sir R. Alcock,* Prest. R. Geog. Soc., May 28.

"Colonel Y— in reply, said: . . . Though I do not know Nain Singh personally, I know his work. . . . He is not a topographical automaton, or merely one of a great multitude of native employés with an average qualification. His observations have added a larger amount of important knowledge to the map of Asia than those of any other living man, and his journals form an exceedingly interesting book of travels. It will afford me great pleasure to take steps for the transmission of the Medal through an official channel to the Pundit."—*Reply to the President,* same date.

SOURCE: Definitions from Colonel Henry Yule and A. C. Burnell, *Hobson-Jobson: A Glossary of Colloquial Anglo-Indian Words and Phrases, and of Kindred Terms, Etymological, Historical, Geographical, and Discursive* (London: J. Murray, 1903).

India

G. W. F. HEGEL

India, like China, is a phenomenon antique as well as modern; one which has remained stationary and fixed, and has received a most perfect home-sprung development. It has always been the land of imaginative aspiration, and appears to us still as a Fairy region, an enchanted World. In contrast with the Chinese State, which presents only the most prosaic Understanding, India is the region of phantasy and sensibility. The point of advance in principle which it exhibits to us may be generally stated as follows:—In China the patriarchal principle rules a people in a condition of nonage, the part of whose moral resolution is occupied by the regulating law, and the moral oversight of the Emperor. Now it is the interest of Spirit that *external* conditions should become *internal* ones; that the natural and the spiritual world should be recognized in the subjective aspect belonging to intelligence; by which process the unity of subjectivity and [positive] Being generally—or the Idealism of Existence—is established. This Idealism, then, is found in India, but only as an Idealism of imagination, without distinct conceptions;—one which does indeed free existence from Beginning and Matter [liberates it from temporal limitations and gross materiality], but changes everything into the merely Imaginative; for although the latter appears interwoven with definite conceptions and Thought presents itself as an occasional concomitant, this happens only through accidental combination. Since, however, it is the abstract and absolute Thought itself that enters into these dreams as their material, we may say that Absolute Being is presented here as in the ecstatic state of a dreaming condition. For we have not the dreaming of an actual Individual, possessing distinct personality, and simply unfettering the latter from limitation, but we have the dreaming of the unlimited absolute Spirit.

There is a beauty of a peculiar kind in women, in which their countenance presents a transparency of skin, a light and lovely roseate hue, which is unlike the complexion of mere health and vital vigor—a more refined bloom, breathed, as it were, by the soul within—and in which the features, the light of the eye, the position of the mouth, appear soft, yielding, and relaxed. This almost unearthly beauty is perceived in women in those days which immediately succeed child-birth; when freedom from the burden of pregnancy and the pains of travail is added to the joy of soul that welcomes the gift of a beloved infant. A similar tone of beauty is seen also in women during the magical somnambulic sleep, connecting them with a world of superterrestrial beauty. A great artist (Schoreel) has moreover given this tone to the dying Mary, whose spirit is already rising to the regions of the blessed, but once more, as it were, lights up her dying countenance for a farewell kiss. Such a beauty we find also in its loveliest form in the Indian World; a beauty of enervation in which all that is rough, rigid, and contradictory is dissolved, and we have only the soul in a state of emotion—a soul, however, in which the death of free self-reliant Spirit is perceptible. For should we approach the charm of this Flower-life—a charm rich in imagination and genius—in which its whole environment and all its relations are permeated by the rose-breath of the Soul, and the World is transformed into a Garden of Love—should we look at it more closely, and examine it in the light of Human Dignity and Freedom—the more attractive the first sight of it had been, so much the more unworthy shall we ultimately find it in every respect.

The character of Spirit in a state of Dream, as the generic principle of the Hindoo Nature, must be further defined. In a dream, the individual ceases to be conscious of self *as such*, in contradistinction from objective existences. When awake, I exist for myself, and the rest of creation is an external, fixed objectivity, as I myself am for it. As external, the rest of existence expands itself to a rationally connected whole; a system of relations, in which my individual being is itself a member—an individual being united with that totality. This is the sphere of *Understanding*. In the state of dreaming, on the contrary, this separation is suspended. Spirit has ceased to exist for itself in contrast with alien existence, and thus the separation of the external and individual dissolves before its universality—its *essence*. The dreaming Indian is therefore all that we call finite and individual; and, at the same time—as infinitely universal and unlimited—a something intrinsically divine. The Indian view of things is a Universal Pantheism, a Pantheism, however, of Imagination, not of Thought. One substance pervades the Whole of things, and all individualizations are directly vitalized and animated into particular Powers. The sensuous matter and content are in each case simply and in the rough taken up, and carried over into the sphere of the Universal and Immeasurable. It is not liberated by the free power of Spirit into a beautiful form, and idealized in the Spirit, so that the sensuous might be a merely subservient and compliant expression of the spiritual; but [the sensuous object itself] is expanded into the immeasurable and undefined, and the Divine is thereby made bizarré, confused, and ridiculous. These dreams are not mere fables—a play of the imagination, in which the soul only revelled in fantastic gambols: it is lost in them; hurried to and fro by these reveries, as by something that exists really and seriously for it. It is delivered over to these limited objects as to its Lords and Gods. Everything, therefore—Sun, Moon, Stars, the Ganges, the Indus, Beasts, Flowers—everything is a God to it. And while, in this deification, the finite loses its consistency and substantiality, intelligent conception of it is impossible. Conversely the Divine, regarded as essentially changeable and unfixed, is also by the base form which it assumes, defiled and made absurd. In this universal deification of all finite existence, and consequent degradation of the Divine, the idea of Theanthropy, the incarnation of God, is not a particularly important conception. The parrot, the cow, the ape, etc., are likewise incarnations of God, yet are not therefore elevated above their nature. The Divine is not individualized to a subject, to concrete Spirit, but degraded to vulgarity and senselessness. This gives us a general idea of the Indian view of the Universe. *Things* are as much stripped of rationality, of finite consistent stability of cause and effect, as *man* is of the steadfastness of free individuality, of personality, and freedom.

Externally, India sustains manifold relations to the History of the World. In recent times the discovery has been made, that the Sanscrit lies at the foundation of all those further developments which form the languages of Europe; *e.g.* the Greek, Latin, German. India, moreover, was the centre of emigration for all the western world; but this external historical relation is to be regarded rather as a merely physical diffusion of peoples from this point. Although in India the elements of further developments might be discovered, and although we could find traces of their being transmitted to the West, this transmission has been nevertheless so abstract [so superficial], that that which among later peoples attracts our interest, is not anything derived from India, but rather something concrete, which they themselves have formed, and in regard to which they have done their best to forget Indian elements of culture. The spread of Indian culture is prehistorical, for History is limited to that which makes an essential epoch in the development of Spirit. On the whole, the diffusion of Indian culture is only a dumb, deedless expansion; that is, it presents no political action. The people of India have achieved no foreign conquests, but have been on every occasion vanquished themselves. And as in this silent way, Northern India has been a centre of emigration, productive of merely physical diffusion, India as a *Land of Desire* forms an essential element in General History. From the most ancient times downwards, all nations have directed their wishes and longings to gaining access to the treasures of this land of marvels, the most costly which the Earth presents; treasures of Nature—pearls, diamonds, perfumes, rose-essences, elephants, lions, etc.—as also treasures of wisdom. The way by which these treasures have passed to the West, has at all times been a matter of World-historical importance, bound up with the fate of nations. Those wishes have been realized; this Land of Desire has been attained; there is scarcely any great nation of the East, nor of the Modern European West, that has not gained for itself a smaller or larger portion of it. In the old world, Alexander the Great was the first to penetrate by land to India, but even he only just touched it. The Europeans of the modern world have been able to enter into direct connection with this land of marvels only circuitously from the other side; and by way of the sea, which, as has been said, is the general uniter of countries. The English, or rather the East India Company, are the lords of the land; for it is the necessary fate of Asiatic Empires to be subjected to Europeans; and China will, some day or other, be obliged to submit to this fate. The number of inhabitants is near 200,000,000, of whom from 100,000,000 to 112,000,000 are directly subject to the English. The Princes who are not immediately subject to them have English Agents at their Courts, and English troops in their pay. Since the country of the Mahrattas was conquered by the English, no part of India has asserted its independence of their sway. They have already gained a footing in the Burman Empire, and passed the Brahmaputra, which bounds India on the east.

SOURCE: In *The Philosophy of History*, trans. J. Sibree (1822; reprint, New York: Colonial Press, 1900).

A Discourse on the Institution of a Society for Inquiring into the History, Civil and Natural, the Antiquities, Arts, Sciences, and Literature of Asia
WILLIAM JONES

[William Jones (1746–1794) was knighted in 1783 and a year later sailed for Calcutta. He had previously studied languages at Oxford and been admitted to the bar. A year after his arrival in India, he founded the Asiatic Society of Bengal. His commitment to comparative law and linguistics has had both political and literary consequences—in terms of questions of governance and the development of the study of comparative literature in the Euro-American academy.]

Gentlemen,

When I was at sea last August, on my voyage to this country, which I had long and ardently desired to visit, I found one evening, on inspecting the observations of the day, that *India* lay before us, and *Persia* on our left, whilst a breeze from *Arabia* blew nearly on our stern. A situation so pleasing in itself, and to me so new, could not fail to awaken a train of reflections in a mind, which had early been accustomed to contemplate with delight the eventful histories and agreeable fictions of this eastern world. It gave me inexpressible pleasure to find myself in the midst of so noble an amphitheatre, almost encircled by the vast regions of *Asia*, which has ever been esteemed the nurse of sciences, the inventress of delightful and useful arts, the scene of glorious actions, fertile in the productions of human genius, abounding in natural wonders, and infinitely diversified in the forms of religion and government, in the laws, customs, and languages, as well as in the features and complexions, of men. I could not help remarking, how important and extensive a field was yet unexplored, and how many solid advantages unimproved; and when I considered, with pain, that, in this fluctuating, imperfect, and limited condition of life, such inquiries and improvements could only be made by the united efforts of many, who are not easily brought, without some pressing inducement or strong impulse, to converge in a common point, I consoled myself with a hope, founded on opinions which it might have the appearance of flattery to mention, that, if in any country or community, such a union could be effected, it was among my countrymen in *Bengal*, with some of whom I already had, and with most was desirous of having, the pleasure of being intimately acquainted.

You have realized that hope, gentlemen, and even anticipated a declaration of my wishes, by your alacrity in laying the foundation of a society for inquiring into the history and antiquities, the natural productions, arts, sciences, and literature of *Asia*. I may confidently foretel, that an institution so likely to afford entertainment, and convey knowledge, to mankind, will advance to maturity by slow, yet certain, degrees; as the Royal Society, which at first was only a meeting of a few literary friends at *Oxford,* rose gradually to that splendid zenith, at which a *Halley* was their secretary, and a *Newton* their president.

Although it is my humble opinion, that, in order to ensure our success and permanence, we must keep a middle course between a languid remissness, and an over zealous activity, and that the tree, which you have auspiciously planted, will produce fairer blossoms, and more exquisite fruit, if it be not at first exposed to too great a glare of sunshine, yet I take the liberty of submitting to your consideration a few general ideas on the plan of our society; assuring you, that, whether you reject or approve them, your correction will give me both pleasure and instruction, as your flattering attentions have already conferred on me the highest honour.

It is your design, I conceive, to take an ample space for your learned investigations, bounding them only by the geographical limits of *Asia;* so that, considering *Hindustan* as a centre, and turning your eyes in idea to the North, you have on your right, many important kingdoms in the Eastern peninsula, the ancient and wonderful empire of *China* with all her *Tartarian* dependencies, and that of *Japan,* with the cluster of precious islands, in which many singular curiosities have too long been concealed: before you lies that prodigious chain of mountains, which formerly perhaps were a barrier against the violence of the sea, and beyond them the very interesting country of *Tibet,* and the vast regions of *Tartary,* from which, as from the *Trojan* horse of the poets, have issued so many consummate warriors, whose domain has extended at least from the banks of the Ilissus to the mouths of the *Ganges:* on your left are the beautiful and celebrated provinces of *Iran* or *Persia,* the unmeasured, and perhaps unmeasurable deserts of *Arabia,* and the once flourishing kingdom of *Yemen,* with the pleasant isles that the *Arabs* have subdued or colonized; and farther westward, the *Asiatick* dominions of the *Turkish* sultans, whose moon seems approaching rapidly to its wane.—By this great circumference, the field of your useful researches will be inclosed; but, since *Egypt* had unquestionably an old connexion with this country, if not with *China,* since the language and literature of the *Abyssinians* bear a manifest affinity to those of *Asia,* since the *Arabian* arms prevailed along the *African* coast of the *Mediterranean,* and even erected a powerful dynasty on the continent of *Europe,* you may not be displeased occasionally to follow the streams of *Asiatick* learning a little beyond its natural boundary; and, if it be necessary or convenient, that a short name or epithet be given to our society, in order to distinguish it in the world, that of *Asiatick* appears both classical and proper, whether we consider the place or the object of the institution, and preferable to *Oriental,* which is in truth a word merely relative, and, though commonly used in *Europe,* conveys no very distinct idea.

If now it be asked, what are the intended objects of our inquiries within these spacious limits, we answer, MAN and NATURE; whatever is performed by the one, or produced by the other. Human knowledge has been elegantly analysed according to the three great faculties of the mind, *memory, reason,* and *imagination,* which we constantly find employed in arranging and retaining, comparing and distinguishing, combining and diversifying, the ideas, which we receive through our senses, or acquire by reflection; hence the three main branches of learning are *history, science,* and *art:* the first comprehends either an account of natural productions, or the genuine records of empires and states; the second embraces the whole circle of pure and mixed mathematicks, together with ethicks and law, as far as they depend on the reasoning faculty; and the third includes all the beauties of imagery and the charms of invention, displayed in modulated language, or represented by colour, figure, or sound.

Agreeably to this analysis, you will investigate whatever is rare in the stupendous fabrick of nature, will correct the geography of *Asia* by new observations and discoveries; will trace the annals, and even traditions, of those nations, who from time to time have peopled or desolated it; and will bring to light their various forms of government, with their institutions civil and religious; you will examine their improvements and methods in arithmetick and geometry, in trigonometry, mensuration, mechanicks, opticks, astronomy, and general physicks; their systems of morality, grammar, rhetorick, and dialectick; their skill in chirurgery and medicine, and their advancement, whatever it may be, in anatomy and chymistry. To this you will add reserches into their agriculture, manufactures, trade; and, whilst you inquire with pleasure into their musick, architecture, painting, and poetry, will not neglect those inferior arts, by which the comforts and even elegances of social life are supplied or improved. You may observe, that I have omitted their languages, the diversity and difficulty of which are a sad obstacle to the progress of useful knowledge; but I have ever considered languages as the mere instruments of real learning, and think them improperly confounded with learning itself: the attainment of them is, however, indispensably necessary; and if to the *Persian, Armenian, Turkish,* and *Arabick,* could be added not only the *Sanscrit*, the treasures of which we may now hope to see unlocked, but even the *Chinese, Tartarian, Japanese,* and the various insular dialects, an immense mine would then be open, in which we might labour with equal delight and advantage.

Having submitted to you these imperfect thoughts on the *limits* and *objects* of our future society, I request your permission to add a few hints on the *conduct* of it in its present immature state.

Lucian begins one of his satirical pieces against historians, with declaring that the only true proposition in his work was, that it should contain nothing true; and perhaps it may be advisable at first, in order to prevent any difference of sentiment on particular points not immediately before us, to establish but one rule, namely, to have no rules at all. This only I mean, that, in the infancy of any society, there ought to be no confinement, no trouble, no expense, no unnecessary formality. Let us, if you please, for the present, have weekly evening meetings in this hall, for the purpose of hearing original papers read on such subjects, as fall within the circle of our inquiries. Let all curious and learned men be invited to send their tracts to our secretary, for which they ought immediately to receive our thanks; and if, towards the end of each year, we should be supplied with a sufficiency of valuable materials to fill a volume, let us present our *Asiatick* miscellany to the literary world, who have derived so much pleasure and information from the agreeable work of *Kæmpfer,* than which we can scarce propose a better model, that they will accept with eagerness any fresh entertainment of the same kind. You will not perhaps be disposed to admit mere translations of considerable length, except of such unpublished essays or treatises as may be transmitted to us by native authors; but, whether you will enrol as members any number of learned natives, you will hereafter decide, with many other questions as they happen to arise; and you will think, I presume, that all questions should be decided on a ballot, by a majority of two thirds, and that nine members should be requisite to constitute a board for such decisions. These points, however, and all others I submit entirely, gentlemen, to your determination, having neither wish nor pretension to claim any more than my single right of suffrage. One thing only, as essential to your dignity, I recommend with earnestness, on no account to admit a new member, who has not expressed a voluntary desire to become so; and in that case, you will not require, I suppose, any other qualification than a love of knowledge, and a zeal for the promotion of it.

Your institution, I am persuaded, will ripen of itself, and your meetings will be amply supplied with interesting and amusing papers, as soon as the object of your inquiries shall be generally known. There are, it may not be delicate to name them, but there are many, from whose important studies I cannot but conceive high expectations; and, as far as mere labour will avail, I sincerely promise, that, if in my allotted sphere of jurisprudence, or in any intellectual excursion, that I may have leisure to make, I should be so fortunate as to collect, by accident, either fruits or flowers, which may seem valuable or pleasing, I shall offer my humble *Nezr* to your society with as much respectful zeal as to the greatest potentate on earth.

SOURCE: "A Discourse on the Institution of a Society" was a pamphlet published in 1784.

Minute on Indian Education
LORD THOMAS BABINGTON MACAULAY

[Thomas Babington Macaulay (1800–1859) was a dominant critic—and advocate as well as historian—of imperial ambitions, both scholastic and political. He wrote voluminously on the topic and its multiple ramifications. His "minute" on Indian education was—and remains—a critical and much-cited contribution to the debate on the respective roles of Indian and English traditions in the issues of governments and instruction. Should the English, for example (and as William Jones argued), learn from and about their Indian subjects? Or vice versa? And what consequences would such considerations bring to the existing relations between colonizer and colonized? Macaulay served in India from 1834 to 1838; he later served as a member of Parliament.]

Shortly after he reached India in 1834, Macaulay found himself embroiled in the struggle over the future of Indian education which had been raging within the General Committee on Public Instruction for some time. The committee was divided into two factions—the "Orientalists" who felt that the British government should continue to foster instruction in Sanskrit and Arabic as well as in English for students in institutions of higher learning sponsored by the committee; and the "Anglicists" who were convinced that the available funds should be employed more or less exclusively for the teaching of English. Both sides believed in varying degrees in the necessity for "Westernization" and in the importance of the Indian vernaculars for carrying out this purpose. But the Anglicist party, unlike the Orientalist, believed strongly that the principal effort on the part of the government had to be put into the teaching of English. Macaulay's minute, written in his capacity of Legal Member of Council, strongly favored the Anglicist side. In the event, the governor-general, Lord William Bentinck, adopted in principle (though not in every detail) the policies recommended by Macaulay. The correctness of these policies is still being argued about today, but there is no doubt that their consequences for India were immense.

As it seems to be the opinion of some of the gentlemen who compose the Committee of Public Instruction, that the course which they have hitherto pursued was strictly prescribed by the British Parliament in 1813, and as, if that opinion be correct, a legislative Act will be necessary to warrant a change, I have thought it right to refrain from taking any part in the preparation of the adverse statements which are now before us, and to reserve what I had to say on the subject till it should come before me as a member of the Council of India.

It does not appear to me that the Act of Parliament can, by any art of construction, be made to bear the meaning which has been assigned to it. It contains nothing about the particular languages or sciences which are to be studied. A sum is set apart "for the revival and promotion of literature and the encouragement of the learned natives of India, and for the introduction and promotion of a knowledge of the sciences among the inhabitants of the British territories." It is argued, or rather taken for granted, that by literature the Parliament can have only meant Arabic and Sanscrit literature, that they never would have given the honourable appellation of a "learned native" to a native who was familiar with the poetry of Milton, the metaphysics of Locke, and the physics of Newton; but that they meant to designate by that name only such persons as might have studied in the sacred books of the Hindoos all the usages of cusa-grass, and all the mysteries of absorption into the Deity. This does not appear to be a very satisfactory interpretation. To take a parallel case; suppose that the Pacha of Egypt, a country once superior in knowledge to the nations of Europe, but now sunk far below them, were to appropriate a sum for the purpose of "reviving and promoting literature, and encouraging learned natives of Egypt," would anybody infer that he meant the youth of his pachalic to give years to the study of hieroglyphics, to search into all the doctrines disguised under the fable of Osiris, and to ascertain with all possible accuracy the ritual with which cats and onions were anciently adored? Would he be justly charged with inconsistency, if, instead of employing his young subjects in deciphering obelisks, he were to order them to be instructed in the English and French languages, and in all the sciences to which those languages are the chief keys?

The words on which the supporters of the old system rely do not bear them out, and other words follow which seem to be quite decisive on the other side. This lac of rupees is set apart, not only for "reviving literature in India," the phrase on which their whole interpretation is founded, but also for "the introduction and promotion of a knowledge of the sciences among the inhabitants of the British territories,"—words which are alone sufficient to authorize all the changes for which I contend.

If the Council agree in my construction, no legislative Act will be necessary. If they differ from me, I will prepare a short Act rescinding that clause of the Charter of 1813, from which the difficulty arises.

The argument which I have been considering affects only the form of proceeding. But the admirers of the Oriental system of education have used another argument, which, if we admit it to be valid, is decisive against all change. They conceive that the public faith is pledged to the present system, and that to alter the appropriation of any of the funds which have hitherto been spent in encouraging the study of Arabic and Sanscrit would be downright spoliation. It is not easy to understand by what process of reasoning they can have arrived at this conclusion. The grants which are made from the public purse for the encouragement of literature differed in no respect from the grants which are made from the same purse for other objects of real or supposed utility. We found a sanatarium on a spot which we suppose to be healthy. Do we thereby pledge ourselves to keep a sanatarium there, if the result should not answer our expectation? We commence the erection of a pier. Is it a violation of the public faith to stop the works, if we afterwards see reason to believe that the building will be useless? The rights of property are undoubtedly sacred. But nothing endangers those rights so much as the practice, now unhappily too common, of attributing them to things to which they do not belong. Those who would impart to abuses the sanctity of property are in truth imparting to the institution of property the unpopularity and fragility of abuses. If the Government has given to any person a formal assurance; nay, if the Government has excited in any person's mind a reasonable expectation that he shall receive a certain income as a teacher or a learner of Sanscrit or Arabic, I would respect that person's pecuniary interests—I would rather err on the side of liberality to individuals than suffer the public faith to be called in question. But to talk of a Government pledging itself to teach certain languages and certain sciences, though those languages may become useless, though those sciences may be exploded, seems to me quite unmeaning. There is not a single word in any public instructions from which it can be inferred that the Indian Government ever intended to give any pledge on this subject, or ever considered the destination of these funds as unalterably fixed. But, had it been otherwise, I should have denied the competence of our predecessors to bind us by any pledge on such a subject. Suppose that a Government had in the last century enacted in the most solemn manner that all its subjects should, to the end of time, be inoculated for the small-pox: would that Government be bound to persist in the practice after Jenner's discovery? These promises, of which nobody claims the performance, and from which nobody can grant a release; these vested rights, which vest in nobody; this property without proprietors; this robbery, which makes nobody poorer, may be comprehended by persons of higher faculties than mine—I consider this plea merely as a set form of words, regularly used both in England and India, in defence of every abuse for which no other plea can be set up.

I hold this lac of rupees to be quite at the disposal of the Governor-General in Council, for the purpose of promoting learning in India, in any way which may be thought most advisable. I hold his Lordship to be quite as free to direct that it shall no longer be employed in encouraging Arabic and Sanscrit, as he is to direct that the reward for killing tigers in Mysore shall be diminished, or that no more public money shall be expended on the chanting at the cathedral.

We now come to the gist of the matter. We have a fund to be employed as Government shall direct for the intellectual improvement of the people of this country. The simple question is, what is the most useful way of employing it?

All parties seem to be agreed on one point, that the dialects commonly spoken among the natives of this part of India contain neither Literary nor scientific information, and are, moreover so poor and rude that, until they are enriched from some other quarter, it will not be easy to translate any valuable work into them. It seems to be admitted on all sides that the intellectual improvement of those classes of the people who have the means of pursuing higher studies can at present be effected only by means of some language not vernacular amongst them.

What, then, shall that language be? One half of the Committee maintain that it should be the English. The other half strongly recommend the Arabic and Sanscrit. The whole question seems to me to be, which language is the best worth knowing?

I have no knowledge of either Sanscrit or Arabic.—But I have done what I could to form a correct estimate of their value. I have read translations of the most celebrated Arabic and Sanscrit works. I have conversed both here and at home with men distinguished by their proficiency in the Eastern tongues. I am quite ready to take the Oriental learning at the valuation of the Orientalists themselves. I have never found one among them who could deny that a single shelf of a good European library was worth the whole native literature of India and Arabia. The intrinsic superiority of the Western literature is, indeed, fully admitted by those members of the Committee who support the Oriental plan of education.

It will hardly be disputed, I suppose, that the department of literature in which the Eastern writers stand highest is poetry. And I certainly never met with any Orientalist who ventured to maintain that the Arabic and Sanscrit poetry could be compared to that of the great European nations. But, when we pass from works of imagination to works in which facts are recorded and general principles investigated, the superiority of the Europeans becomes absolutely immeasurable. It is, I believe, no exaggeration to say, that all the historical information which has been collected from all the books written in the Sanscrit language is less valuable than what may be found in the most paltry abridgments used at preparatory schools in England. In every branch of physical or moral philosophy the relative position of the two nations is nearly the same.

How, then, stands the case? We have to educate a people who cannot at present be educated by means of their mother-tongue. We must teach them some foreign language. The claims of our own language it is hardly necessary to recapitulate. It stands preeminent even among the languages of the West. It abounds with works of imagination not inferior to the noblest which Greece has bequeathed to us; with models of every species of eloquence; with historical compositions, which, considered merely as narratives, have seldom been surpassed, and which, considered as vehicles of ethical and political instruction, have never been equalled; with just and lively representations of human life and human nature; with the most profound speculations on metaphysics, morals, government, jurisprudence, and trade; with full and correct information respecting every experimental science which tends to preserve the health, to increase the comfort, or to expand the intellect of man. Whoever knows that language, has ready access to all the vast intellectual wealth, which all the wisest nations of the earth have created and hoarded in the course of ninety generations. It may safely be said that the literature now extant in that language is of far greater value than all the literature which three hundred years ago was extant in all the languages of the world together. Nor is this all. In India, English is the language spoken by the ruling class. It is spoken by the higher class of natives at the seats of Government. It is likely to become the language of commerce throughout the seas of the East. It is the language of two great European communities which are rising, the one in the south of Africa, the other in Australasia; communities which are every year becoming more important, and more closely connected with our Indian empire. Whether we look at the intrinsic value of our literature, or at the particular situation of this country, we shall see the strongest reason to think that, of all foreign tongues, the English tongue is that which would be the most useful to our native subjects.

The question now before us is simply whether, when it is in our power to teach this language, we shall teach languages in which, by universal confession, there are no books on any subject which deserve to be compared to our own; whether, when we can teach European science, we shall teach systems which, by universal confession, whenever they differ from those of Europe, differ for the worse; and whether, when we can patronise sound Philosophy and true History, we shall countenance, at the public expense, medical doctrines which would disgrace an English Farrier—Astronomy, which would move laughter in girls at an English boarding school—History, abounding with kings thirty feet high, and reigns thirty thousand years long—and Geography, made up of seas of treacle and seas of butter.

We are not without experience to guide us. History furnishes several analogous cases, and they all teach the same lesson. There are in modern times, to go no further, two memorable instances of a great impulse given to the mind of a whole society—of prejudices overthrown—of knowledge diffused—of taste purified—of arts and sciences planted in countries which had recently been ignorant and barbarous.

The first instance to which I refer is the great revival of letters among the Western nations at the close of the fifteenth and the beginning of the sixteenth century. At that time almost everything that was worth reading was contained in the writings of the ancient Greeks and Romans. Had our ancestors acted as the Committee of Public Instruction has hitherto acted; had they neglected the language of Cicero and Tacitus; had they confined their attention to the old dialects of our own island; had they printed nothing and taught nothing at the universities but Chronicles in Anglo-Saxon and Romances in Norman-French, would England have been what she now is? What the Greek and Latin were to the contemporaries of More and Ascham, our tongue is to the people of India. The literature of England is now more valuable than that of classical antiquity. I doubt whether the Sanscrit literature be as valuable as that of our Saxon and Norman progenitors. In some departments—in History, for example—I am certain that it is much less so.

Another instance may be said to be still before our eyes. Within the last hundred and twenty years, a nation which had previously been in a state as barbarous as that in which our ancestors were before the Crusades, has gradually emerged from the ignorance in which it was sunk, and has taken its place among civilised communities—I speak of Russia. There is now in that country a large educated class, abounding with persons fit to serve the state in the highest functions, and in nowise inferior to the most accomplished men who adorn the best circles of Paris and London. There is reason to hope that this vast empire, which in the time of our grandfathers was probably behind the Punjab, may, in the time of our grandchildren, be pressing close on France and Britain in the career of improvement. And how was this change effected? Not by flattering national prejudices; not by feeding the mind of the young Muscovite with the old woman's stories which his rude fathers had believed: not by filling his head with lying legends about St. Nicholas: not by encouraging him to study the great question, whether the world was or was not created on the 13th of September: not by calling him "a learned native," when he has mastered all these points of knowledge: but by teaching him those foreign languages in which the greatest mass of information had been laid up, and thus putting all that information within his reach. The languages of Western Europe civilized Russia. I cannot doubt that they will do for the Hindoo what they have done for the Tartar.

And what are the arguments against that course which seems to be alike recommended by theory and by experience? It is said that we ought to secure the co-operation of the native public, and that we can do this only by teaching Sanscrit and Arabic.

I can by no means admit that, when a nation of high intellectual attainments undertakes to superintend the education of a nation comparatively ignorant, the learners are absolutely to prescribe the course which is to be taken by the teachers. It is not necessary, however, to say anything on this subject. For it is proved by unanswerable evidence that we are not at present securing the co-operation of the natives. It would be bad enough to consult their intellectual taste at the expense of their intellectual health. But we are consulting neither—we are withholding from them the learning for which they are craving; we are forcing on them the mock-learning which they nauseate.

This is proved by the fact that we are forced to pay our Arabic and Sanscrit students, while those who learn English are willing to pay us. All the declamations in the world about the love and reverence of the natives for their sacred dialects will never, in the mind of any impartial person, outweigh the undisputed fact, that we cannot find, in all our vast empire, a single student who will let us teach him those dialects unless we will pay him.

I have now before me the accounts of the Madrassa for one month—the month of December, 1833. The Arabic students appear to have been seventy-seven in number. All receive stipends from the public. The whole amount paid to them is above 500 rupees a month. On the other side of the account stands the following item: Deduct amount realised from the out-students of English for the months of May, June, and July last, 103 rupees.

I have been told that it is merely from want of local experience that I am surprised at these phenomena, and that it is not the fashion for students in India to study at their own charges. This only confirms me in my opinion. Nothing is more certain than that it never can in any part of the world be necessary to pay men for doing what they think pleasant and profitable. India is no exception to this rule. The people of India do not require to be paid for eating rice when they are hungry, or for wearing woollen cloth in the cold season. To come nearer to the case before us, the children who learn their letters and a little elementary Arithmetic from the village schoolmaster are not paid by him. He is paid for teaching them. Why, then, is it necessary to pay people to learn Sanscrit and Arabic? Evidently because it is universally felt that the Sanscrit and Arabic are languages the knowledge of which does not compensate for the trouble of acquiring them. On all such subjects the state of the market is the decisive test.

Other evidence is not wanting, if other evidence were required. A petition was presented last year to the Committee by several ex-students of the Sanscrit College. The petitioners stated they had studied in the college ten or twelve years; that they had made themselves acquainted with Hindoo literatures and science; that they had received certificates of proficiency: and what is the fruit of all this? "Notwithstanding such testimonials," they say, "we have but little prospect of bettering our condition without the kind assistance of your Honourable Committee, the indifference with which we are generally looked upon by our countrymen leaving no hope of encouragement and assistance from them." They therefore beg that they may be recommended to the Governor-General for places under the Government, not places of high dignity or emolument, but such as may just enable them to exist. "We want means," they say, "for a decent living, and for our progressive improvement, which, however, we cannot obtain without the assistance of Government, by whom we have been educated and maintained from childhood." They conclude by representing, very pathetically, that they are sure that it was never the intention of Government, after behaving so liberally to them during their education, to abandon them to destitution and neglect.

I have been used to see petitions to Government for compensation. All these petitions, even the most unreasonable of them, proceeded on the supposition that some loss had been sustained—that some wrong had been inflicted. These are surely the first petitioners who ever demanded compensation for having been educated gratis—for having been supported by the public during twelve years, and then sent forth into the world well-furnished with literature and science. They represent their education as an injury which gives them a claim on the Government for redress, as an injury for which the stipends paid to them during the infliction were a very inadequate compensation. And I doubt not that they are in the right. They have wasted the best years of life in learning what procures for them neither bread nor respect. Surely we might, with advantage, have saved the cost of making these persons useless and miserable; surely, men may be brought up to be burdens to the public and objects of contempt to their neighbours at a somewhat smaller charge to the state. But such is our policy. We do not even stand neuter in the contest between truth and falsehood. We are not content to leave the natives to the influence of their own hereditary prejudices. To the natural difficulties which obstruct the progress of sound science in the East we add fresh difficulties of our own making. Bounties and premiums, such as ought not to be given even for the propagation of truth, we lavish on false taste and false philosophy.

By acting thus we create the very evil which we fear. We are making that opposition which we do not find. What we spend on the Arabic and Sanscrit colleges is not merely a dead loss to the cause of truth: it is the bounty-money paid to raise up champions of error. It goes to form a nest, not merely of helpless place-hunters, but of bigots prompted alike by passion and by interest to raise a cry against every useful scheme of education. If there should be any opposition among the natives to the change which I recommend, that opposition will be the effect of our own system. It will be headed by persons supported by our stipends and trained in our colleges. The longer we persevere in our present course, the more formidable will that opposition be. It will be every year re-inforced by recruits whom we are paying. From the native society left to itself we have no difficulties to apprehend; all the murmuring will come from that oriental interest which we have, by artificial means, called into being and nursed into strength.

There is yet another fact, which is alone sufficient to prove that the feeling of the native public, when left to itself, is not such as the supporters of the old system represent it to be. The Committee have thought fit to lay out above a lac of rupees in printing Arabic and Sanscrit books. Those books find no purchasers. It is very rarely that a single copy is disposed of. Twenty-three thousand volumes, most of them folios and quartos, fill the libraries, or rather the lumber-rooms, of this body. The Committee contrive to get rid of some portion of their vast stock of Oriental literature by giving books away. But they cannot give so fast as they print. About twenty thousand rupees a year are spent in adding fresh masses of water paper to a hoard which, I should think, is already sufficiently ample. During the last three years, about sixty thousand rupees have been expended in this manner. The sale of Arabic and Sanscrit books, during those three years, has not yielded quite one thousand rupees. In the mean time the School-book Society is selling seven or eight thousand English volumes every year, and not only pays the expenses of printing, but realizes a profit of 20 per cent on its outlay.

The fact that the Hindoo law is to be learned chiefly from Sanscrit books, and the Mahomedan law from Arabic books, has been much insisted on, but seems not to bear at all on the question. We are commanded by Parliament to ascertain and digest the laws of India. The assistance of a law commission has been given to us for that purpose. As soon as the code is promulgated, the Shasters and the Hedeya will be useless to a Moonsiff or Sudder Ameen. I hope and trust that, before the boys who are now entering at the Madrassa and the Sanscrit college have completed their studies, this great work will be finished. It would be manifestly absurd to educate the rising generation with a view to a state of things which we mean to alter before they reach manhood.

But there is yet another argument which seems even more untenable. It is said that the Sanscrit and Arabic are the languages in which the sacred books of a hundred millions of people are written, and that they are, on that account, entitled to peculiar encouragement. Assuredly it is the duty of the British Government in India to be not only tolerant, but neutral on all religious questions. But to encourage the study of a literature admitted to be of small intrinsic value only because that literature inculcates the most serious errors on the most important subjects, is a course hardly reconcilable with reason, with morality, or even with that very neutrality which ought, as we all agree, to be sacredly preserved. It is confessed that a language is barren of useful knowledge. We are told to teach it because it is fruitful of monstrous superstitions. We are to teach false history, false astronomy, false medicine, because we find them in company with a false religion. We abstain, and I trust shall always abstain, from giving any public encouragement to those who are engaged in the work of converting natives to Christianity. And, while we act thus, can we reasonably and decently bribe men out of the revenues of the state to waste their youth in learning how they are to purify themselves after touching an ass, or what text of the Vedas they are to repeat to expiate the crime of killing a goat?

It is taken for granted by the advocates of Oriental learning that no native of this country can possibly attain more than a mere smattering of English. They do not attempt to prove this; but they perpetually insinuate it. They designate the education which their opponents recommend as a mere spelling-book education. They assume it as undeniable, that the question is between a profound knowledge of Hindoo and Arabian literature and science on the one side, and a superficial knowledge of the rudiments of English on the other. This is not merely an assumption, but an assumption contrary to all reason and experience. We know that foreigners of all nations do learn our language sufficiently to have access to all the most abstruse knowledge which it contains, sufficiently to relish even the more delicate graces of our most idiomatic writers. There are in this very town natives who are quite competent to discuss political or scientific questions with fluency and precision in the English language. I have heard the very question on which I am now writing discussed by native gentlemen with a liberality and an intelligence which would do credit to any member of the Committee of Public Instruction. Indeed, it is unusual to find, even in the literary circles of the continent, any foreigner who can express himself in English with so much facility and correctness as we find in many Hindoos. Nobody, I suppose, will contend that English is so difficult to a Hindoo as Greek to an Englishman. Yet an intelligent English youth, in a much smaller number of years than our unfortunate pupils pass at the Sanscrit college, becomes able to read, to enjoy, and even to imitate, not unhappily, the composition of the best Greek authors. Less than half the time which enables an English youth to read Herodotus and Sophocles ought to enable a Hindoo to read Hume and Milton.

To sum up what I have said: I think it clear that we are not fettered by the Act of Parliament of 1813; that we are not fettered by any pledge expressed or implied; that we are free to employ our funds as we choose; that we ought to employ them in teaching what is best worth knowing; that English is better worth knowing than Sanscrit or Arabic; that the natives are desirous to be taught English, and are not desirous to be taught Sanscrit or Arabic; that neither as the languages of law, nor as the languages of religion, have the Sanscrit and Arabic any peculiar claim to our encouragement; that it is possible to make natives of this country thoroughly good English scholars, and that to this end our efforts ought to be directed.

In one point I fully agree with the gentlemen to whose general views I am opposed. I feel, with them, that it is impossible for us, with our limited means, to attempt to educate the body of the people. We must at present do our best to form a class who may be interpreters between us and the millions whom we govern; a class of persons, Indian in blood and colour, but English in taste, in opinions, in morals, and in intellect. To that class we may leave it to refine the vernacular dialects of the country, to enrich those dialects with terms of science borrowed from the Western nomenclature, and to render them by degrees fit vehicles for conveying knowledge to the great mass of the population.

I would strictly respect all existing interests. I would deal even generously with all individuals who have had fair reason to expect a pecuniary provision. But I would strike at the root of the bad system which has hitherto been fostered by us. I would at once stop the printing of Arabic and Sanscrit books; I would abolish the Madrassa and the Sanscrit college at Calcutta. Benares is the great seat of Brahmanical learning; Delhi, of Arabic learning. If we retain the Sanscrit college at Benares and the Mahomedan college at Delhi, we do enough, and much more than enough in my opinion, for the Eastern languages. If the Benares and Delhi colleges should be retained, I would at least recommend that no stipend shall be given to any students who may hereafter repair thither, but that the people shall be left to make their own choice between the rival systems of education without being bribed by us to learn what they have no desire to know. The funds which would thus be placed at our disposal would enable us to give larger encouragement to the Hindoo college at Calcutta, and to establish in the principal cities throughout the Presidencies of Fort William and Agra schools in which the English language might be well and thoroughly taught.

If the decision of his Lordship in Council should be such as I anticipate, I shall enter on the performance of my duties with the greatest zeal and alacrity. If, on the other hand, it be the opinion of the Government that the present system ought to remain unchanged, I beg that I may be permitted to retire from the chair of the Committee. I feel that I could not be of the smallest use there—I feel, also, that I should be lending my countenance to what I firmly believe to be a mere delusion. I believe that the present system tends, not to accelerate the progress of truth, but to delay the natural death of expiring errors. I conceive that we have at present no right to the respectable name of a Board of Public Instruction. We are a Board for wasting public money, for printing books which are of less value than the paper on which they are printed was while it was blank; for giving artificial encouragement to absurd history, absurd metaphysics, absurd physics, absurd theology; for raising up a breed of scholars who find their scholarship an encumbrance and a blemish, who live on the public while they are receiving their education, and whose education is so utterly useless to them that, when they have received it, they must either starve or live on the public all the rest of their lives. Entertaining these opinions, I am naturally desirous to decline all share in the responsibility of a body which, unless it alters its whole mode of proceeding, I must consider not merely as useless, but as positively noxious.

SOURCE: In *Miscellaneous Works of Lord Macaulay*, ed. Lady Trevelyan (New York: Harper and Brothers, 1880). Dated 2 February 1835.

The Aryan Section
MAX MÜLLER

[Max Müller (1823–1900), a distinguished "orientalist" of German background but with residence in England, was important in representing the importance of the East in the elaborations of academic and institutional efforts of the empire. His work takes, for example, the early efforts of Jones as proponent of the "Asiatic" school through Lord Thomas Babington Macaulay's arguments on behalf of "Anglicization" to the more procedural directions of latter-nineteenth-century scholars.]

The danger of all scientific work at present, not only among Oriental scholars, but, as far as I can see, everywhere, is the tendency to extreme specialisation. Our age shows in that respect a decided reaction against the spirit of a former age, which those with grey heads among us can still remember, an age represented in Germany by such names as Humboldt, Ritter, Böckh, Johannes Müller, Bopp, Bunsen, and others; men who look to us like giants, carrying a weight of knowledge far too heavy for the shoulders of such mortals as now be; aye, men who *were* giants, but whose chief strength consisted in this, that they were never entirely absorbed or bewildered by special researches, but kept their eye steadily on the highest objects of all human knowledge; who could trace the vast outlines of the kosmos of nature or the kosmos of the mind with an unwavering hand, and to whose maps and guide books we must still recur, whenever we are in danger of losing our way in the mazes of minute research. At the present moment such works as Humboldt's Kosmos, or Bopp's Comparative Grammar, or Bunsen's Christianity and Mankind, would be impossible. No one would dare to write them, for fear of not knowing the exact depth at which the *Protogenes Haeckelii* has lately been discovered or the lengthening of a vowel in the *Samhitapâtha* of the *Rig-veda*. It is quite right that this should be so, at least, for a time; but all rivers, all brooks, all rills, are meant to flow into the ocean, and all special knowledge, to keep it from stagnation, must have an outlet into the general knowledge of the world. Knowledge for its own sake, as it is sometimes called, is the most dangerous idol that a student can worship. We despise the miser who amasses money for the sake of money, but still more contemptible is the intellectual miser who hoards up knowledge instead of spending it, though, with regard to most of our knowledge, we may be well assured and satisfied that, as we brought nothing into the world, so we may carry nothing out.

Against this danger of mistaking the means for the end, of making bricks without making mortar, of working for ourselves instead of working for others, meetings such as our own, bringing together so large a number of the first Oriental scholars of Europe, seem to me a most excellent safe-guard. They draw us out of our shell, away from our common routine, away from that small orbit of thought in which each of us moves day after day, and make us realise more fully, that there are other stars moving all around us in our little universe, that we all belong to one celestial system, or to one terrestrial commonwealth, and that, if we want to see real progress made in that work with which we are more specially entrusted, the re-conquest of the Eastern world, we must work with one another, for one another, like members of one body, like soldiers of one army, guided by common principles, striving after common purposes, and sustained by common sympathies. Oriental literature is of such enormous dimensions that our small army of scholars can occupy certain prominent positions only; but those points, like the stations of a trigonometrical survey, ought to be carefully chosen, so as to be able to work in harmony together. I hope that in that respect our Congress may prove of special benefit. We shall hear, each of us, from others, what they wish us to do. "Why don't you finish this?" "Why don't you publish that?" are questions which we have already heard asked by many of our friends. We shall be able to avoid what happens so often, that two men collect materials for exactly the same work, and we may possibly hear of some combined effort to carry out great works, which can only be carried out *viribus unitis,* and of which I may at least mention one, a translation of the *Sacred Books of Mankind.* Important progress has already been made for setting on foot this great undertaking, an undertaking which I think the world has a right to demand from Oriental scholars, but which can only be carried out by joint action. This Congress has helped us to lay the foundation-stone, and I trust that at our next Congress we shall be able to produce some tangible results.

I now come to the second point. A Congress enables us to tell the world what we have been doing. This, it seems to me, is particularly needful with regard to Oriental studies which, with the exception of Hebrew, still stand outside the pale of our schools and Universities, and are cultivated by the very smallest number of students. And yet, I make bold to say, that during the last hundred, and still more during the last fifty years, Oriental studies have contributed more than any other branch of scientific research to change, to purify, to clear, and intensify the intellectual atmosphere of Europe, and to widen our horizon in all that pertains to the Science of Man, in history, philology, theology, and philosophy. We have not only conquered and annexed new worlds to the ancient empire of learning, but we have leavened the old world with ideas that are already fermenting even in the daily bread of our schools and Universities. Most of those here present know that I am not exaggerating; but as the world is sceptical while listening to orations *pro domo*, I shall attempt to make good my assertions.

At first, the study of Oriental literature was a matter of curiosity only, and it is so still to a great extent, particularly in England. Sir William Jones, whose name is the only one among Oriental scholars that has ever obtained a real popularity in England, represents most worthily that phase of Oriental studies. Read only the two volumes of his Life, and they will certainly leave on your mind the distinct impression that Sir William Jones was not only a man of extensive learning and refined taste, but undoubtedly a very great man—one in a million. He was a good classical scholar of the old school, a well-read historian, a thoughtful lawyer, a clear-headed politician, and a true gentleman, in the old sense of the word. He moved in the best, I mean the most cultivated society, the great writers and thinkers of the day listened to him with respect, and say what you like, we still live in his grace, we still draw on that stock of general interest which he excited in the English mind for Eastern subjects.

Yet the interest which Sir William Jones took in Oriental literature was purely aesthetic. He chose what was beautiful in Persian and translated it, as he would translate an ode of Horace. He was charmed with Kâlidâsa's play of Sakuntala—and who is not?—and he left us his classical reproduction of one of the finest of Eastern gems. Being a judge in India, he thought it his duty to acquaint himself with the native law-books in their original language, and he gave us his masterly translation of the Laws of Manu. Sir William Jones was fully aware of the startling similarity between Sanskrit, Latin, and Greek. More than a hundred years ago, in a letter written to Prince Adam Czartoryski, in the year 1770, he says: "Many learned investigators of antiquity are fully persuaded that a very old and almost primeval language was in use among the northern nations, from which not only the Celtic dialect, but even Greek and Latin are derived; in fact we find πατήρ and μήτηρ in Persian, nor is θυγάτηρ so far removed from *dockter*, or even ὄνομα and *nomen* from Persian *nâm*, as to make it ridiculous to suppose that they sprang from the same root. We must confess," he adds, "that these researches are very obscure and uncertain, and, you will allow, not so agreeable as an ode of Hafez, or an elegy of Amr'alkeis." In a letter, dated 1787, he says: "You will be surprised at the resemblance between Sanskrit and both Greek and Latin."

Colebrooke also, the great successor of Sir William Jones, was fully aware of the relationship between Sanskrit, Greek, Latin, German, and even Slavonic. I possess some curious MS. notes of his, of the year 1801 or 1802, containing long lists of words, expressive of the most essential ideas of primitive life, and which he proved to be identical in Sanskrit, Greek, Latin, German, and Slavonic.

Yet neither Colebrooke nor Sir William Jones perceived the full import of these facts. Sir William Jones died young; Colebrooke's energies, marvellous as they were, were partly absorbed by official work, so that it was left to German and French scholars to bring to light the full wealth of the mine which those great English scholars had been the first to open. We know now that in language, and in all that is implied by language, India and Europe are one; but to prove this, against the incredulity of all the greatest scholars of the day, was no easy matter. It could be done effectually in one way only, viz. by giving to Oriental studies a strictly scientific character, by requiring from Oriental students not only the devotion of an *amateur*, but the same thoroughness, minuteness, and critical accuracy which were long considered the exclusive property of Greek and Latin scholars. I could not think of giving here a history of the work done during the last fifty years. It has been admirably described in Benfey's 'History of the Science of Language.' Even if I attempted to give merely the names of those who have been most distinguished by really original discoveries—the names of Bopp, Pott, Grimm, Burnouf, Rawlinson, Miklosich, Benfey, Kuhn, Zeuss, Whitley Stokes—I am afraid my list would be considered very incomplete.

But let us look at what has been achieved by these men, and many others who followed their banners! The East, formerly a land of dreams, of fables, and fairies, has become to us a land of unmistakeable reality; the curtain between the West and the East has been lifted, and our old forgotten home stands before us again in bright colours and definite outlines. Two worlds, separated for thousands of years, have been reunited as by a magical spell, and we feel rich in a past that may well be the pride of our noble Aryan family. We say no longer vaguely and poetically *Ex Oriente Lux,* but we know that all the most vital elements of our knowledge and civilisation,—our languages, our alphabets, our figures, our weights and measures, our art, our religion, our traditions, our very nursery stories, came to us from the East; and we must confess that but for the rays of Eastern light, whether Aryan, or Semitic, or Hamitic, that called forth the hidden germs of the dark and dreary West, Europe, now the very light of the world, might have remained for ever a barren and forgotten promontory of the primeval Asiatic continent. We live indeed in a new world, the barrier between the West and the East, that seemed insurmountable, has vanished. The East is ours, we are its heirs, and claim by right our share in its inheritance.

I have so far dwelt chiefly on the powerful influence which the East, and more particularly India, has exercised on the intellectual life and work of the West. But the progress of Oriental scholarship in Europe, and the discovery of that spiritual relationship which binds India and England together, has likewise produced practical effects of the greatest moment in the East. The Hindus, in their first intercourse with English scholars, placed before them the treasures of their native literature with all the natural pride of a nation that considered itself the oldest, the wisest, the most enlightened nation in the world. For a time, but for a short time only, the claims of their literature to a fabulous antiquity were admitted, and dazzled by the unexpected discovery of a new classical literature, people raved about the beauty of Sanskrit poetry in truly Oriental strains. Then followed a sudden reaction; and the natives themselves, on becoming more and more acquainted with European history and literature, began to feel the childishness of their claims, and to be almost ashamed of their own classics. This was a national misfortune. A people that cannot feel some pride in the past, in its history and literature, loses the mainstay of its national character. When Germany was in the very depth of its political degradation, it turned to its ancient literature, and drew hope for the future from the study of the past. Something of the same kind is now passing in India. A new taste, not without some political ingredients, has sprung up for the ancient literature of the country; a more intelligent appreciation of their real merits has taken the place of the extravagant admiration for the masterworks of their old poets; there is a revival in the study of Sanskrit, a surprising activity in the republication of Sanskrit texts, and there are traces among the Hindus of a growing feeling, not very different from that which Tacitus described, when he said of the Germans: "Who would go to Germany, a country without natural beauty, with a wretched climate, miserable to cultivate or to look at—*unless it be his fatherland?*"

Even the discovery that Sanskrit, English, Greek, and Latin are cognate languages, has not been without its influence on the scholars and thinkers, on the leaders of public opinion, in India. They, more than others, had felt for the time most keenly the intellectual superiority of the West, and they rose again in their own estimation by learning that physically, or, at all events, intellectually, they had been and might be again, the peers of Greeks and Romans and Saxons. These silent influences often escape the eye of the politician and the historian, but at critical moments they may decide the fate of whole nations and empires.

Now it seems to me that, first of all, our Universities, and I think again chiefly of Oxford, might do much more for missions than they do at present. If we had a sufficient staff of professors for Eastern languages, we could prepare young missionaries for their work, and we should be able to send out from time to time such men as Patteson, the Bishop of Melanesia, who was every inch an Oxford man. And in these missionaries we might have not only apostles of religion and civilisation, but at the same time, the most valuable pioneers of scientific research. I know there are some authorities at home who declare that such a combination is impossible, or at least undesirable; that a man cannot serve two masters, and that a missionary must do his own work and nothing else. Nothing, I believe, can be more mistaken. First of all, some of our most efficient missionaries have been those who have done also the most excellent work as scholars, and whenever I have conversed on this subject with missionaries who have seen active service, they all agree that they cannot be converting all day long, and that nothing is more refreshing and invigorating to them than some literary or scientific work. Now what I should like to see is this: I should like to see ten or twenty of our non-resident fellowships, which at present are doing more harm than good, assigned to missionary work, to be given to young men who have taken their degree, and who, whether laymen or clergymen, are willing to work as assistant missionaries on distant stations; with the distinct understanding, that they should devote some of their time to scientific work, whether the study of languages, or flowers, or stars, and that they should send home every year some account of their labours. These men would be like scientific consuls, to whom students at home might apply for information and help. They would have opportunities of distinguishing themselves by really useful work, far more than in London, and after ten years, they might either return to Europe with a well-established reputation, or if they find that they have a real call for missionary work, devote all their life to it. Though to my own mind there is no nobler work than that of a missionary, yet I believe that some such connection with the Universities and men of science would raise their position, would call out more general interest, and secure to the missionary cause the good-will of those whose will is apt to become law.

Thirdly, I think that Oriental studies have a claim on the colonies and the colonial governments. The English colonies are scattered all over the globe, and many of them in localities where an immense deal of useful scientific work might be done, and would be done with the slightest encouragement from the local authorities, and something like a systematic supervision on the part of the Colonial Office at home. Some years ago I ventured to address the Colonial Secretary of State on this subject, and a letter was sent out in consequence to all the English colonies, inviting information on the languages, monuments, customs, and traditions of the native races. Some most valuable reports have been sent home during the last five or six years, but when it was suggested that these reports should be published in a permanent form, the expense that would have been required for printing every year a volume of Colonial Reports, and which would not have amounted to more than a few hundred pounds for all the colonies of the British Empire, part of it to be recovered by the sale of the book, was considered too large.

SOURCE: In *Transactions of the Second Session of the International Congress of Orientalists* (n.p., 1876).

VI

LAWS AND ORDERS

INTRODUCTION
Ordering "Chaos": Administering the Law
MIA CARTER

EIGHTEENTH- AND NINETEENTH-CENTURY orientalist scholarship, represented here by the works of Robert Orme, William Jones, and Lord Thomas Babington Macaulay, depicts India as a lawless and chaotic land, inhabited by various despotic governments and roving bands of thugs and bandits; characterized by myriad superstitions and contradictory religious beliefs; and troubled by a history of bribery and corruption, which served as poor imitations of civil jurisprudence. Orme concluded that no existing Indian codes of law could amend the nation's elaborate disorder. Jones's work continued this strain of thought while simultaneously marveling at the intricacy, antiquity, and "curious matter" of the legal ordinances of Menu, the son or grandson of Brahma. Jones's scholarship functioned as a double translation: a transcription of Sanskrit and Brahamanic codes into English, and a means of translating Hindu tradition into British legal discourse. The linguistic accessibility of the Indian legal traditions enabled the implementation of "well-mannered" British forms of government, that is, those in accordance with Indians' "ancient usages" and "religious prejudices." Jones described the logic of the ordinances as childish, absurd, and incomprehensible; however, he admired the style in which they were detailed and respected the democratic nature of their admonitions. He reminded his European audience that these imperfect and mystifying beliefs were genuinely and sincerely upheld by the inhabitants of India, which was of vital economic interest to the British Empire. In other words, some incorporation of Indian "superstition" into British law was felt to be potentially profitable, if not wholly rational.

Macaulay, on the other hand, described the pre-existing laws of India as having been implemented by supersuccession; the Indian legal system, he argued, had been imported, put into place by the nation's various conquerors. He suggested that a more aggressive, precise, and consistent penal code be implemented to amend the colonial nation's motley inherited legal traditions. Macaulay declared that the British penal code would be the superior in juridical import; its enlightened qualities would be immediately recognized when translated into native languages.

BIBLIOGRAPHY

Cruikshank, Margaret. *Thomas Babington Macaulay*. Boston: Twayne Publishers, 1977.
Franklin, Michael J. *Sir William Jones*. Cardiff: University of Wales Press, 1995.
Hamburger, Joseph. *Macaulay and the Whig Tradition*. Chicago: University of Chicago Press, 1976.
Lively, Jack, and John Collwyn Rees. *Utilitarian Logic and Politics: James Mill's Essay on Government, Macaulay's Critique, and the Ensuing Debate*. Oxford: Clarendon Press, 1978.
Millgate, Jane. *Macaulay*. London: Routledge and Kegan Paul, 1973.
Morely, William Hook. *The Administration of Justice in British India: Its Past History and Present State*. London: Metropolitan Book Co., 1858.
Srivastava, Ramesh Chandra. *Development of the Judicial System in India under the East India Company, 1833–1858*. Lucknow, India: n.p., 1971.
Stokes, Eric. *The English Utilitarians and India*. Oxford: Clarendon Press, 1959.
Vasu, Siva Chandra. *The Hindus as They Are: A Description of the Manners, Customs, and Inner Life of Hindoo Society in Bengal*. London: E. Stanford, 1881.

Of the Laws and Justice of Indostan
ROBERT ORME

[Robert Orme (1728–1801) was initially employed as a Company writer in 1742; he later became a member of the Madras Council (1754–1758). Orme was also a friend of Robert Clive and his fortunes rose and fell alongside those of the illustrious warrior-merchant and notorious nabob; eventually charges of extortion were leveled against Orme. In 1769 he was employed as the historiographer for the East India Company.]

OF THE LAWS OF INDOSTAN

A government depending upon no other principle than the will of one, cannot be supposed to admit any absolute laws into its constitution; for these would often interfere with that will.

There are no digests or codes of laws existing in Indostan: the Tartars who conquered this country could scarcely read or write; and when they found it impossible to convert them to Mahomedanism, left the Gentoos at liberty to follow their own religion.

To both these people (the lords and slaves of this empire) custom and religion have given all the regulations which are at this time observed in Indostan. The sanction of such impressions continue the policies of this empire, such as they are, with a constancy not exceeded in legislatures founded upon the best of principles.

A detail of these customs and policies is not to be expected. A whole life spent in such enquiries, would at the end remain ignorant of the hundredth part of them: every province has fifty sects of Gentoos; and every sect adheres to different observances. My intent is only to give a general idea of the sources of civil and criminal cases, and of the methods of process by which they are adjudged.

OF CIVIL CASES

It is a maxim, that civil institutions will always be found infinitely more circumscribed, and much less complicated, in despotic States, than in those of liberty. If these in Indostan are found less frequent than in freer governments, they certainly are more than could be expected in one so absolute: and this I shall endeavour to account for.

No property in lands admits of disputes concerning them. The slavery to which the rights of parent and husband subjects the female (who neither amongst the Moors or Gentoos is suffered to appear before any of the other sex, except her nearest relations) abolishes at once all suits of dowries, divorce, jointures, and settlements: but if these two of the fundamental causes of dispute are removed, the other two remain; commerce and inheritances are permitted, and naturally produce contentions.

INHERITANCES AND COMMERCE PERMITTED; AND FROM HENCE CIVIL CASES ARISE IN INDOSTAN

Although the notion of absolute power admits of nothing which can be sanctified from its grasp, whence the king, as in other despotic States, may, if he pleases, become heir to any man in his kingdom; yet custom has not established this right to him in Indostan; and these perhaps are the reasons why neither the Moors or Gentoos have been subjected to it.

1. All the political institutions of the Gentoos are so blended with the idea of religion, that this is generally effected where these are concerned. The softness of manners which these people receive from the climate, has fixed all their attention to the solaces of a domestic life. There are not more tender parents, or better masters, in the world: such a people will make wills in favour of their offspring: and the prince finds himself restrained by policy from establishing a right so utterly shocking to the nature and disposition of the subject. He is likewise restrained by religion: the name of God invoked in the testament of a Gentoo, gives it as sacred an authority as with those who have better notions of a deity; and the Brachman is too much interested, as father of a family, to sanctify a practice which would affect his own property. Thus the Gentoo princes were never seen to assert this right, excepting when avarice had got so far the ascendant, as not only to confound all their notions of policy, but even to make them look on religion as the prejudice of education.

2. The Moors, in the first outrages of conquest, doubtless possessed them-

selves of all kinds of property; but when the Gentoos would not be converted, and were left to the observance of their own rites, the right of testaments was continued, and still subsists amongst them. The Gentoos, by their subtilty and application, find many means of gaining wealth under the Moors; and this wealth they devolve by will to their male children. The obstacles which these may meet with in taking possession, will be explained hereafter.

3. The idea of being fellow-conquerors; the complacency arising from perpetual victories; the immense wealth which these conquests afforded; might have been the causes which prevented the first Mahomedan princes of Indostan, from establishing amongst those of their own religion, this utmost effort of absolute power. They were contented with knowing that they had at all times the power to seize, without declaring that they intended to inherit every man's property.

4. When the kingdom came to be divided into distinct provinces; when many of these provinces rendered their Nabobs almost independant of the throne; it would have been the height of impolicy to have attempted such an institution; it would have been impossible to have effected it.

5. Had the throne attempted such violence upon such subjects as were more immediately within its reach, the next province, or, if not that, one beyond it, would have afforded an asylum, where a part of the persecuted wealth, bestowed with address, could not fail to procure safety and protection to the remainder; especially if the heirs, as they doubtlessly would, took sanctuary with princes, who either were dissatisfied with, or disregarded, the authority of the court; hence confusions and revolts may be strengthened, if not produced.

6. If a Nabob thought his power sufficiently established to perpetrate, and should attempt the violence of such acquisitions, the subject would remove to the government of the neighbouring prince, whom he would probably find in a state of war with him from whose outrages he had fled.

If the right of inheritance in the sovereign were as chimerical a notion as it appears inconsistent with the existence of a powerful nation, I should not have insisted upon these conjectures; but this right is certainly established in the dominions of the Turk: and the emperor of Japan is not only the absolute lord of the property of his subjects, but is likewise so, in the utmost signification of the term, over their persons, which he massacres and tortures at his pleasure, at some times exterminating a whole city for the offence of a single man.

The different methods of inheritance amongst the Gentoos, are settled by their religion, according to the different casts by which they are distinguished. In general, the females are recommended to the care of the brothers; and these are commonly ordered to divide equally: sometimes first cousins, especially if born under the same roof, share equally with the brothers: sometimes the first wife of the deceased is intrusted with the management of the whole estate during life—a custom attended with no consequences prejudicial to the children, as she cannot enter into a second marriage. It is always recommended by the parent, that the house, if in a way of trade, be not divided; and as surely it happens, that divisions ensue amongst the heirs.

If the rights of inheritance are seen to be a source from whence a multiplicity of litigations may arise in Indostan, the free exercise of commerce will be found to produce still more frequent occasions of dispute.

The varied and extensive commerce which exists in Indostan, both by sea and land, is more than can be imagined by those who are unacquainted with the multiplicity and value of the productions of this wealthy empire: the high roads are full of caravans; the navigable rivers of boats; the sea-coasts of barques; and ships with the richest cargoes make voyages from one part of the kingdom to another.

SPIRIT OF THE MOORS AND THE GENTOOS, IN LITIGIOUS CONTENTIONS

It may not be thought unnecessary to view the dispositions of the people of Indostan in litigious contentions.

The Moors hold the office of a scribe in contempt: commerce therefore cannot be held by them in honour. The Moors who engage in it have nothing but the name of the merchant; the business is transacted by some subtle Gentoo, who, when he wants his master to confirm a bargain, is sure to find him in the women's apartment, or falling asleep over his Kaloon.[1] Nothing is so indolent as a Moor out of the track of ambition: he will readily compromise a cause, if he entertains the least doubt of gaining it; and if there is a necessity of prosecuting it, he sends a Gentoo to the Durbar, as his representative solicitor.

That pusillanimity and sensibility of spirit, which renders the Gentoos incapable of supporting the contentions of danger, disposes them as much to prosecute litigious contests. No people are of more inveterate and steady resentments in civil disputes. The only instance in which they seem to have a contempt for money, is their profusion of it in procuring the redress and revenge of injuries at the bar of justice. Although they can, with great resignation, see themselves plundered to the utmost by their superiors, they become mad with impatience when they think themselves defrauded of any part of

---

1. An instrument out of which they smoke tobacco.

their property by their equals. Nothing can be more adapted to the feminine spirit of a Gentoo, than the animosities of a law-suit.

OF THE ADMINISTRATION OF JUSTICE IN CIVIL CASES

The superiority of their numbers in every province of Indostan, may have first given rise to the custom of devolving the office of Duan upon a Gentoo: and the sense of their superior industry and abilities may have confirmed this custom; which nevertheless is not so absolute as to exclude the Moors entirely: if any favourite of the Nabob hath[2] application and capacity equal to the task, his being a Moor will certainly give him that preference, which a kind of necessity alone seems to have established amongst the Gentoos.

The Duan is, by his office, the chief judge of the province: from whose tribunal no appeal is made, as by suffering him to preside in the seat of judgment, it is known that the Nabob will confirm his decrees.

A Nabob, who through humanity is led to inquire into the condition of his subjects, may sometimes be seen to preside at the Durbar in person; during which time the Duan has no authority but what the countenance of his master gives him.

No man is refused access to the Durbar, or seat of judgment; which is exposed to a large area, capable of containing the multitude: here justice, or the appearance of it, is administered upon all but festival days, by the Duan, if the Nabob is absent; or by a deputy, in the absence of the Duan.

The plaintiff discovers himself by crying aloud, Justice! Justice! until attention is given to his importunate clamours. He is then ordered to be silent, and to advance before his judge; to whom, after having prostrated himself, and made his offering of a piece of money, he tells his story in the plainest manner, with great humility of voice and gesture, and without any of those oratorical embellishments which compose an art in freer nations.

The wealth, the consequence, the interest, or the address of the party, become now the only considerations. He visits his judge in private, and gives the jar of oil: his adversary bestows the hog, which breaks it. The friends who can influence, intercede; and, excepting where the case is so manifestly proved as to brand the failure of redress with glaring infamy (a restraint which human nature is born to reverence) the value of the bribe ascertains the justice of the cause.

This is so avowed a practice, that if a stranger should enquire, how much it would cost him to recover a just debt from a creditor who evaded payment, he

2. Read 'have'.

would every where receive the same answer—the government will keep one-fourth, and give you the rest.

Still the forms of justice subsist: witnesses are heard; but brow-beaten and removed: proofs of writing produced; but deemed forgeries and rejected, until the way is cleared for a decision, which becomes totally or partially favourable, in proportion to the methods which have been used to render it such; but still with some attention to the consequences of a judgment, which would be of too flagrant iniquity not to produce universal detestation and resentment.

The quickness of decisions which prevails in Indostan, as well as in all other despotic governments, ought no longer to be admired. As soon as the judge is ready, everything that is necessary is ready: there are no tedious briefs of cases, no various interpretations of an infinity of laws, no methodized forms, and no harangues to keep the parties longer in suspence.

Providence has, at particular seasons, blessed the miseries of these people with the presence of a righteous judge. The vast reverence and reputation which such have acquired, are but too melancholy a proof of the infrequency of such a character. The history of their judgments and decisions is transmitted down to posterity, and is quoted with a visible complacency on every occasion. Stories of this nature supply the place of proverbs in the conversations of all the people of Indostan, and are applied by them with great propriety.

OF ARBITRATIONS

The abuses of public justice naturally produced the preference of private arbitrations: these would soon have removed all causes from the tribunal of the sovereign; all arbitrations are therefore prohibited, excepting under the inspections and restrictions of the Durbar, which confirms such umpire as are desired, or elects such as are dreaded, comfortable to the complacency or displeasure which have been inspired by the address of the parties.

Many of the causes which arise from the intracacies in commercial accounts, are referred to arbitration, as the attention necessary to scrutinize them would employ too much time at the Durbar. These are sometimes decided with sufficient candour, as the umpire capable of such a task are not always the immediate instruments of the government.

AN OBJECTION ANSWERED

It may be objected, that the strict attention given to the forms of justice in Indostan, appears inconsistent with the nature of a government acknowledged to be despotic.

These forms would, without doubt, be despised, were not the inhabitants of the province less subjected to the will of their Nabob, than the vicegerent himself is dependant upon the will of his sovereign.

A government depending upon the will of one, exists no longer if another absolute will exists in any part of it; that part immediately becomes a separate kingdom. This is openly the case in the *revolts of Indostan* whilst they last; and sometimes is secretly so in the dominions of such vicegerents, who, relying on their power, distance, or address, think that they have little to fear from the throne; but at the same time do not openly give defiance to it.

The Nabob is commissioned to represent his prince as a steward, who is bound to take all measures for the preservation and increase of his master's estate. It would be absurd to imagine that the emperor should delegate to any subject the power of plundering and murdering at pleasure: this monstrous privilege is acknowledged in none but himself, and others must use oblique means to attain it. The last resource from injustice lays at the throne, which has been often seen to recall a Nabob, when the cries of a province have been loud enough to penetrate its recesses.

It is well known that the emperor is commonly the most ignorant man in his dominions, of the transactions of his government. The lordly minister who thus excludes all affairs from his master's inspection, subjects them as much to his own. The cabals, the caprice, the revolutions of a court, are every hour to be dreaded by every vicegerent, if not of overgrown authority; and he is never without enemies and rivals ready to exaggerate all pretexts for supplanting him.

From the impression of these restraints, such as they are, the forms of justice are revered in all the governments of Indostan, as much as the reality of it is abused.

MONSTROUS ABUSE OF THE FORMS OF JUSTICE

From the impression of such restraints, we likewise see no act of violence committed but under the mask of justice.

As soon as a man becomes conspicuous for his possessions, and begins to despise keeping measures with the Durbar, by neglecting to supply the voluntary contributions which are expected from him; instead of giving him poison, which would not answer the end proposed, as his treasures are buried, he is beset with spies, commonly of his own domestics, who report even to the minutest of his actions: offers from discontented parties are made to him; a commerce with the enemies of the province is proposed; if he avoids these snares, a profitable post in the government is tendered to him; which if he accepts, his ruin is at hand, as the slightest of the villanies practised in every branch of it, becomes foundation sufficient to render him a public criminal: should he have escaped this too, it remains that some more glaring and desperate measures of iniquitous justice hurry him to destruction. Let the following example suggest and supply the many which might be produced.

A very wealthy house of Gentoo bankers were admonished at Muxadavad of the Nabob's necessities for money: and better versed in the arts of amassing, than in the methods necessary to preserve their riches, they presented a sum much more agreeable to their own avarice, than to the expectations of their persecutors. None of the usual snares were likely to succeed with people of their excessive caution. One of the dead bodies, which are continually floating upon the river Ganges, happened to be thrown ashore under the wall of their dwelling-house; which was immediately surrounded by the officers of the civil magistrate, and nothing heard but execrations against these devoted criminals, who were proclaimed the murderers of a son of Mahomed. The chief of the house was hurried away to a dungeon prepared for his reception; where, after having thrice endured the scourge, he compromised the price of his liberty, and the remission of his pretended crime, for the sum of fifty thousand rupees. This man I personally knew.

Warned by such examples, the more intelligent man of condition sees at once the necessity of ingratiating himself into the favour of his prince by making acceptable offerings, proportioned to his fortune. It would not be credited, that the family of Tuttichchund, shortly after his death, gave in one present to the Nabob of Bengal, the sum of three hundred thousand pounds sterling! were it not known that this man, by having managed the mint and treasury of the province for forty years successively, was become the richest private subject in the empire.

GENERAL IDEA OF THE OPPRESSION OF THE GOVERNMENT

Imitation has conveyed the unhappy system of oppression which prevails in the government of Indostan throughout all ranks of the people, from the highest even to the lowest subject of the empire. Every head of a village calls his habitation the Durbar, and plunders of their meal and roots the wretches of his precinct: from him the Zemindar extorts the small pittance of silver, which his penurious tyranny has scraped together: the Phousdar seizes upon the greatest share of the Zemindar's collections, and then secures the favour of his Nabob by voluntary contributions, which leave him not possessed of the half of his rapines and exactions: the Nabob fixes his rapacious eye on every portion of wealth which appears in his province, and never fails to carry off part of it: by large deductions from these acquisitions, he purchases security from his superiors, or maintains it against them at the expence of a war.

Subject to such oppressions, property in Indostan is seldom seen to descend to the third generation.

OF CRIMINAL CASES, AND OF THE JUSTICE ADMINISTERED IN THEM

It now remains to speak of the justice administered in criminal cases.

These meet with severer and more various punishments amongst the Gentoos, who are guided by their own caprice in appointing them, than amongst the Moors, who are directed by their *Alcoran*—a law which, amongst its absurdities, has not admitted that of cruelty in the punishment of crimes.

The punishment of all offences is executed immediately after conviction; and the proofs of this conviction are generally attended to with more justice than prevails in any other cases: perhaps, because the guilty have seldom any thing but their lives to lose.

Murders and robberies upon the highway incur death; other felonies, labour during life, and the scourge, a mulet, or imprisonment.

The offices in the civil magistrate are comprized in an institution, which is too peculiar to Indostan to be expressed by any word in our language.

In every city, and in every considerable town, is appointed a guard, directed by proper officers, whose duty it is to coerce and punish all such crimes and misdemeanors as affect the policy of that distrct, and are at the same time of too infamous or of too insignificant a nature to be admitted before the more solemn tribunal of the Durbar. These ministers of justice are called the Catwall; and a building bearing the same name is allotted for their constant resort.

At this place are perpetually heard the clamours of the populace: some demanding redress for the injury of a blow, or a bad name; others for a fraud in the commerce of farthings: one wants assistance to take, another has taken a thief: some offering themselves for bondsmen; others called upon for witnesses. The cries of wretches under the scourge, and the groans of expiring criminals, complete a scene of perfect misery and confusion.

After these employments of the day, parties are sent from the Catwall, to patrole and watch through the town by night.

The intelligence which the Catwall constantly receives, of every transaction which passes within the limits of its jurisdiction, renders it very capable of assisting the superior powers of the government in their system of oppressions.

Gentoos who have commerce with public women; Moors who are addicted to drinking spirituous liquors; all persons who hazard money in gaming; — such are subject to be norrowly watched by the Catwall; and, when detected, find that nothing by money can exempt them from public disgrace.

In such governments where the superiors are lost to all sense of humanity, the most execrable of villanies are perpetrated by this institution, designed to prevent them.

The Catwall enters into treaty with a band of robbers, who receive from hence the intelligence necessary to direct their exploits, and in return pay to it a stipulated portion of their acquisitions: besides the concessions necessary to secure impunity when detected, one part of the band is appointed to break into houses, another assaults the traveller upon the road, a third the merchant upon the river: I have seen these regulated villains commit murders in the face of day, with such desperate audacity as nothing but the confidence of protection could inspire.

In jurisdictions of narrow limits and little importance, it is customary to blend the Durbar and Catwall in one tribunal. In these all causes wherein money and property are in contention, those wherein the terror of his presence is necessary to support the intended extortions,—such are brought before the governor of the district, who leaves to inferior ministers the execution of what are properly the duties of the Catwall.

SOME REFLECTIONS

Having brought to a conclusion this essay on the government and people of Indostan, I cannot refrain from making the reflections which so obviously arise from the subject.

Christianity vindicates all its glories, all its honour, and all its reverence, when we behold the most horrid impieties avowed amongst the nations on whom its influence does not shine, as actions necessary in the common conduct of life: I mean poisonings, treachery, and assassinations, in the sons of ambition; rapines, cruelty, and extortions, in the ministers of justice.

I leave divines to vindicate, by more sanctified reflections, the cause of their religion and their God.

The sons of Liberty may here behold the mighty ills to which the slaves of a despotic power must be subject: the spirit darkened and depressed by ignorance and fear; the body tortured and tormented by punishments inflicted without justice and without measure: such a contrast to the blessings of liberty, heightens at once the sense of our happiness, and our zeal for the preservation of it.

SOURCE: In *Historical Fragments of the Mogul Empire* (London: F. Windgrave, 1805). This document was first published in 1782.

Preface to the Institutes of Hindu Law: Or, the Ordinances of Menu
SIR WILLIAM JONES

[William "Oriental" Jones (1746–1794), Welshman and father of comparative linguistics, was a poet and scholar of oriental languages. His *Grammar of the Persian Language* (1771) and *Moallakât* (1782), a translation of seven pre-Islamic Arabic odes, helped to establish his international reputation. Jones was knighted in 1783; he founded the Asiatic Society of Bengal the following year. Jones's significant legal-orientalist scholarship includes *An Inquiry into the Legal Mode of Suppressing Riots* (1780) and his "Essay on the Law of Bailments" (1781).]

THE PREFACE

It is a maxim in the science of legislation and government, that *Laws are of no avail without manners,* or, to explain the sentence more fully, that the best intended legislative provisions would have no beneficial effect even at first, and none at all in a short course of time, unless they were congenial to the disposition and habits, to the religious prejudices, and approved immemorial usages, of the people, for whom they were enacted; especially if that people universally and sincerely believed, that all their ancient usages and established rules of conduct had the sanction of an actual revelation from heaven: the legislature of *Britain* having shown, in compliance with this maxim, an intention to leave the natives of these *Indian* provinces in possession of their own Laws, at least on the titles of *contracts* and *inheritances,* we may humbly presume, that all future provisions for the administration of justice and government in *India,* will be conformable, as far as the natives are affected by them, to the manners and opinions of the natives themselves; an object, which cannot possibly be attained, until those manners and opinions can be fully and accurately known. These considerations, and a few others more immediately within my province, were my principal motives for wishing to know, and have induced me at length to publish, that system of duties, religious and civil, and of law in all its branches, which the *Hindus* firmly believe to have been promulged in the beginning of time by MENU, son or grandson of BRAHMĀ, or, in plain language, the first of created beings, and not the oldest only, but the holiest, of legislators; a system so comprehensive and so minutely exact, that it may be considered as the *Institutes of Hindu Law*, preparatory to the copious *Digest*, which has lately been compiled by *Pandits* of eminent learning, and introductory perhaps to a *Code*, which may supply the many natural defects in the old jurisprudence of this country, and, without any deviation from its principles, accomodate it justly to the improvements of a commercial age.

We are lost in an inextricable labyrinth of imaginary astronomical cycles, *Yugas, Mahāyugas, Calpas,* and *Menwantaras,* in attempting to calculate the time, when the first MENU, according to the *Brāhmens,* governed this world, and became the progenitor of mankind, who from him are called *Mānavāh;* nor can we, so clouded are the old history and chronology of *India* with fables and allegories, ascertain the precise age, when the work, now presented to the Publick, was actually composed; but we are in possession of some evidence, partly extrinsick and partly internal, that it is really one of the oldest compositions existing. From a text of PARĀSARA, discovered by MR. DAVIS, it appears, that the vernal equinox had gone back from the *tenth* degree of *Bharanì* to the *first* of *Āswinì,* or *twenty-three degrees and twenty minutes,* between the days of that *Indian* philosopher, and the year of our Lord 499, when it coincided with the origin of the *Hindu* eclipitck; so that PARĀSARA probably flourished near the close of the *twelfth* century before CHRIST: now PARĀSARA was the grandson of another sage, named VASISHT'HA, who is often mentioned in the laws of MENU, and once as contemporary with the divine BHRIGU himself; but the character of BHRIGU, and the whole dramatical arrangement of the book before us, are clearly fictitious and ornamental, with a design, too common among ancient lawgivers, of stamping authority on the work by the introduction of supernatural personages, though VASISHT'HA may have lived many generations before the actual writer of it; who names him, indeed, in one or two places as a philosopher in an earlier period. The style, however, and metre of this work (which there is not the smallest reason to think affectedly obsolete) are widely different from the languages and metrical rules of CĀLIDĀS, who unquestionably wrote before the beginning of our era; and the dialect of MENU is even observed in many passages to resemble that of the VĒDA, particularly in a departure from the more modern grammatical forms; whence it must at first view seem very probable, that the laws, now brought to light, were considerably older than those of SOLON or even of LYCURGUS, although the promulgation of them, before they were reduced to writing, might have been coeval with the first monarchies established in *Egypt* or *Asia*: but, having had the singular good fortune to procure ancient copies of eleven *Upanishads* with a very perspicuous comment, I am enabled to fix with more exactness the probable age of the work before us, and even to limit its highest possible age, by a mode of reasoning, which may be thought new, but will be found, I persuade myself, satisfactory; if the Publick shall on this occasion give me credit for a few very curious facts, which, though capable of strict proof, can at present be only asserted. The *Sanscrit* of the three first *Vēdas* (I need not here speak of the fourth), that of the *Mānava Dherma Sāstra*, and that of the *Purānas*, differ from each other in pretty exact proportion to the Latin of NUMA, from whose laws entire sentences are preserved, that of APPIUS, which we see in the fragments of the Twelve Tables, and that of CICERO, or of LUCRETIUS, where he has not affected an obsolete style: if the several changes, therefore, of *Sanscrit* and *Latin* took place, as we may fairly assume, in times very nearly proportional, the *Vēdas* must have been written about 300 years before these Institutes, and about 600 before the *Purānas* and *Itihāsas*, which, I am fully convinced, were not the productions of VYĀSA; so that, if the son of PARĀSARA committed the traditional *Vēdas* to writing in the *Sanscrit* of his father's time, the original of this book must have received its present form about 880 years before CHRIST's birth. If the texts, indeed, which VYĀSA collected, had been actually *written*, in a much older dialect, by the sages preceding him, we must inquire into the greatest possible age of the *Vēdas* themselves: now one of the longest and finest *Upanishads* in the second *Vēda* contains three lists, in a regular series upwards, of at most forty-two pupils and preceptors, who successively received and transmitted (probably by oral tradition) the doctrines contained in that *Upanishad;* and, as the old *Indian* priests were students at *fifteen*, and instructors at *twenty-five*, we cannot allow more than *ten* years on an average for each interval between the respective traditions; whence, as there are *forty* such intervals, in two of the lists, between VYĀSA, who arranged the whole work, and AYĀSYA, who is extolled at the beginning of it, and just as many, in the third list, between the compiler and YĀJNYAWALCYA, who makes the principal figure in it, we find the highest age of the *Yajur-Vēda* to be 1580 years before the birth of our Saviour, (which would make it older than the five books of MOSES) and that of our *Indian* lawtract about 1280 years before the same epoch. The former date, however, seems the more probable of the two, because the *Hindu* sages are said to have delivered their knowledge orally, and the very word *Sruta*, which we often see used for the *Vēda* itself, means *what was heard;* not to insist, that CULLŪCA expressly declares the sense of the *Vēda* to be conveyed in the *language* of VYĀSA. Whether MENU, or MENUS in the nominative and MENŌS in an oblique case, was the same personage with MINOS, let others determine; but he must indubitably have been far older than the work, which contain his laws, and, though perhaps he was never in *Crete,* yet some of his institutions may well have been adopted in that island, whence LYCURGUS a century or two afterwards may have imported them to *Sparta.*

There is certainly a strong resemblance, though obscured and faded by time, between our MENU with his divine Bull, whom he names as DHERMA himself, or the genius of abstract justice, and the MNEUES of Egypt with his companion or symbol, *Apis;* and, though we should be constantly on our guard against the delusion of etymological conjecture, yet we cannot but admit that MINOS and MNEUES, or *Mneuis,* have only Greek terminations, but that the crude noun is composed of the same radical letters both in *Greek* and in *Sanscrit.* 'That APIS and MNEUIS', says Analyst of ancient Mythology, 'were both representations of some personage, appears from the testimony of LYCOPHRON and his scholiast; and that personage was the same, who in *Crete* was styled MINOS, and who was also represented under the emblem of the *Minotaur:* DIODORUS, who confines him to *Egypt,* speaks of him by the title of the bull *Mneuis,* as the first lawgiver, and says, 'That he lived after the age of the gods and heroes, when a change was made in the manner of life among men; that he was a man of a most exalted soul, and a great promoter of civil society, which he benefited by his laws; that those laws were unwritten, and received by him from the chief *Egyptian* deity HERMES, who conferred them on the world as a gift of the highest importance. He was the same', adds my learned friend, 'with MENES, whom the *Egyptians* represented as their first king and principal benefactor, who first sacrificed to the gods, and brought about a great change in diet'. If MINOS, the son of JUPITER, whom the *Cretans,* from national vanity, might have made a native of their own island, was really the same person with MENU, the son of BRAHMĀ, we have the good fortune to restore, by means of *Indian* literature, the most celebrated system of heathen jurisprudence, and this work might have been entitled *The Laws of* MINOS; but the paradox is too singular to be confidently asserted, and the geographical part of the book, with most of the allusions to natural history, must indubitably have been written after the *Hindu* race had settled to the south of *Himālaya.* We cannot but remark that the word MENU has no relation whatever to the *Moon;* and that it was the *seventh,* not the *first,* of that name, whom the *Brāhmens* believe to have been preserved in an ark from the general duluge: him they call the *Child of the Sun,* to distinguish him from our legislator; but they assign to his brother YAMA *the office* (which the *Greeks* were pleased to confer on MINOS) *of Judge in the shades below.*

The name of MENU is clearly derived (like *menes, mens,* and *mind*) from the root *men* to *understand;* and it signifies, as all the *Pandits* agree, *intelligent,* particularly in the doctrines of the *Vēda,* which the composer of our *Dherma Sastra* must have studied very diligently; since great number of its texts, changed only in a few syllables for the sake of the measure, are interspersed through the work and cited at length in the commentaries: the Publick may, therefore, assure themselves, that they now possess a considerable part of the *Hindu* scripture, without the dullness of its profane ritual or much of its mystical jargon. DĀRA SHUCŪH was persuaded, and not without sound reason, that the first MENU of the *Brāhmens* could be no other person than the progenitor of mankind, to whom *Jews, Christians,* and *Muselmāns* unite in giving the name of ADAM; but, whoever he might have been, he is highly honoured by name in the *Vēda* itself, where it is declared, that 'whatever MENU pronounced, was a medicine for the soul'; and the sage VRIHASPETI, now supposed to preside over the planet *Jupiter,* says in his own law tract, that 'MENU held the first rank among legislators, because he had expressed in his code the whole sense of the *Vēda;* that no code was approved, which contradicted MENU; that other *Sāstras,* and treatises on grammar or logick, retained splendour so long only, as MENU, who taught the way to just wealth, to virtue, and to final happiness, was not seen in competition with them': VYĀSA too, the son of PARĀSARA before mentioned, has decided, that 'the *Vēda* with its *Angas,* or the six composition deduced from it, the revealed system of medicine, the *Purānas,* or sacred histories, and the code of MENU, were four works of supreme authority, which ought never to be shaken by arguments merely human'.

It is the general opinion of *Pandits,* that BRAHMĀ taught his laws to MENU in a *hundred thousand verses,* which MENU explained to the primitive world in the very words of the book now translated, where he names himself, after the manner of ancient sages, in the third person; but, in a short preface to the lawtract of NĀRED, it is asserted, that 'MENU, having written the laws of BRAHMĀ in a hundred thousand *slōcas* or couplets, arranged under *twenty-four* heads in a *thousand* chapters, delivered the work to NĀRED, the sage among gods, who abridged it, for the use of mankind, in *twelve thousand* verses, and gave them to a son of BHRIGU, named SUMATI, who, for greater ease to the human race, reduced them to *four thousand;* that mortals read only the second abridgement by SUMATI, while the gods of the lower heaven, and the band of celestial musicians, are engaged in studying the primary code, beginning with the fifth verse, a little varied, of the work now extant on earth; but that nothing remains of NĀRED's abridgement, except an elegant epitome of the *ninth* original title *on the administration of justice'*. Now, since these institutes consist only of *two thousand six hundred and eighty-five* verses, they cannot be the whole work ascribed to SUMATI, which is probably distinguished by the name of the *Vriddha*, or ancient, *Mānava*, and cannot be found entire; though several passages from it, which have been preserved by tradition, are occasionally cited in the new digest.

A number of glosses or comments on MENU were composed by the *Munis*, or old philosophers, whose treatises, together with that before us, constitute the *Dhermasāstra,* in a collective sense, or *Body of Law;* among the more modern commentaries, that called *Mēdhātit'hi,* that by GŌVINDARĀJA, and that by DHARANĪ-DHERA, were once in the greatest repute; but the first was reckoned prolix and unequal; the second, concise but obscure; and the third, often erroneous. At length appeared CULLŪCA BHATTA; who, after a painful course of study, and the collation of numerous manuscripts, produced a work, of which it may, perhaps, be said very truly, that it is the shortest, yet the most luminous, the least ostentatious, yet the most learned, the deepest yet the most agreeable, commentary ever composed on any author ancient or modern, *European* or *Asiatick.* The *Pandits* care so little for genuine chronology, that none of them can tell me the age of CULLŪCA, whom they always name with applause; but he informs us himself, that he was a *Brāhmen* of the *Vārēndra* tribe, whose family had been long settled in *Gaur* or *Bengal,* but that he had chosen his residence among the learned on the banks of the holy river at *Cāsi.* His text and interpretation I have almost implicitly followed, though I had myself collated many copies of MENU, and among them a manuscript of a very ancient date: his gloss is here printed in *Italicks;* and any reader who may choose to pass it over as if unprinted, will have in *Roman* letters an exact version of the original, and may form some idea of its character and structure, as well as of the *Sanscrit* idiom, which must necessarily be preserved in a verbal translation; and a translation not scrupulously verbal would have been highly improper in a work on so delicate and momentous a subject as private and criminal jurisprudence.

Should a series of *Brāhmens* omit, for three generations, the reading of MENU, their sacerdotal class, as all the *Pandits* assure me, would in strictness be forfeited; but they must explain it only to their pupils of the three highest classes; and the *Brāhmen,* who read it with me, requested most earnestly, that his name might be concealed; nor would he have read it for any consideration on a forbidden day of the moon, or without the ceremonies prescribed in the second and fourth chapters for a lecture on the *Vēda:* so great, indeed, is the idea of sanctity annexed to this book, that, when the chief native magistrate at *Banares* endeavoured, at my request, to procure a Persian translation of it, before I had a hope of being at any time able to understand the original, the *Pandits* of his court unanimously and positively refused to assist in the work; nor should I have procured it at all, if a wealthy *Hindu* at *Gayà* had not caused the version to be made by some of his dependants, at the desire of my friend Mr. [Thomas] LAW. The *Persian* translation of MENU, like all others from the *Sanscrit* into that language, is a rude intermixture of the text, loosely rendered, with some old or new comment, and often with the crude notions of the translator; and, though it expresses the general sense of the original, yet it swarms with errours, imputable partly to haste, and partly to ignorance: thus where MENU says, *that emissaries are the eyes of a prince,* the *Persian* phrase makes him ascribe *four eyes* to the person of a king; for the word *chār,* which means an *emmissary* in *Sanscrit,* signifies *four* in the popular dialect.

The work, now presented to the *European* world, contains abundance of curious matter extremely interesting both to speculative lawyers and antiquaries, with many beauties, which need not be pointed out, and with many blemishes, which cannot be justified or palliated. It is a system of despotism and priestcraft, both indeed limited by law, but artfully conspiring to give mutual support, though with mutual checks; it is filled with strange conceits in metaphysicks and natural philosophy, with idle superstitions, and with a scheme of theology most obscurely figurative, and consequently liable to dangerous misconception; it abounds with minute and childish formalities, with ceremonies generally absurd and often ridiculous; the punishments are partial and fanciful, for some crimes dreadfully cruel, for others reprehensibly slight; and the very morals, though rigid enough on the whole, are in one or two instances (as in the case of light oaths and of pious perjury) unaccountably relaxed: nevertheless, a spirit of sublime devotion, of benevolence to mankind, and of amiable tenderness to all sentient creatures, pervades the whole work; the style of it has a certain austere majesty, that sounds like the language of legislation and extorts a respectful awe; the sentiments of independence on all beings but GOD, and the harsh admonitions even to kings are truly noble; and the many panegyricks on the *Gāyatrì,* the *Mother,* as it is called, of the *Vēda,* prove the author to have *adored* (not the visible material sun, but) *that divine and incomparably greater light,* to use the words of the most venerable text in the *Indian* scripture, *which illumines all, delights all, from which all proceed to which all must return, and which alone can irradiate* (not our visual organs merely, but our souls and) *our intellects.* Whatever opinion in short may be formed of MENU and his laws, in a country happily enlightened by sound philosophy and the only true revelation, it must be remembered, that those laws are actually revered, as the word of the Most High, by nations of great importance to the political and commercial interests of *Europe*, and particularly by many millions of *Hindu* subjects, whose well directed industry would add largely to the wealth of *Britain*, and who ask no more in return than protection for their persons and places of abode, justice in their temporal concerns, indulgence to the prejudices of their own religion, and the benefit of those laws, which they have been taught to believe sacred, and which alone they can possibly comprehend.

SOURCE: Can be found in *Sir William Jones: A Reader*, ed. Satya S. Pachori (Delhi: Oxford University Press, 1993). This document was originally published in 1794.

Introductory Report upon the Indian Penal Code
LORD THOMAS BABINGTON MACAULAY

[Lord Thomas Babington Macaulay (1800–1859) was a dominant critic—and advocate as well as historian—of imperial ambitions, both scholastic and political. He wrote voluminously on the topic and its multiple ramifications. His "minute" on Indian education was—and remains—a critical and much-cited contribution to the debate on the respective roles of Indian and English traditions in the issues of governments and instruction. Should the English, for example (and as William Jones argued), learn from and about their Indian subjects? Or vice versa? And what consequences would such considerations bring to the existing relations between colonizer and colonized? Macaulay served in India from 1834 to 1838; he later served as a member of Parliament.]

To the Right Honorable George Lord Auckland, O.G.C.B., Governor-General of India in Council.

My Lord,—The Penal Code which, according to the orders of government of the 15th of June, 1835, we had the honor to lay before your Lordship in Council on the 2d of May last has now been printed under our superintendence, and has, as well as the Notes, been carefully revised and corrected by us while in the press.

The time which has been employed in framing this body of law will not be thought long by any person who is acquainted with the nature of the labor which such works require, and with the history of other works of the same kind. We should, however, have been able to lay it before your Lordship in Council many months earlier but for a succession of unfortunate circumstances against which it was impossible to provide. During a great part of the year 1836, the Commission was rendered almost entirely inefficient by the ill-health of a majority of the members; and we were altogether deprived of the valuable services of our colleague, Mr. Cameron, at the very time when those services were most needed.

It is hardly necessary for us to entreat your Lordship in Council to examine with candor the work which we now submit to you. To the ignorant and inexperienced, the task in which we have been engaged may appear easy and simple. But the members of the Indian government are doubtless well aware that it is among the most difficult tasks in which the human mind can be employed; that persons placed in circumstances far more favorable than ours have attempted it with very doubtful success; that the best codes extant, if malignantly criticised, will be found to furnish matter for censure in every page; that the most copious and precise of human languages furnish but a very imperfect machinery to the legislator; that, in a work so extensive and complicated as that on which we have been employed, there will inevitably be, in spite of the most anxious care, some omissions and some inconsistencies; and that we have done as much as could reasonably be expected from us if we have furnished the government with that which may, by suggestions from experienced and judicious persons, be improved into a good code.

Your Lordship in Council will be prepared to find in this performance those defects which must necessarily be found in the first portion of a code. Such is the relation which exists between the different parts of the law that no part can be brought to perfection while the other parts remain rude. The penal code cannot be clear and explicit while the substantive civil law and the law of procedure are dark and confused. While the rights of individuals and the powers of public functionaries are uncertain, it cannot always be certain whether those rights have been attacked or those powers exceeded.

Your Lordship in Council will perceive that the system of penal law which we propose is not a digest of any existing system, and that no existing system has furnished us even with a groundwork. We trust that your Lordship in Council will not hence infer that we have neglected to inquire, as we are commanded to do by Parliament, into the present state of that part of the law, or that in other parts of our labors we are likely to recommend unsparing innovation, and the entire sweeping-away of ancient usages. We are perfectly aware of the value of that sanction which long prescription and national feeling give to institutions. We are perfectly aware that law-givers ought not to disregard even the unreasonable prejudices of those for whom they legislate. So sensible are we of the importance of these considerations that, though there are not the same objections to innovation in penal legislation as to innovation affecting vested rights of property, yet, if we had found India in possession of a system of criminal law which the people regarded with partiality, we should have been inclined rather to ascertain it, to digest it, and moderately to correct it than to propose a system fundamentally different.

But it appears to us that none of the systems of penal law established in British India has any claim to our attention, except what it may derive from its own intrinsic excellence. All those systems are foreign. All were introduced by conquerors differing in race, manners, language, and religion from the great mass of the people. The criminal law of the Hindoos was long ago superseded, through the greater part of the territories now subject to the Company, by that of the Mahometans, and is certainly the last system of criminal law which an enlightened and humane government would be disposed to revive. The Mahometan criminal law has in its turn been superseded, to a great extent, by the British Regulations. Indeed, in the territories subject to the Presidency of Bombay, the criminal law of the Mahometans, as well as that of the Hindoos, has been altogether discarded, except in one particular class of cases; and even in such cases it is not imperative on the judge to pay any attention to it. The British Regulations, having been made by three different legislatures, contain, as might be expected, very different provisions. Thus, in Bengal, serious forgeries are punishable with imprisonment for a term double of the term fixed for perjury;[1] in the Bombay Presidency, on the contrary, perjury is punishable with imprisonment for a term double of the term fixed for the most aggravated forgeries;[2] in the Madras Presidency, the two offences are exactly on the same footing.[3] In the Bombay Presidency, the escape of a convict is punished with imprisonment for a term double of the term assigned to that offence in the two other presidencies;[4] while a coiner is punished with little more than half the imprisonment assigned to his offence in the other two presidencies.[5] In Bengal, the purchasing of regimental necessaries from soldiers is not punishable except at Calcutta, and is there punishable with a fine of only fifty rupees.[6] In the Madras Presidency, it is punishable with a fine of forty rupees.[7] In the Bombay Presidency, it is punishable with imprisonment for four years.[8] In Bengal, the vending of stamps without a license is

1. Bengal Regulation XVII. of 1817, section ix.
2. Bombay Regulation XIV. of 1827, sections xvi. and xvii.
3. Madras Regulation VI. of 1811, section iii.
4. Bombay Regulation XIV. of 1827, section xxiv., Regulation v. of 1831, section i. Bengal Regulation XII. of 1818, section v. clause 1.
5. Bombay Regulation XVI. of 1827, section xviii. Bengal Regulation XVII. of 1817, section ix. Madras Regulation II. of 1822, section v.
6. Calcutta Rule, Ordinance and Regulation; passed 21st August, registered 18th Nov., 1821.
7. Madras Regulation XIV. of 1832, section ii. clause 1.
8. Bombay Regulation XXII. of 1827, section xix.

punishable with a moderate fine; and the purchasing of stamps from a person not licensed to sell them is not punished at all.[9] In the Madras Presidency, the vendor is punished with a short imprisonment; but there also the purchaser is not punished at all.[10] In the Bombay Presidency, both the vendor and the purchaser are liable to imprisonment for five years, and to flogging.[11]

Thus widely do the systems of penal law now established in British India differ from each other; nor can we recommend any one of the three systems as furnishing even the rudiments of a good code. The penal law of Bengal and of the Madras Presidency is, in fact, Mahometan law, which has gradually been distorted to such an extent as to deprive it of all title to the religious veneration of Mahometans, yet which retains enough of its original peculiarities to perplex and encumber the administration of justice. In substance it now differs at least as widely from the Mahometan penal law as the penal law of England differs from the penal law of France. Yet technical terms and nice distinctions borrowed from the Mahometan law are still retained. Nothing is more usual than for the courts to ask the law officers what punishment the Mahometan law prescribes in a hypothetical case, and then to inflict that punishment on a person who is not within that hypothetical case, and who by the Mahometan law would be liable either to a different punishment or to no punishment. We by no means presume to condemn the policy which led the British government to retain, and gradually to modify, the system of criminal jurisprudence which it found established in these provinces. But it is evident that a body of law thus formed must, considered merely as a body of law, be defective and inconvenient.

The penal law of the Bombay Presidency is all contained in the Regulations; and is almost all to be found in one extensive Regulation.[12] The government of that presidency appears to have been fully sensible of the great advantage which must arise from placing the whole law in a written form before those who are to administer and those who are to obey it; and, whatever may be the imperfections of the execution, high praise is due to the design. The course which we recommend to the government, and which some persons may perhaps consider as too daring, has already been tried at Bombay, and has not produced any of those effects which timid minds are disposed to anticipate even from the most reasonable and useful innovations. Throughout a large territory, inhabited, to a great extent, by a newly conquered population,

---

9. Bengal Regulation x. of 1820, section ix. clause 2.
10. Madras Regulation xiii. of 1816, section x. clause 10.
11. Bombay Regulation xviii. of 1827, section ix. clause 1.
12. Bombay Regulation xiv. of 1827.

all the ancient systems of penal law were at once superseded by a code, and this without the smallest sign of discontent among the people.

It would have given us great pleasure to have found that code such as we could with propriety have taken as the groundwork of a code for all India. But we regret to say that the penal law of the Bombay Presidency has over the penal law of the other presidencies no superiority, except that of being digested. In framing it, the principles according to which crimes ought to be classified and punishments apportioned have been less regarded than in the legislation of Bengal and Madras. The secret destroying of any property, though it may not be worth a single rupee, is punishable with imprisonment for five years.[13] Unlawful confinement, though it may last only for a quarter of an hour, is punishable with imprisonment for five years.[14] Every conspiracy to injure or impoverish any person is punishable with imprisonment for ten years;[15] so that a man who engages in a design as atrocious as the Gunpowder Plot, and one who is party to a scheme for putting off an unsound horse on a purchaser, are classed together, and are liable to exactly the same punishment. Under this law, if two men concert a petty theft, and afterwards repent of their purpose and abandon it, each of them is liable to twenty times the punishment of the actual theft.[16] All assaults which cause a severe shock to the mental feelings of the sufferer are classed with the atrocious crime of rape, and are liable to the punishment of rape; that is, if the courts shall think fit, to imprisonment for fourteen years.[17] The breaking of the window of a house, the dashing to pieces a china cup within a house, the riding over a field of grain in hunting, are classed with the crime of arson, and are punishable, incredible as it may appear, with death. The following is the law on the subject, "Any person who shall wilfully and wrongfully set fire to or otherwise damage or destroy any part of a dwelling-house or building appertaining thereto, or property contained in a dwelling-house, or building or enclosure appertaining thereto, or crops standing or reaped in the field, shall be liable to any of the punishments specified in section iii. of this Regulation."[18] The section to which reference is made contains a list of the punishments authorized by the Bombay code, and at the head of that list stands "Death."

But these errors, the effects probably of inadvertence, are not, in our opin-

---

13. Regulation xiv. of 1827, section xlii. clause 2.
14. Regulation xiv. of 1827, section xxxiii. clause 1.
15. Regulation xvii. of 1828.
16. Regulation xiv. of 1837, section xxxix.
17. Regulation xiv. of 1827, section xxix. clause 1.
18. Regulation xiv. of 1827, section xlii. clause 1.

ion, the most serious faults of the penal code of Bombay. That code contains enactments which it is impossible to excuse on the ground of inadvertence—enactments the language of which shows that when they were framed their whole effect was fully understood, and which appear to us to be directly opposed to the first principles of penal law. One of the first principles of penal law is this, that a person who merely conceals a crime after it has been committed ought not to be punished as if he had himself committed it. By the Bombay code, the concealment after the fact of murder is punishable as murder; the concealment after the fact of gang-robbery is punishable as gang-robbery;[19] and this, though the concealment after the fact of the most cruel mutilations, and of the most atrocious robberies committed by not more than four persons, is not punished at all.

If there be any distinction which more than any other it behooves the legislator to bear constantly in mind, it is the distinction between harm voluntarily caused and harm involuntarily caused. Negligence, indeed, often causes mischief, and often deserves punishment. But to punish a man whose negligence has produced some evil which he never contemplated as if he had produced the same evil knowingly and with deliberate malice is a course which, as far as we are aware, no jurist has ever recommended in theory, and which we are confident that no society would tolerate in practice. It is, however, provided by the Bombay code that the "unintentional commission of any act punishable by that code shall be punished according to the court's judgment of the culpable disregard of injury to others evinced by the person committing the said act; but the punishment for such unintentional commission shall not exceed that prescribed for the offence committed."[20]

We have said enough to show that it is owing not at all to the law, but solely to the discretion and humanity of the judges, that great cruelty and injustice is not daily perpetrated in the Criminal Courts of the Bombay Presidency.

Many important classes of offences are altogether unnoticed by the Bombay code; and this omission appears to us to be very ill supplied by one sweeping clause, which arms the courts with almost unlimited power to punish as they think fit offences against morality, or against the peace and good order of society, if those offences are penal by the religious law of the offender.[21] This clause does not apply to people who profess a religion with which a system of penal jurisprudence is not inseparably connected. And from this state of the law some singular consequences follow. For example, a

19. Regulation XIV. of 1827, section i. clause 1.
20. Regulation XIV. of 1827, section i. clause 8.
21. Regulation XIV. of 1827, section i. clause 1.

Mahometan is punishable for adultery: a Christian is at liberty to commit adultery with impunity.

Such is the state of the penal law in the Mofussil. In the mean time the population which lives within the local jurisdiction of the courts established by the Royal Charters is subject to the English Criminal Law, that is to say, to a very artificial and complicated system—to a foreign system—to a system which was framed without the smallest reference to India—to a system which, even in the country for which it was framed, is generally considered as requiring extensive reform—to a system, finally, which has just been pronounced by a Commission composed of able and learned English lawyers to be so defective that it can be reformed only by being entirely taken to pieces and reconstructed.[22]

Under these circumstances we have not thought it desirable to take as the groundwork of the code any of the systems of law now in force in any part of India. We have, indeed, to the best of our ability, compared the code with all those systems, and we have taken suggestions from all; but we have not adopted a single provision merely because it formed a part of any of those systems. We have also compared our work with the most celebrated systems of Western jurisprudence, as far as the very scanty means of information which were accessible to us in this country enabled us to do so. We have derived much valuable assistance from the French code, and from the decisions of the French courts of justice on questions touching the construction of that code. We have derived assistance still more valuable from the code of Louisiana, prepared by the late Mr. Livingston. We are the more desirous to acknowledge our obligations to that eminent jurist, because we have found ourselves under the necessity of combating his opinions on some important questions.

The reasons for those provisions which appear to us to require explanation or defence will be found appended to the Code in the form of notes. Should your Lordship in Council wish for fuller information as to the considerations by which we have been guided in framing any part of the law, we shall be ready to afford it.

One peculiarity in the manner in which this code is framed will immediately strike your Lordship in Council—we mean the copious use of illustrations. These illustrations will, we trust, greatly facilitate the understanding of the law, and will at the same time often serve as a defence of the law. In our definitions we have repeatedly found ourselves under the necessity of sacrificing neatness and perspicuity to precision, and of using harsh expressions

---

22. Letter to Lord John Russell from the Commissioners appointed to inquire into the state of the Criminal Law, dated 19th January, 1837.

because we could find no other expressions which would convey our whole meaning, and no more than our whole meaning. Such definitions standing by themselves might repel and perplex the reader, and would perhaps be fully comprehended only by a few students after long application. Yet such definitions are found, and must be found, in every system of law which aims at accuracy. A legislator may, if he thinks fit, avoid such definitions, and by avoiding them he will give a smoother and more attractive appearance to his workmanship; but in that case he flinches from a duty which he ought to perform, and which somebody must perform. If this necessary but most disagreeable work be not performed by the law-giver once for all, it must be constantly performed in a rude and imperfect manner by every judge in the empire, and will probably be performed by no two judges in the same way. We have therefore thought it right not to shrink from the task of framing these unpleasing but indispensable parts of a code. And we hope that when each of these definitions is followed by a collection of cases falling under it, and of cases which, though at first sight they appear to fall under it, do not really fall under it, the definition and the reasons which led to the adoption of it will be readily understood. The illustrations will lead the mind of the student through the same steps by which the minds of those who framed the law proceeded, and may sometimes show him that a phrase which may have struck him as uncouth, or a distinction which he may have thought idle, was deliberately adopted for the purpose of including or excluding a large class of important cases. In the study of geometry it is constantly found that a theorem which, read by itself, conveyed no distinct meaning to the mind, becomes perfectly clear as soon as the reader casts his eye over the statement of the individual case taken for the purpose of demonstration. Our illustrations, we trust, will in a similar manner facilitate the study of the law.

There are two things which a legislator should always have in view while he is framing laws; the one is, that they should be, as far as possible, precise: the other, that they should be easily understood. To unite precision and simplicity in definitions intended to include large classes of things, and to exclude others very similar to many of those which are included, will often be utterly impossible. Under such circumstances it is not easy to say what is the best course. That a law, and especially a penal law, should be drawn in words which convey no meaning to the people who are to obey it, is an evil. On the other hand, a loosely-worded law is no law, and to whatever extent a legislature uses vague expressions, to that extent it abdicates its functions, and resigns the power of making law to the courts of justice.

On the whole, we are inclined to think that the best course is that which we have adopted. We have, in framing our definitions, thought principally of making them precise, and have not shrunk from rugged or intricate phraseology when such phraseology appeared to us to be necessary to precision. If it appeared to us that our language was likely to perplex an ordinary reader, we added as many illustrations as we thought necessary for the purpose of explaining it. The definitions and enacting clauses contain the whole law. The illustrations make nothing law which would not be law without them. They only exhibit the law in full action, and show what its effects will be on the events of common life.

Thus the code will be at once a statute-book and a collection of decided cases. The decided cases in the code will differ from the decided cases in the English law-books in two most important points. In the first place, our illustrations are never intended to supply any omission in the written law, nor do they ever, in our opinion, put a strain on the written law. They are merely instances of the practical application of the written law to the affairs of mankind. Secondly, they are cases decided not by the judges but by the legislature, by those who make the law, and who must know more certainly than any judge can know what the law is which they mean to make.

The power of construing the law in cases in which there is any real reason to doubt what the law is amounts to the power of making the law. On this ground the Roman jurists maintained that the office of interpreting the law in doubtful matters necessarily belonged to the legislature. The contrary opinion was censured by them with great force of reason, though in language perhaps too bitter and sarcastic for the gravity of a code. "Eorum vanam subtilitatem tam risimus quam corrigendam esse censuimus. Si enim in præsenti leges condere soli imperatori concessum est, et leges interpretari solo dignum imperio esse oportet. Quis legum reningmata solvere et omnibus aperire idoneus esse videbitur nisi is cui legislatorem esse concessum est? Explosis itaque his ridiculosis ambiguitatibus tam conditor quam interpres legum solus imperator juste existimabitur."[23]

The decisions on particular cases which we have annexed to the provisions of the code resemble the imperial rescripts in this, that they proceed from the same authority from which the provisions themselves proceed. They differ from the imperial rescripts in this most important circumstance, that they are not made *ex post facto,* that they cannot therefore be made to serve any particular turn, that the persons condemned or absolved by them are purely imaginary persons, and that, therefore, whatever may be thought of the wisdom of any judgment which we have passed, there can be no doubt of its impartiality.

23. Cod. Just. lib. i. tit. xiv. 12.

The publication of this collection of cases decided by legislative authority will, we hope, greatly limit the power which the courts of justice possess of putting their own sense on the laws. But we are sensible that neither this collection nor any other can be sufficiently extensive to settle every question which may be raised as to the construction of the code. Such questions will certainly arise, and, unless proper precautions be taken, the decisions on such questions will accumulate till they form a body of law of far greater bulk than that which has been adopted by the legislature. Nor is this the worst. While the judicial system of British India continues to be what it now is, these decisions will render the law not only bulky, but uncertain and contradictory. There are at present eight chief courts subject to the legislative power of your Lordship in Council, four established by Royal Charter, and four which derive their authority from the Company. Every one of these tribunals is perfectly independent of the others. Every one of them is at liberty to put its own construction on the law; and it is not to be expected that they will always adopt the same construction. Under so inconvenient a system there will inevitably be, in the course of a few years, a large collection of decisions diametrically opposed to each other, and all of equal authority.

How the powers and mutual relations of these courts may be placed on a better footing, and whether it be possible or desirable to have in India a single tribunal empowered to expound the code in the last resort, are questions which must shortly engage the attention of the Law Commission. But whether the present judicial organization be retained or not, it is most desirable that measures should be taken to prevent the written law from being overlaid by an immense weight of comments and decisions. We conceive that it is proper for us, at the time at which we lay before your Lordship in Council the first part of the Indian code, to offer such suggestions as have occurred to us on this important subject.

We do not think is desirable that the Indian legislature should, like the Roman emperors, decide doubtful points of law which have actually been mooted in cases pending before the tribunals. In criminal cases, with which we are now more immediately concerned, we think that the accused party ought always to have the advantage of a doubt on a point of law, if that doubt be entertained after mature consideration by the highest judicial authority, as well as of a doubt on a matter of fact. In civil suits which are actually pending, we think it, on the whole, desirable to leave to the courts the office of deciding doubtful questions of law which have actually arisen in the course of litigation. But every case in which the construction put by a judge on any part of the code is set aside by any of those tribunals from which at present there is no appeal in India, and every case in which there is a difference of opinion in a court composed of several judges as to the construction of any part of the code, ought to be forthwith reported to the legislature. Every judge of every rank whose duty it is to administer the law as contained in the code should be enjoined to report to his official superiors every doubt which he may entertain as to any question of construction which may have arisen in his court. Of these doubts, all which are not obviously unreasonable ought to be periodically reported by the highest judicial authorities to the legislature. All the questions thus reported to the government might with advantage be referred for examination to the Law Commission, if that Commission should be a permanent body. In some cases it will be found that the law is already sufficiently clear, and that any misconstruction which may have taken place is to be attributed to weakness, carelessness, wrongheadedness or corruption on the part of an individual, and is not likely to occur again. In such cases it will be unnecessary to make any change in the code. Sometimes it will be found that a case has arisen respecting which the code is silent. In such a case it will be proper to supply the omission. Sometimes it may be found that the code is inconsistent with itself. If so, the inconsistency ought to be removed. Sometimes it will be found that the words of the law are not sufficiently precise. In such a case it will be proper to substitute others. Sometimes it will be found that the language of the law, though it is as precise as the subject admits, is not so clear that a person of ordinary intelligence can see its whole meaning. In these cases it will generally be expedient to add illustrations, such as may distinctly show in what sense the legislature intends the law to be understood, and may render it impossible that the same question, or any similar question, should ever again occasion difference of opinion. In this manner every successive edition of the code will solve all the important questions as to the construction of the code which have arisen since the appearance of the edition immediately preceding. Important questions, particularly questions about which courts of the highest rank have pronounced opposite decisions, ought to be settled without delay; and no point of law ought to continue to be a doubtful point more than three or four years after it has been mooted in a court of justice. An addition of a very few pages to the code will stand in the place of several volumes of reports, and will be of far more value than such reports, inasmuch as the additions to the code will proceed from the legislature, and will be of unquestionable authority; whereas the reports would only give the opinions of the judges, which other judges might venture to set aside.

It appears to us also highly desirable that, if the code shall be adopted, all those penal laws which the Indian legislature may from time to time find it necessary to pass should be framed in such a manner as to fit into the code.

Their language ought to be that of the code. No word ought to be used in any other sense than that in which it is used in the code. The very part of the code in which the new law is to be inserted ought to be indicated. If the new law rescinds or modifies any provision of the code, that provision ought to be indicated. In fact, the new law ought, from the day on which it is passed, to be part of the code, and to affect all the other provisions of the code, and to be affected by them as if it were actually a clause of the original code. In the next edition of the code, the new law ought to appear in its proper place.

For reasons which have been fully stated to your Lordship in Council in another communication, we have not inserted in the code any clause declaring to what places and to what classes of persons it shall apply.

Your Lordship in Council will see that we have not proposed to except from the operation of this code any of the ancient sovereign houses of India residing within the Company's territories. Whether any such exception ought to be made is a question which, without a more accurate knowledge than we possess of existing treaties, of the sense in which those treaties have been understood, of the history of negotiations, of the temper and of the power of particular families, and of the feeling of the body of the people towards those families, we could not venture to decide. We will only beg permission most respectfully to observe that every such exception is an evil; that it is an evil that any man should be above the law; that it is a still greater evil that the public should be taught to regard as a high and enviable distinction the privilege of being above the law; that the longer such privileges are suffered to last, the more difficult it is to take them away; that there can scarcely ever be a fairer opportunity for taking them away than at the time when the government promulgates a new code binding alike on persons of different races and religions; and that we greatly doubt whether any consideration, except that of public faith solemnly pledged, deserves to be weighed against the advantages of equal justice.

The peculiar state of public feeling in this country may render it advisable to frame the law of procedure in such a manner that families of high rank may be dispensed, as far as possible, from the necessity of performing acts which are here regarded, however unreasonably, as humiliating. But though it may be proper to make wide distinctions as respects form, there ought in our opinion to be, as respects substance, no distinctions except those which the government is bound by express engagements to make. That a man of rank should be examined with particular ceremonies or in a particular place may, in the present state of Indian society, be highly expedient. But that a man of any rank should be allowed to commit crimes with impunity must in every state of society be most pernicious.

The provisions of the code will be applicable to offences committed by soldiers, as well as to offences committed by other members of the community. But for those purely military offences which soldiers only can commit, we have made no provision. It appears to us desirable that this part of the law should be taken up separately, and we have been given to understand that your Lordship in Council has determined that it shall be so taken up. But we have, as your Lordship in Council will perceive, made provision for punishing persons who, not being themselves subject to martial law, abet soldiers in the breach of military discipline.

Your Lordship in Council will observe that in many parts of the penal code we have referred to the code of procedure, which as yet is not in existence; and hence it may possibly be supposed to be our opinion that, till the code of procedure is framed, the penal code cannot come into operation. Such, however, is not our meaning. We conceive that almost the whole of the penal code, such as we now lay it before your Lordship, might be made law, at least in the Mofussil, without any considerable change in the existing rules of procedure. Should your Lordship in Council agree with us in this opinion, we shall be prepared to suggest those changes which it would be necessary immediately to make.

In conclusion, we beg respectfully to suggest that, if your Lordship in Council is disposed to adopt the code which we have framed, it is most desirable that the native population should, with as little delay as possible, be furnished with good versions of it in their own languages. Such versions, in our opinion, can be produced only by the combined labors of enlightened Europeans and natives; and it is not probable that men competent to execute all the translations which will be required would be found in any single province of India. We are sensible that the difficulty of procuring good translations will be great; but we believe that the means at the disposal of your Lordship in Council are sufficient to overcome every difficulty; and we are confident that your Lordship in Council will not grudge anything that may be necessary for the purpose of enabling the people who are placed under your care to know what that law is according to which they are required to live.

> We have the honor to be, my Lord,
> Your Lordship's most obedient humble servants,
> T. B. Macaulay,
> J. M. Macleod,
> G. W. Anderson,
> F. Millett.
> Indian Law Commission, October 14, 1837.

NOTES

Note (A). On the Chapter of Punishments.

First among the punishments provided for offences by this code stands death. No argument that has been brought to our notice has satisfied us that it would be desirable wholly to dispense with this punishment. But we are convinced that it ought to be very sparingly inflicted, and we propose to employ it only in cases where either murder or the highest offence against the State has been committed.

SOURCE: In *Miscellaneous Works of Lord Macaulay,* ed. Lady Trevelyan (New York: Harper and Brothers, 1880). This report was originally published in 1837.

VII
THUGGEE/THAGI

INTRODUCTION
Decriminalizing the Landscape: Thugs and Poisoners
MIA CARTER

EVIDENCE OF THE DRAMATIC need for British forms of law and government in India could be found in the sensational representations of the subcontinent's criminality. In addition to the alleged inconsistency of native laws, India's landscape was purportedly peopled by "villains as subtle, rapacious, and cruel, as any who are to be met in the records of human depravity." The former description, taken from Captain, later Major-General, W. H. Sleeman's accounts of Indian criminality, combines police surveillance and the practices of orientalist scholarship. Sleeman's "The Ramaseeana, or Vocabulary of the Thug Language" (1839) catalogs the density and variety of the thug vocabulary as a means of displaying the intricacy of the thugs' criminal genius and the totality of India's outlaw culture. In Sleeman's history of "that extraordinary fraternity of assassins," *The Thugs or Phansigars of India* (1839), he described the extensiveness of banditry in the colony and outlined a plan for its suppression: "Every arrest brought to light new combinations and associations of these professed assassins, and discovered new scenes in which their dreadful trade was at work. It was obvious that nothing but a general system, undertaken by a paramount power, strong enough to bear down all opposition by interested native chiefs, could ever eradicate such well-organized villainy." The representations of thuggee/thagi (banditry) served to document the need for an expansive and aggressive police force in the colony; Fanny Parks Parlby's *Wanderings of A Pilgrim* (1850) describes the circulation of an 1829 pamphlet, "The Confessions of a Thug," to the judges of various colonial stations.

The accounts of thugs and poisoners activated administrative policy and stimulated the literary imagination as well; Philip Meadows Taylor's romance, *The Confessions of a Thug* (1837), was inspired by Sleeman's accounts. Meadows Taylor, a civil servant, volunteered to collect evidence against the thugs, which became fictionalized in the novel. Meadows Taylor's florid and romantic prose reveals the intensity of the fascination with thuggee; note, for example, the eroticized description of thug confessor, Ameer Ali. Popular representations of thuggee/thagi were distributed in paintings and etchings and are evident in twentieth-century representations like the films *Gunga Din* and the Beatles' *Help!* The vivid representations and administrative discourses on thuggee/thagi, native criminality, advanced policing systems, and legal reform also inflamed the imaginations of politicians and statesmen in Great Britain. The working class "street Arabs" and Irish "hooligans" at home were the subjects of equally zealous reform campaigns that would, in the near future, receive similar kinds of public interest and administrative scrutiny.

BIBLIOGRAPHY

Buford, Bill. *Among the Thugs*. London: Secker and Warburg, 1991.
Hall, Stuart, et al. *Policing the Crisis: Mugging, The State, and Law and Order*. London: Macmillan, 1978.
Hutton, James. *Thugs and Dacoits of India*. London: W. H. Allen, 1857; reprint, Delhi: Gian Publications, 1981.
Kapur, Shekhar. *The Bandit Queen* (India/U.K., 1994). Film.
Lester, Richard. *Help!* (U.K., 1965). Film.
Metcalf, Thomas R. *Ideologies of the Raj*. Cambridge: Cambridge University Press, 1995.
Singha, Radhika. *A Despotism of Law: Crime and Justice in Early Colonial India*. Oxford: Oxford University Press, 1998.
Srivastava, Ramesh Chandra. *Development of the Judicial System in India Under the East India Company, 1833–1858*. Lucknow: n.p., 1971.
Stevens, George. *Gunga Din* (U.S., 1939). Film.
Wightman, Archibald John. *No Friend for Travelers*. London: Hale, 1959.

The Ramaseeana, or Vocabulary of the Thug Language
CAPTAIN WILLIAM H. SLEEMAN

[Captain William Henry "Thuggee" Sleeman (1788–1856) served as chief agent under Lord William Bentinck, the governor-general of India (1833–35) and a famous reformer. Sleeman combined his orientalist interests with his professional military duties; he solicited incriminating evidence from captured thugs and collected their vocabulary and phrases for his scholarship. Sleeman is credited for having "exterminated" the thugs and bandits of India. Between 1831 and 1837, over three thousand thugs were captured; more than four hundred of them were executed. Close to five hundred thugs gave state evidence, and the remainder were transported or imprisoned for life. Sleeman published his memoirs, *Rambles and Recollections of an Indian Official*, in 1844. He was promoted to major and knighted by Queen Victoria for his Indian service.]

Angjhap: A term used by the Thugs of the Duckun for Rehna, or a temporary burial of bodies.

Ard,hul: Any bad omen; the same as Khurtul. Both terms are confined to Duckun Thugs.

Adhoreea: Any person who has separated himself from a party whom the Thugs have murdered or intend to murder, and thereby escaped them.

Agasse: A turban. A Thug never moves out without his turban, except in Bengal perhaps. If a turban is set on fire, it threatens great evil, and the gang must if near home, return and wait seven days; if at a distance, an offering of goor is made, and the individual to whom the turban belonged, alone returns home. If the turban falls off it is an omen almost as bad, and requires the same sacrifices.

Aulae: A Thug, in contradistinction to Beeto, any person not a Thug. When Thugs wish to ascertain whether the persons they meet are Thugs or not, they accost them with "Aulae Bhae Ram Ram," in Hindoo. This to any

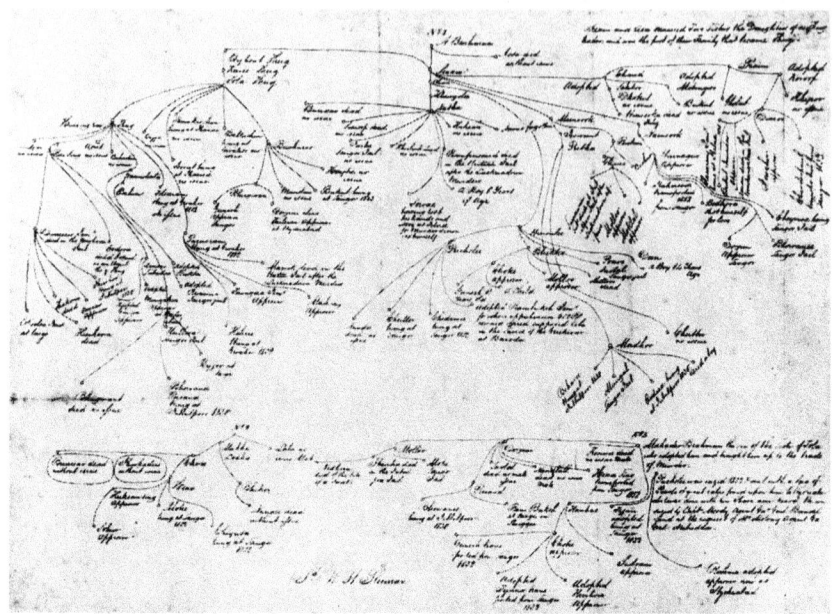

A thug "family tree" (1836). From W. H. Sleeman, "Papers on Thuggee," reproduced in Francis Tuker, *The Yellow Scarf: The Story of the Life of Thuggee Sleeman* (London: J. M. Dent and Sons, 1961).

Thug depradations (1836), by "Thuggee" Sleeman and his staff. Reproduced in Francis Tuker, *The Yellow Scarf: The Story of the Life of Thuggee Sleeman* (London: J. M. Dent and Sons, 1961).

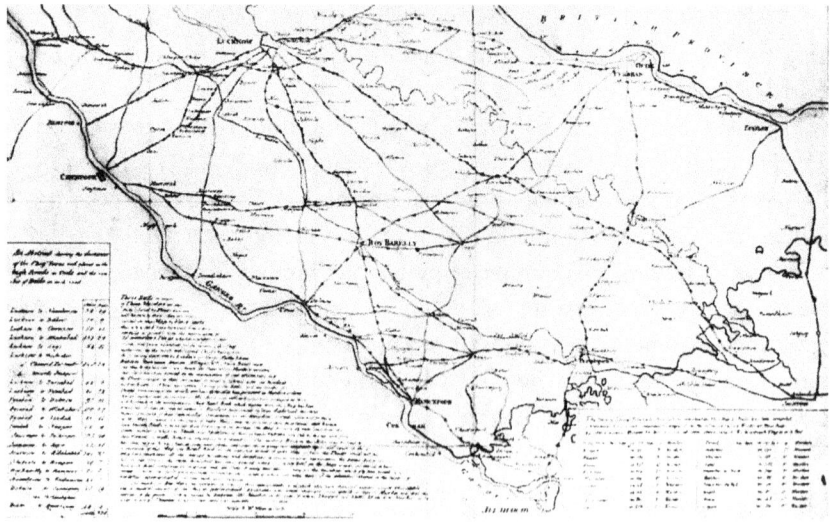

Thugs giving a demonstration of their method of strangulation (1855). Photo by F. Beato. In Francis Tuker, *The Yellow Scarf: The Story of the Life of Thuggee Sleeman* (London: J. M. Dent and Sons, 1961).

one but a Thug would seem the common salutation of "peace to thee, friend," but it would be instantly recognized by a Thug. Any man that should reply in the same manner would be quite safe.

Balmeek: The author of one of the three Ramaens (or histories of the rape of Seeta, the wife of Ram, one of the incarnations of Vishnoo) which after its author is called the Balmeek Ramaen. The Thugs consider Balmeek to have been of their profession; but, though they quote his name with reverence, they do not, I believe, invoke it in their offerings and sacrifices. A sketch of his life is given in each of the three Ramaens. His name was Dojadh,un, and he is said to have been a Brahmin by birth; to have been born at Kunoje in the latter end of the Sutjoog, or golden age; to have lost his parents when he was five years of age, and soon after to have joined some gangs of Bheel robbers, who, armed with bows and arrows, infested the roads about Chutterkote; to have married one of their daughters, and to have become the most noted robber and murderer of his day. From this course of life he is said to have been reclaimed by a miracle. Seven celebrated saints, at their holy place of abode, learned by inspiration that a Brahmin was thus disgracefully employed, and proceeded to the place to admonish him. He saw them approach, and as usual bent his bow, and demanded their money or their lives. "Why do you, a Brahmin by birth, follow this horrible trade, and rob and murder innocent travellers?" "I have a wife and children whom I love, on the top of yonder hill; they want food, and I must provide it for them." "Go and ask those you love, and for whom you provide food by the murder of innocent men, whether they are willing to share with you in the crimes as well as in the fruits." "And in the mean time you will make off. Many a traveller has tried to escape me by similar tricks, but I am not to be deceived." "We swear to remain till you return." He went to his wife and children and asked the questions. They told him that they shared in what he brought to them, but he must be alone answerable for the means by which he acquired it. He returned to the saints, with a contrite heart, and implored their instructions. They told him to tarry where he stood till they should return, and continue to repeat the words, "Mura, Mura, Mura," dead, dead, dead, which was familiar to him; knowing that he would in time convert it into Ram, Ram, Ram, God, God, God; and thinking that his soul was not yet fitted to repeat the holy name. He soon made the expected change, and continued to repeat Ram, Ram, Ram, for twelve thousand years, when the seven saints returned. Nothing but the bones remained, but they were erect, and repeating the holy name of Ram. White ants had built their hill over them, but on hearing their voice the skeleton assumed a form of godlike beauty, and burst forth, as it is said, like the sun from behind a dark cloud. He became a man after God's own heart, and wrote his Ramaen by inspiration. Balmee signifies ant hill, and the *k* affixed signifies, born of, and his name was changed from Dojadhun to Balmeek.

Bajeed: Safe, free from danger. When the Thugs have got their victims at the place where they intend to murder them, if the spies placed around, see all clear, they call out one of the following names, and the work of murder goes on. Bajeed or Bajeed Khan, Deo or Deomun, or Deo-

Bunjaree: A cat. If a cat comes to them at their lodgings at night it promises good fortune.

Bungur: A Thug term peculiar to Duckun Thugs.

Buneana: To stain with blood a cloth or any other thing.

Bunar: Same as Baee. Bad news, untoward discovery of the Thugs' proceedings: also a road become unsafe for Thugs.

Bhurtote: A strangler.

Bhurtotee: The office or duty of strangler. Thugs seldom attain this rank or office till they have been on many expeditions, and acquired the requisite courage or insensibility by slow degrees. At first they are almost always shocked and frightened; but after a time they say they lose all sympathy with the victims. A Thug leader, of most polished manners and great eloquence, being asked one day in my presence by a native gentleman, whether he never felt compunction in murdering innocent people, replied with a smile, "Does any man feel compunction in following his trade; and are not all our trades assigned us by Providence." The native gentleman said, "How many people have you in the course of your life killed with your own hands at a rough guess?" "I have killed none!" "Have you not been just describing to me a number of murders?" "Yes; but do you suppose I could have committed them. Is any man killed from man's killing? *Admee ke marne se koe murta.* Is it not the hand of God that kills him? and are we not mere instruments in the hand of God?" They are first employed as scouts; then as sextons; then as shumseeas or holders of hands; and lastly as Bhurtotes. When a man feels that he has sufficient courage and insensibility for the purpose, he solicits the oldest and most renowned Thug of the gang to make him his cheyla, or disciple. The Thug agrees to become his gooroo, or spiritual preceptor, and when the gang falls in with a man of respectability but not much strength, fitted for the purpose, he tells the gooroo that he is prepared, with his permission, to try his hands upon him. While the traveller is asleep with the gang at their quarters, the gooroo takes his disciple into a neighboring field followed by three or four old members of the gang. On reaching the spot chosen, they all face to the direction the gang intends to move, and the gooroo says, "Oh Kalee, Kunkalee, Bhudkalee. Oh Kalee, Mahakalee, Calcutta Walee.[1] If it seemeth to thee

---

[1]. The Thugs, and I understand all other Hindoos, believe Kalee to have first appeared upon the earth in Calcutta. They believe also that after she had, through the means of the Thugs created by her for the special purpose, destroyed the great Demon "*Rukut beej dana*" at Bindachul, on the eastern extremity of the Vindeya range, she carried the body to Calcutta and there buried it where her temple now stands. That place they consider to be her favourite seat where she *works more miracles* than in all the rest of India. They have got a notion that in Calcutta even the Christians attend her worship, and make offerings to her temple; and I believe the priests have always actually made offerings to her image on great occasions in the name of the Hon'ble Company out of the rents of the land with which government has endowed the temple. European gentlemen and ladies frequently attend the nautches and feasts of her great days in the *Durja Pooja;* and as these feasts are part of the religious ceremonies, this innocent curiosity is very liable to be misconstrued by people at a distance from the scene, and should not therefore be indulged. The Hindoos have a verse which they often repeat in their invocations. "*Kalee! Calcutta walee! tera buchun na jawe Khalee. Oh Kalee, great goddess of Calcutta, may thy promise never be made in vain.*" She is said to delight in the name of *Kunkalee*, or man-eater, and to be always drinking the blood of men and of demons. The term means, I believe, the same thing as *Kunkulin.* They all believe Kalee to have been extremely black, and to have had features so terrifically hideous that no mortal man could dare to look upon them.

When Kalee or Parbuttee appears in company with her husband, Siwa or Mahadeo, she is represented as beautiful and fair, and is commonly called *Gouree,* or the *fair.* It was only when she came to destroy demons, or as the Goddess of war, that she is supposed to have put on these hideous shapes. In a beautiful piece of sculpture at Beragur on the Nerbudda river, she is represented as seated on a bull behind her husband, whose dress and ornaments are, as usual, composed of snakes, very gracefully twisted and suspended around him. This piece of sculpture is called *Gouree Shunkur,* after her name *Gouree,* and that of Mahadco, *Shunkur;* and it is so much superior to any other they are accustomed to see, that the people, from the most learned to the most unlettered, implicitly believe that the God and Goddess came here, mounted as they now

fit that the traveller now at our lodging should die by the hands of this thy slave, vouch-safe us the Thibaoo." If they get the auspice on the right within a certain time (half an hour), it signifies her sanction; but if they have no sign, or the dhilhaoo, (or sign on the left,) some other Thug must put the traveller to death, and the candidate for honour wait for another time.

Davey's sanction having been conveyed in the Thibaoo, they return to their quarters, and the gooroo takes a handkerchief, and, facing to the west, ties the knot in one end of it with a rupee or other piece of silver inserted. This knot they call the Goor Ghat, or classic knot, and no man who has not been thus ordained by the high priest, is permitted to tie it. See *Goor Ghat*. The disciple receives it respectfully from the high priest in his right hand, and stands over the victim, with a shumseea, or holder of hands, by his side. The traveller is roused on some pretence or other, and the disciple passes the handkerchief over his neck, at the signal given by the leader of the gang, and strangles him with the aid of his shumseea. Having finished his work, he bows down before his gooroo, and touches his feet with both hands, and does the same to all his relations and friends present, in gratitude for the honour he has attained. He opens the knot after he has heard or seen the Thibaoo, or auspice on the right, takes out the rupee and gives it, with all the other silver he has, to his gooroo, as a nuzur; and the gooroo adding what money he has at the time, purchases a rupee and a quarter's worth of goor for the Tuponee, and lays out the rest in sweetmeats. The Tuponee sacrifice is now performed under the neem, the mango, or the byr, if they are available, and if not, under any other tree except the babul, the sirsa (mamosa series) and the reonja. The new disciple now takes his seat among the Bhurtotes around the carpet, and receives his share of the consecrated sugar, and the sweetmeats are distributed to all the members of the gang of whatever grade. On his return home after the expedition he gives a feast to his gooroo and his family; and if he has the means, to all his relations; and he presents his gooroo with an entire new suit of clothes for himself and one for his wife, and others for his relations, if he can afford it.

---

are, on a visit to the Nurbudda, from the mountain *Khylas,* and got their earthly parts turned into stone as a memorial of their visit, and will some day resume them.

The whole is cut out of one block of lava from a dyke in the marble rocks through which the Nurbudda flows beneath the temple which is consecrated to them. The wall of the court in which the temple stands is lined all round by the statues of some three scores *Jognies,* or petty goddesses, who attend upon Parbuttee, about the size of life, cut out of rocks of different kinds, with various faces and in various attitudes, and all mounted upon different *Bahuns,* or vehicles of birds and quadrupeds. They are all sadly mutilated, and the God and Goddess within are said to have been saved by a miracle from *Aurungebe* and his army, to whom these things are always attributed. At this temple an annual fair is held in the beginning of November.

The gooroo after a certain interval, returns the compliment to him and his family, and the relation between them is ever after respected as the most sacred that can be formed. A Thug will often rather betray his father than the gooroo by whom he has been knighted.

The Bhurtote is not permitted to bathe on the day he has strangled any one: formerly no member of the gang was permitted to bathe on the day that a murder was committed, but now the stranglers alone are forbidden to do so.

Buhup, Buhupna, Buhapjana: To go, or escape; as a traveller from the snares of the Thugs, or Thugs from pursuit.

Bara Muttee: The call of the lizard. At whatever time and place they hear the call of the lizard, they consider it a very good omen. The fall of a lizard, upon a Thug is considered a very bad omen; and if it falls upon any garment, that garment must be given away in charity. If it falls upon the ground it threatens nothing.

Baroonee: An old and venerable Thug woman, who is much respected by the fraternity.

I have heard of only one woman who has gone herself on Thug expeditions, and that is the wife of Bukhtawur Jemadar, of the Sooseea class of Thugs. She and her husband are still at large in the Jypore territory. She has often assisted her husband in strangling; and on one occasion strangled a man who had overpowered and stunned her husband. Mothers, I know, have often made their sons go on Thuggee when they would not otherwise have gone, and wives on some occasions their husbands; and I have heard of one woman in the Duckun who kept herself a small gang of Thugs; but Bukhtawur's wife is the only woman that has, as far as I can learn, gone on Thuggee herself.

Bunij Ladhna: Literally, to load the goods; technically, to murder the travellers.

Cheeha: A Coward, timid Thug, one who shows sympathy or fear.

Jhirnee: The signal for strangling; this is commonly given either by the leader of the gang, or the Beiha, who has chosen the place for the murder.

Guthonie: A knot in a turban, or any other piece of cloth in which money or jewels may be concealed.

Puthoree or *Kosut:* The loud and continued chirping or calling of the small owl. If made by the bird while sitting, it promises good. If while flying, it threatens evil. The chatter or call when sitting is interpreted according to the rules of the Thibaoo or Pilaoo.

Puteear: The call of the partridge. If heard while the Thugs are travelling, the call on the left promises good, and on the right threatens slight evil. If they are halting at the time, the call on the right is good, that on the left bad.

Putoree: The small owl.

Qulundera: One of the sects of Moltanee Thugs, who travel with bears and monkeys.

Rooh: An affix to the number of persons killed in any affair; a single person killed in an Eeloo, when two persons are killed, the affair is a Bhitree, three Singhore, four Behra, five Puchrooh, six Chehrooh, and so on.

Raba: Any trick of Thugs.

Richee: Behind. Peculiar to a few classes, and obsolete.

Rugon: An omen good or bad.

Rugnoutee: Taking the auspices.

Even the most sensible approvers who have been with me for many years, as well Musulmans as Hindoos, believe that their good or ill success always depended upon the skill with which the omens were discovered and interpreted, and the strictness with which they were observed and obeyed. One of the old Sindouse stock told me yesterday (May 30th, 1835) in presence of twelve others from Hydrabad, Behar, the Dooab, Oude, Rajpootana, and Bundelcund, assembled for the purpose of revising this vocabulary, that had they not attended to these omens they could never have thrived as they did, and that in ordinary cases of murder a man seldom escaped after one of them, while they and their families had for ten generations thrived, though they had murdered hundreds of people. "This," said he, "could never have been the case, had we not attended to omens, and had not omens been intended for us. There were always signs around us to guide us to rich booty and warn us of danger, had we been always wise enough to discern them and religious enough to attend to them." Every Thug present concurred with him from his soul.

Raja: Term among Duckun Thugs for Mahee or Thakur: the loud full call of the large owl. Jungjore Raja: Two large owls responding to each other; at all times and in all situations a bad omen.

Raookar: Sahookar, a banker.

Roukee: A police choukedar or guard—Roukeea, a police-man.

Rukut Beej[2] Dana: The Thugs have a tradition that a demon by name Rukut Beej Dana infested the world and devoured mankind as often as they were born or created; and to enable the world to be peopled Kalee Davey determined to put him to death. This demon they say was so tall that the deepest ocean never reached above his waist; and he could, consequently, walk over the world at his ease. Kalee Davey attacked him, and cut him down; but

---

2. Rukut, blood, and Beej, seed. All Hindoos believe in this demon having been destroyed by the consort of Mahadeo in the form of Kalee, but those who are not Thugs suppose that when she found every drop of blood, as it reached the ground producing another demon to wage war with her, she licked them all off with her enormous tongue as she cut off their heads.

from every drop of his blood another clans, were all that were at Delhie as Thugs; and that they derived their descent from seven brothers. This however is not probable. Musulman Thugs all over India are very proud to trace their descent from one or other of these great stocks, and he who can do so is generally treated as a man of superior birth.

Satha: The first seven days of an expedition, during which the families of those engaged in one expedition admit no visits from the families of Thugs who are absent on another expedition, lest the travellers destined for the one should go over to the other gang; neither must they eat any thing that has belonged to the families of such other Thugs. The Thugs engaged in the expedition do not till the seventh day dress any food in ghee, nor eat any animal food but fish; nor shave, nor allow their clothes to be washed by a dhoby, nor indulge in any sexual intercourse, nor give in charity, not even part of their food to a dog, cat or jackal. They must not bathe nor eat any sugar, except what the leader brought with him on setting out. Formerly they never ate any salt or turmeric, but now they do. On the seventh day they have a good meal of which greens of some kind or other must be a component part. During the whole time the expedition lasts, if within one year, they take no milk, nor do they clean their teeth with a brush (miswak.)

If the Sonrka, or first murder, takes place within the seven days, or Satha, they consider themselves relieved by it from all these restraints. Formerly they never used to murder as the Sonrka (or first victim) any Brahman, or Syad, or any very poor man, nor any man with gold upon him, nor any man who had a quadruped with him, nor a dhobee, nor a sweeper, nor a teylee (oil vender), nor a bhaut (bard), nor a kaet (a writer), nor a blind man, nor maimed persons, nor a leper, nor a dancing woman, nor a pilgrim or devotee. Some classes and individuals neglect these rules and the misfortunes which have fallen upon Thugs lately are attributed principally to this cause.

Setna: To snore when sleeping, or when being strangled.

Seeth: The slight chirp of the small owl three or four times only repeated. This is a very bad omen while the bird is sitting, and still worse when flying.

Santa: A bracelet; confined to the Duckun Thugs.

Siharna: To count.

Sitkala: Gold coins. Term peculiar to Duckun Thugs.

Situk: Gold. Term peculiar to Duckun Thugs.

Sotha: The person employed to inveigle travelers; always the most eloquent and persuasive man they can find.

Sothue: The office of inveigler.

Sootlee: Twenty rupees.

Suthote: Same as Bhurtote; a strangler.

Suthna: A Musulman.

Sutheea dalna: To kill with a sword.

Sutheeana: The same.

Syt: Term used by the Berar Thugs, for phool or parole of rendezvous. Other Thugs of the south call it maulee.

Taw: A gang or party of either travellers or Thugs.

Taw must Chowkaw: Keep out of sight, conceal the gang from view.

Tubae dalna: To kill. Tobae jana, to be killed.

Thibana or *Thibae dena:* To cause travellers to sit down on some pretence or other, that stranglers may conveniently do their work of murder.

Thibaoo: The auspice or omen on the right hand. In opening an expedition the omen must be seen or heard first on the left, Pilhaoo; and be soon followed by one on the right. They will not open their expedition if the omen is first observed on the right, nor when observed on the left, unless followed on the right.

Thibna: To sit down or rest, as a traveller.

Tubae dalna: To strangle. A term peculiar to some classes of Thugs.

Tubae Nakhna: The same.

Tighunee: The eye.

Tighunee kurna: To search.

Togree: The turban. Term confined chiefly to Berar and some other Duckun Thugs.

Taujna: To eat.

Thakur: The loud full call of the large owl, said to be like the word "ghoo ghoo." This they interpret according to the ordinary rules of the Thibaoo and Pilaooo. See also *Gorgareea* and *Kurra.* Duckun Thugs call it Mahee or Raja Teekula.

Teekula: Any suspicious thing taken from a murdered person, which it is dangerous for a Thug to carry.

Teekula purna: To be recognized, as any thing taken from a murdered person and found upon a Thug. Peculiar to Duckun Thugs; same as Purta purna among other Thugs.

[*To strangle*—Dhurdalna, Dhurohurkurna, Jheer Dalna, Leepurna, Ooherna, Parna Khna, Tubae dalna, Wahurna]

SOURCE: In *The Thugs or Phansigars of India: History of the Rise and Progress,* vol. 2 (Philadelphia: Carey and Hart, 1839).

Excerpts from *The Thugs or Phansigars of India:*
History of the Rise and Progress
CAPTAIN WILLIAM H. SLEEMAN

Our readers will almost deem it impossible that such organised gangs of murderers, amounting to several thousands, could carry on their villainy almost undiscovered so long; for two or three centuries at least. The difficulty, however, nearly vanishes when we reflect on the mode of travelling in India, just described, and on the peculiar system of the Thugs. In the first place they seldom murder near their own homes; but even this would be a point of little importance when we consider, secondly, that travellers, and generally from a distant part of the country, are their victims: thirdly, that they invariably murder before they rob.

Lastly, they avoid exciting suspicion by being careful to leave behind them no marks even of a crime having been committed. The travellers who became their victims were men seeking for service; or returning home with the savings of years; merchants going on business to a distant town; or others journeying either for business or pleasure. They might be murdered in the morning twilight within half a mile of the serai or village in which they had passed the night; while the Thugs who watched and had marked them for their prey were encamped at a short distance. No one missed them: the people of the serai or village which they had left took it for granted that they had proceeded on their way; and those of the next halting-place in advance were ignorant of their approach. It is not till days, weeks, months, or even years had passed away that their relations, hearing nothing of their arrival at their intended destinations, make inquiries, and it is seldom that they can ascertain even the place about which the travellers were probably murdered. Unless the inquiry be made within a short time, and there may have been something in the appearance or equipage of the travellers to attract attention, the villagers and others who reside along the road would not recollect whether those inquired for had passed or not. But even supposing (as has occasionally occurred) that the relations succeed in tracing the travellers to a certain spot, beyond which all clue is lost; this gives a moral certainty that they have been murdered at no great distance, that is, within a few miles adjacent.—But how, within such a space, are they to pitch upon the spot where the bodies are interred?—and more,—where are the murderers? probably hundreds of miles away; and even should they by chance be again encamped on the very spot, what means are there of detection? In ordinary thefts, and by local thieves, the tracing and discovery of stolen property affords a very powerful means of bringing the matter home to the perpetrators; but this has but little effect against Thugs. They contrive to obtain full knowledge of the persons, residence, and destination of those they murder, and are careful not to dispose of any recognisable articles where they might by chance be perceived. Such as have any peculiar marks are destroyed.

Considering all these circumstances, it is not astonishing that so little has been done towards suppressing this association of miscreants. The fact is, that until these five or six years, no one had any correct notion of its extent: all that was known up to that period was, that travellers were occasionally enticed and murdered by people called Thugs, who assumed the garb of inoffensive wayfarers. By some extraordinary chance, such as one of the victims having made his escape, or some of the stolen property being unexpectedly recognised, or one of the gang having turned informer in consequence of a quarrel for the division of the spoil, a few of these miscreants were occasionally discovered and punished. Even had the various governments into which India is divided, been aware of the extent of the evil and anxious to destroy it, they would have been unable to do so: insulated efforts would have produced little or no benefit; the jealousies which existed would have prevented their combining for the purpose; and for a century and a half or more, there has not existed any paramount power which could devise a general plan of operations, and compel the rest to submit to it.

Other causes are not wanting which tended to prevent any attempts being made, even in detail, to arrest the proceedings of the different gangs of Thugs. Some of the native chiefs knowingly harboured and protected them as a source of revenue from which they derived considerable sums annually out of the profits of their plunder. The Thugs lived in villages like other people, and generally cultivated small portions of ground to maintain appearances: so that the native chiefs, if questioned, pretended of course to know nothing of their real character; asserting that these people lived, cultivated, and paid their rent like others, and accounting for the absence of most of the male population during several months, by saying that they went for service and returned periodically with the amount of their earnings. In other cases, native chiefs who would have readily punished a gang of thieves when apprehended, were deterred from doing so by superstitious dread. The Thugs always endeavoured to impress the belief that they were acting according to the injunctions of their deity Bhowanee, and that all who opposed them would feel the vengeance of their goddess. The few instances in which Thugs were put to death by native chiefs were generally cases of personal vengeance, because these villains had murdered some relation or dependent of the chief, and were by good fortune apprehended immediately, "in the red-hand." It has unfortunately in several instances occurred that after punishing Thugs, the chief himself, his son, or some relation has died within a short time: whether some of the Thug fraternity took secret means to insure such an occurrence, cannot be ascertained; but they seized all such opportunities to substantiate the belief which they endeavoured to inculcate. In general, a native chief would merely extort a sum of money from the Thugs, or keep them in confinement for a short time, after which they were released; and not unfrequently they were discharged at once. Their own superstition however, as has just been explained, is now beginning to operate against them.

Though the British Indian government was free from the superstitions or the corruptions which prevented the native chiefs from punishing Thugs, it was not the less hampered by prejudices of its own, and by real difficulties which lay in the way of the object desired. Regarding the prejudices alluded to, it is necessary to explain a little of the secret springs that actuated the government. The members at the head of the administration have always had a tolerably correct idea of the oppressive nature of the British rule in India, and of the light in which it is held by the natives; but it has always been a primary object to prevent this knowledge from reaching the English public. To effect this, the reports forwarded to the Court of Directors, have always descanted on the admirable system of internal government which has been established in their territories; the blessings which the native subjects enjoy; and their consequent gratitude. The feeling descends through the various ranks of government servants, who generally take their cue accordingly. It may be observed too, that the majority of the officers of government, civil or military, are extremely ignorant of the natives of India, and of their real sentiments; and are therefore easily misled by a few designing favourites, who alone possess their ear, and have their own ends to serve.

To acknowledge, even had they been fully aware of it, the existence of such an evil as Thuggee over the whole of the British provinces, was by no means agreeable to the government, it would have contradicted their repeated assertions and representations. If an evil could be suppressed quietly and without incurring any additional expense, it would have been a source of deep satisfaction; but the proceedings of government have almost warranted a belief that they would prefer the existence of an evil, provided it were not generally known, even to the discovery of a remedy, if this should tend to produce a considerable sensation and excite inquiry. We could at least instance several public officers who have brought considerable annoyance upon themselves by too broadly bringing to notice the existence of evils, or the enormous extent to which crimes of the deepest dye, such as murders, gang robbery, and others, are perpetrated. Appearances are, however, kept up. The zeal and ability of the officer are praised, and his praiseworthy motives duly appreciated;—but then come certain remarks indicating an "apprehension of his being misinformed;" doubts that "the evil is not so bad as he has represented;" with a concluding observation that copies of the correspondence will be sent to the superintendent of police, judge of circuit, or some superior officer, who will be desired to report on the subject. This individual, if he have any tact, or any thing to hope or fear from the favour of government, frames his report according to what he sees is wished or expected from him; states the district to be not in worse order than others (which perhaps is true enough, owing to the vigorous measures of the magistrate in question, by which crime has been abated); and, by a careful adjustment of words and phrases, contrives to do away entirely with the impression which, in accordance with truth, ought to have been received. Occasionally, where the magistrate has persisted in his representations, the affair has actually ended by his removal, while his successor has reaped the full benefit of his exertions, and gained the entire credit of them.

But even when an insulated gang was actually brought to justice, it was but a drop in the ocean towards the suppression of Thuggee:—nor would, nor will any thing effect this, but a general system, which shall be in operation all over India. Different magistrates might receive information which, if it were combined and compared together, might prove of the greatest value, but which becomes useless when frittered away among separate officers, who have no communication with each other. The whole business too was so little understood, that few could bring themselves to credit the extent of such an organized system of murder. Although sufficient was known, so far back as 1810, to induce the commander-in-chief to issue a general order to the native soldiery who went on leave, urging them to take bills on the different treasuries for the amount of their savings, instead of carrying cash for fear of being robbed on the road, yet year after year passed, and men did not join their corps: but it was always supposed they had deserted, and little suspicion apparently was entertained of their being murdered, which however, was since discovered to have been the case in almost every instance. The scattered residences of the Thugs was another obstacle, and rendered them much more difficult to deal with than ordinary criminals, who inhabit the same locality. The members of a single gang often came from different parts of the country, some of which were hundreds of miles asunder. Numbers of them, perhaps the greater part, were residents of foreign states over which the magistrates had no control; and, although the British government might have requested the co-operation of the different princes, little or no good would have been effected. Even a system of Thug police, such as has now been established, if confined to the British provinces, could have been of no permanent use. The Thugs would have emigrated for the time to the native states, and although the crime might for a while cease in the British territories, as soon as the special Thug police was abolished, those miscreants would all have returned and prosecuted their trade as vigorously as ever.

Occasionally when a gang, residents of a foreign territory, were arrested, and moral proof against them was strong, but legal proof, according to the English system, failing; if the government made them over to their native chief in the hope that he would punish them, this usually ended in their being released by paying a sum of money—sometimes without. On the other hand, when British subjects were apprehended on a Thug expedition in a native state, they sometimes contrived, by flattering English prejudices, to obtain the protection of the functionaries. The established creed of the government is the superior excellence of their own administration, and the blessings enjoyed by their native subjects; and they descant largely on the tyranny and oppression in all native states. This is well known to the native dependents and officials, who play their part accordingly. With many of them the Thugs maintained a good understanding, and when any of those wretches, residents of British territories, were arrested by a native chief, a pitiable story was presented to some English functionary of "poor innocent British subjects on a trading expedition," or something of the sort, having been confined by a tyrannical chief, in order to extort money from them. Of course, a due proportion of compliments and flattery of the English was mixed up with the representation, and this would produce, often without the slightest inquiry, a strong letter from the English functionary to the native chief on the injustice of his proceedings, and generally insured the release of the Thugs.

MEASURES OF THE BRITISH GOVERNMENT IN INDIA FOR THE SUPPRESSION OF THUGGEE

We now proceed to notice the measures taken by the British authorities in India for the suppression of Thuggee. The writer in the Foreign Quarterly Review, upon whose authority as well as that of Captain Sleeman, the following statements are made, seems to have had access to the most authentic original sources of information.

The state of society in India being such as we have just described, it is not surprising that so well organized a system of murder and robbery as that of the Thugs should have remained so long in full vigour.

Things had gone on in this way for years, chequered occasionally by the vigorous attempt of some individual functionary to eradicate the evil, but without any solid benefit. The most notorious of these efforts was an attack made by Messrs. Halhed and Stockwell, in the year 1812, on the stronghold of a large body of Thugs, in the province of Sindouse, in the Gualior territory. They had formed a large village there, whence they issued annually on their excursions, and paid a regular tribute to that state for their protection. Many were killed; but the greater part, being driven away, scattered themselves all over India, joining other gangs or forming new ones wherever they went: so that the enterprize, from not being followed up on a system of information derived from some of those who were captured, actually in its results produced more evil than good.

The next event which occurred, and which ultimately laid the foundation of the successful measures that have been since pursued, was the arrest of a gang of a hundred and fifteen, near Jubulpoor, in 1823; it was accomplished by the following means. A noted leader of Thugs, named Kulian, was in the Jubulpoor gaol. Seeing the proof strong against him, he offered to turn informer to save himself; and was promised his life in the event of his doing good service. He accordingly desired his brother, Motee, to accompany the first large gang he should meet, travelling in that direction; to note well the murders and places where the bodies should be buried: and, as the gang approached Jubulpoor, to give information to Mr. Molony, agent to the governor-general. The gang which Motee joined was that of Dhunnee Khan: he strictly fulfilled his instructions, and caused the apprehension of the whole; this has been already related; and also how Dhunnee Khan contrived to persuade Mr. Molony to order their release. In despair at this, Motee followed the gang, and, by dint of frightening some of them with assurances of speedy re-apprehension, persuaded a few to return with him to Mr. Molony, and declare what they really were. On this additional evidence, a large police force was sent after the gang, and succeeded in capturing a hundred and three, who were safely lodged in gaol. Mr. Molony unfortunately died soon after this: his successor apparently did not know how to proceed in the case, until Mr. F. C. Smith took it up in 1830, shortly after his appointment as governor-general's agent at Jubulpoor; seventy-five were convicted; the others having died in gaol, excepting some who were made informers.

Another considerable gang was apprehended in the same territories in 1826 by Captain Wardlow, employed there as a civil officer; a third by Captain

---

1. For. Quart. Rev. No. xli.

Sleeman, in Bhopal, in the beginning of 1830; and a fourth by Major Borthwick, political agent of Mahidpoor.

Of all these gangs, some of the members, frightened at what had already occurred, turned approvers, in order to save themselves; but the evidence of these men, in particular of a Brahmin approver, named Ferringhea, was perfectly astounding, and laid open a scene of barefaced villainy which could scarcely be credited: nevertheless, every statement hitherto made by them, and by others, have been corroborated.

The disclosures made by these different approvers, and the information given, threw open so fine a field for a general plan of operations, that the matter was warmly taken up by Mr. Smith, agent to the governor-general, and Captain Sleeman, district officer of Nursingpoor, each zealously cooperating with the other. On the 21st September, 1830, Mr. Smith wrote to government, and intimated the necessity of some such plan: but the eyes of the latter had been opened, and before the receipt of Mr. Smith's dispatch, a letter from government, dated 8th October, was addressed to him, requesting his opinion on the subject. In reply, he submitted a plan, of which the following is an outline.

1st. That an officer, to be termed superintendent of operations against Thuggee, should be appointed, with power to send out parties to apprehend those against whom he might have information in any part of the country.

2d. The superintendent to commit all whom he deems guilty for trial, before the governor-general's agent in the Saugor and Nerbudda territories.

3d. Lists to be made out against all upon whom suspicion rests, and sent to the different English functionaries.

4th. The residents at native courts also to give their assistance.

The draught likewise contains several minor provisions regarding the search for dead bodies; rewards to those who deserve such a mark of approbation; penalties for harbouring Thugs; prevention of abuses by approvers; and other clauses not worth enumerating here, although highly useful in practice.

Still, the more that was done the more seemed requisite to do. Every arrest brought to light new combinations and associations of these professed assassins, and discovered new scenes in which their dreadful trade was at work. It was obvious that nothing but a general system, undertaken by a paramount power, strong enough to bear down all opposition by interested native chiefs, could ever eradicate such well-organized villainy; and the other members of government at length succeeded in persuaded Lord William Bentinck that it was incumbent upon a government calling itself enlightened to take the lead in so good a work; and that a moderate expense would be well bestowed in suppressing an association which was causing the annual murder of some thousands of his fellow creatures. In prosecution of the extended system of operations, Captain Sleeman was in January, 1835, relieved altogether from ordinary civil duties, and appointed superintendent; and several additional officers were nominated to act under him in various parts of the country.

Jubulpoor, the residence of the agent to the governor-general in the Saugor and Nerbudda territories, was appointed Captain Sleeman's headquarters. All Thugs apprehended within those territories Jeypoor, Hyderabad, Nagpoor, and other contiguous native states, are tried by the agent at Jubulpoor. Those of Oude and Indore by the residents of those courts; and such as have committed crimes in what are called the regulation provinces, are tried by the officers who are there stationed. Operations have lately extended into Bombay, Madras, the eastern parts of Bengal, and the north westernmost parts of the Indian continent; and there is no doubt that, to ensure complete success it will be necessary to nominate additional superintendents as well as subordinate officers for each of these divisions: to which should be added functionaries specially appointed for the trial of those committed.

The success of the combined operations has been beyond hope; and if properly followed up, it will be almost impossible for a Thug to remain at large. The mode of proceeding is, to take the deposition of those who turn approvers, wherever this may happen to be. These men are then required to give, to the best of their recollection, a full account of every expedition on which they have been, mentioning the dates of every one, and the detail of every murder; together with the names of those who had formed the gangs, their residence, caste, &c., &c. All this is registered in the office of the general-superintendent, and lists of those to be apprehended are sent to the different subordinate officers, who are all provided with approvers and guards. These officers also take the depositions in full of all whom they may apprehend, copies of which are sent to the general-superintendent. It is obvious that when depositions, thus taken almost simultaneously from different people hundreds of miles apart, who have had no means of collusion, and none of them expecting to be apprehended, agree in describing the same scenes and the same actors, it is obviously next to impossible to refuse belief. But another test is applied. When a Thug is arrested, he is brought direct to the officers' residence, and placed in a row between unconcerned people. The approvers, who have been detained at the stations, are then sent for singly, and required to point out any individual of the party whom they may know. If they all fix on the same individual, and their statements also agree with those previously made by others, it is impossible that better evidence can be had.

We mention this, because we are aware that a prejudice has gone forth against the mode of conducting both the previous investigations and the sessions part of the business in Thug trials. That a man who has only seen or heard the latter should have some suspicions is not surprising; for the whole evidence of events long past is given so glibly, that it appears to bear strong marks of fabrication. But in fact the sessions part of the business is the least to be relied on: if that were all a man had before him to enable him to form his judgment, few Thugs would have been punished: before the trials come on, the approvers have all been brought together; have had opportunities of seeing the prisoners, and of fabricating what tales they please. But this they dare not do; they know well that what passes in the sessions, though the actual trial, yet serves chiefly to inspect the papers and operations of the subordinate officers, in order to ascertain that all has been correctly conducted; and that in reality, the previous proceedings form the evidence mainly relied upon. The whole association of Thugs is, in fact, different from that of any other known villains in existence. Their system is such, that they are beyond the reach of the ordinary tribunals of the country, and a special system must be put in force against them. That some petty abuses have been committed, we allow. Money has occasionally been extorted from people, under threat of accusing them of being Thugs; and others, though innocent, have suffered a temporary imprisonment. But there is no system, however well organized, that may not be open to imperfections; and what are such evils as the above, which are the sum total of all that has occurred, to ridding the world of some hundreds of professed assassins.

We are fully convinced, after taking everything into consideration, that there are no trials in which a man may with so safe a conscience pronounce sentence, as those of the Thugs; in proof of which we have only to refer to the table in p. 38 of Captain Sleeman's work. No less than eleven different functionaries, judicial and political, are there mentioned as having held Thug trials; yet the general result is the same in all, as to the proportion found guilty and acquitted. We could mention many individual instances in proof of the correctness of the information obtained and evidence brought forward, but will content ourselves with one very striking case from Hyderabad. About eighty Thugs had been arrested in various parts of that kingdom by different parties of approvers; they were collected into a gang and sent off to Jubulpoor under a guard. As they were passing the residence of the local governor of one of the Hyderabad provinces, he gave in charge to the guard eleven men whom he had apprehended on suspicion. The whole were safely brought to Jubulpoor; but it so happened that the papers and documents relating to their arrest had not been received by the time of their arrival; and the officer commanding the guard made no report as to whence the different men who composed the gang under his charge had been received; they were, therefore, as a matter of course, supposed to be all Thugs who had been arrested by the approvers. Nevertheless the usual form was proceeded in, *i. e.* the approvers who remained at Jubulpoor were sent for singly to inspect the gang; all were recognized to be Thugs excepting eleven men, of whom the approvers said they knew nothing. On the receipt of the documents a few days afterwards, these eleven proved to be the party given in charge to the guard by the local governor, with whose arrest the approvers had no concern.

The success which has attended the exertions of the officers employed to suppress this crime, has hitherto equalled the most sanguine expectations. In most parts of central India, Bundlecund, Boglecund, and from Allahabad to the Himalayah, Thuggee now scarcely exists: the great proof of which is, that the servants of English gentlemen, and Sepahees, who go on leave into those parts of the country, have, during the last three years, all returned in safety; whereas previously, not a year passed without many of them being missed. We mention these two classes, for their movements only can we correctly ascertain; but it is a fair inference that other natives have travelled in equal safety. There can be no doubt that if the British government will pursue vigorous measures for a few years, the system will, with proper supervision on the part of the ordinary police, be completely eradicated, never again to rise; but if exertions are slackened, and any fully initiated Thugs left at large, they would infallibly raise new gangs, and Thuggee would again flourish all over India. It is certainly incumbent on a government which assumes to itself the character of enlightened, and which is now paramount in India, to exert itself for the suppression of such an atrocious system. It is impossible to ascertain with accuracy the extent to which it has been carried annually, and, could it be done, the statement would scarcely be credited. Reckoning the number of Thugs in all India to be ten thousand, and that, on the average, each Thug murders three victims a year, this will give an amount of thirty thousand murders annually committed for many years past, of which, till lately, scarcely any thing was known. Frightfully enormous as this may appear, it is probable that both estimates are under the mark, which is warranted by what appears on the trials, where, of course, but a small portion of the crimes actually committed are proved.

In the sessions of 1836, lately held by the Honourable F. I. Shore at Jubulpoor, two hundred and forty-one prisoners were convicted of the murder of four hundred and seventy-four individuals, of whose corpses three hundred and fourteen were disinterred, and inquests held upon them.

The results have been hitherto highly satisfactory. Within these few years more than two thousand Thugs have been arrested by the officers attached to the Jubulpoor and Central India establishment alone. Of these about three hundred have been made approvers; eighteen hundred and three were committed for trial.[2] Of these four hundred and nineteen were sentenced to death; one thousand and eighty to transportation for life;[3] ninety-five to imprisonment for life; leaving two hundred and nine, who were either sentenced to limited imprisonment, allowed to turn approvers, died in gaol, or were otherwise disposed of. Only twenty-one of the whole have been acquitted; and this proves the extraordinary care with which the cases are prepared by the officers to whom this duty has been intrusted, and the strong nature of the evidence adduced. We cannot but wish them every success in exterminating a system which spares neither sex nor age; whose members never abandon their profession as long as they possess the power to engage in an expedition; who watch for their prey like wild beasts or vultures; and talk of the principal scenes of their crimes as a sportsman would of his favourite preserves. We trust also that no miserable fit of economy on the part of government may arise to thwart the measures in progress, but that every co-operation will be given to those praiseworthy exertions.

SOURCE: Captain William H. Sleeman, *The Thugs or Phansigars of India: History of the Rise and Progress* (Philadelphia: Carey and Hart, 1839).

A Kutcherry or Kachahri
FANNY PARKS PARLBY

The sketch represents the examination of a criminal before the judge of the station, who is taking notes. The fat moonshee on his right hand is reading the deposition, and the native officers of the court are in attendance. The scene of the kachahrī, or court of justice, is a room in the house of the magistrate. The duffadār stooping by the side of the table is putting the seal of office to the paper that will consign the criminal for trial to the suddur dewani. The hooqŭ bārdar with his snow-white beard, standing behind his master's chair, has just brought a fresh chilam for the hooqŭ, which the gentleman has laid aside during the examination of the Thug. The criminal, who appears to have suffered from a blow on the head from one of those iron

---

2. This result reaches to the year 1836, and is consequently greater than that given in a paper of Captain Sleeman's, in a subsequent part of the work.

3. These sentences are at once carried into execution, and not commuted, as is so common in England.

shod lātees, of which a description is given in the next chapter, is attempting to prove his innocence; and the man to the right, who was speaking in his defence to the judge, has stopped in the midst of his sentence, and is cocking his ear to catch the words of the defendant. A sketch of the lātee is in the plate entitled "The Thug's Dice," . . .

Copy of "The Confessions of a Thug," from a circular dated August, 1829, sent by the Governor-general to the judges of the different stations on this subject. The reason for the Governor-general sending this circular to all the judges and magistrates, was to induce them to be on the alert after Thugs, in consequence of a party of them having been seized up the country by Captain Borthwick, four of whom turned evidence against the others. They were examined separately, and their confessions compared.

The following is the confession and statement of the principal witness:—

"My father was a cultivator of land in Buraicha and other neighbouring villages, and I followed the same occupation until I entered my thirtieth year, when I joined the Thugs, with whom I have been more or less connected ever since, a period of upwards of thirty years.

"During this time, however, I have not accompanied them on every excursion; but, on the contrary, for intervals of two, three, and even six years, have remained at home and earned a subsistence by cultivating land, so that I have been engaged in only six predatory excursions: four under a leader, since dead, called Oo-dey Singh, and two under my present chief and fellow-prisoner, Mokhun Jemadar.

"Whilst residing at home during the last interval alluded to, I was apprehended on suspicion of being a Thug, but the proofs I adduced of having been for so many years employed in husbandry were the means which restored me to liberty.

"By this event, however, my circumstances became so greatly embarrassed, that I was forced to go to Salany to borrow money from Mokhun Jemadar, who I knew had generally some at command; but he would not agree to relieve my wants except on condition of my engaging to bring my family to Salany and becoming one of his gang. These conditions I was forced by my destitute state to comply with, and I accordingly accompanied him in his last two excursions.

"Oo-dey Singh my former leader was, at the period of my joining his gang, beyond the prime of life, although, at the same time, active and enterprising; but gradually becoming unfit for the exertion required of him by his situation, and his son Roman being seized, with other Thugs, and cast into prison at Jubbalpore, he abandoned his former course of life, and shortly after died.

"At the time I was serving under Oo-dey Singh, tranquillity had not been established throughout the country, and our excursions were neither carried to so great a distance, nor were they so lucrative or certain as they have since been; for in those days travellers, particularly those possessed of much property, seldom ventured from one place to another unless in large parties, or under a strong escort; and we ourselves held the Pindaries and other armed plunderers in as much dread as other travellers.

"About three months after I had joined Mokhun's gang, which consisted of forty men, we set out from Bundelkund for the Dekkun, this was in the month of Phagoon Summet, 1883 (about March, 1826). We proceeded by regular stages, and crossed the Nerbudda at the Chepanair Ghāt, where we fell in with Chotee Jamadar (a Brahman), who joined us with his gang, the strength of which was about the same as our own.

"We then continued our course towards Mallygaow, and at Thokur, near that cantoonment, celebrated the Hooly; after which we resumed our route and reached Mallygaow, where we struck off by the Nassuk road, intending to turn from Nassuk to Poona and Aurungabad.

"After proceeding a coss or two on this road we met a relation of Mokhun's, belonging to Oomrao and Ruttyram's gangs, who informed us that these two leaders with their gangs were near at hand on the Poona road, engaged in the pursuit of some angriahs with treasure. It was proposed that Mokhun should join them with some of his men, in order to be entitled to a share of the spoil. Mokhun at first thought of going himself, but recollecting that Oomrao and himself were not on good terms, he sent twenty-five men with Chotee Jamadar. On the day following we heard the business was effected, and that they intended to proceed with Oomrao and Ruttyram to Bhoorampore, at which place they requested us to meet them. We accordingly proceeded to that quarter, and found Chotee Jemadar and his party at Bhoorampore, Oomrao and Ruttyram having returned to their homes.

"Here we learnt that the angriahs had been attacked and murdered near Koker (the place where we had celebrated the Hooly), and that no less a sum than 22,000 rupees was found on their persons in gold, bullion, mohurs, and pootlies. Of this 6000 rupees had been received as the share of our two gangs, and was disposed of in the following manner.

"Mokhun received one-third for himself and gang, a third was given to Chotee Jamadar for himself and his gang, and the remainder was reserved for the mutual expenses of the two gangs. Mokhun and Chotee despatched the two-thirds above mentioned to their homes: that sent by the latter reached its destination safely; but one of Mokhun's men in charge of our share having got drunk at Jansy, blabbed that he was a Thug, and returning with others with a large amount of treasure; he was consequently seized by the sirdar of the place, and the money taken from him. We now quitted Bhoorampore, and proceeded to Aurungbad, but, meeting with little or no success, we returned by Dhoolia and Bhopaul to Bundelcund, and reached our several homes before the rains set in. Our next excursion was towards Guzerat, but in this nothing occurred worthy of note.

"I have never, during my connexion with the Thugs, known a single instance of their committing a robbery without the previous destruction of life, which is almost invariably accomplished by strangulation. This is effected either by means of a roomal (handkerchief) or shred of cloth well twisted and wetted, or merely by the hands, though the latter is rarely practised, and only had recourse to from accidental failure in the former and usual mode.

"A preconcerted signal being given, the victim or victims are instantly overpowered, and death, either by the roomal or hands, is the act of a moment. In perpetrating murder it is an invariable rule with the Thugs never, if possible, to spill the blood of their victims, in order that no traces of murder may appear, to awaken suspicion of the deed in the minds of those who may happen to pass the spot, and detection be the consequence. In the hurry in which it is sometimes necessary to dispose of the bodies, holes cannot be dug sufficiently large to contain them in an entire state, particularly when the number of them is great; the bodies are then cut in pieces and packed therein.

"When these holes are near the road side, and especially in an exposed spot, it is usual, after covering them with earth, to burn fires over them, to do away with the appearance of the earth having been newly turned. Murders, in the manner just described, are perpetrated as frequently, and with equal facility and certainty, whilst the victims are walking along the road, as when they have been enticed to our places of encampment, and, unconscious of what is to befal them, are sitting amongst us with every thing carefully and leisurely arranged for their destruction.

"These murders frequently take place near villages where we encamp, and usually during twilight; and always, whilst the business is going on, the hand-drum is beaten and singing commenced, to drown any noise that might be made by the victims.

"The several persons actually engaged commence their operations simultaneously at a preconcerted signal given.

"The signal is an arbitrary one; generally a common, coarse expression is used, not likely to strike the attention of the victims, such as 'Tumbākoo lao,' (bring tobacco).

"I have never seen the phansy (or noose) made of cord employed for strangling, though I am fully aware of the general supposition, that it is with it that we strangle people; but if such has ever been employed, which I greatly doubt, it has long since been laid aside, for the obvious reason, that if a Thug were seized having it about his person, it would inevitably lead to his detection.

"A direct understanding with the local authorities in Bundelcund is constantly kept up by Oomrao, Mokhun, and all the other leaders and jāmadārs, who on their return from their excursions reside in that part of the country, and these authorities are conciliated and their favour gained by suitable presents.

"Assistance and support from the English authorities, being likewise indispensable, are obtained through artifice. This is effected by means of their emissaries, who, by misrepresentation and falsehood, frequently contrive to extricate them from the difficulties in which persons of our habits are constantly involved. A relation of Oomrao's, Motee by name, and Lala Hajain, an inhabitant of Secundra, render important services in this way. Motee, who was himself a Thug formerly, has for some years past discontinued going on predatory excursions. He first brought himself into notice with European gentlemen by informing against a gang, which was seized in consequence, and confined at Jubbulpore, where the greater part still remain.

"Since then Motee has advanced in favour with these gentlemen, who are led to suppose he acts as a check upon the Thugs and other plunderers; at least, he persuades us that such is the case, the consequence of which is, that he exercises great influence over us; making us pay well for his connivance, and the good offices he no doubt frequently performs in our behalf.

"He principally exerts himself in protecting and assisting Oomrao, Ruttyram, Hera Mandeen, and their gangs.

"Lala Hajain, by means of representations to different persons of his acquaintance in the adālut at Cawnpore, renders great assistance to Mokhun in getting him through matters of difficulty. The latter, after his return to Bundelcund from his last excursion but one, when he heard the mishap which had befallen the share of the plunder sent by him to Boorampore, had recourse, as was usual with him, to his patron Lala Hajain. Lala lost no time in waiting on his friend Madee Moonshee, at Cawnpore, to whom he represented matters in such a light, that the moonshee wrote himself, or had instructions sent by his superiors to the Tausy Rajah, intimating that, it having been made known that he, the Rajah, had seized four travellers of respectable and inoffensive character passing through his territories, and plundered them of their property—he was directed to restore them to liberty, with whatever property he had taken from them.

"A day or two before the receipt of the letter containing this order, the Rajah had released Mokhun's men, having first obtained from them an acquittance of the money he had taken; but now, thinking that unless he could prove the men to be Thugs, and that their true characters had been misrepresented, he should get a bad name with Europeans, he immediately sent after them, and had them again apprehended. What became of these men afterwards I have never been able to learn.

"Besides Lala Hajain, who manages matters favourably for him through his acquaintance at the courts and kutcherries at Cawnpore, Etaweh, Humeerpore, Auria, and Mynpoor, Mokhun has a great friend and supporter in the Tauzie Vakeel, Gunesh Lall, who resides at Humeerporah.

"Oomrao may have other patrons besides his relation Motee, who watches over his interests principally at Jubbulpore. Makay Sahib, at Kytah, is a great friend of Motee's, and it was from him that the English pass, which Oomrao showed the horsemen when we were apprehended at Dekhola, was obtained.

"Passing through a country in so numerous a body as our gangs sometimes form, is certainly calculated to awaken suspicion, but when this happens, it is always lulled to rest by our being all prepared with the same story or explanation.

"Few of us carry arms, indeed, amongst fifteen or twenty persons not more than two or three swords may be found.

"When Thugs, though strangers to each other, meet, there is something in their manner which discovers itself; and, to make 'assurance doubly sure,' one exclaims 'Alee khan!' which being repeated by the other party, recognition takes place, but is never followed by a disclosure of past acts.

"In the division of plunder the jāmadārs receive seven and a half per cent., besides sharing equally with the rest of the gang; but, before any division is made, a certain portion is devoted to Bhawānī, our tutelar deity. This applies only to money in gold or silver; for when the plunder consists of diamonds and pearls, the leader draws blood from his hand, and having sprinkled a little over them, the sanction of the goddess to a division is thereby obtained without any other alienation. But the omission of this ceremony, or neglecting, when success attends us, to propitiate a continuance of Bhawānī's favour by laying aside a part of our acquisitions for her service, would, we firmly believe, bring heavy misfortune upon us.

"The office of strangler is never allowed to be self-assumed, but is conferred with due ceremony, after the fitness of the candidate in point of firmness, activity, and bodily strength, has been ascertained, and a sufficient degree of expertness in the use of the roomal has been acquired by long sham practice amongst ourselves.

"When thus qualified, the person on whom the office is to be conferred proceeds to the fields, conducted by his gooroo (spiritual guide), previously selected, who carries with him the roomal (or handkerchief), and anxiously looking out for some favourable omen, such as the chirping of certain birds, or their flight past the right hand, knots the roomal at each end the moment that either occurs, and delivers it to the candidate, imploring success upon him.

"After this they return, when the ceremony is closed by a feast, or distribution of sweetmeats. The seniors only confer this office, generally old Thugs held in some estimation, but who from infirmity or age have ceased to accompany the gangs in their expeditions, and whose chief support is received from the voluntary contributions of those on whom they have conferred the privilege of using the roomal.

"Certain terms, known to ourselves alone, are made use of to distinguish certain circumstances, events, &c., connected with our proceedings: viz.

The persons whose office it is to strangle the victims are called *Luddya*, also *Bullod*.

Those who dig the graves or holes, *Lucka*.

Those who carry away the bodies, *Gutnee Walow*.

A scout or spy, *Tulha*.

A traveller on whom designs are formed, *Betoo*.

If a Musulmān, *Sultan Betoo*.

If a Hindoo, *Bundoo Betoo*.

A murder committed at the halting-place or encampment-ground, *Topa*.

A murder committed whilst the victims are walking along the road—if during the day, *Phoolkee;* if during the night, *Kootul*.

The spot where the bodies are buried, *Kurwa*.

The spot where the murder is committed, *Balee*.

A female victim, *Ecmud*.

A child victim, *Chumota*.

Horse, *Poornkna* or *Pootra*.

Bullock, *Subba*.

Gold, *Sirya*.

Sword, *Lumberee*.

Silver or rupee, *Peeky*.

Matchlock, *Puttakee*.

Gold mohurs, *Tandya*.

Turban, *Kassee*.

A ring, *Pulbya*.

Dhotee, *Kurdhunny*.

Pearls, *Punnyara*.

Diamonds, *Kukreya*.

A knife, *Booky*.

The roomal with which people are strangled, *Phyloo* and *roomal*.

If one person is strangled, it is called *Eloo.*
If two persons are strangled, it is called *Beetsee.*

If three	.	.	.	.	.	*Singod.*
If four	.	.	.	.	.	*Bhurra.*
If five	.	.	.	.	.	*Puckrao.*
If six	.	.	.	.	.	*Chutroo, &c.*

"These terms are used by the Thugs in all parts of the country. The numerals exclusively apply to travellers, and are used to denote the number that fall into the hands of detached parties."

This is the end of the "Thug's Confession."

The other men, on their examination, acknowledged having murdered a bearer, on whom they found four rupees. They also met with twelve seapoys; eight of the soldiers took one road, and the other four another. The Thugs, therefore, divided into two parties, overtook the seapoys, and killed them all.

One Thug said, that on a certain day eleven men were killed and buried. The other Thug said, that on the same day only seven were strangled: on re-examination he replied, "Yes, it it true I only mentioned seven—there might have been eleven, or more, I cannot remember; we strangled people so constantly, that I took little account of the numbers buried, I only know on that day about seven or eleven were buried."

The Thugs never attack Europeans.

SOURCE: Chapter 13 in *The Wanderings of a Pilgrim in Search of the Picturesque* (London: Pelham Richardson, 1850; reprint, Karachi: Oxford University Press, 1975).

Thugs

PHILIP MEADOWS TAYLOR

[Philip Meadows Taylor's romance, *The Confessions of a Thug*, was inspired by Captain William Sleeman's investigations of thuggee/thagi. Meadows Taylor (1806–1876) volunteered to collect evidence in the campaign to suppress thuggee/thagi and served under Sleeman.]

We returned to Hingolee on the 21st June by twelve easy stages, instead of the three we had marched the distance in before. Some rain had fallen, and it was cooler.

Now I became very busy. Those famous discoveries in regard to the practice of Thuggee had recently been made at Jubbulpore and Saugor by (then) Captain Sleeman, which made a sensation in India never to be forgotten. By the confessions of one gang who were apprehended, many Thugs in Central India were brought to justice; and at last the Thugs of the Deccan were denounced by these approvers, and as many lived near Hingolee, they were at once arrested. I volunteered my services in the labour of collecting evidence, and they were accepted. Day after day I recorded tales of murder, which, though horribly monotonous, possessed an intense interest; and as fast as new approvers came in, new mysteries were unravelled and new crimes confessed. Names of Thugs all over the Deccan were registered, and I found one list containing the names of nearly all those whom I had suspected in my old district. The reader will remember my intense anxiety on this subject in 1829, and my conviction that deadly crime existed and was only awaiting discovery; now it was all cleared, but I felt sore that it had not fallen to my lot to win the fame of the affair.

Some men of the artillery and some camp-followers deserted at this time. They were also Thugs; and it was a horrible thought that these miscreants had been in our midst, and it made many in the station, and especially the ladies, very nervous. We had searched for bodies of murdered people wherever we were told to look by the approvers, and invariably found them, sometimes singly, sometimes whole parties, and the details were so sickening we resolved to open no more graves. I wrote and sent home to my father an article on Thuggee, which was shown to Sir Edward Bulwer, who sent me word that had he possessed any local knowledge of India or its people, he would write a romance on the subject; why did I not do so? I pondered over this advice, and hence my novel, 'Confessions of a Thug.'

SOURCE: In *The Story of My Life* (Edinburgh: W. Blackwood and Sons, 1877).

Excerpts from *Confessions of a Thug*
PHILIP MEADOWS TAYLOR

CHAPTER I

The Thug's introduction to the reader,
and an event in his history which
determines his future career

You ask me, Sahib, for an account of my life; my relation of it will be understood by you, as you are acquainted with the peculiar habits of my countrymen; and if, as you say, you intend it for the information of your own, I have no hesitation in relating the whole; for though I have accepted the service of Europeans, in my case one of bondage, I cannot help looking back with pride and exultation on the many daring feats I have performed. Often indeed does my spirit rise at the recollection of them, and often do I again wish myself the leader of a band of gallant spirits, such as once obeyed me, to roam with them wherever my inclination or the hope of booty prompted.

But the time is past. Life, Sahib, is dear to every one; to preserve mine, which was forfeited to your laws, I have bound myself to your service by the fearful tenure of denouncing all my old confederates, and you well know how that service is performed by me. Of all the members of my band, and of those with whom chance has even casually connected me, but few now remain at large; many have been sacrificed at the shrine of justice, and of those who now wander broken, and pursued from haunt to haunt, you have such intelligence as will lead to their speedy apprehension.

Yet Thuggee, capable of exciting the mind so strongly, will not, cannot be annihilated! Look at the hundreds, I may say thousands, who have suffered for its profession; does the number of your prisoners decrease? No, on the contrary, they increase; and from every Thug who accepts the alternative of perpetual imprisonment to dying on a gallows, you learn of others whom even I knew not of, and of Thuggee being carried on in parts of the country where it is least suspected, and has never been discovered till lately.

It is indeed too true, Ameer Ali, said I; your old vocation seems to be as flourishing as ever, but it cannot last. Men will get tired of exposing themselves to the chance of being hunted down like wild beasts, and hung when they are caught; or what is perhaps worse to many, of being sent over the Kala-Panee; and so heartily does the Government pursue Thugs wherever they are known to exist, that there will no longer be a spot of ground in India where your profession can be practised.

You err, Sahib; you know not the high and stirring excitement of a Thug's occupation. To my perception it appears, that so long as one exists, he will gather others around him; and from the relation of what I will tell you of my own life, you will estimate how true is my assertion.

How many of you English are passionately devoted to sporting! Your days and months are passed in its excitement. A tiger, a panther, a buffalo, or a hog, rouses your utmost energies for its destruction—you even risk your lives in its pursuit. How much higher game is a Thug's! His is man: against his fellow-creatures in every degree, from infancy to old age, he has sworn relentless, unerring destruction.

Ah! you are a horrible set of miscreants, said I: I have indeed the experience, from the records of murders which are daily being unfolded to me, of knowing this at least of you. But you must begin your story; I am prepared to listen to details worse than I can imagine human beings to have ever perpetrated.

The whole scene is now before me. The bullocks and their drivers, with the Thugs, were all in a confused group in the bed of the little stream, the men shouting and urging on their beasts: but it was easy to see that every man had a Thug close to him awaiting the signal. They were only a few feet below us, and the stream was so narrow that it was with some difficulty all could stand in its bed, especially when the cart reached the bottom. Above stood my father, Hoosein, and myself,—the Sahoukar, one of his servants, and several other Thugs.

I was eagerly awaiting the signal; I tightly grasped the fatal handkerchief, and my first victim was within a foot of me! I went behind him as being preferable to one side, and observed one of the other Thugs do the same to a servant. The Sahoukar moved a step or two towards the road—I instinctively followed him—I scarcely felt that I stirred, so intensely was I observing him. 'Jey Kalee!' shouted my father: it was the signal, and I obeyed it!

As quick as thought the cloth was round his neck—I seemed endued with superhuman strength—I wrenched his neck round—he struggled convulsively for an instant, and fell. I did not quit my hold, I knelt down on him, and strained the cloth till my hand ached: but he moved not—he was dead! I quitted my hold, and started to my feet; I was mad with excitement!—my blood boiled, and I felt as though I could have strangled a hundred others, so easy, so simple had the reality been. One turn of my wrists had placed me on an equality with those who had followed the profession for years,—I had taken the first place in the enterprise, for I had killed the principal victim! I should receive the praise of the whole band, many of whom I was confident had looked on me as only a child.

CHAPTER XXV

He is a man, take him for all in all,
I shall not look upon his like again.
—*Hamlet,* Act I, Sc. ii.

At the expiration of a week, Ameer Ali sent word to me that he was ready to resume his narrative, and I lost no time in requesting him to repair to my residence. He arrived, and making his usual graceful obeisance, I desired him to be seated.

The reader will perhaps like to know something of the appearance of the man with whom he and I have had these long conversations; and no longer to keep him in the dark on so important a subject, I will describe Ameer Ali to him. He is what would be called a short man, about five feet seven inches in height; his figure is now slender, which may be the effect of his long imprisonment,—imprisonment it can hardly be called, except that to one of his formerly free and unrestrained habits and pursuits, the smallest restraint must of course be irksome in the highest degree and painful to bear. His age may be about thirty-five or forty years, but it sits lightly on him for a native of India, and it has not in the least whitened a beard and mustachios on which he evidently expends great care and pains, and which are always trimmed and curled with the greatest neatness. His figure, as I have said, is slight, but it is in the highest degree compact, agile, and muscular, and his arms are remarkable for the latter quality combined with unusual length and sinewiness. His dress is always scrupulously neat and clean, and put on with more attention to effect than is usual with his brother approvers, his turban being always tied with a smart cock, and his waist tightly girded with an English shawl or a gaily dyed handkerchief, where once a shawl of Cashmere or a handkerchief of brocade was better suited to his pretensions. In complexion he is fair for a native; his face is even now strikingly handsome, and leads me to believe that the accounts of his youthful appearance have not been exaggerated. His forehead is high and broad; his eyes large, sparkling and very expressive, especially when his eloquence kindles and bursts forth in a torrent of figurative language, which it would be impossible to render into English, or if it were rendered, would appear to the English reader, unused to such forms of speech, highly exaggerated and absurd. His cheeks are somewhat sunken, but his nose is aquiline and elegantly formed, his mouth small and beautifully chiselled, and his teeth are exquisitely white and even. His upper lip is graced with a pair of small mustachios, which would be the envy of many a gay lieutenant of hussars; while a beard close and wavy, from which a straggling hair is never suffered to escape, descends nearly to his breast, and hides a throat and neck which would be a study for a painter or a sculptor: to complete all, his chest is very broad and prominent, and well contrasts with the effect of his small waist.

His manner is graceful, bland, and polite,—it is indeed more than gentlemanlike—it is courtly, and I have not seen it equalled even by the Mahomedan noblemen, with many of whom I have associated. Any of my readers who may have been in India, and become acquainted with its nobles and men of rank, will estimate at once how high is the meed of praise on this score which I give to Ameer Ali. His language is pure and fluent, perhaps a little affected from his knowledge of Persian, which, though slight, is sufficient to enable him to introduce words and expressions in that language, often when they are not needed, but still it is pure Oordoo; he prides himself upon it, and holds in supreme contempt those who speak the corrupt patois of the Dukhun, or the still worse one of Hindostan. Altogether Ameer Ali is a character, and a man of immense importance in his own opinion and that of every one else; and the swagger which he has now adopted in his gait, but which is evidently foreign to him, does not sit amiss on his now reduced condition.

Reader, if you can embody these descriptions, you have Ameer Ali before you; and while you gaze on the picture in your imagination and look on the mild and expressive face you have fancied, you, as I was, would be the last person to think that he was a professed murderer, and one who in the course of his life has committed upwards of seven hundred murders. I mean by this, that he has been actively and personally engaged in the destruction of that number of human beings.

Now, Ameer Ali, said I, since I have finished describing your appearance, I hope you are ready to contribute more to the stock of adventures you have already related.

Your slave is ready, Sahib, he replied, and Inshalla Ta-alla! he will not disappoint you. But why has my lord described my poor appearance, which is now miserable enough? But might your slave ask what you have written?—and the tone of his voice implied that he had concluded it could not be favourable.

Listen, said I, and I will read it to you. At every sentence the expression of his face brightened. When I had concluded, he said:

It is a faithful picture, such as I behold myself when I look in a glass. You have omitted nothing, even to the most trifling particulars; nay, I may even say, my lord has flattered me. And he arose and made a profound salam.

No, said I, I have not flattered your external appearance, which is prepossessing; but of your heart I fear those who read will judge for themselves, and their opinions will not be such as you could wish, but such as you deserve.

You think my heart bad then, Sahib?

Certainly I do.

But it is not so, he continued. Have I not ever been a kind husband and a faithful friend? Did I not love my children and wife while He who is above spared them to me? and do I not even now bitterly mourn their deaths? Where is the man existing who can say a word against Ameer Ali's honour, which ever has been and ever will remain pure and unsullied? Have I ever broken a social tie? ever been unfaithful or unkind to a comrade? ever failed in my duty or in my trust? ever neglected a rite or ceremony of my religion? I tell you, Sahib, the man breathes not who could point his finger at me on any one of these points. And if you think on them, they are those which, if rigidly kept, gain for a man esteem and honour in the world.

But the seven hundred murders, Ameer Ali,—what can you say to them? They make a fearful balance against you in the other scale.

Ah! those are a different matter, said the Thug laughing,—quite a different matter. I can never persuade you that I was fully authorized to commit them, and only a humble instrument in the hands of Alla. Did *I* kill one of those persons? No! it was He. Had my roomal been a thousand times thrown about their necks and the strength of an elephant in my arms, could I have done aught,—would they have died,—without it was His will? I tell you, Sahib, they would not, they could not; but as I shall never be able to persuade you to think otherwise, and as it is not respectful in me to bandy words with my lord, I think it is time for me to recommence my tale, if he is ready to listen, for I have still much to relate. I have been so minute in the particulars of my first expedition that perhaps I need not make the narrative of the other events of my life so prolix; indeed, were I to do so, you, Sahib, would be tired of writing and your countrymen of reading, for it would be an almost endless task to follow me in every expedition I undertook. I shall therefore, with your permission, confine myself to the narration of those which I think will most interest you, and which I remember to possess remarkable incidents.

Go on, said I; I listen.

Well then, said the Thug, Khodawund must remember that I told him I passed over three expeditions, and that I had partly determined to go on the third. It is of that expedition I would now speak, as it was marked by an extraordinary circumstance, which will show you at once that it is impossible for any one to avoid his fate if it be the will of Alla that he should die.

At the time I speak of I had been obliged to form another set of intimates in consequence of the loss of Bhudrinath and Surfuraz Khan, for both of whom I had the sincerest regard. Hoosein, though I loved and revered him as my father's dearest friend, was now too old and grave to participate in all my thoughts and perhaps wild aspirations for distinction. So as Peer Khan and Motee-ram, with whose names you are familiar, had now risen to my own rank, and proved themselves to be 'good men and true' in various expeditions, I took them into my confidence, and we planned an enterprise, of which I was to be the leader and they my subordinates. Fifty of the youngest, stoutest, and most active and enterprising of our acquaintance were fixed on as the band; and all having been previously warned, we met a few days before the Dussera of the year 18—in a grove near our village, which was shady and well adapted for large assemblies, and was always used as a place of meeting and deliberation; it was considered a lucky spot, no unfortunate expedition ever having set out from it.

We were all assembled. It was a lovely morning, and the grass, as yet not even browned by the sun and drought, was as if a soft and beautiful carpet had been spread on purpose for us. The surrounding fields, many of them tilled by our own hands, waved in green luxuriance, and the wind as it passed over them in gentle gusts caused each stalk of tall jowaree to be agitated, while the sun shining brightly made the whole glitter so that it was almost painful to look on for a continuance. Birds sang in the lofty banian trees which overshadowed us; hundreds of green parroquets sported and screamed in their branches, as they flew from bough to bough, some in apparent sport, others to feed on the now ripening berries of the trees; and the whole grove resounded with the cooing of innumerable turtle-doves, whose gentle and loving murmurs soothed the turbulence of the heart, and bade it be at peace and rest and as happy as they were.

My father and Hoosein were present to guide us by their counsels and experience, and the matter in hand was commenced by a sacrifice and invocation to Bhowanee; but as I have before described these ceremonies, it is needless to repeat them; suffice it to say that the omens were taken and were favourable in the highest degree; they assured us, and though I had little faith in them, notwithstanding all I had heard to convince me of their necessity, they inspirited the whole band, and I partook of the general hilarity consequent upon them.

My father opened the object of the meeting in a short address. He said he was old and no longer fitted for the fatigues and privations of a journey; he recapitulated all I had done on the former expedition, pointed out the various instances in which I had displayed activity, daring, and prudence beyond my years, and concluded by imploring the men to place implicit confidence in me, to obey me in all things as though himself were present, and above all not to give way to any disposition to quarrel among themselves, which would infallibly lead to the same disastrous results as had overtaken the expedition which had gone out the previous year.

They one and all rose after this address, and by mutual consent swore on the sacred pickaxe to obey me, the most impressive oath they could take, and any deviation from which they all firmly believed would draw down the vengeance of our Protectress upon them and lead to their destruction.

I will not occupy your time, Sahib, by a narration of what I myself said; suffice it to say, I proposed that the band should take the high road to the Dukhun, and penetrate as far as Jubbulpoor or Nagpoor; from thence we would take a direction eastward or westward, as hope of booty offered, and so return to our home. Khandesh I mentioned, as being but little known to us Thugs, and where I thought it likely we might meet with good booty, as I had heard that the traders of Bombay were in the habit of sending large quantities of treasure to their correspondents at Malwa for the purchase of opium and other products of that district. I concluded by assuring them that I had a strong presentiment of great success, that I felt confidence in myself, and that if they would only follow me faithfully and truly, we might return in a few months as well laden with spoil as we had on the former occasion.

Again they rose and pledged their faith; and truly it was a solemn sight to see those determined men nerve themselves for an enterprise which might end happily, but which exposed them to fearful risk of detection, dishonour, and death.

SOURCE: Philip Meadows Taylor, *Confessions of a Thug* (London: R. Bentley, 1837).

Thug Approvers
CAPTAIN WILLIAM H. SLEEMAN

Extracts from Captain W. H. Sleeman's investigations into the customs and beliefs of Thuggee.

Sleeman: Do you ever recollect any misfortune arising from going on when a hare crossed the road before you?

Nasir: Yes. When General Doveton commanded the troops at Jhalna we were advancing towards his camp; a hare crossed the road; we disregarded the omen, though the hare actually screamed in crossing and went on. The very next day, I, with seventeen of our gang, were seized; and it was with great difficulty and delay that we got our release. We had killed some people belonging to the troops, but fortunately none of their property was found upon us.

And you think these signs are all mandates from the deity, and, if properly attended to, no harm can befall you?

Certainly; no one doubts it; ask anybody. How could Thugs have otherwise prospered? Have they not everywhere been protected as long as they have attended religiously to their rules?

But if there was such a deity as Bhowani, and she were your patroness, how could she allow me and others to seize and punish so many Thugs?

I have a hundred times heard my father and other old and wise men say, when we had killed a sweeper and otherwise infringed their rules, that we should be some day punished for it; that the European rulers would be made the instruments to chastise us for our disregard of omens and neglect of the rules laid down for our guidance.

(*The pickaxe is supposed to be possessed of supernatural powers and to fly at call to the hand of the Thug initiate.*)

You have heard this from your fathers, who heard it from their fathers; but none of you have ever seen it, nor is it true?

It is true; quite true. And though we have not seen this, we have all of us seen the sacred pickaxe spring in the morning from the well into which it had been thrown overnight, and come to the hands of the man who carried it at his call. Nay, we have seen the pickaxes of different gangs all come up of themselves from the same well at the same time, and go to their several bearers.

(To Sahib Khan) You are a Muslim?

Yes; and the greater part of the Thugs of the South are Mussulmans.

And you still marry, inherit, pray, eat and drink according to the Koran? And your Paradise is to be the Paradise promised by Mahomed?

Yes, all, all!

Has Bhowani been anywhere named in the Koran?

Nowhere.

(Here a Muslim Thug from Hindustan interposed, and said he thought Bhowani and Fatima, the daughter of Mahomed, and wife of Ali, were one and the same person; and that it was Fatima who invented the use of the *rumal* to strangle the great demon, Rukt Bijdana; which led to a discussion between him and some of my Muslim native officers, who did not like to find the amiable Fatima made a goddess of Thuggee,—an "Iphigenia in Tauris." The Thug was a sturdy wrangler and in the estimation of his associate Thugs had, I think, the best of the argument.)

Then has Bhowani anything to do with your Paradise?

Nothing.

She has no influence on your future state?

None.

Does Mahomed, your prophet, anywhere sanction crimes like yours; the murder in cold blood of your fellow creatures for the sake of their money?

No.

Then do you never feel any dread of punishment hereafter?

Never. We never murder unless the omens are favourable; and we consider favourable omens as the mandate of the Deity.

What Deity?

Bhowani.

Bhowani, you say, has no influence upon the welfare, or otherwise, of your soul hereafter?

None, we believe; but she influences our fates in this world, and what she orders in this world, we believe that God will not punish in the next.

[Here Sleeman gave up the hopeless argument.]

And do you never feel any sympathy for the persons murdered—never any pity or compunction?

Never.

How can you murder old men and young children without some motions of pity—calmly and deliberately as they sit with you and converse with you and tell you of their private affairs, of their hopes and fears, of the wives and children they are going to meet after years of absence, toil and suffering?

From the time that the omens have been favourable, we consider them as victims thrown into our hands by the deity to be killed, and that we are the mere instruments in her hands to destroy them: that if we do not kill them, she will never be again propitious to us, and we and our families will be involved in misery and want.

And you can sleep as soundly by the bodies and over the graves of those whom you have murdered, and eat your meals with as much appetite as ever?

Just the same; we sleep and eat just the same unless we are afraid of being discovered.

Do your wives never reproach you with your deeds?

In the South we never tell our wives what we do lest they should disclose our secrets.

And your children too reverence their Thug fathers like other sons, even after they have become acquainted with their trade?

The same. We love them and they love us.

At what age do you initiate them?

I was initiated by my father when I was only thirteen years of age.

Do they not become frightened?

Not after the second or third expedition.

Feringheea: About twelve years ago my cousin, Aman Subadar, took out with us my cousin, Kurhora, brother of Umrao, a lad of fourteen, for the first time. He was mounted upon a pretty pony, and Harsuka, who had been already on three expeditions, an adopted son of Aman's, was appointed to take charge of the boy. We fell in with five Sikhs and, when we set out before daylight in the morning, Harsuka was ordered to take the bridle and keep the boy in the rear out of sight and hearing.

The boy became alarmed and impatient and got away from Harsuka and galloped up at the instant the *Jhirni*, or signal for murder was given. He heard the screams of the men and saw them all strangled. He was seized with a trembling and fell from his pony. He became immediately delirious, was dreadfully alarmed at the sight of the turbans of the murdered men, and when anyone touched or spoke to him, talked about the murders and screamed exactly like a boy talks in his sleep, and trembled violently if anyone touched or spoke to him. We could not get him on and, after burying the bodies, Aman and I and a few others sat by him while the gang went on; we tried to tranquillize him, but he never recovered his senses and before evening he died. I have seen many instances of people greatly shocked at the first murder, but never one so strong as this. Kurhora was a very fine boy, and Harsuka took his death much to heart, and turned Byragi [monk]; he is now at some temple on the bank of the Nerbudda river.

Was not Jharhu, who was taken with your gang after the Bhilsa murders and hung at Jubbulpore, a brother of his?

Feringheea: Yes, poor Jharhu! You ought not to have hung him; he never strangled or assisted in strangling any man!

(Here the tears ran down over Feringheea's face. Strange as it may seem, I have never heard him speak of his young cousin Jharhu's fate without weeping, and yet all the males of his family have been Thugs for generations and neither he nor any of them would shed one tear for any man or woman whom they had done to death. Another brother of this Jharhu was a very noted Thug leader, at that time still at large, of the name of Phulsa.)

But you worship at Devi's temples? [Devi being the Hindu goddess, consort of the god Siva.]

Yes, of course. All men worship at her temple.

No. We sahib log [folk] never do.

I mean all Hindus and Muslims.

(Here my Mahomedan officers again interposed and declared that they never did: that it was only the very lowest orders of Muslims who did. But, unfortunately, these keen observers of passing events had seen the wives of some very respectable Muslims at Jubbulpore, during the time the smallpox was raging, take their children to her temples and prostrate them before the images of the Goddess of Destruction. The officers admitted this to be sometimes the case, but pretended that it was unknown to their husbands.)

Tell me frankly which oath, now while you are in custody, you who are Muslims deem the strongest—that upon the Koran or that upon the pickaxes?

If we could be allowed to consecrate the pickaxe in the prescribed form, neither the Koran nor anything else on earth could be so binding; but without consecration it would be of no avail.

Above the Nerbudda, chiefs have never had the same dread of punishing Thugs as below it, have they?

They had formerly, and have still in many parts.

Why should they fear? Have there been any instances of suffering from it?

A great many. Was not Nanha, the Rajah of Jalaun, made leprous by Devi for putting to death Budhu and his brother Khumoli, two of the most noted Thugs of their day? He had them trampled under the feet of elephants, but the leprosy broke out upon his body the very next day.

Did he believe that this punishment was inflicted by Devi for putting them to death?

Durgha: He was quite sensible of it.

Did he do anything to appease her?

Everything. Budhu had begun a well in Jalaun. The Rajah built it up in a magnificent style: he had a *chabutra* [tomb] raised to their name, fed Brahmans and consecrated it and had worship instituted upon it but all in vain. The disease was incurable and the Rajah died in a few months, a miserable death. The tombs and well are both kept up and visited by hundreds to this day and no one doubts that the Rajah was punished for putting these two Thugs to death.

Nasir: Ah, Devi took care of them, and why? Was it not that you were more attentive to her orders?

Durgha: The Company's *iqbal* [good fortune] is such that before the sound of your drums, sorcerers, witches and demons take flight, and how can Thuggee stand?

Devi Din: Thuggee! Why it is gone. There are not fifty *Asal* [Thugs of good birth] left between the Ganges and Jumna.

Choti, Brahman: And not more than that number of all our old clans of Gwalior and Bundelkhand. But the Suseas of Rajputana have been untouched, and much is to be done about Delhi and Patiala.

But Nasir and Sahib Khan think it can never be suppressed in the Deccan?

Nasir: I think it never can.

Then by whose killing have all the Thugs who have been hung at Saugor and Jubbulpore been killed?

God's, of course.

You think that we could never have caught and executed them but by the aid of God?

Certainly not.

Then you think that so far we have been assisted by God in what we have done?

Yes.

And you are satisfied that we should not have ventured to do what we have done unless we were assured that our God was working with us, or rather that we were the mere instruments of his hands?

Yes, I am.

Then do you not think that we may go on with the same assurance till the work we have in hand is done; till, in short, the system of Thuggee is suppressed?

God is almighty.

And there is but one God?

One God above all gods.

And if that God above all gods supports us, we shall succeed?

Certainly.

Then we are all satisfied that he is assisting us, and therefore hope to succeed even in the Deccan?

God only knows.

Sahib Khan: If God assists, you will succeed, but the country is large and favourable and the gangs are numerous and well organized.

How is it you Hindustan Thugs kill women with less scruple than the Deccan Thugs?

Feringheea: To that we owe much of our misfortunes. It began with the murder of the Kali Bibi.

Who was the Kali Bibi?

Durgha: I was not present but I have heard that she was on her way from Elichpore to Hyderabad with a gold *chadar* or sheet for the tomb of Daula Khan Nawab, the brother of Salabat Khan of Hyderabad, who had died just before. Shansher Khan and Ghulab Khan strangled her, I believe.

Did any calamity befall you after the murder of the Kali Bibi?

I think not.

And therefore you continued to kill them?

Feringheea: For five years no misfortune befell us and they continued to kill women. But then the misfortunes of my family began.

And you are worse than the Deccan Thugs, for you murder handsome young women as well as the old and ugly?

Not always. I and my cousin Aman Subadar were with a gang of one hundred and fifty Thugs on an expedition through Rajputana about thirteen years ago when we met a handmaiden of the Peshwa's, Baji Rau's, on her way from Poona to Cawnpore. We intended to kill her and her followers, but we found her very beautiful and, after having her and her party three days within our grasp, and knowing that they had a lac and a half of rupees worth of property in jewels and other things with them, we let her and all her party go. We had talked to her and felt love towards her, for she was very beautiful.

And how came you to kill the Moghulani? She also is said to have been very handsome?

We none of us ventured near her palankeen. The Muslims were the only men who approached her before the murder. Madar Bakhsh strangled her.

And you think killing women has been one of the chief causes of your misfortunes?

Yes.

How did you preserve the infant daughter of Banda Ali Munshi for adoption?

Chattar: Ghubbu Khan strangled the mother while her infant was in her arms, and he determined to keep and adopt the child. But, after the bodies had all been put into the grave, Dhanni Khan urged him to kill the child also, or we should be seized on crossing the Nerbudda valley. He threw the child living in upon the dead bodies, and the grave was filled up over it.

And the child was buried alive?

Yes.

How was that affair managed?

We fell in with the Munshi and his family at Chapra, between Nagpore and Jubbulpore, and they came on with us to Lucknadaun, where we found that some Companies of a Native Regiment under European officers were expected the next morning. It was determined to put all of the Munshi's party to death that evening, as he seemed likely to keep with the Companies. Our encampment was near the village, and the Munshi's tent was pitched close to us. In the afternoon some of the officers' tents came on in advance, and were pitched on the other side, leaving us between them and the village. The *Khalasis* [coolies] were all busily occupied in pitching them. Nur Khan and his son, Sadi Khan, and a few others went as soon as it became dark to the Munshi's tent and began to sing and play upon a sitar, as they had been accustomed to do. During this time some of them took up the Munshi's sword on pretence of wishing to look at it. His wife and children were inside listening to the music. The *Jhirni*, or signal, was given, but at this moment the Munshi saw his danger, called out 'Murder!' and attempted to rush through, but was seized and strangled. His wife, hearing him, ran out with the infant in her arms, but was seized by Ghubbu Khan, who strangled her and took the infant. The *Saises* (grooms) were at the time cleaning their horses and one of them seeing his danger, ran under the belly of his horse and called out 'Murder!' but he was soon seized and strangled, as well as all the rest.

How did not the *Khalasis* and others who were pitching the tents close by hear these calls for help?

As soon as the signal was given, those of the gang who were idle began to play and sing as loud as they could, and two vicious horses were let loose and many ran after them calling out as loudly as they could, so that the cries of the Munshi and his party were drowned.

Do you Thugs from Bihar ever murder women?

Bhidda: How could we do so? We do not even murder a person that has a cow with him, for we regard the cow as sacred and his master immune.

Did not the Hindus assist in strangling the women in the Sutrooh and Chalisrooh affairs?

Punna: God forbid! They sinned enough in consenting to share in the booty, but they never assisted in the murder.

Are you never afraid of the spirits of the persons you murder?

Nasir: Never, they cannot trouble us.

Why? Do they not trouble other men when they commit a murder?

Of course they do. The man who commits a murder is always haunted by spirits. He has sometimes fifty at a time upon him, and they drive him mad.

And how do they not trouble you?

Are not the people whom we kill, killed by the orders of Devi?

Kalyan: Yes. It is by the blessing of Devi that we escape evil.

Durgha: Do not all whom we kill go to Paradise, and why should their spirits stay to trouble us?

Inaent: A good deal of our security from spirits is to be attributed to the *rumal* with which we strangle.

I did not know that there was any virtue in the *rumal*?

Inaent: Is it not our sikka [ensign] as the pickaxe is our nishan [standard]?

Feringheea: More is attributable to the pickaxe. Do we not worship it every seventh day? Is it not our standard? Is its sound ever heard when digging the grave by any but a Thug? And can any man even swear to a falsehood upon it?

And no other instrument would answer, you think, for making the graves?

Nasir: How could we dig graves with any other instruments! This is the one appointed by Devi, and consecrated, and we should never have survived the attempt to use any other.

Feringheea: No man but a Thug who had been a strangler, and is remarkable for his cleanliness and decorum is permitted to carry it.

Are the usages of the River Thugs the same as yours?

Moradun: In worship, the same. They strangle in boats and throw the bodies into the river. If they see blood, they must go back and open the expedition anew. They give the Jhirni by first striking on the deck of the boat three times, when the man appointed to give it sees all clear.

Have the River Thugs the same Ramasi [dialect] as you?

Imam Bakhsh: No, totally different. They neither understand our Ramasi, nor do we theirs.

(I then sent for Buktawar.)

You are said to have occasionally gone with the River Thugs. What do you call them?

We call them Pungus. On one occasion only have I ever served with them.

Where do they live?

They live about Beerbohm, Bankura, Kulna-Kutwa, Seori and other places in the district of Burdwan, which is a very large district. Thugs do not live in these or any other towns, as they are there always liable to be a good deal annoyed by police questions, but live in small villages round about them. Annoying police questions are such as, Who's come? Who's gone? Who's born? Who's died? What's your occupation? Whence your income? and so forth. These questions annoy Thugs a good deal, and oblige them to share their incomes with the policemen as well as with the *zumeendars* [landowners].

When you have a poor traveller with you, or a party of travellers who appear to have little property about them, and you hear or see a very good omen, do you not let them go, in the hope that the virtue of the omen will guide you to better prey?

Durgha: Let them go! never, never!—*kabhi nahin, kabhi nahin!*

Nasir: How could we let them go? Is not the good omen the order from Heaven to kill them, and would it not be a disobedience to let them go? If we did not kill them, should we ever get any more travellers?

Feringheea: I have known the experiment tried with good effect. I have known travellers who promised little, let go, and the virtue of the omen brought better.

Inaent: Yes. The virtue of the omen remains, but the traveller who had little should be let go, for you are sure to get a better.

Sahib Khan: Never, never! This is one of your Hindustani heresies. You could never let him go without losing all the fruits of your expedition. You might get property, but it could never do you any good. No success could result from your disobedience!

Morlee: Certainly not! The travellers who are in our hands when we have a good omen must never be let go, whether they promise little or much. The omen is unquestionably the order, as Nasir says.

Nasir: The idea of securing the good will of Devi by disobeying her order, is quite monstrous. We Deccan Thugs do not understand how you got hold of this. Our ancestors were never guilty of such folly.

Feringheea: You do not mean to say that we of Murnai and Sindause were not as well instructed as you of Telingana?

Nasir and Sahib Khan: We only mean to say that you have clearly mistaken the nature of a good omen in this case. It is the order of Devi to take what she has put in your way—at least, so we in the Deccan understand it.

You told Mr Johnstone, the traveller, while he was at Saugor, that the operations of your trade were to be seen in the caves at Ellora?

Feringheea: All! Every one of the operations is to be seen there. In one place you see men strangling: in another burying the bodies: in another carrying them off to the graves. There is not one operation in Thuggee that is not exhibited in the caves of Ellora.

Durgha: In those caves are to be seen the operations of every trade in the world.

Choti: Whenever we passed near, we used to go and see these caves. Every man will there find his trade described, however secret he may think it; and they were all made in one night.

Does any person beside yourself consider that any of these figures represent Thugs?

Feringheea: Nobody else, but all Thugs know they do. We never told anyone else what we thought about them. Everybody there can see the secret operations of his trade, but he does not tell others of them, and no other person can understand what they mean. They are the works of God. No human hands were employed upon them. That everybody admits.

What particular operations are there described in figures?

Sahib Khan: I have seen the *Sotha* [inveigler] sitting upon the same carpet with the traveller, and in close conversation with him, just as we are when we are worming out their secrets. In another place, the strangler [*Bhartote*] has got his *rumal* over his neck and is strangling him; while another, the *Chamochi*, is holding him by the legs. These are the only two operations that I have seen described.

Nasir: These I have also seen, and there is no mistaking them. The *Chamochi* has a close hold of the legs and is pulling at them, *thus*, while the Bhartote is tightening the *rumal* round his neck, *thus*.

Have you seen no others?

Feringheea: I have seen these two, and also the *Lughas* carrying away the bodies to the graves, *in this manner,* and the sextons digging the grave with the sacred pickaxe. All is done just as if we had done it ourselves; nothing could be more exact.

And who do you think could have executed this work?

Feringheea: It could not have been done by Thugs because they would never have exposed the secrets of their trade, and no other human being could have done it. It must be the work of the gods; human hands could never have performed it.

And, supposing so, you go and worship it?

Sahib Khan: No. We go to gratify curiosity, and not to worship. We look upon it as a mausoleum, a collection of curious figures cut by some Demons, who knew the secrets of all mankind, and amused themselves in describing them.

Harnagar: We Hindus go for the same purpose. We never go to worship. We consider it as a Pantheon of unknown Gods.

But where did you fall in with Feringheea and the Moghulani?

Durgha: We fell in with them at Lalsont and came on with them to Somp. She had with her an old female servant, mounted upon a pony, one manservant and six bearers for her palankeen. From Somp we sent on men to select a place for the murder, and set out with her before daylight; but the Thug who selects the place of murder, the *bele*, lost the road in the dark, and we were trying to find it when the young woman became alarmed and began to reproach us for taking her into the jungle in the dark. We told Feringheea to come up and quieten her but, dreading that some of her party might make off, the signal was given and they were all strangled. We got six hundred rupees worth of property from them.

And was this enough to tempt so large a gang to murder a beautiful young woman?

We were very adverse to it, and often said that we should not get two rupees apiece, and that she ought to be let go. But Feringheea insisted upon taking her.

How came you to advise the murder of this young woman?

Feringheea: It was her fate to die by our hands. I had several times tried to shake them off before we met the Muslims, and when we came to Lalsont, I told her to go on, as I had joined some old friends and would be delayed. She then told me that I must go to her home near Agra, or she would get me into trouble; and being a Brahman while she was a Muslim, I was afraid that I should be accused of improper intercourse and turned out of caste.

You were then a young man and she was a beautiful young woman. Had you no pity?

Madar Baksh: *I* had. But I had undertaken the duty and we must all have food. *I have never known any other means of gaining it.*

(It was this last statement that showed me that there might be a gleam of hope in trying to redeem these men, or at least some of them.)

Feringheea: We all feel pity sometimes, but the *goor* [sugar] of the Tuponi[1] changes our nature. It would change the nature of a horse. Let any man once taste of that *goor*, and he will be a Thug, though he knows all the trades and have all the wealth in the world. I never wanted food; my mother's family was opulent, her relations in high office. I have been in high office myself, and became so great a favourite wherever I went that I was sure of promotion, yet I was always miserable while absent from my gang, and obliged to return to Thuggee. My father made me taste of that fatal *goor* when I was yet a mere boy, and, if I were to live a thousand years, I should never be able to follow any other trade.

Kalyan Sing: When our gang was arrested at Hoshungabad, was there not a scramble among the Hill Chiefs and Zamindars to get us released upon their security? Did not many, both there and at Jubbulpore, who had never seen us in their lives, make their agents offer any security that could be demanded for our future good behaviour?

And why did they do this? They no doubt thought you very innocent and respectable men under misfortune?

Not at all. We managed to persuade them that we could by being allowed to follow our old trade under their protection, be made a new source of revenue to them. We told them that we would pay for the little land we might cultivate in their villages more than fifty times its value.

Choti: Did not the Khairo chief stand a long siege from his master, the Jhansi Rajah, before he would give up eight or ten of us?

Qaim Khan: And was not the Maharajah of Gwalior obliged to send two large guns and a great force against Bhume Zamindar of Bahmanpore before he would give us up; and were not several lives lost in the action which continued from daylight till nine in the morning? Bhume was very fond of us, particularly of our Jemadar Ghulab Khan, whose father had been hung the year before at Saugor, and who is now an approver with Mr Thomas, and he said that he would rather die than give us up. But, poor man, he had only sixteen muskets to fight with, and had got into disgrace at Court by

---

1. *Tuponi*, or *Tupounee*, sacrifice of *goor* to Bhowani (Kali). The *goor* or coarse sugar is placed on a clean cloth close to the consecrated pickaxe and a piece of silver. The leader of the gang sits besides these, places some *goor* in a hole in the ground, raises hands and eyes to heaven and prays.

not paying his rents! The Lord Sahib (Lord William Bentinck) must have heard the guns, for he and the Rai Sahib were encamped only a few miles off at the time.

How was it that this lad's father, an old and noted Thug, did not initiate him himself?

Buktawar: His father used to drink very hard, and in his fits of intoxication he used to neglect his *prayers,* and his *days of fast.* All days were the same to him. This lad, Shamshera, was always sober and *religiously disposed,* and separated from his father, living always with his uncle Dundi, *who was a very worthy and good man.*

But he was a Thug also?

Yes, he was, but he did not tell this boy so.

SOURCE: In Sir Francis Tuker, *The Yellow Scarf: The Story of the Life of Thuggee Sleeman* (London: J. M. Dent and Sons, Ltd., 1961).

VIII
SUTTEE/SATI

INTRODUCTION
Sati/Suttee: Observances, Abolition, Observations
BARBARA HARLOW AND MIA CARTER

Like thuggee/thagi, Sati, the customary Hindu practice of widow immolation, captured the attention and imaginations of British administrators and reformers. In his "Minute" proposing its abolition, William Bentinck—governor-general of India from 1828 to 1835—described at some length the several considerations that led him to propose the legislative act. Despite the risks such an action threatened, the beneficial advantages, he claimed, were more substantial. The perils were real, however, and included a certain circumspection with regard to interfering in native religious practices, lest such intrusion arouse among native observers a well-grounded suspicion of further incursion or, more risky still for British rule, lead to open opposition, even resistance from within the ranks of the sepoys in the British army in India. Women-related issues would emerge again in the latter half of the century, when the subjects of polygamy and child marriage figured in the legislature, but for Bentinck, the abolition of sati was a considered response to the authority of a newly established legal/moral precedent and the imperatives of humanity and "civilization"; reform would be carried out not only for the "benefit of the Hindus" themselves, in the establishment of a "purer morality," but would additionally serve to "wash out a foul stain upon British rule" (527).

Although sati had much earlier been prescribed in the annals of Hindu law (which were translated by H. T. Colebrooke) under the rubric of the "duties of a faithful widow," duties that included "dying with or after her husband," there were in India at the time local advocates of its proscription. In petitions and addresses, in particular from the reformer Raja Ram Mohan Roy and his supporters, the argument was that the law itself had been egregiously misapplied in a "system of female destruction": "While in fact fulfilling the suggestion of their jealousy, they [Hindu princes] pretended to justify this hideous practice by quoting some passages from authorities of evidently inferior weight, sanctioning the wilful ascent of a widow on the flaming pile of her husband, as if they were offering such female sacrifices in obedience to the dictates of the Shastrus and not from the influence of jealousy" (Address to Lord Bentinck, 1830, this volume, 370–371).

But if the observance of sati was officially abolished in India in 1829, European depictions of the practice persisted throughout the century, from the writings of thuggee expert William H. Sleeman (*Rambles and Recollections*, 1844) to those of Jules Verne, whose Phileas Fogg saves a Bombay widow from such destruction, a woman who then accompanies Fogg and his companion, Passepartout, through the rest of their journey in *Around the World in Eighty Days* (1873). Hegel, too, had made the practice a part of his "philosophy of history," and Charles Dickens—whose periodical, *Household Words*, had published several articles on the custom—reenacted it, in a fashion, in the immolation of Miss Havisham in *Great Expectations* (1861). Sati's reproduction also became the basis for a midcentury advertisement of Egyptian cigarettes: "With only a Suttee's passion / To do their duty and burn." More recently, Gerald Crich, the zealous and pragmatic modernist antihero of D. H. Lawrence's *Women in Love* (1917), looked back with nostalgia to the "good old days" of Indian widow sacrifice as he contemplated the financial burden of supporting the Crich Coal Mine's dependent widows. Since the nineteenth century, according to Lata Mani, the "abolition of sati (widow immolation) by the British in 1829 has become a founding moment in the history of women in modern India" ("Contentious Traditions," 89).

BIBLIOGRAPHY

Dickens, Charles. "Heathen and Christian Burial." *Household Words* 1, no. 2 (1850).
———. "Suttee in China." *All the Year Round* 127, no. 6 (1861).
Mani, Lata. "Contentious Traditions: The Debate on Sati in Colonial India." In *Recasting Women: Essays in Indian Colonial History*, edited by Kumkum Sangari and Sudesh Vaid, 88–126. New Brunswick, N.J.: Rutgers University Press, 1990.
———. *Contentious Traditions: The Debate on Sati in Colonial India*. Berkeley: University of California Press, 1998.
Peggs, James. *The Suttee's Cry: Containing Extracts from Essays Published in India and Parliamentary Papers on the Burning of Hindoo Widows*. London: Seely, 1827.
Sakuntala, Narasimhan. *Sati: Widow Burning in India*. New York: Penguin Books, 1992.
Sleeman, William H. *Rambles and Collections of an Indian Official*. London: J. Hatchard and Son, 1844.
Spivak, Gayatri Chakravorty. "Can the Subaltern Speak?" In *Marxism and the Interpretation of Culture*, edited by Cary Nelson and Lawrence Grossberg, 271–313. Urbana, Ill.: University of Illinois Press, 1988.

Stratton Hawley, John, ed. *Sati, the Blessing and the Curse: The Burning of Wives in India.* Oxford: Oxford University Press, 1994.

Sunder Rajan, Rajeswari. *Real and Imagined Women: Gender, Culture, and Postcolonialism.* London: Routledge, 1993.

Thompson, Edward. *Suttee: A Historical and Philosophical Enquiry into the Hindu Rite of Widow Burning.* Boston: Houghton Mifflin Company, 1928.

Upreti, Harish Chandra. *The Myth of Sati: Some Dimensions of Widow Burning.* Bombay: Himalaya House, 1991.

Weinberger-Thomas, Catherine. *Ashes of Immortality: Widow-Burning in India.* Chicago: University of Chicago Press, 1999.

Suttee

COLONEL HENRY YULE AND A. C. BURNELL

[Compiled by participants of the "raj" in the latter half of the nineteenth century, *Hobson-Jobson* has since become a standard reference—and a nomer—for the diction and vocabulary of the English lexical reconstructions of nearly two centuries of British history in India.]

Suttee, s. The rite of widow-burning; *i.e.* the burning of the living widow along with the corpse of her husband, as practised by people of certain castes among the Hindus, and eminently by the Rājpūts.

The word is properly Skt. *satī*, 'a good woman,' 'a true wife,' and thence specially applied, in modern vernaculars of Sanskrit parentage, to the wife who was considered to accomplish the supreme act of fidelity by sacrificing herself on the funeral pile of her husband. The application of this substantive to the suicidal act, instead of the person, is European. The proper Skt. term for the act is *sahagamana*, or 'keeping company,' [*sahamarana*, 'dying together'].[1] A very long series of quotations in illustration of the practice, from classical times downwards, might be given. We shall present a selection.

We should remark that the word (*satī* or *suttee*) does not occur, so far as we know, in any European work older than the 17th century. And then it only occurs in a disguised form (see quotation from P. Della Valle). The term *masti* which he uses is probably *mahd-satī*, which occurs in Skt. Dictionaries ('a wife of great virtue'). Della Valle is usually eminent in the correctness of his transcriptions of Oriental words. This conjecture of the interpretation of *masti* is confirmed, and the traveller himself justified, by an entry in Mr. Whitworth's Dictionary of a word *Masti-kalla* used in Canara for a

---

1. But it is worthy of note that in the Island of Bali one manner of accomplishing the rite is called Satis (skt. *satyā*, 'truth,' from *sat*, whence also *satī*). See *Crawford, H. of Ind. Archip.* ii. 248, and *Friedrich*, in *Verhandelingen van les Batav. Genootschap.* xxiii. 10.

monument commemorating a *sati*. *Kalla* is stone and *masti* = *mahd-satī*. We have not found the term exactly in any European document older than Sir C. Malet's letter of 1787, and Sir W. Jones's of the same year (see below).

Suttee is a Brahmanical rite, and there is a Sanskrit ritual in existence (see *Classified Index to the Tanjore MSS.*, p. 135*a*). It was introduced into Southern India with the Brahman civilisation, and was prevalent there chiefly in the Brahmanical Kingdom of Vijayanagar, and among the Mahrattas. In Malabar, the most primitive part of S. India, the rite is forbidden (*Anachdranirnaya*, v. 26). The cases mentioned by Teixeira below, and in the *Lettres Edifiantes*, occurred at Tanjore and Madura. A (Mahratta) Brahman at Tanjore told one of the present writers that he had to perform commemorative funeral rites for his grandfather and grandmother on the same day, and this indicated that his grandmother had been a *satī*.

The practice has prevailed in various regions besides India. Thus it seems to have been an early custom among the heathen Russians, or at least among nations on the Volga called Russians by Maṣ'ūdī and Ibn Fozlān. Herodotus (Bk. v. ch. 5) describes it among certain tribes of Thracians. It was in vogue in Tonga and the Fiji Islands. It has prevailed in the island of Bali within our own time, though there accompanying Hindu rites, and perhaps of Hindu origin,—certainly modified by Hindu influence. A full account of Suttee as practised in those Malay Islands will be found in Zollinger's account of the Religion of Sassak in *J. Ind. Arch.* ii. 166; also see Friedrich's *Bali* as in note preceding. [A large number of references to *Suttee* are collected in Frazer, *Pausanias*, iii. 198 *seqq.*]

In Diodorus we have a long account of the rivalry as to which of the two wives of Kēteus, a leader of the Indian contingent in the army of Eumenes, should perform suttee. One is rejected as with child. The history of the other terminates thus:

B.C. 317.—"Finally, having taken leave of those of the household, she was set upon the pyre by her own brother, and was regarded with wonder by the crowd that had run together to the spectacle, and heroically ended her life; the whole force with their arms thrice marching round the pyre before it was kindled. But she, laying herself beside her husband, and even at the violence of the flame giving utterance to no unbecoming cry, stirred pity indeed in others of the spectators, and in some excess of eulogy; not but what there were some of the Greeks present who reprobated such rites as barbarous and cruel. . . ."—*Diod. Sic. Biblioth.* xix. 33–34.

Suttee/Sati

c. B.C. 30.

"Felix Eois lex funeris una maritis
Quos Aurora suis rubra colorat equis;
Namque ubi mortifero jacta est fax ultima lecto
Uxorum fusis stat pia turba comis;
Et certamen habet leti, quae viva sequatur
Conjugium; pudor est non licuisse mori.
Ardent victrices; et flammae pectora praebent,
Imponuntque suis ora perusta viris."
—*Propertius*,[2] Lib. iii. xiii. 15–22.

c. B.C. 20.—"He (Aristobulus) says that he had heard from some persons of wives burning themselves voluntarily with their deceased husbands, and that those women who refused to submit to this custom were disgraced."—*Strabo*, xv. 62 (E.T. by *Hamilton and Falconer*, iii. 112).

A.D. c. 390.—"Indi, ut omnes fere barbari uxores plurimas habent. Apud eos lex est, ut uxor carissima cum defuncto marito cremetur. Hae igitur contendunt inter sede amore viri, et ambitio summa certantium est, ac testimonium castitatis, dignam morte decerni. Itaque victrix in habitu ornatuque pristino juxta cadaver accubat, amplexans illud et deosculans et suppositos ignes prudentiae laude contemnens."—*St. Jerome, Advers. Jovinianum*, in ed. *Vallars*, ii. 311.

c. 851.—"All the Indians burn their dead. Serendib is the furthest out of the islands dependent upon India. Sometimes when they burn the body of a King, his wives cast themselves on the pile, and burn with him; but it is at their choice to abstain."—*Reinaud, Relation*, &c. i. 50.

c. 1200.—"Hearing the Raja was dead, the Parmâri became a satí:—dying she said—The son of the Jadavani will rule the country, may my blessing be on him!"—*Chand Bardai*, in *Ind. Ant.* i. 227. We cannot be sure that *satí* is in the original, as this is a *condensed* version by Mr. Beames.

1298.—"Many of the women also, when their husbands die and are placed on the pile to be burnt, do burn themselves along with the bodies."—*Marco Polo*, Bk. iii. ch. 17.

c. 1322.—"The idolaters of this realm have one detestable custom (that I must mention). For when any man dies they burn him; and if he leave a

---

2. The same poet speaks of Evadne, who threw herself at Thebes on the burning pile of her husband Capaneus (I. xv. 21), a story which Paley thinks must have come from some early Indian legend.

wife they burn her alive with him, saying that she ought to go and keep her husband company in the other world. But if the woman have sons by her husband she may abide with them, an she will."—*Odoric,* in *Cathay,* &c., i. 79.

c. 1322.—Also in Zampa or Champa: "When a married man dies in this country his body is burned, and his living wife along with it. For they say that she should go to keep company with her husband in the other world also."—*Ibid.* 97.

c. 1328.—"In this India, on the death of a noble, or of any people of substance, their bodies are burned; and eke their wives follow them alive to the fire, and for the sake of worldly glory, and for the love of their husbands, and for eternal life, burn along with them, with as much joy as if they were going to be wedded. And those who do this have the higher repute for virtue and perfection among the rest."—*Fr. Jordanus,* 20.

c. 1343.—"The burning of the wife after the death of her husband is an act among the Indians recommended; but not obligatory. If a widow burns herself, the members of the family get the glory thereof, and the fame of fidelity in fulfilling their duties. She who does not give herself up to the flames puts on coarse raiment and abides with her kindred, wretched and despised for having failed in duty. But she is not compelled to burn herself." (There follows an interesting account of instances witnessed by the traveller.)—*Ibn Batuta,* ii. 138.

c. 1430.—"In Mediâ vero Indiâ mortui comburuntur, cumque his, ut plurimum vivae uxores ... una pluresve, prout fuit matrimonii conventio. Prior ex lege uritur, etiam quae unica est. Sumuntur autem et aliae uxores quaedam eo pacto, ut morte funus suâ exornent, isque haud parvus apud eos honos ducitur ... submisso igne uxor ornatiori cultu inter tubas tibicinasque et cantus, et ipsa psallentis more alacris rogum magno comitatu circuit. Adstat interea et sacerdos ... hortando suadens. Cum circumierit illa saepius ignem prope suggestum consistit, vestesque exuens, loto de more prius corpore, tum sindonem albam induta, ad exhortationem dicentis in ignem prosilit."—*N. Conti,* in *Poggius de Var. Fort.* iv.

c. 1520.—"There are in this Kingdom (the Deccan) many heathen, natives of the country, whose custom it is that when they die they are burnt, and their wives along with them; and if these will not do it they remain in disgrace with all their kindred. And as it happens oft times that they are unwilling to do it, their Bramin kinsfolk persuade them thereto, and this in order that such a fine custom should not be broken and fall into oblivion."—*Sommario de' Genti,* in *Ramusio,* i.f. 329.

c. 1520.—"In this country of Camboja . . . when the King dies, the lords voluntarily burn themselves, and so do the King's wives at the same time, and so also do other women on the death of their husbands."—*Ibid.* f. 336.

1522.—"They told us that in Java Major it was the custom, when one of the chief men died, to burn his body; and then his principal wife, adorned with garlands of flowers, has herself carried in a chair by four men . . . comforting her relations, who are afflicted because she is going to burn herself with the corpse of her husband . . . saying to them, 'I am going this evening to sup with my dear husband and to sleep with him this night.' . . . After again consoling them (she) casts herself into the fire and is burned. If she did not do this she would not be looked upon as an honourable woman, nor as a faithful wife."—*Pigafetta*, E.T. by *Lord Stanley of A.*, 154.

c. 1566.—Cesare Federici notices the rite as peculiar to the Kingdom of "*Beseneger*" (see BISNAGAR): "vidi cose stranie e bestiali di quella gentilità; vsano prima-mente abbrusciare i corpi morti cosi d'huomini come di donne nobili; e si l'huomo è maritato, la moglie è obligata ad abbrusciarsi viva col corpo del marito."—*Orig.* ed. p. 36. This traveller gives a good account of a Suttee.

1583.—"In the interior of Hindústán it is the custom when a husband dies, for his widow willingly and cheerfully to cast herself into the flames (of the funeral pile), although she may not have lived happily with him. Occasionally love of life holds her back, and then her husband's relations assemble, light the pile, and place her upon it, thinking that they thereby preserve the honour and character of the family. But since the country had come under the rule of his gracious Majesty [Akbar], inspectors had been appointed in every city and district, who were to watch carefully over these two cases, to discriminate between them, and to prevent any woman being forcibly burnt."—*Abu'l Fazl, Akbar Námah*, in *Elliot*, vi. 69.

1583.—"Among other sights I saw one I may note as wonderful. When I landed (at Negapatam) from the vessel, I saw a pit full of kindled charcoal; and at that moment a young and beautiful woman was brought by her people on a litter, with a great company of other women, friends of hers, with great festivity, she holding a mirror in her left hand, and a lemon in her right hand. . . ."—and so forth.—*G. Balbi*, f. 82v. 83.

1586.—"The custom of the countrey (Java) is, that whensoever the King doeth die, they take the body so dead and burne it, and preserve the ashes of him, and within five dayes next after, the wiues of the said King so dead, according to the custome and vse of their countrey, every one of them goe together to a place appointed, and the chiefe of the women which was nearest to him in accompt, hath a ball in her hand, and throweth it from her, and the place where the ball resteth, thither they goe all, and turne their faces to the Eastward, and every one with a dagger in their hand (which dagger they call a crise (see CREASE), and is as sharpe as a rasor), stab themselues in their owne blood, and fall a-groueling on their faces, and so ende their dayes."—*T. Candish*, in *Hakl.* iv. 338. This passage refers to Blambangan at the east end of Java, which till a late date was subject to Bali, in which such practices have continued to our day. It seems probable that the Hindu rite here came in contact with the old Polynesian practices of a like kind, which prevailed *e.g.* in Fiji, quite recently. The narrative referred to below under 1633, where the victims were the slaves of a deceased queen, points to the latter origin. W. Humboldt thus alludes to similar passages in old Javanese literature: "Thus we may reckon as one of the finest episodes in the *Brata Yuda*, the story how Satya Wati, when she had sought out her slain husband among the wide-spread heap of corpses on the battlefield, stabs herself by his side with a dagger."—*Kawi-Sprache*, i. 89 (and see the whole section, pp. 87–95).

[c. 1590.—"When he (the Rajah of Asham) dies, his principal attendants of both sexes voluntarily bury themselves alive in his grave."—*Ain*, ed. *Jarrett*, ii. 118.]

1598.—The usual account is given by *Linschoten*, ch. xxxvi., with a plate; [Hak. Soc. i. 249].

[c. 1610.—See an account in *Pyrard de Laval*, Hak. Soc. i. 394.]

1611.—"When I was in India, on the death of the Naique (see *Naik*) of Maduré, a country situated between that of Malauar and that of Choromandel, 400 wives of his burned themselves along with him."—*Teixeira*, i. 9.

c. 1620.—"The author ... when in the territory of the Karnátik ... arrived in company with his father at the city of Southern Mathura (Madura), where, after a few days, the ruler died and went to hell. The chief had 700 wives, and they all threw themselves at the same time into the fire."—*Muhammad Sharif Hanafi*, in *Elliot*, vii. 139.

1623.—"When I asked further if force was ever used in these cases, they told me that usually it was not so, but only at times among persons of quality, when some one had left a young and handsome widow, and there was risk either of her desiring to marry again (which they consider a great scandal) or of a worse mishap,—in such a case the relations of her husband, if they were very strict, would compel her, even against her will, to burn . . . a barbarous and cruel law indeed! But in short, as regarded Giaccamà, no one exercised either compulsion or persuasion; and she did the thing of her own free choice; both her kindred and herself exulting in it, as in an act magnanimous (which in sooth it was) and held in high honour among them. And when I asked about the ornaments and flowers that she wore, they told me this was customary as a sign of the joyousness of the Masti (*Masti* is what they call a woman who gives herself up to be burnt upon the death of her husband)."—*P. della Valle*, ii. 671; [Hak. Soc. ii. 275, and see ii. 266 *seq.*].

1633.—"The same day, about noon, the queen's body was burnt without the city, with two and twenty of her female slaves; and we consider ourselves bound to render an exact account of the barbarous ceremonies practised in this place on such occasions as we were witness to. . . ."—*Narrative of a Dutch Mission to Bali*, quoted by *Crawford, H. of Ind. Arch.*, ii. 244–253, from *Prevost*. It is very interesting, but too long for extract.

c. 1650.—"They say that when a woman becomes a Sattee, that is burns herself with the deceased, the Almighty pardons all the sins committed by the wife and husband and that they remain a long time in paradise; nay if the husband were in the infernal regions, the wife by this means draws him from thence and takes him to paradise. . . . Moreover the Sattee, in a future birth, returns not to the female sex . . . but she who becomes not a Sattee, and passes her life in widowhood, is never emancipated from the female state. . . . It is however criminal to force a woman into the fire, and equally to prevent her who voluntarily devotes herself."—*Dabistān*, ii. 75–76.

c. 1650–60.—Tavernier gives a full account of the different manners of *Suttee*, which he had witnessed often, and in various parts of India, but does not use the word. We extract the following:

c. 1648.—" . . . there fell of a sudden so violent a Shower, that the Priests, willing to get out of the Rain, thrust the Woman all along into the Fire. But the Shower was so vehement, and endured so long, that the Fire was quench'd, and the Woman was not burn'd. About midnight she arose, and went and knock'd at one of her Kinsmen's Houses, where Father *Zenon* and many *Hollanders* saw her, looking so gastly and grimly, that it was enough to have scar'd them; however the pain she endur'd did not so far terrifie her, but that three days after, accompany'd by her Kindred, she went and was burn'd according to her first intention."—*Tavernier*, E.T. ii. 84; [ed. *Ball*, i. 219].

Again:

"In most places upon the Coast of Coromandel, the Women are not burnt with their deceas'd Husbands, but they are buried alive with them in holes, which the Bramins make a foot deeper than the tallness of the man and woman. Usually they chuse a Sandy place; so that when the man and woman are both let down together, all the Company with Baskets of Sand fill up the hole above half a foot higher than the surface of the ground, after which they jump and dance upon it, till they believe the woman to be stifl'd."—*Ibid.* 171; [ed. *Ball,* ii. 216].

c. 1667.—Bernier also has several highly interesting pages on this subject, in his "Letter written to M. Chapelan, sent from Chiras in Persia." We extract a few sentences: "Concerning the Women that have actually burn'd themselves, I have so often been present at such dreadful spectacles, that at length I could endure no more to see it, and I retain still some horrour when I think on't. . . . The Pile of Wood was presently all on fire, because store of Oyl and Butter had been thrown upon it, and I saw at the time through the Flames that the Fire took hold of the Cloaths of the Woman. . . . All this I saw, but observ'd not that the Woman was at all disturb'd; yes it was said, that she had been heard to pronounce with great force these two words, *Five, Two,* to signifie, according to the Opinion of those who hold the Souls Transmigration, that this was the 5th time she had burnt herself with the same Husband, and that there remain'd but *two* times for perfection; as if she had at that time this Remembrance, or some Prophetical Spirit."—E.T. p. 99; [ed. *Constable,* 306 *seqq.*].

1677.—Suttee, described by A. Bassing, in *Valentijn* v. (*Ceylon*) 800.

1713.—"Ce fut cette année de 1710, que mourut le Prince de Marava, âgé de plus de quatre-vingt-ans; ses femmes, en nombre de quarante sept, se brûlèrent avec le corps du Prince. . . . " (details follow).—*Père Martin* (of the Madura Mission), in *Lett. Edif.* ed. 1781, tom. xii., pp. 123 *seqq.*

1727.—"I have seen several burned several Ways. . . . I heard a Story of a Lady that had received Addresses from a Gentleman who afterwards deserted her, and her Relations died shortly after the Marriage . . . and as the Fire was well kindled . . . she espied her former Admirer, and beckned him to come to her. When he came she took him in her Arms, as if she had a Mind to embrace him ; but being stronger than he, she carried him into the Flames in her Arms, where they were both consumed, with the Corpse of her Husband."—*A. Hamilton*, i. 278; [ed. 1744, i. 280].

1727.—"The country about (Calcutta) being overspread with *Paganisms*, the Custom of Wives burning themselves with their deceased Husbands, is also practised here. Before the *Mogul's* War, Mr. *Channock* went one time with his Ordinary Guard of Soldiers, to see a young Widow act that tragical Catastrophe, but he was so smitten with the Widow's Beauty, that he sent his Guards to take her by Force from her Executioners, and conducted her to his own Lodgings. They lived lovingly many Years, and had several Children; at length she died, after he had settled in *Calcutta*, but instead of converting her to *Christianity*, she made him a Proselyte to *Paganism*, and the only part of *Christianity* that was remarkable in him, was burying her decently, and he built a Tomb over her, where all his Life after her Death, he kept the anniversary Day of her Death by sacrificing a Cock on her Tomb, after the *Pagan* Manner."—*Ibid.* [ed. 1744], ii. 6–7. [With this compare the curious lines described as an Epîtaph on "Joseph Townsend, Pilot of the Ganges" (5 ser. *Notes de Queries*, i. 466 seq.).]

1774.—"Here (in Bali) not only women often kill themselves, or burn with their deceased husbands, but men also burn in honour of their deceased masters."—*Forest, V. to N. Guinea*, 170.

1787.—"Soon after I and my conductor had quitted the house, we were informed the suttee (for that is the name given to the person who so devotes herself) had passed...."—*Sir C. Malet*, in *Parly. Papers of* 1821, p. 1 ("Hindoo Widows").

1787.—"My Father, said he (Pundit Rhadacaunt), died at the age of one hundred years, and my mother, who was eighty years old, became a sati, and burned herself to expiate sins."—Letter of *Sir W. Jones*, in *Life*, ii. 120.

1792.—"In the course of my endeavours I found the poor suttee had no relations at Poonah."—Letter from *Sir C. Malet*, in *Forbes, Or. Mem.* ii. 394; [2nd ed. ii. 28, and see i 178, in which the previous passage is quoted].

1808.—"These proceedings (Hindu marriage ceremonies in Guzerat) take place in the presence of a Brahmin.... And farther, now the young woman vows that her affections shall be fixed upon her Lord alone, not only in all this life, but will follow in death, or to the next, that she will die, that she may burn with him, through as many transmigrations as shall secure their joint immortal bliss. Seven successions of suttees (a woman seven times born and burning, thus, as often) secure to the loving couple a seat among the gods."—*R. Drummond.*

1809.—
>"O sight of misery!
>   You cannot hear her cries . . . their sound
>   In that wild dissonance is drowned; . . .
>   But in her face you see
>   The supplication and the agony . . .
>   See in her swelling throat the desperate strength
>   That with vain effort struggles yet for life;
>   Her arms contracted now in fruitless strife,
>   Now wildly at full length,
>   Towards the crowd in vain for pity spread, . . .
>   They force her on, they bind her to the dead."
>   —*Kehama,* i. 12.

In all the poem and its copious notes, the word suttee does not occur.

[1815.—"In reference to this mark of strong attachment (of Sati for Siva), a Hindoo widow burning with her husband on the funeral pile is called sutee."—*Ward, Hindoos,* 2nd ed. ii. 25.]

1828.—"After having bathed in the river the widow lighted a brand, walked round the pile, set it on fire, and then mounted cheerfully: the flame caught and blazed up instantly; she sat down, placing the head of the corpse on her lap, and repeated several times the usual form, 'Ram, Ram, Suttee; Ram, Ram, Suttee.'"—*Wanderings of a Pilgrim,* i. 91–92.

1829.—"*Regulation XVII.* A regulation for declaring the practice of Suttee, or of burning or burying alive the widows of Hindoos, illegal, and punishable by the Criminal Courts."—Passed by the *G.-G. in C.,* Dec. 4.

1839.—"Have you yet heard in England of the horrors that took place at the funeral of that wretched old Runjeet Singh! *Four* wives, and *seven* slave-girls were burnt with him; not a word of remonstrance from the British Government."—*Letters from Madras,* 278.

1843.—"It is lamentable to think how long after our power was firmly established in Bengal, we, grossly neglecting the first and plainest duty of the civil magistrate, suffered the practices of infanticide and suttee to continue unchecked."—*Macaulay's Speech on Gates of Somnauth.*

1856.—"The pile of the sutee is unusually large; heavy cart-wheels are placed upon it, to which her limbs are bound, or sometimes a canopy of massive logs is raised above it, to crush her by its fall. . . . It is a fatal omen to hear the sutee's groan; therefore as the fire springs up from the pile, there rises simultaneously with it a deafening shout of 'Victory to Umbâ! Victory to Ranchor!' and the horn and the hard rattling drum sound their loudest, until the sacrifice is consumed."—*Râs Mâlâ,* ii. 435; [ed. 1878, p. 691].

[1870.—A case in this year is recorded by Chevers, *Ind. Med. Jurispr.* 665.]

1871.—"Our bridal finery of dress and feast too often proves to be no better than the Hindu woman's 'bravery,' when she comes to perform suttee."—*Cornhill Mag.* vol. xxiv. 675.

1872.—"La coutume du suicide de la Sati n'en est pas moins fort ancienne, puisque déjà les Grecs d'Alexandre la trouvèrent en usage chez un peuple au moins du Penjâb. Le premier témoignage brahmanique qu'on en trouve est celui de la *Brihaddevatâ* qui, peut-être, remonte tout aussi haut. A l'origine elle parait avoir été propre à. l'aristocratie militaire."—*Barth, Les Religions de l'Inde,* 39.

SOURCE: Definition from Colonel Henry Yule and A. C. Burnell, *Hobson-Jobson: A Glossary of Colloquial Anglo-Indian Words and Phrases* (London: J. Murray, 1903).

Bentinck's Minute on Sati, 8 November 1829

[Lord William Bentinck (1774–1839) was British governor-general in Madras from 1828 to 1835. As administrator, he introduced numerous innovations and reforms to British rule in India, including financial reforms, representation of Indians in government, and the suppression of such practices as thuggee/thagi and suttee/sati.]

Whether the question be to continue or discontinue the practice of suttee, the decision is equally surrounded by an awful responsibility. To consent to the consignment, year after year, of hundreds of innocent victims to a cruel and untimely end, when the power exists of preventing it, is a predicament which no conscience can contemplate without horror. But on the other hand, if heretofore received opinions are to be considered of any value, to put to hazard, by a contrary course, the very safety of the British empire in India, and to extinguish at once all hopes of those great improvements affecting the condition, not of hundreds and thousands, but of millions, which can only be expected from the continuance of our supremacy, is an alternative which, even in the light of humanity itself, may be considered as a still greater evil. It is upon this first and highest consideration alone, the good of mankind, that the tolerance of this inhuman and impious rite can, in my opinion, be justified on the part of the government of a civilized nation. While the solution of this question is appalling from the unparalleled magnitude of its possible results, the considerations belonging to it are such as to make even the stoutest mind distrust its decision. On the one side, religion, humanity under the most appalling form, as well as vanity and ambition, in short all the most powerful influences over the human heart, are arrayed to bias and mislead the judgment. On the other side, the sanction of countless ages, the example of all the Mussulman conquerors, the unanimous concurrence in the same policy of our own most able rulers, together with the universal veneration of the people, seem authoritatively to forbid, both to feeling and to reason, any interference on the exercise of their natural prerogative. In venturing to be the first to deviate from this practice, it becomes me to shew, that nothing has been yielded to feeling, but that reason, and reason alone, has governed the decision. So far indeed from presuming to condemn the conduct of my predecessors, I am ready to say, that in the same circumstances, I should have acted as they have done. So far from being chargeable with political rashness, as this departure from an established policy might infer, I hope to be able so completely to prove the safety of the measure, as even to render unnecessary any calculation of the degree of risk, which for the attainment of so great a benefit, might wisely and justly be incurred. So far also from being the sole champion of a great and dangerous innovation, I shall be able to prove that the vast preponderance of present authority has long been in favour of abolition. Past experience indeed ought to prevent me, above all men, from coming lightly to so positive a conclusion. When Governor of Madras, I saw, in the mutiny of Vellore, the dreadful consequences of a supposed violation of religious customs upon the minds of the native population and soldiery: I cannot forget that I was then the innocent victim of that unfortunate catastrophe, and I might reasonably dread, when the responsibility would justly attach to me in the event of failure, a recurrence of the same fate. Prudence and self-interest would counsel me to tread in the footsteps of my predecessors. But in a case of such momentous importance to humanity and civilization, that man must be reckless of all his present or future happiness who could listen to the dictates of so wicked and selfish a policy. With the firm undoubting conviction entertained upon this question, I should be guilty of little short of the crime of multiplied murder, if I could hesitate in the performance of this solemn obligation. I have been already stung with this feeling. Every day's delay adds a victim to the dreadful list, which might perhaps have been prevented by a more early submission of the present question. But during the whole of the present year, much public agitation has been excited, and when discontent is abroad, when exaggerations of all kinds are busily circulated, and when the native army have been under a degree of alarm, lest their allowances should suffer with that of their European officers, it would have been unwise to have given a handle to artful and designing enemies to disturb the public peace. The recent measures of government for protecting the interests of the sepoys against the late reduction of companies, will have removed all apprehension of the intentions of government; and the consideration of this circumstance having been the sole cause of hesitation on my part, I will now proceed, paying the blessing of God upon our counsels, to state the grounds upon which my opinion has been formed.

We have now before us two reports of the Nizamat Adalat with statements of suttees in 1827 and 1828, exhibiting a decrease of 54 in the latter year as compared with 1827, and a still greater proportion as compared with former years. If this diminution could be ascribed to any change of opinion upon the question, produced by the progress of education or civilization, the fact would be most satisfactory; and to disturb this sure though slow process of self correction would be most impolite and unwise. But I think it may be safely affirmed, that though in Calcutta truth may be said to have made a considerable advance among the higher orders; yet in respect to the population at large, no change whatever has taken place, and that from these causes at least no hope of the abandonment of the rite can be rationally entertained. The decrease, if it be real may be the result of less sickly seasons, as the increase in 1824 and 1825 was of the greater prevalence of cholera. But it is probably in a greater measure due to the more open discouragement of the practice given by the greater part of the European functionaries in latter years; the effect of which would be to produce corresponding activity in the police officers, by which either the number would be really diminished, or would be made to appear so in the returns.

It seems to be the very general opinion that our interference has hitherto done more harm than good, by lending a sort of sanction to the ceremony, while it has undoubtedly tended to cripple the efforts of magistrates and others to prevent the practice.

I think it will clearly appear, from a perusal of the documents annexed to this minute, and from the facts which I shall have to adduce, that the passive submission of the people to the influence and power beyond the law, which in fact and practically may be and is often exercised without opposition by every public officer, is so great, that the suppression of the rite would be completely effected by a tacit sanction alone on the part of government. This mode of extinguishing has been recommended by many of those whose advice has been asked, and no doubt this, in several respects might be a preferable course, as being equally effectual, while more silent, not exciting the alarm which might possibly come from a public enactment, and from which, in case of failure, it would be easy to retreat with less inconvenience and without any compromise of character. But this course is clearly not open to government, bound by parliament to rule by law, and not by their good pleasure. Under the present position of the British empire moreover, it may be fairly doubted, if any such underhand proceeding would be really good policy. When we had powerful neighbours and had greater reason to doubt our own security, expediency might recommend an indirect and more cautious proceeding, but now that we are supreme my opinion is decidedly in favour of an open, avowed and general prohibition, resting altogether upon the moral goodness of the act, and our power to enforce it, and so decided is my feeling against any half measure, that were I not convinced of the safety of total abolition, I certainly should have advised the cessation or all interference.

Of all those who have given their advice against the abolition of the rite, and have described the ill effects likely to ensue from it, there is no one to whom I am disposed to pay greater deference than Mr. Horace Wilson. I purposely select his opinion, because, independently of his vast knowledge of oriental literature, it has fallen to his lot, as secretary to the Hindu College, and possessing the general esteem both of the parents and of the youths, to have more confidential intercourse with natives of all classes, than any man in India. While his opportunity of obtaining information has been great beyond all others, his talents and judgement enable him to form a just estimate of its value. I shall state the most forcible of his reasons, and how far I do and do not agree with him.

1st. Mr. Wilson considered it to be a dangerous evasion of the real difficulties, to attempt to prove that suttees are not 'essentially a part of the Hindu religion'—I entirely agree in this opinion. The question is, not what the rite is, but what it is supposed to be; and I have no doubt that the conscientious belief of every order of Hindus, with few exceptions, regard it as sacred.

2nd. Mr. Wilson thinks that the attempt to put down the practice will inspire extensive dissatisfaction. I agree also in this opinion. He does not imagine that the promulgated prohibition will lead to any immediate and overt act of insubordination, but that affrays and much agitation of the public mind must ensue. But he conceives, that, if once they suspect that it is the intention of the British government to abandon this hitherto inviolate principle of allowing the most complete toleration in matter of religion, that there will arise, in the mind of all, so deep a distrust of our ulterior designs, that they will no longer be tractable to any arrangement intended for their improvement and that the principles of morality as well as of a more virtuous and exalted rule of action, now actively inculcated by European education and knowledge, will receive a fatal check. I must acknowledge that a similar opinion as to the probable excitation of a deep distrust of our future intentions was mentioned to me in conversation by that enlightened native, Rammohan Roy, a warm advocate for the abolition of suttees, and of all other superstitions and corruptions, engrafted on the Hindu religion, which he considers originally to have been a pure deism. It was his opinion that the practice might be suppressed, quietly and unobservedly, by increasing the difficulties, and by the indirect agency of the police. He apprehended that any public enactment would give rise to general apprehension, that the reasoning would be, 'While the English were contending for power, they deemed it politic to allow universal toleration, and to respect our religion; but having obtained the supremacy, their first act is a violation of their professions, and the next will probably be like the Mahomedan conquerors, to force upon us their own religion.'

Admitting, as I am always disposed to do, that much truth is contained in these remarks, but not all assenting to the conclusions which though not described, bear the most unfavourable import, I shall now enquire into the evil and the extent of danger which may practically result from this measure.

It must be first observed, that of the 463 suttees occurring in the whole of the presidency of Fort William, 420 took place in Bengal, Bihar and Orissa, or what are termed the lower provinces, and of these latter, 287 in the Calcutta division alone.

It might be very difficult to make a stranger to India understand, much less believe, that in a population of so many millions of people, as the Calcutta division includes, and the same may be said of all the lower provinces, so great is the want of courage and of vigour of character, and such the habitual submission of centuries, that insurrection or hostile opposition to the will of the ruling power may be affirmed to be an impossible danger. I speak of the population taken separately from the army, and may add for the information of the stranger, and also in support of my assertion that few of the natives of the lower provinces are to be found in our military ranks. I therefore, at once deny the danger in toto, in reference to this part of our territories, where the practice principally obtains. If, however, security were wanting against extensive popular tumult or revolution, I should say that the permanent settlement, which though a failure in many other respects and its most important essentials, has this great advantage at least, of having created a vast body of rich landed proprietors, deeply interested in the continuance of the British dominion, and having complete command over the mass of the people, and, in respect to the apprehension of ulterior views, I cannot believe that it could last but for the moment. The same large proprietary body, connected for the most part with Calcutta, can have no fears of the kind, and through their interpretation of our intentions, and that of their numerous dependants, and agents, the public mind could not long remain in a state of deception.

Were the scene of this sad destruction of human life laid in the upper instead of the lower provinces, in the midst of a bold and manly people, I might speak with less confidence upon the question of safety. In these provinces the suttees amount to 43 only—upon a population of nearly twenty millions. It cannot be expected that any general feeling, where combination of any kind is so unusual, could be excited in defence of a rite, in which so few participate, a rite also, notoriously made too often subservient to views of personal interest on the part of the other members of the family.

It is stated by Mr. Wilson that interference with infanticide and the capital punishment of Brahmins offer a fallacious analogy with the prohibition now proposed. The distinction is not perceptible to my judgement. The former practice, though confined to particular families, is probably viewed as a religious custom; and as for the latter, the necessity of the enactment proves the general existence of the exception, and it is impossible to conceive a more direct and open violation of the shastras or one more at variance with the general feelings of the Hindu population. To this day, in all Hindu states, the life of Brahmins is, I believe, still held sacred.

But I have taken up too much time in giving my own opinions, when those of the greatest experience, and the highest official authority are upon our records. In the report of the Nizamat Adalat for 1828, four out of five of the judges recommended to the governor-general in council the immediate abolition of the practice, and attest its safety. The fifth judge, though not opposed to the opinions of the rest of the bench, did not feel then prepared to give his entire assent. In the report of this year, the measure has come up with the unanimous recommendation of the court. The two superintendents of police for the upper and lower provinces, Mr Walter Ewer, and Mr. Charles Barwell, have in the strongest terms expressed their opinion that the suppression might be effected without the least danger. The former officer has urged the measure upon the attention of government in the most forcible manner. No documents exist to shew the opinions of the public functionaries in the interior, but I am informed that nine-tenths are in favour of the abolition.

How again are these opinions supported by practical experience?

Within the limits of the supreme court at Calcutta, not a suttee has taken place since the time of Sir John Anstruther.

In the Delhi territory, Sir Charles Metcalfe never permitted a suttee to be performed.

In Jessore, one of the districts of the Calcutta division, in 1824 there were 30 suttees, in 1825—16, in 1826—3, in 1827 and 1828 there were none. To no other cause can this be assigned, than to a power beyond the law, exercised by the acting magistrate, against which, however, no public remonstrance was made. Mr. Pigou has been since appointed to Cuttack, and has pursued the same strong interference as in Jessore, but his course, although most humane, was properly arrested, as being illegal, by the commissioners. Though the case of Jessore is perhaps one of the strongest examples of efficacious and unopposed interposition, I really believe that there are few districts in which the same arbitrary power is not exercised to prevent the practice. In the last week, in the report of the acting commissioner, Mr. Smith, he states that in Ghazipur in the last year 16, and in the preceding years 7 suttees had been prevented by the persuasions, or rather it should be said by the threats of the police.

Innumerable cases of the same kind might be obtained from the public records.

It is stated in the letter of the collector of Gaya, Mr. Trotter, but upon what authority I have omitted to enquire, that the Peishwa (I presume he means the ex-Peishwa Baji Rao) would not allow the rite to be performed, and that in Tanjore it is equally interdicted. These facts, if true, would be positive proofs at least that no unanimity exists among the Hindus upon the point of religious obligations.

Having made enquiries also how far suttees are permitted in the European foreign settlements, I find, from Dr. Carey, that at Chinsurah no such sacrifices had ever been permitted by the Dutch government; that within the limits of Chandernagore itself they were also prevented, but allowed to be performed in the British territories. The Danish government of Serampore has not forbidden the rite in conformity to the example of the British government.

It is a very important fact, that though representations have been made by the disappointed party to superior authority, it does not appear that a single instance of direct opposition to the execution of the prohibitory orders of our civil functionaries has ever occurred. How then can it be reasonably feared that to the government itself, from whom all authority is derived, and whose power is now universally considered to be irresistible, anything bearing the semblance of resistance can be manifest. Mr. Wilson also is of opinion that no immediate overt act of insubordination would follow the publication of the edict. The regulations of government may be evaded, the police may be corrupted, but even here the price paid as hush money will operate as a penalty indirectly forwarding the objects of government.

Suttee/Sati 357

I venture then to think it completely proved that, from the native population, nothing of extensive combination or even of partial opposition may be expected from the abolition.

It is, however, a very different and much more important question, how far the feelings of the native army might take alarm, how far the rite may be in general observance by them, and whether as in the case of Vellore, designing persons might not make use of the circumstance either for the purpose of immediate revolt, or of sowing the seeds of permanent disaffection. Reflecting upon the vast disproportion of numbers between our native and European troops, it was obvious that there might be, in any general combination of the former, the greatest danger to the state, and it became necessary therefore to use every precaution to ascertain the impression likely to be made upon the minds of the native soldiery.

Before I detail to council the means I have taken to satisfy my mind upon this very important branch of the enquiry, I shall beg leave to advert to the name of Lord Hastings. It is impossible but that to his most humane, benevolent, and enlightened mind, this practice must have been often the subject of deep and anxious meditation. It was consequently a circumstance of ill omen and severe disappointment not to have found, upon the records, the valuable advice and direction of his long experience and wisdom. It is true that during the greater part of his administration, he was engaged in war, when the introduction of such a measure would have been highly injudicious. To his successor, Lord Amherst, also the same obstacle was opposed. I am however fortunate in possessing a letter from Lord Hastings to a friend in England upon suttees, and from the following extract, dated 21st November 1825, I am induced to believe that, had he remained in India, this practice would long since have been suppressed. 'The subject which you wish to discuss is one which must interest one's feeling most deeply; but it is also one of extreme nicety. When I mention that in one of the years during my administration of government in India, above eight hundred widows sacrificed themselves within the provinces comprised in the presidency of Bengal, to which number I very much suspect, that very many not notified to the magistrates should be added, I will hope to have credit for being acutely sensible to such an outrage against humanity. At the same time, I was aware how much danger might attend the endeavouring to suppress, forcibly, a practice so rooted in the religious belief of the natives. No men of low caste are admitted into the ranks of the Bengal army. Therefore the whole of that formidable body must be regarded as blindly partial to a custom which they consider equally referable to family honour and to points of faith. To attempt the extinction of the horrid superstition, without being supported in the procedure by a real concurrence on the part of the army, would be distinctly perilous. I have no scruple to say, that I did believe, I could have carried with me the assent of the army towards such an object. That persuasion, however, arose from circumstances which gave me peculiar influence over the native troops.

Lord Hastings left India in 1823. It is quite certain that the government of that time were much more strongly impressed with the risk of the undertaking, than is now very generally felt. It would have been fortunate could this measure have proceeded under the auspices of that distinguished noble-man, and that the state might have had the benefit of the influence which undoubtedly he possessed, in a peculiar degree, over the native troops. Since that period, however, six years have elapsed. Within the territories all has been peaceful and prosperous, while without, Ava and Bharatpur, to whom alone a strange sort of consequence was ascribed by public opinions, have been made to acknowledge our supremacy. In this interval, experience has enlarged our knowledge, and has given us surer data upon which to distinguish truth from illusion, and to ascertain the real circumstances of our position and power. It is upon these that the concurring opinion of the officers of the civil and military services at large having been founded, is entitled to our utmost confidence.

I have the honour to lay before council the copy of a circular addressed to forty-nine officers, pointed out to me by the secretary to government in the military department, as being from their judgement and experience the best enabled to appreciate the effect of the proposed measure upon the native army, together with their answers. For more easy reference, an abstract of each answer is annexed in a separate paper and classed with those to the same purport.

It appears—first, that of those whose opinions are directly adverse to all interference, whatever, with the practice, the number is only five. Secondly, of those who are favourable to abolition, but averse to absolute and direct prohibition under the authority of the government, the number is twelve. Thirdly, of those who are favourable to abolition, to be effected by the indirect interference of magistrates and other public officers, the number is eight. Fourthly, of those who advocate the total, immediate and public suppression of the practice, the number is twenty-eight.

It will be observed also, of those who are against an open and direct prohibition, few entertain any fear of immediate danger. They refer to a distinct and undefined evil. I can conceive the possibility of the expression of dissatisfaction and anger being immediately manifested upon this supposed attack on their religious usages; but the distant danger seems to me altogether groundless, provided that perfect respect continues to be paid to all their innocent rites and ceremonies, and provided also, that a kind and considerate regard be continued to their worldly interests and comforts.

I trust therefore that the council will agree with me in the satisfactory nature of this statement, and that they will partake in the perfect confidence which it has given me of the expediency and safety of the abolition.

In the answer of one of the military officers, Lieutenant-Colonel Todd, he has recommended that the tax on pilgrims should be simultaneously given up, for the purpose of affording an undoubted proof of our disinterestedness and of our desire to remove every obnoxious obstacle to the gratification of their religious duties. A very considerable revenue is raised from this head; but if it were to be the price of satisfaction and confidence to the Hindus, and of the removal of all distrust of our present and future intentions, the sacrifice might be a measure of good policy. The objections that must be entertained by all to the principle of the tax, which in England has lately excited very great reprobation, formed an additional motive for the enquiry. I enclose the copy of a circular letter addressed to different individuals at present in charge of the districts where the tax is collected, or who have had opportunities from their local knowledge of forming a judgment upon this question. It will be seen that opinions vary, but upon a review of the whole, my conviction is that, in connection with the present measure, it is inexpedient to repeal the tax. It is a subject upon which I shall not neglect to bestow more attention than I have been able to do. An abstract of these opinions is annexed to this minute.

I have now to submit for the consideration of council the draft of a regulation enacting the abolition of suttees. It is accompanied by a paper containing the remarks and suggestions of the judges of the Nizamat Adalat. In this paper is repeated the unanimous opinion of the court in favour of the proposed measure. The suggestions of the Nizamat Adalat are, in some measure, at variance with a principal object I had in view of preventing collision between the parties to the suttee and the officers of police. It is only in the previous processes or during the actual performance of the rite, when the feelings of all may be more or less roused to a high degree of excitement, that I apprehend the possibility of affray, or of acts of violence, through an indiscreet and injudicious exercise of authority. It seemed to me prudent, therefore, that the police in the first instance should warn and advise, but not forcibly prohibit, and if the suttee, in defiance of this notice, were performed, that a report should be made to the magistrate, who would summon the parties and proceed as in any other case of crime. The sadar court appear to think these precautions unnecessary and I hope they may be so, but, in the beginning, we cannot, I think, proceed with too much circumspection. Upon the same principle, in order to guard against a too hasty or severe a sentence, emanating from extreme zeal on the part of the local judge, I have proposed that the case should only be cognizable by the commissioner of circuit. These are, however, questions which I should wish to see discussed in council. The other recommendations of the court are well worthy of our adoption.

I have now brought this paper to a close, and I trust I have redeemed my pledge of not allowing, in the consideration of this question, passion or feeling to have any part. I trust it will appear that due weight has been given to all difficulties and objections; that facts have been stated with truth and impartiality; that the conclusion to which I have come is completely borne out, both by reason and authority. It may be justly asserted that the government, in this act, will only be following, not preceding the tide of public opinion, long flowing in this direction: and when we have taken into consideration the experience and wisdom of that highest public tribunal, the Nizamat Adalat, who in unison with our wisest and ablest public functionaries have been, year after year, almost soliciting the government to pass this act, the moral and political responsibility of not abolishing this practice far surpasses in my judgment that of the opposite course.

But discarding, as I have done, every inviting appeal from sympathy and humanity, and having given my verdict, I may now be permitted to express the anxious feelings with which I desire the success of this measure.

The first and primary object of my heart is the benefit of the Hindus. I know nothing so important to the improvement of their future conditions, as the establishment of a purer morality, whatever their belief, and a more just conception of the will of God. The first step to this better understanding will be dissociation of religious belief and practice from blood and murder. They will then, when no longer under this brutalizing excitement, view with more calmness, acknowledged truths. They will see that there can be no inconsistency in the ways of providence, that to the command received as divine by all races of men, "No innocent blood shall be split', there can be no exception, and when they shall have been convinced of the error of this first and most criminal of their customs, may it not be hoped, that others which stand in the way of their improvement may likewise pass away, and that (with) this emancipation from those chains and shackles upon their minds and actions, they may no longer continue as they have done, the slaves of every foreign conqueror, but that they may assume their just places among the great families of mankind. I disavow in these remarks or in this measure any view whatever to conversion to our own faith. I write and feel as a legislator for the Hindus, and as I believe many enlightened Hindus think and feel.

Descending from these higher considerations, it cannot be a dishonest ambition that the government of which I form a part, should have the credit of an act, which is to wash out a foul stain upon British rule, and to stay the sacrifice of humanity and justice to a doubtful expediency; and finally, as a branch of the general administration of the empire, I may be permitted to feel deeply anxious, that our course shall be in accordance with the noble example set to us by the British government at home and that the adaptation, where practicable, to the circumstances of this vast Indian population, of the same enlightened principles, may promote here as well as there, the general prosperity, and may exalt the character of our nation.

SOURCE: This document can be found in *The Correspondence of Lord William Cavendish Bentinck,* vol. 1, 1828–1831, ed. C. H. Philips (Oxford: Oxford University Press, 1977).

Sati Regulation XVII, A.D. 1829 of the Bengal Code, 4 December 1829

LORD WILLIAM CAVENDISH BENTICK

A regulation for declaring the practice of suttee, or of burning or burying alive the widows of Hindus, illegal, and punishable by the criminal courts, passed by the governor-general in council on the 4th December 1829, corresponding with the 20th Aughun 1236 Bengal era; the 23rd Aughun 1237 Fasli; the 21st Aughun 1237 Vilayati; the 8th Aughun 1886 Samavat; and the 6th Jamadi-us-Sani 1245 Hegira.

1. The practice of suttee, or of burning or burying alive the widows of Hindus, is revolting to the feelings of human nature; it is nowhere enjoined by the religion of the Hindus as an imperative duty; on the contrary a life of purity and retirement on the part of the widow is more especially and preferably inculcated, and by a vast majority of that people throughout India the practice is not kept up, nor observed: in some extensive districts it does not exist: in those in which it has been most frequent it is notorious that in many instances acts of atrocity have been perpetrated which have been shocking to the Hindus themselves, and in their eyes unlawful and wicked. The measures hitherto adopted to discourage and prevent such acts have failed of success, and the governor-general in council is deeply impressed with the conviction that the abuses in question cannot be effectually put an end to without abolishing the practice altogether. Actuated by these considerations the governor-general in council, without intending to depart from one of the first and most important principles of the system of British government in India, that all classes of the people be secure in the observance of their religious usages so long as that system can be adhered to without violation of the paramount

dictates of justice and humanity, has deemed it right to establish the following rules, which are hereby enacted to be in force from the time of their promulgation throughout the territories immediately subject to the presidence of Fort William.

II. The practice of suttee, or of burning or burying alive the widows of Hindus, is hereby declared illegal, and punishable by the criminal courts.

III. First. All zamindars, or other proprietors of land, whether malguzari or lakhiraj; ali sadar farmers and underrenters of land of every description; all dependent taluqdars; all naibs and other local agents; all native officers employed in the collection of the revenue and rents of land on the part of government, or the court of wards; and all munduls or other headmen of villages are hereby declared especially accountable for the immediate communication to the officers of the nearest police station of any intended sacrifice of the nature described in the foregoing section; and any zamindar, or other description of persons above noticed, to whom such responsibility is declared to attach, who may be convicted of wilfully neglecting or delaying to furnish the information above required, shall be liable to be fined by the magistrate or joint magistrate in any sum not exceeding two hundred rupees, and in default of payment to be confined for any period of imprisonment not exceeding six months.

Secondly. Immediately on receiving intelligence that the sacrifice declared illegal by this regulation is likely to occur, the police darogha shall either repair in person to the spot, or depute his mohurrir or jamadar, accompanied by one or more burkundazes of Hindu religion, and it shall be the duty of the police-officers to announce to the persons assembled for the performance of ceremony, that it is illegal; and to endeavour to prevail on them to disperse, explaining to them that in the event of their persisting in it they will involve themselves in a crime, and become subject to punishment by the criminal courts. Should the parties assembled proceed in defiance of these remonstrances to carry the ceremony into effect, it shall be the duty of the police-officer to use all lawful means in their power to prevent the sacrifice from taking place, and to apprehend the principle persons aiding and abetting in the performance of it, and in the event of the police-officers being unable to apprehend them, they shall endeavour to ascertain their names and places of abode, and shall immediately communicate the whole of the particulars to the magistrate for his orders.

Thirdly. Should intelligence of a sacrifice have been carried into effect before their arrival at the spot, they will nevertheless institute a full enquiry into the circumstances of the case, in like manner as on all other occasions of unnatural death, and report them for the information and orders of the magistrate or joint magistrate, to whom they may be subordinate.

IV. First. On the receipt of the reports required to be made by the police daroghas, under the provisions of the foregoing section, the magistrate or joint magistrate of the jurisdiction in which the sacrifice may have taken place, shall enquire into the circumstances of the case, and shall adopt the necessary measures for bringing the parties concerned in promoting it to trial before the court of circuit.

Secondly. It is hereby declared, that after the promulgation of this regulation all persons convicted of aiding and abetting in the sacrifice of a Hindu widow, by burning or burying her alive, whether the sacrifice be voluntary on her part or not, shall be deemed guilty of culpable homicide, and shall be liable to punishment by fine or by both fine and imprisonment, at the discretion of the court of circuit, according to the nature and circumstance of the case, and the degree of guilt established against the offender; nor shall it be held to be any plea of justification that he or she was desired by the party sacrificed to assist in putting her to death.

Thirdly. Persons committed to take their trial before the court of circuit for the offence above-mentioned shall be admitted to bail or not, at the discretion of the magistrate or joint magistrate, subject to the general rules in force in regard to the admission of bail.

V. It is further deemed necessary to declare, that nothing contained in this regulation shall be construed to preclude the court of Nizamat Adalat from passing sentence of death on persons convicted of using violence or compulsion, or of having assisted in burning or burying alive a Hindu widow while labouring under a state of intoxication, or stupefaction, or other cause impeding the exercise of her free will, when, from the aggravated nature of the offence, proved against the prisoner, the court may see no circumstances to render him or her proper object of mercy.

SOURCE: In *The Correspondence of Lord William Cavendish Bentinck,* vol. 1, 1828–1831, ed. C. H. Phelps (Oxford: Oxford University Press, 1977).

The Duties of a Faithful Widow

[In addition to his translation of the *Digest of Hindu Law*, Henry Thomas Colebrooke (1765–1837) wrote numerous studies of the history, literature, and religions of ancient India.]

SECTION I: ON DYING WITH OR AFTER HER HUSBAND

123

ANAGIRAS:—That woman who, on the death of her husband, ascends the *same* burning pile with him, is exalted to heaven, as equal in virtue to ARUNDHATI.

2. She who follows her husband *to another world*, shall dwell in a region of joy for so many years as there are hairs on the human body, or thirty-five millions.

3. As a serpent-catcher forcibly draws a snake from his hole, thus, drawing her lord *from a region of torment*, she enjoys delight together with him.

4. The woman who follows her husband *to the pile*, expiates the sins of three generations, on the paternal and maternal side, of that family to which she was given while a virgin.

5. There, having the best of husbands, *herself* best *of women*, enjoying the best delights, she partakes of bliss with her husband *in a celestial abode*, as long as fourteen INDRAS reign.

6. Even though the man had slain a priest, or returned evil for good, or killed an intimate friend, the woman expiates those crimes: this has been declared by ANGIRAS.

7. No other effectual duty is known for virtuous women, at any time after the death of their lords, except casting themselves into the same fire.

8. As long as a woman, *in her successive transmigrations*, shall decline burning herself, like a faithful wife, on the *same* fire with her deceased lord, so long shall she be not exempted from *springing again to life in* the body of some female animal.

9. When their lords have departed at the *fated* time of *attaining* heaven, no other way but entering the *same* fire is known for women whose virtuous conduct and whose thoughts have been devoted to their husbands, and who fear the dangers of separation.

124

The *Mahabharata:*—Those who have slighted their former lord through an evil disposition, or have remained at all times averse from their husbands,

If they follow their lords at the *proper* time, in such a mode are all purified from lust, wrath, fear, and avarice.

125

VYASA:—Learn the power of that widow, who, hearing that her husband has deceased, and been burned in another region, speedily casts herself into the fire:

2. Though he have sunk to a region of torment, be restrained in dreadful bonds, have reached the place of anguish, be seized by the imps of YAMA,

3. Be exhausted of strength, and afflicted and tortured for his crimes; still, as a serpent-catcher unerringly drags a serpent from his hole,

4. So does she draw her husband *from hell*, and ascend to heaven by the power of devotion. There, with the best of husbands, lauded by the choirs of APSARAS,

5. She sports with her husband, as long as fourteen INDRAS reign.

126

The *Brahme-purana:*—No other way is known for a virtuous woman, after the death of her husband; the separate cremation of her husband would be lost, *to all religious intents*.

2. If her lord die in another country, let the faithful wife place his sandals on her breasts, and pure, enter the fire.

3. The faithful widow is pronounced no suicide by the *recited* text of the *Rigveda:* when three days of mourning are passed, she obtained legal obsequies.

127

Vrihat Narediya purana:—Mothers of infant children, pregnant women, they who have not menstruated, and they who are actually unclean, ascend not the funeral pile, O lovely princess!

128

VRIHASPATI:—The mother of an infant child may not relinquish the care of her infant to ascend *the pile;* nor *may* a woman in her courses, not one who *lately* brought forth a child, *burn herself* with her husband; a pregnant widow must preserve the embryo.

The husband may employ, in every sort of business, his wife who has borne a son, when she has bathed after twenty nights from the child-birth; and her who has borne a daughter, when she has bathed after a month.

MENU:—A man of the sacerdotal class becomes pure in ten days; of the warlike, in twelve; of the commercial, in fifteen; of the servile, in a month.

129

GOTAMA:—A woman of the sacerdotal class cannot go *with her husband to another world,* ascending a separate pile.

130

THE *Bhawishya-purana:*—If, indeed, *her* husband die after the third night of her uncleanness, the corpse, O twice-born men, should be kept one night, that she may follow him in death.

131

VYASA:—If the faithful wife reside at a place which may be reached in one day, and notice be given *her of her husband's death,* the ceremony of burning her lord should not be performed so long as her arrival may be *expected.*

SECTION 3: ON THE DUTIES OF WIDOWS CHOOSING TO SURVIVE THEIR HUSBANDS

132

VRIHASPATI:—A wife is considered as half the body *of her husband,* equally sharing the fruit of pure and impure acts: whether she ascend *the pile* after him, or survive for the benefit of her husband, she is a faithful wife.

133

VISHNU:—After the death of her husband, a wife must practise austerities, or ascend *the pile* after him.

134

PRACHETAS:—An anchorite, a student in theology, and a widow, must avoid the leaf of the betel, inunctions, and feeding from vessels of zinc.

The *Ayur Veda:*—When oil is applied to the crown of the head, and reaches all the limbs, if both arms be sufficiently wetted with water, it is called *abhyanga.*

2. If the oil sparingly reach the limbs, and the arms be not sufficiently

wetted, it is *mashti*, a distinct inunction (*abhyanga*) intended for the head (*mastaca*) and the rest of the limbs.

135
Smriti:—Only one meal each day should ever be made *by a widow*, not a second repast by any means; and a widowed woman, sleeping on a bed, would cause her husband to fall *from a region of joy:*

2. She must not again use perfumed substances: but daily make offerings for her husband, with *cusa* grass, *tila,* and water.

3. In the month of *Vaisac'ha, Cartica,* and *Magha,* let her observe special fasts, perform ablutions, make gifts, travel to places of pilgrimage, and repeatedly utter the name of VISHNU.

136
The *Matsya purana* declares veneration due to faithful women:
Therefore should faithful women be venerated like deities by all men; *for,* through their merits, the three worlds are governed by the king.

137
HARITA:—Leaving her husband's favourite abode, keeping her tongue, hands, feet, and *other* organs in subjection, strict in her conduct, *all* day mourning her husband, with harsh duties, devotion, and fasts to the end of her life, a widow victoriously gains her husband's abode and repeatedly acquires the same mansion with her lord as is thus declared:

"That faithful woman who practises harsh duties after the death of her lord, cancels all her sins, and acquires the same mansion with her lord."

138
VRIHASPATI:—Strict in austerities and rigid devotion, firm in avoiding sensuality, and ever patient and liberal, a widow attains heaven even though she have no son.

139
MENU:—Let her emaciate her body, by living voluntarily on pure flowers, roots, and fruit; but let her not, when her lord is deceased, even pronounce the name of another man.

2. Let her continue till death forgiving all injuries, performing harsh duties, avoiding every sensual pleasure, and cheerfully practising the incomparable rules of virtue, which have been followed by such women as were devoted to only one husband.

140

MENU:—Many thousands of *Brahmanas,* having avoided sensuality from their early youth, and having left no issue in their families, have ascended, *nevertheless,* to heaven.

141

MENU:—And, like those abstemious men, a virtuous wife ascends to heaven, though she have no child, if, after the decease of her lord, she devote herself to pious austerity.

142

MENU:—But a widow who, from a wish to bear children, slights her *deceased* husband *by marrying again,* brings disgrace on herself here below; and shall be excluded from the seat of her lord.

143

MENU:—Issue begotten on a woman by any other *than her husband* is here declared to be no progeny of her's, no more than a child begotten on the wife of another man belongs to the begetter; nor is a second husband allowed, in any part *of this code,* to a virtuous woman.

144

YAMA:—Let her continue as long as she lives, performing austere duties, avoiding every sensual pleasure, and cheerfully practising those rules of virtue which have been followed by such women as were devoted to *one only husband.*

2. Neither in the *Veda,* nor in the sacred code, is religious seclusion allowed to a woman; her own duties, practised with a husband of equal class, are indeed her religious rites: this is a settled rule.

3. Eighty-eight thousand holy Sages of the sacerdotal class, superior to sensual appetites, and having left no issue in their families, have ascended, *nevertheless,* to heaven.

4. Like them, a *betrothed* damsel, become a widow, and devoting herself to pious austerity, shall attain heaven, though she have no son: this MENU, sprung from the self-existent, has declared.

145

CATYAYANA:—Though her husband die guilty of many crimes, if she remain ever firm in virtuous conduct, obsequiously honouring her spiritual parents,

2. And devoting herself to pious austerity after the death of her husband, that faithful widow is exalted to heaven, as equal in virtue to ARUNDHATI.

SOURCE: From *Digest of Hindu Law,* trans. H. T. Colebrooke, Esq. (Madras: Higgonbotham and Co., 1874).

Petitions and Addresses on the Practice of Suttee (1818–1831)

[Particularly distinguished among the early participants in "reform" in India under British rule was Ram Mohan Roy (1772–1833). A social and political activist, Roy was also a newspaper editor and educator interested in the introduction of a Western curriculum of study.]

ON CONCREMATION: A SECOND CONFERENCE BETWEEN AN ADVOCATE AND AN OPPONENT OF THAT PRACTICE

The Counter-Petition of the Hindu Inhabitants of Calcutta against Suttee (1818)[1]

To the Most Noble the Marquis of Hastings,
Governor General in Council:
   The humble petition of the undersigned Hindu inhabitants of Calcutta.
   Humbly sheweth,—that your petitioners have with equal surprise and sorrow, perceived a statement in the newspapers, that a petition to your lordship's government, to repeal the orders at present in force against illegal proceedings in burning widows with the bodies of their deceased husbands, was drawn up and had received the signature of the principal inhabitants of Calcutta, and we have since learned that a petition to that effect has actually been transmitted to the honourable the Vice-President in Council.
   That your petitioners do not know by what authority the subscribers to the

---

1. The July number of the Asiatic Journal (1819) has the following note regarding this counter-petition against Suttee:
   "This petition, which explains its own object, was signed by a great number of the most respectable Hindu inhabitants of Calcutta. It will be observed that this document bears no date. From the date of some Mss. transmitted with it for the Asiatic Journal, we consider it to have been presented soon after the Governor General's return to the seat of government, may, the beginning of August 1818". The style, the arguments and sentiments expressed all points to its being written by Raja Ram Mohan Roy.—Ed.

said petition have been so designated; as from the very nature of their petition it appears obvious, that those who signed it must be ignorant.

Address to Lord William Bentinck (1830)[2]

To the Right Hon. Lord William Cavendish Bentinck, &c.
My Lord:

With hearts filled with the deepest gratitude, and impressed with the utmost reverence, we, the undersigned native inhabitants of Calcutta and its vicinity, beg to be permitted to approach your Lordship, to offer personally our humble but warmest acknowledgements for the invaluable protection which your Lordship's government has recently afforded to the lives of the Hindoo female part of your subjects, and for your humane and successful exertions in rescuing us for ever, from the gross stigma hitherto attached to our character as wilful murderers of females, and zealous promoters of the practice of suicide.

Excessive jealousy of their female connexions operating on the breasts of Hindu princes, rendering them despots regardless of the common bonds of society and of their incumbent duty as protectors of the weaker sex, insomuch that, with a view to prevent every possibility of their widows forming subsequent attachments, they availed themselves of their arbitrary power, and under the cloak of religion, introduced the practice of burning widows alive, under the first impressions of sorrow or despair, immediately after the demise of their husbands. This system of female destruction, being admirably suited to the selfish and servile disposition of the populace, has been eagerly followed by them, in defiance of the most sacred authorities, such as the *Opunishuds* or the principal parts of the *Veds*, and the *Bhugvud Geeta*, as well as of the direct commandment of Munoo, the first and the greatest of all the legislators, conveyed in the following words: 'Let a widow continue till death forgiving all injuries, performing austere duties, avoiding every sensual pleasure,' &c, (Ch. 5, v. 158).

While in fact fulfilling the suggestion of their jealousy, they pretended to justify this hideous practice by quoting some passages from authorities of

---

2. On the 16th January, 1830, Lord William Bentinck was presented with addresses on the passing of the regulation abolishing the *Suttee* by Ram Mohan Roy, Callynath Roy, Huree Hur Dutt, and others. The addresses were signed by 300 inhabitants of Calcutta. There were two addresses, one in Bengali read by Baboo Callynath Roy, the other, a translation of the former in English, read by Baboo Huree Hur Dutt. The similarities of style and arguments show that the address was drawn up by Ram Mohan Roy and represented his views and sentiments.—Ed.

evidently inferior weight, sanctioning the wilful ascent of a widow on the flaming pile of her husband, as if they were offering such female sacrifices in obedience to the dictates of the Shastrus and not from the influence of jealousy. It is, however, very fortunate that the British government, under whose protection the lives of both the males and females of India have been happily placed by Providence, has ascertained that even those inferior authorities yielding wilful ascent by a widow to the flaming pile, have been practically set aside, and that, in gross violation of their language and spirit, the relatives of widows have, in the burning of those infatuated females, almost invariably used to fasten them down on the pile, and heap over them large quantities of wood and other materials adequate to the prevention of their escape—an outrage on humanity which has been frequently perpetrated under the indirect sanction of officers, undeservedly employed for the security of life and preservation of peace and tranquillity.

In many instances, in which the vigilance of the magistrate has deterred the native officers of police from indulging their own inclination, widows have either made their escape from the pile after being partially burnt, or retracted their resolution to burn when brought to the awful task, to the mortifying disappointment of the instigators; while in some instances the resolution to die has been retracted on pointing out to the widows the impropriety of their intended undertaking, and on promising them safety and maintenance during life, notwithstanding the severe reproaches liable thereby to be heaped on them by their relatives and friends.

In consideration of circumstances so disgraceful in themselves, and so incompatible with the principles of British rule, your Lordship in Council, fully impressed with the duties required of you by justice and humanity has deemed it incumbent on you, for the honour of the British name to come to the resolution, that the lives of your female Hindoo subjects should be henceforth more efficiently protected; that the heinous sin of males and females may no longer be committed, and that the most ancient and purest system of Hindoo religion should not any longer be set at nought by the Hindoos themselves. The magistrates, in consequence, are, we understand, positively ordered to execute the resolution of government by all possible means.

We are, my Lord, reluctantly restrained by the consideration of the nature of your exalted situation, from indicating our inward feelings by presenting any valuable offering as commonly adopted on such occasions; but we should consider ourselves highly guilty of insincerity and ingratitude, if we remained negligently silent when urgently called upon by our feelings and conscience to express publicly the gratitude we feel for the overlasting obligation you have graciously conferred on the Hindoo community at large. We, however, are at a loss to find language sufficiently indicative even of a small portion of the sentiments we are desirous of expressing on the occasion, we must therefore conclude this address with entreating that your Lordship will condescendingly accept our most grateful acknowledgements for this act of benevolence towards us, and will pardon the silence of those who, though equally partaking of the blessing bestowed by your Lordship, have, through ignorance or prejudice, omitted to join us in this common cause.[3]

Petition to Parliament in Defence of the Regulation
Prohibiting the Practice of Suttee (1830–31)[4]

To the Honourable the Commons of the United Kingdom of Great Britain and Ireland in Parliament Assembled

The humble Petition of the undersigned Natives of India, Sheweth—That a practice has prevailed throughout India, particularly in Bengal, of burning those willing on the funeral piles of their deceased husbands, who could be induced to offer themselves as voluntary sacrifices.

That this barbarous and inhuman practice has been happily abolished by the Government of the Right Honourable Lord William Cavendish Bentinck, who has thus conferred an inestimable benefit on the native population of India.

3. The following was His Lordship's reply:
"It is very satisfactory for me to find that, according to the opinions of so many respectable and intelligent Hindoos, the practice which has recently been prohibited, not only was required by the rules of their religion, but was at variance with those writings which they deem to be of the greatest force and authority. Nothing but a reluctance to inflict punishment for acts which might be conscientiously believed to be enjoined by religious precepts, could have induced the British government at any time to permit, within territories under its protection, an usage violently opposed to the best feelings of human nature who present this address are right in supposing that by every nation in the world, except the Hindoos themselves, this part of their customs has always been made a reproach against them, and nothing so strangely contrasted with the better features of their own national character, so inconsistent with the affections which unite families, so destructive of the moral principles on which society is founded, has ever subsisted amongst a people in other respects so civilized. I trust that the reproach is removed for ever; and I feel a sincere pleasure in thinking that the Hindoos will thereby be exalted in the estimation of mankind, to an extent in some degree proportioned to the repugnance which was felt for the usage which has now ceased."—Asiatic Journal, N.S. Vol II, Asiatic Intelligence, p. 189.

4. This petition was taken to England by Raja Ram Mohan Roy and presented by Lord Lansdown before the House of Lords to counteract the impression sought to be created by the appeal sent to the authorities in England by orthodox advocates of Suttee belonging to the Dhurmu Subha. It is generally known to be, and is probably the production of Raja Ram Mohan Roy. For the text of the petition *Vide Asiatic Journal*, N.S. Vol. V, Asiatic Intelligence pp. 20–21.—Ed.

That the regulation prohibiting the practice has been received with gratitude by many, while the majority of the native population have remained passive and acquiescent, although nearly a twelve month has elapsed since the abolition took place.

That, as a proof of your Honourable House of the feeling entertained on the subject by a numerous portion of the native community, the subjoined address was presented to the Governor General in Council expressive of their thanks for his benevolent interference.

[Here the petitioners recited the address presented by the Native Hindoo gentlemen of Calcutta to Lord William Bentinck, in January, 1830.][5]

That your petitioners have, however, learned that a number of natives, professing to be attached to the ancient practice, have prepared a petition to your Honourable House, soliciting the re-establishment of the rite of burning

---

5. The presentation of the Petition and the Address is thus described by the Asiatic Journal:—
House of Lords, July 1st, 1831.
Suttee. The Marquess of Lansdowne said, he had a petition of a peculiar nature to present to the House, to which he wished to call their lordships' attention. Their lordships, doubtless were acquainted with the fact, that Lord William Bentinck, as Governor General of India, took upon himself some time ago, after giving to the subject that calm and serious attention which is demanded, to issue an order by which a most inhuman practice, that of burning widows on the funeral pile of their deceased husbands, was forbidden the consequence of this, some months after the order a number of Hindus assembled together and sign the document deprecating this intervention with their religious ceremonies and condemning the interference of the company and their efforts, the forbidding, the fulfilment of their ceremonies. The petitioners prayed that the subject might be investigated before the Privy Council. The petition was forwarded to the Privy Council, and if it were the wish of those persons to be heard before that body, it would be the duty of the Privy Council so to hear them. But since that petition was presented, an individual who he believed was known to some of their lordships, and whose abilities were very generally acknowledged in the East—a Brahmin of India, Ram Mohan Roy—called upon him and stated, that, under the impression which existed in India, that such a petition as that which he had described would be presented, not to the Privy Council, but to the House of Lords, a number of the most influential and intellectual natives of India had met together and determined to send a counter-petition (that, which he held in his hand) to the House of Lords. In the petition they expressed the great approbation with which they viewed this act of the government of India; and they stated their decided conviction, after looking into the Shastrus and Vedas, that the inhuman custom which had been abolished was not authorised by the Hindu religion. They observed, that it was first instituted by certain Hindu princes for private and personal reasons; and they further declared, that one of the most important injunctions of Menu was, that widows should live in the observance of purity and virtue after the death of their husbands—that they should lead a life of chastity and austerity, but that they should not destroy themselves. In his opinion, every human mind must rejoice at the abolition of such a custom. Many of those who had governed India were, he believed, shocked at the reflection that a practice of this description prevailed and that they were without the power of preventing such disgusting scenes.

The petition was laid on the table.

their widows; and therefore to prevent your Honourable House from supposing that their sentiments are those of the whole native population, your petitioners respectively present themselves to the notice of your Honourable House, and pray that the Regulation of the local government may be confirmed and enforced.

That your petitioners cannot permit themselves to suppose that such a practice, abhorrent to all the feelings of nature, the obligations of society, and the principles of good government will receive the sanction of your Honourable House much less the British name and character will be dishonoured by its re-establishment.

That your petitioners confidently rely on receiving from your Honourable House a full and final confirmation of the Act of the Governor General in Council abolishing the rite of widow-burning.

And your petitioners will ever pray.

SOURCE: In Mulk Raj Anand, *Sati: A Write-up of Raja Ram Mohan Roy about Burning of Widows Alive* (Delhi: B.R. Publishing Corp., 1908).

On Sati

G. W. F. HEGEL

However pusillanimous and effeminate the Hindoos may be in other respects, it is evident how little they hesitate to sacrifice themselves to the Highest—to Annihilation. Another instance of the same is the fact of wives burning themselves after the death of their husbands. Should a woman contravene this traditional usage, she would be severed from society, and perish in solitude. An Englishman states that he also saw a woman burn herself because she had lost her child. He did all that he could to divert her away from her purpose; at last he applied to her husband who was standing by, but he showed himself perfectly indifferent, as *he had more wives at home.* Sometimes twenty women are seen throwing themselves at once into the Ganges, and on the Himalaya range an English traveller found three women seeking the source of the Ganges, in order to put an end to their life in this holy river. At a religious festival in the celebrated temple of Juggernaut in Orissa, on the Bay of Bengal, where millions of Hindoos assemble, the image of the god Vishnu is drawn in procession on a car: about five hundred men set it in motion, and many fling themselves down before its wheels to be crushed to pieces. The whole seashore is already strewed with the bodies of persons who have thus immolated themselves. Infanticide is also very common in India. Mothers throw their children into the Ganges, or let them pine away under the rays of the sun. The morality which is involved in respect for human life, is not found among the Hindoos. There are besides those already mentioned, infinite modifications of the same principle of conduct, all pointing to annihilation. This, *e.g.*, is the leading principle of the Gymnosophists, as the Greeks called them. Naked Fakirs wander about without any occupation, like the mendicant friars of the Catholic church; live on the alms of others, and make it their aim to reach the highest degree of abstraction—the perfect deadening of consciousness; a point from which the transition to physical death is no great step.

SOURCE: In *The Philosophy of History* (1822) (London: K. Paul, Trench, Trubner and Co., 1892–96, 3 vols).

Death by Fire of Miss Havisham
CHARLES DICKENS

[Dickens's novel *Great Expectations* is often construed as the education of the young Pip, but it also tells the story of the abandoned, sequestered Miss Havisham. Dickens's own writings on the practice of "suttee" in essay form suggest that the stories of both sati and purdah from the East may have contributed to his representation of the woman in his novel.]

I looked into the room where I had left her, and I saw her seated in the ragged chair upon the hearth close to the fire, with her back towards me. In the moment when I was withdrawing my head to go quietly away, I saw a great flaming light spring up. In the same moment I saw her running at me, shrieking, with a whirl of fire blazing all about her, and soaring at least as many feet above her head as she was high.

I had a double-caped great-coat on, and over my arm another thick coat. That I got them off, closed with her, threw her down, and got them over her; that I dragged the great cloth from the table for the same purpose, and with it dragged down the heap of rottenness in the midst, and all the ugly things that sheltered there; that we were on the ground struggling like desperate enemies, and that the closer I covered her, the more wildly she shrieked and tried to free herself; that this occurred I knew through the result, but not through anything I felt, or thought, or knew I did. I knew nothing until I knew that we were on the floor by the great table, and that patches of tinder yet alight were floating in the smoky air, which a moment ago had been her faded bridal dress.

Then, I looked round and saw the disturbed beetles and spiders running away over the floor, and the servants coming in with breathless cries at the door. I still held her forcibly down with all my strength, like a prisoner who might escape; and I doubt if I even knew who she was, or why we had struggled, or that she had been in flames, or that the flames were out, until I saw the patches of tinder that had been her garments, no longer alight, but falling in a black shower around us.

She was insensible, and I was afraid to have her moved, or even touched. Assistance was sent for, and I held her until it came, as if I unreasonably fancied (I think I did) that if I let her go, the fire would break out again and consume her. When I got up, on the surgeon's coming to her with other aid, I was astonished to see that both my hands were burnt; for I had no knowledge of it through the sense of feeling.

On examination it was pronounced that she had received serious hurts, but that they of themselves were far from hopeless; the danger lay mainly in the nervous shock. By the surgeon's directions, her bed was carried into that room and laid upon the great table, which happened to be well suited to the dressing of her injuries. When I saw her again, an hour afterwards, she lay indeed where I had seen her strike her stick, and had heard her say she would lie one day.

Though every vestige of her dress was burnt, as they told me, she still had something of her old ghastly bridal appearance; for, they had covered her to the throat with white cotton wool, and as she lay with a white sheet loosely overlying that, the phantom air of something that had been and was changed was still upon her.

I found, on questioning the servants, that Estella was in Paris, and I got a promise from the surgeon that he would write by the next post. Miss Havisham's family I took upon myself; intending to communicate with Matthew Pocket only, and leave him to do as he liked about informing the rest. This I did next day, through Herbert, as soon as I returned to town.

There was a stage, that evening, when she spoke collectedly of what had happened, though with a certain terrible vivacity. Towards midnight she began to wander in her speech, and after that it gradually set in that she said innumerable times in a low solemn voice: 'What have I done!' And then: 'When she first came, I meant to save her from misery like mine.' And then: 'Take the pencil and write under my name, "I forgive her!"' She never changed the order of these three sentences, but she sometimes left out a word in one or other of them; never putting in another word, but always leaving a blank and going on to the next word.

As I could do no service there, and as I had, nearer home, that pressing reason for anxiety and fear which even her wanderings could not drive out of my mind, I decided in the course of the night that I would return by the early morning coach: walking on a mile or so, and being taken up clear of the town. At about six o'clock of the morning, therefore, I leaned over her and touched her lips with mine, just as they said, not stopping for being touched: 'Take the pencil and write under my name, "I forgive her."'

SOURCE: Chapter 49 in *Great Expectations* (London: Chapman and Hall, 1861).

Fogg Rescues a Sati
JULES VERNE

[The Indian widow rescued by Phileas Fogg in the company of his servant, Passepartout, and the detective Fix finishes with them their journey around the world and eventually marries Fogg on their return to England.]

A group of old fakirs were capering and making a wild ado around the statue; these were striped with ochre, and covered with cuts whence their blood issued drop by drop,—stupid fanatics, who, in the great Indian ceremonies, still throw themselves under the wheels of Juggernaut. Some Brahmins, clad in all the sumptuousness of Oriental apparel, and leading a woman who faltered at every step, followed. This woman was young, and as fair as a European. Her head and neck, shoulders, ears, arms, hands, and toes, were loaded down with jewels and gems,—with bracelets, earrings, and rings; while a tunic bordered with gold, and covered with a light muslin robe, betrayed the outline of her form.

The guards who followed the young woman presented a violent contrast to her, armed as they were with naked sabres hung at their waists, and long damasceened pistols, and bearing a corpse on a palanquin. It was the body of an old man, gorgeously arrayed in the habiliments of a rajah, wearing, as in life, a turban embroidered with pearls, a robe of tissue of silk and gold, a scarf of cashmere sewed with diamonds, and the magnificent weapons of a Hindoo prince. Next came the musicians and a rearguard of capering fakirs, whose cries sometimes drowned the noise of the instruments; these closed the procession.

Sir Francis watched the procession with a sad countenance, and turning to the guide, said, "A *suttee*."

The Parsee nodded, and put his finger to his lips. The procession slowly wound under the trees, and soon its last ranks disappeared in the depths of the wood. The songs gradually died away; occasionally cries were heard in the distance, until at last all was silence again.

Phileas Fogg had heard what Sir Francis said, and, as soon as the procession had disappeared, asked, "What is a *suttee?*"

"A *suttee*," returned the general, "is a human sacrifice, but a voluntary one. The woman you have just seen will be burned tomorrow at the dawn of day."

"Oh, the scoundrels!" cried Passepartout, who could not repress his indignation.

"And the corpse?" asked Mr. Fogg.

"Is that of the prince, her husband," said the guide; "an independent rajah of Bundelcund."

"Is it possible," resumed Phileas Fogg, his voice betraying not the least emotion, "that these barbarous customs still exist in India, and that the English have been unable to put a stop to them?"

"These sacrifices do not occur in the larger portion of India," replied Sir Francis; "but we have no power over these savage territories, and especially here in Bundelcund. The whole district north of the Vindhias is the theatre of incessant murders and pillage."

"The poor wretch!" exclaimed Passepartout, "to be burned alive!"

"Yes," returned Sir Francis, "burned alive. And if she were not, you cannot conceive what treatment she would be obliged to submit to from her relatives. They would shave off her hair, feed her on a scanty allowance of rice, treat her with contempt; she would be looked upon as an unclean creature, and would die in some corner, like a scurvey dog. The prospect of so frightful an existence drives these poor creatures to the sacrifice much more than love or religious fanaticism. Sometimes, however, the sacrifice is really voluntary, and it requires the active interference of the Government to prevent it. Several years ago, when I was living at Bombay, a young widow asked permission of the governor to be burned along with her husband's body; but, as you may imagine, he refused. The woman left the town, took refuge with an independent rajah, and there carried out her self-devoted purpose."

While Sir Francis was speaking, the guide shook his head several times, and now said, "The sacrifice which will take place tomorrow at dawn is not a voluntary one."

"How do you know?"

"Everybody knows about this affair in Bundelcund."

"But the wretched creature did not seem to be making any resistance," observed Sir Francis.

"That was because they had intoxicated her with fumes of hemp and opium."

"But where are they taking her?"

"To the pagoda of Pillaji, two miles from here; she will pass the night there."

"And the sacrifice will take place—"

"Tomorrow, at the first light of dawn."

The guide now led the elephant out of the thicket, and leaped upon his neck. Just at the moment that he was about to urge Kiouni forward with a peculiar whistle, Mr. Fogg stopped him, and turning to Sir Francis Cromarty, said, "Suppose we save this woman."

"Save the woman, Mr. Fogg!"

"I have yet twelve hours to spare; I can devote them to that."

"Why, you are a man of heart!"

"Sometimes," replied Phileas Fogg, quietly; "when I have the time."

SOURCE: Chapter 12 in *Around the World in Eighty Days* (Philadelphia: Porter and Coates, 1873).

Maspero Jingle

Calm in the early morning
Solace in time of woes
Peace in the hush of twilight,
Balm ere my eyelids close.
This will Masperos bring me,
Asking naught in return,
With only a Suttee's passion
To do their duty and burn.

SOURCE: The "Maspero Jingle" appeared in the *Bombay Times and Journal of Commerce*; it was reprinted in Rajeswari Sunder Rajan's *Real and Imagined Women: Gender, Culture, and Postcolonialism* (London: Routledge, 1993).

On Suttee

ERNEST RENAN

[Ernest Renan (1823–1892) was a renowned French philosopher, historian, and religious scholar. Renan argued that study of the history of religions could lead way to a scientific understanding of human natures and cultures. His better known works are *Studies of Religious History* (1857) and "Moral and Critical Essays" (1859).]

The English have imagined that they were furthering the cause of sacred morality by prohibiting in India the processions stained with the blood of voluntary sacrifices, the *suttee*. A strange mistake indeed. Do you really believe that the fanatic who joyfully lays down his head under the wheels of the car of Juggernauth is not happier and more beautiful than you, insipid merchants. Do not you think that he honours human nature more by attesting—in an irrational, but none the less powerful manner, no doubt—that man has within him instincts superior to all the cravings for the finite and the love of self. Undoubtedly if we looked upon those acts as the mere sacrifice to a chimerical deity, they would be simply absurd. But we look upon them as the fascination which the infinite exercises on man, as impersonal enthusiasm, the cult of the suprasensible. And it is upon those magnificent outbursts of the grand instincts of human nature that you would impose limits, with your paltry morality and your narrow common sense. . . . In those sublime and picturesque exaggerations of human nature there is a foolhardiness, a spontaneousness which the healthy and regular exercise of reason, do what it will, will never equal, and which the poet and the artist will always prefer (39). A morbid and exclusive development is more original and shows in greater relief the energy of nature, like an injected vein which stands out more clearly to the inspection of the anatomist. Go and have a look in the Louvre at the marvellous Spanish collection; it is ecstasy and the superhuman incarnated, saints whose feet scarcely touch earth; virgins with necks craned, haggard eyes, staring into space, martyrs who wrench their hearts from their bodies or lacerate themselves, monks undergoing all kinds of self torture, etc. Well, I love those monks of Ribeira and Zurbaran, without which one would fail to understand the Inquisition. It is the moral force of man exaggerated, off the track, but original and bold in its excess. The apostle is certainly not the pure type of humanity, nevertheless, where shall we find a more powerful manifestation for the psychologist from which to study the inmost energy of human nature and its divine outbursts?

SOURCE: In *The Future of Science* (Boston: Roberts Brothers, 1893).

The Reformer's Wife
FLORA ANNIE STEEL

[Flora Annie Steel (1847–1929) was raised in London and Scotland; at age twenty, she went to India where her husband, a civil servant, had been assigned duty in the Punjab. She remained in India for twenty-one years. Steel was a prolific author. Much of her work centered on Indian subjects and themes, including *On the Face of the Waters* (1896), Steel's fictional account of the Indian Uprising/Sepoy Mutiny, and *The Complete Indian Housekeeper and Cook* (co-authored with Grace Gardiner), a handbook for proper and effective management of the Anglo-Indian domicile. She also wrote a collection of tales set in the Punjab, *Wide Awake Stories* (1884), and recounted the tales of the classical Indian myths in *A Tale of Indian Heroes: Being the Stories of the Mahabharata and the Ramayana* (n.d.). For further study, see Lady Violet Georgiana Powell's *Flora Annie Steel: Novelist of India* (London: Heinemann, 1981).]

A Sketch from Life

He was a dreamer of dreams, with the look in his large dark eyes which Botticelli put into the eyes of his Moses; that Moses in doublet and hose, whose figure, isolated from its surroundings, reminds one irresistibly of Christopher Columbus, or Vasco da Gama—of those, in fact, who dream of a Promised Land.

And this man dreamt as wild a dream as any. He hoped, before he died, to change the social customs of India.

He used to sit in my drawing-room, talking to me by the hour of the Prophet and his blessed Fâtma—for he was a Mahomedan—and bewailing the sad degeneracy of these present days, when caste had crept into and defiled the Faith. I shall never forget the face of martyred enthusiasm with which he received my first invitation to dinner. He accepted it, as he would have accepted the stake, with fervour, and indeed to his ignorance the ordeal was supreme. However, he appeared punctual to the moment on the appointed day, and greatly relieved my mind by partaking twice of plum-pudding, which he declared to be a surpassingly cool and most digestible form of nourishment, calculated to soothe both body and mind. Though this is hardly the character usually assigned to it, I did not contradict him, for not even his eager self-sacrifice had sufficed for the soup, the fish, or the joint, and he might otherwise have left the table in a starving condition. As it was, he firmly set aside my invitation to drink water after the meal was over, with the modest remark that he had not eaten enough to warrant the indulgence.

The event caused quite a stir in that far-away little town, set out among the ruins of a great city, on the high bank of one of the Punjab rivers; for the scene of this sketch lay out of the beaten track, beyond the reach of *babus* and barristers, patent-leather shoes and progress. Beyond the pale of civilization altogether, among a quaint little colony of fighting Pathans who still pointed with pride to an old gate or two which had withstood siege after siege, in those old fighting days when the river had flowed beneath the walls of the city. Since then the water had ebbed seven miles to the south-east, taking with it the prestige of the stronghold, which only remained a picturesque survival; a cluster of four-storied purple-brick houses surrounded by an intermittent purple-brick wall, bastioned and loop-holed. A formidable defence, while it lasted. But it had a trick of dissolving meekly into a sort of mud hedge, in order to gain the next stately fragment, or maybe to effect an alliance with one of the frowning gateways which had defied assault. This condition of things was a source of sincere delight to my Reformer Futteh Deen (Victory of Faith) who revelled in similes. It was typical of the irrational, illogical position of the inhabitants in regard to a thousand religious and social questions, and just as one brave man could break through these sham fortifications, so one resolute example would suffice to capture the citadel of prejudice, and plant the banner of abstract Truth on its topmost pinnacle.

For he dreamt excellently well, and as he sate declaiming his Persian and Arabic periods in the drawing-room with his eyes half-shut, like one in presence of some dazzling light, I used to feel as if something might indeed be done to make the Mill of God grind a little faster.

In the matter of dining out, indeed, it seemed as if he was right. For within a week of his desperate plunge, I received an invitation to break bread with the municipal committee in the upper story of the Vice-President's house. The request, which was emblazoned in gold, engrossed on silk paper in red and black, and enclosed in a brocade envelope, was signed by the eleven members and the Reformer, who, by the way, edited a ridiculous little magazine to which the committee subscribed a few rupees a month. Solely for the purpose of being able to send copies to their friends at Court, and show that they were in the van of progress. For a man must be that, who is patron of a 'Society for the General Good of All Men in All Countries.' I was, I confess it, surprised, even though a casual remark that now perhaps his Honour the Lieutenant-Governor would no longer suspect his slaves of disloyalty, showed me that philanthropy had begun at home. For the little colony bore a doubtful character, being largely leavened by the new Puritanism, which Government, for reasons best known to itself, chooses to confound with Wahabeeism.

The entertainment given on the roof amid starshine and catherine-wheels proved a magnificent success, its great feature being an enormous plum-pudding which I was gravely told had been prepared by my own cook. At what cost, I shudder to think; but the rascal's grinning face as he placed it on the table convinced me that he had seized the opportunity for some almost inconceivable extortion. But there was no regret in those twelve grave, bearded faces, as one by one they tasted and approved. All this happened long before a miserable, exotic imitation of an English vestry replaced the old patrician committees, and these men were representatives of the bluest blood in the neighbourhood, many of them descendants of those who in past times had held high offices of state, and had transmitted courtly manners to their children. So the epithets bestowed on the plum-pudding were many-syllabled; but the consensus of opinion was indubitably towards its coolness, its digestibility, and its evident property of soothing the body and the mind. Again I did not deny it. How could I, out on the roof under the eternal stars, with those twelve foreign faces showing, for once, a common bond of union with the Feringhee? I should have felt like Judas Iscariot if I had struck the thirteenth chord of denial.

The Reformer made a speech afterwards, I remember, in which, being wonderfully well read, he alluded to love-feasts and sacraments, and a coming millennium, when all nations of the world should meet at one table, and— well! not exactly eat plum-pudding together, but something very like it. Then we all shook hands, and a native musician played something on the *siringhi* which they informed me was 'God Save the Queen.' It may have been. I only know that the Reformer's thin face beamed with almost pitiful delight, as he told me triumphantly that this was only the beginning.

He was right. From that time forth the plum-pudding feast became a recognized function. Not a week passed without one. Generally—for my gorge rose at the idea of my cook's extortion—in the summer-house in my garden, where I could have an excuse for providing the delicacy at my own expense. And I am bound to say that this increased intimacy bore other fruits than that contained in the pudding. For the matter of that it has continued to bear fruit, since I can truthfully date the beginning of my friendship for the people of India from the days when we ate plum-pudding together under the starshine.

The Reformer was radiant. He formed himself and his eleven into committees and sub-committees for every philanthropical object under the sun, and many an afternoon have I spent under the trees with my work watching one deputation after another retire behind the oleander hedge in order to permutate itself by deft rearrangement of members, secretaries, and vice-presidents into some fresh body bent on the regeneration of mankind. For life was leisureful, lingering and lagging along in the little town where there was neither doctor nor parson, policeman nor canal officer, nor in fact any white face save my own and my husband's. Still we went far and fast in a cheerful, unreal sort of way. We started schools and debating societies, public libraries and technical art classes. Finally we met enthusiastically over an extra-sized plum-pudding, and bound ourselves over to reduce the marriage expenditure of our daughters.

The Reformer grew more radiant than ever, and began in the drawing-room—where it appeared to me he hatched all his most daring schemes—to talk big about infant marriage, enforced widowhood, and the seclusion of women. The latter I considered to be the key to the whole position, and therefore I felt surprised at the evident reluctance with which he met my suggestion, that he should begin his struggle by bringing his wife to visit me. He had but one, although she was childless. This was partly, no doubt, in deference to his advanced theories; but also, at least so I judged from his conversation, because of his unbounded admiration for one who by his description was a pearl among women. In fact this unseen partner had from the first been held up to me as a refutation of all my strictures on the degradation of seclusion. So, to tell truth, I was quite anxious to see this paragon, and vexed at the constant ailments and absences which prevented our becoming acquainted. The more so because this shadow of hidden virtue fettered me in argument, for Futteh Deen was an eager patriot, full of enthusiasms for India and the Indians. Once the sham fortifications were scaled, he assured me that Hindustan, and above all its women, would come to the front and put the universe to shame. Yet, despite his successes, he looked haggard and anxious; at the time I thought it was too much progress and plum-pudding combined, but afterwards I came to the conclusion that his conscience was ill at ease, even then.

So the heat grew apace. The fly-catchers came to dart among the *sirus* flowers and skim round the massive dome of the old tomb in which we lived.

The melons began to ripen, first by ones and twos, then in thousands—gold, and green, and russet. The corners of the streets were piled with them, and every man, woman, and child carried a crescent moon of melon at which they munched contentedly all day long. Now, even with the future good of humanity in view, I could not believe in the safety of a mixed diet of melon and plum-pudding, especially when cholera was flying about. Therefore, on the next committee-day I had a light and wholesome refection of sponge-cakes and jelly prepared for the philanthropists. They partook of it courteously, but sparingly. It was, they said, super-excellent, but of too heating and stimulating a nature to be consumed in quantities. In vain I assured them that it could be digested by the most delicate stomach; that it was, in short, a recognized food for convalescents. This only confirmed them in their view, for, according to the Yunâni system, an invalid diet must be heating, strengthening, stimulating. Somehow in the middle of their upside-down arguments I caught myself looking pitifully at the Reformer, and wondering at his temerity in tilting at the great mysterious mass of Eastern wisdom.

And that day, in deference to my Western zeal, he was to tilt wildly at the *zenâna* system.

His address fell flat, and for the first time I noticed a distinctly personal flavour in the discussion. Hitherto we had resolved and recorded gaily, as if we ourselves were disinterested spectators. However, the Vice-President apologized for the general tone, with a side slash at exciting causes in the jelly and sponge-cake, whereat the other ten wagged their heads sagely, remarking that it was marvellous, stupendous, to feel the blood running riot in their veins after those few mouthfuls. Verily such food partook of magic. Only the Reformer dissented, and ate a whole sponge-cake defiantly.

Even so the final Resolution ran thus: 'That this committee views with alarm any attempt to force the natural growth of female freedom, which it holds to be strictly a matter for the individual wishes of the man.' Indeed it was with difficulty that I, as secretary, avoided the disgrace of having to record the spiteful rider, 'And that if any member wanted to unveil the ladies he could begin on his own wife.'

I was young then in knowledge of Eastern ways, and consequently indignant. The Reformer, on the other hand, was strangely humble, and tried afterwards to evade the major point by eating another sponge-cake, and making a facetious remark about experiments and vile bodies; for he was a mine of quotations, especially from the Bible, which he used to wield to my great discomfiture.

But on the point at issue I knew he could scarcely go against his own convictions, so I pressed home his duty of taking the initiative. He agreed, gently. By and by, perhaps, when his wife was more fit for the ordeal. And it was natural, even the *mem-sahiba* must allow, for unaccustomed modesty to shrink. She was to the full as devoted as he to the good cause, but at the same time— Finally, the *mem-sahiba* must remember that women were women all over the world—even though occasionally one was to be found like the *mem-sahiba* capable of acting as secretary to innumerable committees without a blush. There was something so wistful in his eager blending of flattery and excuse that I yielded for the time, though determined in the end to carry my point.

With this purpose I reverted to plum-puddings once more, and, I fear, to gross bribery of all kinds in the shape of private interviews and soft words. Finally I succeeded in getting half the members to consent to sending their wives to an after-dark at-home in my drawing-room, provided always that Mir Futteh Deen, the Reformer, would set a good example.

He looked troubled when I told him, and pointed out that the responsibility for success or failure now lay virtually with him, yet he did not deny it.

I took elaborate precautions to ensure the most modest seclusion on the appointed evening, even to sending my husband up a ladder to the gallery at the very top of the dome to smoke his after-dinner cigar. I remember thinking how odd it must have looked to him perched up there to see the twinkling lights of the distant city over the soft shadows of the *ferash* trees, and at his feet the glimmer of the white screens set up to form a conventional *zenán-khâna*. But I waited in vain—in my best dress, by the way. No one came, though my ayah assured me that several jealously guarded *dhoolies* arrived at the garden-gate and went away again when Mrs. Futteh Deen never turned up.

I was virtuously indignant with the offender, and the next time he came to see me sent out a message that I was otherwise engaged. I felt a little remorseful at having done so, however, when, committee-day coming round, the Reformer was reported on the sick-list. And there he remained until after the first rain had fallen, bringing with it the real Indian spring—the spring full of roses and jasmines, of which the poets and the bul-buls sing. By this time the novelty had worn off philanthropy and plum-pudding, so that often we had a difficulty in getting a quorum together to resolve anything; and I, personally, had begun to weary for the dazzled eyes and the eager voice so full of sanguine hope.

Therefore it gave me a pang to learn from the Vice-President, who, being a Government official, was a model of punctuality, that in all probability I should never hear or see either one or the other again. Futteh Deen was dying of the rapid decline which comes so often to the Indian student.

A recurrence of a vague remorse made me put my pride in my pocket and go unasked to the Reformer's house, but my decision came too late. He had died the morning of my visit, and I think I was glad of it.

For the paragon of beauty and virtue, of education and refinement, was a very ordinary woman, years older than my poor Reformer, marked with the small-pox, and blind of one eye. Then I understood.

SOURCE: "The Reformer's Wife" is from *The Indian Scene: Collected Short Stories of Flora Annie Steel* (London: E. Arnold and Co., 1933).

IX
THE INDIAN UPRISING/SEPOY MUTINY
1857-58

INTRODUCTION
The "Asiatic Mystery":
The Sepoy Mutiny, Rebellion, or Revolt
MIA CARTER

IN HIS EXHAUSTIVE account of the Cawnpore Massacre, historian Andrew Ward remarked, "Anyone who tries to tell the story of Cawnpore must subsist on a sometimes sparse diet of questionable dispositions, muddled accounts, dubious journals, and narratives of shell-shocked survivors with axes to grind" (*Our Bones Are Scattered*, 555). For these and other reasons, unequivocal representation of the Sepoy Mutiny is, perhaps, an impossible endeavor. Ambiguities and contradictions are evident from the very start, as the descriptions of the events of 1857–1859 are variously referred to as a military mutiny, a national revolt, and a native rebellion or uprising. Were the events the cause of Indian backwardness and native superstition, or were they the result of native treachery, sinister plotting, or anticolonial insurgence? In the days and months after the mutiny, politicians in the House of Commons and the British Parliament argued and debated these questions (see "The Asiatic Mystery") in an attempt to determine whether the rebellious actions were confined to the military, or were they, as Benjamin Disraeli inquired more gravely, "a reflex of the national mind." Were the sepoys' actions "mere barbaric movements" or something greater and less containable? Was the uprising/mutiny an extraordinary event or did the explosion of violence foreshadow the end of empire?

The historians' and statesmen's analyses and representations reveal a wide range of emotional, prejudicial, and inescapably ideological interpretations of the uprising/mutiny. Critics of the East India Company located the origins of the events in the Company's administrative and legislative policies and procedures. In their eyes, the mutiny, and the potential for future unrest, began with Robert Clive's victory at the Battle of Plassey on 23 June 1757 and the Company's subsequent annexation of the materially and culturally rich Bengal region. Many of these critics were progressive orientalists who believed that British rule of India was doomed to fail if Indian rituals and linguistic, legal, and cultural customs and traditions were not respected. Policies involving taxation, land seizure, the absorption of native states, and the disruption of indigenous adoption and inheritance traditions were frequently cited as the Company's most destructive and offensive actions. For example, the adoption restrictions implemented by Lord Dalhousie, governor-general of India (1847–1856), challenged native rulers' system of inheritance. Indian adoption policies guaranteed Indian rulers an heir in the case of the death or murder of the inheritor of the estate; childless couples, like the Raja and Rani or Jhansi, also utilized this tradition. Lord Dalhousie perfected an existing administrative policy that gave the Company the right to refuse an adopted son as the new ruler of a native state. The Company would declare the throne "lapsed"—in other words, vacant—and would then annex the ruler's property and place it under Company "protection" (ownership) and administrative rule. Nana Sahib (Dhoondu Punt), an adopted Indian chief or Peshwa, like the Rani of Jhansi and other Indian rulers, struggled to reverse the British policies that stripped them of their authority and possessions. The Rani of Jhansi attempted to use the force of British law against the Company and failed; she was subsequently fined for the legal debts the Company incurred defending itself against her charges.

Other British reforms, like the Inam Commission's (Bombay Presidency) investigative attempts to locate documentary evidence—titles and deeds—that granted the Indian rulers their rights and territories also alarmed Indian rulers, who recognized such actions as a challenge of their rights to rule. This kind of "land settlement" investigation was initiated in Oudh (Oude), which was supposedly protected by an 1837 treaty that granted the region independence. Company officials signed the treaty, but the Company board in England refused to ratify it. The King of Oudh was never informed of the treaty's illegitimacy. Oudh was one of the only surviving Mohammedan states, an empire some likened to the great Mogul Empire. Dalhousie's annexation of Oudh in 1856, just before Lord Canning's administrative appointment, and the latter's appointment of Coverly Jackson—who was infamous for his mistreatment of the Queen of Oudh and her household—as the British ruler of the region contributed to making Oudh a center of armed revolt.

Some historians discount the Company's political and administrative policies and native reactions to them as significant factors which led up to the uprising/mutiny. The activities of missionary societies and rumors of their attempts at widespread conversion are pointed to as causes for native unrest. Much of the missionary literature of the time reveals overly zealous "uplift and moral rescue" discourses and campaigns. Many missionaries believed that the colonial administrators' respect for Indian religions, customs, and traditions was not only wrong-headed but dangerous. In their view, no stable, rational, or moral form of government could coexist alongside "heathen and barbaric" traditions; aggressive conversion and Christian rule were the cures for India's native problem. In both missionary and military accounts of the uprising, the "Mohammedans"—Indians of Islamic faith—are portrayed as the most treacherous, savage, and unrelentingly seditious of the rebellious sepoys. The depiction may, in part, be understood as being related to the history of British and Islamic mercantile and evangelical competition; Christian zealots and colonial administrators were often haunted by fears of "the good" Indians' Islamic conversion and increasing militancy.

Contemporary historians also suggest that the revolt was provoked by native rulers who were primarily concerned about their waning wealth and power; these rulers are alleged to have duped the masses and utilized India's criminal element in attempt to regain control of their territories. Their "call to arms" was believed to have been disseminated across the land with the use of seditiously encoded chupatties, an Indian bread. Other accounts blame the revolt on Indian "superstition"—a general term assigned to Indian religious beliefs and practices—such as the Hindu and Muslim soldiers' "hysterical" aversion to the pig and cow fat required to grease the cartridges for the Enfield rifles. This interpretation held credence for many, due to its resemblance to the Vellore Mutiny (Madras Presidency) in 1806, which was purportedly provoked by rumors that the hats of the sepoys' newly designed uniforms were made of cow and pig hide. Even Mary Kingsley, who was sympathetic to Irish and African "agrarian grievances," her term for native reactions to land seizure and annexation policies, considered the Indian rebellion to be a symptom of Indian pathology rather than resistance to British rule (see Kingsley, "The Clash of Cultures").

The uprising/mutiny caused a flurry of responses and interpretations and created an explosion of visual and narrative representations. The event was considered an epic moment in the history of the British Empire; narratives of crime and punishment became imperial high drama. The events are recounted in romances, poems, and historical novels, as well as standard histories and official accounts, which in their tone, florid dialogue, and sensational narration closely resemble their fictional counterparts. Governmental response to the uprising/mutiny was swift and decisive: the Company's rule over India would come to an end. For political, practical, and economic reasons, a *better* system of government had to be implemented. The Company's demise established the British Raj and a new era of procedural experimentation and administrative rule.

BIBLIOGRAPHY

Baucom, Ian. "The Path from War to Friendship: E. M. Forster's Mutiny Pilgrimage." In *Out of Place: Englishness, Empire, and the Locations of Identity*. Princeton: Princeton University Press, 1999.

Benegal, Shyam. *Junoon (The Possessed* and *A Flight of Pigeons)*. India, 1978. Film.

Bhatia, Nandi. "Staging the 1857 Mutiny as 'The Great Rebellion': Colonial History and Post Colonial Interventions in Utpal Dutt's *Mahavidroh*." *Theatre Journal* 51, no. 2 (1999): 167–84.

Bhargava, Moti Lal. *Architects of Indian Freedom Struggle*. New Delhi: Deep and Deep, 1981.

Broehl, Wayne. *Crisis of the Raj: The Revolt of 1857 through British Lieutenants' Eyes*. Hanover, N.H.: for Dartmouth College by University Press of New England, 1986.

Buckler, F. W. (Francis William). *The Political Theory of the Indian Mutiny*. London: Transactions of the Royal Historical Society, 1922.

Chaudhuri, Sashi Bhusan. *English Historical Writings on the Indian Mutiny, 1857–1859*. Calcutta: World Press, 1979.

David, Saul. *The Indian Mutiny*. London: Viking, 2002.

Dewar, Douglas. *A Reply to Mr. F. W. Buckler's* The Political Theory of the Indian Mutiny. London: Transactions of the Royal Historical Society, 1924.

Hilton, Richard. *The Indian Mutiny: A Centenary History*. London: Hollis and Carter, 1957.

Hunter, W. W. *The Indian Mussalmans*. London: Indological Book House, 1871.

Hutchinson, David. *Annals of the Indian Rebellion*. London: n.p., 1974.

Kingsley, Mary H. "The Clash of Cultures." In *West African Studies*. London: Macmillan, 1901.

Kinsley, D. A. *They Fight Like Devils: Stories from Lucknow During the Great Indian Mutiny*. London: Greenhill, 2001.

Lahiri, Abani. *The Peasant and India's Freedom Movement*. New Delhi: Manak Publications, 2001.

Lebra-Chapman, Joyce. *The Rani of Jhansi: Study in Female Heroism in India*. Honolulu: University of Hawaii Press, 1986.

Mukherjee, Rudrangshu. *Spectre of Violence: The 1857 Kanpur Massacres*. New Delhi: Penguin Books India, 1998.

Ray, Satyajit. *Shatranj Ke Khiladi (The Chess Players)*. India, 1977. Film.

Roy, Tapti. *The Politics of a Popular Uprising: Bundelkhand in 1857*. Delhi: Oxford University Press, 1994.

Savarkar, Vinayak Damodar. *Indian War of Independence, 1857*. England, 1909; reprint, India: Sethani Kampani, Mumbai, 1949.

Scholberg, Henry. *The Indian Literature of the Great Rebellion*. New Delhi: Promilla and Co., 1993.

Sengupta, Kaylan Kumar. *Recent Writings on the Revolt of 1857: A Survey*. New Delhi: Indian Council Historical Research, 1975.

Sharpe, Jenny. *Allegories of Empire: The Figure of the Woman in the Colonial Text*. Minneapolis, Minn.: University of Minnesota Press, 1993.

Thompson, Edward John. *The Other Side of the Medal*. London: Hogarth Press, 1925.

Tytler, Harriet. *An Englishwoman in India: The Memoirs of Harriet Tytler, 1828–1858*. Oxford: Oxford University Press, 1986.

Viswanathan, Gauri. *Masks of Conquest: Literary Study and British Rule in India*. New York: Columbia University Press, 1989.

Ward, Andrew. *Our Bones Are Scattered: The Cawnpore Massacres and the Indian Mutiny of 1857.* New York: H. Holt and Co., 1996.

NOTEWORTHY FICTIONAL ACCOUNTS OF THE UPRISING/MUTINY

Bond, Ruskin. *A Flight of Pigeons.* Bombay: IBH Publishing Company, 1980.

Collier, Richard. *The Great Mutiny: a Dramatic Account of the Sepoy Rebellion.* New York: Dutton, 1964.

Dhutt, Utpal. *The Great Rebellion 1857.* Calcutta: Seagull Books, 1986.

Farrell, J. G. (James Gordon). *The Siege of Krishnapur.* London: Weidenfeld and Nicholson, 1973.

Grant, James. *Fairer than a Fairy: A Novel.* London: Tinsley, 1874.

Henty, G. A. (George Alfred). *In Times of Peril: A Tale of India.* London: Griffith, Farran, Okeden and Welsh, 1888.

Irwin, H. C. (Henry Crossley). *With Sword and Pen: a Story of India in the Fifties.* London: T. F. Unwin, 1904.

Kaye, M. M. (Mary Margaret). *Shadow of the Moon.* London: Longmans, Green, 1957.

Malgonkar, Manohar. *The Devil's Wind: Nana Saheb's Story: A Novel.* Delhi: Penguin Books, 1988.

Masters, John. *Nightrunners of Bengal: a Novel.* New York: Viking, 1951.

Steel, Flora Annie. *On the Face of the Waters.* London: W. Heinemann, 1897.

Taylor, Lucy. *Sahib and Sepoy, or, Saving an Empire: A Tale of the Indian Mutiny.* London: J. F. Shaw, 1897.

Chronology of Events

1857
May 2	Mutiny of the 7th Irregulars at Lucknow
May 10	Mutiny at Meerut
May 11	Mutineers take Delhi
June 5	Mutiny at Cawnpore
June 30	Seige at Lucknow
July 5	Victory of sepoy army at Shahganj near Agra
July 7	Havelock marches to Cawnpore
July 16	First Battle of Cawnpore
August 13	Defeat of Kunwar Singh at Jagdishpur
September 21	King of Delhi surrenders to Hodson
November 17	Relief of Lucknow by Sir Colin Campbell
December 6	British reclaim Cawnpore

1858
March 20	Canning's Oudh Proclamation
March 21	Final relief at Lucknow
June 1	Tatya Tope and the Rani of Jhansi seize Gwalior
June 17	Death of the Rani of Jhansi
August 2	Transfer of the British East India Company to the Crown
November 1	Queen Victoria's Proclamation

1859
July	Lord Canning declared first viceroy of India

Rulers and Rebels: Some Major Figures

RULERS

Lord Dalhousie, James Andrew Broun Ramsay, 10th earl of Dalhousie, governor-general of India (1847–1856); born 1812, died 1860. Dalhousie was recognized as the maker of modern India. His famous and infamous policies of annexation were cited as one of the primary causes of unrest in India. Dalhousie implemented the Doctrine of Lapse, the policy under which Indian lands and kingdoms were seized and put under British control, with "lapsed" territories defined as those allegedly lacking a legitimate heir— Dalhousie refused to recognize the Indian rulers' practice of adopting a male child to guarantee an heir to the throne. Dalhousie's aggressive annexation policies resulted in the seizure of Satara (1848), Punjab (1849), Jhansi (1854), Nagpur (1854), and Oudh/Oude (1856). Oudh was seized against a living ruler's will based on Dalhousie's accusations of "native" misgovernment. Dalhousie planned the expansion of the Indian railway and telegraph systems, promoted the completion of the Grand Trunk Road, promoted the education of girls, suppressed the practices of infanticide and human sacrifice, and centralized the postal system. However, his annexation policies, and the Indian responses to them, are central to understanding Dalhousie's Indian career.

Sir Colin Campbell ("Old Careful"), commander-in-chief of the British forces during the Sepoy Mutiny/Indian Uprising; born 1792, died 1863. Campbell was born in Glasgow, Scotland, the son of a carpenter. He served in the War of 1812 against the United States and in the Opium War in China in 1842. Despite his distinguished service in both of those wars, Campbell's rise in the military was a slow one, his humble origins probably having affected his career advancement. However, Campbell was eventually knighted for his service in the Second Sikh War (1848–1849) and appointed commander-in-chief at the outbreak of the mutiny/uprising. Campbell acquired his nickname as the result of his military caution and careful protection of the men under his leadership; he was both criticized and praised for these attributes. Campbell was raised to the peerage in 1858 for his service and leadership during the mutiny/uprising. He was buried at Westminster Abbey.

General Henry Havelock (Sir Henry); born 1795, died 1857. General Havelock first distinguished himself while serving in the First Anglo-Burmese War (1824–1826) and, later, during the First Afghan War (1839–1842). He was promoted in 1843 while serving as an interpreter during the first Gwalior Campaign. Havelock also served under Sir James Outram during the Persian Expedition in 1857; he was called to India during the outbreak of the mutiny. General Havelock fought against Nana Sahib at Lucknow, which he reclaimed on his fourth attempt. Havelock was rewarded with a knighthood (the Order of the Bath) for rescuing Lucknow and was promoted to major-general; however, he died from dysentery before learning of his promotion.

John Laird Mair Lawrence, ("Savior of the Punjab") first baron; born 1811, died 1879. Lawrence first served in India as an assistant judge in Delhi, a position he maintained for nineteen years. During these years, Lawrence was renowned for his opposition to the *talukdas* (tax collectors) and their mistreatment of the peasantry; his sympathy for the common people would later become the cause of a rift between Lawrence and his older brother, Henry Lawrence, the president of the board of administration in the Punjab. At age thirty-five, Lawrence was appointed to the newly annexed Jullunder region as a reward for his service during the First Sikh War (1845–1846). Lawrence's nickname paid tribute to the judge's economic, social, and political reforms in the region; he established courts and police posts, and suppressed female infanticide and suttee. Lawrence was made a baronet and knight of the Grand Cross of Bath for successfully negotiating a treaty with the Afghan ruler Dost Mohammad Khan. He was later appointed viceroy and governor-general (1864). While serving in this capacity, Lawrence supported Indian education but resisted the appointment of Indians to high positions in the civil service.

Sir Henry Montgomery Lawrence, born 1806, died 1857 at Lucknow. Henry Lawrence was a distinguished soldier and administrator who was placed in charge of Ferozepur in the Punjab (1839). Lawrence would later be appointed resident of Lahore (1846). He was knighted in 1848 for his reform activities (suttee, forced labor, infanticide) and for his suppression of mutinies in Kangra and the Kasmir. A specialist in Indian and oriental languages (Urdu, Hindi, Persian), Lawrence was appointed president of the board of administration in the Punjab (1849). During this period of service, he and his younger brother, John Lawrence, the finance supervisor of the region, quarreled over financial reforms. John favored the peasants, while Henry championed the Sikh aristocracy. The brothers' disagreement caused John to request a transfer out of the region. In 1857, Henry Lawrence was assigned to Oudh. He was mortally wounded at Lucknow and died before learning that he had been appointed provisional Governor-General.

Viscount Canning ("Clemency Canning"), Charles John, earl, governor-general of India (1857), first viceroy of India (1858); born 1812, died 1862. Viscount Canning began his career as a statesman serving as a member of

Parliament in 1836. He later served as undersecretary for foreign affairs in Sir Robert Peel's cabinet (1841). While serving as governor-general of India, Canning refused to succumb to the public cries of bloodletting and widespread vengeance against the Indians during and after the mutiny/uprising; he was vilified by some for being cowardly and traitorous. His July 1858 policy of conciliation and his insistence on calm and reasonable justice for the Indian rebels and citizens earned him his nickname. Canning became the first viceroy of India when the British East India Company was turned over to the Crown. He received an earldom in 1859.

REBELS

Nana Sahib (Nana Saheb), also known as Dhondu Pant; born 1820, died 1859. Adopted in 1827 by Peshwa (prince) Baji Rao II, the last Maratha peshwa, to inherit his throne. Nana Sahib was an educated Hindu nobleman who became one of the principal military leaders against the British forces. General Sahib's forces held off General Havelock at Lucknow, which was rescued by the British on Havelock's fourth attempt to reclaim it. Sahib has been depicted as a nationalist hero and as the "Butcher of Cawnpore," responsible for killing British women and children in November of 1857. Sahib escaped to the hills after the Battle of Gwalior, where he was believed to have died.

Tatya Tope (Tantia Tope), also known as Ram Chandra Pandurang; born 1814, died 1859. Tope was a Maratha Brahman who was in service to Baji Rao II, and a friend and follower of Nana Sahib. Tope was recognized as the most impressive rebel warrior, despite his lack of military training. He fought alongside the Rani of Jhansi and successfully escaped after the Battle of Gwalior. Tope waged a successful guerrilla war against the British for more than a year; he was finally betrayed by an associate and executed by the British.

The Rani of Jhansi, also known as Rani or Maharani Lakshmi Bai, wife of Raja of Jhansi; born 1835, died 1858. The childless ruling couple adopted a young boy to provide an heir for the kingdom of Jhansi, an adoption that went unrecognized by Governor-General Dalhousie, who planned to annex the Jhansi territories. The Rani wrote a number of letters appealing to the British Parliament and statesmen, protesting the annexation and British mistreatment of the royal family. When these appeals failed to amend the situation, the Rani hired a British attorney, John Lang, to plead her kingdom's cause to Company administrators. The Company granted the Rani a pension and allowed her to remain in residence at the palace at Jhansi. The Rani's refusal to accept the British annexation moved from the legal arena to the military one; her exploits on the battlefield and her renowned "exotic" beauty captured British imaginations. The Rani fought alongside Tatya Tope and Rao Sahib; she was mortally wounded at the battle of Gwalior.

Excerpts from *The Who's Who of Indian Martyrs*

Tatya Tope alias Ram Chandra Pandurang: b. 1814 at v. Gola, Maharashtra; s. of Shri Pandurang Bhat; Follower of Nana Sahib *alias* Dhondupant, who rose to be a General in the latter's army and one of the most important and eminent figures of the Great Revolt of 1857; Organised the rebel forces and planned the strategy of war against the British with great brilliance. Fought against the British army at several places in Uttar Pradesh and Madhya Pradesh, performing great military feats. Captured the towns of Charkhari and Gwalior and inflicted heavy losses on the British. After losing Gwalior to the British, he launched a successful guerilla campaign against the British forces in the Sagar and Narbada regions and in Khandesh and Rajasthan. The British forces failed to subdue him for more than a year. He was, however, betrayed into the hands of the British by his trusted associate Man Singh, Chief of Narwar, while asleep in his camp in the Paron forest. Captured by the British and taken to Sipri. Tried by a military court and executed on the gallows on April 18, 1859.

Tula Ram, Rao: Resident of Rewari, Distt. Gurgaon, Haryana; Chieftan of Rewari and successor to the jagir of his grand-father, Rao Tej Singh; Played a prominent part in the Great Revolt against British rule in 1857. Took up arms against the British and fought a brief engagement on October 7, 1857, against the British troops near the fort of Rampura. Shortly afterwards, a big battle against the British forces was fought by his army at Nasibpur near Narnaul and he was at the point of defeating the British force under Colonel Gerrard when the pro-British Naga Sadhus of Galta (Jaipur) and the Sikh army from Jind, Kapurthala and Patiala came to their rescue. Ordered a retreat and escaped. The leaders of the Great Revolt met at Kalpi to consider the situation and decided to depute Rao Tula Ram as the head of a mission to seek foreign help. Rao Tula Ram led the mission consisting of Ram Pandit (Shalig Ram Tripathi), Tara Singh and Nathwa Ram Mali. They went out of India in disguise aboard a ship from Bombay. Visited Iran to negotiate with the Russian Ambassador in Teheran through the good offices of the Iranian Government. Met Amir Dost Mohammad Khan of Afghanistan at Kandahar. The mission reached Kabul for further negotiations with Dost Mohammad's son, Amir Sher Ali Khan. Fell ill due to the rigorus of the journey and died at Kabul on September 8, 1862. The Afghan Government gave him a State funeral and his body was cremated outside the Delhi Gate in Kabul, where a small memorial was also erected.

Kunwar Singh: b. about 1782 at v. Jagdishpur, Distt. Shahabad, Bihar; Eldest son of Shri Sahibzada Singh; Owner of the large Jagdishpur Estate which he developed and expanded. The management of his estate was taken over by the British as he faced financial difficulties caused by family litigation; Took a very prominent part in the Great Revolt of 1857 as the principal leader of the anti-British forces in eastern India. Joined the revolutionary forces as they reached Arrah on July 26, 1857. Proclaimed himself to be the ruler of Shahabad. Entered into correspondence with other rebel leaders like Nana Saheb and persuaded other chiefs in Bihar to revolt. Defeated the British forces at Arrah, but failed to stop their advance. Dislodged from Jagdishpur, he marched towards Mirzapur and threatened Rewa and part of Allahabad district from a position of vantage. Moved to Banda where the Nawab had already identified himself with the rebel cause. Went to Kalpi on Nana Saheb's invitation to participate in the assault on Kanpur. Visited Lucknow, where he was warmly received by Birjis Qadr, invested with a high position of honour and granted a *firman* for taking over Azamgarh. Occupied the town after defeating the British forces. Decided to return to his ruined home in Jagdishpur as he saw no chance of retaining Azamgarh against the superior British forces. Fought a series of heroic and brilliant rearguard actions during the withdrawal. While crossing the Ganga river, he lost one of his hands which was shattered by a cannon ball. Returned to Shahabad with hardly two thousand battle-weary and ill-armed men. Led another attack on the British forces and inflicted a crushing defeat on them on April 23, 1858. Expired on the following day as a result of the severe wounds received during the battles. The deeds of valour performed by this brave 75-year-old patriot have been the subject of song and legend.

Nana Saheb alias Dhondu Pant: Resident of Bithoor, near Kanpur, Uttar Pradesh; s. of Shri Madhav Rao Narayan Bhat. Adopted by Peshwa Baji Rao II in 1827; Inherited the title and estates bequeathed by the Peshwa in a written testament of 1841. Made a futile appeal to the Court of Directors of the East India Company against the decision of the Governor-General-in-Council to discontinue the grant of a pension of Rs. 8 lakhs to him; Participated in the

402 Indian Uprising/Sepoy Mutiny

"Portrait of Nana Sahib." James Grant, ed. *Cassell's Illustrated History of India*, vol. 2, part 1 (New Delhi: Oriental Publishers and Distributors, 1978).

Great Revolt of 1857 as one of the principal leaders of the revolutionary forces. Defeated the British forces, declared himself the Peshwa and assumed control of the revolutionary government at Kanpur. Reorganised the civil and military administration with the assistance of a Council of Advisers which included Bala Saheb, Baba Bhat, Azimullah Khan and Tatya Tope. Took part in many encounters with the British troops and fought for every inch of the ground during the battle of Kanpur before the British commander, General Havelock, could enter the city on July 17, 1857. Reorganised his army and marched to Avadh where his troops caused severe harrassment to Havelock's force. Sent two envoys to Chandernagore, a French possession in Bengal, to negotiate and conclude an alliance with the French Emperor, Napoleon III.

Proceeded to Kalpi to take charge of the Avadh forces. Launched an attack to recapture Kanpur in December 1857, but could not succeed although his troops surrounded the city in a semi-circle. Proclaimed as the Peshwa in June 1858 by Lakshmi Bai, the patriotic Rani of Jhansi, who led her army against the British at Gwalior. Facing heavy odds, he was forced to retreat. The British troops pursued him for the next six months after the defeat of his forces in quick succession. Escaped into Nepal and is believed to have died of fever on September 24, 1859, in the Dang district of Nepal.

Lakshmi Bai, Maharani: b. November 19, 1835, at Varanasi, Uttar Pradesh; daughter of Shri Moropant Tambe and widow of Raja Gangadhar Rao. Her original name was Manikarnika; Became regent of Jhansi State after the death of her husband in 1835. The British refused to recognise her or her adopted son, Damodar Rao. Took up arms against the British seizure of her State. Attacked the British forces and drove them out of Jhansi in June 1857. Inflicted further defeats on the British at Mauranipur and Barwasagar and became the most powerful rebel leader of the 1857 revolt. Her army was further strengthened when the rulers of Banpur and Shahgarh in Bundelkhand became her allies. Fought valiantly against the attacks by the British forces under Sir Hugh Rose. The battle lasted about two weeks and she had to escape to Kalpi due to British pressure. She was joined at Kalpi by the forces of Rao Sahib and Tatya Tope. Their combined army fought bitter battles at Koonch and Kalpi. Due to adverse circumstances, she had to proceed to Gwalior. Set up the Peshwa's authority at that place. Pursued by the British troops, she decided to have a showdown. Personally commanded her forces wearing male attire. Fought against the superior British forces with great courage and bravery, but was mortally wounded in the battle at Kotahki-Sarai in Gwalior on June 18, 1858. Her body was cremated by her soldiers in the nearby garden of Baba Ganga Das, now known as Phool Bagh. After independence, a memorial was constructed at the spot to perpetuate the memory of her heroic deeds and martyrdom.

Mohammad Amin Khan: b. at Bareilly, Uttar Pradesh: Took part in the Great Revolt of 1857. Joined the rebel forces under the leadership of Khan Bahadur Khan, who had declared himself to be the independent Nawab of Rohilkhand. Fought against the British forces in the Rohilkhand region in May 1857. Captured by the British and executed on March 20, 1850, by hanging from a banyan tree in the Commissioner's office compound at Bareilly. In the mass execution, 243 other patriots were also hanged from the same tree on that day.

404 Indian Uprising/Sepoy Mutiny

SOURCE: These illustrated biographies of the Indian rebels are from P. N. Chopra, ed., *The Who's Who of Indian Martyrs,* 3 vols. (New Delhi: Ministry of Education and Youth Services, Government of India, 1969–1973).

Proclamation to the People of Oude on its Annexation. February 1856

[This document contains the East India Company's rationalization for its annexation of the Bengal region. The Company is depicted as a rescuing party whose gentle and superior government will ensure happiness and protect the Indian people from unjust and exorbitant indigenous practices. The document presents the Company as a humanizing enterprise whose primary concern is civilizing India; the East India Company's trading interests and mercantile mission are not referred to in the announcement.]

By a treaty concluded in the year 1801, the Honourable East India Company engaged to protect the Sovereign of Oude against every foreign and domestic enemy, while the Sovereign of Oude, upon his part, bound himself to establish "such a system of administration, to be carried into effect by his own officers, as should be conducive to the prosperity of his subjects, and calculated to secure the lives and property of the inhabitants." The obligations which the treaty imposed upon the Honourable East India Company have been observed by it for more than half a century, faithfully, constantly, and completely.

In all that time, though the British Government has itself been engaged in frequent wars, no foreign foe has ever set his foot on the soil of Oude; no rebellion has ever threatened the stability of its throne; British troops have been stationed in close promixity to the king's person, and their aid has never been withheld whenever his power was wrongfully defied.

On the other hand, one chief and vital stipulation of the treaty has been wholly disregarded by every successive ruler of Oude, and the pledge which was given for the establishment of such a system of administration as should secure the lives and property of the people of Oude, and be conducive to their prosperity, has, from first to last, been deliberately and systematically violated.

By reason of this violation of the compact made, the British Government might, long since, have justly declared the treaty void, and might have withdrawn its protection from the rulers of Oude. But it has hitherto been reluctant to have recourse to measures which would be fatal to the power and authority of a royal race who, whatever their faults towards their own subjects, have ever been faithful and true to their friendship with the English nation.

Nevertheless, the British Government has not failed to labour, during all that time, earnestly and perseveringly, for the deliverance of the people of Oude from the grievous oppression and misrule under which they have suffered.

Many years have passed since the Governor-General, Lord William Bentinck, perceiving that every previous endeavour to ameliorate the condition of the people of Oude had been thwarted or evaded, made formal declaration to the court of Lucknow, that it would become necessary that he should proceed to assume the direct management of the Oude territories.

The words and the menace which were then employed by Lord William Bentinck were, eight years ago, repeated in person by Lord Hardinge to the king. The sovereign of Oude was, on that day, solemnly bid remember that, whatever might now happen, "it would be manifest to all the world" that he "had received a friendly and timely warning."

But the friendly intentions of the British Government have been wholly defeated by the obstinacy, or incapacity, or apathy of the viziers and kings of Oude. Disinterested counsel and indignant censure, alternating, through more than fifty years, with repeated warning, remonstrance, and threats, have all proved ineffectual and vain.

The chief condition of the treaty remains unfulfilled, the promises of the king rest unperformed, and the people of Oude are still the victims of incompetency, corruption, and tyranny, without remedy or hope of relief. It is notorious throughout the land that the king, like most of his predecessors, takes no real share in the direction of public affairs.

The powers of government throughout his dominions are for the most part abandoned to worthless favourites of the court, or to violent and corrupt men, unfit for their duties and unworthy of trust.

The collectors of the revenue hold sway over their districts with uncontrolled authority, extorting the utmost payment from the people, without reference to past or present engagements.

The king's troops, with rare exceptions undisciplined and disorganized, and defrauded of their pay by those to whom it is entrusted, are permitted to plunder the villages for their own support, so that they have become a lasting scourge to the country they are employed to protect.

Gangs of freebooters infest the districts. Law and justice are unknown. Armed violence and bloodshed are daily events: and life and property are nowhere secure for an hour.

The time has come when the British Government can no longer tolerate in

"The Asiatic Mystery. As Prepared by Sepoy D'Israeli." In *Punch* 33 (8 August 1857): 55.

Opposite, above: "Sepoys, 1757" (1890). In James Grant, ed. *Cassell's Illustrated History of India*, vol. 1, part 1 (New Delhi: Oriental Publishers and Distributors, 1978). This image is a simple representation of Indian soldiers, sketched at the early stages of British enterprise in India. The stasis and rigidity of the image is dramatically contrasted with the melodramatic and dynamic portraits of the sepoys included in many of the illustrated histories of the Indian Uprising/Sepoy Mutiny.

Opposite, below. "Attack of the Mutineers on the Redan Battery at Lucknow, July 30, 1857" (n.d.). In Charles Ball, *The History of the Indian Mutiny* (London: London Publishing and Printing Co., 1858–1859). Charles Ball's *History of the Indian Mutiny* is filled with tigerlike, animalistic representations of Indians with flashing white eyes, bared teeth, daggers, and swords.

Oude these evils and abuses, which its position under the treaty serves indirectly to sustain, or continue to the sovereign that protection which alone upholds the power whereby such evils are inflicted.

Fifty years of sad experience have proved that the treaty of 1801 has wholly failed to secure the happiness and prosperity of Oude, and have conclusively shown that no effectual security can be had for the release of the people of that country from the grievous oppression they have long endured, unless the exclusive administration of the territories of Oude shall be permanently transferred to the British Government.

To that end it has been declared, by the special authority and consent of the Honourable Court of Directors, that the treaty of 1801, disregarded and violated by each succeeding sovereign of Oude, is henceforth wholly null and void.

His Majesty Wajid Alee Shah was invited to enter into a new engagement whereby the government of the territories of Oude should be vested, exclusively and for ever, in the Honourable East India Company; while ample provision should be made for the dignity, affluence, and honour of the king and of his family.

But his Majesty the King refused to enter into the amicable agreement which was offered for his acceptance.

Inasmuch, then, as his Majesty Wajid Alee Shah, in common with all his predecessors, has refused or evaded, or neglected to fulfil the obligations of the treaty of 1801, whereby he was bound to establish within his dominions such a system of administration as should be conducive to the prosperity and happiness of his subjects; and inasmuch as the treaty he thereby violated has been declared to be null and void; and inasmuch as his Majesty has refused to enter into other agreements which were offered to him in lieu of such treaty; and inasmuch as the terms of that treaty, if it had been still maintained in force, forbade the employment of British officers in Oude, without which no efficient system of administration could be established there, it is manifest to all that the British Government had but one alternative before it.

Either it must altogether desert the people of Oude, and deliver them up helpless to oppression and tyranny, which acting under the restriction of the treaty it has already too long appeared to countenance; or it must put forth its own great power on behalf of a people for whose happiness it, more than fifty years ago, engaged to interpose, and must at once assume to itself the exclusive and permanent administration of the territories of Oude.

The British Government has had no hesitation in choosing the latter alternative.

Wherefore, proclamation is hereby made that the Government of the territories of Oude is henceforth vested, exclusively and for ever, in the Honourable East India Company.

All Amils, Nazims, Chuckledars, and other servants of the Durbar; all officers, civil and military; the soldiers of the State; and all the inhabitants of Oude, are required to surrender, henceforth, implicit and exclusive obedience to the officers of the British Government.

If any officer of the Durbar—Jageerdar, Zemindar, or other person—shall refuse to render such obedience, if he shall withhold the payment of revenue, or shall otherwise dispute or defy the authority of the British Government, he shall be declared a rebel, his person shall be seized, and his jageers or lands shall be confiscated to the State.

To those who shall, immediately and quietly, submit themselves to the authority of the British Government, whether Amils or public officers, Jageerdars, Zemindars, or other inhabitants of Oude, full assurance is hereby given of protection, consideration, and favour.

The revenue of the districts shall be determined on a fair and settled basis.

The gradual improvement of the Oude territories shall be steadily pursued.

Justice shall be measured out with an equal hand.

Protection shall be given to life and property; and every man shall enjoy, henceforth, his just rights, without fear of molestation.

SOURCE: In J. J. MacLeod Innes, *Lucknow and Oude in the Mutiny* (London: A. D. Innes, 1895).

Sir Henry Lawrence's Essay of 1843, Forecasting the Events of 1857

[Sir Henry Montgomery Lawrence (1806–1857) was a Company soldier and administrator who was renowned for his consolidation of British rule in the Punjab (1839). Lawrence's military career was distinguished for his success in suppressing native mutinies, for which he was knighted in 1848. He would eventually become president of the Board of Administration in the Punjab region (1849). In 1857 Lawrence was assigned to Oudh; he was mortally wounded in Lucknow during the Indian Uprising/Sepoy Mutiny.]

Asia has ever been fruitful in revolutions, and can show many a dynasty overthrown by such small bands as, on November 2, 1841, rose against our force at Cabul; and British India can show how timely energy, as at Vellore, Benares, and Bareilly, has put down much more formidable insurrections.... Dissensions among our enemies has raised us from the position of commercial factors to be lords over emperors. Without courage and discipline we could not thus have prevailed; but even these would have availed little had the country been united against us, and would now only defer the day of our discomfiture were there anything like a unanimous revolt. The same causes operated for our first success in both India and Afghanistan, and the errors by which we lost the latter may any day deprive us of the former.

Perhaps our great danger arises from the facility with which these conquests have been made—a facility which in both cases has betrayed us into the neglect of all recognized rules for military occupation. Our sway is that of the sword, yet everywhere our military means are insufficient. There is always some essential lacking at the very moment when troops are wanted for immediate service. If stores are ready, they may rot before carriage is forthcoming. If there are muskets, there is no ammunition. If there are infantry there are no muskets for them. In one place we have guns without a man to serve them; in another we have artillerymen standing comparatively idle, because the guns have been left behind.

To come to examples. Is Delhi or Agra, Bareilly or Kurnaul, Benares or Saugor, or, in short, any one of our important military positions better prepared than Cabul was, should 300 men rise to-morrow and seize the town? Take Delhi more especially as a parallel case. At Cabul we had the treasury and one of the commissariat forts in the town; at Delhi we have the magazine and treasury within the walls.

Now suppose that any morning 300 men were to take possession of these. What would follow if the troops in the cantonment (never more than three regiments) were to keep close to their quarters, merely strengthening the palace guards? The palace at Delhi stands much as did the Bala Hissar with respect to the city, except that the former has not sufficient elevation to command the town, as the latter did. What then would be the result at Delhi, if the palace garrison were to content themselves, as Colonel Shelton did, with a faint and distant cannonade from within their walls; not even effectually supporting the king's bodyguards, who had already sallied into the town, nor even enabling or assisting them to bring off their field-guns when driven back from the city, but should suffer these guns to be abandoned at the very palace gates, and there to lie? Let not a single effort be made to succour or bring off the guards at the magazine or treasury; give up everything for lost; suffer unresistingly the communication between the town and cantonment (almost precisely the same distance in both cases) to be closed; let all this happen in Hindoostan on June 2, instead of among the Afghan mountains on November 2, and does any sane man doubt that twenty-four hours would swell the hundreds of rebels into thousands; and that, if such conduct on our part lasted for a week, every ploughshare in the Delhi States would be turned into a sword? And when a sufficient force had been mustered, by bringing European regiments from the hills and native troops from every quarter (which could not be effected within a month at the very least, or in three at the rate we moved to the succour of Candahar and Jellalabad), should we not then have a more difficult game to play than Clive had at Plassey, or Wellington at Assaye? We should then be literally striking for our existence, at the most inclement season of the year, with the prestige of our name vanished, and the fact before the eyes of imperial Delhi, that the British force, placed not only to protect but to overawe the city, were afraid to enter it.

But the parallel does not end here. Suppose the officer commanding at Meerut, when called on for help, were to reply, "My force is chiefly cavalry and horse artillery, not the sort to be effective within a walled town, where every house is a castle. Besides, Meerut itself, at all times unquiet, is even now in rebellion, and I cannot spare my troops." Suppose that from Agra and Umbaila an answer came that they required all the force they had to defend their own posts; and that the reply from Sobathoo and Kussowlee was, "We have not carriage, nor, if we had, could we sacrifice our men by moving them to the plains at this season." All this is less than actually did happen in Afghanistan, when General Sale was recalled, and General Nott was urgently called on for succour; and if all this should occur at Delhi, should we not have to strike anew for our Indian empire?

But who would attribute the calamity to the Civil Commissioners at Delhi? And could not that functionary fairly say to the officer commanding, "I knew very well that there were not only 300 desperate characters in the city, but as many thousands—men having nothing to lose, and everything to gain, by an insurrection. You have let them plunder the magazine and the treasury. They will, doubtless, expect as little resistance elsewhere. A single battalion could have exterminated them the first day, but you let the occasion slip, and the country is now in a blaze, and the game completely out of my hands. I will now give you all the help I can, all the advice you ask, but the Riot Act has been read, and my authority has ceased." Would the civil officer be blamed for thus acting? Could he be held responsible for the way in which the outbreak had been met?

I have endeavoured to put the case fairly. Delhi is nearly as turbulent and unquiet a city as Cabul. It has residing within its walls a king less true to us than was Shah Shoojah. The hot weather of India is more trying to us than the winter of Afghanistan. The ground between the two and cantonment of Delhi, being a long rocky ridge on one side of the road, and the river Jumna on the other, is much more difficult for the action of troops against an insurgent population than anything at Cabul. At Delhi the houses are fully as strong, the streets not less defensible. In short, here as there, we occupy dangerous ground. *Here,* if we act with prudence and intrepidity, we shall, under God's blessing, be safe, as we should have been, with similar conduct, *there.*

But if, under the misfortune that has befallen our arms, we content ourselves with blaming the envoy, or even the military authorities, instead of looking fairly and closely into the foundations of our power, and minutely examining the system that could admit of such conduct as was exhibited in Afghanistan, not in one case, but in many; then, I say, we are in the fair way of reaping another harvest more terrible than that of Cabul.

The foregoing parallel has been drawn out minutely, perhaps tediously, for I consider it important to show that what was faulty and dangerous in one quarter is not less so in another.

I wish, moreover, to point out that the mode of operation so pertinaciously styled "the Afghan system," and currently linked with the name of the late envoy, as if, with all its errors, it had originated with *him,* is essentially *our Indian system;* that it existed with all its defects when Sir William Macnaghten was in his cradle, and flourishes in our own provinces now that he is in his grave. Among its errors are—moving with small parties on distant points without support; inefficient commissariat arrangements; absolute ignorance on all topographical points; and reckoning on the attachment of our allies (as if Hindoo or Mahomedan could love his Christian lord, who only comes before him as master or tax-gatherer; as if it were not absurd to suppose that the chiefs of Burmah, Nepaul, Lahore, and the like could tolerate the power that restrains their rapacious desires and habits, that degrades them in their own and each other's eyes).

Men may differ as to the soundness of our policy, but no one can question its results, as shown in the fact of Hyder Ali twice dictating terms at the gates of Fort St. George (Madras); in the disasters that attended the early period of the Nepaul war; in the long state of siege in which Sir Archibald Campbell was held at Rangoon; in the frightful mortality at Arracan; in the surrender of General Matthews; in the annihilation of Colonel Baillie's detachment; in the destruction of Colonel Monson's force; and in the attacks on the Residencies of Poonah and Nagpoor. These are all matters of history, though seldom practically remembered. Still less is it borne in mind how little was wanting to starve General Harris at Seringapatam, General Campbell in Ava, or Sir John Keane in Afghanistan. All these events have been duly recorded, though they have not withheld us, on each occasion, from retracing our old errors. At length a calamity that we had often courted has fallen upon us; but direful as it is, and wrecked though it has the happiness of numbers, we may yet gather fruit from the thorns, if we learn therefrom how easily an army is paralyzed and panic-stricken, and how fatal such prostration must ever be. If we read the lesson set before us, the wreck of a small army may be the beacon to save large ones.

Our chief danger in India is from within, not from without. The enemy who cannot reach us with his bayonets, can touch us more fatally if he lead us to distrust ourselves, and rouse our subjects to distrust us; and we shall do his work for him if we show that our former chivalrous bearing is fled, that we pause to count the half-armed rabble opposed to us, and hesitate to act with battalions where a few years before companies would have been deemed sufficient.

The true basis of British power in India is often lost sight of, namely, a well-paid, well-disciplined army, relying, from experience, on the good faith, wisdom, and energy of its leaders.

We forget that our army is composed of men like ourselves, quick-sighted and inquisitive on all matters bearing upon their personal interests; who, if they can appreciate our points of superiority, are just as capable of detecting our deficiencies, especially any want of military spirit or soldierly bearing.

At Cabul we lost an army, and we lost some character with the surrounding States. But I hold that by far our worst loss was in the confidence of our native soldiery. Better had it been for our fame if our harassed troops had rushed on the enemy and perished to a man, than that surviving Sepoys should be able to tell the tales they can of what they saw at Cabul.

SOURCE: In J. J. MacLeod Innes, *Lucknow and Oude in the Mutiny* (London: A. D. Innes, 1895).

Letters of Rani Lakshmi Bai

[Rani Lakshmi Bai (1835–1858), also known as the Rani of Jhansi, became the ruler of Jhansi state after her husband, the Raja's death in 1853. After numerous unsuccessful legal and diplomatic appeals to Company administrators and British politicians and statesmen, the Rani militarily rebelled against the annexation of her kingdom. Her beauty and military daring, along with her adoption of male attire on the battlefield, captured the imaginations of the Indians and British. The Rani fought alongside Rao Sahib and Tatya Tope. She was mortally wounded at the battle of Gwalior in June of 1858.]

LETTER I

Translation of a Kureeta [Persian letter] from Her Highness the Lakshme Bai the widow of Gungadhur Rao the late Maharajah of Jhansi to the address of the Marquis of Dalhosie the Most Noble the Governor General of India, 3rd December 1853.

After Compliments—

The services rendered by Sheo Rao Bhao, the father of my late husband, to the British government before its authority in this part of the Country was established are recorded with other State Documents and have been amply rewarded by the unceasing flow of benefits which his family have derived from the acknowledged favour and protection of such a mighty power.

The concluding article of the Treaty with my late husband signed by Colonel Sleeman in 1842 guarantees to the Jhansi Government the continued existence of all the benefits claimable by virtue of a former treaty made with Ramchand Row in 1817 not specifically cancelled by the terms of the new agreement then made.

This treaty was declaredly made in consideration of the very respectable character borne by the late Subhadar Sheo Rao Bhow and his uniform and faithful attachment to the British Government and in deference to his wish expressed before his death that the principality of Jhansi might be confirmed in perpetuity to his grandson Ramchand Rao.

As the means of effecting this and with the view to confirming the fidelity and attachment to the Government of Jhansi the second article acknowledges and constitutes Rao Ramchand his heirs and successors hereditary rulers of the territory enjoyed by the late Sheo Rao Bhow thereby meaning that any party who he adopted as his son to perform the funeral rites over his body, necessary to ensure beatitude in a future world, would be acknowledged by the British Government as his successor and one through whom the name and interests of the family might be preserved.

The Hindu Shastras inculcate the doctrine that the libation offered to the manes of a deceased parent are as efficacious when performed by an adopted as by a real son and the custom of adoption is accordingly found prevalent in every part of Hindostan. My husband therefore, upon the morning of the 19th November last, sent for Dewan Nara Sing, Rao Appa, Lalla Lahori Mull, and Lalla Futteh Chund the Ministers and myself and told us to consult with the Shastra and elect a duly qualified child from his own 'Gote' clan to succeed him as ruler of Jhansi, as he found himself getting worse and the medicines doing him no good.

Ramchand Baba was in consequence summoned, when at his recommendation out of several children of the Gote it was agreed that Anund Rao, a boy of five years of age the son of Bashdeva, was the best qualified for the purpose. My husband then ordered the Shastri to perform the rites of adoption. The next morning Benaik Rao Pandit performed the Saukalpa when Bashdeva the father of Anund Rao having poured water on my husband's hands with the usual ceremonies the boy was named Damodhur Rao Gungadhur when the ceremony was completed.

The Ministers by order of the Raja wrote to Major Ellis who was encamped at Sayer, 6 Cos from Jhansi, and to Major Martin, the officer Commanding the Station, requesting their attendance at the Palace with the view of bearing witness to what had been done. These two Gentlemen came to the Palace at 10 A.M. the next morning, the 20th November, when my husband delivered a letter to Major Ellis requesting him to obtain the sanction of Government to the adoption which was read over in their presence, when Major Ellis promised that he would make known his wishes to your Lordship.

The next day, Monday the 21st November, my husband expired; the different funeral rites required to be performed by a son have all been discharged by Anund Rao styled Damodhur Rao Gungadhur.

My late husband before his death made the boy over to the protection and favour of the British government—and as the adoption made by Parakshata (the late Rajah of Datia), that of Bala Rao (the last Chief of Jaloun) and that of Tej Singh (the last Raja of Urcha) have all been sanctioned by your Lordship—the more strongly as the term 'dawana' (perpetuity) made use of in the Treaty of the Jhansi State is not mentioned in theirs.

LETTER 2

Translation of a Khureeta from Her Highness the Lackmee Bau the widow of Gunghadhur Rao late Maharajah of Jhansi to the address of the Marquis of Dalhousie the Most Honourable the Governor General of India, dated Jhansi, 16th February 1854.

After Compliments

Distress at recent affliction when I addressed your Lordship upon the 3rd December last had prevented by entering as fully as I ought to have done into the circumstances of the adoption made by my late husband, an omission which I now beg leave to supply.

It was the good fortune of Sheo Rao Bhao, the father of my late husband, to be the first of the chiefs in this part of the country who tendered their allegiance to the British Government, which he improved by subsequent exertions in inducing them to follow his example; at which Lord Lake was so pleased that he directed him to submit a paper of requests as to the manner in which the interests of himself and family could be best served. In obedience to these orders a paper, Wajib ul urz ['record of rights'], containing seven different articles, was submitted, thro' Captain John Baillie, the Political Agent for Bundlecund, which were all sanctioned by order of the Most Noble the Governor General of India. Sheo Rao Bhao having omitted to define certain requests in the Wajib ul urz, which he was anxious to make, and having in the mean time had an opportunity of rendering further services, His Lordship entered into a new agreement, for the purpose of rectifying this omission, and thereby becoming an ad-ditional pledge of fidelity and attachment on his part to the Government. The new agreement consisted of nine articles, in which the benefits of two new articles were added to those already derivable from the seven articles of the Wajib ul urz, and having been duly signed and sealed by the Governor General, was delivered to him by Captain John Baillie, at Kotra.

In the 6th article of the Wajib ul urz, Sheo Rao Bhao reports that the Rajas of Urcha, Duttia, Chanderi, and other neighbouring States, are ready to tender their allegiance to the British Government, provided the different places then in their possession was [sic] confirmed to them, and prepared to pay their accustomed tribute to the British Government. Upon which an order was passed, to the effect that any chief who imitated his example in showing obedience and attachment to the British cause should be confirmed in possession of all the advantages then belonging to them; moreover, that other marks of friendship might be expected from service in such a cause.

It was from the same desire to reward past services like these that the British Government entered into a treaty, in 1817, with Rao Ram Chundra Rao, the grandson of Sheo Rao Bhao, the second article of which acknowledges Rao Ram Chundra, his heirs and successors, as hereditary rulers in perpetuity of the Jhansi principality, and guaranteed its protection to them from foreign aggression.

During the Burmese war in 1824, Rao Ram Chundra Rao advanced upwards of 70,000 rupees to banjarahs [suppliers] employed in carrying grain to the troops in Burmah. Mr. Ainslie reported his having done so in favourable terms to the Governor General, who ordered the money to be repaid; but Rao Ram Chundra Rao having declined repayment on the grounds that he was an ally of the British Government, and that the interests of the two States were identical, the Governor General was pleased to send him a dress of honour, with a complimentary Khareeta, thanking him for his services upon the occasion. I regret to say that this Khareeta has been mislaid, and would esteem it a favour if your Lordship would kindly order my being furnished with a copy of it.

Shortly afterwards, during the siege of Bharutapoor, the city Kalpi, in the British Territory, being threatened with an attack from Nannay Pandit, at the time in the rebellion against Jaloun, Mr. Ainslie, the agent, called upon Bhikraji Nana, Kamdar of Jhansi during the minority, to dispatch troops with the utmost expedition to Kalpi, with a view to protect the Kooneh district from plunder; in consequence of which, Bhikraji Nana made immediate arrangements for sending off 2 guns, 4,000 sowars, [cavalry] and 1,000 foot soldiers, to Kalpi, and which arrived in time to save Kalpi from being plundered, and proved the means of restoring general confidence to the people in the Kooneh district. Copies of letters from Mr. Ainslie to Ram Chundra Rao, the minor Rajah, and Bhakaji, his kamdar, thanking them for their services on this emergent occasion, are submitted with the view of showing that Jhansi state was always foremost in the field when opportunity occurred for displaying its loyalty to the Paramount Power.

When Lord William Bentinck was at Jhansi in 1832, he visited Rao Ram Chunder Rao in the fort on the evening of the 19th December, and conferred upon him the title Maharaj Dhiraj Fidwi Badshah Janujah Englistan [King of Kings, Faithful to the Emperor of England], Maharajah Ram Chunder Rao Bahadur, ordering him to have it engraved on his seal, investing him at the same time with the insignia of the Nakara and Chonar, with permission to adopt the British flag, telling him, in open durbar, that of all the chiefs of Budelkund, his uncle, Sheo Rao Bhao, had done the best service, and that the honours now conferred were the reward of his meritorious services to the British Government. On arrival at Saugur, his Lordship was further pleased to send him a complimentary letter in English, having a gold-leaf border, dated 20th December 1832, copy of which is forwarded, repeating what he had stated in Durbar, and adding, that the letter then issued would serve ever afterwards as a patent of his rank and authority.

Raghonath Rao, who succeeded his nephew, Ram Chundra Rao, in 1835, died in 1838, when the right of my husband to the succession was acknowledged; but owing to the State being in debt at the time, it was placed under the superintendence of Captain D. Ross for a period of three years, at the expiration of which it was restored to him, with an agreement on his part by which he ceded Duboh, Talgong, and other districts, valued at 2,55,891 Jhansi rupees, as payment towards a legion to be employed for the purpose of coercing any of his turbulent feudatories who might set his authority at defiance; and one on Colonel Sleeman's part, dated 1st January 1843, confirming to the Jhansi State all of the advantages guaranteed to it by virtue of former treaties.

It cannot be denied that the terms Warisan [wārisan], 'heirs', and Janishnian [jānishin], 'successors', made use of in the second article of the treaty with Ram Chundra Rao, refer to different parties; the term Warisan being confined in meaning to natural or collateral heirs, while Janishnian, on the contrary, refers to the party adopted as heir and successor to the estate, in the event of their being no natural or collateral heir entitled to the succession. Treaties are studied with the utmost care before ratification; and it is not to be supposed that the term Janishnian used in contradistinction to Warisan was introduced in an important document of this kind, of the authority almost of a revelation from Heaven, without a precise understanding of its meaning, the advantages of which are further explained by the clause declaring the gift then made to have been one in perpetuity to the family. It was with this understanding of the terms of the treaty that my husband, the day before his death, summoned Major Ellis and Captain Martin, the officer commanding the station, to the palace, and with his dying breath, in full Durbar, made over Anand Rao, his adopted son, to the care and protection of the British Government, delivering at the same time a kharita, or testament, further declaratory of his wishes on this solemn occasion for communication to your Lordship.

I take the liberty of enclosing a list of some of the precedents which have occurred in Bundlecund in which the right of the native chief or his widow to adopt a successor to the guddi [throne], in default of natural heirs, has been sanctioned; and as it is the firm reliance which they feel in the integrity and justice of the British Government which enables them to pass their days in peace and quietness, without other care than how to prove their loyalty, venture to express a hope that the widow of the son of Sheo Rao Bhao will not be considered undeserving of that favour and compassion which others similarly situated have been declared entitled to. [Attached are the four enclosures referred to in the letter.]

LETTER 3

Letter (supposed to be from the Widow of the Raja of Jhansi to the Governor General), received 22nd April, 1854. [Following compliments, the Rānī requests a delay in the annexation then goes on to say:]

I would make known unto your Lordship that Jhansi is a powerless Native state; that, depending on the protection of the British Government, my late husband devoted his attention to the art of Peace, and not to keeping up even the semblance of a warlike state; and that if Jhansie is to be absorbed during your Lordship's administration, the five thousand rusty swords worn by the people called its Army and its fifty pieces of harmless ordnance (harmless except against a power of equal insignificance) will be delivered over to your Lordship's Agent without any demonstration save that of sorrow—that valuable services should be requited by the confiscation of a puny Kingdom or Raj; which has been ever faithful to the paramount power.

SOURCE: These letters can be found in *The Politics of the British Annexation of India*, ed. Michael Fisher (Delhi: Oxford University Press, 1993). For a book-length study on the Rani of Jhansi, see Joyce Lebra-Chapman, *The Rani of Jhansi: A Study in Female Heroism* (Honolulu: University of Hawaii Press, 1986).

Preface and Excerpt from *The Queen's Desire: A Romance of the Indian Mutiny*
HUME NISBET

PREFACE

To Sir William Wilson Hunter, K.C.S.I.,
C.I.E., M.A. (Oxford), LL.D. (Cambridge).
Dear Sir,

When I first thought about tackling this vast subject, The Indian Mutiny, I turned naturally to the writer whom I had a slight acquaintance with in the past for information, and he responded with promptitude, through that love of the native races which he has ever shewn in his erudite works, by advising me and sending me what he knew would be best for my purpose.

That I have obeyed my own pig-headed instincts throughout this present romance, for romance it is in the most literal sense, must not be wondered at, as I am a dogmatic Scot, who reads the Scriptures according to his 'ain lichts, and will not budge a point for either minister or gravedigger.

Still for all that, I fear many Anglo-Indians will not quite accept my version of this most awful tragedy; some will do so I think, at least I can but hope so, and those who have lived with the Brahmins and Buddhists for the biggest portion of their lives and know what the *real* professors are, I fondly trust will give me credit for my patient investigation and thought.

I fear also that I may offend some with my characters, yet I hope not, for you must always remember, in every class of society, that where two or three are gathered together, there the devil may be also, as well as the spirits of good.

THE QUEEN'S DESIRE

A Romance of the Indian Mutiny

BY

HUME NISBET,

AUTHOR OF
"BAIL UP," "THE SAVAGE QUEEN,"
"THE BUSHRANGER'S SWEETHEART," &C., &C.

LONDON:
F. V. WHITE & CO.,
31, SOUTHAMPTON STREET, STRAND, W.C.
1893

I have had much reading and hard labour, as well as many an anxious hour over this present book, which was not written in a hurry, therefore, I may say, if a hard birth be the sign of a great one, then this child of my fancy ought to grow into a big chap, for I have had great travail with him.

I have gone into many books for my facts, yours Sir William, which I need not enumerate, as they are so widely known, but others I must mention, such as Col. C. B. Mallison's C.S.I., work the "Indian Mutiny," Col. M. Taylor's "Confessions of a Thug," "Pandurang Hugi," and so many more that it would take up too many pages to mention all the authorities which I have gobbled up in order to arrive at the true character of the Indian Natives, Hindoo Buddhist, and Moslem.

Perhaps I have idealized my Hindoo priest; I will confess that I have been swindled in my Eastern travels by the Hindoos, but never by the Buddhists, but then they were not very high-caste Hindoos with whom I had dealings, merchants somewhat after the type of the merchants of Petticoat Lane, therefore, I could not take them as a representative type. I only looked to the great principle of their religion, while I regard our high-caste Christian professors as practising the principles of our Faith, leaving outside of the question those hypocrites and vile traders in religion—the "Stiggins" class.

If I have gone astray, pray forgive me, you who know better. I have tried my hardest to present Indian and Anglo-Indian life of 1857–58 to you in a picturesque and vivid manner, and I can only hope that with all its technical blemishes I may enlist your sympathies with my faulty characters, and that you may say, when you have cast my story aside, that I have entertained you somewhat, even if I fail as a teacher.

With respectful regards, I am yours,
very truly, The Author.
Hogarth Club, 34, Dover Street, Piccadilly, W.
April, 1893.

CHAPTER IV. THE RANEE'S FATE

Six long months of arduous marching, counter-marching, and hard fighting had dragged away since the women and children had parted with their husbands and fathers at Allahabad, and still the rebels have not been overcome.

They are everywhere beaten and driven from stronghold to stronghold, but, like the mythical Hydra, no sooner is one head cut off than another seems to take its place.

Barney McKay, Captains Green and Jackson, with Sammy Tompkins and his hound, Hector, have been retained by General Sir Hugh Rose, while

"The Ranee's Death." In Hume Nisbet, *The Queen's Desire: A Romance of the Indian Mutiny* (London: F. V. White, 1893).

Drill-Instructor Tompkins, with his friends King and Wilson, are with Sir Colin Campbell in Oudh, as is also Major Mortimer.

The natives are disputing every foot of the way, for they have no hope of pardon; when caught they are at once examined and if found guilty, hung or blown in indiscriminate batches from the cannon's mouths; doubtless many innocent ones and friends of the Government share in the fate of the guilty, but these are the chances and horrors of war; the court-martials have no time for legal quirks. In many cases it is Jeddart justice, "hang first and try afterwards."

The English are victorious everywhere, but their labour is intense and unrelaxing, and now that summer is once more upon them with its awful heat and worse rains, even the man fondest of a brush with the enemy, and that is Barney McKay, wishes it was over so that he might have time to finish a decent cigar.

"Boys, I don't mind marching, and sweating, and fighting straight on from sunrise to sunset, year in, year out, if you like, so that I have time to get a wash and a smoke afterwards, but to be at it day and night like this—well, there, I don't mind confessing just this once that it's becoming monotonous, besides being mighty wearing on the swords, to say nothing about the wrists."

Major Barney McKay didn't really mind the hardships and constant work, although to please his companions he pretended to be so sick and tired of it, as he saw they were, for he was the most accommodating of chums so long as no one attempted to impose on his good nature; but in reality if he had not had the distraction of battle and fatigue-tramps, he would have worried out his life arranging the rooms, pictures, and hangings of his friends, for idleness and Major McKay were sworn foes.

There had been a vast amount of slaughter during these past six months, days and nights of battle and pursuit, when the swords of the officers and the bayonets of the rank and file grew blunt and twisted with the cutting and prodding at humanity, when they rode over men's bodies by hundreds, and made the land reek so much with blood that the eagles, vultures and kites grew as bloated and lazy as old maids' cockatoos. The eagles and vultures of Upper India during the past twelve months had become sad epicures, while the jackals went about as sleek and rounded in the paunches as pet poodles.

The Maulavi of Fyzabad, that impetuous and bloody-handed fanatic, was at rest with so many of his countrymen. He had made much trouble, and kept the pot of rebellion boiling for a long time, but at last he had met his doom by the pistol at the hand of his own countryman; but Nana Sahib, with his brother and nephew, were still at large. Tantia Topí, with the Begum of Oudh and the Ranee of Jhansi, defied them still, although most of the other leaders had paid the penalty of their rash folly and cruelty.

To-night, the 17th of June, 1858, they are besieging the rock-built citadel of Gwalior, where Tantia Topí and the Ranee of Jhansi have taken shelter, after the downfall of Jhansi and Morar, within these walls, with the remnant of their former large following, and are in a desperate position.

All day long the British have been battering at this massive fortress, and to-night, with the full moon lighting up their operations, they are at it still. It is at this point of the siege that Major McKay, pausing to light a cheroot, had just taken his first puff, when a bullet from the walls dashed it from his lips; hence the plaintive grumble which he indulged in to his companions, Captains Green and Jackson, who were on the General's staff like himself; Sammy Tompkins, now a full-blown bugler, being, with his dog, beside the chief some few yards away.

Above them swung that great eastern moon in its full lustre, making the landscape almost as distinct as an English daylight scene, only more weird and thrilling in its silver and warm intensity.

The June heat, which had been terrific all day, had toned down somewhat, yet not much, for the earth felt like a baker's oven after the fire had just been taken out, or the floor of the hot room of a Turkish bath, so that even at this hour of midnight to think about sleep was an impossibility, and even to walk barefoot uncomfortable.

A cloudless ocean of sea-green atmosphere spread around that silver circle, that seemed in its dazzling whiteness to float very close to the world; while the planets and stars gathered in brightness as they receded from that greater light, until they flamed out like beacons studding a measureless plain.

It was the sort of night to make young men melancholy; the sort of night to lie rocking within a hammock under the shady branches of a tamarind tree, and think upon far-off England and those who were waiting to welcome them back, and while dreaming of these pleasures enjoy the fragrant and soothing cigar; the sort of night when poetic minds would expect to see the whole court of the elf-king shaking the heavy dew-drops from their gossamer wings, as they flirted, and enjoyed their merry and soulless dancing.

In fact, it was the sort of night suitable to any other sort of game instead of the grim one to which it was at present devoted by those wearied men who had marched over a thousand miles, captured more than a hundred guns, forced their way through artfully-defended mountain passes and intricate jungles, waded and swam over rivers swarming with alligators, and dangerous quicksands, taken strongly-fortified forts, and conquered the enemy wherever they met him, no matter the odds, during the past six months.

As their gallant and wonderfully patient, but now almost broken-down, old general told them, when he thought he was at liberty to disband them, a fortnight before this night:

"Soldiers! I thank you with all my sincerity for your bravery, your devotion, and your discipline. When you first marched I told you that you, as British soldiers, had more than enough of courage for the work which was before you; but that courage without discipline was of no avail, and I exhorted you to let discipline be your watchword. You have attended to my orders. In hardships, in temptations, and in dangers, you have obeyed your general, and have never left the ranks. You have fought against the strong, and you have protected the rights of the weak and defenceless—of foes as well as friends. I have seen you in the ardour of the combat preserve and place children out of harm's way. This is the discipline of Christian soldiers, and this it is that has brought you triumphant from the shores of Western India to the waters of the Jumna, and establishes without doubt that you will find no place to equal the glory of your arms."

This noble farewell address had been delivered a fortnight before, and still the wearied arms of the men had to ply their muskets and rammers, still were at the deadly, hard labour that knows no time for rest; while their leader, Sir Hugh Rose, stood at his post, although hardly able to hold the field-glass to his eyes, watching over them and directing them to further victories.

The great rock upon which the fortress was built rose up before them like the rock of Edinburgh Castle, solid, massive, and impregnable to cannon-balls or shell; each detail and cliff fissure showed out distinctly with the broad-staired pathway leading from the mighty gate, portcullis, and drawbridge, to the plain, dotted in parts with trees, buildings, and mosques. It seemed hopeless to bombard such a place, for the balls only flattened themselves against the granite without doing more damage than a few splinters of dust.

There were about six thousand fugitives inside this fortress, along with Tantia Topí and the Ranee of Jhansi, who had been driven from her own town with heavy losses to here, and as this was their last stand they were defending it desperately. From the walls the guns flamed down on the plain, as the batteries there were doing their utmost to reply; yet, so far, the rebels had the advantage, for they were behind shelter, while the British force lay open at their feet.

Through that serene midnight sky the shells flew, shrieking or exploding like fireworks on all sides, while the roar of cannon made the night, which might have been so romantic, hideous with the hellish din.

"Be Jabbers!" shouted Barney McKay, relapsing into his mother tongue in his excitement, "I have a plan to take that town, for the guns will never do it."

He rushed off red-hot with his scheme to the general, who, after listening patiently, at once gave his permission with the men required, remarking that the plan was extraordinary and daring enough to deserve success.

Sammy Tompkins went with the surprise party, as he could climb like a monkey, while Jackson and Green were deputed with their regiment to guard the main roadway, and while the guns continued to play on heavier than ever to cover McKay's approach, the army drew up in line and prepared for action.

Three hours passed away after this without any signs coming from the bold Barney, and already the grey dawn was beginning to creep along the eastern horizon, when suddenly the great gates were thrown open, the portcullis raised and the drawbridge lowered, and with a rush the besieged poured down the steep road, the cavalry first, and the infantry after them. Barney had succeeded in his plan of alarming the garrison and driving them out.

Then the fiercest battle they had yet experienced took place on that plain under this moonlit and greyling sky; those who still had hopes or meant to keep life as long as possible, such as Tantia Topí, rushed at the weakest portion of the environment, and breaking through it, fled as fast as their horses' legs could carry them, with the troopers after them in hot haste. About five hundred escaped in this fashion, for Sir Hugh Rose had to recall the pursuers to help him with those who, tired of the struggle, were making a final bid for paradise by killing as many as they could before they died themselves.

Those natives who now occupied the field were fighting with a savage disregard for their own lives, fighting as long as they could stand, and even when cut down, in many cases they slashed at the horses' legs as they galloped over them, and managed to do much damage before they gave up the ghost—in fact, before many moments had gone by the field was covered with corpses, and only a remnant of about two hundred left out of the crowd which had fled from the castle.

It was what they hoped would be the final engagement of this campaign, and the British put all their force and energy to get it over quickly, as there could be no question of surrender. Up on that lofty rock, the houses which the McKay party had lit were blazing and spreading into a general conflagration, which soon, in its lurid vividness, blanked out the lustre of the moon, and while they fought, honouring the foes that so bravely fell, the daylight was creeping up every instant stronger and stronger.

Captain Jackson was in the thick of it as usual, distinguishing himself with his sword and agile strength of wrist as well as the managing of his horse. He was working his way through a body-guard of devoted warriors who had surrounded their chief on a small mound, and who was noticeable not only for his fierce activity, but for his splendidly caparisoned white horse.

As Jackson mowed his way towards this warrior, who was armed cap-à-pie with his chain visor over his face and a tiara of blazing jewels on his helmet, a rich prize thought this practical young man as, even in his heat, he took notice of the golden ornaments and gems, and resolved that they should become his property by right of conquest.

As Jackson drew near, the chief evidently divined his purpose, and, signalling with his tulwar for his adherents to stand aside and see to themselves, in another moment the white horse and the black horse which carried Jackson met, while sabre and tulwar joined with a clash.

Jackson was a splendid swordsman, yet for a few seconds he had all his work cut out for him guarding that fierce and scientific onslaught.

Like a lurid flame it played about him, now gleaming pale with the moon's reflection, now scarlet as it caught on its polished surface the firelight from the burning stronghold, while the horses bit savagely at each other, and tore at the dry ground with their iron-shod hoofs.

Then all at once that halo of fierce light was dimmed, for the English captain had seen his advantage, and passed the blade of his sword through chain armour and body, and the native antagonist dropped his sword-arm and head.

A wild shriek burst from the visor as Jackson withdrew his sword from the breast before him, a shrill shriek like a woman's, which made his blood run cold in his veins, as he hastily caught the falling figure and drew it to his own horse's neck, while the riderless white horse stood snorting and shivering for a moment, and then galloped wildly across the bloody corpse-covered field; for while Jackson had been fighting this duel, his comrades had demolished the enemy, so that the night's work was over, and they were all resting now and wiping the stains from their blades.

"Agi Jau," panted that choking voice, so near to his own mouth, "you can uncover me now, for I have got all my desire. Your sword has tasted my heart."

A mighty trembling fell upon George Jackson as he slid from his saddle with his load, and, laying it gently on the ground, removed the helmet and visor, to see what he expected to see—his wife for a month; then, for the first time in all his many butcherings, he felt like a murderer, and grew weak with the horror of the situation.

The lovely dark eyes opened as he uncovered that beautiful face, and the lips that had once so passionately kissed him smiled again tenderly, as she said faintly:

"You are a sure messenger of King Death, Agi Jau, and I am happy, since what I have prayed for has come to pass—your hand the deliverer."

"Who are you? Ah, my poor lass!"

"Your wife, George—your first wife, my lord and master. She who was the Ranee of Jhansi, and gave you her heart to split."

"Oh, my God!"

"Never grieve about that matter, Agi Jau; all good husbands give this last favour to those they love best. And it is well that my heart's blood should flow over you at this time, for it was my best gift, although I have another for you which may please you better. Hold me up, for this blood is choking me."

Without a word he drew up her dying face until it rested on his perjured breast, too much conscience-stricken to utter a word.

The sun was now rising, and the woman once more opened her languid eyes.

"That is better—that is where I want to stay until my soul can enter yours. You know the secret of the treasure-chamber of Jhansi, where I had you—for a time to myself. The vaults lie under the mosque, and Patla is there to show you how to reach them—they are yours as the last gift from—your—first—wife. Farewell, my love—my—"

That passionate, erring, but human heart had pumped out its last drop, and George Jackson, the heir to the Rajah's fortune, held in his arms the inanimate remains of what once had been a queen.

SOURCE: In *The Queen's Desire: A Romance of the Indian Mutiny* (London: F. V. White and Co., 1893).

The King of Oude's Manifesto from the *Delhi Gazette*, 29 September 1857

The question of cause and effect, as it regarded the fact of the Indian mutiny of 1857, was but partially solved, when the curtain fell upon the closing scenes of the great drama which, for more than two years, had absorbed the attention of the civilised world. Throughout the vast provinces of Bengal, the influence of religious fanaticism—the yearnings of disappointed ambition—the impatience of a foreign rule, which coerced, while it did not protect, the people from the tyranny and oppression of its servants; and the reliance of the native races upon the prophetic auguries of their soothsayers and moulvies—had doubtless much to do with the garnering of that vast harvest of discontent, which an alleged intention of the government to interfere with the inviolability of *caste*, at length scattered broadcast over the country. The following statement of grievances, published in the *Delhi Gazette*, as a manifesto issued by the king at an early period of the rebellion, explains very fully to the people the sense entertained by their native princes of the wrongs under which they suffered, and in some degree sheds light upon the causes of the revolt:—

"It is well known to all, that in this age the people of Hindostan, both Hindoos and Mohammedans, are being ruined under the tyranny and oppression of the infidel and treacherous English. It is therefore the bounden duty of all the wealthy people of India, especially of those who have any sort of connexion with any of the Mohammedan royal families, and are considered the pastors and masters of their people, to stake their lives and property for the well-being of the public. With the view of effecting this general good, several princes belonging to the royal family of Delhi, have dispersed themselves in the different parts of India, Iran, Turan, and Affghanistan, and have been long since taking measures to compass their favourite end; and it is to accomplish this charitable object that one of the aforesaid princes has, at the head of an army of Affghanistan, &c., made his appearance in India; and I, who am the grandson of Abul Muzuffer Sarajuddin Bahadur Shah Ghazee, king of India, having in the course of circuit come here to extirpate the infidels residing in the eastern part of the country, and to liberate and protect the poor helpless people now groaning under their iron rule, have, by the aid of the Majahdeens, or religious fanatics, erected the standard of Mohammed, and persuaded the orthodox Hindoos who had been subject to my ancestors, and have been and are still accessories in the destruction of the English, to raise the standard of Mahavir.

"Several of the Hindoo and Mussulman chiefs, who have long since quitted their homes for the preservation of their religion, and have been trying their best to root out the English in India, have presented themselves to me, and taken part in the reigning Indian crusade, and it is more than probable that I shall very shortly receive succours from the west. Therefore, for the information of the public, the present Ishtahar, consisting of several sections, is put in circulation, and it is the imperative duty of all to take it into their careful consideration, and abide by it. Parties anxious to participate in the common cause, but having no means to provide for themselves, shall receive their daily subsistence from me; and be it known to all, that the ancient works, both of the Hindoos and the Mohammedans, the writings of the miracle-workers, and the calculations of the astrologers, pundits, and rammals, all agree in asserting that the English will no longer have any footing in India or elsewhere. Therefore it is incumbent on all to give up the hope of the continuation of the British sway, side with me, and deserve the consideration of the Badshahi, or imperial government, by their individual exertion in promoting the common good, and thus attain their respective ends; otherwise if this golden opportunity slips away, they will have to repent of their folly, as is very aptly said by a poet in two fine couplets, the drift whereof is—'Never let a favourable opportunity slip, for in the field of opportunity you are to meet with the ball of fortune; but if you do not avail yourself of the opportunity that offers itself, you will have to bite your finger through grief.'

"No person, at the misrepresentation of the well-wishers of the British government, ought to conclude from the present slight inconveniences usually attendant on revolutions, that similar inconveniences and troubles should continue when the Badshahi government is established on a firm basis; and parties badly dealt with by any sepoy or plunderer, should come up and represent their grievances to me, and receive redress at my hands; and for whatever property they may lose in the reigning disorder, they will be recompensed from the public treasury when the Badshahi government is well fixed.

"Section I.—Regarding Zemindars.—It is evident that the British government, in making zemindary settlements, have imposed exorbitant jummas, and have disgraced and ruined several zemindars, by putting up their estates to public auction for arrears of rent, insomuch, that on the institution of a suit by a common ryot, a maidservant, or a slave, the respectable zemindars are summoned into court, arrested, put in gaol, and disgraced. In litigations regarding zemindaries, the immense value of stamps, and other unnecessary expenses of the civil courts, which are pregnant with all sorts of crooked dealings, and the practice of allowing a case to hang on for years, are all calculated to impoverish the litigants. Besides this, the coffers of the zemindars are annually taxed with subscriptions for schools, hospitals, roads, &c. Such extortions will have no manner of existence in the Badshahi government; but, on the contrary, the jummas will be light, the dignity and honour of the zemindars safe, and every zemindar will have absolute rule in his own zemindary. The zemindary disputes will be summarily decided according to the Shurrah and the Shasters, without any expense; and zemindars who will assist in the present war with their men and money, shall be excused for ever from paying half the revenue. Zemindars aiding only with money, shall be exempted in perpetuity from paying one-fourth of the revenue; and should any zemindar who has been unjustly deprived of his lands during the English government, personally join the war, he will be restored to his zemindary, and excused from paying one-fourth of the revenue.

"Section II.—Regarding Merchants.—It is plain that the infidel and treacherous British government have monopolised the trade of all the fine and valuable merchandise, such as indigo, cloth, and other articles of shipping, leaving only the trade of trifles to the people, and even in this they are not without their share of the profits, which they secure by means of customs and stamp fees, &c., in money suits, so that the people have merely a trade in name. Besides this, the profits of the traders are taxed with postages, tolls, and subscriptions for schools, &c. Notwithstanding all these concessions, the merchants are liable to imprisonment and disgrace at the instance or complaint of a worthless man. When the Badshahi government is established, all these aforesaid fraudulent practices shall be dispensed with, and the trade of every article, without exception, both by land and water, shall be open to the native merchants of India, who will have the benefit of the government steam-vessels and steam carriages for the conveyance of their merchandise gratis; and merchants having no capital of their own shall be assisted from the public treasury. It is therefore the duty of every merchant to take part in the war, and aid the Badshahi government with his men and money, either secretly or openly, as may be consistent with his position or interest, and forswear his allegiance to the British government.

"Section III.—Regarding Public Servants.—It is not a secret thing, that under the British government, natives employed in the civil and military services, have little respect, low pay, and no manner of influence; and all the posts of dignity and emolument in both the departments, are exclusively bestowed on Englishmen; for natives in the military service, after having devoted the greater part of their lives, attain to the post of subahdar (the very height of their hopes), with a salary of 60r. or 70r. per mensem; and those in the civil service obtain the post of sudder ala, with a salary of 500r. a-month, but no influence, jagheer, or present. But under the Badshahi government, like the posts of colonel, general, and commander-in-chief, which the English enjoy at present, the corresponding posts of pansadi, punjhazari, hafthazari, and sippah-salari, will be given to the natives in the military service; and, like the post of collector, magistrate, judge, sudder judge secretary, and governor, which the European civil servants now hold, the corresponding posts of wuzeer, quazi, safir, suba, nizam, and dewan, &c., with salaries of lacs of rupees, will be given to the natives of the civil service, together with jagheers, khilluts, inams, and influence. Natives, whether Hindoos or Mohammedans, who fall fighting against the English, are sure to go to heaven; and those killed fighting for the English, will, doubtless, go to hell. Therefore, all the natives in the British service ought to be alive to their religions and interest, and, abjuring their loyalty to the English, side with the Badshahi government, and obtain salaries of 200 or 300 rupees per month for the present, and be entitled to high posts in future. If they, for any reason, cannot at present declare openly against the English, they can heartily wish ill to their cause, and remain passive spectators of passing events, without taking any active share therein. But at the same time they should indirectly assist the Badshahi government, and try their best to drive the English out of the country.

"All the sepoys and sowars who have, for the sake of their religion, joined in the destruction of the English, and are at present, on any consideration, in a state of concealment, either at home or elsewhere, should present themselves to me without the least delay or hesitation.

"Foot soldiers will be paid at the rate of three annas, and sowars at eight or twelve annas per diem for the present, and afterwards they will be paid double of what they get in the British service. Soldiers not in the English service, and taking part in the war against the English, will receive their daily subsistence-money according to the rates specified below for the present; and in future the foot soldiers will be paid at the rate of eight or ten rupees, and sowars at the rate of twenty or thirty rupees, per month; and on the permanent establishment of the Badshahi government, will stand entitled to the highest posts in the state, to jagheers and presents:—

	annas a-day
Matchlockmen	2
Riflemen	2 1/2
Swordsmen	1 1/2
Horsemen, with large horses	8
with small	6

"Section IV.—Regarding Artisans.—It is evident that the Europeans, by the introduction of English articles into India, have thrown the weavers, the cotton-dressers, the carpenters, the blacksmiths, and the shoemakers, &c., out of employ, and have engrossed their occupations, so that every description of native artisan has been reduced to beggary. But under the Badshahi government the native artisans will exclusively be employed in the services of the kings, the rajahs, and the rich; and this will no doubt insure their prosperity. Therefore these artisans ought to renounce the English services, and assist the Majahdeens, or religious fanatics, engaged in the war, and thus be entitled both to secular and eternal happiness.

"Section V.—Regarding Pundits, Fakirs, and other learned persons.—The pundits and fakirs being the guardians of the Hindoo and Mohammedan religions respectively, and the Europeans being the enemies of both the religions, and as at present a war is raging against the English on account of religion, the pundits and fakirs are bound to present themselves to me, and take their share in the holy war, otherwise they will stand condemned according to the tenor of the Shurrah and the Shasters; but if they come, they will, when the Badshahi government is well established, receive rent-free lands.

"Lastly, be it known to all, that whoever, out of the above-named classes, shall, after the circulation of this Ishtahar, still cling to the British government, all his estates shall be confiscated, and his property plundered, and he himself, with his whole family, shall be imprisoned, and ultimately put to death."

In this appeal to the people, to whom, as distinguished from the army, it was specially addressed, there was doubtless much of truth mingled with error; and, coming from the highest authority at the time, impressed with the royal seal and titles of the king himself, it confirmed and strengthened the sense of injustice which the natives were already too prone to believe they suffered under. In Oude, the germinating cause of mischief was of another and a loftier character. The people had beheld the sudden prostration of their country, which, by the arbitrary will of strangers, had been reduced from the rank of an independent state to the position of a mere province of Bengal: they knew their king to be a prisoner; their royal family dispersed, and their nobles and chiefs despoiled of wealth and power. In Europe, much less than this would have been held to warrant patriotic resistance to the death; and, in Oude, a natural feeling of indignation, and a resolve to avenge the wrongs of their native princes and of their country, became an inevitable consequence of the proceedings of the Company's government.

SOURCE: In Charles Ball's *The History of the Indian Mutiny,* vol. 2 (London: The London Printing and Publishing Co., Ltd., 1858–59).

Essays on the Indian Uprising
KARL MARX

THE REVOLT IN INDIA

London, July 17, 1857

On the 8th of June, just a month has passed since Delhi fell into the hands of the revolted Sepoys and the proclamation by them of a Mogul Emperor.[1] Any notion, however, of the mutineers being able to keep the ancient capital of India against the British forces would be preposterous. Delhi is fortified only by a wall and a simple ditch, while the hights surrounding and commanding it are already in the possession of the English, who, even without battering the walls, might enforce its surrender in a very short period by the

1. Bahadur Shah II.—*Ed.*

easy process of cutting off its supply of water. Moreover, a motley crew of mutineering soldiers who have murdered their own officers, torn asunder the ties of discipline, and not succeeded in discovering a man upon whom to bestow the supreme command, are certainly the body least likely to organize a serious and protracted resistance. To make confusion more confused, the checkered Delhi ranks are daily swelling from the fresh arrivals of new contingents of mutineers from all parts of the Bengal Presidency, who, as if on a preconcerted plan, are throwing themselves into the doomed city. The two sallies which, on the 30th and 31st of May, the mutineers risked without the walls, and in both of which they were repulsed with heavy losses, seem to have proceeded from despair rather than from any feeling of self-reliance or strength. The only thing to be wondered at is the slowness of the British operations, which, to some degree, however, may be accounted for by the horrors of the season and the want of means of transport. Apart from Gen. Anson, the commander-in-chief, French letters state that about 4,000 European troops have already fallen victims of the deathly heat, and even the English papers confess that in the engagements before Delhi the men suffered more from the sun than from the shot of the enemy. In consequence of its scanty means of conveyance, the main British force stationed at Umballah consumed about twenty-seven days in its march upon Delhi, so that it moved at the rate of about one and a half hours per day. A further delay was caused by the absence of heavy artillery at Umballah, and the consequent necessity of bringing over a siege-train from the nearest arsenal, which was as far off as Phillour, on the further side of the Sutlej.

With all that, the news of the fall of Delhi may be daily expected; but what next? If the uncontested possession by the rebels during a month of the traditionary center of the Indian Empire acted perhaps as the most powerful ferment in completely breaking up the Bengal army, in spreading mutiny and desertion from Calcutta to the Punjaub in the north, and to Rajpootana in the west, and in shaking the British authority from one end of India to the other, no greater mistake could be committed than to suppose that the fall of Delhi, though it may throw consternation among the ranks of the Sepoys, should suffice either to quench the rebellion, to stop its progress, or to restore the British rule. Of the whole native Bengal army, mustering about 80,000 men—composed of about 28,000 Rajpoots, 23,000 Brahmins, 13,000 Mahometans, 5,000 Hindoos of inferior castes, and the rest Europeans—30,000 have disappeared in consequence of mutiny, desertion, or dismission from the ranks. As to the rest of that army, several of the regiments have openly declared that they will remain faithful and support the British authority, excepting in the matter in which the native troops are now engaged: they will not aid the

Indian Uprising/Sepoy Mutiny 435

authorities against the mutineers of the native regiments, and will, on the contrary, assist their "bhaies" (brothers). The truth of this has been exemplified in almost every station from Calcutta. The native regiments remained passive for a time; but, as soon as they fancied themselves strong enough, they mutinied. An Indian correspondent of *The London Times* leaves no doubt as to the "loyalty" of the regiments which have not yet pronounced, and the native inhabitants who have not yet made common cause with the rebels.

> "If you read," he says, "that *all is quiet*, understand it to mean that the native troops have not yet risen in open mutiny; that the discontented part of the inhabitants are not yet in open rebellion; that they are either too weak, or fancy themselves to be so, or that they are waiting for a more fitting time. Where you read of the 'manifestations of loyalty' in any of the Bengal native regiments, cavalry or infantry, understand it to mean that one half of the regiments thus favorably mentioned only are really faithful; the other half are but acting a part, the better to find the Europeans off their guard, when the proper time arrives, or, by warding off suspicion, have it the more in their power to aid their mutinous companions."[2]

In the Punjaub, open rebellion has only been prevented by disbanding the native troops. In Oude, the English can only be said to keep Lucknow, the residency, while everywhere else the native regiments have revolted, escaped with their ammunition, burned all the bungalows to the ground, and joined with the inhabitants who have taken up arms. Now, the real position of the English army is best demonstrated by the fact that it was thought necessary, in the Punjaub as well as the Rajpootana, to establish flying corps. This means that the English cannot depend either on their Sepoy troops or on the natives to keep the communication open between their scattered forces. Like the French during the Peninsular war, they command only the spot of ground held by their own troops, and the next neighborhood domineered by that spot; while for communication between the disjoined members of their army they depend on flying corps, the action of which, most precarious in itself, loses naturally in intensity in the same measure that it spreads over a greater extent of space. The actual insufficiency of the British forces is further proved by the fact that, for removing treasures from disaffected stations, they were constrained to have them conveyed by Sepoys themselves, who, without any exception, broke out in rebellion on the march, and absconded with the

---

2. "Agra, June 3", *The Times*, No. 22733, July 15, 1857.—*Ed.*

treasures confided to them. As the troops sent from England will, in the best case, not arrive before November, and as it would be still more dangerous to draw off European troops from the presidencies of Madras and Bombay—the Tenth regiment of Madras Sepoys, having already shown symptoms of disaffection—any idea of collecting the regular taxes throughout the Bengal presidency must be abandoned, and the process of decomposition be allowed to go on. Even if we suppose that the Burmese will not improve the occasion, that the Maharajah of Gwalior[3] will continue supporting the English, and the Ruler of Nepaul,[4] commanding the finest Indian army, remain quiet; that disaffected Peshawur will not combine with the restless Hill tribes, and that the Shah of Persia[5] will not be silly enough to evacuate Herat—still, the whole Bengal presidency must be reconquered, and the whole Anglo-Indian army remade. The cost of this enormous enterprise will altogether fall upon the British people. As to the notion put forward by Lord Granville in the House of Lords, of the East India Company being able to raise, by Indian loans, the necessary means,[6] its soundness may be judged from the effects produced by the disturbed state of the north-western provinces on the Bombay money market. An immediate panic seized the native capitalists, very large sums were withdrawn from the banks. Government securities proved almost unsalable, and hoarding to a great extent commenced, not only in Bombay but in its environs also.

THE INDIAN QUESTION

London, July, 28 1857

The three hours' speech delivered last night in "The Dead House," by Mr. Disraeli, will gain rather than lose by being read instead of being listened to.[1] For some time, Mr. Disraeli affects an awful solemnity of speech, an elaborate slowness of utterance and a passionless method of formality, which, however consistent they may be with his peculiar notions of the dignity becoming a Minister in expectance, are really distressing to his tortured audience. Once he succeeded in giving even commonplaces the pointed appearance of epigrams.

---

3. Sindhia.—*Ed.*
4. Juṅg Bahadur.—*Ed.*
5. Nasr-ed-Din.—*Ed.*
6. Lord Granville's speech in the House of Lords on July 16, 1857, *The Times*, No. 22735, July 17, 1857.—*Ed.*
1. Here and below Disraeli's speech in the House of Commons on July 27, 1857, *The Times*, No. 22744, July 28, 1857.—*Ed.*

Now he contrives to bury even epigrams in the conventional dullness of respectability. An orator who, like Mr. Disraeli, excels in handling the dagger rather than in wielding the sword, should have been the last to forget Voltaire's warning, that "Tous les genres sont bons excepté le genre ennuyeux."[2]

Beside these technical peculiarities which characterize Mr. Disraeli's present manner of eloquence, he, since Palmerston's accession to power, has taken good care to deprive his parliamentary exhibitions of every possible interest of actuality. His speeches are not intended to carry his motions, but his motions are intended to prepare for his speeches. They might be called self-denying motions, since they are so constructed as neither to harm the adversary, if carried, nor to damage the proposer, if lost. They mean, in fact, to be neither carried nor lost, but simply to be dropped. They belong neither to the acids nor to the alkalis, but are born neutrals. The speech is not the vehicle of action, but the hypocrisy of action affords the opportunity for a speech. Such, indeed, may be the classical and final form of parliamentary eloquence; but then, at all events, the final form of parliamentary eloquence must not demur to sharing the fate of all final forms of parliamentarism—that of being ranged under the category of nuisances. Action, as Aristotle said, is the ruling law of the drama.[3] So it is of political oratory. Mr. Disraeli's speech on the Indian revolt might be published in the tracts of the Society for the Propagation of Useful Knowledge, or it might be delivered to a mechanics' institution, or tendered as a prize essay to the Academy of Berlin. This curious impartiality of his speech as to the place where, and the time when, and the occasion on which it was delivered, goes far to prove that it fitted neither place, time, nor occasion. A chapter on the decline of the Roman Empire which might read exceedingly well in Montesquieu or Gibbon[4] would prove an enormous blunder if put in the mouth of a Roman Senator, whose peculiar business it was to stop that very decline. It is true that in our modern parliaments, a part lacking neither dignity nor interest might be imagined of an independent orator who, while despairing of influencing the actual course of events, should content himself to assume a position of ironical neutrality. Such a part was more or less successfully played by the late M. Garnier Pagès—not the Garnier Pagès of Provisional Government memory in Louis Philippe's Chamber of Deputies; but Mr. Disraeli, the avowed leader of an obsolete faction, would consider even success in this line as a supreme failure. The revolt of the Indian

---

2. "All genres are good except the boring ones" (F. M. A. Voltaire, *L'enfant prodigue*, Preface).—Ed.

3. Aristoteles, *De Poetica*, 6.—Ed.

4. [Ch.-L. de Montesquieu,] *Considérations sur les causes de la grandeur des Romains, et de leur décadance* and E. Gibbon, *The History of the Decline and Fall of the Roman Empire*.—Ed.

army afforded certainly a magnificent opportunity for oratorical display. But, apart from his dreary manner of treating the subject, what was the gist of the motion which he made the pretext for his speech? It was no motion at all. He feigned to be anxious for becoming acquainted with two official papers, the one of which he was not quite sure to exist, and the other of which he was sure not immediately to bear on the subject in question. Consequently his speech and his motion lacked any point of contact save this, that the motion heralded a speech without an object, and that the object confessed itself not worth a speech. Still, as the highly elaborated opinion of the most distinguished out-of-office statesman of England, Mr. Disraeli's speech ought to attract the attention of foreign countries. I shall content myself with giving in his *ipsissima verba*[5] a short analysis of his "considerations on the decline of the Anglo-Indian Empire".

> "Does the disturbance in India indicate a military mutiny, or is it a national revolt? Is the conduct of the troops the consequence of a sudden impulse, or is it the result of an organized conspiracy?"

Upon these points Mr. Disraeli asserts the whole question to hinge. Until the last ten years, he affirmed, the British empire in India was founded on the old principle of *divide et impera*—but that principle was put into action by respecting the different nationalities of which India consisted, by avoiding to tamper with their religion, and by protecting their landed property. The Sepoy army served as a safety-valve to absorb the turbulent spirits of the country. But of late years a new principle has been adopted in the government of India—the principle of destroying nationality. The principle has been realized by the forcible destruction of native princes, the disturbance of the settlement of property, and the tampering with the religion of the people. In 1848 the financial difficulties of the East India Company had reached that point that it became necessary to augment its revenues one way or the other. Then a minute in Council was published, in which was laid down the principle, almost without disguise, that the only mode by which an increased revenue could be obtained was by enlarging the British territories at the expense of the native princes. Accordingly, on the death of the Rajah of Sattara,[6] his adoptive heir was not acknowledged by the East India Company, but the Raj absorbed in its own dominions. From that moment the system of annexation was acted upon whenever a native prince died without natural heirs. The principle of adoption—the very corner-stone of Indian society—was system-

---

5. Very words.—*Ed.*
6. Appa Sahib.—*Ed.*

atically set aside by the Government. Thus were forcibly annexed to the British Empire the Rajs of more than a dozen independent princes from 1848–54. In 1854 the Raj of Berar, which comprised 80,000 square miles of land, a population from 4,000,000 to 5,000,000, and enormous treasures, was forcibly seized. Mr. Disraeli ends the list of forcible annexations with Oude, which brought the East India Government in collision not only with the Hindoos, but also with the Mohammedans. Mr. Disraeli then goes on showing how the settlement of property in India was disturbed by the new system of government during the last ten years.

> "The principle of the law of adoption," he says, "is not the prerogative of princes and principalities in India, it applies to every man in Hindostan who has landed property, and who professes the Hindoo religion."

I quote a passage:

> "The great feudatory, or jaguedar, who holds his lands by public service to his lord; and the enamdar, who holds his land free of all land-tax, who corresponds, if not precisely, in a popular sense, at least, with our freeholder—both of these classes—classes most numerous in India—always, on the failure of their natural heirs, find in this principle the means of obtaining successors to their estates. These classes were all touched by the annexation of Sattara, they were touched by the annexation of the territories of the ten inferior but independent princes to whom I have already alluded, and they were more than touched, they were terrified to the last degree, when the annexation of the Raj of Berar took place. What man was safe? What feudatory, what freeholder who had not a child of his own loins was safe throughout India? [Hear, hear]. These were not idle fears; they were extensively acted upon and reduced to practice. The resumption of jagheers and of inams commenced for the first time in India. There have been, no doubt, impolitic moments when attempts have been made to inquire into titles but no one had ever dreamt of abolishing the law of adoption; therefore no authority, no Government had ever been in a position to resume jagheers and inams the holders of which had left no natural heirs. Here was a new source of revenue; but while all these things were acting upon the minds of these classes of Hindoos, the Government took another step to disturb the settlement of property, to which I must now call the attention of the House. The House is aware, no doubt, from reading the evidence taken before the Committee of 1853, that there are great portions of the land of Indian which are exempt from the land-tax. Being free from land-tax in

India is far more than equivalent to freedom from the land-tax in this country, for, speaking generally and popularly, the land-tax in India is the whole taxation of the State.

"The origin of these grants is difficult to penetrate, but they are undoubtedly of great antiquity. They are of different kinds. Beside the private freeholds, which are very extensive, there are large grants of land free from the land-tax with which mosques and temples have been endowed."

On the pretext of fraudulent claims of exemption, the British Governor General[7] took upon himself to examine the titles of the Indian landed estates. Under the new system, established in 1848,

"That plan of investigating titles was at once embraced, as a proof of a powerful Government, vigorous Executive, and most fruitful source of public revenue. Therefore commissions were issued to inquire into titles to landed estates in the Presidency of Bengal and adjoining country. They were also issued in the Presidency of Bombay, and surveys were ordered to be made in the newly-settled provinces, in order that these commissions might be conducted, when the surveys were completed, with due efficiency. Now there is no doubt that, during the last nine years, the action of these commissions of Inquiry into the freehold property of landed estates in India has been going on at an enormous rate, and immense results have been obtained."

Mr. Disraeli computes that the resumption of estates from their proprietors is not less than £500,000 a year in the Presidency of Bengal; £370,000 in the Presidency of Bombay; £200,000 in the Punjaub, &c. Not content with this one method of seizing upon the property of the natives, the British Government discontinued the pensions to the native grandees, to pay which it was bound by treaty.

"This," says Mr. Disraeli, "is confiscation by a new means, but upon a most extensive, startling and shocking scale."

Mr. Disraeli then treats the tampering with the religion of the natives, a point upon which we need not dwell. From all his premises he arrives at the conclusion that the present Indian disturbance is not a military mutiny, but a national revolt, of which the Sepoys are the acting instruments only. He ends his harangue by advising the Government to turn their attention to

---

7. Dalhousie.—*Ed.*

the internal improvement of India, instead of pursuing its present course of aggression.

BRITISH INCOMES IN INDIA

The present state of affairs in Asia suggests the inquiry, What is the real value of their Indian dominion to the British nation and people? Directly, that is in the shape of tribute, of surplus of Indian receipts over Indian expenditures, nothing whatever reaches the British Treasury. On the contrary, the annual outgo is very large. From the moment that the East India Company entered extensively on the career of conquest—now just about a century ago—their finances fell into an embarrassed condition, and they were repeatedly compelled to apply to Parliament, not only for military aid to assist them in holding the conquered territories, but for financial aid to save them from bankruptcy. And so things have continued down to the present moment, at which so large a call is made for troops on the British nation, to be followed, no doubt, by corresponding calls for money. In prosecuting its conquests hitherto, and building up its establishments, the East India Company has contracted a debt of upward of £50,000,000 sterling, while the British Government has been at the expense, for years past, of transporting to and from and keeping up in India, in addition to the forces, native and European, of the East India Company, a standing army of thirty thousand men. Such being the case, it is evident that the advantage to Great Britain from her Indian empire must be limited to the profits and benefits which accrue to individual British subjects. These profits and benefits, it must be confessed, are very considerable.

First, we have the stockholders in the East India Company, to the number of about 3,000 persons, to whom under the recent charter there is guaranteed, upon a paid-up capital of six millions of pounds sterling, an annual dividend of ten and a half per cent, amounting to £630,000 annually. As the East India stock is held in transferable shares, anybody may become a stockholder who has money enough to buy the stock, which, under the existing charter, commands a premium of from 125 to 150 per cent. Stock to the amount of £500, costing say $6,000, entitles the holder to speak at the Proprietors' meetings, but to vote he must have £1,000 of stock. Holders of £3,000 have two votes, of £6,000 three votes, and of £10,000 or upward four votes. The proprietors, however, have but little voice, except in the election of the Board of Directors, of whom they choose twelve, while the Crown appoints six; but these appointees of the Crown must be qualified by having resided for ten years or more in India. One third of the Directors go out of office each year, but may be re-elected or reappointed. To be a Director, one must be a proprietor of £2,000 of stock. The Directors have a salary of £500 each, and their Chairman and Deputy Chairman twice as much; but the chief inducement to accept the office is the great patronage attached to it in the appointment of all Indian officers, civil and military—a patronage, however, largely shared, and, as to the most important offices, engrossed substantially, by the Board of Control. This Board consists of six members, all Privy Councilors, and in general two or three of them Cabinet Ministers—the President of the Board being always so, in fact a Secretary of State for India.

Next come the recipients of this patronage, divided into five classes—civil, clerical, medical, military and naval. For service in India, at least in the civil line, some knowledge of the languages spoken there is necessary, and to prepare young men to enter their civil service, the East India Company has a college at Haileybury. A corresponding college for the military service, in which, however, the rudiments of military science are the principal branches taught, has been established at Addiscombe, near London. Admission to these colleges was formerly a matter of favor on the part of the Directors of the Company, but under the latest modifications of the charter it has been opened to competition in the way of a public examination of candidates. On first reaching India, a civilian is allowed about $150 a month, till having passed a necessary examination in one or more of the native languages (which must be within twelve months after his arrival), he is attached to the service with emoluments which vary from $2,500 to near $50,000 per annum. The latter is the pay of the members of the Bengal Council; the members of the Bombay and Madras Councils receive about $30,000 per annum. No person not a member of Council can receive more than about $25,000 per annum, and, to obtain an appointment worth $20,000 or over, he must have been a resident in India for twelve years. Nine years' residence qualifies for salaries of from $15,000 to $20,000, and three years' residence for salaries of from $7,000 to $15,000. Appointments in the civil service go nominally by seniority and merit, but really to a great extent by favor. As they are the best paid, there is great competition to get them, the military officers leaving their regiments for this purpose whenever they can get a chance. The average of all the salaries in the civil service is stated at about $8,000, but this does not include perquisites and extra allowances, which are often very considerable. These civil servants are employed as Governors, Councilors, Judges, Embassadors, Secretaries, Collectors of the Revenue, &c.—the number in the whole being generally about 800. The salary of the Governor-General of India is $125,000, but the extra allowances often amount to a still larger sum. The Church service includes three bishops and about one hundred and sixty chaplains. The

Bishop of Calcutta has $25,000 a year; those of Madras and Bombay half as much; the chaplains from $2,500 to $7,000, beside fees. The medical service includes some 800 physicians and surgeons, with salaries of from $1,500 to $10,000.

The European military officers employed in India, including those of the contingents which the dependent princes are obliged to furnish, number about 8,000. The fixed pay in the infantry is, for ensigns, $1,080; lieutenants, $1,344; captains, $2,226; majors, $3,810; lieutenant colonels, $5,520; colonels, $7,680. This is the pay in cantonment. In active service, it is more. The pay in the cavalry, artillery and engineers, is somewhat higher. By obtaining staff situations or employments in the civil service, many officers double their pay.

Here are about ten thousand British subjects holding lucrative situations in India, and drawing their pay from the Indian service. To these must be added a considerable number living in England, whither they have retired upon pensions, which in all the services are payable after serving a certain number of years. These pensions, with the dividends and interest on debts due in England, consume some fifteen to twenty millions of dollars drawn annually from India, and which may in fact be regarded as so much tribute paid to the English Government indirectly through its subjects. Those who annually retire from the several services carry with them very considerable amounts of savings from their salaries, which is so much more added to the annual drain on India.

Besides these Europeans actually employed in the service of the Government, there are other European residents in India to the number of 6,000 or more, employed in trade or private speculation. Except a few indigo, sugar and coffee planters in the rural districts, they are principally merchants, agents and manufacturers, who reside in the cities of Calcutta, Bombay and Madras, or their immediate vicinity. The foreign trade of India, including imports and exports to the amount of about fifty millions of dollars of each, is almost entirely in their hands, and their profits are no doubt very considerable.

It is thus evident that individuals gain largely by the English connection with India, and of course their gain goes to increase the sum of the national wealth. But against all this a very large offset is to be made. The military and naval expenses paid out of the pockets of the people of England on Indian account have been constantly increasing with the extent of the Indian dominion. To this must be added the expense of Burmese, Afghan, Chinese and Persian wars. In fact, the whole cost of the late Russian war may fairly be charged to the Indian account, since the fear and dread of Russia, which led to that war, grew entirely out of jealousy as to her designs on India. Add to this the career of endless conquest and perpetual aggression in which the English are involved by the possession of India, and it may well be doubted whether, on the whole, this dominion does not threaten to cost quite as much as it can ever be expected to come to.

THE ANNEXATION OF OUDE

About eighteen months ago, at Canton, the British Government propounded the novel doctrine in the law of nations that a State may commit hostilities on a large scale against a Province of another State, without either declaring war or establishing a state of war against that other State. Now the same British Government, in the person of the Governor-General of India, Lord Canning, has made another forward move in its task of upsetting the existing law of nations. It has proclaimed that

> "the proprietary right in the soil of the Province of Oude is confiscated to the British Government, which will dispose of that right in such manner as it may seem fitting."[1]

When, after the fall of Warsaw in 1831, the Russian Emperor[2] confiscated "the proprietary right in the soil" hitherto held by numerous Polish nobles, there was one unanimous outburst of indignation in the British press and Parliament. When, after the battle of Novara, the Austrian Government did not confiscate, but merely sequestered, the estates of such Lombard noblemen as had taken an active part in the war of independence, that unanimous outburst of British indignation was repeated. And when, after the 2d December, 1851, Louis Napoleon confiscated the estates of the Orleans family, which, by the common law of France, ought to have been united to the public domain on the accession of Louis Philippe, but which had escaped that fate by a legal quibble, then British indignation knew no bounds, and *The London Times* declared that by this act the very foundations of social order were upset, and that civil society could no longer exist.[3] All this honest indignation has now been practically illustrated. England, by one stroke of the pen, has confiscated not only the estates of a few noblemen, or of a royal family, but the whole length and breadth of a kingdom nearly as large as Ireland, "the inheritance of a whole people," as Lord Ellenborough himself terms it.[4]

1. Here and below Ch. J. Canning, "Proclamation", *The Times*, No. 22986, May 6, 1858.—*Ed.*
2. Nicholas I.—*Ed.*
3. "If Louis Napoleon had proceeded to exercise with judgment . . . ", *The Times*, No. 21021, January 26, 1852.—*Ed.*
4. E. L. Ellenborough's speech in the House of Lords on May 7, 1858, *The Times*, No. 22988, May 8, 1858.—*Ed.*

But let us hear what pretexts—grounds we cannot call them—Lord Canning, in the name of the British Government, sets forth for this unheard-of proceeding: First, "The army is in possession of Lucknow." Second, "The resistance, begun by a mutinous soldiery, has found support from the inhabitants of the city and of the province at large." Third, "They have been guilty of a great crime, and have subjected themselves to a just retribution." In plain English: Because the British army have got hold of Lucknow, the Government has the right to confiscate all the land in Oude which they have not yet got hold of. Because the native soldiers in British pay have mutinied, the natives of Oude, who were subjected to British rule by force, have not the right to rise for their national independence. In short, the people of Oude have rebelled against the legitimate authority of the British Government, and the British Government now distinctly declares that rebellion is a sufficient ground for confiscation. Leaving, therefore, out of the question all the circumlocution of Lord Canning, the whole question turns upon the point that he assumes the British rule in Oude to have been legitimately established.

Now, British rule in Oude was established in the following manner: When, in 1856, Lord Dalhousie thought the moment for action had arrived, he concentrated an army at Cawnpore which, the King of Oude[5] was told, was to serve as a corps of observation against Nepaul. This army suddenly invaded the country, took possession of Lucknow, and took the King prisoner. He was urged to cede the country to the British, but in vain. He was then carried off to Calcutta, and the country was annexed to the territories of the East India Company. This treacherous invasion was based upon article 6 of the treaty of 1801,[6] concluded by Lord Wellesley. This treaty was the natural consequence of that concluded in 1798 by Sir John Shore.[7] According to the usual policy followed by the Anglo-Indian Government in their intercourse with native princes, this first treaty of 1798 was a treaty of offensive and defensive alliance on both sides. It secured to the East India Company a yearly subsidy of 76 lacs[8] of rupees ($3,800,000); but by articles 12 and 13 the King was obliged to reduce the taxation of the country. As a matter of course, these two conditions, in open contradiction to each other, could not be fulfilled by the King at the same time. This result, looked for by the East India Company, gave rise to fresh complications, resulting in the treaty of 1801, by which a cession of

---

5. Wajid Ali Shah.—*Ed.*
6. "Treaty between the Honorable East India Company and His Excellency the Nabob Vizier-ul-Momalik..., 10th November 1801".—*Ed.*
7. "Treaty with the Nabob Vizier Saadet Ali Khan Behauder, 21st February 1798".—*Ed.*
8. Lac = 100,000.—*Ed.*

territory had to make up for the alleged infractions of the former treaty; a cession of territory which, by the way, was at the time denounced in Parliament as a downright robbery, and would have brought Lord Wellesley before a Committee of Inquiry, but for the political influence then held by his family.

In consideration of this cession of territory, the East India Company, by article 3, undertook to defend the King's remaining territories against all foreign and domestic enemies; and by article 6 guaranteed the possession of these territories to him and his heirs and successors forever. But this same article 6 contained also a pit-fall for the King, viz: The King engaged that he would establish such a system of administration, to be carried into effect by his own officers, as should be conducive to the prosperity of his subjects, and be calculated to secure the lives and property of the inhabitants. Now, supposing the King of Oude had broken this treaty; had not, by his government, secured the lives and property of the inhabitants (say by blowing them from the cannon's mouth, and confiscating the whole of their lands), what remedy remained to the East India Company? The King was, by the treaty, acknowledged as an independent sovereign, a free agent, one of the contracting parties. The East India Company, on declaring the treaty broken and thereby annulled, could have but two modes of action: either by negotiation, backed by pressure, they might have come to a new arrangement, or else they might have declared war against the King. But to invade his territory without declaration of war, to take him prisoner unawares, dethrone him and annex his territory, was an infraction not only of the treaty, but of every principle of the law of nations.

That the annexation of Oude was not a sudden resolution of the British Government is proved by a curious fact. No sooner was Lord Palmerston, in 1831, Foreign Secretary, than he sent an order to the then Governor-General[9] to annex Oude. The subordinate at that time declined to carry out the suggestion. The affair, however, came to the knowledge of the King of Oude,[10] who availed himself of some pretext to send an embassy to London. In spite of all obstacles, the embassy succeeded in acquainting William IV., who was ignorant of the whole proceeding, with the danger which had menaced their country. The result was a violent scene between William IV. and Palmerston, ending in a strict injunction to the latter never to repeat such *coups d'état* on pain of instant dismissal. It is important to recollect that the actual annexation of Oude and the confiscation of all the landed property of the country took

---

9. W. C. Bentinck.—*Ed.*
10. Nazir-ed-Din.—*Ed.*

place when Palmerston was again in power. The papers relating to this first attempt at annexing Oude, in 1831, were moved for, a few weeks ago, in the House of Commons, when Mr. Baillie, Secretary of the Board of Control, declared that these papers had disappeared.[11]

Again, in 1837, when Palmerston, for the second time, was Foreign Secretary, and Lord Auckland Governor-General of India, the King of Oude[12] was compelled to make a fresh treaty with the East India Company.[13] This treaty takes up article 6 of the one of 1801, because "it provides no remedy for the obligation contained in it" (to govern the country well); and it expressly provides, therefore, by article 7,

> "that the King of Oude shall immediately take into consideration, in concert with the British Resident, the best means of remedying the defects in the police, and in the judicial and revenue administrations of his dominions; and that if his Majesty should neglect to attend to the advice and counsel of the British Government, and if gross and systematic oppression, anarchy and misrule should prevail within the Oude dominions, such as seriously to endanger the public tranquillity, the British Government reserves to itself the right of appointing its own officers to the management of whatsoever portions of the Oude territory, either to a small or great extent, in which such misrule shall have occurred, for so long a period as it may deem necessary; the surplus receipts in such case, after defraying all charges, to be paid into the King's Treasury, and a true and faithful account rendered to his Majesty of the receipts and expenditure."

By article 8, the treaty further provides:

> "That in case the Governor-General of India in Council should be compelled to resort to the exercise of the authority vested in him by article 7, he will endeavor so far as possible to maintain, with such improvements as they may admit of, the native institutions and forms of administration within the assumed territories, so as to facilitate the restoration of these territories to the Sovereign of Oude, when the proper period for such restoration shall arrive."

---

11. H. J. Baillie's speech in the House of Commons on March 16, 1858, *The Times*, No. 22943, March 17, 1858.—*Ed.*
12. Mohammed Ali Shah.—*Ed.*
13. "Treaty between the Honorable East India Company and His Majesty . . . Mohammud Ali Shah . . ., 11th September 1837".—*Ed.*

This treaty professes to be concluded between the Governor-General of British India in Council, on one hand, and the King of Oude on the other. It was, as such, duly ratified, by both parties, and the ratifications were duly exchanged. But when it was submitted to the Board of Directors of the East India Company, it was annulled (April 10, 1838) as an infraction of the friendly relations between the Company and the King of Oude, and an encroachment, on the part of the Governor-General, on the rights of that potentate. Palmerston had not asked the Company's leave to conclude the treaty, and he took no notice of their annulling resolution. Nor was the King of Oude informed that the treaty had ever been canceled. This is proved by Lord Dalhousie himself (minute Jan. 5, 1856):

> "It is very probable that the King, in the course of the discussions which will take place with the Resident, may refer to the treaty negotiated with his predecessor in 1837; the Resident is aware that the treaty was not continued in force, having been annulled by the Court of Directors as soon as it was received in England. The Resident is further aware that, although the King of Oude was informed at the time that certain aggravating provisions of the treaty of 1837, respecting an increased military force, would not be carried into effect, the *entire abrogation of it was never communicated to his Majesty*. The effect of this reserve and want of full communication is felt to be embarrassing to-day. It is the more embarrassing that the canceled instrument was still included in a volume of treaties which was published in 1845, by the authority of Government."

In the same minute, sec. 17, it is said:

> "If the King should allude to the treaty of 1837, and should ask why, if further measures are necessary in relation to the administration of Oude, the large powers which are given to the British Government by the said treaty should not now be put in force, his Majesty must be informed that the treaty has had no existence since it was communicated to the Court of Directors, by whom it was wholly annulled. His Majesty will be reminded that the Court of Lucknow was informed at the time that certain articles of the treaty of 1837, by which the payment of an additional military force was imposed upon the King, were to be set aside. It must be presumed that it was not thought necessary at that time to make any communication to his Majesty regarding those articles of the treaty which were not of immediate operation, and that the subsequent communication was inadvertently neglected."

But not only was this treaty inserted in the official collection of 1845, it was also officially adverted to as a subsisting treaty in Lord Auckland's notification to the King of Oude, dated July 8, 1839; in Lord Hardinge's (then Governor-General) remonstrance to the same King, of November 23, 1847, and in Col. Sleeman's (Resident at Lucknow) communication to Lord Dalhousie himself, of the 10th December, 1851. Now, why was Lord Dalhousie so eager to deny the validity of a treaty which all his predecessors, and even his own agents, had acknowledged to be in force in their communications with the King of Oude? Solely because, by this treaty, whatever pretext the King might give for interference, that interference was limited to an assumption of government by British officers *in the name of the King of Oude,* who was to receive the surplus revenue. That was the very opposite of what was wanted. Nothing short of annexation would do. This denying the validity of treaties which had formed the acknowledged base of intercourse for twenty years; this seizing violently upon independent territories in open infraction even of the acknowledged treaties; this final confiscation of every acre of land in the whole country; all these treacherous and brutal modes of proceeding of the British toward the natives of India are now beginning to avenge themselves, not only in India, but in England.

SOURCE: Karl Marx's essays on the Indian Uprising—"The Revolt in India," "The Indian Question," "British Incomes in India," "The Annexation of Oude"—appeared between 17 July 1857 and 14 May 1858. Originally published as a series in the *New York Daily Tribune,* these essays are from *Karl Marx Frederick Engels: Collected Works, 1856–58* vol. 15 (New York: International Publishers, 1986).

Final Orders to the Musketry Schools
COLONEL C. CHESTER

The Adjutant-General of the Army to Major-General Hearsey
Adjutant-General's Office, Simlah, April 13, 1857.

"Sir,—Referring to the telegraph message from this office dated the 23rd ultimo (and your acknowledgments of the 25th idem), communicating the Commander-in-Chief's orders to postpone the target practice of the Native soldiers at the Rifle Depôt at Dum-Dum, pending further instructions from this Department, I am now desired to request you will be good enough to inform the officer commanding at Dum-Dum, and through him the Depôt authorities concerned, that the course of instruction is to be completed by the Native details, and that their target practice is to be commenced as soon as practicable after the Government General Order disbanding the Nineteenth Regiment of Native Infantry has been read to the troops at the station, including the detachments of Native regiments at the Depôt.

"2. The grease for the cartridge is to be any unobjectionable mixture which may be suited for the purpose, to be provided by selected parties comprising all castes concerned, and is to be applied by the men themselves.

"3. The paper of which the cartridges are constructed having been proved by chemical test, and otherwise, to be perfectly free from grease, and in all respects unobjectionable; and all possible grounds for objection in regard to the biting of the cartridge, and the nature of the grease to be used, having been removed, it is not anticipated that the men will hesitate to perform the target practice; but, in the event of any such unexpected result, the Commander-in-Chief desires that their officers may be instructed to reason calmly with them, pointing out the utter groundlessness for any objection to the use of the cartridges now that biting the end has been dispensed with, and the provision and application of the necessary greasing material has been left to themselves; and, further, to assure them that any one who shall molest or taunt them on return to their corps, shall be visited with severe punishment.

"4. The officer commanding the Depôt will be held responsible that the above directions respecting the greasing mixture, and those recently issued in regard to the new mode of loading, are strictly observed.

"5. If, notwithstanding all these precautions and considerate measures, any disinclination to use the cartridges shall be manifested, the parties demurring are to be warned calmly and patiently, but firmly, that a persistence in such unjustifiable conduct will be viewed as disobedience of orders and insubordination, and treated accordingly, and in the event of any individuals after such warning obstinately refusing to fire, the officer commanding at Dum-Dum will at once place such parties in arrest or confinement, according to the rank of the offenders, and cause them to be tried by Court-Martial.

"6. If, however, the entire Depôt shall combinedly refuse to fire, which is very improbable, the Commander-in-Chief, under such circumstances, empowers you to place all the Native officers in arrest pending his Excellency's further orders, which you will immediately apply for; to deprive the non-commissioned officers and Sepoys of their arms and accoutrements, and to pay them up and summarily discharge them on the spot, excepting, of course, any ringleaders in these latter grades or parties whose refusal may be accompanied by insolence or insubordination, who are to be placed under arrest or confinement, in view of their being arraigned before a District or General Court-Martial, as the case may require.

"7. This communication is to be considered purely confidential, and his Excellency relies implicitly on your carrying out the instructions it contains with the utmost caution and discretion.

"I have the honour to be, Sir,
"Your most obedient servant,
"C. Chester, Col.
"*Adjt.-Gen. of the Army.*"

SOURCE: In John William Kaye, *The History of the Sepoy War in India, 1857–1858* (London: W. H. Allen, 1880–1888).

Selected Documents from John William Kaye's *The History of the Sepoy War in India, 1857–1858*

THE CHUPATTIES

[It is stated at page 571 that Mr. Ford, Magistrate and Collector of Goorgaon, was the first to call the attention of the Government of the North-Western Provinces to this subject. His letter, addressed, in official course, to the Commissioner of Delhi, is appended:]

"Goorgaon Magistracy, February 19, 1857.

"Sir,—I have the honour to inform you that a signal has passed through numbers of the villages of this district, the purport of which has not yet transpired.

"The Chowkeydars of the villages bordering on those belonging to Mutra have received small baked cakes of atta, with orders to distribute them generally through this district.

"A Chowkeydar, upon receiving one of these cakes, has had five or six more prepared, and thus they have passed from village to village; so quickly has the order been executed, that village after village has been served with this notice.

"This day, cakes of this description have arrived and been distributed in the villages about Goorgaon, and an idea has been industriously circulated that Government has given the order.

"W. Ford, Magistrate.
"To Simon Fraser, Esq., Commissioner, Delhi."

[In the course of the trial of the King of Delhi great pains were taken to extract from the witnesses, both European and Native, some explanation of the "Chupatty mystery;" but nothing satisfactory was elicited. The following opinions, however, were recorded:]

From the Evidence of Jat Mall,
News-writer to the Lieutenant-Governor

"Q. Did you ever hear of the circulation of chupatties about the country some months before the outbreak; and if so, what was supposed to be the meaning of this?

A. Yes, I did hear of the circumstance. Some people said that it was a propitiatory observance to avert some impending calamity; others, that they were circulated by the Government to signify that the population throughout the country would be compelled to use the same food as the Christians, and thus be deprived of their religion; while others, again, said that the chupatties were circulated to make it known that Government was determined to force Christianity on the country by interfering with their food, and intimation of it was thus given that they might be prepared to resist the attempt.

Q. Is sending such articles about the country a custom among the Hindoos or Mussulmans; and would the meaning be at once understood without any accompanying explanation?

A. No, it is not by any means a custom; I am fifty years old, and never heard of such a thing before.

Q. Did you ever hear that any message was sent with the chupatties?

A. No; I never heard of any.

Q. Were these chupatties chiefly circulated by Mahomedans or Hindoos?

A. They were circulated indiscriminately, without reference to either religion, among the peasantry of the country."

From the Evidence of Sir Theophilus Metcalfe

"Q. Can you give the Court any information about the chupatties which were circulated from village to village some months before the outbreak; and has it been ascertained how they originated, or what was the purport of their being circulated?

A. There is nothing but conjecture regarding them, but the first suggestion made by the Natives in reference to them was, that they were thus sent about in connexion with some sickness that prevailed; but this was clearly an error, as I took the trouble of ascertaining that these chupatties were never sent into any Native States, but were confined always to Government villages; they were spread through only five villages of the Delhi territory, when they were immediately stopped by authority, and they never proceeded farther up-country. I sent for the men who had brought them from the district of Bolundshuhr, and their apology for circulating them was that they believed it to be done by order of the English Government, that they had received them elsewhere, and had but forwarded them on. I believe that the meaning of the chupatties was not understood in the Delhi district; but originally they were to be taken to all those who partook of one kind of food, connecting a body of men together in contradistinction to those who lived differently and had different customs. I think these chupatties originated at Lucknow, and were, no doubt, meant to sound a note of alarm and preparation, giving warning to the people to stand by one another on any danger menacing them."

From the Evidence of Chuni, News-writer

"Q. Do you recollect the circumstance of chupatties being circulated from village to village?

A. Yes, I remember hearing of it before the outbreak.

Q. Was the subject discussed in the Native newspapers; and if so, what was considered the meaning of it?

A. Yes, it was alluded to, and it was supposed to portend some coming disturbance, and was, moreover, understood as implying an invitation to the whole population of the country to unite for some secret objects afterwards to be disclosed.

Q. Do you know whence these chupatties originated, or to what quarter general opinion among the Natives attributed them?

A. I have no knowledge as to where they were first started, but it was generally supposed that they came from Kurnaul and Paneeput."

From the Evidence of Captain Martineau

"Q. Had you any conversation with these men (*i.e.* with the men assembled at Umballah for musketry instruction) relative to some chupatties that were circulated to different villages in these districts before the outbreak?

A. Yes, I had frequent conversations with various Sepoys on this subject. I asked them what they understood in reference to them, and by whom they supposed that they were circulated; they described them to me as being in size and shape like ship biscuits, and believed them to have been distributed by order of Government through the medium of their servants for the purpose of intimating to the people of Hindoostan that they should all be compelled to eat the same food, and that was considered as a token that they should likewise be compelled to embrace one faith, or, as they termed it, 'One food and one faith.'

Q. As far as you could understand, was this idea generally prevalent among all the Sepoys of the various detachments at the Depôt?

A. It was prevalent, as far as I could judge, among all the Sepoys of every regiment that furnished a detachment to the Depôt at Umballah.

Q. Was there any report of the Government having mixed ground bones with flour for the purpose of having it distributed to the Sepoys, and so destroying their caste?

A. Yes, I heard of this in the month of March. It was told me that all the flour retailed from the Government Depôts for the supply of troops on the march was so adulterated.

Q. Do you think the Sepoys generally firmly believed this?

A. I have seen correspondence from various men, which the Sepoys of the Depôt voluntarily placed in my hands, the writers of which, themselves Sepoys, evidently believed that such was the case.

Q. Did the Sepoys ever speak to you about any other cause of complaint, or points on which they sought information?

A. Their complaints, or rather fear, was this: they apprehended that Government was going forcibly to deprive them of their caste.

Q. Did any of them ever speak about Government interference regarding the re-marriage of Hindoo widows?

A. Yes, they alluded to that as an invasion of their social rights."

From the Statement of Hakim Ahsan Ullah, Confidential Physician to the King of Delhi

"Nobody can tell what was the object of the distribution of the chupatties. It is not known who first projected the plan. All the people in the palace wondered what it could mean. I had no conversation with the King on the subject; but others talked in his presence about it, wondering what could be the object.

"I consider that the chupatty affair probably originated with the Native troops, and the distribution first commenced in Oude. I also wondered what it was, but considered that it implied something.

"I consider that the distribution of the chupatties first began in Oude.

"It was the opinion of some that the Native troops had designed these chupatties as emblematical of some particular object. Others believed that there was some charm attached to them, inasmuch as they were distributed unknown all over the country, and without it being known who first originated the idea, and whence they were first sent out. People also believed that these chupatties were the invention of some adept in the secret arts, in order to preserve unpolluted the religion of the country, which, it was reported, the Government had proposed to themselves to subvert in two years."

[The following extracts from published works bear upon the subject of inquiry. In the first, the preceding statement that the circulation of the chupatties commenced in Oude, is corroborated:]

"Some time in February, 1857, a curious occurrence took place. It began on the confines of Oude. A Chowkeydar ran up to another village with two chupatties. He ordered his fellow-official to make ten more, and give two to each of the five nearest village Chowkeydars with the same instructions. In a few hours the whole country was in a stir, from Chowkeydars flying about with these cakes. The signal spread in all directions with wonderful celerity. The magistrates tried to stop it, but, in spite of all they could do, it passed along to the borders of the Punjab. There is reason to believe that this was originated by some intriguers of the old Court of Lucknow. Its import has not been satisfactorily explained, and was probably not understood by many who helped it along. But the same thing occurred in Behar and about Jhansi in connexion with the discontent caused by the new income-tax. It has been stated by a Native authority, published by Mr. Russell of the *Times* (see *Friend of India*, March 10, 1859), that the first circulation of the chupatties was made at the suggestion of a learned and holy pundit, who told Rajah Madhoo Singh that the people would rise in rebellion if it were done, and that the person in whose name the cakes were sent would rule all India. This, however, is very doubtful."—*Siege of Delhi, by an Officer who served there.*

"That remarkable and still unexplained passage through Oude, and elsewhere, of the chupatty symbol, occurred early in 1857, and, from the first movement of its advent into Oude, spread with such amazing rapidity, that it was calculated ten days more than sufficed for every village Chowkeydar in Oude to have received the little bread-cake, and made and passed on similar little bread-cakes to every village Chowkeydar within the ordinary radius of his travels. The Natives generally may have viewed this sign-manual flying through their villages—so common a method amongst men in the early stages of civilisation to warn all for either peace or war—as a forerunner of some universal popular outbreak, but by whom or with what class the standard of rebellion would be raised certainly was not generally known."—*Narrative of the Mutinies in Oude, compiled from Authentic Records, by Captain G. Hutchinson, Military Secretary to the Chief Commissioner, Oude.*

"In the North-West Provinces it was discovered that chupatties were being circulated throughout the country in a somewhat mysterious manner.[1] The fact was duly reported from various quarters; inquiries were ordered to be set on foot, but nothing further could be traced as to their origin or object, and they were suffered to travel on from village to village with little let or hindrance. Some fifty years before a similar appearance in Central India had perplexed the authorities,[2] but no solution of the mystery had been gained, and as nothing had then resulted from it, the hope was grasped at that in the present instance also, if not meaningless, it might prove equally harmless: it might be some superstitious spell against disease, for cholera had ravaged several districts during the previous autumn, or against some impending calamity, for the whole country teemed with forebodings of coming trouble. At all events, the idea was scouted of its having any political meaning; and far-seeing old Indians, who dared to look gravely on the 'chupatty mystery,' were denounced as croakers."—*The Punjab and Delhi in 1857, by the Rev. T. Cave-Browne, Chaplain of the Punjab Moveable Column.*

"The leaders and promoters of this great rebellion, whoever they may have been, knew well the inflammable condition, from these causes, of the rural society in the North-Western Provinces, and they therefore sent among them the chupatties, as a kind of fiery cross, to call them to action. The cakes passed with the most amazing rapidity over the length and breadth of the land.

---

1. One district officer, who saw a chupatty-laden messenger arrive in a village, and observed him breaking his cake into pieces and distributing them among the men of the village, asked what it meant; he was told that there was an old custom in Hindoostan, that when their *malik*, or chief, required any service from his people, he adopted this mode to prepare them for receiving his orders, and every one who partook of the chupatties was held pledged to obey the order whenever it might come, and whatever it might be. "What was the nature of the order in the present case?" he asked. The answer, accompanied by a suspicious smile, was, "We don't know yet."
2. Mr. Browne, in his very interesting and trustworthy work, quotes, as his authority for this, "Kaye's Life of Metcalfe;" but I have no recollection of the statement, and I have caused a diligent search to be made through the work, but with no success. I remember, however, to have read in the papers of Sir John Malcolm a statement to the effect that, at a time of political excitement, I believe just before the mutiny of the Coast Army in 1806, there had been a mysterious circulation of sugar. There was also, in 1818, a very perplexing distribution of cocoanuts in Central India; but it subsequently appeared to have been the result of a mere accident.— J. W. K.

Where they came from originally, it is impossible to say, but I believe Barrackpore was the starting-point, where large masses of mutinous Sepoys were congregated. The chupatties entered my district from the adjoining one of Shajehanpoor, a village watchman of that place giving to the watchman of the nearest Budaon village two of the cakes, with an injunction to make six fresh ones, retain two for his own, and give the others to the watchman of the next village, who would follow the same course, and continue the manufacture and distribution. I truly believe that the rural population of all classes, among whom these cakes spread, were as ignorant as I was myself of their real object; but it was clear they were a secret sign to be on the alert, and the minds of the people were through them kept watchful and excited. As soon as the disturbances broke out at Meerut and Delhi, the cakes explained themselves, and the people at once perceived what was expected of them."—*Personal Adventures during the Indian Rebellion in Rohilcund, Futtehghur, and Oude, by William Edwards, Esq., B.C.S., Judge of Benares, and late Magistrate and Collector of Budaon, in Rohilcund.*

THE BONE-DUST STORY

[The following translations from Native letters and papers show how general was the belief among the Sepoys in all parts of the country that the Government had mixed ground bones with the flour, and purposed to compel or to delude them to eat it:]

Translation of an Anonymous Petition sent, in March, 1857, to Major Matthews, commanding the 43rd Regiment at Barrackpore.

"The representation of the whole station is this, that we will not give up our religion. We serve for honour and religion; if we lose our religion, the Hindoo and Mahomedan religions will be destroyed. If we live, what shall we do? You are the masters of the country. The Lord Sahib has given orders, which he has received from the Company, to all commanding officers to destroy the religion of the country. We know this, as all things are being bought up by Government. The officers in the Salt Department mix up bones with the salt. The officer in charge of the ghee mixes up fat with it; this is well known. These are two matters. The third is this: that the Sahib in charge of the sugar burns up bones and mixes them in the syrup the sugar is made of; this is well known—all know it. The fourth is this: that in the country the Burra Sahibs have ordered the Rajahs, Thakurs, Zemindars, Mahajans, and Ryots, all to eat together, and English bread has been sent to them; this is well known. And this is another affair, that throughout the country the wives of respectable men, in fact, all classes of Hindoos, on becoming widows, are to be married again; this is known. Therefore we consider ourselves as killed. You all obey the orders of the Company, which we all know. But a king, or any other one who acts unjustly, does not remain.

"With reference to the Sepoys, they are your servants; but, to destroy their caste, a council assembled and decided to give them muskets and cartridges made up with greased paper to bite; this is also evident. We wish to represent this to the General, that we do not approve of the new musket and cartridge; the Sepoys cannot use them. You are the masters of the country; if you will give us all our discharge we will go away. The Native officers, Soubahdars, Jemadars, are all good in the whole Brigade, except two, whose faces are like pigs: the Soubahdar Major of the 70th Regiment, who is a Christian, and Thakur Misser, Jemadar of the 43rd Regiment Light Infantry.

"Whoever gets this letter must read it to the Major as it is written. If he is a Hindoo and does not, his crime will be equal to the slaughter of a lakh of cows; and if a Mussulman, as though he had eaten pig; and if a European, must read it to the Native officers, and if he does not, his going to church will be of no use, and be a crime. Thakur Misser has lost his religion. Chattrees are not to respect him. Brahmins are not to salute or bless him. If they do, their crime will be equal to the slaughter of a lakh of cows. He is the son of a Chumar. The Brahmin who hears this is not to feed him; if he does, his crime will be equal to the murdering of a lakh of Brahmins or cows.

"May this letter be given to Major Matthews. Any one who gets it is to give it, if he does not, and is a Hindoo, his crime will be as the slaughter of a lakh of cows; and if a Mussulman, as if he had eaten pig; and if he is an officer he must give it."

SOURCE: In John William Kaye, *The History of the Sepoy War in India, 1857–1858* (London: W. H. Allen, 1880–1888).

Act No. XIV. of 1857

Passed by the Legislative Council of India.
*(Received the assent of the Governor-General
on the 6th June, 1857.)*

An Act to make further provision for the trial and punishment of certain offences relating to the Army, and of offences against the State.

Whereas it is necessary to make further provision for the trial and punishment of persons who endeavour to excite mutiny and sedition among the Forces of the East India Company, and also for the trial of offences against the State: It is enacted as follows:

I. Whoever intentionally seduces or endeavours to seduce any Officer or Soldier in the service or pay of the East India Company from his allegiance to the British Government or his duty to the East India Company, or intentionally excites or stirs up, or endeavours to excite or stir up, any such Officer or Soldier, or any Officer or Soldier serving in any part of the British Territories in India in aid of the Troops of the British Government, to commit any act of mutiny or sedition; and whoever intentionally causes, or endeavours to cause, any other person to commit any such offence—shall be liable upon conviction to the punishment of death, or to the punishment of transportation for life, or of imprisonment with hard labour for any term not exceeding fourteen years; and shall forfeit all his property and effects of every description.

II. Whoever shall knowingly harbour or conceal any person who shall have been guilty of any offence mentioned in the preceding section, shall be liable to imprisonment, with or without hard labour, for any term not exceeding seven years, and shall also be liable to fine.

III. It shall be lawful for the Governor-General of India in Council, from time to time, by Order in Council, to empower every General or other Officer having the command of Troops in the Service of Her Majesty or of the East India Company, or any of such General or other Officers, to appoint General Courts-Martial for the trial of any person or persons charged with having committed an offence punishable by this Act or by Section I. or Section II. of Act XI. of 1857, and also to confirm and carry into effect any sentence of such Court-Martial.

IV. Any General Court-Martial, which may be appointed under the authority of this Act, shall be appointed by the Senior Officer on the spot, and shall consist of not less than five Commissioned Officers, the number to be fixed by the General or other Officer appointing the Court-Martial. The Order in Council may direct that a General Court-Martial to be appointed under the provisions of this Act shall consist wholly of European Commissioned Officers or wholly of Native Commissioned Officers, or partly of European Commissioned Officers, and partly of Native Commissioned Officers; and in such case the Officer appointing the Court-Martial shall determine whether the same shall consist wholly of European Officers or wholly of Native Officers, or partly of European Officers and partly of Native Officers.

v. Sentence of death or other punishment to which the offender is liable by law, may be given by such Court-Martial, if a majority of the members present concur in the sentence; and any such sentence may be confirmed by, and carried into effect immediately or otherwise by order of, the Officer by whom the Court-Martial shall have been appointed, or, in case of his absence, by the Senior Officer on the spot.

vi. It shall be lawful for the Governor-General in Council to countermand or alter any Order in Council which may be issued under the authority of this Act.

vii. It shall be lawful for the Governor-General in Council, or for the Executive Government of any Presidency or place, or for any person or persons whom the Governor-General in Council may authorise so to do, from time to time to issue a Commission for the trial of all or any persons or person charged with having committed within any district described in the Commission, whether such district shall or shall not have been proclaimed to be in a state of rebellion, any offence punishable by Sections I. and IIX. of Act XI. of 1857, or by this Act, or any other crime against the State, or murder, arson, robbery, or other heinous crime against person or property.

viii. The Commissioner or Commissioners authorised by any such Commission, may hold a Court in any part of the district mentioned in the Commission, and may there try any person for any of the said crimes committed within any part thereof, it being the intention of this Act that the district mentioned in the Commission shall, for the purpose of trial and punishment of any of the said offences, be deemed one district.

ix. Any Court held under the Commission shall have power, without the attendance or futwa of a Law Officer, or the assistance of Assessors, to pass upon every person convicted before the Court of any of the aforesaid crimes any sentence warranted by law for such crime; and the judgment of such Court shall be final and conclusive; and the said Court shall not be subordinate to the Sudder or other Court.

x. If a Commission be issued under the authority of this Act, any Magistrate or other Officer having power to commit for trial within the district described in the Commission may commit persons charged with any of the aforesaid crimes within such district for trial before a Court to be held under this Act.

XI. Nothing in this Act shall extend to the trial or punishment of any of Her Majesty's natural born subjects born in Europe, or of the children of such subjects.

XII. This Act shall not extend to the trial or punishment of any person for any offence for which he is liable to be tried by the Articles of War.

XIII. The word "Soldier" shall include every person subject to any Articles of War.

XIV. This Act shall continue in force for one year.

SOURCE: In John William Kaye, *The History of the Sepoy War in India, 1857–1858* (London: W. H. Allen, 1880–1888).

Summary Justice
CHARLES BALL

The opportunities afforded for recounting incidents of such bloodless ebullitions of disaffection as those exhibited at Jullundur and Phillour, are but rare throughout the wild progress of the Indian rebellion; the pages of its history being far oftener shaded by the sombre hues of a desolating and indiscriminating vengeance, than brightened by the lighter tints of human feeling, or the recognised usages of modern warfare.

In connection with the mutiny at Jullundur, the following graphic letter of an officer of the 60th regiment of native infantry, stationed at Umballah, will probably be deemed entitled to attention. We shall best preserve the interest of the narrative by following the text of the gallant writer, without interrupting it by comment. Writing on the 15th of July, from Umballah, he says

> —"One day I was hastily summoned to a council of war, and learnt that the troops at Jullundur had mutinied, consisting of three regiments, a cavalry corps, and two guns, and that they were marching on us; so, with my 100 men, I was ordered to defend the left flank of cantonments—not a pleasant duty, as I should be a mile away from the rest of the Europeans in the fort, and my men had been whispering ominously among themselves. The next afternoon some troops were perceived advancing; the dust was so great, that their numbers could not be ascertained. Directly

the alarm was sounded, every man took refuge in the church, while I rode away to my lines. However, I put on a good face, and being mounted on a capital horse of Colonel Seaton's, I soon reached the lines, and turned the men out. They were very eager, and talked amazingly of what they would do; but I thought very differently, and determined to fight on horseback. However, it turned out a false alarm, the troops being friends; but as they filed under the guns of the fort, a European artilleryman requested leave to give them some 'grape,' saying, 'Sure they are niggers.' All that night I patrolled by myself, being more afraid of my own sentries than any enemy; however, like all nights, it at last came to an end; and I felt like another man when daylight came and no enemy; for I do not think I am maligning my men when I say, that had an enemy appeared, they would have shot me and joined the rebels. That morning information was received, that General Johnstone, from Jullundur, was pursuing them, and that the 61st native infantry had separated, and was sneaking along the foot of the hills by by-roads, and thus trying to get to Delhi. Two companies of Europeans were immediately ordered in carts to intercept them in the Malka-road, and I volunteered to go with them, and was appointed aide-de-camp and quartermaster to the force. I had previously volunteered for Delhi, for a volunteer troop of cavalry and a volunteer troop of infantry, and had been invariably refused. We did not start till 1 P.M., a wind blowing as hot as the breath from a furnace. There were no carts for us, and we had to ride. The officer commanding got struck by the sun, and two others fell sick, so at last I was left by myself. We did not halt all day; and at about 11 P.M., my pony having outstepped the carts, I was about a mile ahead, and passing through a nasty brushwood, and thinking what a place it would be for a surprise, when a volley of musketry came on one side. I pulled up, clutched that invaluable weapon 'Colt,' and listened. The night was as dark as ink, and all quiet and still again. I listened for the carts, but could not hear them, and was surprised to find how I had unconsciously wandered away from them. Just then I faintly heard the bugle sounding the 'assembly,' followed by the 'double:' putting spurs to my 'tat' I flew back, and found that the enemy were close by, and we were going to foot it after them. A party was put on some elephants and sent ahead, but those on foot declared they would get on first, and set off at about five miles an hour. I got off my elephant and fell-in with them, and we have a hottish walk, beating the elephants hollow. I was afterwards called out, and sent on ahead to where the commissioner was to give orders; so I galloped off, and found the said gentleman in an unpleasant state of fear, and so disordered in mind that he could give no orders, except that Mr. Forsyth (civilian) had come upon the rebels, and that his men had all bolted, and Forsyth had taken refuge in a walled town. I took the liberty of ordering dinner for six, sharp, and carried back this intelligence, and strongly advised pushing on eight miles more to relieve Forsyth. We all arrived at the bungalow, and then the commissioner kept saying that we were too late by three hours. So we ate our dinner at 1 A.M., and, putting my saddle for a pillow, I turned-in on the floor. In about an hour I was awoke, and told we were going on to relieve Forsyth; so we all got up, weary and tired, having had just enough sleep to make us wish for more. We reached Forsyth, and heard we were just too late again; but he had carriage for fifty men, he said, if we were game to pursue, and he offered fifty rupees for every head brought in; so of course all volunteered, but only fifty were chosen, and the officers drew lots for it. The commanding officer told me to do as I liked, so I volunteered and attached myself to Forsyth as deputy-assistant, and found him a jolly companion, and a resolute, energetic man. He mounted me on his elephant, and, the men being all likewise mounted, we started at 6 A.M. after the rebels. The heat was fearful that day, and the road nothing more than a track over dazzling, drifting sand. After marching for two hours, a temporary halt for water was called, and I was thinking how lucky I was to have a flask of brandy with me, when Forsyth offered me claret. I was delighted of course to find myself attached to one who marched with claret. We did not halt again till 12 P.M., and then found the rebels still ahead, but very close.

"Forsyth then asked me to make a 'dour' twenty miles on horseback, and try to reach a police-station before the rebels, and check them till the Europeans could arrive. As I had no good horse, he lent me a government artillery horse, as it was imperatively necessary to be well mounted in case of having to bolt. He rode a beautiful Arab, and, buckling on swords and pistols, and slinging our rifles on our backs, away we went as hard as we could, with an escort of ten mounted natives. We were meeting the wind, and the heat was insufferable; the wind dried me up, and blistered my face almost to suffocation; still, 'forward' we cried, and in a state of mad excitement we hammered along, our poor horses suffering greatly, mine especially; however, I never mounted a gamer animal; he would not allow the Arab to be one inch ahead of him. The escort had fallen to the rear, and were nowhere. Still we flew along, and at least reached a fort, and, summoning up the head man, demanded intelligence. He lied to us, and tried to break our scent, so he was hung there and then, and another fined 1,000 rupees. After having been so merciful we started afresh, and actually rode right through the 61st native infantry, who were eating their dinners, when a cry arose of 'Two Europeans!' They immediately fled to the jungle. We, observing places for cooking, and fires burning, thought they must be just ahead, and dashed forwards with renewed speed. I never could understand why they spared us, except that they were chased off their legs, and had lost all pluck and heart. Just beyond we came to a nullah, with steep banks. We charged it abreast, without looking to see what it was, and took it exactly together; but my horse had not the blood of the Arab, and was done. He reached the other side, but his hind legs slipped back, and over he went to the bottom. I got bruised from the lock of the rifle entering my back; but it was softish ground, so I scrambled up and soon remounted; but the horse was nearly done for; still he gallantly held out for five miles more, when we entered the police-station, and then he lay down and died. I got some rice to eat, almost the first thing I had tasted since I left Umballah. We laid down and got a bit of rest, all owing to my poor horse; for if he had not failed, we should have ridden on and destroyed a bridge over the Jumna. The detachment soon arrived, and we let them rest a little, seeing nothing of any rebels. After our dinner, Forsyth and I were once more in the saddle, and ready to proceed. I was on my white pony. No mounted men would come with us unless we promised to ride like men in their senses. As it was pitch dark, we promised, and off we went for fifteen miles more. We went very quietly at first, Forsyth's Arab as fresh as if he had not been out of the stable for a month. We soon increased our speed, and at last were in a sharp canter, to the horror of the men behind. One man was very troublesome, and would persist in keeping close by me, making my pony very fidgety and warlikely inclined; so, at last, I paid him out beautifully, though quite by accident. We came suddenly on a great fissure across the road. It was too late to stop, so I rode at it, and reached the other side all right. The native behind me did not see it, and rode right into it. I heard a heavy fall and cry of 'I'm killed!' but we only laughed, and rode on and saw no more of the escort. Just before we arrived at the little station we rode through a clump of trees, and a low bough caught Forsyth, who was thrown. I caught his horse, and we rode quietly on, and got in just in time to warn Plowden (civil servant.) The next morning, the fall, combined with fatigue and heat, prostrated Forsyth, and, not willing to leave him in the jungle, I stayed with him, and returned to Umballah the next night, having been out three days, two of which, night and day, had been incessant marching; but the sun had no effect upon me, and no one stood it better, if so well, as I did. I only changed the skin on my face and hands. Perhaps the excitement is good for me; but certainly it seems to me to be the coolest hot weather altogether that I have experienced. On my return, I heard the news of the mutiny of our regiment. They are all gone! The men that we so trusted; my own men, with whom I have shot, played cricket, jumped, and entered into all their sports, and treated them kindly. They mutinied at Bhotuck. It was a hard trial their being sent there, only three marches from Delhi. While there they received hundreds of letters from the rebels to come over to them. So, on the 11th of June, they rushed on the drummers. The officers were collected in the mess-tent when the regiment came up, fired a volley through it, miraculously hitting no one, and then off they went. The officers rushed out, got on their horses, and bolted to Delhi to join the camp. Shebbeare refused to leave them at first, hoping to bring them round again, and trusted to his great popularity to get off; but their looks were so murderous that he soon walked off, and, when told by them to quicken his pace, told them that he would not put himself out for any of them. They then looted the mess, smashed all the messplate, carried off all our silver of every description, plundered the wine, took the treasure chest, and, after hanging a policeman who had hid their camels, they marched for Delhi. But the officers arrived first, and gave information, and all the guns were laid for the gate by which they would enter; so as they approached they were awfully cut up, and the 9th lancers swept down upon them, so that the left wing was annihilated. The next day the rebels made a fierce attack upon the camp, and the 60th were told to lead, and were cut up almost to a man. Miraculous to say, this is the only station that has escaped a massacre, and it was a touch-and-go here; few knew their danger until it was over; even now we dare not go to church. Sunday here is a day when revolvers and two-barrelled guns are by our sides. What has kept us afloat so long is the constant passing of Europeans, and the rajah of Putteala, who is for us at present; but if he were to go we should have to fight our way either to Delhi or Loodiana—the latter is only six marches, and then we can drop down the Sutlej to Mooltan; but I hope it will not come to that; for fancy the ladies, who have all been ordered up to the hills! some thousands of them.

"I have got into the habit of sleeping so lightly, that a cat walking across the room would wake me. Under my pillow is a revolver and a suit of mud-coloured clothes, in which I am at night nearly invisible; my sword by the bed, and rifle and gun in the corner; so I think I could manage a few of them if they came. All I want now is a good horse, and then I am game for anything. *** We have had that terrible scourge the cholera. It has been raging here with frightful violence for two months; but, thank God, has now left us without harming the 'sahibs.' It seemed a judgment on the natives. They were reeling about and falling dead in the streets, and no one to remove them. Now it is all over. It is the only time we have looked on it as an 'ally,' though it has carried off many soldiers, two native officers, and six policemen, who were guarding prisoners. All fell dead at the same place. As one dropped another stepped forward and took his place, and so on the whole lot. We have just disarmed the natives here, and got three cartloads of weapons from them. I have applied for leave of absence for all the men left here under my command. If granted, I shall be free and able to join my officers in the camp. I am looking forward to my furlough, or rather sick certificate, or something—sick, indeed, of India and its army of murderers. This dâk is going round by Mooltan, Kurrachee, and back to Bombay. Three sepoys to be executed this evening. We have blown away a great number from guns; in fact, we show them every week what they will get."

The hand of retributive justice was by this time uplifted, and the sword ready to fall upon the guilty perpetrators of unprovoked and hitherto unparalleled crimes; and it was at Ferozepore and Peshawur that the presence of the avenger was first impressively manifested to the actors and abettors of a career of treason and murder. At the former place, it will be remembered, the men of the 45th regiment of native infantry had broken into revolt, and attacked the Magazine fort during the morning of the 13th of May. They were, however, repulsed by a detachment of her majesty's 61st regiment, and finally driven out of the cantonment; but not before they had committed great depredation, and wantonly destroyed much property of the Europeans at the station. Some of the mutineers were taken prisoners; and as an example was necessary, to deter the other troops from following their example, a number of them were tried by court-martial, and sentenced to death.

On the morning of the 13th of June, exactly one month from the mutinous outbreak by which the destruction of the whole European community at Ferozepore was to have been accomplished, a huge gallows was erected at the south-east end of the Suddur Bazaar, and north of the Old Fort, the side at which the rebels had effected an entry. All the available troops, and persons belonging to public departments at the station, were collected to witness the scene. On three sides of the area, of which the gallows formed the centre, the troops were stationed in the following order:—On the east a squadron of the 10th native light cavalry, the remnant of the disbanded 37th regiment of native infantry, and some persons belonging to the commissariat and magazine departments: on the south, her majesty's 61st regiment and the artillery, with twelve guns loaded and portfires lighted: and, on the west, the city and cantonment armed police. When the hour arrived for the execution of the sentence, twenty-four of the mutineers, wearing irons, were brought into the centre of the area by a guard of the 61st regiment, one of them being carried in a dhooly, in consequence of a wound received by him in the attack upon the fort. Lieutenant Hoggan, adjutant of the 61st, then, by order of the brigadier, read aloud the proceedings and sentence of the court-martial, and, at its close, announced to the condemned, that if any among them would become queen's evidence, the brigadier would reprieve them. The sight of the preparations for an otherwise inevitable punishment, had an instantaneous effect upon twelve of the miserable wretches, who declared their readiness to inform against the ringleaders of the movement, and also to divulge the secret as to the origin and object of the revolt. These men were immediately marched to the rear of the artillery, from whence they were compelled to witness the fate of their more inflexible comrades. Of the latter, two were then led, or rather taken to the gallows, one of them being the wounded man. Each of them ascended the ladder with a firm step, and without betraying the slightest indication of terror at the fate they had provoked. On gaining the platform, they coolly adjusted the ropes with their own hands in silence; their arms were then pinioned, and their eyes bandaged, and in another second they were suspended in the air. With one, death appeared to be instantaneous; but the wounded culprit struggled for some time, as the knot had slipped from its position, and the hangman had to readjust it, and again launch him from the platform before his death was accomplished.

As soon as this, the first act of the tragedy, had been performed, the remaining ten prisoners were marched up to the guns, and their irons were struck off, previous to their being bound to the muzzles of the terrible implements of destruction. While being freed from their shackles, some of them appealed to the brigadier for mercy, exclaiming, "Do not sacrifice the innocent for the guilty!" Two others indignantly cried out to these, "Hold your tongues!—die like men, not cowards! You defended your religion, why then do you crave your lives? Sahibs!—they are not sahibs, they are dogs!" Others upbraided the commanding officer, saying, "He released the havildar-major, who was chief of the rebels." By this time the process of fastening them to the guns had been completed. The commandant then gave the word, "Ready—Fire!"—and instantaneously the ten miserable wretches were scattered in bloody fragments over the ground.

As the smoke cleared away from the horrible scene, the view to the spectators was overpowering: many of the firmest nerved were shaken by a glance at the carnage that lay around and before them. The native lookers-on—and they were numerous—appeared awe-stricken, and, according to the description of one of the officers, "not only trembled like aspen-leaves, but their colour actually changed into unnatural hues." Unfortunately, this execution was attended by a series of accidents, that rendered it painfully impressive upon others than those for whose just punishment it was required.

In the first place, precaution had not been taken to remove the sponge and loadmen from their proper station near the muzzle of the guns; and the consequence was, that they were bespattered with blood, and bruised by the scattered limbs of the prisoners—one man in particular being struck down by a heavy fragment of one of the mutilated bodies, and severely injured by the contusion. The next mishap was yet more disastrous in its consequences. An order had been given that the guns should be loaded with blank cartridge only; but, by oversight or neglect, one or two of them were charged with grapeshot. In the direction in which the guns were pointed, a number of spectators, supposed to be out of the range of blank cartridge, had assembled, and amongst them the grapeshot was scattered with distressing effect. Five were carried off the ground, severely, if not dangerously, wounded; two others were shot through the thigh, and three more in various parts. All were promptly conveyed to the station hospital; and of some, the limbs had to suffer amputation.

The execution of these mutineers was but an instalment of the just vengeance that the crimes of their race had provoked. In the evening of the same day, two ruffians, who had taken advantage of the disturbed state of the district to commit depredations upon the roads, were summarily tried, convicted, and hung at the gaol: from their capture to their death, three hours had not elapsed! On the 14th of June, the trials of the deserters from the 16th and 49th native regiments were proceeded with, and the various sentences accorded to them were instantly carried into execution. Some mitigating circumstances in the conduct of the men of the 57th regiment, rendered a sentence of imprisonment sufficient, in their case, to satisfy the requirements of justice.

Peshawur.—At this place also, although as yet preserved from the ferocious outrages of a sepoy revolt, there were sufficient reasons, about the beginning of June, for apprehending that the immunity from danger would not be of long continuance. It had, by some means, been made known to the officer in command of the station, that a total massacre of the Europeans was contemplated, and that its execution had been fixed for the 23rd of May; but, for some reason not explained, had been deferred. With a conviction of the perfect truth of this information, it would have been perfectly suicidal to have allowed the troops implicated in the frightful project to retain possession of their arms, if ever they were allowed to be at liberty; but the disarming of four regiments was not a feat to be undertaken without some danger of failure, or without precautions for neutralising its effect, should the failure actually occur. At the time this necessary step was resorted to, the position of the 2,000 Europeans at this station was as follows:—

The native force in cantonments at Peshawur consisted of the 21st, 24th, 27th, 51st, and 64th regiments of Bengal native infantry, and the 5th light cavalry. The cantonment in which this host was quartered, was filled to repletion with vagabonds and camp-followers of the vilest description. The city itself was thronged with a disaffected rabble, ripe for any atrocity; and in a chain of forts surrounding the station, were four other native regiments, all animated by the same spirit of hostility to the Europeans, and only waiting the signal to concentrate upon their prey, and carry out the sanguinary purpose of the whole body. Beyond the line of forts the station was again encircled by hills, swarming with Mohammedan fanatics, who thirsted for the blood of the Christians, and were known to be in communication with the embryo mutineers; and to add to the difficulty of the European residents, the country people, to whom the intended rising of the 22nd of May was well known, had refused to furnish supplies of provisions; and, being in daily expectation of the destruction of the Feringhees, no longer cared to have any intercourse with them, or to minister to their wants. It was obvious this state of existence could not be endured long after its reality had become apparent; and, by the judicious and energetic measures adopted, the evil was remedied, and the cause of disquietude removed. It yet, however, remained to punish such of the guilty contemplators of a wholesale massacre, as, by their conduct, had put themselves beyond the pale of forgiveness.

At the time the regiments in Peshawur were deprived of their arms without offering resistance, the men of the 56th native infantry, occupying the adjacent fort of Murdan, were also required to surrender their arms; and the result was a furious mutinous outbreak, during which a reckless disregard of life and property was as usual exhibited. Upon the arrival of Colonel Nicholson with a sufficient force of Europeans to compel obedience, it was found, that in addition to other calamities produced by the misconduct of the regiment, its commanding officer, Colonel Spottiswoode, had, in a paroxysm of frenzy and disgust, terminated a life of honour by an act of suicide. The rebels had the audacity to offer battle to the men with Colonel Nicholson, and the offer was eagerly accepted to their cost; for after the first discharge of musketry, their hearts failed them, and they sought to escape in every direction. This, however, could not be permitted; 150 of them were shot down in the momentary contest; others were made prisoners; and of these, several were tried by drumhead court-martial as soon as the contest had ceased, and were at once consigned to the death they merited. Some few of the mutineers fled before their pursuers into the hills, and were dispatched by the hill-men for the sake of a reward of ten rupees per head.

Of the prisoners taken during this affair, it became of course requisite, for the better instruction of the inhabitants of Peshawur and the adjacent district, that an example should be made; and, like that at Ferozepore, it was a terrible one. On the 11th of June, forty of the sanguinary demons that would have revelled in the hearts' blood of their too long confiding friends, were marched to the parade-ground of the cantonment at Peshawur, where a square of troops had been formed, with ten guns loaded and pointed outward. The usual formalities were observed as to the proceedings of the court-martial, the sentence, &c., and then ten of the miscreants were bound to the guns, and, at a signal, the horrible salvo was fired. Without clearing away the mutilated and shattered fragments that lay around, the guns were again prepared—a second ten were bound—and again a shower of blood and human fragments marred the light of the sun. Twice more was this awful scene repeated; and twice again was retributive justice exhibited in its most fearful aspect. In one of the sections of ten that were thus to be destroyed, there were two prisoners who, from terror or, it might have been, some yet lingering hope of mercy, refused to be bound to the guns, and, in their desperation, struggled hard with the men appointed to place them before the engines of destruction. With this insane conduct there could be but one way of dealing; and the painful scene, thus aggravated by unavailing resistance, was terminated by throwing the two men upon the ground, and discharging the contents of two muskets through their heads. The appalling business of the morning was then proceeded with; and at its close, such of the native troops as were present, were marched round the field of slaughter, and dismissed to their lines, thoroughly, if not usefully, impressed with the importance of the terrible lesson they had received. The result of this decisive conduct on the part of the commandant, Colonel Edwardes, C.B., was quickly apparent in the altered demeanour of the native inhabitants and the people of the valley, who now hastened to renew a friendly intercourse with the Europeans, and evinced wonderful activity in furnishing supplies of all kinds of necessaries almost gratuitously, that a few days previous they would not produce for any amount of money, or, in short, for any consideration whatever, if they were required by the Europeans, or by those connected with them.

Of the terrible exhibition thus briefly described, the following account is rendered in a letter from Peshawur, which appeared in *Blackwood's Magazine* for November, 1857:—

"It was an awfully imposing scene. All the troops, European and native, armed and disarmed, loyal and disaffected, were drawn up on parade, forming three sides of a square; and drawn up very carefully, you may be sure, so that any attempt on the part of the disaffected to rescue the doomed prisoners would have been easily checked. Forming the fourth side of the square, were drawn up the guns (9-pounders), ten in number, which were to be used for the execution. The prisoners, under a strong European guard, were then marched into the square, their crimes and sentences read aloud to them, and at the head of each regiment; they were then marched round the square, and up to the guns. The first ten were picked out, their eyes were bandaged, and they were bound to the guns—their backs leaning against the muzzles, and their arms fastened to the wheels. The portfires were lighted, and at a signal from the artillery-major, the guns were fired. It was a horrid sight that then met the eye; a regular shower of human fragments of heads, of arms, of legs, appeared in the air through the smoke; and when that cleared away, these fragments lying on the ground—fragments of Hindoos and fragments of Mussulmans, all mixed together—were all that remained of those ten mutineers. Three times more was this scene repeated; but so great is the disgust we all feel for the atrocities committed by the rebels, that we had no room in our hearts for any feeling of pity; perfect callousness was depicted on every European's face; a look of grim satisfaction could even be seen in the countenances of the gunners serving the guns. But far different was the effect on the native portion of the spectators; their black faces grew ghastly pale as they gazed breathlessly at the awful spectacle. You must know that this is nearly the only form in which death has any terrors for a native. If he is hung, or shot by musketry, he knows that his friends or relatives will be allowed to claim his body, and will give him the funeral rites required by his religion; if a Hindoo, that his body will be burned with all due ceremonies; and if a Mussulman, that his remains will be decently interred, as directed in the Koran. But if sentenced to death in this form, he knows that his body will be blown into a thousand pieces, and that it will be altogether impossible for his relatives, however devoted to him, to be sure of picking up all the fragments of his own particular body; and the thought that perhaps a limb of some one of a different religion to himself might possibly be burned or buried with the remainder of his own body, is agony to him. But notwithstanding this, it was impossible for the mutineers' direst hater not to feel some degree of admiration for the way in which they met their deaths. Nothing in their lives became them like the leaving of them. Of the whole forty, only two showed any signs of fear; and they were bitterly reproached by the others for so disgracing their race. They certainly died like men. After the first ten had been disposed of, the next batch, who had been looking on all the time, walked up to the guns quite calmly and unfalteringly, and allowed themselves to be blindfolded and tied up without moving a muscle, or showing the slightest signs of fear, or even concern. Whence had these men this strength? Their religion, bad as it may be and is, in all other points, at least befriends them well at the hour of death; it teaches them well that great and useful lesson, how to die."

The beneficial effect of the plan adopted at Peshawur for the instruction of the disaffected, was not confined to the immediate locality, or to the population around it, as may be inferred from a communication of Colonel Edwardes, dated from that place between the 21st of June and the 6th of July, in which the gallant officer thus expresses his view of the state of local affairs at that period:—

"This post, so far from being more arduous in future, will be more secure. Events here have taken a wonderful turn. During peace, Peshawur was an incessant anxiety. Now it is the strongest point in India. We have struck two great blows—we have disarmed our own troops, and raised levies of all the people of the country. The troops are confounded; they calculated on being backed by the people. The people are delighted, and a better feeling has sprung up between them and us in this enlistment than has ever been obtained before. I have also called on my old country, the Deragât, and it is quite delightful to see how the call is answered. Two thousand horsemen, formerly in my army at Mooltan, are now moving on different points, according to order, to help us in this difficulty; and every post brings me remonstrances from chiefs as to why they have been forgotten. What fault have they committed that they are not sent for? This is really gratifying. It is the heart of a people. It does one good all through. The Peshawurees had often heard that I had been grateful in getting rewards for my followers after the Mooltan war; but they were not prepared to see such a demonstration from the other end of the Soolimanee mountains. It excites their better feelings, and will do them good too. All yesterday I was busy fitting out 700 horse and foot levies (Mooltanee) to reinforce Nicholson at Jullundur. How all the liberality shown to these Mooltanese after the war of 1848—'49 is now repaid, in the alacrity with which they rush to our side again to help us! They are now invaluable, and so glad to see me again; it is quite a pleasure in the midst of this howling wilderness."

Rhonee: About the time the stern but imperatively called-for measures we have recorded were progressing in one division of the great presidency of Bengal, ample grounds for the introduction of somewhat similar correction were daily obtruded upon the attention of government in other directions. At Rhonee (Deoghur), a small station in the Sonthal district, garrisoned by a company of the 32nd regiment of native infantry, and a portion of the 5th irregular cavalry (the whole under the command of Major Macdonald, of the latter corps), a sudden and murderous attack was made, in the evening of the 12th of June, upon three of the officers at the station, which resulted in the death of one, and the severe and dangerous mutilation of the others, under the following extraordinary circumstances:—

On the evening mentioned, the three officers—namely, Major Macdonald, Lieutenant Sir Norman Leslie, and assistant-surgeon Grant, also of the 5th irregulars—were sitting together in the verandah of the major's house. The night was dark and cloudy, and the moon was not yet up, when, shortly before nine o'clock, as Dr. Grant rose from his seat, and was turning to enter the house, his attention was attracted by hasty footsteps. He had scarcely time to exclaim, "Who can these fellows be?" when, on the instant, three men, in the undress of troopers, rushed into the verandah with their swords drawn, and furiously attacked the three unarmed men. The assassin who struck Sir Norman Leslie, threw such vigour into his blow, that the unfortunate gentleman was cut down from the shoulder to the chest; another aimed at the head of the major, whose scalp was completely taken off; and the third selected for his victim Dr. Grant, whom he severely wounded in the arm and hip. The lieutenant, deprived of all power by the magnitude of the injury, fell from his chair to linger a short time and die. Major Macdonald seized the chair on which he had been seated, and used it to defend himself against successive attacks of the murderers, one of whom he struck a blow that induced him to retreat from the place: the miscreant was quickly followed by his companions; and the major and Dr. Grant made their way, streaming with blood, into the house, and gave an alarm. The whole affair was so sudden, and so entirely unexpected, that, at the moment, pursuit of the assassins was unthought of.

Upon recovering from the surprise occasioned by the attack, the major and Dr. Grant went back to the verandah, to see after Lieutenant Leslie, whose condition is thus described by his gallant commander:—

> "We found poor Leslie stretched on the ground, in a dying state. He must have received his death-blow the first cut, and have fallen forward on his face, for he was cut clean through his back into his chest, and breathing through the wound in the lungs; also many cuts on the head: he was quite sensible, and said, as I bent over him, 'Oh, Macdonald, it is very hard to die in this manner!'—and added, 'My poor wife and children! what will become of them?' I told him he had only a few minutes to live, and to make his peace with God, and that all should be done for his poor wife and family that could be done. Under such fearful circumstances he then applied himself to make his peace with God, poor fellow! and breathed his last in about half-an-hour afterwards."

The surprise and consternation occasioned by this sanguinary attack was so great, that some time elapsed before the servants of the house could be prevailed upon to go to the lines (a short distance from the house) and alarm the soldiers. To the credit of the latter, the major states that, as soon as the men were acquainted with the cowardly transaction, every man off duty crowded round his bungalow, all evincing sympathy, and expressing horror and detestation of the murderous act that had perilled the life of their commandant, and had actually deprived another officer of existence.

Any attempt to trace or pursue the ruffians by whom the savage attack had been perpetrated, was now useless. Some of the troopers, nevertheless, rode off to Deoghur, about two miles from Rhonee, where they found everything perfectly quiet. A detachment of the 32nd regiment (of which the headquarters were established at Deoghur) were immediately marched over for the protection of the major and his station; but the former at once sent them back, as he considered the hundred men he already had in the lines, quite sufficient for that purpose; and the men themselves declared they were more than a match for any odds that might appear, composed of such miscreants.

Neither Major Macdonald or Dr. Grant were dangerously, although badly wounded. One of the blows aimed at the major took off his scalp, which was found next morning near the scene of outrage. For a short time, it was supposed the three assassins were some of the disbanded sepoys who were prowling about the district, and trying to instil their mischievous doctrines into the Sonthals; the object being to induce the troops to join them by first removing the obstacles in the way of revolt, presented by the watchfulness of the European officers, who were, therefore, to be murdered out of the way.

On the 14th of June, an official communication referring to this lamentable affair, was made to the adjutant-general by Captain Watson, second in command of the 5th irregular cavalry. In this report, the incidents of the murderous attack are related; and the detail thus proceeds:—"Major Macdonald had his head cut open and was insensible when the express was dispatched to me, four hours after the occurrence; the assistant-surgeon received two cuts, one on the arm and one on the leg; and Lieutenant Sir Norman Leslie was cut down from both shoulders to the waist, and expired in about half-an-hour. A guard was at the major's quarters; but the sentry says he saw nothing of the men, who escaped immediately after attacking the officers. The Woordie major of the regiment assembled all the men who were present, and examined their swords, which were perfectly clean. As far as I can judge, none of the men seem to have been implicated in any way."

On the 15th, Captain Watson forwarded to the adjutant-general a copy of a letter sent him on the 13th by Major Macdonald, describing the murderous affair thus:—

"I am as fairly and neatly scalped as any Red Indian could do it. Grant got a brace of ugly cuts, but Leslie was literally cut to ribbons; he lived half-an-hour, poor fellow, and quietly died. We were sitting in front of my house, as usual, at 8 P.M., taking our tea, when three men rushed quickly upon us, and dealt us each a crack. I was scalped; Grant cut on the elbow; Leslie, sitting in his easy chair, appeared to fall at the first blow. I got three cracks on the head in succession before I knew I was attacked. I then seized my chair by the arms, and defended myself successfully from two of them on me at once; I guarded and struck the best I could, and, at last, Grant and self drove the cowards off the field. God only knows who they were and where they came from, but they were practised swordsmen. Leslie was buried with military honours, and had the burial service read over him at Deoghur, in Ronald's garden. This is against my poor head writing; but you will be anxious to know how matters really were. I expect to be in high fever to-morrow. I have got a bad gash into the skull, besides being scalped. Grant and I have had the most miraculous escape from instant death. The men of the regiment are most attentive, and would sit up all last night round us. My poor head is aching, so I can write no more."—Captain Watson adds to this communication, that he has received a report of the occurrence from the civil commissioner of the district, and that he has great satisfaction in repeating the opinion of the latter official, "that the men of the 5th irregular cavalry are loyal, and not in the smallest degree suspected."

The mystery, however, that darkness had thrown around the perpetrators of the savage act, was not of long endurance. On the 15th, it was discovered that three troopers of the major's own regiment were the assassins by whom Sir Norman Leslie was foully murdered. The means by which they were detected, or the motives upon which they acted, are not stated; but summary justice was awarded the miscreants by drum-head court-martial on the 16th, and they were immediately hung in the presence of their comrades, within view of the scene of their butchery, and under the eyes of their surviving victims. Major Macdonald, whose good spirits, like his high courage, appear to have been indomitable, wrote on the same day to Captain Watson thus:—

> "I received your kind note as I was sitting in my verandah, seeing the last struggles of our friends (the three assassins.) To tell you the truth, when we were attacked, I felt convinced that our own men did the deed, and I told the Woordie major so; but Grant thought otherwise, and I was only too glad to think our own men could not have had a hand in it. Yesterday evening two of the fellows were found with bloody clothes; and the third, who lived with a sick sowar, confessed he had done for Leslie; and this was evidence enough. I had them in irons in a crack, held a drum-head court-martial, and convicted and sentenced them to be hanged this morning. I took on my own shoulders the responsibility of hanging them first and asking leave to do so afterwards. One of the fellows was of very high caste and influence; and this man I determined to treat with the greatest ignominy by getting the lowest caste man to hang him. To tell you the truth, I never for a moment expected to leave the hanging scene alive; but I was determined to do my duty, and well knew the effect that pluck and decision had on the natives. The regiment was drawn out: wounded cruelly as I was, I had to see everything done myself, even to the adjusting the ropes; and saw them looped to run easy. Two of the culprits were paralysed with fear and astonishment, never dreaming that I should dare to hang them without an order from government. The third said he would not be hanged, and called on the prophet and on his comrades to rescue him. This was an awful moment; an instant's hesitation on my part, and probably I should have had a dozen of balls through me; so I seized a pistol, clapped it to the man's ear, and said, with a look there was no mistake about, 'Another word out of your mouth, and your brains shall be scattered on the ground.' He trembled and held his tongue. The elephant came up; he was put on his back, the rope adjusted, the elephant moved, and he was left dangling. I then had the others up, and off in the same way; and after some time, when I had dismissed the men of the

regiment to their lines, and still found my head on my shoulders, I really could scarcely believe it. However, it is now all over. I have had a sad time of it, and but little able to go through such scenes, for I am very badly wounded; but, thank God, my spirits and pluck never left me for a moment. Grant says I am playing the dickey with my head, with all this work and bother. Certainly not! any strange officer with the men. I'd rather stay and die here first. There will be no more such scenes, depend upon it. You must make the report to army head-quarters. I think I must come in for fever. Thanks be to God for such a miraculous escape, and enabling me to go through all I have done. When you see my poor old head, you will wonder how I could hold it up at all. I have preserved my scalp in spirits of wine; such a jolly specimen!—I had hopes our men had no hand in it; but, after all, two were only recruits."

A correspondent of the *Hurkaru*, writing upon the subject of the execution, says—

"When these scoundrels were being executed, they gave utterance to expressions that were most mutinous in their character. One of them cried, 'Which of you, my brethren, have the courage to rescue me from the hands of these dogs!' But the brave old major, who, despite his wounds, was sitting in his chair with his pistol in his hand, instantly and sternly exclaimed, as he pointed his weapon at the miserable assassin, 'One word more, and I will fire.' This decisive act settled the affair; not a voice was heard, and the execution proceeded without any further effort to interrupt it."

Throughout this extraordinary business, nothing appeared at the time upon which to found suspicion that it was in any manner connected with the object for which the mutineers of the Bengal army were in a state of general revolt; yet as, within two months of the occurrence, the sowars of the 5th irregular cavalry (to which regiment the assassins belonged) broke into mutiny at Bhaugulpore, Deoghur, Rhonee, and their other stations, it is more than probable, that the murderous attack upon their commanding officer and adjutant, was only part of a more comprehensive design, by which the lives of all the European officers would have been jeopardised, but which was happily frustrated by the impetuosity and subsequent cowardice of the miscreants employed to strike the first blow. At all events, the conduct of the regiment was so unexceptionable at the time, that the confidence of Major Macdonald in its loyalty was unshaken; and to mark his sense of their soldierlike behaviour, three of the non-commissioned officers were promoted, and rewarded with handsome gratuities; while, upon his recommendation, the Woordie major was presented by government with a handsome sword and belt, as a token of its approbation. The head-quarters of the regiment was then removed from Rhonee to Bhaugulpore, where it remained quietly until the period of its mutiny and desertion in the following August.

SOURCE: Chapter 21 in *The History of the Indian Mutiny*, vol. 1 (London: The London Printing and Publishing Co., Ltd., 1858–1859).

Selected Correspondence of Queen Victoria

27 June 1857
To Palmerston

The Queen has just received Lord Palmerston's letter and is likewise much alarmed at the news from India.[1] She has for some time been very apprehensive of the state of affairs in the army there, and her fears are now fully realised. She trusts that Lord Palmerston and Lord Panmure will consult with the Duke of Cambridge [the Commander-in-Chief] without delay as to what measures should be taken to meet this great danger and that no time will be lost in carrying them out.

Buckingham Palace, 29 June 1857
Queen Victoria to Lord Panmure

The Queen has to acknowledge the receipt of Lord Panmure's letter of yesterday. She had long been of opinion that reinforcements waiting to go to India ought not to be delayed. The moment is certainly a very critical one, and the additional reinforcements now proposed will be much wanted. The Queen entirely agrees with Lord Panmure that it will be good policy to oblige the East India Company to keep permanently a larger portion of the Royal Army in India than heretofore. The Empire has nearly doubled itself within the last twenty years, and the Queen's troops have been kept at the old establishment. They are the body on whom the maintenance of that Empire depends, and the Company ought not to sacrifice the highest interests to love of patronage. The Queen hopes that the new reinforcements will be sent out in their Brigade organisation, and not as detached regiments; good Com-

---

1. In May 1857 sepoys in the Bengal army of the East India Company had mutinied at Meerut and had seized Delhi and other nearby towns; and by the middle of June the revolt had spread to the Ganges valley.

"Justice." In *Punch* 33 (12 September 1857): 109.

manding Officers knowing their troops will be of the highest importance next to the troops themselves.

The Queen must ask that the troops by whom we shall be diminished at home by the transfer of so many regiments to the Company should be forthwith replaced by an increase of the establishment up to the number voted by Parliament, and for which the estimates have been taken, else we denude ourselves altogether to a degree dangerous to our own safety at home, and incapable of meeting a sudden emergency, which, as the present example shows, may come upon us at any moment. If we had not reduced in such a hurry this spring, we should now have all the men wanted!

The Queen wishes Lord Panmure to communicate this letter to Lord Palmerston. The accounts in today's papers from India are most distressing.

5 July 1857
To Lady Canning, wife of the Governor-General
of India and a Former Lady-in-Waiting

I had long intended writing . . . when I received your last of 19th May with all the sad and alarming news of the insurrection at Meerut and Delhi. It is an anxious moment but we have great confidence in Lord Canning and in General Anson (the Commander-in-Chief in India who had, in fact, already died of cholera) and trust to hear soon of the fall of Delhi. Still I fear that there is a dangerous spirit amongst the Native Troops and that a fear of their religion being tampered with is at the bottom of it. I think that the greatest care ought to be taken not to interfere with their religion—as once a cry of that kind is raised amongst a fanatical people—very strictly attached to their religion—there is no knowing what it may lead to and where it may end.

11 July 1857
To Palmerston

The Queen has just received Lord Palmerston's letter and highly approves the proposed appointment of Sir Colin Campbell as commander-in-chief in India and thinks it very handsome of this distinguished, loyal and gallant general to be ready to start at once on so important and arduous a mission. The Queen likewise approves of . . . the intention of sending out more troops forthwith.

22 August 1857

The Queen is afraid from the telegram of this morning that affairs in India have not yet taken a favourable turn . . . Delhi seems still to hold out . . . The

Queen must repeat to Lord Palmerston that the measures hitherto taken by the Government are not commensurate with the magnitude of the crisis.

2 September 1857
To King Leopold

We are in sad anxiety about India, which engrosses all our attention. Troops cannot be raised fast or largely enough. And the horrors committed [at Cawnpore] on the poor ladies—women and children—are unknown in these ages, and make one's blood run cold. Altogether, the whole is so much more distressing than the Crimea—where there was glory and honourable warfare, and where the poor women and children were safe. Then the distance and the difficulty of communication is such an additional suffering to us all. I know you will feel much for us all. There is not a family hardly who is not in sorrow and anxiety about their children, and in all ranks—India being the place where every one was anxious to place a son!

8 September 1857
To Lady Canning

I have to thank for several kind and interesting letters . . . That our thoughts are almost solely occupied with India and with the fearful state in which everything there is—that we feel as we did during Crimean days and indeed far more anxiety, you will easily believe. That my heart bleeds for the horrors that have been committed by people once so gentle—(who seem to be seized with some awful mad fanaticism [for that is what] it is there cannot be a doubt) on my poor Country Women and their innocent little children—you, dearest Lady Canning who have shared my sorrows and anxieties for my beloved suffering Troops will comprehend. It haunts me day and night. You will let all who have escaped and suffered and all who have lost dear ones in so dreadful a manner know of my sympathy;—you cannot say too much. A Woman and above all a Wife and Mother can only too well enter into the agonies gone through of the massacres. I ask not for details, I could not bear to hear more, but of those who have escaped I should like to hear as much about as you can tell me.

I feel for you and Lord Canning most deeply! What a fearful time for you both, but what a comfort for Lord Canning to have such a wife as he has in you.

The deaths of Sir H Lawrence—Sir Hugh Wheeler and Sir H Barnard (the latter an old acquaintance of mine who seemed to be doing so well with his small force) are most grievous, and the loss of Sir H. Lawrence irreparable. The retribution will be a fearful one, but I hope and trust that our Officers and Men will show the difference between Christian and Mussulmen and Hindoo—by sparing the old men, women and children. Any retribution on these I should deeply deprecate for then indeed how could we expect any respect or esteem for us in future?

Those Troops (Native) who have remained faithful deserve every reward and praise for their position must be very trying and difficult. The accounts of faithfulness and devotion on the part of servants are also touching and gratifying. I cannot say how sad I am to think of all this blood shed in a country which seemed so prosperous—so improving and for which, as well as for its inhabitants, I felt so great an interest.

Balmoral Castle, 23 September 1857
Queen Victoria to the Earl of Clarendon

The Queen hopes that the arrival of troops and ships with Lord Elgin will be of material assistance, but still it does not alter the state of affairs described by the Queen in her letter, which she wrote to Lord Palmerston, and which she is glad to see Lord Clarendon agrees in. Though we might have perhaps wished the Maharajah to express his feelings on the subject of the late atrocities in India, it was hardly to be expected that he (naturally of a negative, though gentle and very amiable disposition) should pronounce an opinion on so painful a subject, attached as he is to his country, and naturally *still* possessing, with all his amiability and goodness, an *Eastern nature;* he can also hardly, a deposed Indian Sovereign, *not very* fond of the British rule as represented by the East India Company, and, above all, impatient of Sir John Login's tutorship, be expected to *like* to hear his country-people called *fiends* and *monsters,* and to see them brought in hundreds, if not thousands, to be executed.

His best course is to say nothing, she must think.

It is a great mercy he, poor boy, is not there.

Calcutta, 25 September 1857
Viscount Canning to Queen Victoria

One of the greatest difficulties which lie ahead—and Lord Canning grieves to say so to your Majesty—will be the violent rancour of a very large proportion of the English community against every native Indian of every class. There is a rabid and indiscriminate vindictiveness abroad, even amongst many who ought to set a better example, which it is impossible to contemplate without something like a feeling of shame for one's fellow-countrymen.

Not one man in ten seems to think that the hanging and shooting of forty or fifty thousand mutineers, besides other Rebels, can be otherwise than practicable and right; nor does it occur to those who talk and write most upon the matter that for the Sovereign of England to hold and govern India without employing, and, to a great degree, trusting natives, both in civil and military service, is simply impossible. It is no exaggeration to say that a vast number of the European community would hear with pleasure and approval that every Hindoo and Mohamedan had been proscribed, and that none would be admitted to serve the Government except in a menial office. That which they desire is to see a broad line of separation, and of declared distrust drawn between us Englishmen and every subject of your Majesty who is not a Christian, and who has a dark skin; and there are some who entirely refuse to believe in the fidelity or goodwill of any native towards any European; although many instances of the kindness and generosity of both Hindoos and Mohammedans have come upon record during these troubles.

To those whose hearts have been torn by the foul barbarities inflicted upon those dear to them any degree of bitterness against the natives may be excused. No man will dare to judge them for it. But the cry is raised loudest by those who have been sitting quietly in their homes from the beginning, and have suffered little from the convulsions around them, unless it be in pocket. It is to be feared that this feeling of exasperation will be a great impediment in the way of restoring tranquillity and good order, even after signal retribution shall have been deliberately measured out to all chief offenders.

Balmoral, 28 September 1857
Queen Victoria to the Earl of Clarendon

The Queen is much surprised at Lord Clarendon's observing that "from what he hears the Maharajah was either from nature or early education cruel." He must have changed very suddenly if this be true, for if there was a thing for which he was remarkable, it was his extreme gentleness and kindness of disposition. We have known him for three years (our two boys intimately), and he always shuddered at hurting anything, and was peculiarly gentle and kind towards children and animals, and if anything rather timid; so that all who knew him said he never could have had a chance in his own country. His valet, who is a very respectable Englishman, and has been with him ever since his twelfth year, says that he never knew a kinder or more amiable disposition. The Queen fears that people who do not know him well have been led away by their present very natural feelings of hatred and distrust of all Indians to slander him.

What he might turn out, if left in the hands of unscrupulous Indians in his own country, of course no one can foresee.

22 October 1857
To Lady Canning

Thank God—the accounts are much more cheering and those of Lucknow are a very great relief. The continued arrival of Troops will I trust be of great use, and that no further mutinies and atrocities will take place. As regards the latter I should be very thankful if you and Lord Canning could ascertain how far these are true. Of course the mere murdering—(I mean shooting or stabbing) innocent women and children is very shocking in itself—but in civil War this will happen, indeed I fear that many of the awful insults etc. to poor children and women are the inevitable accompaniments of such a state of things—and that the ordinary sacking of Towns by Christian soldiers presents spectacles and stories which if published in Newspapers would raise outbursts of horror and indignation: Badajoz and St Sebastian I fear were two examples which would equal much that has occurred in India and these the Duke of Wellington could not prevent—and they were the acts of British Soldiers, not of black blood. I mention this not as an excuse but as an explanation of what seems so dreadful to our feelings. Some of these stories certainly are untrue—as for instance that of Colonel and Mrs. Farquarson who were said to be sawn asunder and has turned out be a sheer invention, no such people existing in India! What I wish to know is whether there is any reliable evidence of eye witnesses—of horrors, like people having to eat their children's flesh—and other unspeakable and dreadful atrocities which I could not write? Or do these not rest on Native intelligence and witnesses whom one cannot believe implicitly. So many fugitives have arrived at Calcutta that I'm sure you could find out to a great extent how this really is.

I am delighted to hear that that most loyal excellent veteran Hero Sir Colin Campbell is well and that you like him; I was sure you would, for it is impossible not to do so—and we never for a moment credited the shameful lies of disagreement between him and Lord Canning. If he is still with you say everything most kind to him. I am glad to hear that he does not share that indiscriminate dislike of all brown skins which is very unjust—for the Inhabitants have, it appears, taken no part in this purely Military Revolution—and while summary punishment must alas! be dealt out to the mutinous sepoys—I trust he will see that great forbearance is shown towards the innocent and that women and children will not be touched by Christian soldiers. I hope also that some rule may be laid down as to Ladies in future living in such an unprotected way as they have done in many of those stations and that at the first alarm they will be sent away to places of security, for really they must be dreadfully in the way and it must be so paralysing to the Officers and Men if they have their wives and children in danger.

Now that the rebellion had been suppressed, the Queen continued to oppose harsh reprisals and to support Lord Canning whose clement policies had led to calls for his recall.

SOURCE: Queen Victoria's letters dated June 29, September 23, September 25, and September 28 are from *The Letters of Queen Victoria: A Selection from Her Majesty's Correspondence between the Years 1837 and 1861,* vol. 3, ed. Arthur Christopher Benson and Viscount Esther (New York: Longmans, Green, 1907). The letters dated June 27, July 5, July 11, August 22, September 2, September 8, and October 22 are from *Queen Victoria: In Her Letters and Journals,* ed. Christopher Hilbert (New York: Viking, 1985).

How to Make an Indian Pickle

[The "Indian Pickle" poem highlights many of the charges of corruption and unfair governmental practices leveled against the East India Company, which is directly blamed for the unrest in India. The "Ellenborough" remark refers to Viscount (Edward Law) Ellenborough, who was president of the Board of Control for India on four different occasions (1828–1830, 1834–1835, 1841, 1858). Ellenborough was appointed governor-general of India in 1841, serving in this capacity until 1844. He fell out of favor with Company directors when he reportedly became influenced by Sir Charles Napier. Napier's suspicions about the Indian rulers in Sindh led to war in the region (February–March 1843) and the annexation of Sindh. After a subsequent war broke out in Gwalior (1844), Ellenborough was recalled from India. On his return to England, however, he was made an earl and viscount. Ellenborough would later be called on to draft a new policy for the government of India after the uprising/mutiny in 1858; his hostility toward the newly appointed Viceroy Charles John Canning hastened the end of his political career.]

Entrust the selection of materials and the whole management of affairs to a commercial company, like (for instance) the East India Company. Allow them to make use of as much corruption as they please. Throw in various green things, such as incompetent judges, cruel tax-gatherers, and overbearing military officers. Stir up the above with a large Spoon of the Ellenborough pattern. Mix the above with native superstitions, and by no means spare the official sauce. Allow the above quietly to ferment for several years without taking any notice of how matters are going on. When you come to look into the state of things, you will find that you have as fine an Indian Pickle as you could wish. You need not trouble yourself about the jars, for they will be supplied to you afterwards, gratis. For further particulars, inquire of the great Indian Pickle Warehouse, in Leadenham Street. N.B. No pickle is genuine, unless there is the mark of "John Company" plainly visible on the face of it.

SOURCE: Anonymous, "How to Make an Indian Pickle," *Punch* (15 August 1857).

The Punishment of Allahabad
ATTRIBUTED TO BHOLANAUTH-CHUNDER

[Some of the illustrated histories of the Indian Uprising/Sepoy Mutiny contain graphic narratives and illustrations of the sepoys being "blown from the guns." For those members of the British public who clamored for aggressive punishment of the rebellious Indian soldiers, the sensational executions were the soldiers' just desserts; others, however, voiced concerns about whether or not the condemned were actually or positively guilty. Administrators like Governor-General Charles John "Clemency" Canning called for reason and restraint and voiced concern over the moral and ethical implications of the excessive retribution. The graphic impression of the sepoy executions is mirrored in the *Punch* cartoon of 15 August 1857, which documents the dissolution of the British East India Company and its administrative transfer of powers to the British Crown.]

Edited by a Government Secretary, and dedicated to the Governor-General of India.

"They speak of it as a fearful epoch of unexampled atrocities on the one side, and of an unparalleled retaliation on the other. There were the Sepoys with the blood of murdered officers on their heads, and budmashes and bullies, and cut-throats and cut-purses, all acknowledging a fraternal tie, and holding a bloody carnival. But it was impossible that twenty uncongenial parties, divided by quarrels about caste, quarrels about religion, quarrels about power, and quarrels about plunder, could long act together in an undisturbed concert. Soon as batch after batch of Englishmen arrived to re-establish the Saxon rule, they were driven like chaff before the wind. Then followed a dreadful sequel—the horror of horrors. The martial law was an outlandish demon, the

"The British Lion's Vengeance on the Bengal Tiger." In *Punch* 33 (22 August 1857): 76–77.

like of which had not been dreamt of in Oriental demonology. Rampant and ubiquitous, it stalked over the land devouring hundreds at a meal, and surpassed in devastation the rakhasi, or female carnival of Hindoo fables. It mattered little whom the red-coats killed; the innocent and the guilty, the loyal and the disloyal, the well-wisher and the traitor, were confounded in one promiscuous vengeance. To 'bag the nigger,' had become a favourite phrase of the military sportsmen of that day. 'Pea-fowls, partridges, and Pandies rose together, but the latter gave the best sport. Lancers ran a tilt at a wretch who had taken to the open for his covert.' In those bloody assizes, the bench, bar, and jury were none of them in a bland humour, but were bent on paying off scores by rudely administering justice with the rifle, sword, and halter, making up for one life by twenty. The first spring of the British Lion was terrible, its claws were indiscriminating.

"One's blood still runs cold to remember the soul-harrowing and blood-freezing scenes that were witnessed in those days. There were those who had especial reasons to have been anxious to show their rare qualifications in administering drum-head justice, scouring through the town and suburbs, they caught all on whom they could lay their hands, porter or pedlar, shopkeeper or artisan, and hurrying them on through a mock trial, made them dangle on the nearest tree. Near six thousand beings had been thus summarily disposed of and launched into eternity, their corpses hanging by twos and threes from branch and sign-post all over the town, speedily contributed to frighten down the country into submission and tranquillity. For three months did eight dead-carts daily go their rounds from sunrise to sunset, to take down the corpses which hung at the cross-roads and market-places, poisoning the air of the city, and to throw their loathsome burdens into the Ganges. Others, whose indignation had a more practical turn, sought to make capital out of those troublesome times. The martial law was a terrible Gorgon in their hands to turn men into stone, the wealthy and timid were threatened to be criminated, and they had to buy up their lives as best they could under the circumstances."

SOURCE: In John William Kaye's *The History of the Sepoy War in India, 1857–1858* (London: W. H. Allen, 1875–76).

Pity for the Poor Sepoys!

"Mr. Punch,

"'Spare while you strike.' 'Blend mercy with justice.' I wish, Sir, you would tell the twaddlers who keep beating these copy-book moralities, to hold their tongues. 'Hang not at all,' is a doctrine I can understand; but, if you are to hang at all, hang every Sepoy you can catch. And let us have no more idle deprecation of the public cry for vengeance. Do not hang, if you object to death punishment but, anyhow, don't hang and cant. Let us not talk of mercy and forgiveness toward the criminal while we throttle him. Execution *or* vengeance, whatever we may call it. Chapter and verse are quoted against revenge. But chapter and verse must be construed reasonably. Chapter and verse, if understood literally, would oblige us to send out pale ale and preserved meat to our enemies, the Indian mutineers. Chapter and verse are to be read, not only with grammar in view, but also with rhetoric. Hyperbole is one of the figures for which allowance must be made in reading chapter and verse. Private and personal revenge are doubtless forbidden by chapter and verse, and individuals are counselled to disarm attack by concession. But the public is not required to put up with outrages upon human nature; and doubtless the burning indignation which such crimes excite arises from a sentiment implanted in man, on purpose to secure the punishment of serious criminals. Let us, Sir, in this, as in all other affairs, regard

"THINGS RATHER THAN WORDS."

"P.S.—Poor Nena Sahib! If he should be captured, and vengeful authorities cannot be prevailed on to spare him, might he *not* be allowed to expiate his little offenses against English women and children—under the influence of chloroform!"

SOURCE: Editorial letter in *Punch* (10 October 1857): 154.

Excerpts from A Memorial of the
Futtehgurh Mission and Her Martyred Missionaries:
With Some Remarks on the Mutiny in India

REV. J. JOHNSTON WALSH

CHAPTER I

Futtehgurh described—cantonment—city—villages—population and sects—Hindus—Mahammadans and Sadhs.

Futtehgurh, since the fearful scenes of the late mutiny, has become a name of familiar sound throughout the world. Before this lamentable revolt, it was known to all, who took an interest in the operations of the Presbyterian Board of Foreign Missions, as one of the most favoured and interesting of all our Mission stations in the North-west Provinces of India.

It is situated on the west side of the river Ganges, and is about seven hundred miles from Calcutta. It is the capital of a large district, known as the Zillah of Furrukhabad, and the seat of the European Courts for the district. It is bounded by the Rohilkund on the north, Oudh on the east, Bundlekund on the south, and Agra on the west. The banks of the Ganges on the Futtehgurh side are high, and the river scenery, especially during the rainy season, when the water rises to its greatest height, is quite picturesque. Though there is not much variety in the scenery of the plains in India, as the same features, more or less, characterize the different stations, yet Futtehgurh will not suffer in comparison with the most favoured; and, owing to its remarkably healthy climate and the variety of its productions, it has been regarded with especial favour by the European portion of the community.

The city of Furrukhabad contains three distinct classes of people—Hindus, Mussalmans, and Sadhs. Of these classes the first may be considered the best, and the other two in the descending scale as mentioned. As a race, the Hindus are mild, courteous, and intelligent, and not the unfeeling and savage people many suppose them to be from the developments made of their character during the late mutiny. That there are individual exceptions to this general rule will, of course, be admitted. Being heathen, they have many of the vices peculiar to all heathen races. For example, they are very superstitious and credulous, and consequently addicted to vice in every form, but withal mild and tolerant. Revenge is a strong and marked trait of Hindu character, having a full development in the people of Bengal, and becoming less as we go north.

The Mussalmans of India are the same everywhere, and characterized by those traits which are almost the opposites of the Hindus. They are proud, insolent, and sensual. Being the last native reigning authority, they feel very keenly the loss of power, and have never manifested submission to their position. During the Seikh rebellion in 1845–'46, whilst the author was stationed at Mynpoorie, it was a notorious fact that the Mussalmans met every day to pray for the defeat of the English and the entire overthrow of the British power; and that, too, when the prominent leaders were occupying important positions as Assistant Magistrates and Police Officers. Their former position and their knowledge of Arabic and Persian, the learned languages of the Mahammadans, have induced in them an overweening conceit of their attainments and power, and a most supercilious contempt for their Hindu neighbours. These, with their admitted superior religious knowledge, make them both arrogant and insolent. They evince a perfect detestation of idolatry, and ridicule it in every conceivable manner. Boastful of their religious superiority, and especially of their correct knowledge of the attributes of God, as taught in their Koran, (and copied from our Bible,) they hate Christians for their views of the Trinity and the doctrine of the Atonement, quite as much as they despise and detest the Hindus for their idolatry. This is intensified by the fact that Christians are more than able to meet them in argument, and exert their greater knowledge and power for the overthrow of Islamism. The very essence of their religion is hate and malignity, and where they enjoy the power, as up to a recent period they did in Turkey and still do in Persia, they exercise their avowed right of destroying every opposing system and doctrine. There is and can be no toleration where there is Mahammadanism; for the Koran teaches that every infidel should suffer death, and every one is an infidel who is not *ex animo* a believer in Mahammad and his teachings. This is the distinguishing element of Islamism, and has always been its development in Turkey and Persia, and would be now in India were it not restrained by a strong Christian power. That this has been one of the causes, and a chief one too, of the mutiny must be apparent to any one conversant with India and the character and restlessness of its Mahammadan population for the past few years.

Differing from both Hindus and Mussalmans, there is another class of religionists at Futtehgurh, who are called Sadhs. They are very peculiar as a class, and very strict and rigid in their observance of little things: such as tying up their mouths to prevent the inhaling of insects, in straining the water they drink through many fine cloths for the same purpose, and in rejecting all the usual forms of salutation. They reject all external rites, and assert that they believe only in God, but in reality are Atheists. They have no book like our Bible or the Koran of the Mahammadans and Shastras of the Hindus; nor have they any particular place of worship as the temple and mosque. This sect is not very large, though they have considerable wealth. Their meetings being secret, but little is known of them, and that little does not warrant much hope of winning them to a better belief.

CHAPTER XII

*Memoirs of the Rev. Albert Osborne Johnson,
and Mrs. Amanda Joanna Johnson.*

As Mr. and Mrs. Johnson had only been in India about eighteen months, and most of their time had been occupied with the study of the native languages, we have deemed it best to unite their memoirs in one chapter.

Mr. Johnson's birth place is in Cadiz, Ohio. His father, Dr. William Johnson, was a practising physician, having studied medicine at Washington, Pa. During his residence there he married Miss Elizabeth Orr, daughter of the late James Orr, Esq., a ruling elder in the Presbyterian Church of that place. Soon after their marriage, they removed to Greensburg, Westmoreland County, Pa., but remained only a short time, when they changed their place of residence for Cadiz. Albert was born on the 22d June, 1833, and was the fourth of a family of six children, of whom three only are now living.

Albert's parents were exemplary members of the Presbyterian Church, and dedicated their child to God in a public and solemn covenant, whereby they promised to bring him up in the nurture and admonition of the Lord. The privilege of having our children embraced with us in the bonds of the everlasting covenant in Christ, is of such an inestimable value—of such binding force, and followed with such precious results, that we love to dwell on the goodness of God, in permitting us to dedicate our little ones to his service in the ordinance of baptism. From a child, Albert was carefully instructed in the Holy Scriptures, and both by precept and example, taught to feel and acknowledge his peculiarly solemn obligations to God.

In the year 1850, and whilst a member of Jefferson College, he made a public profession of religion. He graduated with distinction at Jefferson, in 1852, and in the fall of the same year, entered the Western Theological Seminary at Allegheny: After completing his full course of three years' study, he graduated, and was married on the same day, May 9th, 1855, to Miss

Amanda J. Gill, of Pittsburgh. Soon after his marriage, Mr. Johnson was ordained by the Presbytery of Ohio, to the work of the ministry, on the 12th June, 1855. At what time, or by what means, the minds of Mr. and Mrs. Johnson were directed to the foreign field, we are unable to determine. But personal knowledge enables us to state, that it was from a settled conviction of duty, and after long and prayerful consideration.

During the last year of the Author's sojourn in India, Mr. Johnson and he were most intimately associated in the Mission work at Futtehgurh. And he now recalls, with melancholy pleasure, the daily conversations held whilst seated in the new Church, superintending its erection. His new field of labour, his position, and his future prospects for usefulness, were constant themes of familiar discourse. His efforts to acquire the language, and his interest in the people, were manifested in all his actions and words. He seemed to rejoice that God had so directed his steps, and permitted him to engage in the great work of preaching Christ to the heathens of India.

Mrs. Johnson was a daughter of the Rev. Jonathan Gill, a distinguished minister of the Reformed Presbyterian Church, and one of the Professors at the old Western University, in Pittsburgh, during the time Dr. Bruce had charge of that Institution. In the early part of his ministry, Mr. Gill received a call to Green County, Ohio, and during his settlement at that place, Amanda was born. She is therefore a native of that state. In her infancy, her father removed to his native state, Pennsylvania, where she remained until her departure for India. Having an Academy at home, for the instruction of students in the languages, and higher branches of English; a good opportunity was afforded for the education of the family. Under the direction of her learned and excellent father, she acquired a finished education, and in early life formed those habits which fitted her for usefulness in her future career, at home and abroad.

A little more than two months after their marriage, and on the 17th of July, 1855, Mr. and Mrs. Johnson, in company with the Calderwoods and Herons, sailed from Boston in the ship "*Brutus,*" Captain Meacom. In our notice of their short future career, we purpose combining their memoirs, and will quote from their letters without following each separately. Mr. Johnson, writing from the ship, speaks of their last parting from their native land, as follows:—

"As the pilot boat rounds and turns her prow homewards, a few wafts of the hand, a few waves of the handkerchief, and the sound of voices as they sweetly sing, 'The Lord is our Shepherd,' is borne upon the breeze, and gently dies away along the receding shore. Alone upon the quarter deck of our vessel sit our missionary company. Not a word is spoken. Each seems busy with his own thoughts. I now for the first time realized the heartfelt partings of the foreign missionary. The scenes of my youth, and the paths trod in more mature days, never before seemed so delightful as now, at the moment of quitting them for ever. The recollections of kind and true companions, of near and cherished relatives, of the pleasures of Christian and intelligent society, and of an American Sabbath and sanctuary, present themselves to my mind with a force and charm which I never experienced before. Despite myself, a feeling of sadness passes through my mind, and I begin to inquire, must one leave *all* for Christ and his cause? Are his claims superior to all others? Must all the endearments of a cherished home and beloved country be given up? And if so, what is the reward? Ah! then come the all-sustaining promises, 'Lo, I am with you always, even unto the end of the world,' and 'When thou goest through the waters, I will be with thee.' Blessed promises! What true consolation for the true believer in Christ!"

Their voyage was a delightful one, more than is usually the case from having a Captain whose views and feelings were so much in unison with their own, and who gave the fullest opportunity to his passengers to engage in spiritual labours for the good of the poor sailors.

Mr. Johnson, under date of September 17th, and near St. Paul's Island, expresses his appreciation of these privileges, as follows:—"Our voyage thus far has been one of pleasure, and calls forth the overflowings of warm and grateful hearts to Him who has said, 'I will never leave thee nor forsake thee.' Oh! for a full appreciation of the blessings we have hitherto enjoyed.

> 'Oh to grace how great a debtor,
> Daily I'm constrained to be!
> Let that grace, Lord, like a fetter,
> Blind my wandering heart to thee.'"

Mrs. Johnson exhibited the same spirit of cheerfulness and gratitude, and thus refers to her ocean life and arrival at Futtehgurh:—"We arrived at our northern home on the 6th of December, and on looking back to the dangers both seen and unseen of our voyage, we feel thankful to a merciful heavenly Father for his care and protection of us over the ocean. Our passage was exceedingly pleasant. Each one of our party can look back with pleasure to the happy and profitable hours spent together on the good ship Brutus."

Mr. and Mrs. Johnson entered on their labours with great zeal and delight. Happy in the consciousness that they were in the path of duty and labouring in a glorious cause, they seem to have resolved to live and die amid those for whose good they had severed so many and precious ties, binding them to friends and country.

On the 12th of February, and a little over two months after his arrival at

Futtehgurh, Mr. Johnson writes to his friends:—"We are living very happily together, and are in excellent health. I am so well pleased with this climate and country that I do not care very much whether I ever return to America or not. My dear friends, when you bow around your domestic altars, to ask God for his protection over yourselves, do not forget to remember your little army that is this day fighting the battle of life on the sunny plains of India. Think of their sacrifices and privations for the sake of Christ, and remember that they are not surrounded with Sabbaths and sanctuaries, or friends and Christian sympathies as you are. Oh! pray that their faith may not fail, their lives may be prolonged, and their usefulness increased, until the whole world shall sing the loud hosannahs of the great Jehovah."

In similar strains Mrs. Johnson writes to her friends under a later date:—"I have," she says, "no desire to return to my own land again, until I have accomplished something for these poor heathen. I wish that I could tell you all that I feel for them. May they speedily be brought to a knowledge of the Saviour, and rejoice in Him as their God. Soon, very soon, may they cease to seek cleansing virtue in the muddy waters of the Ganges, and seek it in the cleansing blood of the Prince of Peace. Sister, a great change has been wrought in my feelings since I came to this heathen land. I desire nothing else than to do good and promote the cause of Christ among this people. I trust that we can say, in the full assurance of faith, 'the love of Christ hath constrained us' to leave home, friends, and country, to make known to these poor heathen the glorious plan of salvation through a crucified Redeemer. I trust that we shall be found labourers worthy of our hire, and that Jesus will give us many souls for a crown of joy and rejoicing in the day of his great power. I trust that you will not soon forget us. We can hardly expect all to meet again in this world, but may we so live that at the last we shall have a happy meeting in heaven, where we shall never part, is the prayer of your sister far away. Yet, I am happy, very happy, in my Indian home."

Both Mr. and Mrs. Johnson commenced the study of the native language almost immediately after their arrival at their station, and were making rapid progress. Mr. Johnson also took part in the instruction of the young men in the City High School. Some of these dear youth were studying English, and this afforded Mr. Johnson an opportunity for usefulness. But his mouth was closed as yet to the great body of the native population, and he resolved to benefit them through the children of the Sabbath-schools in America.

The following letter is given with the hope that his effort may have still greater effect, and interest the children of all our Sabbath-schools in behalf of the heathen at Futtehgurh, and throughout India. Missionaries love Sabbath-school children, and are very anxious to secure their valuable co-operation:—

Dear Children:—It is a bright, pleasant Sabbath morning with you, and the great bells of your city are ringing out the hour for Sabbath-school. With nice clean clothes, a nice little pocket-Bible, and sundry school books, you hurry away, after having received upon your cheek the impress of a mother's warmest affection, to take your place in time, for you have been taught that it is wrong to be late.

Your teacher is a very nice person, who takes great delight in hearing you recite your catechism, and in telling you stories about other good little boys and girls. Or, perhaps, he may commence by telling you that this is the Lord's day, and that little book from which you read is the Bible; that it was written by holy men a long time ago, as they were directed by God himself. Then he tells you stories about these men; that they belonged to very different classes of society. Some of them were very learned, and some very ignorant; some of them were very rich, and some very poor. Moreover, he tells you that this wonderful book was written by such men as Moses and David, shepherds; Joshua, the commander of an army; Samuel, Isaiah, Ezekiel, and Jeremiah, prophets; Solomon, the wisest man that ever lived, and a king; Daniel, a statesman; Ezra, a priest; Matthew, a tax collector; Peter and John, fishermen; and Paul, the great apostle, a tent-maker and lawyer. Then he tells you that this book teaches you how old the world is, who our first parents were, how God destroyed mankind, and all beasts, and birds, and fishes, by sending a great flood upon the earth; how he saved Noah and his family in a great ship, when all the rest were drowned; how he afterwards preserved and protected his people. Then he tells you particularly about that wonderful man Jesus Christ, God's only-begotten Son, how he was born, how he lived, how he died; how he arose from the grave on the third day, and after forty other days ascended in a cloud up to heaven; how he made a sacrifice for your sins, and for mine. Then he tells you that one day, perhaps long after you and I are dead, that Jesus will come again to the earth in the clouds, and will say to those that are in their graves, "Arise, and come to judgment." Then he tells you that good children he will take to heaven where they will be forever happy, but bad children shall go to hell and be forever miserable.

All these things your teacher tells you; not only once, but many times has he told you. Are you not always glad when Sabbath morning comes, so that you may go and hear what Jesus Christ did? Are you not also glad that you have a kind father and mother to teach you how you may escape going to that place where all bad boys, bad men, bad girls and bad women go? Are you not glad, also, that God has told you so many good things in his wonderful book, the Bible? Yes, I am sure you are, or you would not care about Sabbath-school.

But do you ever think as you study your geography lesson, and see that there is on the other side of the world two great countries, called *India* and *China*, whether the little boys and girls there have the same Bible which you have? Perhaps you do; but if you will read carefully, I will tell you a great deal about their Bible. It is a very different book from your Bible. It says it is the oldest book in the world, that it was even written many thousand years before the world was created. It says there are many gods. First, there is Kartikeya, the god of war and bloodshed, who had six faces, that he might see all his enemies, and twelve hands that he might fight them, and who always rode on a peacock. Then there is Shiva, a white man with five faces, and who always rode on a huge bull. Then there is Vishnu, a black man, who had four arms, and rode upon a young man who had wings, and a beak like a bird. Besides these three principal gods, there are many hundreds of incarnations of the same gods.

Then their Bible says a poor man must not eat with a rich man, nor the people of different castes with each other. Then it tells the mothers how to drown their little daughters in a great river, called Ganges; how, when any one dies, he must be carried to the banks of this river and have the flesh burnt off of his face, or, if he have money enough, they burn the whole body, and the ashes are scattered by the winds. Then their Bible tells us that when parents grow old and unable to work, their children must carry them away into the woods or to the bank of the river, and leave them there to die. Then it tells us how they pray. They must repeat the same prayer many thousand times, or walk many hundred miles with great sharp nails in their shoes, or else have an iron hook thrust through their backs, and then swung high up in the air; or else parents must throw their little children into the Ganges, to be eaten by furious crocodiles; or else they must cast themselves under the wheels of an immense car, called Juggernaut, and be crushed to pieces. Then again it says, that it is wrong to take the life of any animal, even for food; that in order to have their sins forgiven, they must go almost naked, and cover themselves all over with filthy dirt, and roll about in the streets and roads, and have all their hair cut off, except one lock on the back of the head, by this they are to be dragged into heaven when they die. Then it tells us that there is no Sabbath, no Sabbath-school, that it is not wrong to swear, and lie, and cheat as much as one pleases. Then it tells us how they worship the sun, moon, and stars, and images made of wood and stone.

Then it tells us even how the gods used to steal, and lie, and quarrel, and murder, and eat little children, and do everything that was bad.

Such, my dear little boys and girls, are the things that are written in the Bible of the people in India. Do you not all say that this is certainly a very different Bible from mine? Yes, it is very different. Do you think it can be true? No; I know you will all say it is a very bad book, and so it is. Now, what can you do for these people? You can pray for them, ask God to send them your Bible, so that they may not do such wicked things any more, and he will do it. Don't forget the missionary-box when it comes around at Sabbath-school, but give what you can to send these poor people your Bible, and God will bless you, and make you feel happy all your days.

A. O. Johnson.

Mr. Johnson was also desirous of enlisting the feelings and co-operation of the adult as well as the youthful portion of the church in the great work of Missions, and as he looked upon the class of religious beggars, who are so common in every part of India, he penned the following communication, which we commend to the perusal of our readers:—

There is no class of persons under the sun more deserving of human sympathy and christian prayers than the *Fakirs in India*. The word *Fakir* is used in two different senses. The first represents seclusion from the world, and the second is synonymous with the English word *beggar*. To both classes is applied the word *yogis,* from *yog,* signifying devotion. Sometimes they receive the appellation "sitters in a corner," *gymnosophists,* or naked philosophers. It is their religious views and acts principally, from which they derive their notoriety. They profess entire contempt of life and the world. Not satisfied with rejecting luxury, they inflict upon themselves penance, and covet all manner of trials and self-denial. Their avowed object is to divest themselves of every human passion, and detach the feelings from every means of pleasure and gratification. Whilst some prefer to spend their days in solitude, amid the great jungles inhabited by wild beasts, and sometimes by still wilder men, others, more degraded if possible, roll their naked skeleton forms in the dust and offal of the streets of cities, and on the highways, throughout the whole land. Some dwell among the tombs of the dead, cutting and lacerating their bodies with stone, as in the days of our Saviour; others betake themselves to long pilgrimages, and no persuasion can deter them from executing their purpose.

Many of these persons give undeniable testimony of insanity; but, strange as it may appear, they are permitted to wander about every large city, with scarce a hand's-breadth of clothing to cover their loathsome bodies. By the lower castes they are extolled for their meritorious acts, and are considered the most holy and virtuous of God's creatures. They would not dare to oppose their will in the least matter; if they did, they think surely the most dire calamities would inevitably follow. Both classes live principally on charity, and their clamor and entreaties for money meet you everywhere. The self-inflicted tortures of these poor deluded creatures are truly revolting to refined sensibilities. Though civilization, the handmaid to Christianity, furthered by English rule, has done much to decrease the number of these religious mendicants, still the number of subjects and the enormities of their practices, are sufficient to call forth the sympathy of every Christian heart, even at this enlightened and progressive period. It would be impossible to give anything like a correct estimate of the number of these devotees; yet I think I may safely say, without the fear of contradiction, that there are many thousands.

It is difficult to conceive of a more shocking or humiliating spectacle than these poor deluded souls present in their acts of worship. Some expose themselves for days, naked to the rays of the sun, which in this tropical climate are very powerful and unhealthy. Others, not contented with what nature has done for their ease as well as their comfort, hold one or both arms in an upright position, until the muscles become stiffened, and it is impossible to restore the limb to its proper position. Some sit in one posture until their limbs lose their power, and they are maimed for life. Others besmear their bodies with the most filthy offal, and clot their hair with the excrement of the cow. Some go almost naked, in order to show that they have subdued their passions, and have no reason to be ashamed. Others, with their great propensities to make beasts of themselves, are clothed in tiger skins, or have their bodies tattooed to resemble that animal, to show that they reside chiefly in the jungles. Some abstain from food until they become frightful moving skeletons; others must drink their water from a human skull; with many more acts too revolting to be recorded. Even women are to be found among these misanthropic mendicants, and present even a more obscene and degraded spectacle than the men. There is every reason to believe that these unfortunate outcasts are often really sincere in what they do, and that they really consider this the only sure path to eternal bliss.

I fear but little can be done directly to better the condition of this class, owing in part to their seclusion and besotted ignorance of everything reasonable; yet we have every reason to believe, judging from the past, that their numbers will gradually decrease as the light increases.

Oh! that the Lord would cause his people in Christian lands to open their ears to the entreaties of woe and of sorrow that come from this heathen land! Oh! that he would bow his heavens and come down, to teach the nations their responsibilities, to bear witness to the truth, and give a helping hand to further his great cause! Oh! that Christians could only realize the corruption and the self-debasing practices of thousands of their fellow-creatures; that they are dying of hunger, whilst there is bread enough and to spare, in our Father's house above—for then might we expect a cheerful and universal response to the many entreaties sent forth from this land. Let us hope—let us work—let us pray, remembering what God has promised: "Ask of me, and I will give *thee* the heathen *for* thine inheritance, and the uttermost parts of the earth for thy possession."

A. O. Johnson

Mr. and Mrs. Johnson made very rapid progress in the language, and their interest in the work and people seemed to grow with the increase of their knowledge. Mr. Johnson prepared short addresses in Hindústání, which he committed to memory and accompanied by Dhoukal Pershad, the head teacher in the city school, went out into the villages to preach to the people. This work interested him very much, and when he was left alone by the removal of one of our missionaries, he wrote:—

"I am the only missionary for one hundred thousand souls! pray for me. I would now say to come out here is no child's-play, considering the length of time one must be on the way, the number of storms to be encountered, and the dangers surrounding you on every side; yet, on the other hand, it is a great privilege to encounter these for the sake of Christ and his gospel. I am glad that I came, and hope the Lord will give me health and strength to accomplish his will." Mr. Johnson had now acquired the language sufficiently well to make known his thoughts, but not in a very fluent manner. And as our annual meeting was to be held at Allahabad, he itinerated to that place, and the extracts we now give are from a journal he kept and sent home. He left Futtehgurh just one week previous to the author's departure. He writes:—

It is now just a year since, in the kind providence of God, we were permitted to set foot on these dark and benighted shores, during which time the study of the language has engaged the principal part of my time and energies; and I now find a change of place and air very pleasant and invigorating, after having experienced the first very trying hot season in the plains. The distance I am to travel is about two hundred and forty miles, thus affording ample opportunity for proclaiming to thousands the glad tidings of the ever blessed gospel, and to become better acquainted with the real condition and wants of the heathen. Our party consists of Mrs. Johnson, myself, John F. Houston, and Robert J. Breckinridge, catechists.

Having every thing, as I thought, in readiness for camp life, at an early hour, the carts moved off for the first encamping ground, with strict orders to have the tent pitched, and all things in readiness by the time we should arrive in the evening. Breakfasting at nine o'clock, Mrs. Johnson and myself set out in my buggy for the camp, where we arrived at four; and imagine my surprise to find the carts all on the ground, loaded as if ready for another march, whilst the men were quietly sitting beneath a large mangoe-tree, discussing the probabilities of the tent being pitched that night. Upon inquiry I learned that the men whose business it was to pitch the tents had not arrived, and as it was not the work of any one else, of course, it could not be pitched until they arrived. Here, thought I, with the beginning of our journey, also begin a new series of troubles. Having procured a seat for Mrs. Johnson beneath the same large tree, I determined to see if something could not be done towards pitching the tent, whether it was our work or not, as night was fast approaching, and the heavy dews which are deposited here at this season render it dangerous to health to be exposed to them. Mounting a cart myself, the men, through shame, soon were at hand, and we had one cart unloaded in a trice, and went to work with might and main to raise the tent. After repeated trials, we succeeded in raising it upon the poles, and were just fitting on the sides of the room, when, to my inexpressible joy, the arrival of the tent-pitchers was announced, who, understanding their business thoroughly, and being active men, the tent was soon ready for our reception, and we were released from our troubles at this time.

November 18th

At seven o'clock we were on our way for Bewar, a large village distant eleven miles, where we arrived in time to breakfast, and were rejoiced to find every thing in good order, which was a promise for no more troubles of the same kind as we had experienced the day previous. During the day, accompanied by the catechists, we went into a village in order to preach and distribute books and tracts, and soon collected a good number of persons, to whom we discoursed for more than an hour, upon the new and living way appointed by God for the salvation of his people. They heard us in silence, and seemed to think all we said might be true, but as it was new to them they could not say. This village contained about seventy inhabitants, not one of whom could read a word in any language. The ignorance of a large majority of the inhabitants of this country is truly deplorable, their sensibilities seem so benumbed as to be almost incapable of understanding the simplest argument. "Darkness covers the earth, and gross darkness the people." No prophet's saying is more applicable to this people than these words. The scene presented to the gaze of the Christian eye is really gloomy, painful, and revolting beyond description. The most absurd and superstitious systems of idolatry everywhere prevail. From the paying of religious homage to dumb idols of wood and stone, it descends even to brutes and crawling reptiles. The most cruel and debasing religious rites and ceremonies are practised even at this day, and that, too, before the very light of truth.

November 19th

Just as gray morning was dawning in the east, we were off on the Grand Trunk road, (the longest and best in the world, being eleven hundred miles long and well stoned,) for the village of *Chabramow*, distant fifteen miles. To-day we visited three villages in the neighbourhood, in two of which we were permitted to preach to interested groups the glad tidings of the gospel, and in the third we found all the males at work in their fields, so that we did not succeed in collecting a crowd; not so much, however, from an unwillingness to hear us as to quit their work at that time of day. It was the more pleasing to us, as we found in both the former villages schools established for the training of the youthful mind; and notwithstanding the avowed object was to fit them for government employment, yet it is hoped that the instruction received may prove as a means of leading them to see the inconsistency of their false systems of religion, and finally bring them to worship the only living and true God.

November 20th

Marched fifteen miles and encamped at a village called *Gursahai-gunge*. Here we preached twice, once in a Hindu village and once in a Mussalman village. Just as we were about to enter the Mussalman village we came upon the men where they were busily employed preparing indigo seed for the market; the head-man of the village seeing us, said, "Ha! these are Christians, some of them were here before," pointing to one of the catechists; "well, we are very busy now and don't wish to hear any thing about your religion, we are all very well satisfied with ours."

Here then was opposition, and the first, too, with which we had met. I thought a little, what we had better do under the circumstances, Is it best to turn our backs upon them—or at least make an attempt to converse with them? Finally, I determined, if possible, to have a conversation with them and see what could be done; accordingly, I commenced by asking the *Jemadur,* or head-man, a few questions about his work, temporal prospects, &c., &c., and strange to say, in less than half an hour one of the catechists was addressing quite a respectable congregation on that very subject most of all detested by a Mahammadan—Jesus Christ, the Mediator. They heard us through attentively, and before leaving, we had the privilege of distributing some of our books among them, which were very thankfully received. God grant that our words and books may be blessed to them in removing their deep-seated prejudices against the holy child Jesus. I believe it is true that the Mahammadans in this country manifest even more repugnance to the Christian religion than the Hindus.

November 25th

Moved our camp twelve miles to the village of Ramnuger, where we preached twice during the day. At one of the villages we had an unusually large and attentive audience, to whom I was discoursing when a Brahman made his appearance in the crowd, and listening for a few moments, desired the assembly to disperse forthwith, saying, that our words were unsound and not fit to be heard; no one, however, paid any attention to him; this enraged him, and he in a very authoritative tone desired me to stop speaking, and leave the village. I told him when I had done I should leave, but no sooner, and desired him to listen, and perhaps he might hear something that would be of benefit to him. He still persisted that I should leave, and became very boisterous. I then told him he must either keep quiet, or I should have him punished for his insolence; that when I was done, if he desired to be heard before the crowd, we should be glad to hear him. Finding that he could accomplish nothing he immediately left, saying, if it was government's order, I might go on; (he supposing we were preaching by government order;) thus we got rid of one of those famous impostors, and preached and talked until we were tired.

The next day Mr. and Mrs. Johnson reached *Cawnpore,* which in less than eight months was to be the scene of their bloody death. How little he thought then, whilst spending two days near the very place of his execution, and within sight of it, that he and his wife should be made to stand during the hottest month in India, as a mark for the sepoys, whose faith and good-will none could then dispute!

November 26th

Marched sixteen miles and encamped at Cawnpore, where we were detained until the 28th. This is one of the principal cities in India. Besides a very large native population, there is also a large number of English residents. The city has every advantage for commerce and trade, having the River Ganges, the Canal, and the Grand Trunk Road, and will in a short time have the Railroad, now in construction, from Allahabad. There are several very fine tasteful church edifices here, belonging to the Church of England, together with a number of missionaries of the same denomination. As the city is just at the entrance to the large and densely populated province of Oude, the Government have always stationed here several regiments of soldiers, in order to check any egress or assault that might be made.

December 1st

Came fourteen miles to the city of Futtehpore, and encamped in the compound of the Rev. Gopee Nath Nundy, where we remained until the 3d. The Rev. Gopee Nath Nundy, as is well known to the readers of the *Record,* was one of the first converts from heathenism of the Rev. Dr. Duff, and has served our Board for a number of years as a faithful steward. Here he has collected around him a nice little congregation of some thirty persons, principally the fruits of his own labours. Whilst here, we were pleased to see that the cultivation of the soil was in successful operation, conducted entirely by the native converts, and the most sanguine expectations are entertained of its future results. I had the pleasure also of visiting two very large and flourishing schools, under the superintendence of this native brother, one for boys and the other for girls, in both of which the Bible and Shorter Catechism are made text books. During our stay we accompanied Gopee Nath to the bazar, where we had a most pleasant season, discussing with the heathen the prior claims of Christianity. Gopee Nath is peculiarly adapted to the work; having himself once been a heathen, he knows just how to meet their arguments, and put to silence the most forward and boisterous of their brahmans.

We now approach the year 1857, the last year of their sojourn in India. Mrs. Johnson, writing on the 28th Feb., remarks: "How swift the wheels of time roll on! 1856 has been superseded by 1857, and with it has closed the toils and cares of another year. But what shall we say of the one on which we have just entered? Perhaps ere its close, some of us may be sleeping in the cold and silent grave, and numbered it may be with the forgotten dead. It is often a serious thought with me, Shall we all live to see each other, face to face, in this world again? *Somethings tell me it is doubtful."*

How significant is this sentence, though penned without the most remote conception of what was to take place, in view of what has occurred! Long before 1857 or the half of it, had passed away, not only they, but all their associates, had found a resting place in the Heavenly Mansions of their loved and loving Saviour.

We are now brought to the period when the news of the mutiny reached our dear friends, and excited their alarm. Mr. Johnson, in writing to his sister, reviews the state of things from the commencement, and adds:—"Three days ago we were all thrown into the greatest consternation by a letter received from Agra, stating that the Insurgents had burnt Delhi, and were marching upon Agra, five thousand strong, with a great army of thieves and plunderers. We are only eighty miles from Agra, and as all communication between us was stopped, the excitement here was intense. We have a native regiment, but no reliance could be placed on the sepoys. As our bungalows were so far away from the station, we at once left all and took refuge with the English residents, though without the slightest expectation of escape, should the insurgents come. To increase our fears, we heard that three or four of the largest jails had been broken open, and some thousands of the most desperate characters had been set free to assist in the work of plunder and murder. The next report was that Mynpoorie, only thirty miles from us, had been burnt, and all the Europeans murdered. Believing that the enemy were only ten miles from us, and would be on us in a few hours, we all thought our time had come, and as there is no way of escape, we expected every moment to be murdered. This, you will think, is a dark picture, but it is a true one. It is now passed, and we are filled with exceeding joy."

Mrs. Johnson, writing by the same mail to her sister, but two days' earlier date, says:—"Should they reach us to-day or to-morrow, their work must be short among us, for we have no protection but that of the Almighty. There is, humanly speaking, no hope for us but to submit to the awful fate which awaits us. To-morrow is the holy Sabbath, and God only knows whether we will be permitted to see its morning light. If it be the will of a gracious God that we fall by their hands, oh! that it may be a happy transition to be with Jesus! Our only hope is in Him, and He will not disappoint us." And two days later, she adds, "It is Monday morning, and a brighter sky dawns upon us in this land, though all danger is not yet past."

Before we submit the last letters ever penned by Mr. and Mrs. Johnson, let us glance for a moment at their characters and position. Mr. Johnson was a man of very genial influences, and of fine social qualities. As a Christian, he was zealous and devoted, a man of prayer and faithful in all his duties. As a missionary, he bade fair to excel in every department of labour. His qualifications were of a high order, and his desire to be useful was apparent to all. As a friend, he was firm and resolute, and one who could be depended on.

Mrs. Johnson was a woman of good mind, early trained and well cultivated. She had not only strength of mind, but was very energetic and active in all she undertook. Anxious to instruct some little ones, she gathered together the children of some of our native Christians whom she taught, and she adopted every expedient to get the families of her servants to come to her for instruction; and was at last successful in forming a Bazar-school for females. Her industry was remarkable, and when engaged in any particular work, we have known of more than one instance of her leaving her bed before day and resuming her work by candle-light. Her piety is evidenced in her letters, and needs not the eulogium of any one.

Their position, when the mutiny reached Futtehgurh, was a painful one. They could not escape to Agra, as the Mynpoorie district, through which they must pass, was in a most disturbed state and under the control of the insurgents. Their only hope was to make an effort to reach Allahabad, but Lucknow and Cawnpore presented difficulties almost equally as bad as that of Mynpoorie. With extracts of their last letters, we conclude their memoirs.

Mr. Johnson writes, "Dear sister, you cannot imagine the anxiety of mind this insurrection has caused us. We are living every day in expectation that it may be our last, but we have the blessed consolation that if we are to die it will be as missionaries to the heathen. Who would desire a more glorious death? May God in his mercy prepare us for whatever awaits us! The friends of Missions at home will be sorry to hear that all missionary labour is suspended for the present. What the future will be we cannot tell, but we trust that this insurrection will result in opening still wider the door for the spread of the gospel of Christ.

"*June 2d.*—Bad news, all is growing worse. The insurgents have arisen all around us, and we are trying to get a boat in which to make our escape to Cawnpore. My dear sister, this is perhaps my last letter; if so, good-bye—may we both meet above when our work is done."

Mrs. Johnson writes in her last letter, as follows:—"Every thing seems dark and doubtful, but God sometimes works by a mysterious providence. He can bring light out of darkness, and peace out of confusion; and that which seems so mysterious now, may be but the bringing about of a brighter day for poor benighted India. Even should it please Him for a time to allow the suppression of a Christian government in this land, yet the seed which has here been sown shall spring up and bring forth fruit; and the Church which is here established in the midst of the heathen is, we trust, a vine of his own planting, and He will care for it. Although trials and sorrows may assail us in this dark land, and we be called upon to *part with life for Christ and his cause,* may we not glorify Him more by our death than by our life? May the perils through which we have already passed be the means of bringing us nearer to Him! We must only wait the will of God respecting us. We look upon each day now as our last. But oh! how delightful are our seasons of prayer, together imploring the care and protection of that God who alone can save us!

"*June 2d.*—In a few hours we fly. The whole country is now in arms. Farewell, farewell! Perhaps you may *never* hear from me again."

We are certainly better enabled to understand why God has dealt so severely with his servants, and permitted India to be drenched with the blood of Christians, shed by the hands of wicked and heathen men. There are some who are ready to conclude that there must have been something radically and fearfully wrong in the management of affairs in India, else God would not have suffered such a fearful calamity to fall on so many innocent people, and such a disastrous reverse to retard the work of Christianity, even for a time. But this is quite unnecessary, and can be explained in other ways, which are more consistent with the facts of the case. And yet there can be no doubt that the Government of India has been in many things at great fault, and its course, in matters pertaining to religion, unworthy of Christian rulers. Let us then look at the probable effects on the government; and to do this, we must refer to the last policy, and ascertain wherein it was defective.

1. There can be no doubt that the whole spirit of government has been to pet and patronize superstitions, and to discourage every attempt to disturb or alter them. Toleration and neutrality have been the avowed views, and its settled polity was noninterference in religious matters; and there can be no question but that this was, all things taken into consideration, the best and wisest plan that could be adopted. But then the avowed policy was one thing, and the practice another and quite different. According to the latter, government lent its aid and influence to the support and encouragement of idolatry and false religion; for not only were grants made to heathen temples, but the sepoys were allowed to worship their regimental colours, and display their Rám Lílá exploits on the different parade-grounds. Besides all this, there has

been a great favouritism shown to men of high caste, and the native army was almost exclusively made up of men of this character. And that which has been so fostered, even to infatuation, has sprung up and resulted in untold misery and desolation. God has, by the mutiny, spoken in an unmistakable manner to the India government, and we trust that the lessons taught will not pass by without being duly considered. We cannot believe that India is to be lost, but rather benefitted greatly by the changes which are now to be inaugurated and carried on to completion. It is only such a development as has been made, and made too in such a manner as to impress all classes, that could convince the governing powers in Leadenhall street, London, of the folly and sinfulness of their former course and opinions. The government must no longer mislead the people by false statements, wicked compliances, or the repression of any truth whatever. All that tends to foster superstition and encourage false religions, must be discontinued, and perfect liberty of conscience must be allowed to all classes, independent of all aid or sanction from the powers that be. Let the Temples of Kalee and Juggernath receive no more or less protection and encouragement than the Churches of Christians. What is required is that all classes, whatever be their religion, should enjoy equally the most perfect freedom of worship, consistent with good morals, and every degree of proper toleration. And with respect to government schools, high or low, we must insist on no more exclusion of the word of God. This is a point of vital importance to the welfare of India and her rulers. We must have no more such graduates as Náná Sáhib to go forth into the world, to sow the seeds of rebellion, and imbrue their hands in the blood of Christians, whom they have been taught to despise and hate in the nurseries of infidelity, supported and encouraged by government. This may be regarded as strong language, but for its truth and propriety we appeal to facts to sustain us; and on such an occasion we think truth ought to be spoken boldly and honestly. The exclusion of God's word, and the expurgation of the name of the Saviour from the books taught in these schools, is a stigma under which good men have withered and suffered.

We fear there are many in the Church who think that the heathen are sincere, and their sincerity will be accounted sufficient in the last great day. They do not believe that they are exposed to eternal misery, and that their moral state is one of the most deplorable character, being given up to work all kinds of iniquity, falsehood, dishonesty, and uncleanness, with greediness. The sepoy revolt has resulted, we trust, in opening the eyes of Christians to their true character. The Bible declares that the dark places of the earth are full of the habitations of cruelty, and we have seen how true this description is of the people of India. We need no better evidence that they are everywhere earthly, sensual, and devilish. We now see for ourselves how thoroughly Satan has blinded the minds and hardened the hearts of the Hindus, during the centuries he has had them in his power. We regard the impression made by these facts as a most important result, for unless the people of God are convinced of the lost and ruined condition of the heathen, they will not see the necessity, or feel the importance of prayer and other efforts for their salvation. And will we not now realize, as never before, that nothing but the Holy Spirit, operating through the instrumentality of his truth, can accomplish the change which is unto life, and make the heathen meek, humble, and holy? The Church should humbly and thankfully acknowledge the severity of the discipline inflicted, and turn to the Lord. Her martyred sons and daughters now plead with her to dismiss all former apathy, and lean no longer on an arm of flesh, but to arise in the greatness of her strength, and lay hold on the power of God. If there is one truth more important than another, it is that God's Spirit is essential to the success of his work in the conversion of the world. We are not without warning on this subject, and are told expressly that it is not by might or by power, but by his Spirit, that the work is to be accomplished. And this, to be effective, must not be a mere conception or formal acknowledgment of a great truth, but must be of a practical nature in its workings. We believe that there has been a great neglect of prayer for the prosperity of Zion throughout the world, and especially for the influences of the Holy Spirit on missionaries and the work committed to their care. The missionary, above all others, is one who requires the presence of God's Spirit in his soul.

Another of the lessons to be impressed on us deeply by the mutiny is, that we are bound to identify ourselves more than we have ever done, and feel more our deep responsibility. Is it not true that many conceive the missionary work to be one of supererogation—a work in which they may or may not engage at pleasure? We know it is true. Such are ready to award their meed of praise to those who devote themselves more particularly to the work of Foreign Missions, but are not willing to acknowledge that this work has any claims on them as individuals. Now this is all wrong, for we are all under the deepest obligations to glorify God in body and spirit, with our intellects, affections, and all our means to the fullest extent. It is an error, and one, too, that is paralyzing in its effects, to suppose that Christians are under no obligations to propagate his word, and make known the way of salvation to those who are sitting in darkness and exposed to eternal misery. Too long has this been regarded as an optional service, as if engaging in it was meritorious, and refusing to engage in it sinless. It is not so, for every man is a debtor, and we are all bound to consecrate ourselves and our all to the service of God and the promotion of his glory; and if we cannot go in person, we are bound the more to assist and pray for those who are privileged to engage personally in evangelizing the heathen world. We are said to be the light of the *world*, and the salt of the *earth*, and not of the places or country in which we are born. Our influence is to be co-extensive with the human race and the expanse of the wide, wide world. By the very terms of the covenant and profession we have made in entering the Church of Christ, we bind ourselves to the performance of this duty. Looking at the matter in this light, or rather in the light of God's word, do we not see cause why he has touched us in our very heart of hearts, and thus caused us to re-consecrate ourselves to his holy cause? May our Church find in this afflictive dispensation, by means of which God has spoken so solemnly to us all, an admonition and warning that will not pass unheeded! Let none imagine for a moment that He intends us to withdraw our efforts to benefit the people of India. We have now a special call to prosecute our labours there, for the seed of martyrdom has been sown, and the harvest to be gathered is such as we have never been permitted to see before. Let us rather redouble our efforts, and show the heathen that we feel for them a love that is unquenchable, and the greater because nothing but the gospel can soften and change their vile and polluted hearts. May God endow us more and more with this spirit of love for the poor, degraded, and bloodthirsty heathen of India!

SOURCE: Reverend J. Johnston Walsh, *A Memorial of the Futtehgurh Mission and Her Martyred Missionaries: With Some Remarks on the Mutiny in India* (Philadelphia: Joseph M. Wilson, 1859; London: James Nisbet and Co., 1859).

England's Great Mission to India

PART I

Retrospect

Facts are not wanting, from the state of things as they have existed ever since the British came to India, to the time of the great rebellion of the Indian Army in 1857, which proclaim most unmistakably that the Government has been ashamed of its religion in relation to the inhabitants of this empire.

Testimonies of the most reliable kind can be adduced in abundance on this subject; and though it is not necessary here to enlarge much on these facts, yet a few quotations from the writings of eminent men are needed in illustration

"The Execution of 'John Company.'" In *Punch* 33 (15 August 1857): 65.

of the subject in hand. The highest eccleciastical authority in India has said, in a little pamphlet entitled "A Sermon delivered in St. Paul's Cathedral, on Friday, July 24th, 1857, by Daniel Wilson, Bishop of Calcutta and Metropolitan in India, dedicated to the Right Hon'ble Viscount Canning, Governor-General of India:"

"India would seem too much to have been ruled in former times on the theory that God is not the Governor of the world; but that Satan is the power whom it is wiser and safer to fear. It has long appeared to thoughtful persons, that one of the chief sins of India is the close connection with the vices and idolatry of Brahmanism, and the detestable licentiousness and bitter hatred to Christianity of the followers of the false prophet. In this opinion I concur. I am far from thinking that the causes of the extraordinary insurrection now raging, are to be sought in the conduct of the present age only. The Lord accumulates, as it were, His wrath, or in mercy forbears His chastisements, until at length they fall on one particular generation, which goes on in some of the same sins, though possibly it may not in all respects be so abandoned as some of their ancestors. We have a hundred years of offences to answer for—those of Lord Clive, and Warran Hastings, as well as of our rulers since.

"I fear we have too much continued in the spirit, if not in the acts of our fathers. Even in our own times, I remember well the struggle of twenty long years under the great and eminent Wilberforce, that was necessary to secure a free admission of our Missionaries into India. I remember the cruel treatment of Doctor and Mrs. Judson, whom I knew at Moulmein; the forced resort of Dr. Carey and his pious companions to the Danish settlement of Serampore; the prohibition to Dr. Buchanan to publish his Sermons on the Prophecies; the disgraceful delay in disconnecting Government with the pilgrimages to Juggernath; and the salutes to idols and other ceremonies at Madras, which compelled the brave and noble Sir Peregrine Maitland to resign. Even my amiable and beloved friend and brother Bishop Corrie, was rebuked by the Madras Government in 1836 for the mildest exercise of what he considered his appropriate duty in expressing his sympathy with Sir Peregrine on that occasion.

"Further, in our Regulations both at Madras and in Bengal, Hindoo and Mahommedan endowments were, and I fear are, declared to be endowments 'for pious and beneficial purposes,' and were placed in the special charge of the Collectors of the district, instead of being left to the Native priests to manage, or rather mismanage, as they could; which would have gradually extinguished them. Offerings in the name of Government at famous shrines were presented; and by the pilgrim tax, the duty of keeping up some of the shrines was allotted to our Christian authorities.

"All this is going far beyond non-interference—which is right, and our duty. No force can ever be properly used in diffusing Christianity; nor has it ever. But these Acts and Regulations went to the discountenancing of Christianity, and the support of the grossest idolatries and superstitions, which we now find have imperiled our empire. Let it never be forgotten that the first sepoy who was baptized by my late friend the Revd. Mr. Fisher, Chaplain of Meerut, was on that account alone, and though he was admitted to be a good soldier, dismissed the service! This Mr. Fisher told me himself.

"Thanks be to God many remedial measures have been passed of late years, and are now being in preparation, but it is our duty to examine the matter to the bottom, and remove all remaining suspicions of our indifference to Christianity, and of our approbation of the Native abominations. It is our duty to show on all occasions our intense conviction *that Christianity is the only true religion—in fact, the only religion in the world—* and that we adhere to it with all our influence and strength; and surely the present awful visitation for our sins is the proper moment for new and decisive measures to be taken—to which I am sure our present rulers will lend willing attention."

. . .

"Another grievous sin, too prevalent in British India, is the profanation of the Lord's Day. Much improvement has, thank God, taken place of late years. In the time of Bishop Corrie, Dr. Buchanan, and Henry Martyn, the Sunday was almost unknown. And still, a right conception of the absolute duty of devoting the whole day to public and private religious exercises, with rest from all labour (real works of necessity and mercy excepted) is not generally entertained."

. . .

"Few comparatively *turn away their foot from the Sabbath, from doing their pleasure on God's holy day, and call the Sabbath a delight, holy of the Lord and honorable; not doing their own ways, nor finding their own pleasure, not speaking their own words.*

"Few consider, as they ought, the Fourth Commandment, as equally binding with the second or fifth, or any of the other precepts of the Decalogue."

. . .

Indian Uprising/Sepoy Mutiny 513

"Who can think of the licentiousness, to open fornication, the connection with native women under the fraudulent pretence of marriage or otherwise, the increase of wretched European and native prostitutes in Calcutta and elsewhere, without grief and consternation"

. . .

"But there is a wider class of evils to be confessed and forsaken, than any I have adverted to—the deadly slumber of a practical infidelity; the indifference to the immense blessings of the Gospel of Christ;

. . .

our maintaining only a *negative* religion, instead of producing the *positive* fruits of righteousness; our enmity against God in His spiritual character; our dislike and even hatred of true vital Christianity, and the peculiar doctrines of the Gospel; our unfaithfulness to our convictions; our fear of the reproach of the world if we become religious; and our resting satisfied with the slight amount of a superficial religious profession, if reputable in the circle where we move."

. . .

"We should examine ourselves, whether we have understood and preached as we ought, and as St. Paul and St. John in their divine writings prescribe, the full and clear gospel of salvation by grace, and nothing else; whether we have shunned, as a serpent, Satan's snares laid for us; whether we have avoided the errors so prevalent in the present day of Semi-Popery, and a pretended Rationalism—of over statements on external forms and ecclesiastical traditions on the one hand, and the evaporation of vital religion and of revelation itself by the sentimental follies of what is sometimes called Broad Church, on the other?"

It has all along been the firm belief of godly men that the hand of God set up the British rule in India for His own wise and gracious purposes, and these purposes of God have been made manifest to earnest and pious men. In fact, God Himself raised up witnesses from time to time to remind and exhort the rulers of the land as to what His will was; but no heed has ever been given to them,—nay, such men have been treated by the Government with an amount of severity almost bordering upon persecution, as history abundantly proves.

The manifest will of God, as declared by Himself, is, "that all men should be saved," and this salvation can be obtained only through faith in His word. His will cannot be known unless the Divine command be earnestly and faithfully carried out, *viz.*, "Go ye into all the world and preach the Gospel of peace to every creature."

In order to make this practicable in India, Almighty God, "who ruleth in the kingdoms of men and giveth it to whomsoever He will," opened a way for the British nation, and gradually, little by little, gave them dominion and power over the length and breadth of this extensive empire, in a way, and with a stability, that never was possessed by any other king or potentate before. Alas, the rulers of the land, forgetful of their great mission to India, entirely hid the glory of God from the knowledge of the inhabitants, and only sought honor and greatness for themselves.

The following extracts are given here in illustration of this point. They are from "A Memoir of Colonel Stephen Wheler, by Major Conran, of the Indian Army":—

If the domestic life of Britons was so questionable, equally disgraceful was their connection with the idolatrous customs of the native army. From the familiar fact of high-caste Brahmins and Mohammedans having been the favourite element for recruiting, the native regiments at the time of the Mutiny had become the very schools of the false prophet; and, under the patronage and influence of their nominally Christian officers, their saturnalia at the annual idolatrous festivals, continuing a month each, became a nuisance even to many of the native inhabitants, Government property of all kinds—tents, guns, ammunition, regimental bands and colours, etc., were all given for the occasion, the Christian bandsmen were ordered to attend, and not a few officers and ladies frequently helped to swell the procession, and add grandeur to the scene.

Military duties were on such occasions at a standstill, the regiments were in a state of utter disorganization, and the cantonment a perfect pandemonium. In such stations as possessed no church, chaplain, or other representative of religion, and where, perhaps, the entire influence emanated from some native female favourite, all castes and outcasts, Hindoo, Mohammedan, and professing Christian, combined in one heterogeneous mob under the patronage of the representatives of the State.

It is doubtful if even these periodical out-bursts were so demoralizing as the more insidious but ever-present and all pervading atmosphere of idolatry. Its effect may be estimated from the current opinion of European officers that Mohammedanism (which always took precedence of Hindooism) was more suitable than Christianity for the natives of India, and that the moral character of its professors equalled, or was superior to, that of Christians. With an amiable leaning towards native interests, everything connected with the habits and customs of the country (which were all interwoven and impregnated with idolatry), was zealously affected by some of our countrymen, who were thus gradually becoming denationalized. Nor could the natives doubt but that some of those who lived all their lives in India, and died there, were as genuine converts to Hindooism as the converts of our missionaries are to Christianity. No uncommon thing was it also for European professors of Christianity to withstand the native converts with the utmost virulence, on the ground that they were apostates from the faith of their fathers.

Another proof of the predominance of this anti-christian principle was manifested by scurrilous attacks on missionaries by the Indian press, or by Indian officers at home. The feeling of enmity to vital Christianity was equally visible in conversation, and in public and private intercourse. As for the hostility of most who exercised authority in regiments, or held a military command, their latent feelings were only kept in abeyance by the circumstance that missionary effort in the Upper Provinces of India was yet almost unknown. *The hatred manifested by the sepoys towards Christians during the Mutiny too well indicates how thoroughly they had shared these feelings with their quondam associates and guides.*

The well-known instance of the native soldier converted to Christianity at Meerut (for such an event once happened!) shows how the military authorities "stamped out" all such things. He was brought before a military court, reported to the Government as a dangerous character, and removed from the regiment. The European convert, like his congener the native, soon found the place made too hot for him in a native regiment, and was glad of the earliest opportunity to leave the service.

Thus it is clear that the Christian Government whom God had so highly honored in India, did not in return seek the honor and glory of God, and, having little or no trust in his Almighty power, they sought for safety and stability under the policy of conciliating the Indian Army by taking part in all their shameful practices, and without reserve—nay, under the highest sanction—mingling themselves with the vices and idolatry of the heathen. Under the groundless apprehension that as their vast possessions in India were *guarded* by the Native Army, composed entirely of high cast Hindoos and Mahomedans, it would be offensive to them to be brought to a clear knowledge of the Christian religion, or to see any particular manifestation of the claims of that religion exhibited in the lives and conduct of the rulers of the land. Hence the prevailing order of the day, and the earnest care of the Government was "not to preach the Gospel of Christ to men in the Army;" any attempt on the part of a godly man to do so was visited with marks of the highest displeasure from all in authority.

The result of this policy of Government, as might have been expected, was to keep the people grossly ignorant of the nature and requirements of the Christian religion, hence their persuasion that the Government had designs upon their religion. This notion, though perfectly groundless, was taken advantage of by the designing Mahomedans and worked up by them to such a degree, that, in course of time, no doubt was left in the minds of the Hindoos that the time had come when the British Government would have recourse to force and compel them and all India to become Christians. The Province of Oudh, that great nursery and home of the flower of the Indian Army, having been annexed to the Government, all chance of resistance would seem to be at an end.

Two causes helped to give colour and permanence to this most absurd and groundless belief, and they were very gigantic ones in themselves.

1st.—Perfect ignorance of the tenets of the Christian religion.

2nd.—Painful recollection and experience of what the Mahomedans had done in the name of God and religion to the Hindoo population during the period of their Government in India.

With reference to the first of these causes very little remains to be said. Had the Bible been permitted to be preached extensively in all parts of the British possessions, and its principles carefully explained to the native army at large, with the clear understanding that its precepts, unlike the Mahomadan religion, did not authorize the employment of any coercive measures to make proselytes;—had Government authorized, nay, introduced text-books containing in concise and clear terms all the fundamental doctrines and gracious purposes as revealed to mankind by God, and caused these books to become standards for all Government schools and colleges, it is clear that all classes of people in India would have been so far enlightened in regard to the Christian religion, as to know how to avoid being deceived by the misrepresentations of the Mahomedans that the British nation wished to take away the caste of the Hindoos by force.

"The other cause may be briefly stated thus. When the Mahomedans held sway over India, in accordance with the express command of their religion, as contained in the Koran, they lost no time to inculcate in right earnest their own faith, and unhesitatingly set about, by force of arms and with the edge of the sword, to make proselytes of Hindoos and others without the least regard for their feelings; thousands of the descendants of these proselytes are at this day to be found in all parts of India, who follow the rites and ceremonies, and join in all the festivities of both the Hindoos and Mahomedans.

These facts having become a matter of history, and the subject of painful recollection to the Hindoos, it is not to be wondered at that the biased mind of this ignorant people readily allowed itself to be led away into the belief above stated. Bishop Daniel Wilson, in the Sermon quoted above, states:—

"Our case in British India is no doubt most peculiar. I can recal no part of history in modern times which resembles it. The civil wars in England two centuries ago, and the horrors of the first French Revolution, which I myself remember, were quite of a different character.

"The pillars of our power in India have been, and are shaken. Thirty millions of ruthless Mussalmans have been engaged in a conspiracy, and been working on the feeble minds of one hundred and fifty millions of Hindoos for a number of years, and have at last broken out into open rebellion against the comparatively inconsiderable number of the Europeans. Murders and atrocities unheard of in civilized warfare have been perpetrated by a savage and brutal Native soldiery. House-breakers and criminals of every class have been let loose by thousands upon thousands from our jails, to pillage and destroy the peaceable inhabitants of our towns and villages. *The high-ways* of the Mofussil *have been, and are, unoccupied, and our travellers walk through bye-ways.* The minister of religion, the tender female, the child hanging on the breast, have been butchered with unparalleled cruelty. Many of *our holy and beautiful houses where we praised God, have been burned up with fire, and all our pleasant places have been laid waste.* Unnumbered families at home and in this country have been plunged into grief almost inconsolable, for the sudden loss of husbands, wives and children, who have been cut down. The lawful pursuits of commerce and agriculture have been paralysed. Poverty and destitution stare multitudes in the face. We know not yet, and never shall know, a hundredth part of the miseries and horrors which are taking place; but the incidental letters we receive are utterly heart-rending. Still there is hope in the *everlasting God,* if we truly humble ourselves before Him, and repent of our sins."

The Lord Almighty speaks through his Prophet Jeremiah:—

"Hath a nation changed their gods, which are yet no gods? but my people have changed their glory for that which doth not profit. Be astonished, O ye heavens, at this, and be horribly afraid; be ye very desolate, saith the Lord, for my people have committed two evils: they have forsaken me, the fountain of living waters, and hewed them out cisterns, broken cisterns, that can hold no water."

Should the Lord say, I gave my Holy Law, the Bible, to England and ye became a Christian nation, a chosen people, peculiarly my own people, blessed of the Lord. I then sent you out to India to do my work among the heathen; a handful of you, by my power, possessed yourselves of a vast country, and ye have sought out your own glory and pride. Ye have made my Gospel to be a despised Book among the people, and my holy name to be dishonored in their sight by your conduct and life. Your great influence and example could have made my religion both attractive and honorable in the eyes of this benighted people, and would have led them to hear my voice and come to me. By this means ye would have fulfilled the great mission on which I sent you to India, and thus my holy name would have been glorified and magnified in the face of all the earth. But ye have forgotten your high calling, and not only left undone what ye should have done, but have actually ignored and disclaimed my religion and debased yourselves to the level of the heathen themselves.

"Give an account of they stewardship."

How hast thou helped my cause? What aid hast thou afforded to my poor servants who, from time to time, have laboured in my field? How hast thou cared for the poor of my flock—the converts who have left their all to follow me? Missionary enterprize apart—hast thou done any thing directly to honor and diffuse the Christian religion? And the Lord said—

"Thou mayest be no longer steward."

In a moment the Honorable East India Company fell, and became extinct in India. This was the Lord's doing—the wrath of God was kindled, and He consumed the Government and their pampered army together.

> "Alas! we were warned, but we recked not the warning,
>   Till our warriors grew weak in the day of despair;
> And our glory was fled, as the light-cloud of morning
>   That gleams for a moment, and melts into air.
> As the proud heathens tramped o'er Zion's sad daughter,
>   She wept tears of blood o'er her guilt and her woe,
> For the voice of her God had commissioned the slaughter—
>   The rod of his vengeance had pointed the blow."
> Revd. Thomas Dale

PART III

In Connection with the Eurasians and Anglo-Indians

A little thoughtful consideration will make it evident to most minds that the above class of people are destined to take an active, if not a prominent, part in this work of "England's Mission to India." "The day of small things is not to be despised;" from *small beginnings* great things do come to pass; it has been so since the world was created.

The Eurasians are essentially a *new nation in embryo*—as it were, an undeveloped infant—or, as the germ of some gigantic plant, which progresses very slowly and almost imperceptibly for a time, but ultimately out-grows all the trees round about it. God, in his inscrutable providence, has caused this *germ of a peculiar nation* to be planted in the soil of India, and has permitted it to take root. For a century and a quarter this community has been growing, slowly but surely. Rulers of various dispositions and minds have come and gone in quick succession, but, with a very few exceptions, all have passed away without giving that consideration to this subject which it demanded. Nay, men in power—many of whom manifestly rule India, not for God, but for themselves, have tried to hinder God's purpose; while, on the other hand, God-fearing men, and numberless other conscientious people, have, from time to time, prominently and earnestly brought the state of this growing community to the notice of the Government, suggesting various plans whereby their condition might be improved which would save them from that degradation and vice which poverty and starvation foster, but hitherto without effect. Much that is at present blamable and improper in their conduct has been picked up from the example set them by those who should have guided them; the people have never been in a position to feel their responsibility as a body, or to see the necessity of forming social organizations in order to be united as Christians, and be enabled to develop their good qualities. But it is not too late yet; with a little judicious management *on the part of Government,* this community would undoubtedly become a source of blessing to India; whereas, as matters now stand, it is actually being driven to become a curse, and will be so in a few years hence, unless remedial measures be adopted.

It is very evident that India can never again be under the dominion of a heathen power; the way has been preparing step by step for the "Sun of Righteousness" to shine forth in his glory, so that "the people which sit in darkness may see a great light." This country is "no home" for Europeans, and God Himself is manifestly maturing a plan by which a great want may be supplied, *i.e.,* the fixed settlement of a Christian people who may take a lively interest in the land of their birth and heartily engage in this special work of God. India is essentially the home of the Eurasians as well as of the "Anglo-Indians" who are so closely connected with each other that (although the latter very foolishly try to ignore the former) they may be accounted for under the same "general head," and upon this body it is evident will eventually devolve the said special work by God's blessing.

By the term Anglo-Indian, it is to be understood here those Europeans who have no chance or desire to return "Home," and more especially the descendants of the same who must abide in India, but have no Indian blood in their veins. Whereas the term "Eurasian" is derived by joining the names of two great countries together, *i.e.* Europe and Asia, and is, not only in itself demonstrative of its origin, but is a most appropriate designation for those who are thus connected by blood with both countries. History declares "that the ancient Hindoos were the ancestors not only of the Hindoos who afterwards came to India, but also of the Europeans who went to live in Europe, and of the Persians who went to live in Persia." It may not be that the Eurasians are very closely connected with the said ancient Hindoos called "Aryans," yet it cannot be denied that they are a link between Europe and Asia, claiming direct ancestral descent from the English, Irish, and Scotch, truly British-born subjects—at once the representatives of both countries, brought into being by the *direct action of England,* and for whose existence the British nation is most clearly responsible to God.

The greater portion of the Eurasian body of the present day can clearly prove (even at this late date) that they are the descendants of legally married couples; that on one side the parentage was pure European, and on the other side—mother and grandmother were from well-recognized Christian communities, though these may have been originally the offsprings of pure native converts several generations back; for such communities did exist in India, at least for a hundred years previous to the British rule, whose lives and social habits were of a most strictly moral character.

Having rights and claims of a twofold nature, both Europe and Asia being their ancestral home, they should be entitled to respect from all others as being a "peculiar people," raised up under the providence of God for some wise and good purpose; instead of this, the most enlightened of the two countries is the foremost in bringing them into contempt, calling them "half-castes" and other opprobrious names, while the natives are but too prone to copy the example thus set before them; yet it is a known and acknowledged fact that the Eurasians have one peculiarity in them, *i.e.* that under all circumstances they identify themselves as one with the rulers of the land, "having a deep interest in the country, with all the talent and principle of the European race," ever maintaining the character for being trustworthy, respectable, and well-conducted; ready to distinguish themselves in various walks of life, as may be amply verified from the public records, and the testimony of retired officers. The Government of India is fully cognizant of the fact that a large class of this body now exists whose loyalty and services to the State have extended over two or three generations in this country, and that it was the exertions of their progenitors which enabled Great Britain to acquire and hold its possessions in India, for they were the men who were engaged in every battle fought, every fort taken, enduring every hardship and privation, ever ready to shed their blood in the cause of England; while their descendants are not a whit behind them, wanting but the opportunity to prove their loyalty and attachment to the Government; for a proof, one has only to look back to the events which transpired during the mutinies of 1857–58, when in every station or post every individual of this body readily joined himself in the cause of the British, and in most cases rendered important service, and would again and again do the same if needed. Thus it is very clear that the Eurasians no sooner brought into existence but have commenced playing a most prominent part in this great drama, and no argument would appear to be necessary to shew that they deserve well of the British Government. Alas! the action of the last few years clearly indicates that the present rulers entirely ignore their just claim upon the Government. The course now being pursued leaves no room to doubt that the future of the Eurasian is dark and gloomy in the extreme. Every avenue to gain a respectable and honest livelihood is gradually but surely being closed against them in all and every department under the Government.

This state of things is being brought about since the abolition of the Hon'ble East India Company's Government, and it is appalling to contemplate what is to become of this class of Her Majesty's loyal subjects. No status, no prospects, no interest in the soil of India; not a foot of which they can call their own, although their forefathers have had a direct hand in helping to acquire and retain the same; and it is in reference to members of this class whose present sufferings and privations draw the sympathy of well-disposed and right-thinking Hindoos and others who have known them of old to be an upright, deserving set of people, now unable to procure the means of subsistence, large numbers of whom are daily being reduced to a state of starvation, and while commiserating the state of such, the said natives cannot help remarking that a Government which thus tramples under foot the claims of those who are clearly of their own nation, religion, and caste (in India caste rules the day,) it can never be true to the people of India, whatever its professions may be to the contrary. It matters not how much the Government may see fit to idolise and promote the interests and condition of the people—*they know well* that "charity begins at home," and while those of England's own progeny and creed, for whom the English nation is evidently responsible as parents are responsible for their children, are being trampled down under foot, there is every cause of apprehension, and good reasons to doubt the sincerity of those measures so openly being adopted for the good of the natives. True wisdom comes from God alone, therefore truly God-fearing men are absolutely necessary to be placed in the administration—men who will ever pray to God as did King Solomon (I Chron. 8 10) "Give me now wisdom and knowledge, that I may go out and come in before this people, for who can judge this thy people that is so great."—"*Behold the fear of the Lord, that is wisdom.*" (Job xxviii-28). India's greatest need at present undoubtedly is a large increase among the rulers, who feel themselves *accountable to God* for what they do, and who will as a matter of obligation strive to do their duty as God commands—"walking righteously and speaking uprightly." Everything that is as yet good and creditable to Government is due to such men, of whom there is still a goodly number in the country, although the open profession of religion is "not reputable in the circle where they move." Their influence, however, prevents much evil, and helps to keep in check those who would otherwise follow the bent of their own minds.

It is a fact that the Eurasians have to struggle under certain disadvantages, which under existing circumstances they know not how to remedy, not that they claim any exception from the evils with which every state of society is full to repletion; but it is highly discouraging when the vices of others are saddled upon them and brings them into disfavour; for instance, when natives who are not in the remotest degree connected with Europeans by blood, are received as orphans, or converts, and baptised with European names, they are encouraged to assume European costume and to ape European manners; having also the advantage of English education they are enabled to fill various offices, but in most cases behave so badly as to draw the attention of their superiors upon their low and mean habits; while at the same time claiming an identity with those of European discent, they reflect discredit upon the Eurasians. Thus reproaches are levelled at the latter, and *all* are put down as undeserving of respect. As natives the said converts have no right to appear in false colours; no honest man will affect the style of dress or habits of a community when he knows that by doing so he will *seem* to be what he is not, especially if it is done, as it is the case with many, to convey the impression that they are the off-spring of Europeans, and it becomes clearly a case of fraud on their part, an unlawful personation of character with intent to deceive, and is highly reprehensible when by their acts disgrace and contempt is brought upon those whom they personate.

Hitherto all have, however, been allowed to mingle in one heterogeneous mass, the evil-disposed being at liberty to disgrace the entire body by their perverse and unscrupulous-conduct. A little care and judicious interference on the part of the rulers (as parents who use their influence to bring their children in the right path) would no doubt set matters on a better footing, and incite the people to seek their own welfare as a community destined to perform a great work for God in India. Whereas, if rendered helpless as they are at present, discouraged, humiliated, weighed down by poverty, with nothing before them for which to aspire, they must run rapidly down to a state when they will beome a pest and nuisance to India, a standing disgrace to England, and a source of much annoyance to the Government.

Justice demands that those families who have deserved well of the Government, whose proginitors have rendered good services, and to whom England is assuredly in a great measure indebted for its conquest and settlement here, should be dealt with in such a way as will not only benefit the people themselves, but will redound to the honor and praise of a just and equitable Government ruling the destinies of so vast an empire, for it is but reasonable to consider that the offspring of the above have a natural and an indefensible right to higher considerations, whether social or political, than have ever yet been conceded.

Instead of this, however, the idea of late is gaining ground that when this people is sufficiently crushed and humbled, then their children, both boys and girls, must of necessity go as menial servants to officers and their families! Can it be possible that their own and their forefathers' devoted services of so many years will be so completely ignored by a just Government as to bring down their posterity to the level of menial servants in this country?—for whatever such a position may be in Europe, here in India it is of all things the most undesirable. Would it not be far better if the English nation were to take their case into consideration, and devise means whereby the rising generation might be saved this utter degradation, *for which there is no obvious necessity in a country like India,* since native menial servants are always very plentiful and cheap.

The question may honestly be asked, is there any justifiable reason for taking measures to alienate the attachment of this hitherto most loyal of all Her Majesty's subjects in India, when their adherence to Government may, with a little good management, be for ever preserved, and the community be made a source of great strength to the British Crown? Having been brought into being in the manner described above, they have hitherto been in the condition of children who look up entirely to their parents for every provision and means of subsistence, and nothing has been done by the parental Government, in whose service they have grown up to their present state, to wean them of its support by training them in a way to be able to earn a living by their own independent exertions, by pursuing any of the industrial trades or professions of the country; millions of money have been, and are being, spent in various ways. How much is lost in the miscarriage of projects, designs, and experiments of the public works, &c.? What immence sums have these cost, and how frequently have they collapsed? Yet these heavy losses are borne by the Government without much concern; whereas the expenditure of a few thousands for the amelioration of the condition of a people who are well deserving of consideration, is begrudged.

The army can easily absorb a large portion of this class in separate army corps. The educated classes would no doubt find means to shift for themselves under the privileges which place all Her Majesty's subjects on a par; *if care is taken* that the unreasonable prejudices which so much prevail among heads of departments in regard to this community be removed once and for ever, for it is an easy matter for men in power to set aside the most equitable laws, and assign plausable reasons for carrying out the bent of their own inclinations. Others may be directed to form colonies in the lower plateau along the foot of the Hills, where, by clearing out jungles and improving waste lands with the aid of Government, they would find employment as well as support, and would in time be enabled to add to the revenues of the State. A certain percentage might still be permitted to hold posts of trust and responsibility in co-ordination with political justice. By such and other means the present misery and the fearful out-look of the future would soon give place to joy and satisfaction, and the blessing of every heart and home flow in a perennial stream on our most gracious Empress and Her Government.

The loyalty of the Eurasians and Anglo-Indians may be ever relied upon, for their interests are in every respect one and the same. Did the mutineers in 1857 seek the lives of the rulers and spare the country-born? No! they suffered alike with the Europeans, not even a child of theirs was spared. In *all* respects the very being of this community is blended with them. What, then, may it be asked, is the cause which prevents the employment of thousands of deserving men of this class in the only way in which their services can be profitably utilized by the Government, and the means whereby they can maintain a respectable and honest life? Poverty is the source of every evil, and where there is so large a body in all parts of India, once respectable, now going down rapidly into poverty, with no prospect of better times to come, and that in a land like India, it is time that the rulers of the country take their case into favorable consideration, especially when it is considered that poverty cannot prevent the population from increasing, and that it must increase in a much larger scale than it has ever done hitherto. The sacred records give the account of a heathen nation "who made the lives of the children of Israel bitter, and the more they afflicted them the more they multiplied and grew, until the king directed them saying, Every son that is born unto you, ye shall cast them into the river." The actions and disposition of many Europeans at present in India, however limited their authority, too plainly indicate a similar line of policy if it were at all practicable; and one cannot help believing, that however atrocious such a wish may appear to some, it would positively benefit the people themselves if carried out to the letter, as it would certainly save them a vast amount of misery and degradation, which is certainly impending, if England and the Government of India do not over-rule the present policy of those in authority.

To an ungodly European in power the sight of a Christian man is an eye-sore—indeed a constant reproach, and he prefers one whose principles and religion are different, even if it cause him inconvenience. With such men, a subordinate who has no voice in any matter, and, above all, one who can easily be brow-beaten and bullied into holding his tongue when his master is disposed to indulge in any dishonorable practices,—in a word, a man submissive and yielding in every thing,—is the one to be preferred by all means to any who is at all upright or uncompromising. But a reaction in the feelings of the natives of India is fast taking place; and with a clearer knowledge of things which education is imparting—("knowledge is power,")—as soon as the surprise, which the change in the established and well-defined usages and practices in native society, as regards positions and places, is fairly got over, which the present administration is fast bringing about, then these very submissive people will be a sure, and a vast deal greater, source of annoyance to their superiors. But then those who have laboured to sow to the wind shall have gone away, like birds of passage as they are, and taken refuge in a far-away country.

The education of natives costs immense sums of money, but the benefit arising from it seems to be simply to abuse and ridicule the acts of the rulers; if not, where would have been the necessity for limiting the freedom of the Native Press? Moreover, the indiscriminate education of all classes of natives, without right views of its object, has engendered false hopes and ideas in the minds of individuals who have entirely neglected the calling of their forefathers; and in the firm belief that Government situations, with better emoluments, were of easy attainment, they have prosecuted their studies of the

English language with that one object in view, and now find nothing but disappointment and wretchedness awaiting them! Being unable to realize their long-cherished object in the shape of a lucrative post under Government, they would fain revert back to the profession of their progenitors, but cannot do so from want of the necessary training: thus rendered miserable, it is but natural that imprecations and curses should arise in their hearts against the policy which has so disturbed the harmony hitherto existing among the circle to which they belonged.

That there is at present much cause of discontent and apprehension, and that the minds of all classes of people in India are being gradually but surely alienated from the British Government, cannot be a secret to the rulers of the land; but no steps in the right direction is taken to bring about a better state of things. It is admitted that the natives generally feel and acknowledge that the peace and security of life and property obtaining under the British rule can never be hoped for under any other Government, and yet it is an undeniable fact that dissatisfaction—nay, hatred—towards that Government exists to a fearful extent in the minds of all classes of people.

The well-wishers of Britain and men of loyal feelings towards the Government are filled with grief and concern when they see things drifting down from *bad* to *worse*. Misrepresentations often appear in administration reports and other documents which convey wrong impressions in the minds of the public. It is apprehended that the state of things now existing in India, if allowed to be continued in for any length of time, will, without fail, bring most disastrous results. The public journals endeavour to do their duty by often drawing attention to such points, but no one heeds their representations. As an instance, the following extract is taken from the *Indian Railway Service Gazette* of 1st March 1879:—

> "The only thing that will save India is a Government conducted on sound and honest principles. That the interest of India have for many years been made subservient to a class of Englishmen, many of whom are little better than adventurers, and have no real regard for the welfare of the people among whom they are called for a brief period to administer justice (according to their light) is now notorious, and if the communities of this vast empire do not exert themselves, but rely upon the beneficence of a Government largely composed of such men, to do ought that may improve the condition of the country, they will find eventually that they have been living in a fool's paradise."

If it be true—and there is no reason to doubt it—that the laws of England (being founded upon the laws of God), when rightly used, are calculated to bring contentment and happiness to mankind, then it is but right, and the manifest duty of all in power, both here and in England, to earnestly and heartily strive to ascertain the cause of the discontent referred to above. Very reliable and correct information in this matter cannot be obtained, for obvious reasons, in the way similar information is usually collected. Native subordinates and paid servants of Government have their own ideas and views in matters of this kind, and seldom like to enlighten their European superiors in any way which does not serve their own purpose. Who can count the number of those holding positions under the Government, who show their loyalty outwardly but at heart harbour the bitterest enmity, and would like to see the administration in its worst state? There are others who, while they have good feelings, and wish the Government well, nevertheless like to adhere to the precept contained in the following Persian verse:—

> "Agar shah roze ra goyed shub ust een,
> Babayed gooft eenuk mah wa purween;"

i.e., should the king affirm the day to be night, it is proper to respond, "Yea, my Lord—behold the moon and stars!" Under these circumstances, in order to obtain correct information, quite a different mode would have to be adopted whereby the mind of the inhabitants in every position could be ascertained. How few there are among the foreign rulers of the country who ever care to sound the real feelings of the people? or endeavour to secure their unreserved confidence? Facts in abundance may be obtained to prove the absolute necessity of immediate reformation in the present administration as well as in the existing laws of the Government, for there are many things in the latter which, however suitable to Europe, are no doubt the reverse when considered in reference to the inhabitants of India, and stand in urgent need of being modified.

The same journal, in its issue of 5th April, 1879, called the subjoined paragraph from the *Standard*, containing suggestions which, if adopted, would greatly benefit India:—

> "One of the advantages of war, Lord Palmerston used to remark, is that it teaches people geography. In like manner recent events have contributed to establish a more real intimacy between this country and India. The truth has been forced upon us that if we desire to retain our great Eastern dependency, and to give it institutions which shall ensure its future prosperity, we must interest ourselves seriously in its welfare. The delusion that India is a rich country has been rudely dispelled. Instead of being an El Dorado, as was at one time vainly imagined, it is generally

understood now that it contains an enormous but exceedingly poor population, exposed to the periodic recurrence of famine, and that its financial position is one of almost chronic deficiency. Indeed, the management of Indian finance has been, more or less, a stumbling block to every administration since the transfer of the empire to the dominions of the Crown. The situation at the present moment is undoubtedly both delicate and grave. Without taking the extreme view urged last evening by Mr. Bright and Mr. Fawcett, that the advance of two millions of money, without interest, to the Indian Government, for the expenses of the Afghan war, is equivalent to a proclamation of bankruptcy, we are ready to admit that the time has arrived when a thorough investigation into the whole system of finance and government in India might be profitably undertaken."

It cannot be denied that in the government of no other country in the world are men paid, as a rule, on so high a scale as are the *covenanted servants* in India. The drain of so many years has impoverished the country and brought it to its present state. Natives compare the transaction to a rich "*honey comb,*" incessantly and vigorously attacked by thousands of strange creatures merely for the sake of its coveted stores; or, in other words, numerous foreigners, with no feeling of attachment or regard for the people, under the ostensible title of *administrators,* are for ever attacking this honey-comb, and taking away rich portions from it to their country, then levying taxes and other means of distress, which adds to the misery of the poor.

An entire revision of the scale of salaries throughout India, in all the grades of Government employment, would appear to be absolutely and urgently necessary. How many posts at present filled by men drawing large salaries might with great advantage, and without inconvenience, be done away with! One simple fact addresses itself to every right-thinking person—though, of course, ignored by the self-interested—and that is, that were but one-fifth of all salaries from Rs. 1,000 and upwards to be struck off, and one-eighth from all salaries below it down to Rs. 300, there would be no taxes ever heard of—no deficits. The solvency of a State is the only proof of good government. Whenever the subject of reduction crops up, the sheers are in most cases applied to men of the ministerial grades and other poor fellows—with many mouths to fill at home—whose names are struck off the rolls, and a list exhibited! the aggregate salary of perhaps a hundred such individuals would scarce equal that of *one* covenanted servant, who *must* be kept on whether of much use or not! Facts of this nature may be multiplied in great numbers, but such is not the province of this book. The above brief remarks, however, were unavoidable in connection with the Eurasians and Anglo-Indians, whose case is becoming one of great hardship, and deserves consideration.

In conclusion it may be added, that Britain truly believes her greatness to be due to the Christian Bible, but sends out men to administer her Indian possessions without due regard to the requirements of that Holy Book. "While the superior governing minds of England are filled with philanthropic impulses, the inferior governing agents in India are petty tyrants."

Will the Statesmen of Great Britain pause for a moment, and reflect upon what foundation are they building the Indian empire. Is it upon a rock, or upon the sand? Mundane plans are unstable; but the purpose of God, that shall stand for ever." God's word declares:—"He that ruleth over men *must be just, ruling in the fear of God!*" and the example of the king mentioned in II Chron. xix. 6, is greatly needed in India, for "he set judges in the land, city by city, and said to the judges, take heed what ye do: for ye judge not for man but for the Lord."

"So shall they fear the name of the Lord from the west, and His glory from the rising of the sun, and when the enemy shall come in like a flood, the Spirit of the Lord shall lift up a standard against him."—Isaiah lix. 19.

England's great Mission to India will only be fulfilled when that country is governed with the sole object and desire of bringing honor and glory to the Great and Gracious Ruler of the Universe, whose are all things, "who sitteth upon the circle of the earth, and the inhabitants thereof are as grasshoppers; who bringeth the princes to nothing, and maketh the judges of the earth as vanity."—Isaiah xl. 22, 23.

SOURCE: In the anonymously authored book, *The Guilty Men of 1857: The Failure of England's Great Mission in India* (London: London Printing Press, 1879). The author is identified as William Jonah Shepherd in Andrew Ward's *Our Bones Are Scattered: The Cawnpore Massacres and the Indian Mutiny* (New York: H. Holt and Co., 1996), 542–44.

Doubts and Forebodings
HENRY GILBERT

For a hundred years 'John Company' had reigned in India. Beginning, about the year 1612, with a few humble factories on the west coast, "The Governors and Company of Merchants in London trading to East India" (a long-winded title quickly shortened to "The East India Company") gradually built up its power, its main interest being the increase of its trade, which yielded enormous profits. The clerks employed by the Company had to know how to use a sword as well as a quill pen, for they often had to throw down the one and snatch up the other to defend their warehouses. As the years went on the lands of the Company increased, until, in the year 1757, the greatest soldier who has ever worked as a clerk at a desk in India—Robert Clive—carved out for his masters an Empire which embraced the rich provinces of Bengal, Behar, and Orissa. From that year the natives reckoned that the British *raj,* or dominion, had struck its roots deep in the land; year after year since then the pride and wealth and power of the British had grown, until the shadow of their name stretched over the continent from the snowy peaks of the Himalayas to the green seas washing the shores of Ceylon.

In 1857 a hundred years had passed, and because of the increasing pride and power of the British all was not well. The seeds of discontent had been sown, and thoughts of rebellion against the power of the white man were shooting up in dark places. In what rank and terrible growths these thoughts were to end it is the purpose of this book to relate.

"Colonel Jacob says that the Bengal Army is rotten to the core, and that it doesn't know what discipline is."

"You do wrong to read the book, my boy. I think it disgraceful that such wild opinions should be allowed to be published."

It was the afternoon of a day early in January, 1857. Three men were seated talking in the big sitting-room of a bungalow at Barrackpore, a town not far from Calcutta. Two of the men were elderly; one, in the undress of an officer of the 34th Native Infantry, was Major Trent; the other was a prominent member of the Indian Civil Service, by name James Douglas. He was Political Officer; in other words, he represented the interests of the British Government (who, since the time of Pitt, had taken over the political control of the territories possessed by the East India Company) in a small native State on the southern border of Bengal. The younger man, who had made the reference to Colonel Jacob's opinion, was the son of Mr Douglas, and was a young lieutenant in the Bengal Army.

For more than a year rumours had been brought by every spy in the Government service, and reports had been docketed and stored up in many pigeon-holes in Government offices, concerning the strange and unaccountable unrest which was said to exist among the 200,000 native troops who formed the Bengal Army. A good many of the officials of the Civil Service, and almost the whole of the military officers, looked on such rumours as inventions of foolish alarmists or of weak-minded individuals, and the generality of Army officers were offended and scandalized at any hint of suspicion that perhaps the sepoys of their own regiments, who drilled so smartly on the parade-ground every morning, were perhaps not so reliable, not so loyal, not so satisfied with their officers and rulers as they were supposed to be. The *Views and Opinions* of Colonel John Jacob, published as far back as 1851, had especially called forth the wrath of every officer from Meerut to Calcutta, and rarely did two or three of them meet without levelling scorn and disgust at the criticisms he had passed in his pages on the military conditions in the army of Bengal.

Major Trent's opinion as expressed in reply to the young subaltern's quotation was the view usually taken by Army men of the work in question.

"My dear Trent, I don't agree," said Mr Douglas. "If things are not what they should be, it would be the height of folly for us to blind ourselves to the truth. I share the opinions of Sir Henry Lawrence, as he has often expressed them. Government under Lord Dalhousie has been moving very fast. There has been too great an impatience to force Western methods and practices upon the natives, and many of the prejudices both of Hindus and Mussulmans have thereby been wounded."

"But, my dear Douglas," said Major Trent, "whatever the late Governor-General may have done to incur the resentment of native princes, I do not, on my word, understand why people should be so quick to question the loyalty of our sepoys."

"I am quite willing to admit," replied Mr Douglas, "that there are many fine and loyal fellows among our sepoys; that on the whole we have reason to be proud of the record of the Army; but things have changed of late. Many officers are like yourself, who treat your men with courtesy and kindness, and they in return look up to you with affection and confidence. But tell me, how many officers are there who dislike their work and strive all they can to get promotion to a civil berth; who take no interest in their men, and get through their duties with as little trouble as possible?"

"No doubt your are right as regards some officers," was the reply. "The men soon see when and if an officer cares for them; but I refuse to believe that disloyalty and corruption are as rampant in our Army as some alarmists affect to believe."

"Very well," returned Mr Douglas; "but you must allow that several changes and events of recent years have shaken the confidence of the sepoy in his faith concerning us."

"In what way? I suppose you refer to the refusal by Headquarters to give the extra pay for foreign service in Scinde? I agree that that was a bad business. The men were justly entitled to it?"

"What did they do?" asked young Douglas.

"Some of them mutinied, and refused to march into the Scinde country," was the reply. "They had been accustomed to receive extra pay and allowances when engaged in foreign service. Scinde was not annexed then. The Government refused to grant the extra money, and as result the Bengal Army was shaken in its belief in the word of honour of the English Government."

"Since I've been out here, too," went on the young man, "I've heard it said that the fact of our taking several English regiments out of the country to fight against the Russians in the Crimea three years ago excited the surprise of many keen-witted natives. 'What,' they said, 'has the English *raj* so few white soldiers that they have to take them from India?'"

"Then, again, I must admit," said Major Trent, who spoke with evident reluctance of the sins of his beloved *baba-log*, or children, the sepoys, "that Lord Dalhousie's command to the 38th Native Regiment to go for service across the sea to Burma was utterly indefensible. The men had enlisted on condition that they were not to cross the 'Black Water,' which they feared and hated; but instead of calling for volunteers, who no doubt would eventually have come forward, he insisted on sending them willy-nilly. Dalhousie had to give in, and of course the story was in all the native lines and bazaars through the length and breadth of Bengal in a day or two."

"Such things shake the confidence of the native soldiers," said Mr Douglas, "who after all are only simple fellows, in many ways very like children."

Major Trent rose to go. "Well," he said, "I must be off. I shall see you both to-night at the Brigadier's dinner."

"I can see, father," said young Douglas when the Major had left the room, "that you feel more keenly on this matter than you were willing to allow the Major to see. Are things really in a bad way?"

"I will not say they are in a bad way exactly, my boy," replied Mr Douglas, after a thoughtful pause; "but there is evidently immense unrest throughout the native quarters and in the Army. In fact, large sections of the people are in a state of bitter hostility to us, and I am assured are only waiting a favourable opportunity to rise against us. The authorities have been warned for months past, but they ignore all warnings, and are so confident of themselves and of the power of the English Government that they seem to despise all you can say. Except, I should say, our two wisest and greatest men, the most sagacious rulers we have—Sir John and Sir Henry Lawrence. They know India and the Indian mind as no one else knows them; they are forewarned, but even their voices are powerless to open the ears of these other men in whose hands lies the government of this country."

"How do you know this, father? What is being done that makes you sure that this unrest is working up to some outburst?"

"I know it from two sources," replied Mr Douglas; "not only from my spies, who keep me informed of what is said in the bazzars, but from intelligent and friendly Hindu and Mussulman gentlemen. You know, my boy, from your reading of history that the most bitter wars have been those waged by reason of religious hatred. God forbid that it should ever come to bloodshed here in India, but many of the natives are convinced that we are determined to force them to become Christians."

"But such a belief is absurd," said the young man. "No Englishman wishes to force his religion upon the natives."

"No Englishman?" was the retort. "I wish I could believe that. But the missionaries have recently sent circulars to many prominent natives trying to prove that the Christian faith will absorb all native faiths. Moreover, Colonel Wheler, of the 34th Native Infantry, has for years been forcing his religion on the sepoys, and preaching to natives everywhere in and out of season. But in other ways the suspicion of such a plot has been encouraged by our own actions. The Brahmin priests hate us, and the Mohammedan *maulevis*, or learned men, suspect us. We know and we teach too much. Their young men are learning Western ideas from us, and begin to despise their own priests and teachers. Once the Brahmin priest was able to say that all good usages, all good inventions, came from God by their special intercession. To gain further good things the priests were paid by their ignorant flocks, and so waxed rich and fat. But we have brought in the 'fire-carriage' or locomotive on the iron road, and the 'lightning post' or telegraph, and men are carried at marvellous speed, and messages are sent to and from great distances in a few minutes. Then, again, the natives remember how we tried to make the prisoners in the jails give up cooking their own food and wished to put in cooks to prepare the food. That, they said, was a treacherous attempt to defile them, and there were riots in the persons and the towns. A prisoner killed a judge with the brass drinking-vessel which, as you know, every native carries about with him, and which no one but himself must use. We tried to take it away in the prisons and to make the fellows use earthenware vessels. That also led to riots. In these and in other ways we have disturbed the mind of the native, until there seems to be a great fear throughout the Presidency, which gives rise to all manner to wild rumours and evil tales."

"But surely all these things by themselves, though of course they indicate unrest and discontent, will not lead to any outbreak?" asked the young man.

"By themselves they are not much to be feared," said Mr Douglas, "but I greatly fear that they are being turned to account by people whom we have made our enemies—and we have many among the princes and aristocracy of the Mahrattas and Mohammedans."

"You mean in connexion with the recent annexation of Oudh?"

"My dear boy," returned his father, "Oudh is only the last of a long series of usurpations (as I fear I must call them) committed by our late Governor-General, Lord Dalhousie, who, together with much that is praiseworthy, has caused and done much that has sowed seeds of trouble the results of which we shall reap later. It was he who began to deny the right which native princes always possessed of adopting a successor when they had no natural male heirs. In such cases he considered the princely line had lapsed and thereupon annexed the country. Satarah was acquired in that way in 1849, then followed Sambhalpore, Nagpore, and Jhansi. How have the natives taken these annexations, as we call them? They would be quite willing to accept them as the result of conquest, but the refusal of the right of adoption was looked upon as greed and injustice. The result has been that every prince in the country trembles, and wonders if his princedom will be seized next; and the people who have been dispossessed and whose palaces and goods have been sold up hate us bitterly."

"But surely, dad, you must allow that Oudh was most wretchedly governed by the weak king?"

"Admitted," was the reply; "but we should have followed the advice of our greatest administrator, a man for whom my admiration is unbounded, I mean Sir Henry Lawrence. There is no man in India who can approach him for far-sighted statesmanship, knowledge of the natives, their thoughts, their weaknesses, and their fine points. He has condemned the annexation of Oudh in no uncertain terms. He has advised that we should govern the country for the benefit of its people, and should make no profit out of its revenues. But we have ignored his advice. The King of Oudh, feeble-minded though he was, had always been our friend. Why, then, ask the natives, should we have annexed his country? In Oudh this action has created thousands of enemies, not only among people in the province itself, but in the ranks of our Bengal Army, the greater part of which has been recruited from Oudh."

"So that you think we are estranging both our Hindu and our Mohammedan subjects?"

"Both; according to what I learn, are deeply resentful toward us. Our new system of land settlements, under which we have dispossessed thousands of little aristocrats and have thrust into penury multitudes of old families who have hitherto been proud of their position and of their wealth, has roused the passions of anger and revenge among both Hindus and Mussulmans. We have made no difference between either; both equally have felt the crushing weight of our Western system of government, which has been too heavily applied to a people who have ever been used to quite different forms of government."

"I am very sorry indeed to hear what you say, father," said young Douglas; "but I know you do not speak without being able to justify all you state. Indeed, what you tell me now only confirms what I read the other day in an old volume of the *Calcutta Review,* in an article written by Sir Henry Lawrence. It struck me as most strange that the warnings of so great an authority should be so long ignored by the powers that be. He said that a revolt of the sepoys will assuredly come unless we take steps to prevent it."

"That has been his opinion for the last twelve years," replied Mr Douglas. "To some it implies that any disturbance will be merely of a military character. But he is also alive to the fact that any outbreak will be wider than that: it will be taken up by the princes and aristocrats—it will be political as well. There is one disaffected person whom I mistrust deeply. We have refused to give him the pension which we gave his adopted father, the Peishwa of Bithoor. I refer to Nana Sahib. He affects to be our sincere friend, but my spies tell a different tale. If I am not greatly mistaken he is the centre of a deep plot which may wreck our Indian Empire. Believe me, we shall hear more of that man."

SOURCE: Chapter 1 in *The Story of the Indian Mutiny* (New York: Thomas Y. Crowell, n.d.). The mutiny novel also lists Gilbert as the author of other popular-historical novels, including *The Conquerors of Peru* (no information available), *The Book of Pirates* (no information available), and *The Conquerors of Mexico* (New York: T.Y. Crowell, 1914).

What the Native Thought
HENRY GILBERT

A few days after the conversation which is recorded in the previous chapter a native workman, or 'classie,' went out of the cartridge manufactory at Dum-Dum, a place not far from Calcutta, and passed a sepoy soldier of the 2nd Grenadiers. The classie was a man of low caste, while the sepoy was a high-class Brahmin. The latter walked aside as the classie approached him, as if he feared to be contaminated. The low-caste workman stopped and smiled with a sneer.

"Give me a drink from your *lotah,* soldier," he said, pointing to the brass drinking-vessel which was hung at the sepoy's belt. This was never allowed to leave the soldier's possession, since if it was used by a person of lower caste the owner became contaminated.

"Thou fool," replied the sepoy. "How can I let thee drink from that which thy touch would defile?"

"You think much of your caste," said the workman with a sneer; "but wait a little. The *sahib-log* [white gentlemen] will soon make high and low caste on one level."

"How meanest thou?"

"In the factory there they are making a new kind of cartridge. Beef fat and hogs' lard are being used in the paper which your holy lips will have to touch, and all you sepoys will have to use them. Then where will be your caste?"

The classie walked off with a mocking laugh, while the Brahmin soldier gazed at him with horror on his face.

To a high-class Hindu such a piece of news was worse than a condemnation to death. The bullock was a sacred animal to him, and to eat or touch any part of its flesh was impious, and would instantly bring about the loss of caste. To lose his caste was to be thrust out from amid his relatives and friends like a pariah dog; no kinsman would own him, his very children would avoid him, and he would have to live with the street-sweepers, the grass-cutters, the water-carriers—men and women who, to his Brahminical mind, were so low of caste as to be like the dogs.

The horrified grenadier rushed away to the cantonments where, each in his little hut, the soldiers of his regiment lived, with wives and children and numerous relatives, who lived upon their pay. Soon the news spread through the lines of huts, and every one fell to talking of it with anger and fear in their hearts. Few of them disbelieved the tale; to most it seemed to confirm what their priests and wise men, both Hindu and Mussulman, had long asserted, namely, that it was the intention of the *sahib-log* to rob them treacherously of their caste, and thus compel them to come into the only religion left open to them, that of the Christians. The latter were eaters of pigs and cattle, they disbelieved in the gods of both the Hindu and the Mohammedan, and were therefore unclean heathens. Rather than embrace their religion, the sepoys of the Indian Army would suffer death.

The distressing news quickly circulated throughout Bengal, and in every cantonment was sullenly accepted as the truth. In the old days, when the sepoy had confidence in his white officer, the native soldier would have gone to that officer and asked why this cartridge was being made. But now the soldiers whispered among themselves; they kept their feelings to themselves, and the white men knew nothing of the anger, the panic terror, and the disgust which were gradually filling the ranks of the Bengal Army with the seeds of mutiny.

If, indeed, the sepoys had asked whether a change so repugnant to the ideas of both Hindu and Mussulman was really to be introduced into the musketry instruction of the Army, their officers would have had to confess that such a tremendous blunder *was* contemplated. The musket hitherto used in the

Indian Uprising/Sepoy Mutiny 537

Indian Army, commonly known as 'Brown Bess,' required that the paper cartridge to be used with it should be bitten off at the end before being rammed down the barrel of the gun. It was proposed to introduce an improved fire-arm, the Enfield rifle, which required that the cartridge should be greased. This also had to be bitten or torn before being used. By some almost incredible oversight the fat of cows and pigs was used for the purpose of greasing the new cartridges, though as yet none of them had actually been given out.

The mere report, however, that the grease used was formed of the fat of the animals mentioned was sufficient to instill terror in the minds of the ignorant and suspicious native soldiers.

Those who had long nursed enmity against the British rule now seized an opportunity so favourable for their schemes. The sepoys were already infuriated against the Government by real grievances, and in this blunder concerning the cartridges the agitators saw the match that would set ablaze the smouldering passions of the people.

The conversation which went on one day a little later in January, in the shadow of a big banyan-tree on the outskirts of a village not far from Delhi, was being reduplicated over and over again every day throughout the length and breadth of Bengal.

The elders of the village were seated discussing the strange rumours which were passing from village to village in these days. Among them were two of their sons, sepoys on leave of absence, one of Meerut and the other from Cawnpore. It was these men who were confirming by what they said the vague fears of the villagers.

"The *sahib-log* are traitors—they are sly as foxes," said one soldier, Shumshoodeen Khan. "Once they were guardians of the poor and givers of benefits, but now they stint and scrape like a very housewife. Also, they mean evil to our religion, for it is their plan that all Hindus shall be made Christians."

"Once, also," said the other, by name Teeka Sing, "they loved us—we were their *baba-log*, their children—but now they love those wolves, the Sikhs, whom we helped them to conquer. They despise us so much that they are raising an army of thirty thousand Sikh dogs, and when that is done they will disband us."

"Surely, brother," said one of the old villagers, "it is not true what is said, that the sahibs have a plan to destroy our religion?"

"It is true, Siddu," replied Shumshoodeen Khan, the soldier from Cawnpore. "I heard it from Azimoolah himself, the princely friend of Nana Sahib, Peishwa of Bithoor. The Queen has sent out this Lord Sahib Canning for that express purpose—the Hindus and Mussulmans of India are to be made

Christians, come what may. 'But,' said the Lord Sahib, 'it will be a huge task. I shall first have to slay three hundred thousand holy and learned men, the teachers of both religions, our *moulvies* and *pundits*.' 'Nevertheless,' said the Queen, 'let it be done!' And," ended the speaker, "it is to be done."

"Why is it," asked the other, speaking with passion in his voice, "that now they have made a new oath for young soldiers joining our ranks—an oath that they shall go across the Black Water and fight wherever the sahibs desire them? They know that by so doing we risk the losing of our caste. Why do they make a law that our widows may remarry? Why has the Mem-Sahib done so much to get our native women converted to the Christian faith, and why have their colonel sahibs preached to every one to become Christians and brothers, and their missionaries sent abroad a printed paper telling us all to be of the faith of those that brought in the lightning wire and the fire carriage?"

"And these evil cartridges, smeared with the fat of pigs and cows!" cried the other, "what does that mean? We bite them every time we fire our guns, and thus we are defiled."

"But," said one old village elder, who had himself served in the Bengal Army, and had been servant to an English officer and learnt much of the ways of the sahibs, "I am told that none of the evil cartridges has yet been issued, except to those few who are learning to shoot with the new rifle."

"That is what the sahibs say," replied the soldier from Cawnpore; "but their minds are deep and their lies are sly. All their cartridges are things of defilement, and we men of the 2nd Cavalry have sworn—"

The soldier checked himself. Toward them a stranger was coming, a villager from some distant place. In one hand he held a spear, while in the other was a round cake, flat and small, similar to those which every Hindu makes for himself for his daily food. He approached the white-bearded headman of the village and greeted him. Then, handing him the cake, or *chupatti*, he said:

"It is for the elders. From the south to the north, from the east to the west."

"Whence and why?" asked the elder.

"That is all," replied the messenger. "Do thou pass it on as we do."

Men looked at the *chupatti* and then at each other in silence. Then one of the sepoys, having muttered to the other, spoke aloud:

"It is the sign," he said. "The holy Mussulman, the Moulvie of Fyzabad, and the Nana Sahib, Lord of Bithoor, have sent this as a sign that all hearts should take courage. The time is near now."

"What time?" asked one.

The soldier smiled and replied grimly:

"*Sub lal hoga hi*—when everything is to become red."

"Nay," said Doorga Sing, the headman; "it is an ancient way of sending on news. My father's father has told me of it."

"And what is the news this sends, Doorga Sing?" asked the man from Cawnpore ironically.

"We shall learn anon," said the headman gravely.

"You will indeed," was the answer. "But, meanwhile, it is a sign that you should keep yourself prepared, with loins girded up, your spear sharp and your flintlock well oiled. For something great is in the air."

"I heard a saying two days ago," said the other; "it was in the bazaar, and a holy fakir uttered it, and it was something in these words: 'The Kumpani came in 1757. Look for its end in a hundred years.' For a hundred years have the sahibs ruled us and oppressed us."

"Ay, ay," added Shumshoodeen Khan, as he got up from his squatting position and swaggered away, "the Mussulmans have a prophecy:

'Fire worship for a hundred years,
A century of Christ and tears,
Then the True God shall come again
And every infidel be slain.'"

SOURCE: Chapter 2 in *The Story of the Indian Mutiny* (New York: Thomas Y. Crowell, n.d.).

The Grave of the Hundred Head
RUDYARD KIPLING

*There's a widow in sleepy Chester
Who weeps for her only son;
There's a grave on the Pabeng River,
A grave that the Burmans shun,
And there's Subadar Prag Tewarri
Who tells how the work was done.*

A Snider squibbed in the jungle—
Somebody laughed and fled,
And the men of the First Shikaris
Picked up their Subaltern dead,
With a big blue mark in his forehead
And the back blown out of his head.

Subadar Prag Tewarri,
Jemadar Hira Lal,
Took command of the party,
Twenty rifles in all,
Marched them down to the river
As the day was beginning to fall.

They buried the boy by the river,
A blanket over his face—
They wept for their dead Lieutenant,
The men of an alien race—
They made a *samádh* in his honour,
A mark for his resting-place.

For they swore by the Holy Water,
They swore by the salt they ate,
That the soul of Lieutenant Eshmitt Sahib
Should go to his God in state;
With fifty file of Burman
To open him Heaven's gate.

The men of the First Shikaris
Marched till the break of day,
Till they came to the rebel village,
The village of Pabengmay—
A *jingal* covered the clearing,
Calthrops hampered the way.

Subadar Prag Tewarri,
Bidding them load with ball,
Halted a dozen rifles
Under the village-wall;
Sent out a flanking-party
With Jemadar Hira Lal.

The men of the First Shikaris
Shouted and smote and slew,
Turning the grinning *jingal*
On to the howling crew.
The Jemadar's flanking-party
Butchered the folk who flew.

Long was the morn of slaughter,
Long was the list of slain,
Five score heads were taken
Five score heads and twain;
And the men of the First Shikaris
Went back to their grave again;

Each man bearing a basket
Red as his palms that day,
Red as the blazing village—
The village of Pabengmay.
And the "*drip-drip-drip*" from the baskets
Reddened the grass by the way.

They made a pile of their trophies
High as a tall man's chin,
Head upon head distorted,
Clinched in a sightless grin,
Anger and pain and terror
Writ on the smoke-scorched skin.

Subadar Prag Tewarri
Set the head of the Boh
On the top of the mound of triumph
The head of his son below,
With the sword and the peacock-banner
That the world might behold and know.

Thus the *samádh* was perfect,
Thus was the lesson plain
Of the wrath of the First Shikaris—
The price of a white man slain;
And the men of the First Shikaris
Went back into camp again.

Then a silence came to the river,
A hush fell over the shore,
And Bohs that were brave departed,
And Sniders squibbed no more;
For the Burmans said
That a *kullah's* head
Must be paid for with heads five score.

> *There's a widow in sleepy Chester*
> *Who weeps for her only son;*
> *There's a grave on the Pabeng River,*
> *A grave that the Burmans shun,*
> *And there's Subadar Prag Tewarri*
> *Who tells how the work was done.*

SOURCE: This poem is from an anthology of Rudyard Kipling's military poems, *Departmental Ditties and Ballads and Barrack Room Ballads* (New York: Doubleday, 1899).

The Defence of Lucknow
ALFRED TENNYSON

First printed in 'The Nineteenth Century' for April, 1879, and included in the 'Ballads,' 1880.

The events recorded in the poem occurred during the Sepoy Rebellion in British India, in 1857. 'Sir Henry Lawrence took charge of Lucknow as Resident in March of that year. The spread of rebellion in June confined him to the defence of the city, where he died of wounds on July 4. Brigadier Inglis, in succession, then defended Lucknow for twelve weeks until it was relieved on September 25 by General Havelock, to whom Sir James Outram (who accompanied as volunteer) had generously ceded the exploit' (Palgrave).

I
Banner of England, not for a season, O banner of Britain, hast thou
Floated in conquering battle or flapt to the battle-cry!
Never with mightier glory than when we had rear'd thee on high
Flying at top of the roofs in the ghastly siege of Lucknow—
Shot thro' the staff or the halyard, but ever we raised thee anew,
And ever upon the topmost roof our banner of England blew.

II
Frail were the works that defended the hold that we held with our lives—
Women and children among us, God help them, our children and wives!
Hold it we might—and for fifteen days or for twenty at most.
'Never surrender, I charge you, but every man die at his post!' (10)
Voice of the dead whom we loved, our Lawrence the best of the brave;

Cold were his brows when we kiss'd him—we laid him that night in his
    grave.
'Every man die at his post!' and there hail'd on our houses and halls
Death from their rifle-bullets, and death from their cannon-balls,
Death in our innermost chamber, and death at our slight barricade,
Death while we stood with the musket, and death while we stoopt to the
    spade,
Death to the dying, and wounds to the wounded, for often there fell,
Striking the hospital wall, crashing thro' it, their shot and their shell,
Death—for their spies were among us, their marksmen were told of our
    best,
So that the brute bullet broke thro' the brain that could think for the rest;
                                                                (20)
Bullets would sing by our foreheads, and bullets would rain at our feet—
Fire from ten thousand at once of the rebels that girdled us round—
Death at the glimpse of a finger from over the breadth of a street,
Death from the heights of the mosque and the palace, and death in the
    ground!
Mine? yes, a mine! Countermine! down, down! and creep thro' the hole!
Keep the revolver in hand! you can hear him—the murderous mole!
Quiet, ah! quiet—wait till the point of the pickaxe be thro'-!
Click with the pick, coming nearer and nearer again than before—
Now let it speak, and you fire, and the dark pioneer is no more;
And ever upon the topmost roof our banner of England blew!   (30)

III

Ay, but the foe sprung his mine many times, and it chanced on a day
Soon as the blast of that underground thunder-clap echo'd away,
Dark thro' the smoke and the sulphur like so many fiends in their hell—
Cannot-shot, musket-shot, volley on volley, and yell upon yell—
Fiercely on all the defences our myriad enemy fell.
What have they done? where is it? Out yonder. Guard the Redan!
Storm at the Water-gate! storm at the Bailey-gate! storm, and it ran
Surging and swaying all round us, as ocean on every side
Plunges and heaves at a bank that is daily drown'd by the tide—
So many thousands that, if they be bold enough, who shall escape?   (40)
Kill or be kill'd, live or die, they shall know we are soldiers and men!
Ready! take aim at their leaders—their masses are gapp'd with our grape—
Backward they reel like the wave, like the wave flinging forward again.

Flying and foil'd at the last by the handful they could not subdue;
And ever upon the topmost roof our banner of England blew.

IV

Handful of men as we were, we were English in heart and in limb,
Strong with the strength of the race to command, to obey, to endure,
Each of us fought as if hope for the garrison hung but on him;
Still—could we watch at all points? we were every day fewer and fewer.
There was a whisper among us, but only a whisper that past: (50)
'Children and wives—if the tigers leap into the fold unawares—
Every man die at his post—and the foe may outlive us at last—
Better to fall by the hands that they love, than to fall into theirs!'
Roar upon roar in a moment two mines by the enemy sprung
Clove into perilous chasms our walls and our poor palisades.
Rifleman, true is your heart, but be sure that your hand be as true!
Sharp is the fire of assault, better aimed are your flank fusillades—
Twice do we hurl them to earth from the ladders to which they had clung,
Twice from the ditch where they shelter we drive them with hand-grenades;
And ever upon the topmost roof our banner of England blew. (60)

V

Then on another wild morning another wild earthquake out-tore
Clean from our lines of defence ten or twelve good paces or more.
Rifleman, high on the roof, hidden there from the light of the sun—
One has leapt up on the breach, crying out: 'Follow me, follow me!'—
Mark him—he falls! then another, and *him* too, and down goes he.
Had they been bold enough then, who can tell but the traitors had won?
Boardings and rafters and doors—an embrasure! make way for the gun!
Now double-charge it with grape! It is charged and we fire, and they run.
Praise to our Indian brothers, and let the dark face have his due!
Thanks to the kindly dark faces who fought with us, faithful and few, (70)
Fought with the bravest among us, and drove them, and smote them, and slew,
That ever upon the topmost roof our banner in India blew.

VI

Men will forget what we suffer and not what we do. We can fight!
But to be soldier all day, and be sentinel all thro' the night—
Ever the mine and assault, our sallies, their lying alarms,

Bugles and drums in the darkness, and shoutings and soundings to arms,
Ever the labor of fifty that had to be done by five,
Ever the marvel among us that one should be left alive,
Ever the day with its traitorous death from the loopholes around,
Ever the night with its coffinless corpse to be laid in the ground, (80)
Heat like the mouth of a hell, or a deluge of cataract skies,
Stench of old offal decaying, and infinite torment of flies,
Thoughts of the breezes of May blowing over an English field,
Cholera, scurvy, and fever, the wound that *would* not be heal'd,
Lopping away of the limb by the pitiful-pitiless knife,—
Torture and trouble in vain,—for it never could save us a life.
Valor of delicate women who tended the hospital bed,
Horror of women in travail among the dying and dead,
Grief for our perishing children, and never a moment for grief,
Toil and ineffable weariness, faltering hopes of relief, (90)
Havelock baffled, or beaten, or butcher'd for all that we knew—
Then day and night, day and night, coming down on the still-shatter'd walls
Millions of musket-bullets, and thousands of cannon-balls—
But ever upon the topmost roof our banner of England blew.

VII

Hark cannonade, fusillade! is it true that was told by the scout,
Outram and Havelock breaking their way through the fell mutineers?
Surely the pibroch of Europe is ringing again in our ears!
All on a sudden the garrison utter a jubilant shout,
Havelock's glorious Highlanders answer with conquering cheers,
Sick from the hospital echo them, women and children come out, (100)
Blessing the wholesome white faces of Havelock's good fusileers,
Kissing the war-harden'd hand of the Highlander wet with their tears!
Dance to the pibroch!—saved! we are saved!—is it you! is it you?
Saved by the valor of Havelock, saved by the blessing of heaven!
'Hold it for fifteen days!' we have held it for eighty-seven!
And ever aloft on the palace roof the old banner of England blew.

SOURCE: This poem is from Alfred Tennyson's collection *Ballads and Other Poems* (Boston: James R. Osgood, 1880).

English War-Song
ALFRED TENNYSON

Who fears to die? Who fears to die?
Is there any here who fears to die?
He shall find what he fears; and none shall grieve
For the man who fears to die;
But the withering scorn of the man shall cleave
To the man who fears to die.

CHORUS.
Shout for England!
Ho! for England
George for England!
Merry England!
England for aye!

The hollow at heart shall crouch forlorn,
He shall eat the bread of common scorn;
It shall be steeped in the salt, salt tear,
Shall be steeped in his own salt tear:
Far better, far better he never were born
Than to shame merry England here.
CHO.—Shout for England! etc.

There standeth our ancient enemy;
Hark! he shouteth—the ancient enemy!
On the ridge of the hill his banners rise;
They stream like fire in the skies;
Hold up the Lion of England on high
Till it dazzle and blind his eyes.
CHO.—Shout for England! etc.

Come along! we alone of the earth are free;
The child in our cradles is bolder than he;
For where is the heart and strength of slaves?
Oh! where is the strength of slaves?
He is weak! we are strong: he a slave, we are free;
Come along! we will dig their graves.
CHO.—Shout for England! etc.

There standeth our ancient enemy;
Will he dare to battle with the free?
Spur along! spur amain! charge to the fight:
Charge! charge to the fight!
Hold up the Lion of England on high!
Shout for God and our right!
CHO.—Shout for England! etc.

SOURCE: This poem is from Alfred Tennyson's collection *Ballads and Other Poems* (Boston: James R. Osgood, 1880).

The Indian Mutiny
M. B. SYNGE

[A useful companion piece to Synge's English children's history is *The Children's History of India* (Delhi: Publications Division, Ministry of Information and Broadcasting, 1962); the chapter "The Great Revolt" is especially interesting.]

"Handful of men as we were, we were English in heart and in limb,
Strong with the strength of the race to command, to obey, to endure."—Tennyson

But while the Queen was presenting the Victoria Cross on that summer day of 1857 to those of her brave soldiers who had distinguished themselves in the Crimea, alarming news was reaching England of a native revolt in another part of her Dominions, a revolt known to history as the Indian Mutiny.

"There are times in the history of every nation when she must either fight or go down."

Such a time had come now. Swiftly, silently the blow fell, and heroically, alone, without an ally, against odds too great to be counted, England in the face of the world set to work to re-conquer India.

Discontent had long been simmering thoughout the country; Lord Dalhousie, one of the most famous Governor-Generals India has ever seen, had brought province after province under British rule. He had added Satara in 1848, the first year of his residence, and the Punjab in the following year. Later, the Rajah of Nagpur died without heirs and that Principality was likewise added to the British Dominions, being known to-day as the Central

Provinces. After this the kingdom of Oudh was annexed—a country as large as Belgium and Holland—until Lord Dalhousie had increased England's possessions in India by more than a third. A colossal worker, he sought to bind together the scattered parts by telegraph and railway. To this same end, he made the largest of Indian canals, he carried the Grand Trunk road through the Punjab, and only returned home to die, when his physical strength failed to bear the burden.

Utterly worn out with his efforts on behalf of the British Empire, he "tottered on crutches down the banks of the Hugli (Calcutta) to embark for England, predicting that troubles were ahead for India. England had increased her land, but there was no increase of English men to hold it.

This was because every one, both in India and at home, believed in the loyalty of the native soldiers, or Sepoys as they were called. When the Mutiny broke out, there were just five times as many Sepoys as British soldiers in India. At the death of Queen Victoria there was a large proportion of English soldiers, so that a repetition of this terrible catastrophe in English history is impossible.

But in 1857 there was a growing feeling among the natives that the old state of things was passing away; they thought the English wanted to make them Christians, and they believed the native prophecy that a hundred years after Plassey, English rule should cease. The anniversary fell on June 23, 1857, and but for the grand courage of Havelock, the fierce energy of Nicholson, the unsleeping toil and forethought of Lawrence, this prophecy would have come true.

Matters reached a climax at last.

Up to this time the Sepoys had been armed with a musket popularly known as "Brown Bess." In 1857 an improved rifle, known as the Enfield, was substituted. It was rumoured that the new rifles required greased cartridges, and that they were greased with hog's lard, forbidden to Mohammedans. A panic of religious fear ran from regiment to regiment, from village to village.

Early in May some cartridges were served out to a native regiment at Meerut, near Delhi. They were refused by eighty-five Sepoys, who were tried, disarmed, publicly paraded, and marched in chains to the local prison, which was guarded by native officials.

The following day was Sunday. The weather was fiercely hot, but as evening wore on, the little English community made ready for church. They little thought that the church bells were to mark the beginning of the great Indian Mutiny. It was the arranged signal for the Sepoys to revolt.

They burst open the prison, released the eighty-five martyrs, and then proceeded to fire on their officers. Some thirty English against two thousand angry mutineers had little chance, and soon the dusky natives were marching forth in full battle array for Delhi, some thirty-eight miles distant.

Delhi, one of the oldest and stateliest towns in the newly acquired Punjab, on the sacred Jumna, was surrounded by a wall pierced by seven gates, about a mile distant one from the other. In the centre stood the Imperial Palace, where lived the last King of Delhi—the descendant of the Great Mogul. The mutineers arrived early on the morning of May 11th, shouting defiantly and slaying any English they met. Delhi was entirely held by Sepoys officered by Englishmen.

These Englishmen with their wives and children were now butchered without mercy or pity, and in a few days the mutineers had possession of the whole city, which they held till September, besieged by a mere handful of British. On June the 7th an English officer named Willoughby, in "heroic despair," blew up the powder-magazine to save it from falling into the hands of the enemy.

It has been said that "nothing in British history is a more kindling tale of endurance and valour than the story of how for months a handful of British clung to the Ridge outside Delhi, fighting daily with foes ten times more numerous than themselves," besieging the great city, which was the heart of the whole Mutiny, till at the last John Nicholson bought it with his life.

Meanwhile the Mutiny was breaking out in other parts of India. Cawnpore, on the banks of the Ganges, was 270 miles from Delhi, an important military station with vast magazines and a rich treasury. It was held only by Sepoys and a mere handful of British soldiers. An old man of seventy-five, Sir Hugh Wheeler, was in command.

On June 4th the Sepoys revolted, secretly roused by Nana Sahib, a powerful Hindu, who pretended to be on friendly terms with the English, while playing the villain's part of a traitor. The little white population entrenched themselves as best they might behind low mud walls and here for three long and dreary weeks a few Englishmen defended themselves, their wives, and children against the onslaught of the enemy. By the third day all shelter had been destroyed and the hot Indian sun beat pitilessly down on the sick and wounded.

"The annals of warfare contain no episode so painful as the story of this siege," says Sir George Trevelyan. "The sun never before looked on such a sight as a crowd of women and children cooped within a small space and exposed, during twenty days and nights, to the concentrated fire of thousands of muskets and a score of heavy cannon."

The days passed heavily by, each with its deeds of heroism, its acts of self-sacrifice, its pitiful record of wasted life. In three weeks no less than 250 had died from hunger, thirst, and wounds. On June 23rd—the anniversary of Plassey—a determined assault was made by the enemy, but in vain. The following day found the little garrison in despair. "The British spirit alone remains," wrote the old General, "but it cannot last for ever." This was true, and when, on the twenty-first day, Nana Sahib offered a safe passage to Allahabad to those willing to surrender, he felt obliged to accept for the sake of the women and children.

Slowly the feeble remnant of the besieged, "speechless and motionless as spectres" tottered from their forlorn shelter, to make their way to the banks of the Ganges, for them "the Valley of the Shadow of Death." They had not reached the boats, when suddenly a bugle rang through the silent air and from the banks of the river a murderous fire was poured into the hapless crowd. Sir Hugh Wheeler was among the first to perish. Happy were those whose sufferings were not prolonged.

Some hundred and twenty survivors were dragged back to Cawnpore, where a yet more terrible fate awaited them. Here they were crowded into a small building with two rooms, no bedding, and no furniture; the English ladies were made to grind corn for the traitor Nana, who had already murdered all the men, their husbands, brothers, and sons. Sickness and death thinned their ranks day by day. They did not know of the help even now approaching. General Havelock, a little iron-grey man, no longer young, with the "tiniest force that ever set forth to the task of saving an empire" was marching hard from Allahabad to the relief of Cawnpore. "If India is ever in danger," it had been said, "let Havelock be put in command of an army and it will be saved."

These words were ringing true now. On July 7th he began his march at the head of 1,500 men in a gallant if vain attempt to save the English women and children imprisoned at Cawnpore. The ground over which they marched was swampy with the first furious rains of summer, the skies were white with the glare of an Indian sun in July; but Havelock inspired his men with his own scorn of ease, his strong sense of duty, and deep earnestness, and "Havelock's Saints" as they have been called, never wavered in their allotted task.

They were resting at Futtehpore after five days of hard marching, when, with wild shouts, a huge mass of native cavalry rushed upon them. Fiercely and swiftly the little English band advanced; in ten minutes they had captured the rebel guns and the Nana's troops were in full flight. It was not till the 17th that, having marched 126 miles and fought four battles, Havelock reached the outskirts of Cawnpore.

But he was too late. A grim and awful massacre of the women and children had just taken place, by orders of Nana Sahib, from which not one soul had escaped alive, and all the bodies had been thrown into a well in the courtyard hard by. When Havelock and his men entered the room where their fellow-countrywomen had been butchered so lately, the scene was both horrible and pitiful. The floor was strewn with relics: there were pinafores, little shoes and hats, the fly-leaf of a Bible, and some children's curls—all speaking of a time of anguish unspeakable.

To-day over the well at Cawnpore where the poor bodies were thrown stands a white marbel angel by Marochetti with clasped hands and outspread wings—a memorial of those sufferings, which are part of the price of Empire.

SOURCE: Chapter 21 in *The Great Victorian Age for Children* (London: Hodder and Stoughton, 1908).

X
THE SUEZ CANAL:
THE GALA OPENNG

INTRODUCTION
Spectacular Suez: The Opening Gala of the Suez Canal
MIA CARTER

A whole world must be set in motion.—Auguste Mariette, Egyptologist.

THE INAUGURATION of the Suez Canal was a spectacular theatrical event, designed to display the canal as one of the world's more recent wonders, a feat envisioned by European genius and accomplished by European technology. Ismail Pasha, the Khedive of Egypt under whose administration the canal was completed, considered the Suez Canal Egypt's passage to Europe and the modern world. Hans Busch, a Verdi scholar, reports that Pasha proclaimed, "My country is no longer in Africa. I have made it part of Europe" (*Verdi's Aida*, 6). Ismail Pasha, educated in Paris and enamored of things European, was willing to pay any price to present Egypt as *the* cultural capital of the African continent. He instituted a museum for Egyptian antiquities, ordered the building of the Cairo Opera House, and funded the inauguration to celebrate his reign and Egypt's glorious future. Ismail Pasha, Ferdinand De Lesseps, and Auguste (Bey) Mariette, the famous archaeologist and Egyptologist who conceived the original outline for *Aida*, similarly considered Egypt—its land, its architectural and cultural history—a stage, a site in which splendid and magnificent possibilities could be realized. Even the surrounding countryside was incorporated into the grand production; for example, the extant roadway from Cairo to the pyramids was rushed to completion in six weeks to coincide with the canal's opening. Historian Arnold Wilson reports that this feat was accomplished "by forced labour urged on by the lash" (*Suez Canal*, 40).

Ismail Pasha's economic confidence was understandable. The Civil War in the United States had enabled Egypt to corner the world's cotton market; Egyptian profits were considerable. The Pasha's plans for Egypt were as visionary and ambitious as De Lesseps's plans for the canal and Mariette's for the opera that would celebrate the canal's existence. The Egyptian ruler expanded Egyptian commerce and industry and reformed his nation's courts, schools, and universities; his political desires and investments were, in part, influenced by friends like De Lesseps, who convinced him that the canal would revivify Egypt. But the canal was also a massive financial burden for the Egyptian people, whose taxes and labor assisted its completion; Pasha's political designs thus bankrupted his country and jeopardized its future. The grave results of the high expenditures, however, were not in plain sight during the inaugural festivities. As the etchings of the canal celebrations and the staging designs for Verdi's opera suggest, the canal and its cultural constellations were indeed grand—a whole world *was* set in motion, as the canal itself had changed the map of the political future.

BIBLIOGRAPHY

Budden, Julian. *The Operas of Verdi, Volume Three: From Don Carlos to Falstaff.* New York: Oxford University Press, 1981.
Busch, Hans. *Verdi's Aida: The History of an Opera in Letters and Documents.* Minneapolis: University of Minnesota Press, 1978.
Osborne, Charles. *Verdi: A Life in the Theatre.* London: Weidenfeld and Nicolson, 1987.
Phillips-Matz, Mary Jane. *Verdi: A Biography.* New York: Oxford University Press, 1993.
Said, Edward. *Culture and Imperialism.* New York: Knopf, 1993.
Wilson, Arnold. *The Suez Canal: Its Past, Present, and Future.* London: Oxford University Press, 1939.

Selected Correspondence of Giuseppe Verdi

[Giuseppe Verdi (1813–1901) was born the impoverished son of an Italian tavern-keeper and grocer. His youthful musical talents attracted the attention of Antonio Barezzi, a music amateur who paid for Verdi's education and served as his patron. Verdi was a well-known and successful composer by the time the Khedive contacted him to write *Aida;* his grand operas—*Macbeth* (1847), *Rigoletto* (1851), *Il Trovatore* (1853), *La Traviata* (1853)—had already been written and produced. Verdi accepted the invitation to compose the opera for the Suez Canal's opening, but rejected the invitation to write the inaugural hymn for the opening. *Aida* debuted at the newly built Cairo Opera House two years after the inaugural opening on Christmas Eve, 1871.]

Auguste Mariette to Camille Du Locle

Boulaq,[1] 27 April 1870
My dear friend,

I received your two letters.[2] I expected M. Verdi's refusal, which will rather annoy the Viceroy. But try to see our viewpoint. If M. Gounod accepts, we would be very happy. With regard to Prince P.,[3] I think that there are some clouds involved and that the Viceroy would only hesitatingly enter into an agreement.

1. A suburb of Cairo. See biographical note on Auguste Mariette.
2. These two letters, obviously written during Verdi's stay in Paris, are missing.
3. Joseph Michael Xavier Poniatowski (1816–73), Polish singer and composer, great-nephew of Stanislas Augustus, King of Poland. He was born in Rome, composed a number of Italian operas for Italy, Paris, and London, became the Prince of Monterotondo, and followed his friend Emperor Napoleon III into exile in England.

"Opening of the Suez Canal at Port Said: Presence of the Imperial and Royal Visitors." In *London Daily Illustrated*, 11 December 1869, pp. 588–89.

"Opening of the Suez Canal: The Procession of Ships in the Canal." In *London Daily Illustrated*, 18 December 1869, p. 608.

In the meantime I am sending you an outline. Don't be shocked by the fancy printing—I have no secretary. I wanted to have four sets of the manuscript copied out; that would have cost 100 francs.[4] So I had four copies printed for 40 francs. This typographical luxury is, therefore, quite a bonus and the result of economy. Consequently regard the enclosed copy as the most modest of manuscripts.[5]

I need not tell you that the editing is mine. If I have intervened, it is, in the first place, because of the Viceroy's order and, in the second place, because of my belief that I could give the work true local color, which is the indispensable condition for an opera of this kind. Indeed I repeat to you that what the Viceroy wants is a purely ancient and Egyptian opera. The sets will be based on historical accounts; the costumes will be designed after the bas-reliefs of Upper Egypt. No effort will be spared in this respect, and the *mise-en-scène* will be as splendid as one can imagine. You know the Viceroy does things in a grand style. This care for preserving local color in the *mise-en-scène* obliges us, by the same token, to preserve it in the outline itself. In fact, there is a special phraseology for this—a frame of mind, an inspired note which only a thorough acquaintance with Egypt can provide. It is in this capacity that I have intervened and continue to intervene.

Here, my dear friend, is where we stand.

Now if the outline suits you, if you agree to write the libretto, if you find a composer, this is what must be done. You must write me that the subject in question is so archaeologically Egyptian and Egyptological that you cannot write the libretto without an advisor at your side at all times and that my presence in Paris is furthermore indispensable for the sets and costumes. I ask no more of you. If I could go to Paris this summer, my goal would be attained.

It goes without saying that I am not bringing any kind of personal vanity into this matter and that you can change, turn around, and improve the outline as you see fit.

I forgot to tell you that the Viceroy has read the outline, that he has completely approved it,[6] and that I am sending it to you by his order.

Don't be alarmed by the title. *Aida* is an Egyptian name. Normally it would be *Aita*. But that name would be too harsh, and the singers would irresistibly soften it to *Aida*. Moreover I care no more for this name than for the other.

---

4. At this time 100 French francs were the equivalent of 20 American dollars and 100 Italian lire.
5. See note 5, Document I.
6. Note that Mariette mentions only the Viceroy's approval of the outline, not coauthorship. See Du Locle's letter to Verdi of 29 May 1870.

For the second scene of the second act and the chant of the priests there is in the *Ritual* a hymn to the sun which exudes poetry and local color. Perhaps it will inspire you.

I know my place, my dear friend, and I would be very happy if in my humble role I may have been able to show you from far away the road we must travel. For the rest I rely on your talent as a poet. With this I press your hand.

Auguste Mariette to Camille Du Locle[7]

[Cairo,] 28 April [1870]
My dear friend,
   This instant I have left H.H., the Viceroy, to whom I have given your letter.
   I shall not hide from you the fact that H.H. is extremely annoyed and chagrined by the idea of forgoing the collaboration of M. Verdi whose talent he holds in the highest esteem.[8]
   Under the circumstances he makes the offer that rehearsals be held in Paris or in Milan, at the Maestro's choice; the artists of the Cairo Theatre would then receive the order to betake themselves wherever M. Verdi wishes. See if this plan might be agreeable. I have time to write you only these few words in order not to miss the mail.
P.S. One final word. If Maestro Verdi should not accept, H.H. asks you to knock at another door.[. . .] We are thinking of Gounod and even Wagner. If the latter should accept, he could do something grandiose.

Auguste Mariette to Camille Du Locle

Alexandria, 29 May 1870
My dear friend,
   Since my mail from France ran after me to Cairo and caught up with me only in Alexandria, I received your letter containing Verdi's letter[9] only yesterday.

7. Du Locle forwarded this letter to Verdi on 14 May 1870.
8. On 19 August 1867, during the Exposition in Paris, the Viceroy had attended a performance of *Don Carlos* at the Opéra. See Günther, p. 29.
9. Du Locle's letter to Mariette is missing, as is Verdi's letter to Du Locle that was enclosed. Presumably Verdi's missing letter to Du Locle is the one acknowledged by Du Locle in his letter to Verdi of 14 May 1870.

I have not yet been able to see the Viceroy. But I have been authorized for a long time to tell you to go ahead. Everything will be arranged according to your wishes. The Viceroy is ready for anything, and rather extraordinary circumstances would be required to give you cause to complain about him. Therefore put the opera boldly in the works. The Viceroy will be enchanted with Verdi's acceptance. He was particularly eager that the opera should be written by him, since he is a great admirer of the Maestro.

The opera will be performed for the first time in Cairo in Italian. But I know the Viceroy would be very proud if thereafter the opera were performed in French at our foremost lyric theatre. On this point there is no difficulty whatsoever. To the contrary.

Nothing will be neglected here for the *mise-en-scène*, which the Viceroy wants to be as splendid and magnificent as possible. Everything will be made in Paris, sets and costumes.

As for me, I sincerely hope to leave here one of these days. As soon as I see the Viceroy, I shall bluntly pose the question of my true purpose. I am the one who did the outline; I am the one, of all his employees, who knows Upper Egypt best, as well as the question of costumes and sets. Consequently, I am the one he must send to France. I hope this argument will decide the matter. [. . .] If there is any news, I shall inform you by telegraph.

P.S. The Viceroy is most anxious to have *Aida* performed in Cairo, at the latest during February of next year.

Camille Du Locle to Verdi

Paris, 31 May 1870

[. . .] I have requested from you, in complete confidence, the conditions you desire for the Egyptian business. They write and telegraph me without respite, asking me for these conditions; they declare themselves *ready for everything*. The Viceroy passionately wishes to conclude the affair. I have already been asked to take charge of the sets and costumes, etc., etc. Nothing is lacking but your *yes* and a good contract. [. . .]

Verdi to Camille Du Locle

St. Agata, 2 June 1870
Dear Du Locle,
  Here I am at the Egyptian affair, and first of all I must set aside time to

compose the opera, because this is a work of the broadest proportions (as though it were for the *grande boutique*), and because the Italian poet must first find the thoughts to put into the mouths of the characters and then fashion the verses from them. Assuming that I am able to finish all of this in time, here are the conditions:

1. I shall have the libretto done at my expense.

2. I shall send someone to Cairo, also at my expense, to conduct and direct the opera.

3. I shall send a copy of the score and the music for use only in the Kingdom of Egypt, retaining for myself the rights to the libretto and to the music in all other parts of the world.

In compensation, I shall be paid the sum of 150,000 francs, payable at the Rothschild Bank in Paris at the moment the score is *delivered*.

Here's a letter for you, as cut and dried as a promissory note. It's business, and you will forgive me, my dear Du Locle, if for now I don't digress to other things.

Auguste Mariette to Paul Draneht

Paris, 15 July 1870
My dear Bey,

I received your telegram,[10] for which I thank you, and I hasten to send you the letter I have brought for you.

Since Verdi accepted the offer the Viceroy made to him, the opera (the outline of which you know) will be done. Now this business must be started.

It is toward this end that H.H., the Viceroy, has deigned to send me to France. The Viceroy wants the opera to retain its strictly Egyptian color, not only in the libretto but in the costumes and the sets; and I am here to attend to this essential point.

On my part I am not losing an hour. But it is a difficult thing. In the operas we already know, the task is not as great because one has the traditions to follow. But here everything must be created. Add to this the exotic quality of the *mise-en-scène*. It is in the costumes, above all, that we shall encounter difficulty. To create imaginary Egyptians as they are usually seen in the theatre is not difficult; and if nothing else were needed, I would not be involved.

---

10. Like most of Draneht's correspondence with Mariette, this telegram is missing.

But to unite in proper measure the ancient costumes shown in the temples and the requirements of the modern stage constitutes a delicate task. A king may be quite handsome in granite with an enormous crown on his head. But when it comes to dressing one of flesh and bone and making him walk and sing . . . that becomes embarrassing and, it is to be feared, makes people laugh. In addition, the most consistent principle of Egyptian costume is the absence of beards—a principle observed even more because it was imposed by the religion. Now do you feel up to forcing all your people to cut off their beards? And from another point of view, can you see Naudin[11] dressed as a Pharaoh with a short beard, like the Emperor Napoleon? Obviously the short beard will destroy all the effect and all the harmony of the costumes, no matter how exact we make them. So we must not ignore the fact that the job is difficult and that to mount an opera under the conditions the Viceroy demands is a task to be considered twice. On my part, I am putting my whole heart into it. As for you, I am counting on your arrival in Paris soon. In the meantime I am working vigorously. Verdi has promised to have the opera ready by the end of January. (The Viceroy *expressly* desires that.) But the costumers and scene painters have declared that they do not have a day to lose. Believe me . . . in order to follow the instructions the Viceroy has given me, to make a scholarly as well as a picturesque *mise-en-scène*, a whole world must be set in motion.

Verdi to Giuseppe Piroli[12]

[St. Agata,] 16 July 1870

[. . .] I am busy. Guess! . . . Writing an opera for Cairo!!! *Oof.* I shall not go to stage it because I would be afraid of being mummified; but I shall send a copy of the score and retain the original for Ricordi.

I must tell you, however, that the contract has not yet been signed (and therefore do not talk about it for now); but since my conditions—and they were tough—have been accepted by telegram, it must be considered as done. If anyone had told me two years ago, *You will write for Cairo*, I would have considered him a fool; but now I see that I am the fool. [. . .]

---

11. Emilio Naudin (1823–90), the leading Italian tenor at the Cairo Opera during its first season. After making his debut in Cremona in 1843, he became the first Vasco da Gama in Meyerbeer's *L'Africaine,* and he sang during several seasons in London.
12. Lawyer and politician, and Verdi's close friend in Rome.

Suez Canal: The Gala Opening

Auguste Mariette to Paul Draneht

Paris, 19 July 1870[13]

My dear Bey,

I received your two letters of 16 and 17 July[14] at almost the same time and I am replying quickly.

You are perfectly correct to demand that you be informed of what is happening in regard to the progress of Verdi's opera; the letter from H.H. that I sent you was meant to keep you posted, and naturally I have nothing to add to it.

Actually a grand opera in the ancient Egyptian style was commissioned by H.H. from Verdi, who has agreed to undertake it. The only condition H.H. made, a condition *sine qua non,* is that the opera must be presented in Cairo at the end of next January. Moreover Verdi is already at work, since all the arrangements have been made with Verdi directly from Alexandria at the personal suggestion of H.H., the Viceroy.

With regard to the mission that now calls me to France, it has as its point of departure the Viceroy's desire to see the opera composed and executed in a *strictly Egyptian* style. According to the most formal orders that H.H. has given me, I must first place myself at the disposal of the composer and the librettist in order to supply these gentlemen with all the proper information to enlighten them about the local color to be given to the work. Second, I must also take charge of everything pertaining to the *mise-en-scène,* that is, the sets and the costumes. The sets and the costumes, according to H.H.'s orders must be drawn and executed under my eyes; and for greater accuracy H.H. has directed me to choose the scene painter and the costumer whom I judge the most capable. [. . .] This, in short, is the goal of my mission here—a mission which, with your assistance, my dear Bey, I hope to fulfill to the satisfaction of H.H.

I am quite embarrassed to reply to your second letter on the subject of M. Zuccarelli.[15] When I arrived in Paris you were not here; and since I had the instructions of H.H., I had to get in touch with the scene painters at once and begin the task. What would you have me do now? To find a pretext to put an end to the work already begun is impossible. The task is horribly intricate,

---

13. Mariette wrote this letter on the very day that France formally declared war on Prussia. Like many of his countrymen he was unaware of the consequences of that event.
14. Both letters are missing.
15. Giovanni Zuccarelli, scenic designer at La Scala. Apparently he had worked at the Cairo Opera during its first season. In the missing letter of 17 July 1870 Draneht seems to have questioned Mariette's engagement of other designers for *Aida.*

and my attention is needed everywhere all the time. The subject is completely new; and at every moment one has to do, undo, and redo, so that I am beginning to believe that we shall only half succeed—even here in Paris with the world's foremost scene painters. I would have to go to Cairo, then, break off the proposals already exchanged, and, in a word, do in Egypt what the Viceroy directed me to come to Paris to do. You will understand that I do not undertake any extra responsibilities.

As for the credit of 250,000 francs that the Viceroy has sent you, it is intended to pay for the initial expenses incurred by the opera in France. If you wish more information on this subject, I shall (to the best of my knowledge) furnish it to you on your return here, which, I hope very much, will not be delayed any longer.

There, my dear Bey, is the information I have been able to furnish you. It is a question of mounting, of creating, a completely new opera. The task will be very difficult and bristling with obstacles caused by the novelty of the subject. But the honor your administration will derive from this will be all the greater. Therefore, I shall be happy to contribute to it to the extent of my abilities.

Auguste Mariette to Paul Draneht

Paris, 21 July 1870
My dear Bey,
   I have this instant received your letter of 19 July.[16]
   There was no need for you to tell me the contents of the letter from H.H. that I sent you, because, for the good of the mission that I am performing here, H.H. deemed that I should know about it and even charged me to add some less urgent details, which I shall soon be able to communicate to you in person.
   You are so right to call the work we are planning a colossal work. As I believe I told you there is really no tradition whatever to follow, and everything must be created. I am not embarrassed to also admit to you that I did not suspect the immensity of the details and that I am literally losing my mind.
   Furthermore come to Paris as soon as possible. The two of us are not too many to carry this very heavy burden.
   I take the opportunity, my dear Bey, to tell you that you may count on me completely. From now until the end of January, for our dear and illustrious master [the Viceroy], we have to achieve a work of consequence which, to a

16. Missing.

certain extent, will help to augment the renown Egypt has already acquired for herself. It is essential that we not produce a fiasco. Therefore, just as the Viceroy appealed to the most illustrious living composer, we must do everything possible to make the *mise-en-scène* worthy of this initial step. Until now I have neglected nothing to arrive at that result, and I have proceeded in my research without haste. I hope you will be pleased and that the opera, presented for the first time in Cairo this winter, will bring you great honor. As for myself, I declare in advance that with regard to the libretto and all artistic aspects of the work my name should not even be mentioned.

SOURCE: This selection of Verdi letters from 1870 are from Hans Busch, *Verdi's Aida: The History of an Opera in Letters and Documents* (Minneapolis: University of Minnesota Press, 1978).

Excerpt from *An Englishman's Recollections of Egypt 1863 to 1887*
BARON SAMUEL SELIG DE KUSEL

During the year 1869 we were exceedingly busy; not only in connection with our regular line of steamers, but also owing to the fact that we had undertaken the pilgrim traffic, which was generally confined to tramp steamers; the great majority of pilgrims were bound for Morocco, Tripoli, and Tunis, returning home through Alexandria from Mecca, and we generally managed to put from four to five hundred aboard each vessel. The steamer would anchor just opposite the railway station at Gabbarí, and as the trains arrived the pilgrims were promptly put into large barges and towed alongside; a barrier was fixed up half-way across the steamer, and as the Arabs came aboard they had to pay their passage money before passing it. If I remember rightly the fare was about five or six dollars, and each pilgrim, when he paid his money, received a tally which he had to keep and deliver up at his destination as he left the ship. When most of them had paid and gone through to the other side of the barrier, at which sailors were always posted to prevent a rush, there invariably remained a certain number, both male, and female, who pretended that they only possessed one or two dollars in the world, others would swear that they had not even a piastre left, and the scene became indescribable, as they refused to leave the ship, and commenced to scream and howl.

The first time I saw this I felt quite sorry for them; but in that I was alone, for our people thoroughly understood the pleasant little ways of pilgrims.

The stevedore, Hassan, who attended to all our steamers, had two stalwart negroes under him, who looked after and kept the pilgrims in order; their special duty, however, was to search those who refused to pay their fare, and these were generally seized, one at a time, and taken below, where they were stripped and searched thoroughly, the result being that money was found hidden in the most inexplicable places, generally more than enough to pay their passages. It was not only the men one had to treat in this way, for it was more often than not females who were the worst offenders, submitting to be stripped and searched, rather than pay up.

In the end there were usually a few who really had nothing, and these were allowed a free passage; however, the steamers were always detained several hours by these manœuvres.

By this time, having pretty well mastered Italian, I set to work to learn French, and having had a certain amount driven into me at school, before long I was able to converse fairly easily.

On November 16, 1869, the Suez Canal was formally opened; this great work had taken ten years to complete at a cost of about seventeen million sterling. It was my good fortune to be present, having had the honour to be invited as one of the guests of His Highness the Khedive. I left Alexandria on the 15th in one of the Rubattino steamers, which had come specially from Italy with a number of distinguished guests on board. As we steamed out of the harbour the French Imperial yacht *Aigle* was preparing to leave. I remember as we passed alongside seeing Her Majesty, the Empress Eugénie, standing on the bridge, surrounded by her suite, and I may safely say that all eyes were centred upon her.

The next day, Tuesday, November 16, we arrived at Port Said, where we found the harbour crowded with vessels, chiefly French, Italian, and Austrian, whilst outside were anchored five British men-of-war, *Lord Warden* (with Sir A. Milne's flag flying), *Royal Oak, Prince Consort, Caledonia, Bellerophon,* and *Rapid* despatch boats, two Austrian ironclads, and some Italian ships.

When the *Aigle* arrived at about eight o'clock in the morning, the fleet manned yards and fired a grand salute. She anchored alongside the Khedival yacht, *Mahroussah,* on the other side of which lay the Austrian Imperial yacht.

At three in the afternoon a benediction was pronounced by the Ulemas of the Mussulman religion, by the Coptic, Roman Catholic, and Greek clergy. A pavilion had been erected on the seashore for the purpose, the front of which was lined by Egyptian troops.

Other pavilions were erected for the Khedive and his royal guests, and as they were about a quarter of a mile away from the landing stage, quite a procession was formed. The Heir Apparent of Egypt led the way with the Princess of Holland, the Empress Eugénie on the arm of the Emperor of Austria, the Khedive Ismail and the Crown Prince of Prussia walking on each side, the Grand Duke Michael of Russia, the Prince of Holland, the Archduke Victor, brother of the Emperor of Austria, the Princes Augustus of Sweden, Amadeus of Savoy, and Louis of Hesse, following with a brilliant staff of French, Austrian, Italian, and Egyptian officers, amongst whom walked Monsieur de Lesseps and Colonel Staunton, the British Consul-General, and many other notable people.

After the religious ceremony, Monsignor Bauer, the Empress Eugénie's confessor, made a most eloquent speech.

Port Said that night, town as well as harbour, was brilliantly illuminated, a glorious moon adding to the splendour of this scene. The next day, Wednesday, November 17, at 8 a.m., the Suez Canal was opened formally, and a procession of about seventy steamers of various nationalities passed, headed by the Imperial yacht *Aigle* with the Empress of the French. The following were the names of the ships, none of which drew more than thirteen feet of water:—

Austrian Imperial yacht, with Emperor of Austria; Prussian frigate with Crown Prince; Swedish yacht with Prince Oscar of Sweden; Russian warship with Grand Duke Michael; Russian Admiral's ship; Dutch gunboat with Prince and Princess of Holland; *Psyche*, English despatch boat with English Ambassador from Constantinople; Swedish vessel; *Peluse*, French Messageries Maritime steamer; *Rapid*, English gunboat; a French Messageries Maritime steamer; *Vulcan*, Austrian warship; *Forbin*, French gunboat; a French steamer; *Cambria*, English yacht with owner, Mr. Ashbury; *Dido*, English telegraph steamer: English steam yacht; Swedish vessel; British sloop-of-war; Messageries steamer; Austrian Lloyd steamer; *Hawk*, English steamer carrying to Suez the shore-end of the British Indian Telegraph; Russian merchant steamer; Messageries steamer; *Lynx*, English steamer; *Principe Tomaso* and *Principe Oddone*, Italian steamers; *Principe Aurades*, Italian steamer; Austrian steamers; *Scilla*, Italian war frigate; Austrian Lloyd steamer; *Chabin*, Egyptian Government steamer; *Fayoun*, Egyptian Government steamer; and these followed by about as many more.

The Imperial yacht *Aigle* and the Khedive's yacht after a passage of twelve hours arrived at Ismailia, the others followed later on.

As the Royal guests landed, they were conducted by the Khedive to the new palace, which he had had built specially for this occasion.

Shortly after this, the Empress Eugénie and the Emperor of Austria, on camels, accompanied by Monsieur de Lesseps on a white pony, rode past the Arab camp toward the desert, and on returning entered a small pony chaise, and drove for some time about the streets.

The guests of less importance had not been forgotten, and in different parts of the town large marquees had been erected, in which tables beautifully decorated awaited those who wished to eat or drink; every delicacy from all parts of the world had been imported, while wines of all kinds, and of the most recherché quality, were supplied to any guest who happened to pass by.

Waiters and attendants, dressed in the most gorgeous Khedival liveries, attended to the slightest wishes of all present.

I shall never forget the magnificence of the ball at the new Khedival palace that evening, for it was one of the most brilliant sights I have ever witnessed, especially the Royal procession, as it passed through the principal ball-room, on its way to a supper, which was in itself a thing to be long remembered.

On the following day, most of the Royal guests left Ismailia for Suez, but many of the others proceeded direct to Cairo by train, where some remained two or three weeks, sight-seeing, and enjoying themselves at the expense of the Khedive, even the carriages hired by them being paid for by Ismail, and so ended the fêtes given on the occasion of the opening of the Suez Canal. The expense to the Khedive must have been enormous.

The title of Khedive was granted to Ismail Pasha by the Sultan in 1867, since when it has been used by the latter as his official title; the word (pronounced as a dissyllable) is derived from Persian Khidiv and means sovereign, it is therefore a more dignified title than the former one of Vali—Viceroy.

Those people who have never travelled through this canal might be interested in the following details of this great work. On leaving Port Said, one crosses the Menzaleh lake, a shallow body of salt water, something like the Venetian lagoons, and then proceeds for about twenty-seven miles to El Kantarah, which was formerly the chief caravan station on the road from Egypt to Syria.

At Ismailia, one encounters another lake five miles in length, and this is the central point, or half-way home of the canal; at the time of the opening there were only a few houses there, but very soon afterwards a pleasant little town had sprung up with villas, shops, cafés, hotels, etc., and fine streets and squares.

Now there is a central railway station there from whence passengers can travel to Suez, Cairo, or Alexandria.

Besides this great navigable canal which shortens so splendidly the distance between Europe and the Far East, there is a fresh water canal, constructed on purpose to supply the population at various points on the line, this runs from the Nile to Ismailia on Temsah Lake, from Ismailia to Suez on the west side of the canal, and from Ismailia to Port Said. This last is not really a canal, like the first two sections, but consists of a large iron pipe through which the water is conveyed to the sundry stations.

When the canal was first started in 1859, it was very difficult to procure fresh water, as it had to be brought across Lake Menzaleh, from Damietta, in Arab boats, and it was only in 1863 that the iron pipe was laid down between Port Said and Ismailia. The great advantage of the canal is the shortening of the distance between Europe and the Far East. From London to Bombay by the Suez Canal it is about 6300 miles, whilst by the Cape it is about 11,000 miles. From Marseilles to Bombay by the Cape it is 10,000 miles, and by the Suez Canal 4600 miles. The steamers generally pass through the canal at the rate of 5 to 6 knots.

I might mention that, in 1875, the British Government purchased from the Khedive his shares in the canal, paying four million sterling for 176,602 shares, out of a total of 400,000, and they made a very good investment.

On November 25, 1869, the Austrian and German colony in Alexandria gave a ball to His Majesty the Emperor of Austria. It took place in the rooms of the Mohammed Ali Club, which were at that time on the first floor of a fine building, the ground floor of which was occupied by the Alexandria Bourse. I was present at this function and enjoyed it immensely.

I remember meeting about this time a Captain George Hyde commanding the P. and O. steamer, *Pera*. He was a great favourite with most of the Anglo-Indians, and was a well-known celebrity throughout the service, his soubriquet in the P. and O. was "Magnificent George," and really he was a very fine, handsome man. He often gave little luncheons and dinners on board his vessel, and being rather a gourmet, he took care that they were really good. He had a smattering of Italian, of which he was very proud, airing it whenever an opportunity occurred, adding at the end of some very high-sounding sentence, "This is from Dante."

Sometimes he would write his menus in Italian, and one of the items generally found was "Nightingales' tongues, stewed in the dew of roses." His guests, of course, expected to see some marvellous culinary concoction; but when the dish appeared, it was only a dish of cream, with pieces of sponge cake floating about. However, his sparkling Moselle cup was a dream, and a boon on a hot summer's day. He, poor fellow, died some years ago at Lord's whilst watching a cricket match.

I was always very enthusiastic in regard to everything connected with music, and when it was announced that the Khedive Ismail Pasha had commissioned Verdi to write an opera, taking his subject fom Egypt, all of us looked forward with considerable excitement to the first production, which took place at the Opera House in Cairo on December 24, 1871. Verdi was expected to come to Cairo to direct this first performance of "Aida" himself; but, unfortunately, his horror and dread of the sea prevented him accepting

Ismail Pasha's invitation. I went specially to Cairo in order to be present at what for me was a great event.

A most brilliant audience literally crowded the house; the Khedive with all the princes were there, and the Khedivah was present, and the Egyptian princesses were in the Royal Harem boxes, the fronts of which were covered in with thin lattice work, through which one could see, hazily, the forms of the ladies, with their diamonds and precious stones sparkling as they moved to and fro in the large royal box. All the Consul-Generals and their wives were present, the ministers and the Khedival staff officers in their brilliant uniforms, while in every box were many lovely women, resplendent with jewels. This premier performance of "Aïda" was simply perfect, and it was in the early hours of the morning that I left the theatre after an evening which, to me, had been divine.

The caste was as follows:

Il Re	Tommaso Costa, *basso.*
Amneris	Eleonora Grossi, *mezzo-soprano.*
Aïda	Antonietta Pozzoni, *soprano.*
Radames	Pietro Mongini, *tenore.*
Ramfis	Paolo Medini, *basso.*
Amonatio	Francesca Steller, *baritone.*
Un Messaggiero	Stecchi Bottordi, *tenore.*

The Conductor was Mæstro Bottesini, the famous violinist.

SOURCE: Baron Samuel Selig de Kusel, "Chapter Three," *An Englishman's Recollections of Egypt 1863 to 1887* (London: John Lane, 1915).

XI
THE SUEZ CANAL: THE BUILDER, FERDINAND DE LESSEPS

INTRODUCTION
"The Master Builder" and His Designs:
Ferdinand De Lesseps

MIA CARTER

FERDINAND DE LESSEPS's career, like Warren Hastings's, was characterized by soaring accomplishments, great notoriety, and scandal. The indomitable visionary who was nicknamed "Le Grand Francais," was bold enough to implement Napoleon Bonaparte's dream of building across the isthmus of Suez a canal that would serve as a "short cut" to the riches of the East. For some, De Lesseps was a great diplomatic genius; for others, he was a devious schemer, double-dealer, and cheat. De Lesseps's letters and journal entries represent him as a major player, an unswervingly confident man who was fully aware of his charms and absolutely unafraid of using them in pursuit of his goals. De Lesseps saw himself as someone who was destined for greatness, which, in his eyes, was the family tradition. In his journal entries, De Lesseps read Egyptian meteors and ancient texts as evidence that he, and he alone, was destined to build the canal.

De Lesseps's uncle Barthélemy was a military hero of the grand manner who became civil governor of Moscow; he was also a favorite in the court of Louis XVI. His father Mathieu was Napoleon's commissary-general at the Port of Cadiz in Egypt and, later, at Alexandria. Napoleon made the senior De Lesseps a count for his patriotism and loyal service; young Ferdinand grew up in the atmosphere of national glory, great comfort, and wealth. De Lesseps's childhood contacts assisted him in his adult endeavors. Mohammed Said Pasha had been a close associate of his father's, and De Lesseps and Ismail Pasha had been youthful friends. De Lesseps took advantage of this intimacy to convince the Egyptian leaders that they should financially support his canal plan. He impressed Ismail Pasha with fantastic images of Egypt's restored glory; the Suez Canal would be a monument that would rival the Great Pyramids.

De Lesseps campaigned all over Europe, advertising the international and universal benefits of the Suez Canal. Commerce was the primary reason the

European nations should invest in the canal, and commerce would also be the answer to the Western nations' concerns about competition and control in times of peace and war. The nations' self-interest and determination to protect their trade would, he argued, be the ideal deterrent to war. The journalists' and politicians' uncertainties about the Suez Canal and its political consequences appear to have been related to the wars of their recent past and the volatility of the alliances that had emerged after the wars. De Lesseps's early campaign, during which he presented his canal proposal to Britain's merchants and politicians, took place in May 1857, before the far-reaching outbreak of the Indian Uprising/Sepoy Mutiny. Some of De Lesseps's audience also seemed to be concerned about the smooth-talking Frenchman himself.

When the canal was completed, the English were among its primary users and beneficiaries. Despite the originally vehement objections of Prime Minister Palmerston and numerous other politicians to the canal, England soon demonstrated its appreciation. The canal enabled Great Britain to market commercial goods and products more effectively and, in times of trouble, to transport its military far more rapidly and efficiently than had been possible during the Crimean War or Indian Uprising (see Karl Marx's letters on the uprising/mutiny in section IV). In 1870 De Lesseps was awarded the Grand Cross of the Star of India by Queen Victoria; he was also ordained a freeman by the City of London and presented a gold medal at the Crystal Palace by Albert, Prince of Wales. The glorious celebrations that inaugurated the canal's opening, however, would soon dissipate and the difficult job of administering its use and determining rights of passage, taxation, and ownership would cloud the horizon for years to come.

De Lesseps's success with the building of the Suez Canal also dramatically affected his future. Unable to rest on his laurels, De Lesseps felt compelled to outdo his own legacy and took on the project of building the Panama Canal. De Lesseps's questionable financial maneuverings and dramatic but extremely dangerous and costly engineering decisions doomed the second canal project and thousands of its workers, and proved catastrophic for its shareholders and the French government as well. When the Company was forced to liquidate in 1889, France was nearly bankrupted; many individual fortunes were ruined. De Lesseps and his son, Charles, were accused of bribery, found guilty, and later acquitted. De Lesseps's life reflected the productive and destructive nature of his, and the era's, enterprising energies.

BIBLIOGRAPHY

Anonymous. "The Suez Canal." *Edinburgh Review* 103, no. 219 (January 1856): 235–67.
Anonymous. "Suez and Euphrates Routes." *Quarterly Review,* 102, no. 204 (July–October 1857): 354–97.
Beatty, Charles. *Ferdinand De Lesseps: A Biographical Study.* London: Eyrean Spottiswoode, 1956.
Bolt, Jonathan. *To Culebra: A Play in Two Acts.* Salt Lake City, Utah: Peregrine Smith Baks, 1989.
Kinross, Lord John Patrick Balfour. *Between Two Seas: The Creation of the Suez Canal.* London: Murray, 1968.
Marlowe, John. *World Ditch: The Making of the Suez Canal.* New York: Macmillan, 1964.

"Ferdinand De Lesseps Bestrides His Canal" (n.d.). In Lord John Patrick Douglas Balfour Kinross, *Between Two Seas: The Creation of the Suez Canal* (London: J. Murray, 1968).

Chronology of Events

1830	French invade Algeria.
1834	Egyptian-Syrian War.
1842	Spanish Civil War.
1850	Mohammed-Ali dies.
	Abbas Pasha succeeds him.
1853	Crimean War.
1854	Viceroy approves De Lesseps plan for Suez Canal.
	Act of Concession granted to De Lesseps.
1855	Lord Palmerston becomes British prime minister.
1856	Commission approves of De Lesseps's plan.
	End of Crimean War.
1857	Sepoy Mutiny/Indian Uprising.
1858	Lord Derby becomes British prime minister.
	Canal debated in the House of Commons; majority opposes canal.
	Universal Company of the Maritime Suez Canal founded.
	Lord Palmerston again prime minister.
1863	Said Pasha dies.
	Ismail Pasha succeeds him.
1865	Cholera plague in Egypt.
	Palmerston dies.
	Lord John Russell succeeds him.
	De Lesseps's grandson dies of cholera.
1864	Riots on the isthmus of the Suez Canal.
1866	Sultan ratifies Act of Concession.
1869	Suez Canal completed.
	The Canal Inauguration.
1870	De Lesseps honored by Queen Victoria in London.
1871	Debut of Verdi's *Aida* at the Cairo Opera House.

Inquiry into the Opinions of the Commercial Classes of Great Britain on the Suez Ship Canal

FERDINAND DE LESSEPS

DEDICATION

To the Members of the British Parliament

My Lords and Gentlemen,—

To you, individually, I dedicate, and to the earnest consideration of your illustrious assemblies I submit, the following pages. They contain a faithful record of a series of discussions held, and resolutions adopted, in the principal cities of the United Kingdom, whose commercial and municipal bodies have in due form, and under the presidency of their elected authorities, given expression to their opinion as to the interest which the commerce and shipping of Great Britain and her colonies had in the projected Ship Canal across the Isthmus of Suez uniting the Mediterranean and Red Seas, and presenting, without the necessity of transhipment, a short route for merchandise to the East.

Delivered thus from all doubt as to the opinion of the merchants, ship-owners, and manufacturers of England, so competent in the matter, and being now about to pursue the execution of this undertaking, in favour of which I claim exclusively neither the protection nor the assistance of any single Government, I address myself with entire confidence, for the removal of any opposition on the part of the British Ambassador at Constantinople, to the political assemblies of a free country, which, under other circumstances, have already won the glory of setting above all considerations of personal interest, or national rivalry, the great principles of civilization and of free trade.

I remain, My Lords and Gentlemen,
Your most Obedient and Humble Servant,
Ferdinand de Lesseps.
London, June, 1857.

OPINIONS OF THE COURT OF EAST INDIA DIRECTORS AND PENINSULAR AND ORIENTAL STEAM NAVIGATION COMPANY

Two years ago I visited England, and in a first publication laid before the public of this country the early draught of the project for effecting a communication between the Red Sea and Mediterranean by a Ship Canal across the Isthmus of Suez, for the execution of which I have obtained a concession from His Highness the Viceroy of Egypt. It was my object to learn how this great undertaking would be regarded by that nation whose vast possessions in the East, and ever-increasing commercial relations with the whole world, placed her foremost among those who would be affected by the important revolution which would thence result in the conditions of trade and navigation throughout the globe. As the highest authority that could be consulted in all that concerned the interests of the British possessions in India, I submitted the results of our preliminary studies to the Court of Directors of the East India Company; and as an excellent practical guide as to the immediate consequences of the project on the existing mercantile traffic with the East, I referred them also to the Peninsular and Oriental Steam Navigation Company, whose vessels already pursue, in disjointed fragments, the course it is intended to render continuous and unbroken. The expression of opinion which I solicited in both cases was freely, and at once given, and I subjoin the letters in which it was conveyed, as here fitly finding their place, at the commencement of a record which presents the collected verdict of British commercial interests on the Isthmus of Suez Canal.

"East India House, 16th August, 1855.

"Sir,—I have received and laid before the Court of Directors of the East India Company your letter dated the 7th instant, and in conveying to you their acknowledgment for your work entitled 'The Isthmus of Suez Question,' I am commanded to inform you with reference to the important enterprise to which it relates, that the Court must always feel a deep interest in the success of any undertaking that would facilitate the means of communication between this country and India.

"I am, Sir,
"Your most obedient, humble Servant,
"J. C. Melvill, Secretary."

"Peninsular and Oriental Steam Navigation Company.
Offices 122, Leadenhall-street, London, 15th August, 1855.

"Sir,—I have, by order of the Directors, to acknowledge the receipt of your letter, dated 6th inst., and to express their best thanks for the copy of the interesting work on the Isthmus of Suez question, by which it was accompanied.

"With reference to your request to be made acquainted with the opinion of the Directors on the subject, I am desired to state, that, in the absence of more specific data, they cannot venture on prognostications as to the probable success of the scheme, or the plan proposed by you.

"The importance of the results that would attend the junction of the Mediterranean and Red Seas by a navigable canal is, however, so potent, that no second opinion can exist in the matter; and, should the project be carried to a successful issue, this company must of necessity participate in the effect it will produce not only upon the commerce of this country, but of the whole world.

"I am, Sir,
"Your most obedient Servant,
"C. W. Howell, Secretary."

Encouraged by this unequivocal approbation of the advantages of the proposed undertaking if carried into execution, and noting that the practicability of the project remained still, from traditional and inveterate prejudice, subject to doubts which might act unfavourably and render less emphatic that general expression of opinion as to the benefits to be anticipated from it which it was my desire to obtain from the commercial classes of this country, I proceeded at once to set this part of the question at rest as far as human foresight, aided by the highest skill and experience, could determine. Accordingly, in the course of last year, I formed the International Scientific Commission on the Isthmus of Suez Ship Canal, constituted by the most experienced hydraulic engineers and nautical men that Europe could afford, and presenting, from the admixture of all nations, a tribunal the most perfectly impartial that could be formed. The ground was visited and again explored, the details of the early project reviewed under the light of the fresh material resulting from later and more extended observations and researches, and a modified plan was determined on, which is now before the public of Europe in the Report of the International Scientific Commission, whose names attached form a guarantee of its soundness and practicability, which could not easily be surpassed, and which no individual opinion can invalidate.

On my return to England this year, immediately upon the publication of this report, which now cleared and simplified the question I had to submit to the training and shipping interests of England, I commenced a tour through the principal seaports and commercial centres of the three kingdoms, with a view to obtain from each an authentic expression of opinion on a subject which concerned them so nearly. My visit to each place was preceded by the issue of the following circular, announcing its object:—

"To the Bankers, Merchants, Shipowners, and Manufacturers of——.

"Gentlemen,—In inviting your attention to the condition and progress of the Suez Ship Canal scheme, I advocate not only my interest as the promoter and concessionary of that great undertaking, but the interests of all commercial communities, in the measure of their trading and industrial activity, and consequently in the highest degree those of ——:

"By a Charter of His Highness the Viceroy of Egypt, I am empowered to carry out the necessary arrangements for a junction of the Mediterranean with the Red Sea, by a Canal navigable for the largest ships, and for the opening by this means of a safe maritime route to India, China, and Australia.

"The route which will thus be opened to commerce is shorter by 5,000 miles, as respects England, than that at present followed round the Cape of Good Hope. Its track lies through seas of all others most easy of navigation, and it skirts the coasts of countries rich in natural products, though, at present, for all mercantile purposes, beyond the reach of European enterprise.

"Engineers of the highest repute, in England and the chief countries of Europe, have examined and approved the technical features of the scheme. An important accessory work, consisting of a branch canal, is now in actual progress, and the greater part of the capital required has been subscribed among the commercial classes of the several European nations, whose Governments have readily sanctioned a project of such manifest importance to the development of commerce and civilization.

"My object in shortly coming amongst you will be to ascertain the feelings which exist in the financial and commercial classes of —— with respect to this great enterprise, and personally to furnish full information as to its objects and details, well knowing that your countrymen yield only to the most solid arguments and after the most mature and circumspect examination.

"In the principal cities throughout Europe where this scheme has been brought forward to public notice, it has elicited on the part of the chief municipal, commercial, and scientific bodies, manifestations of the most signal interest and sympathy. I am, therefore, naturally desirous to complete this general expression of approval with the crowning sanction of the greatest commercial and manufacturing nation in the world, who, above all others, is called to participate in the incalculable advantages inevitably resulting from a work which, by concentrating her vast colonial possessions in the East and in the South, must increase and consolidate her prosperity.

"I have the honour to subscribe,
"Gentlemen,
"Your most obedient and humble Servant,
"Ferdinand de Lesseps.
"London, May, 1857."

SOURCE: Ferdinand De Lesseps, "Inquiry into the Opinions of the Commercial Classes of Great Britain on the Suez Ship Canal," 1857 pamphlet.

Excerpts from *The Suez Canal: Letters and Documents Descriptive of Its Rise and Progress in 1854–56*
FERDINAND DE LESSEPS

To the Members of the Academy of Sciences, Paris.

I owe the distinguished honour of my seat in the Academy of Sciences to the execution of the Suez Canal.

My colleagues have expressed a wish to know the history of the labours they have so frequently aided by their assistance and influence, and which, spread over a period of twenty years, have resulted in a successful completion of the work, supported as it has been by the verdict of Science and the progress of Civilisation.

It is not for me to compile a complete history of an enterprise in which much opposition and contest, years before the formation of a financial company, necessarily compelled me to make myself conspicuous.

But, in order to prepare an outline of the history and to comply with the wish of the Academy, I have collected my private and official correspondence, together with such of my notes as have been written according to the requirements of events as they occurred.

This collection contains an account of the principal circumstances which occurred during and after the opening of the Egyptian Bosphorus to navigation, an occasion honoured by the presence of a numerous deputation of members of the Institute of France.

Ferd. De Lesseps.
Paris, May 1875.

THE SUEZ CANAL

I. To M. S. W. Ruyssenaers, Consul-General for Holland in Egypt.
Paris, July 8, 1852.

Three years ago, after my mission to Rome as Envoy Extraordinary, I asked for and obtained leave from my office as Minister Plenipotentiary.

Since 1849 I have studied incessantly, under all its aspects, a question which was already in my mind when we first became friends in Egypt twenty years ago.

I confess that my scheme is still a mere dream, and I do not shut my eyes to the fact that so long as I alone believe it to be possible, it is virtually impossible.

To make the public take it up it requires a support still wanting to it, and I ask for your assistance with a view to obtaining that support.

The scheme in question is the cutting of a canal through the Isthmus of Suez. This has been thought of from the earliest historical times, and for that very reason is looked upon as impracticable. Geographical dictionaries inform us indeed that the project would have been executed long ago but for insurmountable obstacles.

I enclose a minute, the result of my former and more recent studies, which I have had translated into Arabic by my friend Duchenoud, the best interpreter to the Government. It is strictly confidential, and you must judge whether the present Viceroy, Abbas Pacha, is likely to recognise its importance for Egypt and to aid in its execution.

II. To the Same.
Paris, November 15, 1852.

When you wrote to me that there was no chance of getting Abbas Pacha to entertain the idea of the Suez Canal, I communicated my project to my friend M. Benoit Fould, the financier, who was about to take part in the formation of a Crédit Mobilier at Constantinople. He was struck with the grandeur of the scheme and with the advantage of including the privilege of making the Suez Canal amongst the concessions to be demanded of Turkey.

The agent sent to Constantinople met with such difficulties as led to the abandonment of the project. One argument brought to bear against it was the impossibility of taking the initiative in a work to be executed in Egypt, where the Viceroy alone has a right to undertake it.

Under these circumstances I shall lay aside my minute on the Canal until a more convenient season, and occupy myself meanwhile with agriculture and in building a model farm on a property recently acquired by my mother-in-law, Madame Delamalle.

III. To the Same.
La Chenaie, September 15, 1854.

I was busy amongst bricklayers and carpenters, superintending the addition of a storey to Agnes Sorel's old manor house, when the postman, bringing the Paris mail, appeared in the courtyard. My letters and papers were handed up to me by the workmen, and my surprise was great on reading of the death of Abbas Pacha and the accession to power of the friend of our youth, the intelligent and warm-hearted Mohammed Said. I hurried down from the scaffolding, and at once wrote to congratulate the new Viceroy. I told him that I had retired from politics, and should avail myself of my leisure to pay my respects to him as soon as he would let me know the date of his return from Constantinople after his investiture.

He lost no time in replying, and fixed the beginning of November for our meeting at Alexandria. I wish you to be one of the first to know that I shall be punctual at the place of meeting. How delightful it will be for us to be together again in dear old Egypt! Not a word to any one, before I arrive, on the Canal project.

IV. To Madame Delamalle, Paris. (*Journal.*)
Alexandria, November 7, 1854.

I landed at Alexandria at eight o'clock a.m., from the Messageries packet *Le Lycurgue*. I was met, on behalf of the Viceroy, by my friend Ruyssenaers, Consul-General for Holland, and Hafouz Pacha, Minister of Marine. I got into a state carriage, which was to take me to one of his Highness's villas, a league from Alexandria, on the Mahmoudieh Canal; and thinking it as well not to pass through Alexandria without calling at the French Consulate, I delivered some despatches to M. Sabatier, of which I had taken charge in Paris, where nothing had been said of my Canal project, as I had mentioned it to no one, not even to my brother, secretary to the Minister of Foreign Affairs. I was very well received by M. Sabatier, who begged me, should I remain a night in Alexandria, to take up my quarters in the French palace, which had been commenced under my own superintendence in 1835, when I was at the head of the French Consulate-General.

I then proceeded on my way to Villa Cérisy, with my escort of Kawas and Sais, and on my arrival I found an entire staff of servants drawn up on the staircase, who saluted me three times by stretching their right hand to the ground and then raising it to their forehead. They were Turks and Arabs, under the control of a Greek *valet de chambre* and a Marseillaise cook named Ferdinand.

Here is a description of my residence, of which I myself witnessed the construction by M. de Cérisy, the celebrated French naval engineer, founder of the Arsenal of Alexandria, from which he has turned out twelve vessels of the line and twelve frigates in a short space of time. Under Mehemet Ali, M. de Cérisy contributed much to the enfranchisement of Egypt. The chief pavilion rises from the centre of a beautiful garden between two avenues, one leading to the plain of Alexandria, on the side of the Rosetta Gate, the other to the Mahmoudieh Canal. This pavilion was occupied a few days back by the princess who has recently presented Said Pacha with a son, named Toussoum. The reception-rooms and dining-room are on the ground floor; and on the first storey we have the drawing-room, a very cheerful apartment, with luxurious divans all round and four large windows overlooking the two avenues; the bedroom, with a soft canopied couch and fine yellow lampas curtains, fringed and embroidered with gold, and supplemented by double inner curtains of worked net; a first dressing-room, well stocked with perfumes and with rosewood and marble furniture; and beyond that again a second dressing-room, not less elegant, provided with a large basin, a silver ewer, and long soft towels, embroidered with gold, hanging from pegs.

I had just inspected my quarters when some friends of the Viceroy came in. I made them talk of the habits of Said Pacha since his accession; of his tastes, his mental tendencies, the persons about him, who was in favour and who in disfavour: all matters which it is well to be informed of beforehand when the guest of a prince. These gentlemen told me that since his return from Constantinople the Viceroy has often spoken of my visit, and has talked to those about him of his old friendship for me. I was informed that he had waited for me to accompany him on a journey he is about to make to Cairo, by way of the Desert of Libya, at the head of an army of 10,000 men. This trip will certainly be interesting, and will take eight or ten days. The start is fixed for next Sunday.

Presently additional servants arrived, including a Kaouadji bachi (chief coffee-maker), accompanied by several assistants; and a Chiboukchi bachi (superintendent of pipes), escorted by four acolytes with their insignia, consisting of a dozen long pipes with large amber bowls set with diamonds. The office of these men is no sinecure, for in well-ordered homes, belonging to great Turkish seigneurs, fresh pipes and little cups of coffee (findjanes) are served to every visitor.

Now came one of the Viceroy's officers to inform me that his Highness would receive me at noon in his palace of Gabbari.

I reflected that, having known the prince when he was in a totally different position, it would be desirable to treat him with the respectful deference always so acceptable to the human heart. I therefore wore my dress coat, with my medals, decorations, and orders.

The Viceroy received me very cordially, and talked about his childhood: of the way in which I had sometimes protected him from his father's severities; of the persecution and misery he had endured in the reign of Abbas Pacha; and, lastly, of his desire to do good and restore prosperity to Egypt. I congratulated him on his intentions, adding that it must be for some good end that Providence had entrusted the most despotic Government in the world to a prince who had received a good education when young, and had subsequently been sorely tried by adversity. I also expressed my conviction that he would be worthy of his mission.

The approaching march through the desert, amongst the Bedouin tribes, was discussed, and it was agreed that I should join the expedition without having to make any preparations myself.

I returned by way of Alexandria, and paid a second visit to M. Sabatier, meeting at his house all the officers of the Consulate-General and some old French friends, who, one and all, welcomed me enthusiastically.

Later I went to the French Post-office, still presided over by M. Gérardin, whom I had myself appointed eighteen years ago, at the time of the inauguration of the packet-boat service by M. Philibert Conte, son of the celebrated Postmaster-General.

Then came a grand dinner at the hospitable mansion of the Pastrés, who had invited the "ban" and "arrière-ban" of my old friends in Egypt to meet me.

On returning to my pavilion at eleven at night I found my entire staff of servants drawn up as before, and the head cook called my attention to a well-spread table decked with flowers. He told me he had orders to serve a similar meal morning, and evening, and I replied that I should only require breakfast, and was now going to my room. Two footmen offered to assist me to ascend the brilliantly-illuminated staircase, and I accepted their services with the gravity and indifference proper to the guest of a Sovereign accustomed to similar attentions.

November 8th.

I was up at five this morning, and opened the two windows of my room, shaded by the branches of trees the names of which I am unable to give. The air was laden with the scent of their blossoms and of the jasmines lining the avenue leading to the canal, beyond which, though the sun had not yet risen, I could see Lake Mareotis swept by a deliciously soft fresh breeze.

I went to make a morning visit to the Viceroy, and he left his apartments as soon as he heard of my arrival. We seated ourselves on a comfortable sofa in a gallery opening on to the garden. After we had had a pipe and some coffee my host led me to the balcony of the gallery to show me a regiment of his guard, which was to accompany him on his journey. We then went into the garden to try some revolving pistols I had brought him from France.

Our walk ended I told Mohammed Said I must leave him to receive some people at his house, whom I had invited in his name. He thanked me for doing the honours of *my* house so well.

Later I called on the Viceroy's brother, Halim Pacha, whose house is near my own. The young prince speaks French fluently, and said that, from what he had heard of me, he was sure we should soon be good friends, as we were both fond of riding and hunting. He is to be of our party in the desert, and will take his falcons and greyhounds with him. He placed his servants and weapons at my disposal.

November 9th.

I went this morning to see the Viceroy at his father's palace at Raz-el-Tyn, on the further side of the port, and he invited me to assist at the first audience of the new Consul-General for Sardinia, who was about to present his credentials.

After the ceremony we retired to the private apartments, where we had a long and very interesting conversation on the best principles of government; but not a word was said about the Suez Canal, a subject I shall not broach until I am quite sure of my ground and the scheme is sufficiently matured for the prince to adopt it as his own rather than mine.

I must act with the greater prudence that Ruyssenaers remembers having heard Said Pacha remark, before his accession to power, that if ever he became Viceroy of Egypt he should follow the example of his father, Mehemet Ali, who had declined to have anything to do with cutting a canal across the Isthmus because of the difficulties it might lead to with England.

This is not an encouraging precedent; but I am confident of success.

November 11th.

This morning I received a fine horse from the Viceroy, for which he sent to Syria, and I was informed that there would be a review of troops this morning on a plain between Alexandria and Lake Mareotis. I mounted and joined my host. Soliman Pacha superintended the manæuvres, which included field exercise. As we were galloping along, a diamond ornament fell from the prince's cartridge-box; but he would not have it picked up, and we rode on.

November 12th.

The Viceroy sent me word that his troops are to begin their march to Cairo, under his leadership, to-day, and he has given orders to his aide-de-camp to bring me to his first halting-place to-morrow.

November 14th.

I was on foot at five o'clock this morning; the soldiers were beginning to leave their tents; and the vast moonlit plains, though bare and desolate, were not entirely without beauty.

Hearing the Viceroy's voice I went to wish him good morning. We smoked a pipe together, drank some coffee, and mounted our horses ready to receive the expected troops, who soon came up, fresh and in good condition, having left Alexandria yesterday morning with only three biscuits for each man. The Arabs are very temperate, and seem to thrive on their abstinence. The review over, we all returned to our tents.

I was interrupted by a visit from Halim Pacha, the Viceroy's brother, who has pitched his tent a league from our camp. He tells me that his Bedouin scouts report having sighted herds of gazelles two or three hours' march off, and that he proposes arranging a hunt for the day on which we resume our journey.

At ten o'clock we were summoned to breakfast by the Viceroy, and went to his tent with Halim Pacha.

Directly after our meal, Prince Halim's horses were brought round, and he returned to his camp. We retired at the same time, and, saddling my horse, I galloped about over the level plains and occasional hills near the camp. On one side the desert stretched away as far as the eye could reach, whilst on the other it was bounded by Lake Mareotis, with the sea beyond. Presently a large jackal started up almost from beneath my horse's feet, and I followed it at close quarters for some ten minutes, nearly touching it with the end of my whip, but finally losing sight of it in the brushwood. It had probably taken up its position at a good starting-point for nocturnal visits to our camp in search of food.

On my return I found the Viceroy outside his tent, and, dismounting, I went with him to an howitzer, planted 450 mètres from a target, on which two companies of light infantry were trying their skill. Several shells had been thrown, but, though often near the mark, none had actually hit it.

And now night closed in upon the camp, and the watchfires were lit. The Viceroy's military band struck up airs and marches of every nationality, including the "Marseillaise" and the "Hymn of Riégo." The Egyptians, the most lively nation on earth, grouped themselves before their tents and sang their national airs, beating time with their hands. The Viceroy, who had lost his appetite, probably because of the failure of his gunners, retired to his own tent, and sent his dinner to me in mine!

November 15th.

I was not dressed at five o'clock this morning. Any one who had happened to see me outside my tent in my red dressing-gown, like the robe of a Scherif of Mecca, washing my arms up to the elbows, would have taken me for a true believer, and in the time of the Inquisition I should have been burnt alive; for you know that washing the arms to the elbow was one of the high misdemeanours punishable with tortures and *autos da fé*.

The camp soon began to show signs of life, and the freshness of the air gave notice of the approaching sunrise. I put on something warmer than my dressing-gown, and returned to my observatory. The horizon was already illuminated by the first rays of the dawn, and the east, on the right, was clear and bright, whilst the west was still dark and cloudy.

Suddenly to the left of my tent I beheld a rainbow of the most brilliant colours, the ends dipping, one into the east, the other into the west. I confess that my heart beat violently, and I was obliged to check myself from jumping to the conclusion that this sign of the covenant alluded to in the Scriptures was a proof of the moment having arrived for the true union of the West and East, and that this day was marked out for the success of my scheme.

The Viceroy's approach roused me from my dream, and we wished each other good morning with a hearty shake of the hand, in thoroughly French style. He told me he thought of adopting my suggestion of yesterday, and riding to some of the neighbouring heights to examine the dispositions of his camp. We mounted, preceded by two lancers and followed by an aide-de-camp. Arrived on a prominent hill, strewn with relics of ancient stone constructions, the Viceroy decided that it would be a good place from which to arrange the start of to-morrow; so he sent an aide-de-camp to order his tent and carriage to be brought to him. The latter is a kind of omnibus, with sleeping accommodation inside, and is drawn by six mules. The mules brought the carriage to the top of the hill at a gallop, and we sat down beneath its shade.

The Viceroy had a circular parapet of stones, picked up on the spot, erected opposite to us by some of his light infantry. An embrasure was then made, through which a cannon was pointed, and a salute fired for the benefit of the rest of the troops arriving from Alexandria. The heads of the columns could be seen beyond the camp.

At half-past ten, the Viceroy having breakfasted before he started, I went to get something to eat with Zulfikar Pacha. I wanted to show my host that his horse, the sturdy qualities of which I had proved on the first day of the journey, was a first-rate jumper; so, as I saluted him, I made my steed clear the stone parapet with one bound, and gallop down the slope to my tent. As you will see, this piece of imprudence probably had something to do with my winning the necessary approbation of the Viceroy's suite for my scheme. The Generals, with whom I breakfasted, complimented me, and I noticed that I had gained greatly in their esteem by my boldness.

I thought the Viceroy was now sufficiently prepared by my previous conversations to recognise the advantage to every Government of having great works of public utility executed by financial companies, and, encouraged by the happy omen of the rainbow, I hoped that the day would not pass over without a decision on the subject of the Suez Canal.

At five p.m. I remounted and returned to the Viceroy's tent, again clearing the parapet. His Highness was in a very good humour, and taking my hand, which he held for a moment in his own, he made me sit down beside him on his divan. We were alone, and through the door of the tent we could see the beautiful setting of that sun the rising of which had affected me so deeply in the morning. I felt strong in my composure and self-control at a moment when I was about to broach a question on which hung my whole future. My studies and reflections on the Canal between the two seas rose clearly before my mind, and the execution seemed to me so practicable that I did not doubt I should be able to make the prince share my conviction. I propounded my scheme without entering into details, laying stress on the chief facts and arguments set forth in my minute, which I could have repeated from end to end. Mohammed Said listened with interest to my explanations, I begged him if he had any doubts to be good enough to communicate them to me. He brought forward several objections with considerable intelligence, to which I replied in a satisfactory manner, for he said at last: *"I am convinced; I accept your plan. We will talk about the means of its execution during the rest of the journey. Consider the matter settled. You may rely upon me."*

Thereupon he sent for his Generals, made them sit down on chairs opposite to us, and repeated the conversation he had just had with me, inviting them to give their opinion on the proposals of *his friend*. These impromptu counsellors, better able to pronounce on an equestrian evolution than on a vast enterprise of which they could not in the least appreciate the significance, opened their great eyes, and, turning toward me, seemed to be thinking that their master's friend, whom they had just seen clear a wall on horseback with so much ease, could not but give good advice. Whilst the Viceroy was speaking to them they raised their hands to their foreheads every now and then in sign of assent.

The dinner-tray now appeared, and with one accord we plunged our spoons into the same bowl, which contained some first-rate soup. This is a faithful account of the most important negotiation I ever made or am ever likely to make.

Toward eight o'clock I took leave of the Viceroy, who told me we should start again to-morrow morning, and I returned to my tent. Zulfikar Pacha guessed my success as soon as he saw me, and rejoiced with me. The Viceroy's playmate in his childhood and the most intimate friend of his mature years, he has done much to contribute to the favourable result just obtained.

I was not inclined for sleep, so I set about working up my notes on the journey, and putting the finishing touches to an *impromptu* minute asked for by the Sultan, which had already been drawn up for two years.

This is the minute, dated Mareia Camp, November 15, 1854, and addressed to his Highness Mohammed Said, Viceroy of Egypt and its dependencies:—

> The scheme of uniting the Mediterranean and the Red Sea, by means of a navigable canal, suggested itself to all the great men who have ruled over or passed through Egypt, including—Sesostris, Alexander, Cæsar, the Arab conqueror Amrou, Napoleon I., and Mohammed Ali.
>
> A canal effecting a junction between the two seas, via the Nile, existed for a period of unknown duration under the ancient Egyptian dynasties; during a second period of 445 years, from the first successors of Alexander and the Roman conquest to about the fourth century before the Mohammedan era; and, lastly, during a third period of 130 years, after the Arab conquest.
>
> On his arrival in Egypt Napoleon appointed a commission of engineers to ascertain whether it would be possible to restore and improve the old route. The question was answered in the affirmative; and when M. Lepère presented him with the report of the commission, the Emperor observed: "It is a grand work; and though I cannot execute it now, the day may come when the Turkish Government will glory in accomplishing it."
>
> The moment for the fulfilment of Napoleon's prophecy has arrived. The making of the Suez Canal is beyond doubt destined to contribute more than anything else to the stability of the Ottoman Empire, and to give the lie to those who proclaim its decline and approaching ruin by proving that it is possessed of prolific vitality and capable of adding a brilliant page to the history of civilization.

Why, I ask, did the Western nations and their rulers combine as one man to secure the possession of Constantinople to the Sultan? Why did the Power which menaced that possession meet with the armed opposition of Europe? Because the importance of the passage from the Black Sea to the Mediterranean is such, that the European Power commanding it would dominate over every other, and would upset the balance of power, which it is to the interest of each one to maintain.

But suppose a similar though yet more important position be established on some other point of the Ottoman Empire; suppose Egypt to be converted into the highway of commerce by the opening of the Suez Canal; would not a doubly impregnable situation be created in the East? for, afraid of seeing any one of themselves in possession of the new passage at some future date, would not the European Powers look upon the maintenance of its neutrality as a vital necessity?

Fifty years ago M. Lephère said he should require ten thousand men for four years and thirty or forty million francs for the restoration of the old indirect canal. He thought, moreover, that it would be possible to cut across the isthmus from Suez to Pelusium in a direct line.

M. Paulin Talabot, who was associated, as surveying engineer for a maritime canal society, with the equally celebrated Stephenson and Negrelli, advocated the indirect route from Alexandria to Suez, and proposed using the *barrage* already existing for the passage of the Nile. He estimated the total cost at 130 million francs for the canal and twenty million for the port and roadstead of Suez.

Linant Bey, the able director for some thirty years of the canal works of Egypt, who has made the Suez Canal question the study of his life in the country itself, and whose opinion is therefore worthy of serious respect, proposed cutting through the isthmus, at its narrowest part, in an almost direct line, establishing a large internal port in the basin of Lake Timsah, and rendering the harbours of Suez and Pelusium accessible to the largest vessels.

Gallice Bey, general of engineers and founder and director of the fortifications of Alexandria, presented Mohammed Ali with a canal scheme coinciding entirely with that proposed by Linant Bey.

Mougel Bey, director of works at the *barrage* of the Nile and chief engineer *des ponts et chaussles*, also had some conversation with Mohammed Ali on the possibility and desirability of making a maritime canal; and in 1840, at the request of Count Walewski, then on a mission in Egypt, he was commissioned to take some preliminary measures in

Europe, which were, however, prevented by political events from leading to any definite results.

A careful survey would decide which would be the best route; and the scheme having once been recognised as possible, nothing remains to be done but to choose the readiest means for carrying it out.

None of the necessary operations, difficult though they may be, are really formidable to modern science. There can be no fear nowadays of their failure. The whole affair is, in fact, reduced to a mere question of pounds, shillings, and pence—a question which will, without doubt, be readily solved by the modern spirit of enterprise and association, that is to say, if the advantages to result from its solution are at all proportionate to the cost.

Now it is quite easy to prove that the cost of the Suez Canal, even on the largest estimate, will not be out of proportion with its value, shortening, as it must do, by more than half the distance between India and the principal countries of Europe and America.

To illustrate this fact I add the following table, drawn up by M. Cordier, Professor of Geology:—

Names of the Chief Ports of Europe and America	Distance from Bombay (in Leagues)		Difference
	Viá the Suez Canal	Viá the Atlantic	
Constantinople	1800	6100	4300
Malta	2062	5800	3778
Trieste	2340	5980	3620
Marseilles	2374	5650	3276
Cadiz	2224	5200	2976
Lisbon	2500	2350	2830
Bordeaux	2800	6650	2850
Havre	2824	5800	2976
London	3100	5950	2850
Liverpool	3050	5900	2850
Amsterdam	3100	5950	2850
St. Petersburg	3700	6550	2850
New York	3761	6200	2439
New Orleans	3724	6450	2726

With such figures before us comment is useless, for they demonstrate that Europe and the United States are alike interested in the opening of the Suez Canal and in the maintenance of its strict and inviolable neutrality.

Mohammed Said is already convinced that no scheme can compare either in grandeur or in practical utility with that in question. What lustre it would reflect upon his reign! What an inexhaustible source of wealth it would be to Egypt! Whilst the names of the sovereigns who built up the pyramids, those monuments of human vanity, are unknown or forgotten, that of the prince who should inaugurate the great maritime canal would go down from age to age, and be blessed by the most remote generations!

The pilgrimage to Mecca henceforth rendered not only possible but easy to all Mussulmans, an immense impulse given to steam navigation and travelling generally, the countries on the Red Sea, Persian Gulf, the east coast of Africa, Spain, Cochin China, Japan, the empire of China, the Philippine Islands, Australia, and the vast archipelago now attracting emigration from the Old World brought 3000 leagues nearer alike to the Mediterranean, the north of Europe, and to America, such would be the immediate results of the opening of the Suez Canal.

It has been estimated that six million tons of European and American shipping annually pass round the Cape of Good Hope and Cape Horn; and if only one-half went through the Canal, there would be an annual saving to commerce of 150 million francs.

There can be no doubt that the Suez Canal will lead to a considerable increase of tonnage; but counting upon three million tons only, an annual produce of thirty million francs will be obtained by levying a toll of ten francs per ton, which might be reduced in proportion to the increase of traffic.

Before closing this note, I must remind your Highness that preparations are actually being made in America for making new routes between the Atlantic and Pacific, and at the same time call your attention to the inevitable results to commerce generally, and that of Turkey in particular, should the isthmus separating the Red Sea from the Mediterranean remain closed for any length of time after the opening of the proposed American lines.

The chief difference between the Isthmus of Panama and that of Suez would appear to be that the mountainous nature of the former presents insuperable difficulties to the construction of a continuous ship canal, whereas on the latter such a canal would be the best solution of the difficulty. For America a kind of compromise has been made, the route consisting partly of a canal and partly of a railway. Now if, with a view to effecting only a partial success, the nations chiefly interested have come forward at once in a case where the advantages to be obtained are fewer and the expenses far greater than they would be in the Suez Canal scheme, and if the conventions for insuring the neutrality of the American route were accepted without difficulty, are we not forced to conclude that the moment has come for considering the question of the Isthmus of Suez? that the scheme for a canal which is of far more importance to the whole world than the Panama line, is perfectly secure from any real opposition, and that, in our efforts to carry it out, we shall be supported by universal sympathy and by the active and energetic co-operation of enlightened men of every nationality?

(Signed) Ferdinand De Lesseps.

ix. To Richard Cobden, Esq., M.P., London.
Cairo, December 3, 1854.

As the friend of peace and of the Anglo-French alliance I am going to tell you some news which will aid in realising the words, *Aperire terram gentibus.*

I arrived in Egypt a short time back, as the invited guest of the Viceroy, with whom, since his boyhood, I have been on terms of friendship, and I have had an opportunity of calling his attention to the advantages which would result to the commerce of the world and the prosperity of Egypt from the opening of a maritime canal between the Mediterranean and the Red Sea. Mohammed Said has understood the importance of this great enterprise, and wishing to see it carried into execution, he has authorised me to form a company of capitalists of all nations. I forward you a translation of the Firman of Concession. The Viceroy has requested me to communicate it to her Britannic Majesty's Agent and Consul-General as well as to the other Consuls-General in Egypt.

Some people maintain that the Viceroy's project will meet with opposition in England. I cannot believe it. Under existing circumstances your statesmen must be too enlightened for me to admit such an hypothesis. What! England monopolises half the general commerce with India and China; she possesses an immense empire in Asia; she can reduce by one-third the charges on her commerce and the distance from her metropolis by one half, and she will not have it done! And why? In order to prevent the countries on the Mediterranean from profiting by their geographical situation to carry on a little more commerce in the Oriental seas than they do at present, she will deprive herself of the advantages, material and political, of this new communication, merely because others are more favourably situated than herself, as if geographical position were everything, as if, having regard to all the circumstances, England had not more to gain by this work than all the other Powers put together. Lastly, England deprecates, it is said, the diminution in the number of vessels trading with India which will result from the reduction by more than one-third of the length of the voyage. Has not our experience with railways proved, in a manner surpassing the expectations of the most sanguine, that the abbreviation of distances and of the duration of journeys lead to an immense increase in the number of passengers and the amount of traffic?

It is difficult to understand why those who admit this last objection do not advise the English Government to compel vessels for India to take the Cape Horn route, for it would employ more ships and turn out better sailors than that of the Cape of Good Hope.

If, though it seems impossible, the difficulties with which we are threatened have actually arisen, I hope that public spirit, so powerful in England, will soon have done justice to interested opposition and superannuated objections.

Allow me, in case of need, to count upon your legitimate influence. I have already written to our friend M. Arles Dufour, Secretary-General to the Imperial Commission at the Universal Exhibition of Paris, asking him to communicate with you.

XII. To M. Arles Dufour, Paris.
Cairo, December 14th.

The Viceroy wrote by the very first mail after his arrival at Cairo to inform the Sultan of his intention to open the Suez Canal.

The Porte has recently spoken in the most complimentary terms with regard to the assistance now being rendered to its cause by the Viceroy, adding an expression of regret for the loss of two Egyptian men-of-war in the Black Sea and the death of Admiral Hassan Pacha. To this the Viceroy replied that he had nothing left to desire so long as the Sultan's own valuable life was spared, and he was able to come to his assistance; adding, that he was now more ready than ever to make fresh sacrifices for the common cause. Then followed some remarks on the railway the Viceroy proposes making between Cairo and Suez, in which England takes a great interest; and, after alluding to the unfortunate condition of the national Exchequer, as left by the late Abbas Pacha, his Highness pointed out the advantages which might ensue from the formation of international financial companies for the execution of useful works in the Ottoman Empire—the making of the Suez Canal, for instance.

He added that he had no doubt of the Sultan's acquiescence in the two schemes, for a railway and a canal.

He thought it useless to enter into longer explanations, which he is, however, prepared to give if necessary, by forwarding all the documents in support of the scheme. Such an act of respectful courtesy, to which the conventions relating to the Government of Egypt do not strictly bind Mohammed Said, will doubtless be appreciated as it deserves at Constantinople, where the maintenance of the present friendly relations with the Viceroy is much desired.

My previsions on the subject of certain foreign susceptibilities have been soon enough realised. Influenced probably by the presence in Cairo of Mr. Murray, late English Consul-General in Egypt and now Minister in Persia, who has too long carried on the old policy of antagonism and jealous rivalry between France and England, Mr. Bruce has begun to make some opposition. For instance, he has told the Viceroy that he is in too much of a hurry about the Suez Canal affair. His Highness replied firmly that in a question of civilisation and progress he could not believe that he should meet with opposition from any European Power, but that if any foreign agent should presently have objections to make *on the part of his Government,* he should request that they be stated in writing, so that he might *draw up his document.*

The English mail is just going, so I cannot give you my ideas to-day about the formation of our company, in which the money kings of Paris and London will be able to make their profits for the common good, although it will not do to let them have their own way entirely. Subscription lists, open for a certain time, will allow of the public taking shares at par.

The survey of the isthmus is put off until the 24th, that the necessary preparations may be made. Canvass opinion in England. Heaven helps those who help themselves.

XXVI. To the Viscount Stratford de Redcliffe.
Constantinople, February 28, 1855.

My Lord,—There are questions which, to be properly settled, should be frankly entered into, just as there are wounds which must be laid bare in order to be cured. The straightforward manner in which you received the remarks I made in the first instance on a subject, the importance of which I do not attempt to conceal, encourages me to submit to your appreciation a point of view which, I think, it would be useful to consider with regard to the Isthmus of Suez. The great influence which your character and your long experience entitle you to exercise in the decisions of your Government in all questions concerning the East, renders it a matter of the highest importance, in my eyes, that your Excellency's opinion should be based on a full knowledge of the facts.

The results already obtained through the close alliance of France and England, prove sufficiently how beneficial it is that the two nations should be united in the interest of the balance of power in Europe and of civilisation. The future and the welfare of all nations depend, therefore, upon the perfect maintenance and preservation of a state of things which, to the everlasting credit of the Government by which it was established, can alone, with time, secure to humanity the blessings of progress and peace. Hence the necessity of getting rid beforehand of every cause of dissension, or even of coolness, between the two nations; hence, therefore, it becomes a matter of positive duty to seek in future contingencies what causes would be likely to arouse feelings of antagonism which are the growth of centuries and produce in either nation explosions against which the wisdom of Governments is powerless. Motives of hostile rivalry are gradually making way for that generous emulation from which grand results inevitably follow.

If the matter, as it stands, be looked at in a general manner, it is difficult to see any ground or motive for renewing a struggle which has cost so much bloodshed to the world. Could financial and commercial interests be a source of dissension between the two nations? But the general investment of British capital in French enterprises and the immense impulse given to international trade, create between them bonds of union which daily become closer. Can it be a matter of political interest, or of principle? But both nations have now one and the same object, one and the same ambition, viz., the triumph of right over might, of civilisation over barbarity. Can it be some petty jealousy connected with territorial aggrandisement? But it is now admitted by both that the world is large enough to satisfy the spirit of enterprise of either nation, that there are countries to be turned to account and human beings to be rescued from a state of barbarism; besides, if both flags keep together, the activity of one must profit by the conquests of the other.

Hence, at first sight, there is nothing in the general aspect of matters that would seem likely to affect our good understanding with England.

Yet, on closer inspection, a contingency becomes apparent, which, by allowing the most enlightened and moderate Governments to be influenced by popular prejudices and passions, might revive old enmities, thus compromising the alliance and its good fruit.

There is a spot in the world the free passage through which is directly connected with the political and commercial power of Great Britain, a spot which France, on the other hand, had, in days gone by, been ambitious to possess. This spot is Egypt, the direct route from Europe to India—Egypt, where Frenchmen have fought and bled.

It is unnecessary to dwell upon the motives which make it impossible that England should allow Egypt to pass into the hands of a rival Power without offering the most determined resistance; but what should also be taken into full account is that France, though not so directly interested, but acting under the influence of glorious traditions and of other feelings more instinctive than rational, and for that very reason most powerful in the case of an impressionable race, would not, on her side, allow England to assume the peaceful mastery of Egypt. It is clear that so long as the route to India through Egypt is open and safe, and that the state of the country guarantees easy and rapid communication, England will not voluntarily create for herself difficulties of the most serious nature for the sake of appropriating a territory which, to her, is only valuable as a means of transit.

It is equally evident that France, whose policy for the last fifty years has consisted in contributing to the prosperity of Egypt, both by means of advice and the co-operation of many Frenchmen distinguished in science, in matters of administration, and in all the arts of peace or of war, will not try to carry out there the ideas of another age, so long as England does not interfere.

But supposing that a crisis should occur such as those which have so often convulsed the East, that a circumstance should take place which would render it imperative for England to get a footing in Egypt in order to prevent another Power from stealing a march on her, can it be maintained for a moment that the alliance could possibly survive the complications which would result from such an event? And why should England be placed in such a position? Why should England think herself bound to be mistress of Egypt, even at the risk of breaking off her alliance with France? For the simple reason that Egypt is the shortest, the most direct, route from England to her Eastern possessions, that this route must always remain open to her, and that, as regards a matter of such vital interest, she can make no compromise. Thus, through the position which nature has assigned to her, Egypt may again become the subject of a conflict between France and England; so that this possibility of dissension would disappear if, by a providential event, the geographical conditions of the Old World were changed, and the route to India, instead of passing through the heart of Egypt, were to be brought back to the boundary, and, being open to all, were the sole privilege of no one. Well, this event, which must be within the views of Providence, is now in the power of man. It can be accomplished by human industry. It can be realised by piercing the Isthmus of Suez, an undertaking to which nature presents no obstacle, and in which available capital from England as well as from other countries will undoubtedly be invested. Let the isthmus be cut through, let the waves of the Mediterranean mingle with the waters of the Indian Ocean, let the railway be continued and finished, and Egypt, whilst acquiring more importance as a productive and commercial country, as a market and as a medium of transit generally, will lose her dangerous reputation as a means of uncertain and disputed communication. The possession of her territory being no longer a matter of interest to England, ceases to be the cause of a possible struggle between that Power and France; the union of the two nations is thenceforth assured for ever, and the world is saved from the misery which would be entailed by a quarrel between them.

This result offers such guarantees for the future that it will be sufficient to point to it, to secure for the undertaking by which it is to be obtained the sympathy and encouragement of those statesmen who are striving to place the Anglo-French alliance on an imperishable basis. You are one of those men, my Lord, and the part you take in the discussion of matters of the highest political moment, with which I am not familiar, is too important a one for me not to seek to make known to you my wishes.

In sending you, with my note of the day before yesterday, my papers relating to the Suez affair, my intention was to leave them at your disposal. I, therefore, beg your Excellency will keep them.

LXVI. Letter Delivered by the Empress to the Emperor.
(Report of my visit to London.)

My first act was to come to an arrangement with Mr. Rendel, chief engineer for harbour works in England. This gentleman, who fully understands the importance which the construction of a canal through the Isthmus of Suez will be for his country, will devote his attention to the realisation of the scheme. He has agreed to join the commission of European engineers for examining the preliminary designs of the Viceroy's engineers, and will visit Egypt in the course of two months, in order to decide on the spot on the practicability of the scheme.

I next published in London a pamphlet in English, accompanied by all the documents relating to the scheme, and supported by the opinions of English travellers and *savants* who have written on the subject. This pamphlet has been sent to the members of both Houses of Parliament, to the papers and reviews, to the merchants and shipowners connected with Indian commerce in London, Liverpool, Manchester, Glasgow, &c. It was accompanied at the same time by a circular making known the proposal for submitting the question of its execution to the decision of European science, announcing the adherence of Mr. Rendel, and pointing out that the two houses Baring Brothers and Rothschild are my London correspondents.

The *Times* of the 6th of August, in the money market article, after making a favourable digest of the pamphlet, thus expresses its opinion:—

> M. de Lesseps may be assured that the national belief in the special advantages which England derives from every circumstance tending to accelerate exchanges between different parts of the world, will be favourably disposed towards all his ideas.

The following are extracts from the answers which have been sent to me by the Peninsular and Oriental Steam Navigation Company and the East India Company:

> 1st. By order of the Directors of the Peninsular and Oriental Steam Navigation Company:
>
> The importance of the results, which would be attained by connecting the Mediterranean to the Red Sea by a navigable canal is so evident that there can be no two opinions on the matter, and if the scheme is realised, this company will be greatly benefited by the important results to the commerce, not only of England but of the whole world.
>
> 2nd. By order of the Court of Directors of the East India Company:
>
> With reference to the importance of the enterprise of piercing the Isthmus of Suez, I am directed to inform you that the Court takes the greatest interest in the success of such an enterprise, destined to facilitate the means of communication between this country and India.

The replies which are daily sent to me by English statesmen and politicians all express the same opinion, of which the *Times* is the medium. This paper must shortly publish a leading article on the question. Other papers are preparing articles which will leave no doubt as to the general feeling of the country.

The Indian papers, especially the *Bombay Gazette*, have expressed their sympathy with the construction of a canal through the Isthmus of Suez.

SOURCE: Ferdinand De Lesseps, *The Suez Canal: Letters and Documents Descriptive of Its Rise and Progress in 1854–56,* trans. N. D'Anvers (London: Henry King and Co., 1876; reprint, Penn.: Scholarly Resources, 1976).

Excerpt from *From Pharaoh to Fellah*
CHARLES FREDERIC MOBERLY BELL

[Charles Moberly Bell (1847–1911) was born in Alexandria, Egypt, and at different periods in his life, lived in England and Egypt. Bell was a journalist and *London Times* correspondent. In 1880 he helped to found the *Egyptian Gazette;* he was also the founder of the *Times Literary Supplement* (1902).]

The last night had arrived; the *Maris* was due early next morning at Alexandria, and our little party were pouring forth their stores of information or imagination regarding Egypt for mutual benefit. The young Patrician was naturally a violent Radical; and the Turtle, having made his money in soap, as decided a Conservative. "We should never have touched the country, sir, but for your fatal Conservative interference," said the first. "We should never have made ourselves contemptible there, if we had been in power," replied the other.

"Now that," said the Sketcher, "is the peculiarity of your English party politics. I invariably find that the party in power, and the party in opposition, are agreed on one point, and that is, that whatever has been done, has been done badly and under pressure from the party out of office. 'Why did you go to Egypt?' says one. 'Because you compelled us,' replies the other. The idea that any one party, ministry, or man should have a policy of their own, is absent from English politics."

"Yes," said Ulster. "'Please, sir, 'twasn't me, 'twas t'other boy,' would summarise most of our debates on foreign politics. But perhaps it's as dignified as sending in an ultimatum one week and going off to Jaffa the next, to the tune of '*Partant pour la Syrie,*' as your fleet did, my good friend."

"Leaving to the British fleet the sole glory of bombarding a helpless town," said the Frenchman.

"The town was not helpless, and was not bombarded," replied the other. "The forts were silenced one day, and only one shot was fired the next day, while the 'helpless' soldiery were firing the town, massacring Christians, and ill-treating even native women. On the whole, throughout this Egyptian business we behaved with singular clemency and good faith."

The discussion became general and was getting warm. The Gallic blood of the Sketcher had been aroused against Ulster, and the Turtle and the Patrician were gradually working their way back into the Middle Ages, in an attempt to fix the origin of our intervention in Egypt.

The Scribbler, who had gravely followed the discussion with the silence becoming a person of authority, summed up the debate with cynical impartiality. "As for the origin of the whole matter, it would be about as useful to discuss the origin of the siege of Troy. Put it down as the offspring bred by human nature out of geographical position nursed by national imbecility. Let us go back a little. Palmerston, so far as I know, never read history, but *knew* it, so avoided logical will-o'-the wisps with a true instinct. Perhaps you don't know that he refused the Protectorate of Egypt when Abbas offered to throw over the Sultan, but it's a fact."

"You mean from the Czar Nicholas?" said the Turtle.

"No, I don't; that was another offer refused; but I refer to a distinct, specific offer on the part of Abbas, then Viceroy of Egypt, to place himself under the protection of England instead of that of the Sultan. Palmerston refused; he said that we did not require Egypt; but when Abbas's successor encouraged the Suez Canal, Palmerston saw as clearly as Alexander that, if the project succeeded, Egypt would become of vital importance to the mistress of India. Did he believe all he said about the certain failure of Lesseps and his visionary schemes? I don't know; but in any case, the wish was father to the thought, and there is no better proof of his foresight than the cautious answer he gave as an explanation of his opposition to the scheme: 'Remote speculations with regard to easier access to our Indian possessions, only requiring to be indistinctly shadowed forth to be fully appreciated.' He recognised, and even predicted, that if a practical waterway were created between the two seas, England would be compelled, sooner or later, to annex Egypt,—that, in fact, we must either hold Egypt or lose India."

The Turtle opined that the Canal could never be depended upon, and that England would have to rely on quick transports by the Cape.

"Excuse me," said the Scribbler, "if I point out that that argument is the result of a singular confusion of ideas. The ordinary British mind can only take in one idea at a time, and that very slowly. It took it a long time to realise that the Suez Canal had altered the situation as regarded Egypt itself. Having at last grasped the importance of the Suez Canal, it dropped all idea of Egypt, just as a monkey drops one nut when you offer it another, though a smaller one. *1st idea:* Egypt is of no importance; *2nd idea:* Egypt is of importance because of Suez Canal; *3rd idea:* Therefore Suez Canal is of importance; *4th idea;* Therefore Egypt is of no importance. Now, because we realise that the Suez Canal is of importance, surely there is no need to forget the importance of Egypt's land route; and if we cannot rely on the Suez Canal (which is an open question), there is all the more reason to hold on to the alternative. If we found our advantage in transporting troops across Egypt during the Indian

Mutiny, when there was no Canal, does that advantage disappear because there is another doubtful route running parallel to it? And when you talk of quick steamers round the Cape, you forget that there is nothing to prevent the same speed in the Mediterranean and the Red Sea. Quicken your transport either way, by all means; but you cannot get over the 4300 miles difference between the two routes, and, even at thirty miles an hour, that is six days. Six days in which you may lose or save your Empire! Besides, if Egypt is useless to you,—if the Mediterranean is a *cul de sac,* leading to nowhither, through seas where you have to run the gauntlet of hostile fleets,—of what use are Gibraltar, Malta, and Cyprus? Be consistent; and when you give up Egypt, give up those also. A year later you will have no trouble in getting rid of India too."

"Stop a bit," said the Patrician. "You said that we sent troops through Egypt during the Mutiny. Well, we didn't garrison Egypt then; why should we not withdraw from the country now, and still be able to cross it if we wished to?"

"Because, my dear boy, 1857 is not 1887. The Crimean war was just over then; France was our ally; Turkey our humble servant; Russia temporarily exhausted; Germany and Italy non-existent. Is that the position to-day? And, lastly, if you want another reason, because we were not in possession then, and we are in legal occupation now. To take is one thing, to give up is another."

"For a somewhat reserved son of honest Britain, I think," said the Sketcher, "that that is a very fair exposition of England's declared policy of retirement from Egypt."

"I am not called upon," replied the Scribbler, "to expound or to subscribe to the absurd engagements entered into by a Government which made two contradictory and equally impossible promises. I might, if I chose, refer you to Mackenzie Wallace's argument, and say that in such a case the less important promise must give way to the other; but not being politicians, let's do away with casuistry, and the cant—pardon me, Ulster—of 'singular clemency and good faith.' We showed just the same amount of the latter as you do when you pay an overdue bill under pressure. As to clemency, it's true that we only *fired* at the forts; but as our shells riddled that lighthouse, which by special order the gunners were instructed to avoid, perhaps it's of more importance to consider what we hit than what we fired at. We certainly didn't do much damage to the inhabited quarters of the town *directly,* but *in*directly, by failing to send troops, or even to land four hundred marines, we are morally responsible for all that happened and the burning of Alexandria must remain, what Wolseley called it, 'a lasting disgrace to the British navy.' As to our not firing the next day, let's be silent about it. There's not much merit in it when you happen to have fired away the last shot from your locker; and seeing that there were representatives of some half-dozen doubtfully friendly fleets within a few miles, it's not pleasant to think that if one or two had turned on us, we should have had to make a bolt for it."

"Is that true?" asked Ulster.

The Scribbler rose. "You had better ask the Admiralty, who, to save a few pounds in coal, sent the *Hecla* with the ammunition from Malta under canvas, so that she arrived twenty-four hours too late. Of course they'll deny it, as they denied sending the marines without arms, and the *Orontes* without troops on board, but it's true none the less."

"Scribbler," said the Sketcher solemnly, as they left the deck, "I have a favour to beg. To-morrow we land at Alexandria, and yonder light on Pharos is the morning star that heralds me to the glorious East. Let me entreat you to abstain from immoderate indulgence in Blue Books. Put your spirit in unison with the surroundings with which we shall be environed. Remember that we shall land amidst the ruins of Ptolemy; that we shall breathe the air of Cleopatra, and be pacing the groves of the Platonists. A few days more, and we shall have plunged into the dreamland of Haroun el Raschid; and yet a few weeks will see us in the temples of Osiris, amidst the shades of Ramses. Remember that the difference between life and death is only accordance or want of accordance with our environments; and let me live!"

The Scribbler was touched by the agonised tone of the appeal. "There doesn't happen," he said, "to be any light on Pharos, but only ruins, not of Ptolemy, but of Beauchamp Seymour. Your morning star is rising and setting every two minutes in a rather ugly lighthouse of the nineteenth century. You will find the air of Cleopatra very much like that of most other decomposed matter; and the groves of the Platonists are converted into peculiarly ugly buildings, mostly tenanted as *café-chantants* of a third-rate order. I might then ask you to put yourself in accordance with these environments, and become a practical travelling companion; but I will not ask impossibilities. I will do my best, and to-morrow shall see me a changed character."

SOURCE: Charles Frederic Moberly Bell, *From Pharaoh to Fellah* (London: Wells Gardner, Darton, 1888).

XII
THE SUEZ CANAL:
THE CANAL AND ITS CONSEQUENCES

INTRODUCTION
The Battlefield of the Future:
The Canal and Its Consequences

MIA CARTER

IN THE 1850s, as Ferdinand De Lesseps tirelessly campaigned on behalf of *his* canal in the academies, civic halls, and geographical institutes of Europe, his plan aroused anxieties and excitement in equal measure. Shipping magnates, trading companies, captains of industry, commercial speculators, colonial administrators, and military leaders enthusiastically supported the Suez Canal plan because it would provide quicker passage to the East, thereby expanding and easing trade and providing the British navy an emergency route in times of trouble, like the recent Indian Uprising/Sepoy Mutiny. Others like Prime Minister Palmerston, who passionately lobbied against the building of the canal, predicted that the new passage to India would be the cause of unrest for years to come. The Suez Canal would, in other words, further complicate the Eastern question—the ongoing challenge to manage and control the Ottoman Empire (Turkey) and Russia—by adding to Britain's already complicated imperial agenda the Egyptian question, the matter of how control of the Suez Canal would be determined in times of peace and war, and to whom authority over the canal would be granted. In his study of the region, *Egypt in the Nineteenth Century* (1898), D. A. Cameron reports that a Monsieur (Ernest?) Renan responded to De Lesseps's canal boosterism by warning the Frenchman and his audience, "The isthmus cut becomes a strait, a battlefield. . . . You have marked the field of the great battles of the future"—words that ring true for the remainder of the nineteenth century and into the twentieth, as the Suez Crisis of 1956 would demonstrate.

A grand canal across the isthmus had been envisioned in the days of the pharaohs; when Napoleon set his sights on Egypt in the eighteenth century, the plan for building the modern canal was conceived. Napoleon's designs on the region were part of his grand plan to seize Indian colonial possessions from the British. In the 1840s Mehemet Ali, the viceroy of Egypt, contemplated building a canal; however, the Egyptian leader shared Palmerston's spectral vision of such a project. The possibility of increased revenue for his government could not put to rest fears that a canal through the isthmus would attract global attention; he decided that the canal would jeopardize his nation's autonomy and well-being. Neither Mehemet Ali nor his successor Abbas Pasha approved of the canal project. Abbas Pasha's successor, Mohammed Said Pasha, and his successor, Ismail Pasha, however, eventually embraced the Frenchman's canal scheme.

In 1854 Mohammed Said Pasha granted De Lesseps a concession for the construction of the canal; the concession inaugurated the Compagnie Universelle du Canal Maritime de Suez, which was directed by De Lesseps. The company was granted administrative control of the Suez Canal for a term of ninety-nine years from the day of the canal's opening; after the term's expiration, control of the canal would revert to the Egyptian government. "The Original Firman of Concession" (1854) permitted the company to extract from the mines and quarries belonging to the public, gave the company uncultivated public lands and the use of private lands adjacent to the Suez Canal (with compensation to be determined by the company), and granted the company tax-free status. "The Charter of Concession" (1856) virtually indentured the Egyptian *fellahs* (peasants) by promising that four-fifths of the workmen would be Egyptians. These extremely generous (or foolishly granted) gifts were made conditional to the sultan's approval, which was eventually granted in 1866 after De Lesseps's sale of public subscriptions to the canal (1858). Pro-expansionist Prime Minister Benjamin Disraeli would purchase 44 percent of these stocks (see "The Lion's Share") with 4,000,000 pounds borrowed from the Rothschild's Bank in 1875 in an attempt to insure that Great Britain would hold the "key to India." The gifts granted to De Lesseps by Mohammed Said Pasha would later cripple the Egyptian economy. Ismail Pasha paid over 2,000,000 pounds sterling to fulfill his predecessor's founder's shares, which was only a small portion of the duties paid to the company to support the Suez Canal through to its completion in 1869. D. A. Cameron estimates that Mohammed Said Pasha's gift cost Egypt over sixteen million pounds sterling—a number that cannot address the costs paid by the Egyptian people.

Once the Suez Canal was completed, the battles for its control began in earnest. The English journalistic essays on the Egyptian question reflect the era's fiscal and political conservatism. The war in Crimea was a reminder of the possibility of political alliances between former competitors; however, the events of the past also highlighted the fragility and impermanence of such alliances. The canal was sure to generate aggressive competition between the

English and the French. Recent troubles in India were also ominous reminders of native discontentment and unrest; the unrest in Ireland also made politicians and statesmen aware of the possibility of forthcoming and potentially troublesome land and home rule issues. For the bold celebrants of imperialism, like Prime Minister Disraeli and the Jingoists, the promises of increased capital and expanded commerce outweighed the logic of cautionary discourses. Whether England was to seize the Suez Canal outright, to build its own canal, or to buy out the French and all other competitors, the Jingoes considered Egypt England's predestined acquisition. In their eyes, England's military-naval strength and financial might made the Egyptian question a moot one.

BIBLIOGRAPHY

Anonymous. "Egypt." *Westminster Review* 127 (April 1887): 23–27.
Arliss, George. *Disraeli* (U.S., 1929). Film.
Avram, Benno. *The Evolution of the Suez Canal Status from 1869 to 1956: A Historio-Juridical Study.* Geneva: Librarie E. Droz, 1858; reprint, Paris: Librarie Minard, 1958.
Baker, Benjamin, and John Fowler. "A Sweet-Water Ship-Canal through Egypt," *Nineteenth Century* 12 (January 1883): 166–72.
Blakesley, J. W., Reverend. "M. De Lesseps and the Suez Canal." *Macmillan's* 1 (March 1860): 407–16.
Cameron, D. A. *Egypt in the Nineteenth Century: Or, Mehemet Ali and His Successors until the British Occupation in 1882.* London: Smith, Elder and Co., 1898.
Dusany, Admiral Lord. "England and the Suez Canal." *Nineteenth Century* 12 (December 1882): 839–60.
Dwan, Allan. *Suez* (U.S., 1938). Film.
Magniac, C. "The Pretensions of M. De Lesseps." *Nineteenth Century* 15 (January 1884): 13–27.
Obieta, Joseph A. *The International Status of the Suez Canal.* The Hague: Martinus Nijhoff, 1960.
Schonfield, Hugh J. *The Suez Canal in Peace and War.* Coral Gables, Fla.: University of Miami Press, 1962.
Society of Comparative Legislation and International Law. *The Suez Canal: A Selection of Documents Relating to the International Status of the Suez Canal and the Position of the Suez Canal Company, November 30, 1854–July 26, 1956.* London: Stevens and Co., 1956; New York: Frederick Praeger, 1956.
Walsh, Raoul. *East of Suez* (U.S., 1925). Film.
Wilson, Arnold Talbot. *The Suez Canal: Its Past, Present, and Future.* London: Oxford University Press, 1939.

"A Stretch of the Canal Is Hollowed Out / The Men Who Have Hollowed It" (n.d.). In Lord John Patrick Douglas Balfour Kinross, *Between Two Seas: The Creation of the Suez Canal* (London: J. Murray, 1968).

Latest—From the Sphinx

Across the desert's sandy sea
   Though sorely battered brows I rear,
Still with my stony eyes I see,
   Still with my stony ears I hear.

Thousands of years this resting place
   Betwixt the Pyramids I hold,
And still their daily shadow trace,
   Broadening o'er me, blue and cold.

And many wonders have I known,
   And many a race and rule of men,
Since first upon the desert's zone
   I fixed my calm, unwinking ken.

'Neath these same orbs that still revolve
   Above my granite brows sedate,
I forged the riddles, which to solve
   Was fame, wherein to fail was fate.

But darker riddle never yet
   I framed for Œdipus the wise,
Than those that to the world I set,
   Touching these things before my eyes.

What of this piercing of the sands?
   What of this union of the seas?
This grasp of unfamiliar hands,
   This blending of strange litanies?

Aves and Allah-hu's that flow
   From ulemas and monsignors—
These *feridjees* and *robes-fourreau,*
   These eunuchs and ambassadors—

This *pot-pourri* of East and West,
   Pillau and *potage à la bisque;*—
Circassian belles whom WORTH has drest,
   And Parisiennes *à l'odalisque!*

Riddles that send no Sphinx to put,
   But more than Œdipus to read—
What good or ill from LESSEPS' cut
   Eastward and Westward shall proceed?

Whose loss or profit? War or peace?
   Sores healed, or old wounds oped anew?
Upon the loosing of the seas,
Strife's bitter waters let loose too?

The Eastern question raised, at last?
   The Eastern question laid for aye?
Russian ambition fettered fast?
   Or feathered but for freer play?

The shattering of the Sultan's throne?
   Or the Khedivè's rise, to fall?
England and France, like hawks let flown?
   Or *Aigle* on perch and Bull in stall?

Answer in vain the Sphinx invites;
   A darkling veil the future hides:
We know what seas the work unites,
   Who knows what sovereigns it divides?

RULE BRITANNIA OR NO?

Mr. Punch extends the right hand of fraternal congratulation to M. Lesseps, because M. Lesseps has made a Large Cut through the Isthmus of Suez. That Large Cut, however, is a Channel, and *Mr. Punch* hopes there will be no difficulty about the command of the Channel Fleet.

Suez Canal: Its Consequences

"From the Great Pyramid. (A Bird's-Eye View of the Canal and Its Consequences.)" In *Punch* 57 (27 November 1869): 212–13.

AN OFFER TO CLOSE WITH.

That famous old vineyard, the Clos Vougeot, has just changed hands for £62,000. Mr. Nathan, on hearing of this, remarked that it was the largest amount ever realised in the Old Clos' line.

PALMAM QUI MERUIT FERAT.

The Suez Canal is opened, and its projector, we are told, is to be made a Senator and a Duke of France, in commemoration of the great event. We congratulate M. De Lesseps on two things—on getting through the Deserts, and on getting his deserts.

SOURCE: In *Punch* 57 (27 November 1869): 210.

The Sultan's Complaint

"Here's Ismail, regardless
  Of *meum* and *tuum*,
Thinks this Suez Canal
  Has made everything *suum!*

Suez Canal: Its Consequences

"Midst crown'd heads at Cairo,
  O'ercrows Stamboul's wassail!
Spends more than his Sovereign,—
  The impudent vassal!

"Then to make both ends meet
  His poor *fellaheen* pinches,
Fain to eke out his ell
  By the aid of their inches.

"But for each pound so squeezed
  He sends three times the money,
And the more bees he plunders
  The more he wants honey.

"In his greed for the golden eggs
  Kills off the ganders;
Drains *my* Egypt dry
  With the millions he squanders.

"Then when quite out-at-elbows,
  His pockets swept clean,
He at ten per cent, borrows,
  While I pay fifteen!

"Now, thus to have pockets
  Sans fond as a sieve is,
And thus, without limit,
  Beg, borrow, and thieve, is
A Sultan's prerogative,
  Not a Khedivès'!"

SOURCE: In *Punch* 57 (18 December 1869): 240.

Report to His Highness the Viceroy of Egypt on the Fellah Workmen to be Employed by the International Suez Canal Company.

FERDINAND DE LESSEPS

Alexandria, July 20, 1856.

The Act of Concession for the Suez Canal gives complete authority to the International Company to obtain the artisans necessary to carry out the work. Article 2 provides that, in every case, four fifths at least of the hands employed shall be Egyptians. Article 22 promises the company the loyal and hearty cooperation of the Government and its officers. It enrolls the two chief engineers of the Viceroy in the company, who are to manage the works, superintend the workmen, and carry out the regulations relative to the work in hand. The practical application of this principle, and adhering to the conditions and clauses attached to its execution, is most essential to the company's interest and the surest guarantee that the work will be promptly and economically executed.

The company has now to secure for the works a sufficient number of efficient, strong, and acclimatised hands, and to fix the maximum of wages, that the estimate of expenses the engineers of the international scientific commission are going to draw up may be complete and accurate.

In order to be quite sure of enough men, it must also concentrate the labourers in one place, under regulations for their order, discipline, and welfare, which will allay all apprehensions and present reciprocal advantages to labour, on the one hand, and capital on the other.

With reference to this matter, Mohammed Said has entrusted me to draw up a decree, which I think it will be well to publish, in order to reassure all interests and answer many of the objections raised against the feasibility of making the Canal without difficulty.

Thanks to the decree, the company will henceforth have at its disposal such workmen as the chief engineers shall think necessary, without resorting to large importations from the European labour market; to which we ought never to have recourse, although our so doing has been gratuitously suggested as a material difficulty and political inconvenience.

In the interest of the company the rate of wages should be two-thirds less than those given in similar enterprises in Europe.

In the interests of the men, it should exceed by one-third the daily pay they are now receiving in Egypt.

Besides cash payment, food and shelter are guaranteed to the hands, as well as free medical attendance in case of illness or accidents. Moreover, the sick and wounded are to receive an indemnity equivalent to half a day's pay daily. We believe this to be the first time that such a thoughtful and humane measure has been officially introduced in workshops (*sic*) even in Europe.

The solicitude shown by the Viceroy in this important particular in favour of the labouring classes, who up to this time have been too little considered in the East, with the guarantees insisted on for their protection and assistance, will perhaps be the best proof, to those who know the old customs of the East, of the progress that Egypt, under a generous impulse, has made in the ideas of Western civilisation. Mohammed Said, who is as well acquainted with his own religion as he is with European learning, well knows that the Mussulman law in no way opposes progress; he often says that it is the bad government, evil customs, and bad habits of the East that want reform more than the laws. In short, the book which proclaims love as the rule of life, and says that in the eyes of God the best man is he who does most good to his fellows, can never oppose measures taken in the interests of the highest civilisation.

We, Mohammed Said Pacha, Viceroy of Egypt, anxious to assure the execution of the works for the Suez Maritime Canal, to arrange that the Egyptian working men who shall be employed shall be well treated, and anxious at the same time to protect the interests of the cultivators, proprietors, and contractors of the country, have drawn up, in conjunction with M. Ferdinand de Lesseps, founder and president of the International Company of the said Canal, the following code:

Article 1.—The men to be employed on the company's works shall be supplied by the Egyptian Government, when applied for by the chief engineer, as they shall be required.

Article 2.—Fixed pay will be allotted to the workmen, according to the average pay fixed in private undertakings, at from two and-a-half to three piastres a day, not including food, which shall be paid in kind by the company, to the value of one piastre. Hands under twelve years of age will only receive one piastre, but full rations.

The rations shall be given out every day, or every two or three days, in advance; and in cases where it shall be found that the workmen are in a position to provide their own food, the value of their rations shall be given in money.

The money payments shall be made every week.

The company, however, will not give out more than half-pay for the first month, till it has accumulated a reserve of fifteen days' pay, after which full pay will be given to the men.

The care of providing plenty of drinkable water for all the wants of the men is undertaken by the company.

Article 3.—The task imposed on the men shall not exceed that fixed in the Egyptian *Ponts et Chausslés* contract, which has been adopted in all canal works undertaken in the last few years.

The number of men employed will be regulated with reference to seasons, and agricultural pursuits.

Article 4.—The police in the workyards will be Government officers and agents, acting under the chief engineer's orders, in accordance with regulations approved by us.

Article 5.—Workmen who shall not have completed their task will have their pay reduced by not less than a third, and in proportion to the amount of work left undone.

Defaulters will entirely lose the fifteen days' pay in reserve. Their share will be devoted to the hospital, which is treated of in the next article. Men giving any trouble in the workyards will be docked of a proportionate part of the fifteen days' pay in reserve; they will also be liable to a fine, which will go to the hospital fund.

Article 6.—The company will find shelter for the workmen, either in tents, sheds, or suitable houses. It will provide a hospital and ambulances, with all necessary appliances for treating the sick, at their expense.

Article 7.—The traveling expenses of the men engaged and their families, from the time of their leaving home till they arrive at the workyards, will be defrayed by the company.

Every workman who is ill will receive, whether in the hospital or in the ambulances, besides everything to restore his health, a pay of one and-a-half piastre during the whole of the time he is unable to work.

Article 8.—Artisans, such as masons, carpenters, stonecutters, blacksmiths, &c., will receive the usual pay the Government allots for their work, exclusive of food, or its equivalent.

Article 9.—When soldiers of the line are employed on the works, the company will give each of them a sum equal to the pay of civilians at the works, on account of the high rate of their ordinary pay, and of their dress.

Article 10.—Everything necessary for the transport of soil, materials, or powder for blasting purposes, will be supplied by the company or the

Government, at net cost, which will be demanded three months (at least) in advance.

Our engineers, Linant Bey and Mougel Bey, whom we place at the disposal of the company to direct and conduct the works, will superintend the workmen, and act in concert with the administrator appointed by the company to remove any difficulties that may arise in carrying out this decree.

Given at Alexandria July 20, 1856.

(L. S.) Viceroy's Signet.
(Translated from the Turkish.)

SOURCE: In *The Suez Canal: Letters and Documents Descriptive of Its Rise and Progress in 1854–56,* trans. D. Anvers (London: Henry S. King, 1876; reprint, Wilmington, Del.: Scholarly Resources, 1976).

The Original Firman of Concession Granted by the Viceroy of Egypt Mohamed Said, to Ferdinand De Lesseps, 1854.

Our friend Monsieur Ferdinand de Lesseps, having called our attention to the advantages which would result to Egypt from the junction of the Mediterranean and Red Seas, by a navigable passage for large vessels, and having given us to understand the possibility of forming a company for this purpose composed of capitalists of all nations, we have accepted the arrangements which he has submitted to us, and by these presents grant him exclusive power for the establishment and direction of a Universal Company, for cutting through the Isthmus of Suez, and the construction of a canal between the two Seas, with authority to undertake or cause to be undertaken all the necessary works and erections, on condition that the Company shall previously indemnify all private persons in case of dispossession for the public benefit. And all within limits, upon the conditions and under the responsibilities, settled in the following Articles.

Art. 1.—Monsieur Ferdinand de Lesseps shall form a company, the direction of which we confide to him, under the name of the Universal Suez Maritime Canal Company, for cutting through the Isthmus of Suez, the construction of a passage suitable for extensive navigation, the foundation or appropriation of two sufficient entrances, one from the Mediterranean and the other from the Red Sea, and the establishment of one or two ports.

Art. 2.—The Director of the Company shall be always appointed by the Egyptian Government, and selected, as far as practicable, from the shareholders most interested in the undertaking.

Art. 3.—The term of the grant is ninety-nine years, commencing from the day of the opening of the Canal of the two Seas.

Art. 4.—The works shall be executed at the sole cost of the Company, and all the necessary land not belonging to private persons shall be granted to it free of cost. The fortifications which the Government shall think proper to establish shall not be at the cost of the Company.

Art. 5.—The Egyptian Government shall receive from the Company annually fifteen per cent of the net profits shown by the balance sheet, without prejudice to the interest and dividends accruing from the shares which the Government reserves the right of taking upon its own account at this issue, and without any guarantee on its part either for the execution of the works or for the operations of the Company; the remainder of the net profits shall be divided as follows: Seventy-five per cent, to the benefit of the Company; ten per cent, to the benefit of the members instrumental in its foundation.

Art. 6.—The Tariffs of dues for the passage of the Canal of Suez, to be agreed upon between the Company and the Viceroy of Egypt, and collected by the Company's agents, shall be always equal for all nations; no particular advantage can ever be stipulated for the exclusive benefit of any one country.

Art. 7.—In case the Company should consider it necessary to connect the Nile by a navigable canal cut with the direct passage of the Isthmus, and in case the Maritime Canal should follow an indirect course, the Egyptian Government will give up to the Company the uncultivated lands belonging to the public domain, which shall be irrigated and cultivated at the expense of the Company, or by its instrumentality. The Company shall enjoy the said lands for ten years free of taxes, commencing from the day of the opening of the canal; during the remaining eighty nine years of the grant, the Company shall pay tithes to the Egyptian Government, after which period it cannot continue in possession of the lands above mentioned without paying to the said Government an impost equal to that appointed for lands of the same description.

Art. 8.—To avoid all difficulty on the subject of the lands which are to be given up to the Company, a plan drawn by M. Linant Bey, our Engineer Commissioner attached to the Company, shall indicate the lands granted both for the line and the establishments of the Maritime Canal and for the alimentary canal from the Nile, as well as for the purpose of cultivation, conformably to the stipulations of Article 7.

It is moreover understood that all speculation is forbidden from the present time, upon the lands to be granted from the public domain, and that the land previously belonging to private persons and which the proprietors may hereafter wish to have irrigated by the waters of the alimentary canal, made at the cost of the Company, shall pay a rent of . . . per feddan cultivated (or a rent amicably settled between the Government and the Company).

Art. 9.—The Company is further allowed to extract from the mines and quarries belonging to the public domain, any materials necessary for the work of the Canal and the erections connected therewith, without paying dues; it shall also enjoy the right of free entry for all machines and materials which it shall import from abroad for the purposes of carrying out this grant.

Art. 10.—At the expiration of the concession the Egyptian Government will take the place of the Company, and enjoy all its rights without reservation, the said Government will enter into full possession of the Canal of the two Seas, and of all the establishments connected therewith. The indemnity to be allowed the Company for the relinquishment of its plant and movables shall be arranged by amicable agreement or by arbitration.

Art. 11.—The statutes of the Society shall be moreover submitted to us by the Director of the Company, and must have the sanction of our approbation. Any modifications that may be hereafter introduced must previously receive our sanction. The said statutes shall set forth the names of the founders, the list of whom we reserve to ourselves the right of approving. This list shall include those persons whose labours, studies, exertions or capital have previously contributed to the execution of the grand undertaking of the Canal of Suez.

Art. 12.—Finally, we promise our true and hearty co-operation and that of all the functionaries of Egypt in facilitating the execution and carrying out of the present powers.

Cairo, 30th of November 1854.

To my attached friend, of high birth and
elevated rank, M. Ferdinand de Lesseps

The grant made to the Company having to be ratified by His Imperial Majesty the Sultan, I send you this copy that you may keep it in your possession. With regard to the works connected with the excavation of the Canal of Suez, they are not to be commenced until after they are authorised by the Sublime Porte.

3 Ramadan, 1281. (Said, Viceroy.)

SOURCE: In *White Paper on the Nationalisation of the Suez Maritime Canal Company* (Cairo: Ministry for Foreign Affairs, Government Press, 1956).

Charter of Concession and Book of Charges for the Construction and Working of the Suez Grand Maritime Canal and Dependencies.

We Mohammed Said-Pacha Vice-Roy of Egypt,

Considering our charter bearing date the 30th November 1854, by which we have granted to our friend M. Ferdinand de Lesseps exclusive power to constitute and direct a Universal Company for cutting the Isthmus of Suez, opening a passage suitable for large vessels, forming or adapting two sufficient entrances, one on the Mediterranean, the other on the Red Sea, and establishing one or two ports, as the case may be:

M. Ferdinand de Lesseps, having represented to us that in order to constitute a company as above described under the forms and conditions generally adopted for companies of that nature, it is expedient to stipulated beforehand by a fuller and more specific document, the burthens, obligations and services to which that company will be subjected on the one part, and the concessions, immunities, and advantages to which it will be entitled, as also the facilities which will be accorded to it for its administration, on the other part:

Have decreed as follows the conditions of the concession which is the subject matter of these presents.

I. CHARGES

Art. 1.—The Company founded by our friend M. Ferdinand de Lesseps in virtue of our charter of the 30th November 1854, shall execute at its own cost, risk and damage all the necessary works and construction for the establishment of:

(1) A canal navigable by large vessels between Suez on the Red Sea, and the Gulf of Pelusium on the Mediterranean;

(2) A canal of irrigation adapted to the river traffic of the Nile, joining that river to the above-mentioned Maritime Canal;

(3) Two branches for irrigation and supply, striking out of the preceding Canal, and in the direction respectively of Suez and Pelusium.

The works shall be completed within the period of six years, unavoidable hinderances and delays excepted.

Art. 2.—The Company shall have the right to execute the works they have undertaken, themselves and under their own management, or to cause them to be executed by contractors by means of public tender or private contract under penalties. In all cases, four-fifths of the workmen employed upon these works shall be Egyptians.

Art. 3.—The Canal navigable by large vessels shall be constructed of the depth and width fixed by the scheme of the International Scientific Commission.

Conformably with this scheme, it will commence at the port of Suez; it will pass through the basin of the Amer Lakes and Lake Timsah, and will debouche into the Mediterranean at whatever point in the Gulf of Pelusium may be determined in the final plans to be prepared by the engineers of the Company.

Art. 4.—The Canal of Irrigation adapted to the river traffic, according to the terms of the said scheme, shall commence in the vicinity of the city of Cairo, follow the valley (Ouadée) of Tomilat, (ancient land of Gessen), and will fall into the Grand Maritime Canal at Lake Timsah.

Art. 5.—The branches from the above Canal shall strike out from it above the debouchure into Lake Timsah, from which point they shall proceed, on one side to Suez, and on the other to Pelusium, parallel to the Grand Maritime Canal.

Art. 6.—Lake Timsah shall be converted into an inland harbour capable of receiving vessels of the highest tonnage.

The Company shall moreover be bound, if necessary; first, to construct a harbour of refuge at the entrance of the Maritime Canal into the Gulf of Pelusium; secondly, to improve the port and road-stead of Suez so that it shall equally afford a shelter to vessels.

Art. 7.—The Maritime Canal, the ports connected therewith, as also the Junction Canal of the Nile and the branch Canals, shall be permanently maintained in good condition by the Company and at their expense.

Art. 8.—The owners of contiguous lands desirous of irrigating their property by means of water-courses from the Company's canals shall obtain permission so to do in consideration of the payment of an indemnity or rent, the amount whereof shall be fixed according to Article 17 hereinafter recited.

Art. 9.—We reserve the right of appointing at the official head quarters of the Company a special commissioner, whose salary they shall pay and who shall represent at the Board of Direction the rights and interests of the Egyptian Government in the execution of these presents.

If the principal office of the Company be established elsewhere than in Egypt, the Company shall be represented at Alexandria by a superior agent furnished with all necessary powers for securing the proper management of the concern and the relations of the Company with our Government.

II. CONCESSIONS

Art. 10.—For the construction of the Canals and their dependencies mentioned in the foregoing articles, the Egyptian Government grants to the Company, free of impost or rent, the use and enjoyment of all lands not the property of individuals which may be found necessary.

It likewise grants to the Company the use and enjoyment of all uncultivated lands not the propery of individuals which shall have been irrigated and cultivated by their care and at their expense, with these provisions:

(1) The lands comprised under the latter head shall be free of impost during ten years, only to date from their being put in a productive condition.

(2) That after that period, they shall be subject for the remainder of the term of concession, to the same obligations and imposts to which are subjected under like circumstances, the land in other provinces of Egypt.

(3) That the Company shall afterwards, themselves or through their agents, continue in the use and enjoyment of these lands and the watercourses necessary to their fertilisation, subject to payment to the Egyptian Government, of the imposts assessed upon lands under like conditions.

Art. 11.—For determining the area and boundaries of the lands conceded to the Company under Article 10, reference is made to the plans hereunto annexed, in which plans the land conceded for the construction of the Canals and their dependencies free of impost or rent, conformably to Clause 1, is coloured black, and the land conceded for the purpose of cultivation, on paying certain duties conformably with Clause 2, is coloured blue.

All acts and deeds done subsequently to our charter of the 30th November, 1854, the effect of which would be to give to individuals as against the Company, either claims to compensation which were not then vested in the ownership of the lands, or claims to compensation more considerable than those which the owners could then justly advance, shall be considered void.

Art. 12.—The Egyptian Government will deliver to the Company, should the case arise, all lands the property of private individuals, whereof possession shall be necessary for the execution of the works and the carrying into effect of the concession, subject to the payment of just compensation to the parties concerned.

Compensation for temporary occupation or definitive appropriation shall as far as possible be determined amicably; in case of disagreement the terms shall be fixed by a court of arbitration deciding summarily and composed of:

(1) An arbitrator chosen by the Company;

(2) An arbitrator chosen by the interested parties;

(3) A third arbitrator appointed by us.

The decisions of the court of arbitration shall be executed without further process, and subject to no appeal.

Art. 13.—The Egyptian Government grants to the leasing Company, for the whole period of the concession, the privilege of drawing from the mines and quarries belonging to the public domain, without paying duty, impost or compensation, all necessary materials for the construction and maintenance of the works and buildings of the undertaking. It moreover exempts the Company from all duties of customs, entrance dues and others, on the importation into Egypt of all machinery and materials whatsoever which they shall bring from foreign countries, for employment in the construction of the works or working the undertaking.

Art. 14.—We solemnly declare for our part and that of our successors, subject to the ratification of His Imperial Majesty the Sultan, that the Grand Maritime Canal from Suez to Pelusium and the ports appertaining thereto, shall always remain open as a neutral passage to every merchant ship crossing from one sea to another, without any distinction, exclusion, or preference of persons or nationalities, on payment of the dues and observance of the regulations established by the Universal Company lessee for the use of the said Canal and its dependencies.

Art. 15.—In pursuance of the principle laid down in the foregoing article, the Universal Company can in no case grant to any vessel, company, or individual, any advantages or favour not accorded to all other vessels, companies or individuals on the same conditions.

Art. 16.—The term of the Company's existence is fixed at 99 years, reckoning from the completion of the works and the opening of the Maritime Canal to large vessels.

At the expiration of the said term, the Egyptian Government shall enter into possession of the Maritime Canal constructed by the Company, upon condition, in that event, of taking all the working stock and appliances and stores employed and provided for the naval department of the enterprise, and paying to the Company such amount for the same as shall be determined either amicably or by the decision of sworn appraisers.

Nevertheless, if the Company should retain the concession for a succession of terms of 99 years, the amount stipulated to be paid to the Egyptian Government by Article 18, hereinafter recited, shall be raised for the second term to 20 per cent, for the third term to 25 per cent, and so on augmenting at the rate of 5 per cent for each term, but so as never to exceed on the whole 35 per cent, of the net proceeds of the undertaking.

Art. 17.—To indemnify the Company for the expenses of construction, maintenance and working, charged upon them by these presents, we authorize the Company henceforth, and during the whole term of their lease, as determined by clauses 1 and 3 of the preceding Article, to levy and receive for passage through and entrance into the canals and ports thereunto appertaining, tolls and charges for navigation, pilotage, towage to harbour dues, according to tariffs which they shall be at liberty to modify at all times, upon the following express conditions:

(1) That these dues be collected, without exception or favour, from all ships under like conditions;

(2) That the tariffs be published three months before they come into force, in the capitals and principal commercial ports of all nations whom it may concern;

(3) That for the simple right of passage through the Canal, the maximum toll shall be 10 francs per measurement ton on ships and per head on passengers, and that the same shall never be exceeded.

The Company may also, for granting the privilege of establishing watercourses, upon the request of individuals by virtue of Article 8, receive dues, according to tariffs to be hereafter settled, proportionable to the quantity of water diverted and the extent of the lands irrigated.

Art. 18.—Nevertheless, in consideration of the concessions of land and other advantages accorded to the Company by the preceding Articles, we reserve on behalf of the Egyptian Government a claim of 15 per cent, on the net profits of each year, according to the dividend settled and declared by the General Meeting of Shareholders.

Art. 19.—The list of Foundation Members who have contributed by their exertions, professional labours, and capital to the realization of the undertaking before the establishment of the Company, shall be settled by us.

After the said payment to the Egyptian Government, according to Article 18 above recited, there shall be divided out of the net annual profits of the undertaking, one share of 10 per cent, among the Foundation Members or their heirs or assigns.

Art. 20.—Independently of the time necessary for the execution of the works, our friend and authorized agent, M. Ferdinand de Lesseps, shall preside over the direct the Company, as original founder, during ten years from the first day on which the term of concession for 99 years shall begin to run, by the terms of Article 10 above contained.

Art. 21.—The Articles of Association hereunto annexed of the Company, established under the title of THE SUEZ MARITIME CANAL UNIVERSAL COMPANY, are hereby approved, and the present approval shall have force as an authority for its constitution in the form of Sociétés Anonymes, to date from the day when the entire capital of the Company shall be completely subscribed.

Art. 22.—In witness of the interest which we feel in the success of the undertaking, we promise to the Company the loyal co-operation of the Egyptian Government; and we expressly, by these presents, call upon the functionaries and agents of all our administrative departments to give aid and protection at all times to the Company.

Our engineers, Linant Bey and Mougel Bey, whose services we place at the disposal of the Company for the direction and conduct of the works ordered by the said Company, shall have the superintendence of the workmen, and shall be charged with the enforcing of regulations respecting the execution of the works.

Art. 23.—All provisions of our Charter of the 30th November 1854, and others which are inconsistent with the clauses and conditions of the present book of charged, which alone shall constitute the law in respect of the concession to which it applies, are hereby revoked.

Done at Alexandria, January 5, 1856.

To my devoted friend, of high birth and rank,
M. Ferdinand de Lesseps

The grant bestowed upon the Universal Company of the Maritime Canal of Suez having to be ratified by H.I.M. the Sultan, I forward you this authentic copy that you may constitute the said financial Company.

As to the works relating to the boring of the Isthmus, the Company can execute them itself as soon as the authorization of the Sublime Porte has been accorded to me.

Alexandria, the 26 Rebi El-Akhar 1272. (January 5th., 1856).

Seal of His Highness the Viceroy.

A true translation from the original Turkish, deposited in the State Archives.

The Secretary of the commands of His Highness the Viceroy.
(Signed) Koenig Bey.

SOURCE: In *White Paper on the Nationalisation of the Suez Maritime Canal Company* (Cairo: Ministry for Foreign Affairs, Government Press, 1956).

Agreement of February 22, 1866, Determining the Final Terms as Ratified by the Sublime Porte

1. Abolition of forced labour from the Canal works.

Art. 1.—Shall be entirely abolished, all references in the Regulations dated July 20, 1856, pertaining to the employment of fellaheen in the works of the Suez Canal. In consequence, shall be considered null and void the provisions of Art. 2 of the Act of Concession dated January 5, 1856, which provides:—"In all cases, four fifths of the workmen employed upon these works shall be Egyptian."

The Government of Egypt shall, in compensation for the abolition of the Regulations dated July 20, 1856, and the privileges involved thereon, pay the Company 38 million francs.

And henceforth, the Company shall, without any privileges or hindrance, employ the necessary workmen for the enterprise according to the common law.

2. Curtailing the Area of the ceded lands and certain privileges:

Art. 2.—The Company renounces the benefits of provisions of Arts. 7 and 8 of the Act of Concession dated November 30, 1854, as well as Arts. 11 and 12 of the Act dated January 5, 1856. The area of the lands capable of irrigation which had been ceded to the Company under the said 1854 and 1856 Acts and which was receded to the Government is fixed, by mutual agreement, at 63,000 hectares from which shall be deducted 3,000 hectares which form part of the site assigned for the requirements of the Maritime Canal.

Art. 3.—Since, as provided in Articles 7 and 8 of the 1854 Act of Concession and Articles 10, 11 and 12 of that of 1856, remain annulled, the compensation due to the Company from the Government of Egypt for the reclamation of these lands shall amount to 30 million francs, at the rate of 500 francs per hectare.

Art. 4.—Considering the necessity of determining the area of lands required for the establishment of the maritime canal and its working under proper conditions as will insure the prosperity of the enterprise; that this area must not be limited to the space which will be materially occupied by the canal itself, by its freeboards and by the towing paths; considering that, to give full and complete satisfaction to working requirements, it is necessary that the

Company shall be able to establish, within the proximity of the maritime canal, depots, warehouses, workshops and ports where their usefulness will be acknowledged, and, finally, appropriate habitations for the guardians, superintendents, workmen charged with maintenance work, and for all administration officials; that it is also appropriate that lands be annexed to the said habitations which might be cultivated as gardens to provide certain agricultural provisions in such places as are entirely deprived of these supplies.

And, finally, it is absolutely necessary that the Company shall have at its disposal sufficient lands for cultivation and establishment thereon of works intended to protect the maritime canal against invading sand and ensure its maintenance; but it should not be granted more than is necessary to amply meet the needs of the various works indicated above;

Considering that the Company can have no claim to obtain any areas of land whatsoever for speculation purposes, whether by putting it under cultivation, establishing buildings thereon or by sale to others when the population increase;

Being bound by these considerations in determining the boundaries of the lands lying along the length of the maritime canal whose possession shall be necessary, throughout the duration of the concession, for the establishment, working and maintenance of the canal, the Two Contracting Parties mutually agree that these lands be determined in conformity with the plans and tables drawn up, preconcerted, signed and appended to this effect by the present.

Art. 5.—The Company shall return to the Government of Egypt the second part of the fresh water canal situated between El Wadi, Ismailia and Suez; just as it had already returned the first part of the said canal, lying between Cairo and El Wadi Domain under the agreement dated March 18, 1863.

The return of the second part of this canal is made under the following terms and conditions:

(1) The Company undertakes to complete the remaining works to have El Wadi—Ismailia—Suez Canal comply with the dimensions agreed upon, and in a suitable condition for taking over;

(2) The Government of Egypt shall take over the fresh-water canal, the technical constructions and the land dependent thereon as soon as the Company is in a position to deliver the canal according to the preceding conditions.

This delivery, which implies acknowledgement of receipt on the part of the Government of Egypt, shall take place contradictorily between Government engineers and those of the Company, and shall be recorded in a procès-verbal showing in detail the points where the state of the Canal departs from the conditions which it ought to have fulfilled.

(3) As from the date of delivery, the Government of Egypt shall undertake the maintenance of the said Canal, i.e.:

I.—To carry out during the proper time all plantation and cultivation work as well as the necessary fortifications to prevent the delapidation of the banks and the settling of sand; and to maintain feeding the Canal from the Zagazig canal until such feeding can be ensured directly from Cairo water intake.

II.—To carry out the works pertaining to the part returned to it under the Agreement of March 8, 1863; and to connect this first part to the second at El Wadi junction point.

III.—To ensure navigation during all the seasons by maintaining the canal water level at 2.50 metres during high Nile water, at 2 metres during middle water level and at 1 metre during lowest water level.

IV.—Moreover, to supply the Company with 70,000 cubic metres of water daily for supplying the population living alongside the maritime canal, for watering the gardens, for driving the machinery designed for the maintenance of the maritime canal and machinery of industrial establishments connected with its working; for the irrigation of seed plots, sand hill plantations as well as other lands among the dependencies of the maritime canal which cannot be naturally irrigated; and, lastly, to supply vessels passing through the said Canal.

V.—To carry out all the necessary clearing and other works so as to maintain the fresh-water canal and its technical constructions in good condition.

On this account, the Government of Egypt shall substitute the Company in all the charges and obligations that befall it as a result of insufficient maintenance; taking into account the condition on which the canal will be on delivery, and the delay necessary for carrying out such works as would have been demanded by that condition.

3. The Company is Subject to Egyptian Sovereignty and to Laws and Customs of the Country.

Art. 9.—The Maritime Canal shall remain under the Egyptian Police who will have free authority over it as is exercised elsewhere in the Egyptian territory, with a view to maintaining order and public security and ensuring the enforcement of the country's laws and regulations.

The Government of Egypt shall enjoy the right of passage across the Maritime Canal, where this passage is judged necessary, whether to insure its communications or free circulation for commerce and the public. The Company shall under no pretext whatsoever levy any charges or other dues.

Art. 10.—The Government of Egypt shall occupy, within the boundaries of lands reserved as dependencies to the Maritime Canal, any position or strategic point which it judges necessary for the defence of the country. This occupation should not prejudice navigation, nor easements attached to the free-boards of the Canal.

Art. 11.—The Government of Egypt may, under the same reservations, occupy for the use of its administrative services (post, customs, barracks, etc.) any available place it deems convenient; taking into account the exigencies of operating the services of the Company. In this case, the Government shall, where this is necessary, repay the Company the sums which this latter might have spent on the creation or appropriation of the lands which the Government proposes to dispose of.

Art. 16.—Since the Universal Company of the Maritime Suez Canal is an Egyptian Company, it remains subject to the laws and usages of the country. However, regarding its constitution as a Company and the relation of shareholders among themselves, it is—in virtue of a special convention—governed by the laws regulating joint stock companies. It has been agreed that all disputes resulting thereof will be submitted to arbiters in France for judgment and with appeals before the Imperial Court of Paris as being a superarbiter.

As regards the disputes that arise in Egypt between the Company and individuals of whatever nationality, these must be referred to Egyptian courts, and their procedure be subject to Egyptian law, usages and treaties.

As regards the disputes that may arise between the Company and the Egyptian Government, these must in like manner be referred to Egyptian judiciary and settled in accordance with Egyptian law.

Workers and other individuals subject to the administration of the Company will be tried before Egyptian courts and in accordance with Egyptian laws and treaties. This applies to all contraventions and disputes where either or both parties concerned would be Egyptian. Should all parties to the dispute be foreigners, the case will be subject to the established procedure.

All notifications addressed to the Company by any of the parties interested in Egypt will be valid when dispatch to the Company's Office at Alexandria.

4. The Canal is an Egyptian Public Domain.

This is apparent from all the provisions of the Convention (1866) and, in particular from article 13:

Art. 13.—In the interest of commerce, industry and the successful operation of the Canal, every individual shall have the right to settle down either alongside the Maritime Canal or within the villages set up along its course, provided permission is obtained from the Government beforehand, and being subject to the administrative and municipal regulations of the local authority as well as to laws, customs and taxes system of the country.

Shall be excepted, the free-boards, banks and towing paths which shall remain open for free circulation under the regulations governing their use.

This settling down is not permissible except in such places as declared by the Company's engineers as being unnecessary for the working of its services.

Beneficiaries shall repay the Company such sums as it might have spent in the creation or appropriation of these places.

THE OBJECT OF THE CONCESSION

From the foregoing, it will be clearly seen that the Universal Suez Maritime Canal Company is a commercial company operating a public utility enterprise as determined in the act of concession.

The object of this concession forms the target of the company and the field of its activities as indicated in Article 2 of the company's organic law, which was approved by the Government of Egypt on January 5, 1856.

Article 2. The Object of this Company:

(1) The establishment of a canal navigable by large vessels between the Red Sea and the Mediterranean, from Suez to the Gulf of Pelusium.

(2) Establishment of a canal of irrigation adapted to the river traffic of the Nile, joining the Nile to the maritime canal, from Cairo to Lake Timsah.

(3) Establishment of two branches striking out of the preceding canal at its inlet into Lake Timsah and proceeding on one side to Suez, and on the other to Pelusium.

(4) Utilisation of the said Canal and branches and other dependencies.

(5) Utilisation of lands granted to the Company.

The above will be governed by the conditions and stipulations provided for in the two Firmans dated November 20, 1854 and January 5, 1856.

The first Firman grants M. Ferdinand de Lesseps exclusive power to establish and direct a company to carry out the above works in his capacity of being the original founder of the Company and its managing director. The second Firman grants the Company a concession to carry out the establishment of the above canals and dependencies under the provisions set therein with all the attendant costs, obligations, rights or privileges envisaged by the Government.

THE CANAL IS AN EGYPTIAN TERRITORY

The Canal is dug in Egyptian Public Domain. This is evidenced by the following provisions of Firman dated January 5, 1856:

Art. 10.—For the construction of the Canals and their dependencies mentioned in the foregoing articles, the Egyptian Government grants to the Company, free of impost or rent, the use and enjoyment of all lands not the property of individuals which may be found necessary.

It likewise grants to the Company the use and enjoyment of all uncultivated lands not the property or individuals which shall have been irrigated and cultivated by their care and at their expense, with these provisoes:

(1) The lands comprised under the latter head shall be free of impost during ten years, only to date from their being put in a productive condition.

(2) That after that period, they shall be subject for the remainder of the term of concession, to the same obligations and imposts to which are subjected under like circumstances, the land in other provinces of Egypt.

(3) That the Company shall afterward, themselves or through their agents, continue in the use and enjoyment of these lands and the water-courses necessary to their fertilisation, subject to payment to the Egyptian Government, of the imposts assessed upon lands under like conditions.

Art. 11.—For determining the area and boundaries of the lands conceded to the Company under Article 10, reference is made to the plans hereunto annexed, in which plans the land conceded for the construction of the Canals and their dependencies free of impost or rent, conformably to Clause one is coloured black, and the land conceded for the purpose of cultivation, on paying certain duties conformably with Clause two is coloured blue.

All acts and deeds done subsequently to our charter of the 30th November, 1954, the effect of which would be to give to individuals as against the Company, either claims to compensation which were not then vested in the ownership of the lands, or claims to compensation more considerable than those which the owners could then justly advance, shall be considered void.

Art. 12.—The Egyptian Government will deliver to the Company, should the case arise, all lands the property of private individuals, whereof possession shall be necessary for the execution of the works and the carrying into effect of the concession, subject to the payment of just compensation to the parties concerned.

Compensation for temporary occupation or definitive appropriation shall as far as possible be determined amicably; in case of disagreement the terms shall be fixed by a court of arbitration deciding summarily and composed of:

(1) An arbitrator chosen by the Company;
(2) An arbitrator chosen by the interested parties;
(3) A third arbitrator appointed by us.

The decisions of the court of arbitration shall be executed without further process, and subject to no appeal.

Art. 13.—The Egyptian Government grants to the leasing Company, for the whole period of the concession, the privilege of drawing from the mines and quarries belonging to the public domain, without paying duty, impost or compensation, all necessary materials for the construction and maintenance of the works and buildings of the undertaking. It moreover exempts the Company from all duties of customs, entrance dues and others, on the importation into Egypt of all machinery and materials, whatsoever which they shall bring from foreign countries, for employment in the construction of the works or working the undertaking.

Art. 16.—The term of the Company's existence is fixed at 99 years, reckoning from the completion of the works and the opening of the Maritime Canal to large vessels.

At the expiration of the said term, the Egyptian Government shall enter into possession of the Maritime Canal constructed by the Company, upon condition, in that event, of taking all the working stock and appliances and stores employed and provided for the naval department of the enterprise, and paying to the Company such amount for the same as shall be determined either amicably or by the decision of sworn appraisers.

Nevertheless, if the Company should retain the concession for a succession of terms of 99 years, the amount stipulated to be paid to the Egyptian Government by Article 18, hereinafter recited, shall be raised for the second term to 20 per cent, for the third term to 25 per cent, and so on augmenting at the rate of 5 per cent for each term, but so as never to exceed on the whole 35 per cent of the net proceeds of the undertaking.

This is also evidenced by article 4 of the agreement dated February 22, 1866 which provides:

Art. 4.—Considering the necessity of determining the area of lands required for the establishment of the Maritime Canal and its working under proper conditions as will insure the prosperity of the enterprise; that this area must not be limited to the space which will be materially occupied by the canal itself, by its free-boards and by the towing paths; considering that, to give full and complete satisfaction to working requirements, it is necessary that the Company shall be able to establish, within the proximity of the Maritime Canal, depots, warehouses, workshops and ports where their usefulness will be acknowledged, and, finally, appropriate habitations for the guardians, superintendents, workmen charged with maintenance work, and for all administration officials; that it is also appropriate that lands be annexed to the said habitations which might be cultivated as gardens to provide certain agricultural provisions in such places as are entirely deprived of these supplies.

And, finally, it is absolutely necessary that the Company shall have at its disposal sufficient lands for cultivation and establishment thereon of works intended to protect the Maritime Canal against invading sand and ensure its maintenance; but it should not be granted more than is necessary to amply meet the needs of the various works indicated above.

Considering that the Company can have no claim to obtain any areas of land whatsoever for speculation purposes, whether by putting it under cultivation, establishing building thereon or by sale to others when the population increase;

Being bound by these considerations in determining the boundaries of the lands lying along the length of the Maritime Canal whose possession shall be necessary, throughout the duration of the concession for the establishment, working and maintenance of the canal, the Two Contracting Parties, mutually agree that these lands be determined in conformity with the plans and tables drawn up, preconcerted, signed and appended to this effect by the present.

SOURCE: In *White Paper on the Nationalisation of the Suez Maritime Canal Company* (Cairo: Ministry for Foreign Affairs, Government Press, 1956).

Why Not Purchase the Suez Canal?
EDWARD DICEY

[Edward Dicey (1832–1911) was a prominent journalist who wrote numerous articles on Egypt, South Africa, and British colonialism; many of his essays can be found in *Nineteenth Century, Macmillan's,* and *Fortnightly Review.* Dicey's works include *After the Present War* (1899), on the Boer War; *The Confederation of South Africa* (1900); and *The Egypt of the Future* (1907).]

The convention, by which M. de Lesseps proposed to construct a second Suez Canal at the cost of England, is at an end. It has died prematurely, and its decease is, I suspect, scarcely regretted even by its responsible parents. Indeed, the only persons who have much cause to deplore the untoward result of this abortive negociation are speculators for a rise in Suez Canal shares. It would, however, be a grave mistake to suppose that the idea of a second Suez Canal will be allowed to drop because this particular attempt to carry it out has proved a failure. On the contrary, it may be taken for granted that the new Canal will be made, and that, too, at no distant period. Whatever difficulties may stand in the way, the interests demanding the increase of transit accommodation across the Isthmus of Suez are too powerful to be resisted. In as far as anything is certain in this uncertain world, it may be assumed as an axiom that trade forces its way just as water finds its level. In view of the enormous and increasing traffic between the East and the West, and of its urgent demand for greater facilities of transit between the Mediterranean and the Red Sea, it may safely be predicted that the supply of accommodation will somehow or other be made equal to the demand. The ultimate result is, I repeat, certain, but it may be brought about in many ways; and my object in this paper is to point out the way which, in my judgment, would be most conducive to the interests of all parties concerned in the Canal.

Now, the party chiefly concerned is England. This is the broad fact on which all discussions on the subject must be based, if they are to be of any practical value. The interest of the shareholders, though it is one I should be the last to ignore, is, after all, a purely pecuniary one. In common with all other investors, they desire most reasonably and most properly to obtain the highest interest and the best security possible for their investments; but, so long as this object is secured, it is a matter of indifference to them whether they convey many ships or few by their Canal, whether they charge high rates or low, whether they develop or cripple the trade between the East and the West. With England the case is entirely different. Our Government, it is true, is the largest shareholder in the Canal, and owns close upon half the whole amount of the shares. But the question as to what dividend we may receive upon our holding is utterly insignificant to us in comparison with our interest in the development of the Canal as the highway between India and Europe. In the first place, we as a nation are the carriers of the world's commerce. More than one-half the tonnage of the shipping on the face of the globe is owned by England. Our carrying trade is the very backbone of the maritime supremacy upon which we depend for our prosperity, our power, if not our existence as an independent nation. It follows, therefore, that England has a right of voice in all questions concerning the passage of the seas, such as no other nation, and not even all other nations combined, can possibly pretend to possess. In the second place, we have a special right to claim a paramount interest in the Suez Canal. More than four-fifths of the whole traffic passing through the Canal is carried under the Union Jack. But for our trade the receipts of the Canal would not suffice to pay the cost of its maintenance. During last year, 3,108 steamers passed between Suez and Port Said. Of them 2,565 were British ships. France stands next to us in the list, and the total of her contribution consisted of 165 ships. If, therefore, England were in the position of the United States, without a single colony of dependency in the world, she would have an interest in the Canal far surpassing all other powers. But, as it happens, England is the centre of a vast empire, the most important of whose possessions lie in the Eastern seas, to which the Suez Canal gives access. For England, as the master of India, as the owner of Australia and New Zealand, as the possessor of countless settlements scattered all over the Antipodes, the Canal has an importance which cannot be overrated. Other European Powers, it may be said, have possessions in the East as well as England; but these possessions put all together are so small and insignificant compared with those of England, that, according to any standard based upon the comparison of material and political interests in the East, England has, or rather ought to have, a voice in all matters affecting the Canal paramount to that of all other nations. The above assertions are statements of hard plain facts, to be verified, if need be, by a reference to maps and trade-registers; and as facts they must be taken into account in all discussions about the future of the Suez Canal. I admit most fully that our predominant and overwhelming interest in the Canal does not give us the right to ignore the claims of the shareholders or the reasonable requirements of other nations. But I do assert that the possession of such an interest gives us a right to a position in the undertaking distinct from, and superior to, that of all other nations.

As my chief object in writing this paper is to clear away, if possible, certain misconceptions which seem to me to stand in the way of a reasonable solution of the Suez Canal difficulty, I think it well to refer here to a fallacy I often see put forward in connection with this subject. We are told that England is out of court in pleading her interests as a ground for interfering in the administration of the Canal, because as a country she opposed its construction. Now, the character of Lord Palmerston's opposition is, as a rule, very much misrepresented. He held that the creation of a water-route across the Isthmus would be detrimental to British political and commercial interests, and on this ground, as a British statesman, he did his best to hinder the Canal from being made. Whether he was right or wrong in his opinion is a question the future must decide. The course of trade does not alter in a year or many years; and it is far too early yet to say whether British commerce will or will not benefit in the end by the opening of a new route between East and West which renders other ports than those of England the natural depots for the trade of India and China. If Lord Palmerston was mistaken, he was not alone in his delusion; for, in the opinion of the Continent, the opening of the Suez Canal was regarded as certain to prove a death-blow to our commercial and maritime supremacy.

That it has not so proved is due partly to the energy and enterprise of our race, still more to the lack of these qualities on the part of the nations who might otherwise have competed with us for the trade of the East. Still, the fact remains that, by the cutting of the Isthmus, the course of trade has been diverted in a manner not calculated in the long run to prove beneficial to our interests as a trading nation. But even granting that England's opposition to the construction of the Suez Canal was as short-sighted, selfish, and irrational as you please, it does not follow that England has no right to complain later because the Canal is conducted in a way to injure her interests. Some forty years ago the county of Kent exerted all its influence to hinder a railroad being made between London and Dover. Recently the Kentish towns have been agitating for a reduction of the rates charged by the South Eastern and the Chatham and Dover railways. Yet, amidst the arguments submitted to the Railway Commission on behalf of the lines in question, no plea was ever put forward that the inhabitants of Chatham, Dover, and Deal had no right to ask for a reduction of fares and rates on the railways which serve their towns, because their predecessors a generation ago had put these railways to needless and vexatious expense by opposing their construction. Such a contention would at once be laughed out of court; yet it is not a whit less tenable than the argument that England's bygone opposition to the Suez Canal bars her right to insist on increased facilities being provided for the accommodation of her trade across the Isthmus. Nor can any serious weight be attached to the sentimental plea that, because M. de Lesseps made the Canal, therefore we have no right to interfere with his undertaking. Nobody proposes to deprive the founder of the Suez Canal of the credit or the profit to which he is fairly entitled for his great achievement. But England has neither the right nor the power to subordinate the interests of her Empire and her commerce to the personal susceptibilities of any individual, even if he had a tenfold stronger claim upon her gratitude that any which M. de Lesseps can possibly establish.

It is clear, therefore, that, putting aside for the moment the question of the legal rights conferred upon the Canal Company in virtue of their concession, England has an absolute and indefeasible right to insist upon the water-route between the Mediterranean and the Red Sea being conducted in the manner most conducive to the interests of trade, which are practically identical with her own. That it is not so conducted is a matter which hardly requires proof. In the first place, the Canal is managed by French officials, is governed by

French principles of administration, and is under the exclusive jurisdiction of French law and French courts. Now, any Englishman who has ever visited a French colony, or who for his sins has ever had any business with French officials, is aware that the whole system of French administration, though it may suit the genius of the French nation, is utterly inapplicable to foreign use. The passion for logical uniformity, the want of pliability, the rigid and almost servile adherence to hard and fast regulations, the authoritative impatience of opposition, which are the characteristics of all French administration, have always rendered their administrative system a dead failure in foreign lands where French ideas and French habits do not prevail. There is probably no nation in the world less fitted than the French to administer a great enterprise such as the Suez Canal, whose chief customers are captains and shipowners of British nationality. On à priori grounds one would predict that the French administration of the Canal was certain to give general dissatisfaction, and this antecedent probability is confirmed by the test of experience. There is probably not a body of men in the world who care less about logical anomalies or abstract inequalities than the shipowners of Great Britain. When we find, therefore, that, with scarcely an exception, they complain of the vexations and annoyances to which their ships are subject in passing through the Canal, we may safely assume that they have valid causes of complaint. Nobody but the owner knows where the shoe pinches, and it is idle for the advocates of the company to assert that British shipowners have no ground of complaint, when, as a matter of fact, there is not a single British ship which passes through the Canal, whose officers have not some grievance or other to which they consider themselves to have been subjected at the hands of the company's officials.

Apart from these general complaints, about which there is and must be necessarily room for dispute, the shipping trade of England has certain grievances to complain of at the hands of the Suez Canal Company which are not open to discussion. The transit dues are so heavy as to eat up an enormous proportion of the profit on freights between India and England, and as to absolutely prohibit the carrying of goods which cannot afford to pay high rates of transport. For instance, of late years India has made great progress as a wheat-growing country. Indian grain could be sold in England cheaper than American grain to the great advantage of the Indian grower and the English consumer, if it were not for the heavy cost of freight between the two countries caused by the expense of traversing the Canal. If the Canal Company consider it pays them letter to charge ten shillings a ton on a hundred thousand tons than five shillings on two hundred thousand, they have a perfect right to do so. But, on the other hand, our shipowners have an equal right to see if, by the employment of competition, they cannot force the company to reduce its charges. It is obvious, on general grounds, that the tolls raised upon any public highway, whether by land or sea, ought, in the interest of the public at large, to be as low as is consistent with paying for the construction and maintenance of the highway. The interest of the company as a commercial speculation is to charge the maximum tolls consistent with not driving trade away from the Canal. In agitating, therefore, for a reduction of rules far beyond any point, hitherto contemplated by the company, our shipowners are acting in the interest of the public as well as in their own.

Then, again, there can be no question as to the accommodation provided by the Canal being utterly inadequate to the exigencies of the present traffic, and still more to the requirements of the future. In 1870, 486 steamers went through the Canal; in 1882 the number was 3,198. In the same period of time the tonnage increased from under half a million of tons to over seven millions. Every year the proportion of ships engaged in the traffic with the East which go by the Isthmus route increases, while the proportion of those which go round the Cape diminishes. The distance between Port Said and Suez is about eighty miles. This distance, over perfectly still water, ought to be traversed, as a rule, in eight hours. Instead of this the passage of the Canal, owing to the narrowness of the channel, the impossibility of ships passing each other in mid-stream, and the low rate of speed rendered necessary by the importance of avoiding any wash of water against the crumbling sand-banks, occupies on an average from forty to sixty hours. Blocks are of constant occurrence in the Canal, and these blocks impose long delay and heavy loss upon all vessels which happen to be traversing the Canal when the block occurs. Moreover, the liability to these unforeseen stoppages, even when they do not occur, acts as a serious impediment to the development of the trade between Europe and the East. Thus there is an urgent and imperative demand for increased accommodation; and yet this demand the Suez Canal Company has hitherto refused to comply with, except upon conditions which would involve the perpetuation of its monopoly, the maintenance of its excessive tolls, and the recognition of the exclusively French character of its administration.

Moreover, England has an interest of her own in the Canal which is quite independent of her commercial requirements, and which would continue to exist if our mercantile marine were swept off the face of the seas. So long as we hold India the command of the Suez Canal is to us a matter of paramount necessity. Upon this point, however, I feel a certain difficulty in dwelling. It is now six years since I first advocated in the pages of this Review the necessity for England to make herself master of Egypt, in order to secure her highway to India. This mastership has at length been secured, and I am conscious that I am open to the charge of inconsistency, if, after our troops are encamped in Egypt, I plead the necessity of guaranteeing our highway to India as a ground for appropriating the Canal. The inconsistency, however, is only apparent. I feel no doubt myself that the logic of facts which brought our troops to Cairo will of necessity retain them there; and I see no cause to waver in my opinion that, so long as we hold Cairo, we have, for military and Imperial purposes, the absolute and complete command of the Canal in the event of war. If once our protectorate over Egypt were clearly established, I should be the first to admit that, whatever other grounds there might be for altering the conditions under which the Canal is administered, we could not plead as a reason the danger to which our communications with India are exposed by the Canal belonging to a French company. But our protectorate, though, as I hold, it exists in fact, does not exist in theory or in name. On the contrary, the Ministers of the Crown lose no opportunity of declaring that our occupation is only temporary, and that they look forward at no distant date to the withdrawal of our troops from Egyptian rule. Personally I utterly disbelieve in the possibility of these declarations being carried out in practice, although they are made in good faith. But in the face of such utterances on the part of the Government, the British public are fairly entitled to ask that precautions should be taken to secure our right of way to India in the event of our troops being withdrawn from Egypt. The experience of last year's campaign suffices to show how dangerous the antagonism of the Canal Company might easily be, under certain very possible contingencies, to our free access to India across the Isthmus. Even last year M. de Lesseps hostility would have been formidable instead of ludicrous if the action of France had not been paralyzed by her internal dissensions and by her fear of Germany. Notwithstanding, I feel that this argument—though unanswerable on the hypothesis that we are only temporarily in possession of Cairo—does not carry conviction with those who hold with me that our protectorate of Egypt is in reality an accomplished fact; and on that account I lay more weight than I should do otherwise on the commercial considerations which necessitate our taking the Suez Canal under our own control and management.

If, therefore, I have made my meaning intelligible, it is clear that what England requires is such an increase of the transit accommodation through the Suez Canal as will meet the exigencies of her Eastern trade, and such a modification of the constitution of the company as will secure the administration of the Canal being conducted in accordance with English ideas and English interests. Supposing no prior rights, either legal or equitable, stood in the way, there is nothing unreasonable or unfair in the above requirements on the part of England. When once the possibility of effecting a junction between the Mediterranean and the Red Sea was demonstrated by experience, it became inevitable that England, as the owner of India and the virtual possessor of the transit trade between the East and the West, should desire to control, if not to own, the channel by which this trade has to pass. As soon, therefore, as it was found that the dimensions of the present Canal were utterly inadequate to the exigencies of our trade, the idea of making a second canal between the two seas found favour in England. A variety of schemes were proposed long before the despatch of our troops to Egypt was even dreamt of, the object of which was to provide a competing route to that supplied by M. de Lesseps' Canal. It would be foreign to my present purpose to discuss the respective merits of these various projects. It is enough to say that, in the opinion of the most competent authorities, the best, if not the sole, route available for the purpose is across the Isthmus of Suez. About this route there is absolutely no engineering difficulty. The desert of the Isthmus is broad enough to be traversed, not by two alone, but by half-a-dozen parallel ship-canals, all debouching, at no great distance from each other, into the Red Sea and the Mediterranean. Those canals, constructed as they would be under far more favourable conditions than the old canal, and with the benefit of experience, could be made at a comparatively small cost, and could therefore be worked at a far smaller profit. In fact, I may safely say that if the providing of transit accommodation across the Isthmus were regulated by the ordinary laws of supply and demand, a sufficient number of ship canals would have been already constructed to bring down the cost of transit to the amount required to give the ordinary rate of interest on industrial enterprises; and that most, if not all, of these competing canals would have been constructed with English capital and conducted by English management.

The sole obstacle which prevents the natural development of the trans-Isthmus traffic by the creation of new channels between sea and sea lies in the opposition of the Suez Canal Company. This company enjoys a monopoly *de facto*, and claims to enjoy one *de jure;* and in common with all monopolists its instinct is to charge the maximum of price for the minimum of service. I have not the slightest wish to accuse the company of being exceptionally greedy of gain. They only act after the nature of shareholders all over the world in seeking to get the most they can for their money. An English Board would, it is true, have done more to develop trade, and have devoted more money to the improvement of the Canal. This result, however, would be due not to any moral superiority on the part of English, as compared with French, directors, but simply to the fact that Englishmen have larger and sounder views of business, and are more impressed with the wholesome truth that no monopoly in the world can hold its own if it runs counter to the public interest. So long as the existing Canal sufficed fairly well for the accommodation of trade, the question whether it had or had not a monopoly was one which nobody had any strong interest in discussing. But now, when the creation of a new channel has become a matter of urgent necessity, the question is one which demands careful investigation.

Now, the question at issue is one to be determined not so much by the legal bearing of certain words and phrases as by the light of certain general considerations, about which the law officers of the Crown have no special means of forming an opinion. It would be absurd for me, or any other layman, to declare that my reading of a disputed clause in an English title-deed was as likely to be correct as that propounded by our highest legal authorities. But with regard to the meaning of an Egyptian concession I, or any one acquainted with Egypt, am, to say the least, as competent to form an opinion as the Attorney-General or the Lord Chancellor of England. Now, the view I hold is this. When M. de Lesseps obtained his original concession from Said Pasha, the possibility of a competing canal being made was a contingency not even contemplated. The construction of the original canal seemed so problematical, the difficulties to be overcome before the idea could be carried into execution were so grave and so numerous, that to guard against the eventuality of a competing canal must have seemed to the promoters of the project the most idle and superfluous of precautions. Moreover, the danger was one which the founders may reasonably have deemed that they had it in their own hands to avert. According to the original conception, the Canal was to have been an undertaking of Said Pasha himself, carried out by M. de Lesseps acting as the *mandataire* or agent of the Viceroy. Now, in those days, everything in Egypt was a monopoly, and the one monopolist was the Viceroy. The Canal, therefore, was to be the monopoly of Said Pasha subject to the claims of his European associates; and as he alone could grant permission for a competing canal to be made, the risk of competition must have seemed to be absolutely illusory. If Ismail Pasha had not entered on the improvident expenditure which led directly to his own deposition, and indirectly to the British occupation of Egypt, he would still be seated on the throne as the autocratic ruler of Egypt, and the holder of the shares purchased from him by the British Government. To suppose that under these circumstances the Khedive would have entertained the idea of any competing canal is manifestly absurd. The Viceroys, in short, according to M. de Lesseps' original conception, were to be the chief partners in the concern; no competition was possible without their consent; and therefore there was no object in providing against a contingency which it was thought, with good reason, could never possibly arise.

Besides this, everybody is influenced by the *milieu* in which he lives; and the idea of competition, in the European sense of the word, is foreign to the Oriental mind. I remember speaking some years ago to one of the oldest of the European residents in Egypt about a monopoly I was then anxious to obtain for an Egyptian undertaking in which we were both interested. His answer was: 'There is only one monopoly which is worth thinking about in Egypt, and that is the monopoly of priority. Once get your concern established, and you need not be afraid of anybody seeking to establish a rival enterprise.' This remark expressed the sentiment of all who, like M. de Lesseps, had been conversant with Egyptian affairs from the days of Mehemet Ali. On the other hand, though the risk of competition may have seemed imaginary, the risk of dismissal by caprice was very real and appreciable. It was quite in accordance with Egyptian traditions and usages for the execution of a work to be given to one contractor, and then to be suddenly taken from him and assigned to some rival who might chance to supplant him in the favour of the Viceroy. It was therefore of vital importance to M. de Lesseps to guard against the execution of his great enterprise being taken from him at any moment by a change of purpose on the part of his capricious patron, and this object was fully secured by the terms of the original concession, which conferred upon him personally 'an exclusive power to constitute and to *direct* a company for piercing the Isthmus of Suez, with power to undertake the works of construction.'

Thus the natural interpretation of the words 'pouvoir exclusif,' on which, and on which alone, the Suez Canal Company rely for their alleged monopoly, is that they refer to M. de Lesseps' personal position as constructor and director of the undertaking, not to the immunity of the company from any possible competition hereafter. If the object of the clause in question had been to give the company an exclusive power to construct ship-canals across the Isthmus, it is incredible that no care should have been taken to define what the Isthmus was, or what was the area over which the prohibition extended. Does the clause forbid the construction of any ship-canal across Egyptian territory joining the Mediterranean with the Red Sea? This, I understand, is not the allegation of M. de Lesseps, who admits that a ship canal might be constructed across the Delta from Suez to Alexandria without violation of his concession, though on other grounds he disputes the feasibility of the project. Yet if this is so, what are the lines within which the alleged monopoly extends? On this point the concession is absolutely and entirely silent. Yet the addition of twenty words stating that no other canal could be constructed within a certain specified distance of the projected canal would have settled the whole question in dispute. The absence of any such statement is a strong *à priori* argument in favour of the view that the concession did not contemplate any exclusive monopoly. It is urged, however, that this omission is a mere oversight; that M. de Lesseps, if he had thought of it, could have easily had his concession so worded as to secure an absolute monopoly; and that it is ungracious on our part to take advantage of an accidental error. Now, I confess that I fail to understand the plea for generosity. If I am at variance with a neighbour about matters affecting my own interests alone, I have a perfect right to give him the benefit of any presumption which tells in his favour. But if the interests in question are those of third parties, for whom I am acting as trustee, I have clearly no right to concede anything which the law does not compel me to grant; and in this matter the British Government is acting as trustee, not only for the present generation, but for unborn generations of Englishmen. Moreover, I dispute the assertion that M. de Lesseps had only to ask in order to obtain an absolute monopoly. Such a request, if clearly formulated, would have proved fatal to his enterprise. Lord Palmeston had taken his stand upon the ground that the Suez Canal, if it was to be constructed at all, must not give France any permanent footing in Egypt. Indeed, when our great Foreign Minister is held up to obloquy for his opposition to the Canal, it is well to remember that we owe it to his wisdom and his foresight that the Isthmus of Suez was not converted into a French settlement commanded by French forts. It is wellnigh certain that any proposal to give the Canal Company an exclusive right to construct canals in any part of the Isthmus would have been absolutely vetoed by the British Government of the day. It is, therefore, intelligible enough that even if M. de Lesseps contemplated at the time the possibility of rival canals being constructed hereafter, he should not have deemed it wise to guard against this remote contingency by insisting upon as privilege being accorded to him the demand for which would have intensified the immediate opposition he had to encounter at the hands of England. I may be told, however, that M. de Lesseps, who drew up the convention himself, must be credited with knowing what the concession meant. The point is a delicate one to argue without doing what I should be most reluctant to do—that is to say, without using language which might give umbrage to M. de Lesseps personally. All I need say is that no man can expect to be accepted as a conclusive witness in his own favour in a matter in which his interests are deeply concerned; that the wisest and fairest-minded of mankind are apt to have their recollections of bygone events biased by personal considerations; and that, amidst the many and signal merits of the founder of the Suez Canal, even his warmest friends would scarcely assign to him a judicial temperament or absolute impartiality of judgment. Indeed, the value of M. de Lesseps' interpretation of his own privileges under the concession is shown by the fact that only last year he seriously argued that the Canal Company had sovereign rights over its own waters which justified him in refusing access to troops acting under the authority of the Khedive for the suppression of a domestic insurrection.

I am prepared, however, to go further than this. Even admitting for the sake of argument that the words of the concession did give, and were intended to give, the Canal Company an absolute monopoly, I should still dispute the validity of the claim. The British Government was in no sense a party to the contract; and even if it had been, it had no power to bind itself irrevocably to such a compact. All treaties, concessions, and contracts in the world are made subject to the possibility of modification if circumstances should alter, or if paramount public necessity should demand their rescission. Common experience justifies this assertion. This principle cannot well be contested, at any rate by a Government which has just deprived the Irish landlords of property secured to them by law and statute, on the ground that such a sacrifice was demanded by the interests of the commonwealth. If jurists declare that M. de Lesseps' monopoly, as guaranteed by his interpretation of the concession, is good for another eighty years, common sense replies that it is absurd to suppose that the interests of England and India can be sacrificed for wellnigh a century, our trade crippled, and our communications interrupted, in virtue of an agreement between Said Pasha and M. de Lesseps. In such a case the law of contract, even supposing it to be binding, is and must be set aside in favour of the higher law of public necessity.

The conclusion that the foregoing remarks are intended to confirm is that M. de Lesseps' claim is not valid in law, and, if valid in law, is untenable in equity. If, therefore, England is so minded, she would be guilty of no violation of right, of no disregard of public morality, in ignoring the claim of the company to forbid the construction of a second canal across the Isthmus. To establish this point is important, because upon it I should base the solution I shall venture to suggest. England has a great interest in upholding the strength of international obligations, and, apart from any higher considerations, it is not our policy to set an example of cynical disregard for the right of public contracts. But, if my contention is correct, the Suez Canal Company, though it has strong moral claims to liberal and even generous compensation, has no legal or equitable right to bar the construction of a competing canal. There is, therefore, no abstract reason why England should not herself undertake, or allow others to undertake, the work of digging a new and more convenient ship-canal across the Isthmus of Suez. It is not enough, however, that we should possess an abstract right: the real question is whether we have a practical right, and, if so, whether it is wise to exercise that right.

Now, the first question must be answered in the affirmative. There is room for any amount of discussion as to what we ought or ought not to do in Egypt. But it is simple waste of breath to discuss what we can or cannot do there. We are for the time being the masters of the country, the Government is under our control, and no European nation has both the power and the will to interfere in any way with our liberty of action. If, therefore, the British Government chose to say to-morrow that, in their opinion, the construction of a second canal across the Isthmus had become desirable, the requisite authority would be at once provided by the Khedive. Personally, I consider any recognition of the shadowy suzerainty of the Porte over Egypt an anachronism and a blunder. But if the sanction of the Porte to the Khedivial concession should be deemed desirable, that sanction can be easily obtained for a consideration, or, if not, it can be still more easily dispensed with. Once the concession granted, there is no material difficulty about the execution of the project. The capital could be found at once; the work would present no serious engineering obstacles; and if the enterprise were commenced in earnest, we might reckon on possessing, within the next three or four years, a canal of our own, greatly superior to the existing canal in width, depth, and general facilities for the accommodation of ship traffic, and which would have been constructed at less than half the cost. No doubt M. de Lesseps would protect against the construction of this canal as an infraction of his rights; and it is possible, though by no means certain, that his protest might be endorsed by the French Government. But any protest of this nature, however deserving of consideration, is in itself a mere *brutum fulmen,* of the same value as the judgment of a court which has no power to enforce its decisions. It is, of course, theoretically possible that the Government of the Republic might adopt M. de Lesseps' case as their own, and might declare that any attempt to construct a competing canal would be regarded by them as a *casus belli.* But this possibility is simply an imaginary one. Even if France—which for my own part I utterly disbelieve—cared enough about the Canal to make her prepared to fight in its defence, she is not in a position—and she knows that she is not in a position—to run the risk of the foreign complications which a war with England must entail. This is the plain truth; and it is upon facts as they are, not as we might wish them to be, that our action as a nation must be based.

I shall be told, however, that though France may not be in a position to run the risk of war under present circumstances, yet that the fact of our having taken advantage of her weakness to appropriate the Suez Canal would outrage French national sentiments so profoundly as to make France our enemy at heart if not in name. Now, the assertion in question is one which it is impossible either to prove or disprove. Englishmen, as I believe, make a mistake in supposing that Frenchmen regard the Suez Canal with the same feeling as a similar work would be regarded by us if it had been constructed by this country. The self-concentration which constitutes the strength of France renders her almost incredibly indifferent to all interests which lie outside her own area. On such an issue any individual opinion derived from personal observation is of no great value. Still I may say that for some years past I have been in constant communication with Frenchmen in connection with Egyptian affairs; and the conclusion I have come to is that, as a class, they are perfectly indifferent about the political relations between France and Egypt, except in as far as these relations affect their pecuniary interests. About six years ago, when the idea of a British protectorate over Egypt began to be first talked about, M. Waddington came over to London on a sort of semi-officious mission, and had interviews with our leading statesmen both in the Ministry and in the Opposition. To one and all he held the same language. France, he urged, is not able to resist any action England may take in Egypt; but the feeling in France about Egypt is so intense that any attempt to dislodge her from the position she now occupies conjointly with England at Cairo will give rise to a bitterness of resentment against England which will render any co-operation between the two countries impossible for years to come. These utterances were, I am convinced, made with perfect good faith; and they produced, as I am aware, considerable effect upon the persons to whom they were addressed. The result proved that they were based on a complete misconception. When sentiment was brought to the test of reality, it appeared that the French were not prepared to run the slightest risk or make the least sacrifice in order to uphold their ascendency in Egypt; and though they would have been gratified, as a nation, if we had been defeated at Tel-el-Kabir, they acquiesced with singular unconcern in the establishment of our supremacy as the virtual masters of Egypt. I say this in no disparagement of France; but when I am assured, as I am now, that, though France may possibly be unable to hinder us from acting as we like with respect to the Suez Canal, yet any disregard of M. de Lesseps' claims will secure us her lifelong resentment, I am justified in remarking that before this I have been met with a similar assertion, and found it baseless.

I contend, therefore, that it lies practically in our power to construct a second canal of our own if we so think fit, and that we are not debarred from so doing by any claim the existing company can legally establish. Whether it would be wise to do so is another question. My own opinion is that we should do better to settle the matter by an amicable compromise, even at the cost of having to pay heavily. Though the Suez Canal Company has, in my judgment, no right in law or equity to complain of competition, yet the company, and still more its illustrious president, have a very strong claim to generous treatment at the hands of England. That there exists a water-highway between the Mediterranean and the Red Sea is due to the courage, energy, and perseverance of M. de Lesseps, and to the loyalty with which, through good and evil fortune, he was supported by his shareholders; and this fact England is bound to take into account. I can, however, see no possibility of any satisfactory settlement being come to upon the basis of the Suez Canal Company retaining possession of their monopoly. The insignificant concessions obtained during the recent negotiations, conducted as they were with singular ability and skill on the part of Sir Rivers Wilson, show how little M. de Lesseps is prepared to yield. Moreover, the real object that England has in view—the transfer of the management of the Canal to British hands, and the subsequent control of the undertaking with a view to promote the development of trade rather than the enrichment of the shareholders—are objects in which neither M. de Lesseps nor the company can ever be expected to cooperate. There is one way, and one way only, in which England can obtain these objects without constructing a competing canal of her own, and thereby inflicting most grievous injury on the existing company, and that is by becoming the possessor of the Canal by purchase.

Now, it would be impossible within the limits of the present paper to enter on any detailed scheme for the purchase of the Canal. It is my purpose only to indicate very briefly the general outlines on which such a scheme might be based. The Suez Canal Company possesses the power by its statutes to wind up the concern by voluntary liquidation. My proposition, therefore, would be that the existing company should be wound up, and its rights and property transferred to an English company, who would pay off the existing shareholders and bondholders upon terms whose execution would be guaranteed by the British Government. I have reason to suppose that both the direction and the proprietariate of the company would not be indisposed to entertain such a proposition if the terms of purchase were satisfactory. The difficulty would lie, not in the admission of the principle of purchase, but in the settlement of the terms. Leaving aside minor questions, the capital of the Suez Canal Company may be said in round numbers to be 14,000,000*l*., of which 6,000,000*l*. consists of bonds and debentures bearing a fixed preferential interest, while the remainder consists of shares whose interest fluctuates with the earnings of the concern. Now, of this 8,000,000*l*. of ordinary shares half are, thanks to Lord Beaconsfield, the property of the British Government. The value of the bonds and debentures is easily ascertained, and, including the 100,000 founder's shares at their present value, would be covered by 10,000,000*l*. As the British Government would be, under the arrangement

I suggest, either directly or indirectly the actual purchaser of the reversion of the Suez Canal Company, the 4,000,000*l.* of British shares may be left out of account. Indeed, the only item whose appraisement would be matter of serious difficulty is the 4,000,000*l.* of ordinary shares owned by the general public, the great majority of these shares being held, I may add, in France.

Now, if M. de Lesseps' contention is not only right in law, but, what is much more important, is not likely to be disputed in fact, it is difficult to say what figure these shares may not be calculated as capable of attaining. The 20*l.* share is now quoted at about 100*l.* No doubt this price is above the present actual value of the shares, as upon a dividend of 6 per cent, the highest which has yet been reached, a purchaser to-day would receive only a little over 4 per cent on his investment. On the other hand, the prospect of an increased dividend in years to come is more than probable. Unless anything should occur to stop the progress of the world's trade, the traffic between East and West must grow with giant strides, and a larger and larger proportion of the shipping engaged in this traffic must every year pass through the Canal and pay toll to its owners. In consequence, the Suez Canal shares command a price calculated upon that prospective, not upon their actual, earnings. The holders, as a body, are not anxious to sell, and if the British Government went into the market to buy up the shares, they would be forthwith run up to an exorbitant and impossible price. It is this consideration which seems to me in itself a fatal objection to the idea that England might obtain what she desires by buying up any Suez Canal shares which come into the market, and thus gradually making herself mistress of the enterprise. This process, even if it could be carried out without extravagant cost, would be slow and unsatisfactory. By the charter no one shareholder can command more than fifteen votes, however large his holding may be; and though the Government might, in theory, delegate its votes to a number of nominees, such a process would be impossible in practice. Moreover, even if our Government had got a large workable majority of the votes, it could not carry out the object of its purchase—that is, insist upon the shareholders adopting a policy beneficial to England, but, *ex hypothesi*, injurious to the company—without placing itself in an untenable and invidious position. If England is to buy up the Suez Canal at all, the purchase of the shares must be effected *en bloc*, and without any attempt at concealment. Is it possible to effect this end? It can, I think, be effected in one way, and one way only.

The whole prospective value of the Suez Canal shares depends upon the maintenance of the monopoly claimed by the company. Now, according to the view I have endeavoured to put forward, the following conclusions may fairly be sustained as matters of argument. First, that the alleged monopoly has no existence in fact, was never contemplated at the foundation of the company, and only exists, if it exist at all, in virtue of a forced interpretation placed upon an obscure phrase in an obsolete concession; secondly, that the rescission of the monopoly, even admitting its existence, is demanded on grounds of general utility in the interest of the world's trade, of which England is the chief representative; and, thirdly, that the position of England as master of India and occupier of Egypt makes the possession of the Canal a matter of such importance to her as to justify her in insisting upon the water-highway to the East being placed under her control. Now, upon the assumption that the monopoly is, to say the least, open to grave question, the price of 100*l.* per share is far above the value the shareholders could ever hope to get in the open market. If, therefore, the British Government were to propose to pay the ordinary shareholders, on the liquidation of the company, 20,000*l.* for their 4,000,000*l.* of shares—that is, at the rate of 500 per cent profit on the original price—the bargain would, from a business point of view, be one to which no exception could be taken on the score of liberality. Thus, allowing 10,000,000*l.* for the repayment of the bonds, debentures, founder's shares, and other liabilities, the British Government would become possessed of the Canal for about 30,000,000*l.*, exclusive of the amount paid for the Khedive's shares in 1875. As a mere speculation, the bargain would be a losing one for England. Our object in getting the Canal into our own hands would be to increase the accommodation and reduce the tolls; and therefore the utmost we could reasonably hope, with a largely increased capital and with greatly diminished tolls, would be to make a sufficient profit to pay the interest on the money the country would have to borrow for the purchase of the Canal. But even if we lost by the transaction in itself, our direct loss would be more than compensated by the indirect commercial and political advantages we should acquire by the possession of the Canal.

At the same time, however reasonable and liberal such an offer might be if judged upon its own merits, the Suez Canal Company would not accept it if it were not for the fear of competition. If, therefore, the proposal is made, it must be made in the form of an alternative. What I would propose is that the British Government should say to the Suez Canal Company: 'The time has come when transit accommodation, such as you are not in a position to supply, must be provided across the Isthmus of Suez. If you are disposed to sell, we are willing to buy up your concern on reasonable terms; if you are not willing, we have no option except to allow the construction of a competing canal or canals constructed and managed by independent companies.'

If this alternative were presented in such a manner as to leave no doubt in the public mind that England was in earnest, I have very little doubt myself the company would prefer to sell, sooner than run the risk of a competition which, whatever its other results, must prove fatal to the prospect of increased profits in the future. If the company did not accept, then England, with a clear conscience and with the sense of having acted liberally, might provide means to facilitate the construction of a second canal. The figures I have given above are, of course, mere rough estimates. The actual price must be matter for careful investigation. All I need say in conclusion is that, in as far as I can judge, there is no reasonable price Englishmen would not gladly pay in order at once to get possession of the Canal and to avoid the appearance even of not dealing liberally with the Canal Company. But in one way or the other we are bound to get the Canal into our own hands. This, to use an Americanism, is the bottom-fact on which all negotiations in future must be based. It is England's manifest destiny to become mistress of the Canal as she has already become mistress of Egypt; and against manifest destiny gods and men fight in vain, whether in Suez or in Panama.

Edward Dicey.

SOURCE: In *Nineteenth Century* 14, no. 78 (August 1883): 189–205.

De Lesseps and the Canal
CHARLES ROYLE

The history having now been brought to the period when the Suez Canal was occupied by the British forces, it may be interesting to refer to the attitude assumed by M. Ferdinand de Lesseps, the President of the Canal Company, and to show how his communications with the rebel leaders led the latter to postpone until too late the steps resolved on for the destruction of the Canal.

De Lesseps from the first opposed any interference with the Canal by the British forces. The earliest indication of his views was afforded immediately before the Alexandria bombardment. When that operation was impending, Admiral Seymour warned British ships not to enter the Canal in case of hostilities. In consequence of this warning eleven ships were stopped at Port Saïd and Suez on the 10th July. M. Victor de Lesseps, the Company's agent at Ismailia, thereupon protested against what he termed "this violation of the neutrality of the Canal."

On the same day, M. de Lesseps, then in Paris, communicated to the British Ambassador there and to all the other representatives of the Powers, a copy of the telegraphic instructions which had on the 8th July been sent to the agent of the Company at Ismailia. Their effect was that any action or warlike demonstration, in the Canal was forbidden, and that "its neutrality had been proclaimed by the Firman of Concession, and had been recognized and acted upon during the two last wars between France and Germany and Russia and Turkey."

A very slight examination of the question will suffice to show that the Canal had absolutely nothing of the neutral character so persistently claimed for it by M. de Lesseps at this time and during the subsequent operations.

Its claim to neutrality was based solely on a clause in the Concession, in which the Canal was declared by the Sultan to be "a neutral highway for the ships of all nations." This clause, inserted apparently to indicate the peaceful and industrial character of the enterprise, was an expression of intention no doubt binding upon the parties to the Concession, but upon no one else. This, it is obvious, was a totally different matter from construing it, as De Lesseps sought to do, as laying down for the rest of the world a law under which, for all time and all circumstances, the Canal should be considered as outside the range of belligerent operations. No one can contend that the ruler of a country, by a mere *à priori* declaration of his own, can confer the quality of neutrality upon any particular part of his territory irrespective of future eventualities. This is a matter where the rights of other States come in. Whether a country is or is not neutral is a matter which, on war breaking out, has to be determined by the application of certain well-known principles of International Law, and does not depend upon the mere declaration of the ruler, unless followed by a strict observance of neutrality.

Assuming that, as was practically the case, England was at war with the *de facto* ruler of Egypt, which was Arabi, any declaration that the Sultan might choose to make that this or that portion of Egyptian territory should be considered as neutral, and therefore exempt from warlike operations, would clearly be illusory.

The most that could be done towards the so-called neutralization of the Canal was subsequently effected in December, 1888, when, by an agreement between Egypt and the principal Powers, it was arranged that (subject to certain reservations made by Great Britain) no hostilities on the part of any of the contracting Powers should take place in the Canal, nor, in the event of the territorial Power being itself a belligerent, should the ships of that Power attack, or be attacked, in the Canal, nor were the entrances to the Canal to be blockaded. This, it will be seen, is "neutralization" only in a limited and vague sense of the term, the employment of which was carefully avoided in the agreement.

The precedents invoked by M. de Lesseps from the Franco-German and the Russo-Turkish wars, in reality, were worth nothing. When France and Germany were at war, Egypt was at peace, and her neutrality had to be respected, neither Turkey nor Egypt being in any way mixed up with the dispute. As regards the Russo-Turkish war, it is incontestable that if Russia, in the exercise of her undoubted rights as a belligerent, had seized on the Canal as a piece of Ottoman territory, no other Power would have had reason to complain. Whether by doing so Russia would have made an enemy of England, and so have caused her to take part against her, was another matter; and, influenced probably by considerations of this kind, Russia was induced to abstain. This, however, in no way affects the principle involved.

But, apart from the general reasoning above mentioned, there were certain special circumstances affecting the matter which made the case of De Lesseps still weaker, and rendered the ordinary rules regarding neutrality inapplicable. By the terms of the Concession, although the Canal itself was to be the property of the Company for a term of years, the land through which it ran remained none the less Egyptian territory, and by Article 9 it was expressly declared that the Government should have the same right of acting for the maintenance of public security and the enforcement of the law within the limits of the Company's property as might be exercised at any other point of the Khedive's dominions. Arabi at this time was a rebel, and his forces were occupying positions in the immediate neighbourhood of the Canal. This gave the Khedive an undoubted right to act against him, whether on the Canal or elsewhere. To assert that the ruler of Egypt was not at liberty to suppress a revolt in his own dominions would be too startling a proposition for even M. de Lesseps to bring forward. Whether the Khedive interfered by himself or by his agent, who in this case was Sir Garnet Wolseley, comes to exactly the same thing. What took place was a simple matter of police, and if, in the course of suppressing Arabi, certain points on the Canal had to be occupied, the case came expressly within the terms of Article 9. This being so, of what had De Lesseps to complain, and where does the question of neutrality arise?

Regarded, then, from any point of view, the fallacy of the claim to neutrality advanced on behalf of the Canal is so clear that it is difficult to imagine how it could ever have been seriously put forward.

Here, too, it may be remarked that not only was the Canal not a "neutral" concern, but it never possessed any of the "international" or "universal" character claimed for it. It was, in fact, no more "international" or "universal" than a tramway or a dry goods store, to which the citizens of all nations could have access on payment for the accommodation or goods supplied. Viewed in this light, the pretensions of the President of the Company appear simply ridiculous, and in any less distinguished individual would only have excited ridicule.

The question of neutrality having now been dealt with, it only remains to relate the steps taken by the President of the Canal Company.

According to his published memoirs:—

"On his arrival in Egyt with his son Victor, on the 19th July, he found that everything had been prepared by the French and English Commanders for the joint occupation of Port Saïd, with a view to protect the population. De Lesseps hastened to the French Admiral's flagship, and was informed by that officer that he had been asked by two of the French residents to land troops for their protection. After some difficulty De Lesseps prevailed on the French Commander to confide to him the petition, which was signed by two names he knew very well. As the document was legalized by the French Consul, he went straight to his house and got that official to summon the two petitioners. They were soon found, and De Lesseps rated them soundly for what he called their stupidity. He told them that now he was at Port Saïd they might sleep without fear; that he would be responsible for the safety of every one; and then, taking the petition, he tore it up in their faces, threw the pieces on the floor, and told the men who had signed it that as it was withdrawn they might go home. They did so, and De Lesseps, returning to the French Admiral, informed him that the petition no longer existed, and that, therefore, he had no reason for landing. The French Admiral not having yet been informed by his Government of their determination not to co-operate with the English, De Lesseps found it no easy matter to persuade him to alter his decision with regard to the projected landing. The fact that the French fleet had withdrawn from Alexandria when it was bombarded by the English aided De Lesseps in prevailing on the French Commander to abstain. When at last he had attained that object, it was De Lesseps himself who informed the English Commander of the fact."

According to the official journal of the Canal Company ("Le Canal de Suez"), which, however, must not always be regarded as an accurate record of events, De Lesseps found both the native and European population of Port Saïd much disturbed at the idea of the projected landing, and he called a meeting of the native Notables and Sheikhs to reassure them.

After these incidents he received from Arabi a telegram, of which the following is a translation:—

"Thank you for what you have done to prevent the landing of foreign troops at Port Saïd, and for your efforts to restore tranquillity of mind to the natives and the Europeans."

De Lesseps then went through the Canal to Suez, returning again as far as Ismailia, from which place, on the 26th, he sent a telegram to M. Charles de Lesseps, the Company's agent in Paris, to the effect following:—

"The English Admiral having declared to me that he would not disembark without being preceded by the French Navy, and a disembarkation being possibly ruin to Port Saïd, I have had to reassure the numerous Arab population, without whom we should be forced to suspend our works. In the presence of the Ulemas and Notables, I have sworn that not a Frenchman shall disembark whilst I am here, and that I will guarantee public tranquillity and the neutrality of our Universal Canal. The Government of my country will not disavow me."

This was followed by another telegram, of which the following is a translation, to the same person:—

"*Ismailia, 29th July,* 1882.
"To disembark at Ismailia, where there is not a solitary Egyptian soldier, is to determine to take possession of our Canal. The only persons here are a chief of native police and some agents. The inhabitants are our employés, their families, and some refugees. The invaders will find us unarmed at the head of our *personnel* to bar their passage with 'protests.'"

And by yet another, on the 4th August:—

"The English Admiral at Port Saïd writes me that he has decided to take, in spite of my protests, such measures as he judges necessary to occupy the Canal. I have decided to oppose any warlike operation on the Canal."

On the same day, M. de Lesseps went on board H.M.S. *Orion* at Ismailia. He was in evening dress, and wore his Order of the Star of India, and was attended by his son Victor and M. de Rouville, the Canal Company's agent. He demanded the intentions of the English towards the Canal, and protested energetically and with much excitement against any landing as "a violation of international rights."

On the day following, M. de Lesseps telegraphed to Paris as follows:—

"The English Admiral having announced the occupation of Ismailia, I went yesterday on board the *Orion* with Victor. We have signified verbally our resolution to resist to prevent serious disorder and interruption in navigation of the Canal. We have obtained a declaration that a landing should only take place on our demand."

In consequence of this last telegram, Admiral Hoskins was desired to report on the statement that he had promised only to land a force on the Canal upon being asked by De Lesseps. The Admiral replied that the statement was "quite unwarranted."

The Council of the Canal Company assembled on the 5th August, and passed resolutions supporting their President, and declaring that "the Company could not lend itself to the violation of a neutrality which was the guarantee of the commerce of all nations."

On the 15th the Khedive issued a Proclamation declaring that the Commander-in-Chief of the British forces was authorized to occupy all points on the Isthmus necessary for the operations against the rebels.

On the 19th Admiral Hoskins gave orders that no ship or boat was to enter the Canal, and announced that he was prepared to resort to force to prevent any attempt to contravene these orders. M. de Lesseps replied that he protested against "this act of violence and spoliation."

On the 20th August Lord Lyons telegraphed Lord Granville as follows, omitting irrelevant passages:—

"We communicated to M. Charles de Lesseps last night a memorandum in the terms of your Lordship's despatch to us of the 14th instant; and we requested, at the same time, that the transports should pay dues at Ismailia, and that the regular traffic through the Suez Canal should be suspended during the short period necessary for the passage of these vessels. M. Charles de Lesseps declined to express any opinion of his own, but it was plain to us that he did not expect that the wishes of Her Majesty's Government would be acceded to by his father."

As the sequel showed, M. de Lesseps' acquiescence was not deemed by the English Government essential to the carrying out of the operations decided on.

M. de Lesseps, ever since his arrival in Egypt, had continued to assure Arabi that if he let the Canal alone the English would also respect it. His theory was, "Le Canal est la grande route ouverte à tous les pavillons. Y toucher amenerait contre nous l'Europe, le monde entier." Towards the end of July, M. de Lesseps, having learned that the blocking of the Canal had been decided at the Egyptian camp, telegraphed to Arabi to do nothing to it, adding the words, *"Jamais les Anglais n'y pénétreraient, jamais, jamais."* Nevertheless, secret orders were given to Mahmoud Pasha Fehmi to prepare everything for the military occupation of the Canal jointly with Mahmoud Choukri Bey, another engineer of the National Party. This was on the evening of the 17th August.

On the 20th, after a simulated attack by the British on the lines of Kafr Dowar, intended to cover the expedition to Port Saïd, Arabi's look-outs signalled the movement of the English fleet in the direction of the Canal.

The day following, M. de Lesseps having been informed of the presence of thirty-two English ships of war and transports in the waters of Port Saïd, sent to Arabi a telegram, the substance of which was as follows:—

"Make no attempt to intercept *my* Canal. I am there. Not a single English soldier shall disembark without being accompanied by a French soldier. I answer for everything." On receipt of this message, a Council of War was held, which, with the exception of Arabi, who still hesitated, unanimously decided to act. The answer to M. de Lesseps was as follows:—"Sincere thanks, assurances consolatory, but not sufficient under existing circumstances. The defence of Egypt requires the temporary destruction of the Canal." Fortunately the despatch ordering the destruction of the Canal was sent by a roundabout route by way of Cairo, and when men and material were ready to carry out the work, the English were already in occupation, in spite of M. de Lesseps' positive declarations. The fifteen hours' delay caused by M. de Lesseps' communication prevented the execution of the orders of the Council.

SOURCE: Chapter 18 in *The Egyptian Campaigns, 1881–1885* (London: Hurst and Blackett, 1900).

The Suez Canal
D. A. CAMERON

The story of the Suez Canal may be briefly told. In 1841 Lord Palmerston was blamed by some for having curtailed the independence of Egypt, yet his policy was justified by the inheritance of Mehemet Ali falling into the weaker hands of Abbas, Said, and Ismail. He continued loyal to that settlement till his death, in 1865. He was anxious for peace with the French empire, and, seeing that he could not effectually counteract the influence of M. de Lesseps without destroying the semi-independence guaranteed to the pashalik after

Acre, he was obliged to let matters slowly take their course. He did not want a Suez Canal because he did not want an Egyptian Question, but he could not prevent it because the French were our allies in the Crimea, and because De Lesseps enjoyed high favour at the Imperial Court. All he could do was to delay the issue as long as possible, and he warned the French that a state of affairs might arise which would lead to complications. The French persisted in making the canal route to India, and thereby forced an English occupation only thirteen years after its completion. Indeed, as M. Renan said in his answer to the Academy speech of De Lesseps—

> "The isthmus cut becomes a strait, a battle-field. A single Bosphorus has hitherto sufficed for the troubles of the world; you have created a second much more important one. In case of naval war it would be of supreme interest, the point for the occupation of which the whole world would struggle to be first. You have marked the field of the great battles of the future."

As early as 1796 Napoleon entertained the idea of a maritime canal from Suez, but his chief engineer, Lepère, stated that the Red Sea level was thirty feet above the Mediterranean. This error was rectified by another Frenchman, M. Linant de Bellefonds, who submitted his plans to De Lesseps, at that time French consul-general, in 1833.

> "In 1840," M. Linant writes, "England and the East India Company wished for a canal. In 1841 I signed a contract to that effect with the Peninsular and Oriental Company, and in 1842 the Indian Government accepted my project with enthusiasm."

In 1847 a mixed commission, of which Robert Stephenson was a member, surveyed the isthmus with Linant, and agreed that there was no difference of level between the two seas. Mehemet Ali doubted whether the scheme would succeed, but (to his glory be it recorded) one of his last acts was to render the commissioners every official assistance. Nothing further was done till the accession of Said Pasha, and in November, 1854, M. de Lesseps obtained that viceroy's formal consent. This promise was ratified in January, 1856, by a second Act of Concession. A lease was granted for ninety-nine years, to count from the opening of the canal. De Lesseps was to make also a freshwater canal from Cairo to Ismailia, with branches north and south to Port Said and Suez. For this purpose he was given the lands necessary for buildings and works gratis and free from taxation; the lands, not private property, brought under cultivation gratis and free from taxation for ten years; the right to charge landowners for fresh-water which he was bound to supply; all mines found on the company's lands, and the right to work State mines and quarries free of cost or tax; exemption from customs duties on imports for the service of the company; the whole enterprise to be completed, save for unavoidable delays, within six years. Native labour was to be employed to the extent of four-fifths, a special convention settling the terms on which the pasha was to supply relays of thousands of fellaheen diggers every three months. The tolls were fixed at ten francs per passenger and ten francs per ton of "capacity"—an ambiguous word, which led to trouble later on. The company was to be Egyptian, and subject to local jurisdiction. The profits were to be thus divided, after payment of five per cent interest to shareholders and five to reserve fund; namely, fiften per cent to the Egyptian Government, ten per cent to founders, and seventy-five per cent to shareholders, directors, and staff. At the end of the lease the canal and its appurtenances were to revert to the Egyptian Government, the company retaining its material and stores.

Such was the princely gift of Said to De Lesseps when the enterprise began in 1858. The capital was fixed at 200 million francs (eight millions sterling) in twenty-pound shares, interest at five per cent. Owing, however, to sundry loans, the capital had risen to 458 million francs in 1887.

In 1855, while the concession was still doubtful, De Lesseps posed as the friend of England, of English free-trade and honesty. British honour, he said, forbad that we should oppose the canal on the selfish grounds that we should lose our monopoly round the Cape, and have to share the profits of transit through the Mediterranean. But on April 7th, 1856, after obtaining the concession, he wrote—

> "I found Lord Palmerston just as he was in 1840, defiant and prejudiced against France and Egypt. He believed France had for a long time been carrying on a Machiavellian policy against England in Egypt, and he saw the result of this in the canal scheme. Then he persisted that it was impossible to make the canal, and that he knew better about it than all the engineers of Europe, and their opinions would not shake his. Then he delivered a long tirade about the inconveniences which would result for Turkey and Egypt if the viceroy's demands were conceded by the sultan, and the enterprise carried out. He told me frankly that he opposed me. I listened, asking myself whether he was a maniac or a statesman. Not one of his arguments was worth a minute's serious consideration. I answered all his objections as he brought them forward; but, as I was arguing with one whose mind was already made up, I found it only waste of time to prolong the interview."

Again on April 21st he wrote—

"We now know the real motive of Lord Palmerston's opposition. He is afraid of assisting the development of Egypt's prosperity and power. I have suspected this a long time, and mentioned it to Said Pasha last year with reference to a despatch from a late governor-general of India, in which he stated that if England one day came into possession of Egypt, as she had done of India, she would be the mistress of the world.

"The viceroy will see by my advice and conduct how desirous I am not to compromise him. *If I thought more of the canal than I do of him*, nothing would be easier than to give up the scheme into the hands of great capitalists who would quickly carry it out by absorbing him. *But I want him to remain master of the situation,* and *for the canal to be a means of consolidating and strengthening his political position.*"

How did M. de Lesseps act up to this moral engagement? After Said, Ismail Pasha was in favour of the scheme, and paid up some two millions sterling due for 177,642 founder's shares subscribed for by his predecessor. In 1863 he referred an important question to the arbitration of Napoleon the Third, with the result that in July, 1864, the latter delivered an award for an indemnity of £3,360,000 to be paid by Ismail to the company, namely, £1,520,000 for the withdrawal of native forced labour, £1,200,000 for the resumption by the Egyptian Government of land bordering on the canal, except two hundred mètres on either bank, and £640,000 for the fresh-water canal from Ismailia to Suez. This was paid off by 1869. Again, in 1866, the company obtained a further payment of over £300,000 for the cession of Wadi Tumilat (land of Goshen), which it had bought in 1861 for some £74,000. Altogether, Said Pasha's gift cost Egypt an ultimate total of more than sixteen millions sterling paid to the company before the canal was opened in 1869.

Meanwhile, how had the enterprise been prospering since 1858? Lord Palmerston was fully justified in predicting that, if made, the canal would be only a stagnant ditch. The Suez Canal, it must be remembered, was intended for sailing vessels. M. de Lesseps, when trying to raise money in England, said: "It is not your steamers that I am wooing, but your fleet of sailing ships now going round the Cape." He asserted that ordinary steamers, not men-of-war or mail-packets, could not afford to go to India under steam because of the great quantity of coal required. Palmerston had before his eyes the expedition of 1801, when Baird's ships were three months sailing from Bombay to Kosseir. Even at the present time it would take a fast clipper ship the better part of a month to beat up from Perim to Suez, because of the narrowness of the Red Sea. This difficulty was overcome by the invention of the compound engine for steamers, which saved nearly half the fuel, and enabled them to utilize the canal. In the opinion of Sir John Stokes, had the canal been opened in 1862 it would have been a financial failure, because the ships of that day could not have used it. Only the invention of the compound engine gave it a chance of success. Yet another factor must be mentioned—the extraordinary growth of our mercantile steam marine, owing to this invention before the canal was opened. Nevertheless, the enterprise was bankrupt. In 1871–72 its twenty-pound shares had fallen to seven, and no dividends could be paid. Then it was that England came to the rescue by persuading the Powers at the Constantinople Conference to allow the company a surtax of 40 per cent on the tolls. Combine these separate strokes of good luck derived from England, add the sixteen millions received from Ismail, and we see why the Suez Canal became a success.

Another point merits attention. Speaking in 1887, Sir John Stokes said—

"I have found on the part of the *Egyptian Government* a very deep-rooted opinion that the canal has injured Egypt from a national point of view. No doubt their large indemnities might lead to this impression, but the real injury arose from improvident sacrifice of the royalties, which amounted to 15 per cent of the net receipts. These profits were abandoned in 1880 to a French syndicate to cover a debt of £700,000. During the last seven years the syndicate has encashed £1,212,000, and, supposing the receipts did not increase, the company would pay to the syndicate 14 millions sterling up to 1968 for that trifling debt of £700,000. Probably the payment will be three times that amount. I think the Egyptian Government has no right to complain, for at the time of doing it they had already received £83,000 in five bad years, so that they must have known they had got a valuable property."

In this unanswerable and business-like statement Sir John Stokes lays bare the weak point of the case when he speaks of an "Egyptian Government." The only Government was the will of Said Pasha, or of Ismail, who pledged the future of Egypt; and it was this which Lord Palmerston feared when he predicted to De Lesseps the "inconveniences" which might arise later on. But what becomes of M. de Lesseps' promises made in April, 1856? *He* has neither made the khedive master of the situation, nor has he consolidated the power of the dynasty. On the contrary, he established for a time an autocracy of his own, aspiring to the rights and privileges of an independent maritime Power unknown to international law. When British shipowners protested against his high tariff for "capacité" of tonnage, he so prevaricated that on July 7th, 1874, Lord Derby wrote: "This is a specimen of M. de Lesseps' mode of representing facts." A display of force was threatened by Ismail, and the company accepted the inevitable, agreeing to charge on the net, and not on the gross tonnage of vessels.

But the climax was reached during the British expedition of 1882. By charter the company was Egyptian, and not French or "universal;" it could not be neutral so long as Turkey was neutral, it could not be "neutral" when the khedive was in danger from internal rebellion. For the first time, in repayment for the concession and sixteen millions sterling, there was an opportunity for the khedive to derive some personal benefit by turning Aràbi's position at Kafr Dowàr, to become master of the situation, and consolidate his power, as De Lesseps promised in 1856. When, however, the British appeared at Port Said, in order to restore the dynasty, M. de Lesseps and his son Victor protested against their entering the canal. According to father and son, it was no longer an Egyptian, but a De Lesseps canal. Nevertheless, Admiral Hoskins smiled at these protests, and passed on to Ismailia, while M. Charles de Lesseps, at Paris, assuming the status of a maritime power, addressed a circular letter to the ambassadors, inveighing against the violation of his family canal. The French Government did not support him, and begged us to deal gently with a man who enjoyed so high a reputation as "le grand Français," and we were magnanimous. But though he failed to thwart us, M. de Lesseps made himself ridiculous. He telegraphed to Aràbi to leave his canal alone, adding, "Jamais les Anglais n'y pénétreront, jamais, jamais."

Again he insisted—

"Make no attempt to intercept *my* canal. *I* am there. Not a single English soldier shall disembark without being accompanied by a French soldier. *I* answer for everything."

Aràbi replied—

"Sincere thanks. Assurances consolatory, but not sufficient under the existing circumstances. The defence of Egypt requires the temporary destruction of the canal."

From an English point of view we cannot blame him. He was really a great Frenchman, a redoubtable foe, who believed in Egypt as a French appanage, and had worked for his country's interests there during fifty years. Then came the British occupation, and his life's work was undone in a moment. At the fatal crisis France abandoned him, as she had abandoned Dupleix, Labourdonnais, Montcalm, and other great Frenchmen, who fought us in the last century. "His" canal will remain as his monument, and the painful incidents of the enterprise will be forgotten by the admirers of his work.

His sin was against Egypt, the khedivial dynasty, the fellaheen. He turned the document of concession into a bond, and exacted the last drop of blood with his pound of flesh. However much, therefore, we may criticize the profuse expenditure of Said and of Ismail as against the fellaheen, we are bound to give them credit for their generosity toward Europe, especially when it is remembered that the canal ruined the railway transit for troops, mails, and passengers, a traffic which brought a large revenue into their treasury. If our commerce has benefited, our thanks are due to Said and Ismail, our pity for the fellaheen, whose taxes paid more than half the cost of the enterprise. If we apply the one weight and the one measure between Egypt and Europe, the glory of the Suez Canal belongs to the two viceroys, because they made a free gift to their own disadvantage, because they were ever the munificent patrons of De Lesseps, as Mehemet Ali was of the English Waghorn.

And now, having briefly sketched its past history, we may fairly ask what is likely to be the future of the canal? It may safely be answered that it is an instrument on behalf of peace. There is no historic precedent of such another artificial passage at so important a point on the earth's surface. It may be difficult to keep it open during the next naval war between great powers, and it may be very easy to close it by accident or design; the discussion of these alternatives can at present, therefore, be purely academical. On the other hand, as the value of the canal is yearly increasing for all the nations of Europe, anxiety for their commerce must assuredly act as a deterrent from war. This is more particularly the case as between England and France. The French people and the British Government are the chief shareholders, and two-thirds of the tonnage in transit is British. The two chief sufferers in revenue and commerce from the closing of the canal would be ourselves and the French. Thus it is to our mutual interests to make the canal a bond of alliance, the strength of which shall increase with the steady prosperity of De Lesseps' work. We cannot, however, become real allies if we remain ignorant of the past or shirk the problems of the future. What is most needed by Englishmen as a first step towards the peaceful solution of the "Egyptian Question" is an accurate study of the history of Egypt during the nineteenth century, our victories and defeats and drawn battles, whether in war or diplomacy. Then alone will they acknowledge the force of "accomplished facts," both in favour of England and against her, and fully realize that there is no more powerful argument working for peace in Europe than the commercial safety of the Suez Canal.

Waghorn's Overland Route, De Lesseps' Canal, the revolt of Aràbi, and Lord Wolseley's triumph at Tell-el-Kebir. These, again, would cluster into one fact, the long struggle between England and France for the control of the

Egyptian route to India. Mehemet Ali, though a great man, was a "hero" but in a limited sphere, because the work of his life will not bear rigid and impartial criticism. England and her commercial policy in the East is the real plot of this Egyptian drama during the nineteenth century, and the Great Pasha has to be fitted into it as one of the leading characters, not English policy into the life of Mehemet Ali. For two generations, and more, Canning, Peel, Palmerston, and Gladstone determined that there should not be an Egyptian Question. As Waghorn asserts, Canning discouraged Englishmen from settling at Alexandria; Palmerston promptly stifled the trouble by bombarding Acre and bringing the pasha to his knees; Beaconsfield, alive to the growing danger of the canal, bought up the shares offered for sale, and Gladstone was forced to intervene. Such is the British occupation—a logical sequence of Napoleon's expedition, dreaded by Mehemet Ali as early as 1814, prophesied by Kinglake in "Eôthen" in 1835, and forced upon us by Waghorn and De Lesseps.

What the future has in store for England in Egypt?

If, now, we could regard this period of 1798–1882 from a distance—as it were a mediæval century of the Byzantine empire—the minor incidents fully described in the preceding chapters would be lost to view, and we should see merely the chief episodes and actors—Nelson and Napoleon, Mehemet's Ali's massacre of the Mamelukes, Ibrahim's victory at Konia, Napier at Acre, no man can tell, for it depends on the power of France, of Russia, and the fate of Constantinople. It is, above all, a naval question; and though at present we possess a certain supremacy in the Mediterranean, that would be modified by the establishment of a new Byzantine empire on the Bosphorus, with hostile arsenals at the Dardanelles, Smyrna, and Alexandretta. On the other hand, it must not be forgotten that the Red Sea is a continuation of the Canal, and that not Suez, but Perim and Aden, form the true strategic entrance from the south under British control. In 1827, at Navarino, England, France, and Russia defeated Turkey and Egypt. In 1833 Egypt invaded Turkey, the czar aided the sultan, while France and England effected a compromise. In 1840 England and Russia supported the sultan against France and Egypt. In 1882 France and Russia held aloof, and England began her military occupation. As early as Navarino Palmerston was on his guard against an alliance between Russia and France. Seventy years have passed, and such an alliance is now become a notorious fact.

In 1807 England was defeated by Mehemet Ali at El-Hamàd. In 1840 Palmerston assured Egypt to the pasha as an hereditary principality. In 1882 we restored the dynasty at Tell-el-Kebir. That our generosity has not been wasted is shown in the acts of the lamented Tewfik Pasha until his death, in

1892. A great burden had been thrown on that prince—a mad revolt of ignorant Arabs who had some just grievances that cried for reform, and a gigantic debt of nearly a hundred millions sterling due to foreign bondholders, who, as honest buyers in the open market, demanded the payment of their interest. Only England could restore the situation, because she alone possessed the two necessary qualities, supremacy at sea and supremacy in financial credit. No one knew better than Tewfik Pasha the vices of Ismail's Government which had led to the revolt of Aràbi. That *régime,* of course, could never return; but he also bore other facts in mind: he was the descendant of Mehemet Ali, and he owed his dynasty to the British. Loyalty to his ancestor prompted him to save the family name; loyalty to the British, to whom he owed his restoration, led him to cordially support the work of reform. He was like a man succeeding to a mortgaged estate in the hands of administrators; the military force and the financial credit needed for its rehabilitation belonged to England, and not to himself; he was paying the penalty for Ismail and Said, and he did so with a patient equanimity and self-denial deserving of the highest praise. Of Tewfik Pasha it may be said that he was a beloved and popular khedive, who, choosing the path of safety, succeeded in handing on the heritage to his eldest son.

India has been spoken of as the land of regrets. Egypt, on the other hand, is a land of promise, a country with a great future in the twentieth century. The Nile will have been opened up from Nyanza to the sea. We shall have railroads and steamers through the heart of the Soudan, the canal will revert to the State at the end of the concession in 1969, the public debt will have been reduced to moderate dimensions, and, for its size, the province of Egypt will have become the most valuable domain on the face of the globe. At present we are but on the threshold of this new era, and it behoves us as Englishmen, and the heirs of Nelson, to study its possibilities and to prepare for its development.

SOURCE: Chapter 22 in *Egypt in the Nineteenth Century: Or, Mehemet Ali and His Successors Until the British Occupation in 1882* (London: Smith, Elder, 1898).

"Mosé in Egitto!!!" In *Punch* 69 (11 December 1875): 245.

A Day on the Suez Canal (1905)
LORD HERBERT EDWARD CECIL

[At the time these notes were written, Lord Edward Cecil was in the Egyptian Army.]

According to my promise, I write again to tell you the result of the explosion expedition. Unluckily, it was decided to postpone the event until after the British mail had passed through the Canal. In the interval the Suez Canal authorities, who are exclusively foreign, consulted each other and let their minds dwell on the more sombre side of the question. A darker tinge was given to their thoughts by the daily Press, which apparently employed the lineal descendants of Ananias to write up the question; and finally the Suez Canal Board in Paris sent urgent instructions to them to save as many lives as possible, but to die like men and Frenchmen.

During this time they communicated frequently with the Native Governor of Port Said, who at first treated the matter in a most philosophical spirit, until they explained to him that probably his town would be wrecked, but in any case it was his duty to be present on the scene of action, as it was in his province. He then not only took a deep interest in the whole question, but firmly announced his intention of remaining in Port Said to calm the terror-stricken populace.

As we all know, prolonged discussion of a subject from a pessimistic point of view only increases depression; and when your humble servant came on the scene, "Melancholy had marked them for her own."

I was first brought into the matter by being informed by the Prime Minister that the Canal authorities wanted me to furnish a military cordon round the scene of the cataclysm. This appeared to me to be a wise precaution as long as the Egyptian Army were not allowed to meddle with the actual explosives, but hardly as useful in a desert as in a populous country. However, I asked if I was to make my own dispositions or to take my instructions from the Canal authorities. The answer was that I was to carry out the wishes of the Canal Company, who desired that the cordon should be at least five kilometres from the explosion. A moment's thought showed me that the cordon would have to be thirty kilometres in length, and allowing one man to ten yards, it would take three thousand and odd men, which was rather more than I had in Cairo. But, as I wisely reflected, they would not have any one to stop if they wanted to, and it really did not matter how far apart they were, except for the dullness of the thing. I said I would do as they wished, and after discussing the matter with our only expert, who was once ploughed in a special examination on explosives, we decided that a hundred men would be quite enough to line from the Canal to the nearest sandhill, and that, following the practice of the manœuvres and field-days of our native land, the rest of the cordon should be "imaginary," because, unless the Lost Tribes returned by the way they set out, no one would think of coming in from that part of the desert. Our only danger was that an excited Canal man should take it into his head to inspect the cordon.

I started the troops off at eleven on Wednesday, as the explosion was fixed for dawn on Thursday, and had them camped for the night on the scene of prospective carnage. I had been for the last few days honoured by various communications from the Governor of Port Said, who seemed to have a vague idea that explosives could be kept in order by the military like a disorderly crowd. He had a strong opinion that I ought to do something vigorous to make the dynamite understand that it could not explode as it liked in the Khedive's dominions, but must do so, if at all, decently and in order. I expressed my willingness to assist his Excellency in any way in my power, but generally held that his dynamite was essentially civil, being for mining purposes. This was to avoid any suggestion that the Egyptian Army should have anything to do with the matter, as I have explained above. On Wednesday the Governor began to feel more concerned than ever about his poor frightened populace, and suggested that he should come to Cairo to discuss the matter and stop over Thursday morning. After the troops had left for their post, he wired that it had been decided to make the radius of the cordon ten kilometres instead of five, so as to save what we could of our troops; he added that this was on the advice of the great French experts, who had telegraphed from Paris. At first I was annoyed, as it seemed to me to be a half-measure. Why not really play for safety and let the cordon stay in Cairo? A moment's thought, however, showed me how little it mattered, owing to our great foresight in employing the "imaginary" system. Once you accept this great principle, you can make a cordon of any size you like with any number of men. Here we were providing a first-rate cordon of sixty kilometres in length (which would have needed six thousand men at least under the old-fashioned systems) with one hundred men! It only shows what a lot of nonsense is talked about our War Office when they say that they never invented anything but new buttons. I am sure if the Boers had really grasped that system the war would have been much shorter, but they were stupid folk. So I wired back agreeing cordially with the French experts' idea, and sent telegraphic orders to the Officer in Command to "imagine" another thirty kilometres of cordon of the finest description.

As the o.c. is naturally a truthful man, I thought I had better go down and help him, and also see the explosion. I got there late on Wednesday night, and sent one of our party to find out from the British expert (who had been sent out by Nobel's) what was going to be done.

He appeared to be in a somewhat irritable condition, as he disliked receiving different orders every hour, and I could see was not at all the man to be happy under the Canal Company or our War Office, or any really up-to-date body like that. He was the one grim touch in our farce. He knew that the dynamite had, owing to the action of the sea water and some chemical manure which formed part of the cargo, become unstable and dangerous. The least shock might send it off. He had, knowing this, to go and lay two mines in the ship, and connect them by an electric wire with the firing battery. He was confident that the explosion would be very local in its effect, as the high explosives usually are, and in his benighted ignorance put the danger zone down at one mile, at the outside.

The inhabitants of Port Said disagreed profoundly with him: some left for Cairo, some sat on the beach in sort of bomb-proof shelters, and some actually put out to sea. By order of the Canal Company the ships in the harbour were double cabled, and all windows were to be left open, though the actual scene of the explosion was twenty kilometres away.

On the fatal morning we proceeded to the railway station, where we found the senior officials of the Canal assembled. Only the seniors were allowed to come, on the old Hatfield Station principle that only people of some local importance may cross the line in front of an express, and, accompanied by twenty members of the local Press, we got into a special train that was waiting to run us out. I was glad to notice that we took out two ambulance waggons, but the absence of any coffins struck me as evidence of carelessness on the part of somebody. The Governor was unluckily detained by business of importance, which report says he conducted on his face in a cellar.

On arriving at the scene of action we alighted, and I was pleased to see how well the cordon looked, and quite regretted that they had no one to keep back. In this I was wrong, as I found out afterwards.

I now devoted myself to answering the various questions of the Canal authorities, which were summed up by the Agent Supérieur, who said, "Then, milor, one can be assured that the military preparations are complete?" I assured him that everything that the most modern science of war could suggest had been done, and we bowed. It was an impressive sight—we two great men having our final interview, surrounded by the members of the Press, note-book in hand. I then was interviewed by the remaining Canal authorities in order of seniority, who each drew my attention to some point they wished me to consider, and after replying in suitable terms we bowed. I now decided to cross the Canal, partly to get a better view and partly to avoid an attack of hysterics, of which the premonitory symptoms had begun. I also was developing a severe form of lumbago: punctuating all your remarks by a bow needs a practised back if it is to be done with impunity.

I got into a small boat and crossed over. The Canal authorities begged me to be quick, and to have the boat removed from the water as soon as I could, as a tidal wave would sweep down the Canal, wrecking all ships, both great and small, in its path. Getting the boat out was a business; and the Canal Company was nearly a Commissaire-Général, or something like that, short over the job, as in his enthusiasm he lent a hand and had the boat deposited on his toe by the willing but clumsy Egyptian privates. He murmured "*Sapristi!*" in a tone of deep anguish, and sat down in the Canal, producing a magnificent tidal wave on his own account. We helped him out and bowed, and he bowed, maimed and wet as he was.

After a breathless period of suspense, enlivened by the French doctor's reminiscences, which might have been entitled "Operations I Have Performed," suddenly a great column of vapour shot up into the air and then expanded into a great mushroom, from the edges of which we could see tiny black specks (you must remember we were six miles off) falling. Through our glasses we could see the waters seething and boiling in an indescribable way at the foot of the huge mushroom.

We remained listening for what seemed to be an interminable time, and at last we heard a tremendous thud, as if something soft had fallen from a great height. Meanwhile, we had been nerving ourselves for the explosion wind and the tidal wave. We were, so our foreign experts had warned us, to be blown forward on our faces as the air rushed in to fill the vacuum caused by the detonation of the dynamite, and then swept from our sandy bed into the Canal by a tidal wave twenty feet high, which would rush down the Canal at the pace of a galloping horse. I had already selected a position where I should not be crushed under the flabby but massive form of one of the Agents Supérieurs, but at the same time near enough to him to use him as a life-buoy during the tidal wave part of the programme. The maimed Commissaire remained in a prone position in anticipation. He was a kindly man who wished to give as little trouble as possible, even to hurricanes and tidal waves. We waited in constrained attitudes which gradually relaxed as each individual decided in his own mind that he was looking a trifle silly, and we attempted to induce the remainder of our fellow-creatures present to believe that we usually looked on at interesting ceremonies with our teeth clenched and our heads bent. It was a beautiful sight to see successive smiles light up those monumental French faces and the natural ruddy hue steal back to the leaden cheeks. It reminded me of a sunrise in the Alps, when peak after peak catches the golden glow. We re-crossed the Canal humming little songs in a nonchalant manner, as if we had been waiting for nothing in particular. Launching the boat was difficult to do with dignity, but we let the soldiers do it while we looked at the view, and only turned round when she was in the water. It really was a little hard. If only there had been a gust of wind from any quarter we could have pretended it was the result of the explosion; if there had been one ripple our faces would have been saved; but no! I have never seen in Egypt so absolutely still a day, and the waters of the Canal were as smooth as glass. Once over, things went better, and we mounted the train to be carried nearer to the scene of destruction. I was glad to notice that a tactful railway official had got rid of the hospital car.

We were prepared for the worst now, and it was lucky. Mile after mile was passed and no sign of the explosion was visible. In fact, until we came within the danger zone according to the despised Briton, the face of nature was unchanged, except where the Canal Company had pulled things down to avoid their being broken. When we did get close there was much to look at, and it was very interesting. Everything was shredded, after the manner of dynamite. It seems to tear things up into small pieces. Great pieces of iron and steel, torn, not broken, lay about in all directions, and the wood was in many cases literally pulped. We spent a most interesting hour there examining the effects of the shock. A mass of earth two hundred feet long by sixty wide had been blown clean out of the solid bank against which the ship had lain, *and that earth had disappeared.* Where it went to I don't know; but I suppose it was scattered abroad in small fragments. Great fish were picked up in the desert a hundred yards from the Canal bank, and some of the heavier pieces of iron flew a thousand yards before they came to a standstill.

On one thing we—I mean the British portion of the onlookers—congratulated ourselves, and that was that the *entente cordiale* had been preserved unclouded throughout the day. I remarked on this with much satisfaction to the English head of the railways, who was with us, as we ran up the line in our "special" to visit the southern limit of the danger zone. He cordially agreed, when, as we slowed down preparatory to stopping at the point where the cordon crossed the line, we heard a terrible sound. There was no mistaking it. It was the voice of a Frenchman hoarse with rage objurgating some one, and the first words we made out were—well, I cannot translate them, but they included the expression *sales Anglais*. I rushed to the window and beheld a scene far more terrible than any explosion. About twenty yards from the train stood our newest subaltern, who hails from the Far West of Ireland, with his legs apart, with an amused but tolerant smile on his face, and the general attitude and expression of some one passing a few idle minutes by teasing an irritable lap-dog. In front of him, I cannot say stood, as he was never still for one second, the most *supérieur* of all the Agents. He was a very small, very fat and very fussy little man, who had often made me wonder how he contained such an enormous opinion of himself in so small a body. At that moment he was not looking his best. He was a rich crimson with rage and exertion, and he was performing a sort of war dance which, though, as I was subsequently informed, it had begun as a sort of lively polka, had now from pure exhaustion degenerated into a kind of negro shuffle. His voice was nearly gone, and it seemed merely a question of seconds before he had a fit. As I scrambled out of the train, I heard my Irish subordinate sum up the case as follows: "It is no good, monsieur; I have told you you cannot go through the cordon, and you're not going; but if you like dancing in the sun and screaming I shan't stop you." Here he was cut short by a yell of fury which eclipsed all the previous efforts of the enraged little man. In the background stood a mob of Greeks, half-castes, and natives, who were all jabbering at the top of their voices like a stage crowd.

I hastened forward, accompanied by my railway friend, who in the excitement of the moment began talking fluently in a mixture of French, German, Arabic, and Hindustani. On seeing me, the Frenchman rushed forward and launched a torrent of hoarse whispers at me. He was nearly inaudible, and when he was not, one wished he had been. As far as I followed, he proposed taking the case into the Consular Court, sending for the French Fleet, driving the English into the sea, and shooting my Irishman at seven the next morning. In the midst of the tornado I had time to be thankful that my Milesian did not know a solitary word of French; as if he had done so we should have probably had to fish the Agent out of the Canal, always supposing that he was not in bits. He (the Frenchman) walked up and down raving, and I perspired after him, never getting a word in; and I began to think we should go on until his fit began or he dropped down from sheer exhaustion. But at last I remembered being told never to give way to a man in this condition. So I bellowed in my best French: "It appears, sir, you forget to whom you are speaking." At first it looked as if my experiment was going to be a failure. He changed from crimson to purple, but luckily he was quite unable to speak. At this juncture a less *supérieur* Agent rushed forward and murmured that I was the Minister. It was not true, and seemed to me an absolutely futile contribution to the

Suez Canal: Its Consequences 677

"The Lion's Share." In *Punch* 69 (26 February 1876): 69. The caption for the Punch cartoon reads, "Gare à qui la touche!" (Beware whoever touches!), the key to India (a metaphorical representation of the Suez Canal), which is securely fastened beneath the British Lion's claw. In the background, Benjamin Disraeli pays Ismail Pasha, grandson of Mehemet Ali and viceroy of Egypt (1863–1879), for the Egyptian government's stock in the Suez Canal Company.

conversation; but I had forgotten a Frenchman's respect for a Minister. By an effort which must have permanently strained him, he recovered himself, and muttering that I must excuse him, as he was outside himself, he fled into an adjoining hut. After a decent interval I followed, and we made speeches to each other and were very dignified. Keeping in front of the window in order to prevent his seeing the culprit, I pointed out that he, the offender, was cut to the heart at the way he had been treated for merely doing his duty and obeying the orders, not of myself, but the Canal Company, etc. I could hear the young ruffian whistling airs from *The Little Michus*, with variations, and my only hope was the Frenchman would not hear him too. However, all went well, and he admitted that he had misunderstood my officer, which was luckily quite true. The culprit was called in, and shook the Agent by the hand with a bright smile in which no form of penitence appeared. We then drank weird drinks together, and parted full of mutual esteem and with as many compliments as my exhausted French could put into words. So we fared gaily back to Cairo and agreed, as my Irishman said: "Rum beggars, those Froggies, but quite decent when you get to know them and they keep their hair on."

SOURCE: In *The Leisure of An Egyptian Official* (New York: G. H. Doran, 1921).

XIII
THE ARABI UPRISING

INTRODUCTION
The Arabi Uprising:
"Egypt for the Egyptians" or British Egypt

BARBARA HARLOW

EGYPT IS READY still, nay desirous, to come to terms with England, to be fast friends with her, to protect her interests and keep her road to India, to be her ally. But she must keep within the limits of her jurisdiction" (this volume, 708). In these terms Arabi Pasha appealed to England's Prime Minister Gladstone on 2 July 1882, just days before the bombardment of Alexandria on 11 July. Arabi, who hailed from an Egyptian *fellah*, or peasant, background to become a colonel in the Egyptian Army, had led an army mutiny—or, as was also argued, a nationalist movement—against the Khedive Tawfiq and his English supporters on 9 September of the preceding year, and from January 1882 had been acting as Egypt's minister of war. What was to become of England's jurisdiction? In June the London government had ordered General Wolseley and the English fleet to the area and threatened military action against the nationalist opposition. That threat was carried out in the 11 July bombardment of Alexandria, followed by the seizure of Ismailia on 29 July, then consummated in the devastating destruction of Egyptian forces at the Battle of Tel al-Kebir on 29 September. Arabi and his associates were arrested and tried, and Arabi sentenced to exile in Ceylon. And with that, the British formally occupied Egypt.

For Arabi and his followers, the Suez Canal had become part of the pilgrimage route to Mecca and Medina; for England, however, it had assumed significance by allowing shortened passage to India. In both cases, however, the canal had burdened Egypt and the Egyptians with a colossal debt. During Mehemet Ali's reign as viceroy of Egypt from 1805 to 1848, and through those of his successors Ibrahim (1848), Abbas (1848–1854), Said (1854–1863), and Ismail (1863–1879), Egypt's commitments to European interests in Egypt had been costly, including the financing of the canal's building and the expenses of the ceremonies that celebrated its opening. Those costs were exacted through ever-increasing taxations, but the Egyptian economy continued to deteriorate, and in 1876 the French and the English took over, in name of the "Dual Control," the Khedive's government. With dual control, the "relationship of ruler and ruled was placed under the official notice of Europe" (Hourani, *History*, 275). Various investments were at stake in ensuring the stability and dependency of Egypt. Economically, European financial and commercial groups competed and cooperated with indigenous merchant and landowning classes, with an eye toward increased trading advantages, while the rural population and the impoverished inhabitants of the cities suffered under the mounting pressures of fiscal extraction. Politically, England and France were concerned with maintaining their alliance against both Russia and the Ottoman Empire with regard to control of the Mediterranean and the routes to the East.

Arabi's uprising, then, claimed to represent the interests of Egypt and the Egyptians in these contests: "Egypt for the Egyptians." What was to become of England's jurisdiction following the threat to the even then precarious status quo? Already in 1877 Gladstone had raised that question in his article "Aggression on Egypt and Freedom in the East," arguing that "enlargements of the Empire are for us an evil fraught with serious, though possibly not immediate danger." But there were other members of his government and among public policy and opinion makers who insisted that direct intervention in Egyptian affairs, if not outright territorial occupation, was incumbent on an empire that needed to maintain both its suzerainty and its access to territory, trade, and expansion. If the occupationists seemed to have won the day in the immediate aftermath of the Arabi uprising, the debate nonetheless continued. Should England restore order and withdraw quickly to its previous role of a "moral influence," or remain in Egypt to ensure reform following the restoration of order? How long, that is, would/should the occupation last? In the event, it continued until 1956 and the Suez Canal War, in which France, England, and Israel sought to contest Abdel Nasser's nationalization of the waterway.

But if England were to assume control of Egypt, Arabi and his followers had first to be dealt with. Arabi was arrested in fall 1882, and his trial took place shortly thereafter. There were those in England and Egypt alike who clamored for his immediate and summary execution. Others argued just as adamantly for the imperative of a fair trial and due process. It was perhaps not just the man but his example that needed to be disposed of. Lord Cromer, or Sir Evelyn Baring, considered it urgent to cancel the effects of insubordination such as Arabi's, asking in his memoirs, "at what point the sacred right of revolution begins or ends . . . at what stage a disturber of the peace passes from a common rioter . . . to the rank of a leader of a political movement" (Cromer,

Modern Egypt, 1:334). For Cromer, the Arabi uprising marked neither such a point nor such a stage, and, he would maintain, the English had had practical experience in contending with "mutinies." Following his own assignment in the India Service, Cromer had in September 1883 only recently taken over the consul-generalship of Egypt. His admirers and detractors alike emphasized his administrative prowess and discipline in carrying out his politically mandated work—whether in India or Egypt. According to his colleague in the service, Lord Milner, for example, "It would be difficult to overestimate what the work of England in Egypt owes to the sagacity, fortitude, and patience of the British Minister" (*England in Egypt,* 438). Wilfrid Scawen Blunt, by contrast, had earned the reputation, as he himself proudly admitted, of having a "nonconformist conscience." A champion of Arabi and his cause of self-government for the Egyptians, Blunt challenged the attempt to criminalize the work of the national leader, and organized legal counsel through Mark Napier and A. M. Broadley to represent Arabi throughout his trial. As it happened, Arabi was not executed but exiled to Ceylon—where Blunt would later visit him on the occasion of his visit to India in the interests of establishing an institute of Muslim higher education there, even as he championed the rescue mission to Gordon in Khartoum in 1885 (see *Archives of Empire: Volume II. The Scramble for Africa*). Thereafter denied entry into British Egypt, Blunt's subsequent engagements as a "nonconformist conscience" would include a period in Galway Jail in consequence of his support of Irish claims for Home Rule and self-government.

Meanwhile, the British did occupy Egypt, requiring further development of the attributes of the "Anglo-Egyptian official." As Cromer pointed out, "The efficient working of the administrative machine depends . . . mainly on choosing the right man for the right place" (Cromer, *Modern Egypt,* 2:300). Many of those same officials, however, saw the "right place" for the "right men" as at "office, club and dinner." But the larger place, Egypt—representing for some the "key to India," for others "the Gate of the East"—had for the time being become British Egypt.

BIBLIOGRAPHY

Blunt, Wilfrid Scawen. *The Secret History of the English Occupation of Egypt.* London: T. F. Unwin, 1907.
—. *India Under Ripon.* London: T. F. Unwin, 1909.
—. *Gordon at Khartoum.* London: Swift, 1911.
—. *The Land War in Ireland.* n.p., 1913.
Berque, Jacques. *Egypt: Imperialism and Revolution.* Translated by Jean Stewart. 1967. London: Faber and Faber, 1972.

Broadley, A. M. *How We Defended Arabi and His Friends: A Story of Egypt and the Egyptians.* London: A. M. Bradley, 1884.
Cole, Juan Ricardo. *Colonialism and Revolution in the Middle East: Social and Cultural Origins of Egypt's 'Urabi Movement.* Princeton, N.J.: Princeton University Press, 1993.
Cromer, Earl of. *Modern Egypt.* London: Macmillan, 1908.
Daniel, Norman. *Islam, Europe, and Empire.* Edinburgh: Edinburgh University Press, 1966.
Farwell, Brian. "Wolseley Versus Arabi and the Queen, 1881–82." In *Queen Victoria's Little Wars.* 1972. Reprint, New York: Norton, 1985.
Hourani, Albert. *A History of the Arab Peoples.* Cambridge, Mass.: Harvard University Press, 1991.
Landes, David S. *Bankers and Pashas: International Finance and Economic Imperialism in Egypt.* 1958. Reprint, New York: Harper and Row, 1969.
Lytton, Earl of. *Wilfrid Scawen Blunt: A Memoir by his Grandson.* London: Macdonald, 1961.
Mayer, Thomas. *The Changing Past: Egyptian Historiography of the Urabi Revolt.* Gainesville, Fla.: University of Florida Press, 1988.
Milner, Alfred. *England in Egypt.* London: Edward Arnold, 1893.
Mitchell, Timothy. *Colonising Egypt.* Cambridge: Cambridge University Press, 1988.
Robinson, Ronald, and John Gallagher, with Alice Denny. *Africa and the Victorians: The Climax of Imperialism.* 1961. Reprint, New York: Doubleday/Anchor, 1968.
State Information Service Press. *The Orabi Revolution: Features of Egyptian People's Struggle.* Cairo: State Information Service Press, 1988.
Urabi, Ahmad. *The Defense Statement of Ahmad "Urabi, the Egyptian": From the Blunt Manuscript at the School of Oriental and African Studies.* Cairo: American University in Cairo Press, 1982.

Chronology of Events

1869
November Opening of the Suez Canal.

1876 Dual control established.

1879 Ismail deposed and Tewfiq appointed as Khedive.

1881
September 9 Mutiny of the Egyptian Army.

1882
January Arabi appointed minister of war.
June 11 Riots in Alexandria.
July 11 Bombardment of Alexandria.
September 13 Battle of Tel el-Kebir.
September 15 Cairo occupied by British troops; Arabi arrested.
December 3 Arabi condemned to exile.

Important Figures

Viceroys of Egypt

    Mohammed Ali, 1805 to 1848
    Ibrahim Pasha (as Regent), 1848 (four months)
    Abbas Pasha (grandson of Mohammed Ali), 1848 to 1854
    Said Pasha (third son of Mohammed Ali), 1854 to 1863
    Ismail Pasha (second son of Ibrahim Pasha and grandson of Mohammed Ali), raised to dignity of Khedive, 1863 to 1879

Khedives of Egypt

Ismail Pasha, 1863 to 1879
Tewfik Pasha, 1879 to 1892
Abbas Pasha, 1892 to 1914
British Protectorate proclaimed 17 December 1914

British Agents and Consuls-General to Egypt

General Stanton, 1865 to 1876
Lord Vivian, 10 May 1876 to 10 October 1879
Sir Edward Malet, 10 October 1879 to 11 September 1883
Lord Cromer, 11 September 1883 to 6 May 1907
Sir Eldon Gorst, 6 May 1907 to 12 July 1911
Lord Kitchener, September 1911 to July 1914

De War in Egypt
BOB MCGEE

Egyp' kickin' up er row—
    Pullin' on de trigger!
F-r-e-e-z-e, my honey, to de plow,
    Fotch er yell, ole nigger!
Cotton ain't gwine hab no show
    Whar de people's fightin';
Grass is gwinter to walk de row
    Sen' de crop er-kitin'.
Ebberbody on dis side
    Make er mighty tussle,
Take advantage ob de tide,
    Strain de bone and mussle!
Make ole Kit mule plum' de line,
    Keep old Pete er-prancin',
Set yer head ter cut er shine,
    Keep dem hoes er-dancin'!
Prices going up after while—
    Make de nigger "fussy";

Make him feel so happy, chile,
Oh, Lawdy, Lawdy, mussy!

SOURCE: In *Puck* 11, no. 284 (16 August 1882): 379.

Aggression on Egypt and Freedom in the East
W. E. GLADSTONE

[W. E. Gladstone (1809–1898) alternated with Benjamin Disraeli as prime minister between 1868 and 1885, and served again as prime minister in 1886 and from 1892 to 1894.]

Any one whose thought and action have been engaged, like my own, for a twelvemonth past, with the Eastern Question in its very sorest place, namely, the point of contact between the race dominant while inferior, and the races superior yet subject, may well experience a sense of relief when the scene is shifted from Bulgaria, or from Constantinople, to Egypt. He passes at once from a tainted and stifling atmosphere to one which allows of respiration, and which is by comparison free and almost fragrant. It was therefore not without a qualified and relative pleasure that I found a writer eminently competent for the task was about to raise, in this Review, the Egyptian question. This phrase does not signify, as the uninstructed in modern diction might suppose, the question how Egypt should be handled for her own interests and the welfare of her people, but the question whether, and how, her and their political condition is henceforward to be determined by our interests, and for the welfare of our people. An investigation this, not particularly inviting from a moral point of view; but one which Mr. Dicey has twice approached[1] with a candour and a courage equal to the desire he shows to accommodate conflicting interests and claims, so far—and it is not very far—as the necessities of his case will permit.

Mr. Dicey is confident in the support of his countrymen. The occupation of Egypt by England, he thinks, is generally acknowledged both at home and abroad to be only a question of time.[2] He lifts the subject out of the wide whirlpool of the general controversy. He does not join in the wild, irrational

---

1. *Nineteenth Century*, June 1877, Art. X, and August, 1877, Art. I.
2. P. 1.

"Hold On!" In *Punch* 82 (10 June 1882): 271.

"The Neddy of the Nile." In *Punch* 82 (24 June 1882): 295.

denunciations of Russia, so dear not to the people but to the clubs; and he appears to think we could not be justified in upholding a vicious government of European Turkey by any considerations of our own advantage.

It may be that he is correct in his estimate of the tendency and probable verdict of public opinion. It is not to be denied, that the territorial appetite has within the last quarter of a century revived among us with an abnormal vigour. The race of statesmen who authoritatively reproved it are gone, or have passed into the shade; and a new race have succeeded, of whom a very large part either administer strong incentives, or look on with indifference. The newspaper press, developed in gigantic proportions, and, in its action on domestic subjects, absolutely invaluable, is to a great extent wanting in checks and safeguards to guide its action on our foreign affairs, where all the weights are in one scale, and we are, as it were, counsel, judge, and jury for ourselves. Nations are quite as much subject as individuals to mental intemperance; and the sudden flush of wealth and pride, which engenders in the man arrogant vulgarity, works by an analogous and subtler process upon numbers who have undergone the same exciting experience. Indeed, they are the more easily misled, because conscience has not to reproach each unit of a mass with a separate and personal selfishness. With respect to the Slav provinces, the 'strong man' of British interests, of traditional policy, and of hectoring display, has been to a great degree kept down by a 'stronger man;' by the sheer stern sense of right and wrong, justice and injustice, roused in the body of the people by manifestations of unbounded crime. But it may be very doubtful whether, in questions where ethical laws do not so palpably repress the solicitations of appetite, the balance of forces will be so cast among us as to insure the continuance of that wonderful self-command, with which the nation has now for so long a time resisted temptation, detected imposture, encouraged the feeble virtues, and neutralized the inveterate errors of its rulers.

I am sensible, then, of the good which a discussion about Egypt may effect, as a counter-irritant, in abating inflammatory action nearer to a vital organ. I nevertheless incline to believe that every scheme for the acquisition of territorial power in Egypt, even in the' refined form with which it has here been invested, is but a new snare laid in the path of our policy. I will then endeavour succinctly, and I hope temperately, to test the proposal upon the several particulars of Mr. Dicey's argument, to which I must now briefly refer.

His first and fundamental proposition is that the preservation of our dominion in the East is only less important to us than the preservation of our national independence.[3] His next, that the bare possibility of Russia's obtain-

---

3. *Nineteenth-Century*, vol. i, p. 666.

ing the command of the Bosphorus makes it matter of urgent necessity (or again of 'absolute imperative necessity'[4]) that we should secure our route to India. The third step in the argument is joined with the second: the route, of which we must thus be masters, is the route of the Suez Canal.[5] Fourthly, it is held that the Canal 'must be kept open to our ships at all times and under all circumstances.'[6] And fifthly, the 'command of the Canal' involves the 'occupation of the Delta' of the Nile. This is called, in some passages, the occupation of Egypt; and I believe there is a closer connection between the two than Mr. Dicey seems to imagine. But, in strictness, he scarcely means more than the Delta. And, for the benefit of those among us who are nervous at the visions of responsibility and charge thus evoked from the mist of the years to come, he holds that nothing will be required of us 'for the future but—[7]

1. The erection of a few forts on the Syrian side of the Isthmus (query, with nobody in them?).

2. The presence of a small British garrison at Alexandria (query, in the presence of the rather large and very respectable army of the country?).

3. An ironclad at Port Said. (But why nothing at the other end, when our dangers from Russia through the valley of the Euphrates and the Persian Gulf are about to be so formidable?)

4. A Resident at Cairo; or the transfer of the governing power to an Administrator appointed with our consent.[8]

Now I must, in fairness, at once tender some admissions.

First, that there are foreign Powers, and Russia in all likelihood among them, who would with pleasure see us engaged in this operation.

Secondly, it is recommended by the benevolent consideration that the government of Egypt is bad, and that if we were its masters we ought to be able to seal more speedily the doom of slavery, and to relieve the people from much of severe and grinding oppression.

Lastly, that I myself approach the question under adverse prepossessions. It is my firm conviction, derived, I think, from my political 'pastors and masters,' and confirmed by the facts of much experience, that, as a general rule, enlargements of the Empire are for us an evil fraught with serious, though possibly not with immediate danger. I do not affirm that they can always be avoided; but, that they should never be accepted except under circumstances

4. Ibid. p. 684.
5. Ibid. p. 668.
6. Ibid.; also p. 669.
7. *Supra*, p. 10.
8. Vol. 1, p. 682, and *supra*, pp. 10, 11.

of a strict and jealously examined necessity. I object to them because they are, rarely effected except by means that are more or less questionable, and that tend to compromise British character in the judgment of the impartial world; a judgment, which I hope will grow from age to age more and more operative in imposing moral restraint on the proceedings of each particular State. I object to them, because we already have our hands too full. We have undertaken responsibilities of government, such as never were assumed before in the whole history of the world. The cares of the governing body in the Roman Empire, with its compact continuity of ground, were light in comparison with the demands now made upon the Parliament and Executive of the United Kingdom. Claims made, and gallantly, or confidently at least, confronted; yet not adequately met. We, who hail with more than readiness annexations and other transactions which extend and complicate our responsibilities abroad, who are always ready for a new task, yet leave many of the old tasks undone. Forty years have passed since it was thought right to reform fundamentally our municipal corporations; but the Corporation of London, whose case called out for change much more loudly than any other, we have not yet had time or strength to touch. Our currency, our local government, our liquor laws, portions even of our taxation, remain in a state either positively discreditable, or at the least inviting and demanding great improvement; but, for want of time and strength, we cannot handle them. For the romance of political travel we are ready to scour the world, and yet of capital defect in duties lying at our door we are not ashamed.

I protest upon another ground, which, if not more broad and solid than the two foregoing grounds, is yet at least more palpable. The most pacific of prudent men must keep in his view the leading outlines of the condition which we shall have to accept in future wars. As regards the strength, the spirit, the resources of the country, we have nothing to fear. Largely dependent at other times on timber, hemp, and metal of foreign origin for the construction of our navy, we now find ourselves constituted, by the great transition from wooden to iron ships, the principal producers of the one indispensable raw material, and the first ship-manufacturers of the world. But one subject remains, which fills me with a real alarm. It is the fewness of our men. Ample in numbers to defend our island-home, they are, with reference to the boundless calls of our world-wide dominion, but as a few grains of sand scattered thinly on a floor. Men talk of humiliation: may we never be subjected to the humiliation of dependence upon vicarious valour, bought dear and sold cheap in the open market. Public extravagance does not with us take the humour of overpay to our soldiers and our sailors. In war time, we must ungrudgingly add (and it is no easy matter) to the emoluments of the services. But after we have done all that is possible, we shall not have done enough. It will still remain an effort beyond, and almost against, nature, for some thirty millions of men to bear in chief the burden of defending the countries inhabited by near three hundred millions. We must not flinch from the performance of our duty to those countries. But neither let us, by puerile expedients, try to hide from ourselves what it involves. To divest ourselves of territory once acquired is very difficult. Where it is dishonourable, it cannot be thought of. Even where it is not, it is likely to set in action some reasonable as well as many unreasonable susceptibilities. If then we commit an error in adding to territory, it is an error impossible or difficult to cure. It fills me with surprise that the disproportion between our population and our probable duties in war is so little felt, especially (so far as I know) by professional men, as a prudential restraint upon the thirst for more territory. The surrender of the Ionian Protectorate was not founded on a desire to husband our military means; but, even as estimated by that result, it was one of the very best measures of our time.

I must now frankly demur to each and all, in succession, of the arguments, which are supposed to render some kind of occupation in Egypt expedient, and even imperative.

The first of them is, that the retention of our Indian dominion is a matter comparable in some sense with, and next in importance to, our national independence. Now I do not wish to stimulate our national pride. Ministrations at that altar are already far too much in request. But I confess my belief that a high doctrine of the dependence of England upon India is humiliating, and even degrading. I admit, in whole or in part, no such dependence. I hold, firmly and unconditionally, that we have indeed a great duty towards India, but that we have no interest in India, except the wellbeing of India itself, and what that wellbeing will bring with it in the way of consequence. If, in a certain sense and through indirect channels, India is politically tributary to England, the tribute is one utterly insignificant: it is probably not near a hundredth part of the sheer annual profits of the nation, nor near a fourth part of the unforced gains of our commercial intercourse with that country. India does not add to, but takes from our military strength. The root and pith and substance of the material greatness of our nation lies within the compass of these islands; and is, except in trifling particulars, independent of all and every sort of political dominion beyond them. This dominion adds to our fame, partly because of its moral and social grandeur, partly because foreigners partake the superstitions, which still to no small extent prevail among us, and think that in the vast aggregate of our scattered territories lies the main secret of our strength. Further, it imposes upon us the most weighty and solemn duties; duties, nowhere so weighty and solemn as in India. We have of our own motion wedded the fortunes of that country, and we never can in honour solicit a divorce. Protesting, then, against the sore disparagement which attaches to this doctrine of dependence, I am so far in practical agreement with the argument on the other side, that I fully aver we are bound to study the maintenance of our power in India, under the present and all proximate circumstances, as a capital demand upon the national honour.

But, alas! this agreement is but for a moment; and it 'starts aside like a broken bow' when we observe an assumption which underlies all the arguments for an occupation in Egypt, namely, the assumption that the maintenance of our power in India is after all, in its Alpha and its Omega, a military question; though subject, we may hope, to the condition, that it is to be maintained without violation of the moral laws. Now this appears to me to be an inversion of the due order of ideas; an inversion dangerous to us and most degrading to India. I hold that the capital agent in determining finally the question whether our power in India is or is not to continue, will be the will of the two hundred and forty millions of people who inhabit India, their positive or their negative will, their anxiety, or at least their willingness, to be in connection with us rather than encounter the mischiefs or the risks of change. The question who shall have supreme rule in India is, by the laws of right, an Indian question; and those laws of right are from day to day growing into laws of fact. Our title to be there depends on a first condition, that our being there is profitable to the Indian nations; and on a second condition, that we can make them see and understand it to be profitable. It is the moral, and not the military, question which stands first in the order of ideas, with reference to the power of England in India, as much as with reference to the power, in England itself, of the State over the people.

The situation is indeed one charged with mixed and checquered elements. I do not mean merely for those who, like myself, can never escape from the smarting recollection that we have dishonourably abandoned our solemn obligations to the subject races of Turkey; obligations which nothing could satisfy short of a real and constant effort to organise an European concert, and, by this potent and resistless organ, to effect a clean removal of their grievances. I do not here, however, dwell on the repudiation of our duties, but on the loss of our opportunities. The task, which for many was both safe and easy, is arduous and perilous for one. I am jealous enough of Russia to grudge to her the unparalleled position, which has been secured to her by our thoroughly ignoble conduct. I am suspicious enough of Russia to be wholly uncertain—as uncertain as if I were speaking of the English Cabinet—whether the higher or the lower influences that act within and upon her will prevail. Who can say whether, with a sagacious forethought and a lofty self-denial, she will in the making of the peace be modest for herself and rigid only for the subject races, or whether she will mar the more than knightly mission she has taken in hand by diverting her prodigious efforts to selfish ends? If she does the second, we shall have to reflect with remorse, that we gave her the opportunity she abuses. If she has the moral force to work out the first, what coals of fire she will heap upon our head! We may turn over with pious care every leaf in our new 'gospel of selfishness,' but we shall find there no anodyne for the pain.

Among secondary, but still very weighty, reasons why we ought not to have left to the solo charge of Russia an European responsibility, was the high likelihood, to say the least, that in Bulgaria, at any rate, the operations of the war would be tainted with barbarity. It may have been observed that we have no trustworthy evidence to show that this contingency has been realised on the Russian side in the Armenian campaign; and, in that country, the war had not been preceded by any but the normal misconduct of the governing power. But, upon the south bank of the Danube, the land bristled with stinging and exasperating recollections. The Bulgarians are men, as I believe, of at any rate the average humanity of Christendom; but, had they foregone every opportunity of retaliation after the frightful massacres of 1876, they would have been angels. For weeks past the Porte has published official accounts of cruelties inflicted on the Mohammedan population; cruelties very far short of those which it had itself commanded and rewarded, but still utterly detestable. To these utterances, except by a few fanatics, little heed was given; for the world had learned, on conclusive evidence, that the arts of falsehood have received a portentous development in Turkey, and have become the very basis and mainspring, so to say, of Ottoman official speech. As late as on the 15th of July the Correspondent of the *Daily News*[9]—and the title is now one of just authority—declared his conviction that there had not then been a single case in Bulgaria of personal maltreatment of a Turkish civilian by a Russian soldier. I can hardly hope this is now the fact. While I have little fear that there has been, on the part of Russians, widely extended cruelty, there must be among them, at least here and there, ruffians whom discipline will ill restrain; and we have also to bear in mind the diversity of races and civilisations in their army. The subject is one that calls for the closest attention. We have first to wait, as we waited last year, for a full exhibition of the facts; and then, without

---

9. *Daily News*, July 17.

respect of persons, to estimate them as they deserve. Above all, we shall then have to observe, and honestly to appreciate, the conduct of the Russian Government in reference to proved barbarity. I have shown at large[10] that the essence of the case of 1876 lies, not in the massacres themselves, but in the conduct of the Porte about the massacres; the falsehood, the chicane, the mockery and perversion of justice, the denial of redress, the neglect and punishment of the good Mohammedans, and finally the rewards and promotions of the bad, in pretty close proportions to their badness. If the Russian Government descends to the same guilt, I heartily hope it will be covered with the same, or more than the same, infamy. But if it actively assists or boldly undertakes the detection of crime, if, above all, it inflicts prompt and condign punishment on the offenders, of whatever race or land they be, it will then have done all that such a woful case admits to clear its own character, and to vindicate the honour of Christian civilisation.

In the face of these great events, of the gigantic military movements on the surface, of the subtler and deeper changes that are apparently in preparation underneath, the daring of human speculation is abashed, and we seem to see how the hand of the Most High has lifted the vast human interests of the case far above the level of the vacillations of Cabinets, the confused and discordant utterances of a journalism reflecting bewildered opinion, the intrigues of the schemer, and the dreams of the enthusiast. More and more, however, does the great Emancipation, which, twelve months back, friends did but hope for and every adversary scoffed at, mount above the horizon in a form growing more defined from day to day, and promise to take its place in the region of accomplished facts. No such deliverance has for centuries blessed the earth. We of this country may feel, with grief and pain, that, after setting off our *plus* and *minus*, we have, on the whole, done nothing to promote it. Whatever happens, may nothing still worse than this lie at our door. Even now, after all the efforts of the country to instruct its Government, there seem to be, from time to time, flickerings[11] of a fitful purpose not to rest content with having defeated the project of a noble policy, but even to mar the good we had refused to make. Let us hope that they are flickerings only; and that to abdicated duty we may not have to add a chapter of perpetrated wrong.

W. E. Gladstone.

SOURCE: In *Nineteenth Century* (August 1887): 149–66.

10. *Lessons in Massacre,* London, 1877, *passim.*
11. Such flickerings are to be discerned in the recent return of the fleet to Besika Bay, and in the ostentatious reinforcement of the garrison of Malta: perfect examples of the art of disquieting and annoying one side without conferring the smallest advantage on the other.

The Mutiny of the Egyptian Army
LORD CROMER

JANUARY—SEPTEMBER 1881

[Evelyn Baring, the first Earl of Cromer (1841–1917) and a member of the Baring banking family, was consul-general in Egypt from 1883 to 1907, having previously served the empire in India.]

Discontent amongst the officers—They petition Riaz Pasha—Mutiny of February 1—Dismissal of the Minister of War—Imprudent conduct of the Khedive—Conduct of the French Consul-General—Increase of discontent in the army—Mutiny of September 9—Sir Auckland Colvin—Demands of the mutineers—Dismissal of the Ministers—Reluctance of Chérif Pasha to accept office—Nomination of the Chérif Ministry—Chérif Pasha supports the European Control—Arábi is the real ruler of Egypt—His conduct due to fear—Situation created by the mutiny.

Sir John Bowring wrote in 1840: "The situation of the Osmanlis in Egypt is remarkable; they exercise an extraordinary influence, possess most of the high offices of state, and, indeed, are the depositories of power throughout the country. . . . They are few, but they tyrannise; the Arabs are many, but obey."

After Sir John Bowring wrote these lines, the Egyptians, properly so called, gradually acquired a greater share in the administration of the country, but in 1881, as in 1840, the Turks were the "paramount rulers." In the army, however, the number and influence of the Turks sensibly diminished as time went on. During the reigns of Abbas, Said, and Ismail, the Egyptian element amongst the officers had increased to such an extent as to jeopardise the little that remained of the still dominant Turco-Circassian element.

The large number of officers who were placed on half-pay in 1878 were, for the most part, Egyptians. The discontent due to this cause was increased by the fact that, whilst great and in some degree successful efforts were made to improve the civil administration of the country, nothing was done to improve the condition of the army. The prevailing discontent eventually found expression in a petition addressed by certain officers of the army to Riaz Pasha on January 15, 1881.

Ahmed Arábi, an Egyptian of fellah origin, who was colonel of the 4th Regiment, soon took the lead in the movement which was thus begun. But the prime mover in the preparation of the petition was Colonel Ali Bey

Fehmi, who commanded the 1st Regiment. His regiment had been the object of special attention on the part of the Khedive. It guarded the palace. For some time previously, however, there had been a marked cessation of friendly relations between the Khedive and Ali Bey Fehmi. In the East, to be in disgrace is to be in danger. Ali Bey Fehmi determined to strengthen his position by showing that the Egyptian portion of the army could no longer be treated with neglect, and that he himself could not with impunity be dismissed or exiled.

The petition set forth that the Minister of War, Osman Pasha Rifki, had treated the Egyptian officers of the army unjustly in the matter of promotions. He had behaved "as if they were his enemies, or as if God had sent him to venge His wrath on the Egyptians." Officers had been dismissed from the service without any legal inquiry. The petitioners, therefore, made two demands. The first was that the Minister of War should be removed, "as he was incompetent to hold such a high position." The second was that an inquiry should be held into the qualifications of those who had been promoted. "Nothing," it was said, "but merit and knowledge should entitle an officer to promotion, and in these respects we are far superior to those who have been promoted."

This petition was presented by the two Colonels in person to Riaz Pasha. Riaz Pasha was ignorant of military affairs, and had never interfered with the administration of the army, which he considered to be a prerogative of the Khedive. He endeavoured unsuccessfully to induce the Colonels to withdraw their petition, promising at the same time that inquiry should be made into their grievances. A fortnight was allowed to elapse, during which time further unsuccessful efforts were made in the same direction. In the meanwhile, the Colonels had learnt that their petition was viewed with disfavour by the Khedive and his Turkish surroundings. Riaz Pasha received a hint from the palace that the dilatory manner in which he was treating the question was calculated to throw some doubts on his loyalty. He determined, therefore, to provoke an immediate decision. The matter was discussed at a meeting of the Council of Ministers held under the presidency of the Khedive on January 30, from which Sir Auckland Colvin and M. de Blignières were most unwisely excluded. All idea of compromise was rejected. It was resolved to arrest the Colonels, and to try them by Court-martial. Subsequently, an inquiry would be made into their grievances. An order was drawn up and countersigned by the Khedive, summoning the Colonels to the Ministry of War on February 1.

One peculiarity of Egyptian official life is that no secrets are ever kept. The Colonels were immediately informed of the decision at which the Council of Ministers had arrived. Everything was, therefore, arranged for the action which followed. It was settled that, in the event of the Colonels not returning in two hours, the officers and men of their regiments should go to the Ministry of War and deliver them if they were under arrest. At the same time, a message was sent to Toura, about ten miles distant from Cairo, with a view to securing concerted action on the part of the regiment quartered there. This programme was faithfully executed. The Colonels were summoned to the Ministry of War on the pretext that certain arrangements had to be made for a procession which was to accompany one of the princesses on the occasion of her marriage. They obeyed the summons. On their arrival at the Ministry of War, they were arrested and placed on their trial. Whilst the trial was proceeding, the officers and men of their regiments arrived, and broke into the room where the Court was sitting. They treated the Minister of War roughly, destroyed the furniture, and delivered the Colonels, who then marched with their troops to the Khedive's palace, and demanded the dismissal of the Minister of War. The Ministers and other high functionaries soon gathered round the Khedive. Some counselled resistance, but the practical difficulty presented itself that no force was available with which to resist. The only sign of fidelity given by any of the troops belonging to the Cairo garrison was that the regiment quartered at Abbasieh, two miles distant from the town, refused to join the mutineers, but the most their Turkish officers could do was to keep them where they were. They would not have defended the Khedive against the mutinous regiments. The regiment stationed at Toura marched to Cairo, according to previous arrangement, and insisted on continuing its march, although messengers were sent to dissuade the men from advancing after the obnoxious Minister had been dismissed.

Under these circumstances, resistance was impossible. After some hesitation, the Khedive sent for the Colonels and informed them that Osman Pasha Rifki was dismissed and Mahmoud Pasha Baroudi[1] named Minister of War in his place. This announcement was received with cheers. The troops dispersed and tranquillity was for the time being restored. The mutinous Colonels were allowed to remain in command of their regiments. They waited on the Khedive, asked his pardon for their past misconduct, and gave assurances of unalterable fidelity and loyalty to his person.

This was the second mutiny of the Egyptian Army. It had followed the same course as the first. It originated with legitimate grievances to which no attention was paid. The next stage was mutiny. The final result was complete submission to the will of the mutineers. The whole affair was mismanaged, and for this mismanagement the Khedive appears to have been largely re-

---

1. Baroudi was the family name. He was also frequently called Mahmoud Pasha Sami.

sponsible. Two courses were from the first open to the Khedive. Either he should have endeavoured to rally to his side a sufficient force to crush the mutineers, or, if that was impossible, he should have made terms with the officers before discontent developed into mutiny. Unfortunately, he adopted neither of these courses. The attempt to decoy the Colonels away from their troops and to punish them without any trustworthy force behind him to ensure effect being given to the decisions of the Court-martial, was probably the most unwise course which could have been adopted. Sir Edward Malet expressed his opinion that the officers were treated "in the way best calculated to destroy all confidence in the Khedive and his Government, although it was in harmony with the traditions of Oriental statesmanship."

The Egyptian officers and soldiers now learnt for the second time that they had only to assert themselves in order to obtain all they required. With this encouragement, they would not be slow to mutiny a third time, should the necessity for doing so arise.

For the moment, however, a truce was established between the Khedive and his mutinous officers; but suspicions and fears were rife on both sides. The Khedive and his Ministers were afraid to disband the disaffected regiments, or even to remove them from Cairo. The officers, on the other hand, although their victory had been complete, were fearful of the consequences of their own action. They mistrusted the Khedive and thought that, should an opportunity occur, the reluctant pardon which they had received would be cancelled, and that they would be visited with condign punishment. They felt even greater resentment against Riaz Pasha than against the Khedive, and began a series of intrigues with a view to bringing about a change of Ministry.

These intrigues were encouraged by Baron de Ring, the French Consul-General, who had frequent interviews with the mutinous Colonels. The action of Baron de Ring increased the difficulties of the situation. If, in addition to financial embarrassments, defective administration, and a mutinous army, there was to be superadded hostile intrigue on the part of the representative of the French Government, the position of the Egyptian Ministry would clearly become untenable. Riaz Pasha wished to resign, but was dissuaded from doing so. The Khedive eventually wrote to the President of the French Republic to complain of Baron de Ring's conduct. The result was that he was recalled. He left Egypt on February 28. The Khedive then summoned the principal officers of the army to the palace, and expressed the confidence he entertained in Riaz Pasha, of whom he spoke in eulogistic terms. Already the pay of the unemployed Egyptian officers had been increased, and a public declaration had been made by the Khedive to the effect that for the future every class of officer, whether Turk, Circassian, or Egyptian, would be treated on the same footing. These measures somewhat improved the position of the Ministry. When Sir Edward Malet left in May on a short leave, he "had reason to believe that confidence was being restored; that the officers had, in fact, nothing to fear from intrigue; that they were gradually relaxing measures for their own protection, and beginning to feel that the Khedive and the Ministers no longer aimed at their lives."

It is unnecessary to give the detailed history of the next few months. The officers still entertained a deep-rooted mistrust of the intentions of the Khedive and his Ministers. "The traditions of the days of Ismail Pasha," Sir Edward Malet wrote, "stalked like spectres across their paths." They thought that their lives were in danger. Insubordination increased daily. A Commission was appointed to inquire into the grievances of the army. Arábi Bey was one of its members. His language to the Minister of War was very disrespectful. In the month of July, an artilleryman was run over by a cart and killed in the streets of Alexandria. His comrades bore his dead body to the palace, and forced an entrance in defiance of the orders of their officers. They were tried and the ringleaders condemned to punishment. About the same time, nineteen officers brought charges against their Colonel (Abdul-Al). These charges formed the subject of inquiry. They were found to be groundless. The officers were in consequence dismissed from the active list of the army, but were shortly afterwards restored to their former positions by the Khedive. The Colonels were greatly offended. They believed that the Khedive's action had been taken with the intention of encouraging the insubordination of their junior officers towards them. About the same time, Mahmoud Pasha Baroudi, the Minister of War, who sympathised with the officers concerned in the mutiny of February 1, was dismissed, and the Khedive's brother-in-law, Daoud Pasha, was appointed in his place. This measure also caused great dissatisfaction.

Within the Ministerial circle, a good deal of dissension reigned. The relations between Riaz Pasha and M. de Blignières became strained. The Khedive's confidence in Riaz Pasha was impaired. It was whispered that His Highness favoured the return to power of Chérif Pasha.

It was clear that another crisis was not far off, but at the moment it was about to occur, the Government were hopeful that their main difficulties had been overcome. "At no period," Sir Edward Malet wrote, "since February 1 had the confidence of the Khedive and his Government been so complete as immediately before the outbreak of September 9. On the very eve, and on the morning itself of that day, Riaz Pasha assured those with whom he conversed that the Government were masters of the situation, and that the danger of a military movement had passed away. But, in fact, all the terrors of the Colonels for their personal safety had been again aroused. A story had got abroad that the Khedive had obtained a secret Fetwa, or decree from the Sheikh-ul-Islam, condemning them to death for high treason. There was absolutely no foundation for this story, but it is currently believed, and at this moment the position of the Sheikh-ul-Islam is precarious in consequence of it. Spies were continually hovering about the residences of the Colonels, and on the night of the 8th September a man presented himself at the house of Arábi Bey, was refused admittance, and was afterwards followed and seen to return to the Prefecture of Police. There was no doubt in the mind of Arábi Bey that he was to be murdered; he left his house and went to that of the other Colonels, to whom a similar incident had just occurred. It is my belief that then only were measures taken for immediate action, that it was concerted and planned that night, as it was executed on the following day."

On September 9, the 3rd Regiment of Infantry, which was stationed at Cairo, was ordered to Alexandria. This order produced a mutiny. Arábi Bey, with 2500 men and 18 guns, marched to the square in front of the Abdin Palace. The Khedive was at the Ismailia Palace, distant about a quarter of a mile from Abdin. He did the wisest thing possible under the circumstances. He sent for Sir Auckland Colvin.

Sir Auckland Colvin was a member of the Indian Civil Service. In the hour of trial he did not belie the proud motto, *Mens aequa in arduis,* inscribed under the picture of Warren Hastings which hangs in the Calcutta Council Chamber. It is one which might fitly apply to the whole of that splendid body of Englishmen who compose the Indian Civil Service. The spirit of the Englishman rose high in the presence of danger. It was not the first time he had heard of mutiny. He knew how his own countrymen had met dangers of this sort. The example of Lawrence and Outram, of Nicholson and Edwards, pointed the way to the Indian Civilian. His duty was clear. He must endeavour at the risk of his own life to impart to the Khedive some portion of the spirit which animated his own imperial race. He spoke in no uncertain terms. "The Viceroy," he subsequently wrote, "asked my opinion on what should be done. I advised him to take the initiative. Two regiments in Cairo were said by Riaz Pasha to be faithful. I advised him to summon them to the Abdin Square, with all the military police available, to put himself at their head, and, when Arábi Bey arrived, personally to arrest him. He replied that Arábi Bey had with him the artillery and cavalry, and that they might fire. I said that they would not dare to, and that if he had the courage to take the initiative, and to expose himself personally, he might succeed in overcoming the mutineers. Otherwise, he was lost. Stone Pasha[2] warmly supported me. . . . While his carriage was coming Sir Charles Cookson[3] arrived, expressed to the Viceroy his concurrence in my views, and returned to the Agency to telegraph to his Government."

What followed may best be told in Sir Auckland Colvin's words. "I accompanied the Viceroy," he wrote, "in a separate carriage; the Ministers also, and some five or six native officers of rank, with Stone Pasha. We went first to the Abdin barracks, where the regiment of the guard turned out, and with the warmest protestations swore loyalty. Thence we drove to the Citadel, where the same occurred; but we learnt that this regiment, previous to our arrival, had been signalling to the regiment (Arábi Bey's) in the Abbassieh barrack. The Viceroy then announced his intention of going to the Abbassieh barrack. It was already 3.30; I urged him to return to the Abdin Square taking with him the Citadel Regiment, and when he arrived at the square to put himself at the head of that regiment, the regiment of the guard and the military police. He drove off, however, to Abbassieh. It was a long drive, and when we got there about 4 (the Ministers having left us at the Citadel and returned direct) we found Arábi Bey had marched with the regiment to Cairo. We followed, and on entering the town the Viceroy took a long *détour*, and arrived at the Abdin Palace by a side door. I jumped out of my carriage, and urged him on no account to remain in the palace, but to come into the square. He agreed at once, and we went together, followed at a considerable distance by four or five of his native officers, Stone Pasha, and one or two other European officers. The square was entirely occupied by soldiers drawn up round it, and keeping all spectators at a distance. The Viceroy advanced firmly into the square towards a little group of officers and men (some mounted) in the centre. I said to him, 'When Arábi Bey presents himself, tell him to give you his sword, and to give them the order to disperse. Then go the round of the square and address each regiment separately, and give them the order to disperse.' Arábi Bey approached on horseback; the Viceroy called out to him to dismount. He did so, and came forward on foot, with several others and a guard with fixed bayonets, and saluted. I said to the Viceroy, 'Now is your moment.' He replied, 'We are between four fires.' I said, 'Have courage.' He took counsel of a native officer on his left, and repeated to me: 'What can I do? We are between four fires. We shall be killed.' He then told Arábi Bey to sheathe his sword. The order was obeyed; and he then asked Arábi Bey what

---

2. An American officer in the Egyptian army.
3. Sir Charles Cookson was acting as Consul-General during the temporary absence of Sir Edward Malet.

all this meant; Arábi Bey replied by enumerating three points, adding that the army had come there on the part of the Egyptian people to enforce them, and would not retire till they were conceded. The Viceroy turned to me and said, 'You hear what he says.' I replied that it was not fitting for the Viceroy to discuss questions of this kind with Colonels, and suggested to him to retire into the Palace of Abdin, leaving me to speak to the Colonels. He did so, and I remained for about an hour till the arrival of Sir Charles Cookson, explaining to them the gravity of the situation for themselves, and urging them to retire the troops while there was yet time."

The three points to which Sir Auckland Colvin alluded as constituting the demands of Arábi were: (1) that all the Ministers should be dismissed; (2) that a Parliament should be convoked; and (3), that the strength of the army should be raised to 18,000 men.

Sir Charles Cookson then entered into negotiations with the mutineers. The Khedive consented to dismiss his Ministers on the understanding that the other points demanded by the officers should be left in suspense until reference could be made to the Porte. Arábi agreed to these terms. The question then arose of who should be President of the Council. One or two names were put forward by the Khedive, and rejected by Arábi and his followers. The Khedive then intimated that he would be prepared to nominate Chérif Pasha. This announcement "was received with loud and universal shouts of 'Long live the Khedive!' . . . Arábi Bey then asked to be allowed to see the Khedive and make his submission. This favour was granted to him and the other Colonels, and then the troops were drawn off in perfect quietness to their respective barracks."

Some difficulty was encountered in inducing Chérif Pasha to accept office. He objected to becoming Prime Minister as the nominee of a mutinous army. Sir Charles Cookson, M. Sienkiewicz (the French Consul-General), and Sir Auckland Colvin endeavoured to overcome this reluctance, which was in no degree feigned. They so far succeeded that Chérif Pasha consented to enter into negotiations with the leaders of the military movement. At first, there appeared but little prospect of an arrangement. Chérif Pasha asked that, on condition of his undertaking the government, and guaranteeing the personal safety of the leaders of the movement, the mutinous regiments should withdraw to the posts assigned to them. The more violent amongst the officers had, however, got the upper hand. They did not fear Turkish intervention, the probability of which now began to be discussed. Indeed, there was some reason to suppose that the mutineers had received encouragment from Constantinople. Chérif Pasha's terms were rejected, and he declared that he would not undertake to form a Ministry.

Under these circumstances, the Khedive intimated that he was "ready to yield everything in order to save public security." Suddenly, however, on September 13, things took a turn for the better. The relief came from an unexpected quarter. Arábi had summoned to Cairo the members of the Chamber of Notables. When they arrived, "they proved more capable of appreciating the true situation than their military allies. Informed of the negotiations going on with Chérif Pasha, they in a body went to him, and entreated him to agree to form a Ministry, offering him their personal guarantee that, if he consented, the army should engage to absolute submission to his orders. The military leaders seem to have been more struck by this conduct than by all the previous representations made to them." Seeing that public opinion was not altogether with them, Arábi and his followers modified their tone. They tendered their "absolute submission to the authority of Chérif Pasha as the Khedive's Minister." They only made two conditions. One was that Mahmoud Pasha Sami should be reinstated in office. The second was that the Military Law recommended by the Commission, which had been recently sitting, should be put into immediate execution. "To both of these demands," Sir Charles Cookson wrote, "Chérif Pasha, most reluctantly, was compelled to yield, but as to the latter, he expressly reserved to himself the liberty of omitting the most important article, which proposed to raise the army to 18,000 men."

This incident was significant. It showed that there were two parties in opposition to the Khedive. These were, first, a mutinous army half-mad with fear of punishment, and secondly, a party, the offspring of Ismail Pasha's dalliance with constitutionalism, who had some vague national aspirations, and who, as representing the civil elements of society, shunned the idea of absolute military government. Under statesmanlike guidance, this tendency to separation between the two parties might perhaps have been turned to account. The main thing was to prevent amalgamation. If the national party were once made to believe that the only hope of realising its aspirations lay in seeking the aid of the soldiers, not only would the authority of the Khedive disappear altogether, but all hope of establishing a régime under which the army would be subordinate to the civil Government would have to be abandoned.

One of the many political apophthegms attributed to Prince Bismarck is the following: "La politique est l'art de s'accommoder aux circonstances et de tirer parti de tout, même de ce qui déplaît." It would have been wise for the Khedive at this moment to have acted on the principle set forth in this maxim. The military party and the national party were alike distasteful to him. The interests both of his dynasty and of his country pointed, however, to the necessity of conciliating the latter in order to keep in check the former of these two parties. Unfortunately, the Khedive did not possess sufficient political insight to grasp whatever opportunities the situation offered to him.

The new Ministry was nominated on September 14. Chérif Pasha was assured of the support of the British and French Governments. At his own request, he was further assured that "in case the army should show itself submissive and obedient, the Governments of England and France would interpose their good offices with the Sublime Porte in order to avert from Egypt an occupation by an Ottoman army." The usual exchange of letters took place between the Khedive and his Prime Minister setting forth the principles which were to guide the new Ministry. These letters contained only one remark which is noteworthy. Chérif Pasha was no friend to European interference in Egypt. But he had learnt that it might be productive of some good. His letter to the Khedive, therefore, contained the following passage: "The institution of the Control, at first criticised from different points of view, has greatly assisted towards the re-establishment of the finances, at the same time that it has been a real support for the Government of Your Highness. In this twofold capacity, it is important to maintain it as instituted by the Decree of November 15, 1879." To this, the Khedive replied as follows: "A perfect understanding between the Control and my Government is necessary; it must be maintained and strengthened."

The new Ministry, therefore, began work with such props from without as were possible under the circumstances. But for all that, it was clear that the real masters of the situation were the leaders of the mutinous army. Arábi had already treated on equal terms with the representatives of the Powers. He had issued a Circular on September 9 signed "Colonel Ahmed Arábi, representing the Egyptian army," in which he assured the Consuls-General that he and those acting in concert with him "would continue to protect the interests of all the subjects of friendly Powers." There could be no mistaking this language. It was that of a ruler who disposed of power to assert his will, and who intended to use his power with that object.

Yet, whilst Arábi was heading a mutiny against his Sovereign, and employing language which could only lawfully proceed from the Khedive or from one of his Ministers, there can be little doubt that his conduct was mainly guided by fear of the Khedive's resentment and vengeance. Sir Charles Cookson thought that the officers had "exclusively regarded their own safety and interest throughout the agitation." Sir Edward Malet entertained a similar opinion. Every word and deed of the mutineers showed, indeed, that fear was the predominating influence at work amongst them. In the Circular which Arábi addressed to the representatives of the Powers, he said: "Since the

Khedive's return to Cairo, intrigues have been on the increase, while we have been threatened both openly and secretly; and they have culminated in an attempt to create disunion among the military, in order to facilitate the object in view, namely, to destroy and avenge themselves upon us. In this state of things, we consider it our duty to protect our lives and interests." Sir Edward Malet was informed by "a Musulman gentleman, who had had long and frequent conversations" with Arábi, that the latter thought that action had become absolutely necessary in self-defence. At a later period, Arábi said that he believed that a party of Circassians agreed together to kill him, as well as every native Egyptian holding a high appointment, on October 1, 1881. "We heard," he said, "that three iron boxes had been prepared into which to put us, so that we might be dropped into the Nile."[4] Men in this frame of mind would probably not, at an early stage of the proceedings, have been uncontrollable. But, in order to control them, one condition was essential. They might have been treated with severity, or, if that was impossible or undesirable, with leniency, but in either case it was essential that they should be treated in a manner which would leave no doubt in their minds as to the good faith of their rulers. Moreover, the practices which until a recent period had existed in Egypt, notably the fate of Ismail Pasha's Finance Minister,[5] the naturally suspicious character of Orientals, and their belief, which is often well founded, that some intrigue lies at the bottom of every action of the Government, should have rendered it clear to the Khedive that the slightest whisper imputing bad faith would be fatal to his reputation for loyalty. The utmost caution was, in fact, necessary. A bold, straightforward conduct, and a stern repression of all palace intrigues, might perhaps have quieted the fears of the officers. Riaz Pasha, although he may not have grasped the whole situation, had sufficiently statesmanlike instincts to appreciate the true nature of the danger. He warned the Khedive frequently not to do or say anything which could give rise to the least suspicion as to his intentions. It is improbable that the Khedive had any deliberate plan for wreaking vengeance on the mutineers. It is certain that his humane nature would have revolted at any idea of assassination, such as was attributed to him. At the same time, if he had considered himself sufficiently powerful to act, he would not improbably have made his displeasure felt in one form or another, in spite of the pardon which had been reluctantly wrung from him. Like Macbeth, he would not play false, but yet would wrongly win. It would be in harmony with the inconsistency even of an honest Oriental to pardon fully, and at the same time

---

4. "Instructions to my Counsel," *Nineteenth Century*, December 1882.
5. *Vide ante*, p. 26.

to make a mental reserve, which would enable him at some future time to act as though the pardon had only been partial. He allowed his surroundings, which almost always exercise a baneful influence in an Oriental court, to intrigue and to talk in a manner which was calculated to excite the fears and suspicions of the mutineers. Arábi, in his Circular to the Consuls-General, made special allusion to the intrigues of Yousuf Pasha Kemal, the Khedive's agent, and Ibrahim Aga, the Khedive's Tutunji (Pipe-bearer), who, he said, "had been sowing discord." National proclivities and foreign intrigue may, therefore, have had something to do with the mutiny of September 9, but there can be little doubt that the main cause was truly stated by Arábi. It was fear.

This was the third mutiny of the Egyptian army. On each occasion, the mutineers gained confidence in their strength. On each occasion, the submission of the Government was more complete than previously. The first mutiny was quelled by the sacrifice of an unpopular Minister (Nubar Pasha), whom the ruling Khedive did not wish to maintain in office. On the second occasion, the War Minister (Osman Pasha Rifki) was offered up to appease the mutineers. On the third occasion, the mutineers dictated their own terms at the point of the bayonet; they did not rest satisfied without a complete change of Ministry. "Things bad begun make strong themselves by ill." No remnant of military discipline was now left. The khedive was shorn of all real authority. The smallest incident would suffice to show that the Ministers only held office on sufferance from the mutineers. No long time was to elapse before such an incident occurred.

SOURCE: Chapter 11 in *Modern Egypt*, vol. 1 (London: Macmillan, 1908).

Arabi's Appeal to Gladstone

To the Right Hon. W. E. Gladstone, M.P.
Alexandria, July 2, 1882

Sir,—Our Prophet in his Koran has commanded us not to seek war nor to begin it. He had commanded us also, if war be waged against us, to resist, and under penalty of being ourselves as unbelievers to follow those who have assailed us with every weapon and without pity.

Hence England may rest assured that the first gun she fires on Egypt will absolve the Egyptians from all treaties, contracts, and conventions, that the control and debt will cease, that the property of Europeans will be confiscated, that the canals will be destroyed, the communications cut, and that use will be made of the religious zeal of Mahomedans to preach a holy war in Syria, in Arabia, and in India. Egypt is held by Mahomedans as the key of Mecca and Medina, and all are bound by their religious law to defend these holy places and the ways leading to them. Sermons on this subject have already been preached in the mosques of Damascus, and an agreement has been come to with the religious leaders of every land throughout the (Mahomedan) world. I repeat it again and again that the first blow struck at Egypt by England or her allies will cause blood to flow through the breadth of Asia and of Africa, the responsibility of which will be on the head of England.

The English Government has allowed itself to be deceived by its agents, who have cost their country its prestige in Egypt. England will be still worse advised if she attempts to regain what she has lost by the brute force of guns and bayonets.

On the other hand there are still more humane and friendly means to this end. Egypt is ready still, nay desirous, to come to terms with England, to be fast friends with her, to protect her interests and keep her road to India, to be her ally. But she must keep within the limits of her jurisdiction. If, however, she prefer to remain deceived and to boast and threaten us with her fleets and her Indian troops, it is hers to make the choice. Only let her not underrate, as she has done, the patriotism of the Egyptian people. Her representatives have not informed her of the change which has been wrought among us since the days of Ismail's tyranny. Nations in our modern age make sudden and gigantic strides in the path of progress.

England, in fine, may rest assured that we are determined to fight, to die martyrs for our country—as has been enjoined on us by our Prophet—or else to conquer and so live independently and happy. Happiness in either case is promised to us, and when a people is imbued with this belief their courage knows no bounds.

Ahmed Arabi

SOURCE: Published in the *London Times*, which wrote, "The following letter was addressed by Arabi Pasha to Mr Gladstone a few days before the bombardment of Alexandria, but did not reach his hands until after that event."

"Rioters at Alexandria." In *London Illustrated News* 81, no. 2252 (Saturday, 1 July 1882): 1.

"The Crisis in Egypt." In *London Illustrated News* 81, no. 2254 (Saturday, 15 July 1882): 1.

The Bombardment of Alexandria (1882)

E. M. FORSTER

[E. M. Forster (1879–1970), distinguished novelist and critic, wrote in the introduction to the third edition of *Alexandria* that it "was written by me during the First World War when I was stationed in Alexandria as a result of volunteering for the Red Cross."]

Thus the city developes quietly under Mohammed Ali and his successors—one of whom, Said Pasha, is buried here. Attention was rather diverted from her by the cutting of the Suez Canal, and it is not until 1882 that anything of note occurs. She is in this year connected with the rebellion of Arabi, the founder of the Egyptian Nationalist Party. Arabi, then Minister of War, was endeavouring to dominate the Khedive Tewfik, and to secure Egypt for the Egyptians. Alexandria, which had held a foreign element ever since its foundation, was therefore his natural foe, and it was here that he opened the campaign against Europe that ended in his failure at Tel-el-Kebir. The details—like Arabi's motives—are complicated. But four stages may be observed.

(1). RIOT OF JUNE 11TH.

This began at about 1.0 p.m. in the Rue des Soeurs; it is said that two donkey boys, one Arab and one Maltese, had a fight in a café, and that others joined in. The rioters moved down toward the Square, and at some cross roads near the Laban Caracol the British Consul was nearly killed. They were joined in the Square by two other mobs, one from the Attarine Quarter and one from Ras-el-Tin. British and other warships were in the harbour, but took no action, and the Egyptian troops in the city refused to intervene without orders from Arabi, who was in Cairo. At last a telegram was sent to him. He responded and the disorder ceased. There is no reason to suppose that he planned the riot. But naturally enough he used it to increase his prestige. He had shown the foreign communities, and particularly the British, that he alone could give them protection. In the evening he came down in triumph from Cairo. About 150 Europeans are thought to have been killed that day, but we have no reliable statistics.

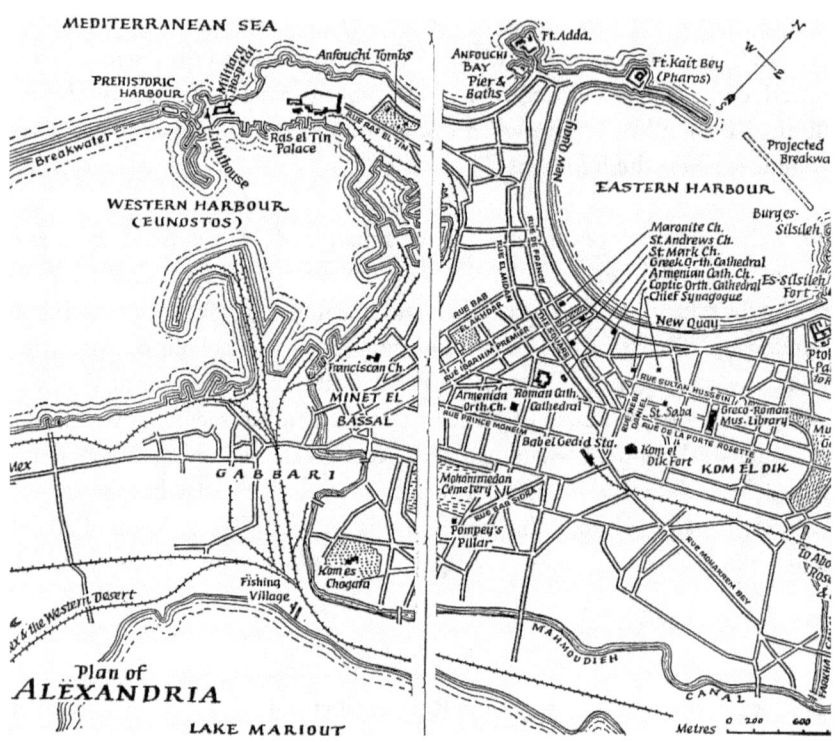

In E. M. Forster, *Alexandria: A History and a Guide*
(Garden City, N.J.: Anchor Books, 1961).

(II). BOMBARDMENT OF JULY 11TH.

British men-of-war under Admiral Seymour had been in the harbour during the riot, but it was a month before they took action. In the first place the British residents had to be removed, in the second the fleet required reinforcing, in the third orders were awaited from home. As soon as Seymour was ready he picked a quarrel with Arabi and declared he should bombard the city if any more guns were mounted in the forts. Since Arabi would not agree he opened fire at 7.0 a.m. July 11th. There were eight iron-clads—six of them the most powerful in our navy. They were thus distributed:—*Monarch, Invincible* and *Penelope* close inshore off Mex; *Alexandria, Sultan* and *Superb* off Ras-el-Tin; while the two others the *Temeraire* and *Inflexible* were in a central position outside the harbour reef, half way between Ras-el-Tin and Marabout; and off Marabout were some gun-boats, under Lord Charles Beresford. The bombardment succeeded, though Arabi's gunners in the forts fought bravely. In the evening the *Superb* blew up the powder magazine in Fort Adda. Fort Kait Bey was also shattered and the minaret of its 15th cent. Mosque was seen "melting away like ice in the sun." The town, on the other hand, was scarcely damaged, as our gunners were careful in their aim. Arabi and his force evacuated it in the evening, marching out by the Rue Rosette to take up a position some miles further east, on the banks of the Mahmoudieh Canal.

(III). RIOT OF JULY 12TH.

Unfortunately Admiral Seymour, after his success, never landed a force to keep order, and the result was a riot far more disastrous than that of June. With the withdrawal of Arabi's troops the native population lost self-control. The Khedive had now broken with Arabi, but during the bombardment he had moved from Ras-el-Tin Palace to Ramleh and his authority was negligible. Pillaging went on all day on the 12th, and by the evening the city had been set on fire. The damage was material rather than artistic, the one valuable object in the Square, the statue of Mohammed Ali, fortunately escaping. Rues Chérif and Tewfik Pacha—indeed all the roads leading out of the Square—were destroyed, and nearly every street in the European quarter was impassable through fallen and falling houses. Empty jewel cases and broken clocks lay on the pavements. Every shop was looted, and by the time Admiral Seymour did land it was impossible for his middies to buy any jam; one of them has recorded this misfortune, adding that in other ways Alexandria, then in flames, was "well enough." Meanwhile the Khedive had returned to his Palace, and order was slowly restored. It is not known how many lives were lost in this avoidable disaster.

(IV). MILITARY OPERATIONS.

A large British force was despatched under Lord Wolseley to the Suez Canal—the force that finally defeated Arabi at Tel-el-Kebir. But, until it reached Egypt, Alexandria remained in danger, for Arabi might attack from his camp at Kafr-el-Dawar. So the city had to be defended on the east. In the middle of July General Alison arrived with a few troops, including artillery, and occupied the barracks at Mustapha Pacha, the hill of Abou-el-Nawatir, and the water works down by the canal. He could thus watch Arabi's movements. And he had a second strongly fortified position at the gates of the Antoniadis Gardens, in case he was attacked from the south. Here he was able to hold on and to harry the enemy's outposts until pressure was relieved. His losses were slight; the regiments involved are commemorated by tablets in the English church. Next month Wolseley arrived, and having inspected the position re-embarked his troops and pretended that he was going to land at Aboukir. Arabi was deceived and prepared resistance there. Wolseley steamed past him, and landed at Port Said instead. Arabi then had to break up his camp, and the danger for Alexandria was over.

SOURCE: In *Alexandria: A History and a Guide,* 3d ed. (Woodstock, N.Y.: Overlook Press, 1961).

The Arabi Trial
WILFRED SCAWEN BLUNT

[What Benjamin Disraeli called "peace with honour," Wilfred Scawen Blunt referred to as "peace with plunder." Blunt (1840–1922) was a close friend and defender of Ahmed Arabi who he had met during his first visit to Egypt. Blunt's interest in Egyptian affairs continued throughout his life, and he maintained a residence in Egypt as well as an attachment to Arabian horses and poetry. His wife, Anne Blunt, shared his commitments. He was also a committed critic in print and practice of Britain's imperial policies generally, and he eventually became a member of Parliament. The four volumes of his diaries describe his activism relating to Egypt, India, the Sudan, and Ireland.]

While these great events were happening on the Nile, I at my home at Crabbet spent the summer sadly enough. My sympathies were, of course, still all with the Egyptians, but I was cut off from every means of communication with them, and the war fever was running too strongly during the first weeks of the fighting for further words of mine to be of any avail. Publicly I held my peace. All that I could do was to prepare an "Apologia" of the National movement and of my own connection with it—for this was now being virulently attacked in the press[1]—and wait the issue of the campaign.

Nevertheless, though in dire disgrace with the Government, I did not wholly lose touch with Downing Street. I saw Hamilton once or twice, and submitted proofs of my "Apologia" to him and Mr. Gladstone before it was published, and this was counted to me by them for righteousness. It appeared in the September number of "The Nineteenth Century Review," and at a favourable moment when the first sparkle of military glory had faded, and reasonable people were beginning to ask themselves what after all we were fighting in Egypt about. Written from the heart even more than from the head, my pleading had a success far beyond expectation and, taken in connection with an anti-war tour embarked on in the provinces by Sir Wilfrid Lawson, Mr. Seymour Keay and a few other genuine Radicals, touched at last what was called the "Nonconformist" conscience of the country and turned the tide of opinion distinctly in my favour. This encouraged me. About the same time, too, a letter reached me from General Gordon, dated "Cape Town, the 3rd of August," in which he avowed his sympathy with the cause I had been advocating, and which elated me not a little. It was as follows:

---

1. One of the matters principally laid to my charge was due to a Reuter's telegram announcing that my country house near Cairo had been broken open by Arabi's order, and that seventeen cases of firearms had been found in it. The foundation of this story was as follows: In 1881, when I was on my way, as I intended, to Arabia, I had brought with me some Winchester rifles and revolvers for the journey, amounting to seventeen rifles in all, as well as a small brass cannon of the kind used on yachts, as a present, if I should find a way to send it him, to Ibn-Rashid at Hail. These were still stored in my house, and some one having announced the fact to the provincial authorities, they had taken possession of them, and removed them to the Cairo citadel. In the confusion after the war I could gain no intelligence of what had become of my property except the story which was afloat in London that my brass cannon had been taken there as a trophy of war, and was forming an ornament at the Admiralty. It was not till some ten years afterwards that having lunched one day with my cousin, Colonel Wyndham, at the citadel at Cairo, he took me afterwards to visit the arsenal, where I soon recognized my cannon and other property intact. As the box containing the rifles had my name on it, no difficulty was made in restoring all to me.

"Cape Town, 3, 8, 82.
"My Dear Mr. Blunt,

"You say in 'Times' you are going to publish an account of what passed between you and the Government. Kindly let me have a copy addressed as enclosed card. I have written a MS. bringing things down from Cave's mission to the taking of office by Cherif, it is called 'Israel in Egypt,' and shall follow it with a sequel, 'The Exodus.' I do not know whether I shall print it, for it is not right to rejoice over one's enemies. I mean *official* enemies. What a fearful mess Malet and Colvin have made, and one cannot help remarking the *finale* of all Dilke's, Colvin's, and Malet's secretiveness. Dilke, especially, in the House evaded every query on the plea that British interests would suffer. Poor thing. I firmly believe he knows no more of his policy than the Foreign Office porter did; he had none. Could things have ended worse if he had said everything? I think not. No more Control—no more employés drawing £373,000 a year—no more influence of Consuls-General, a nation hating us—no more Tewfik—no more interest—a bombarded town, Alexandria—these are the results of the grand secret diplomacy. Colvin will go off to India, Malet to China—we shall know no more of them. All this because Controllers and Consuls-General would not let Notables see the Budget when Cherif was in office. As for Arabi, whatever may become of him individually, he will live for centuries in the people; they will never be 'your obedient servants' again.

"Believe me, yours sincerely,
"C. G. Gordon."

The value to me of this letter I saw at once was great, for, though out of favour with the Foreign Office, Gordon's name was one to conjure with in the popular mind, and especially with that "Non-conformist conscience" which, as I have said, was beginning now to support me, and consequently I knew with Gladstone; and it was on the text of it that I began a fresh correspondence with Hamilton. Mr. Gladstone had stated in Parliament that I was the "one unfortunate exception," among Englishmen who knew Egypt, to the general approval of the war; and I sent him, through Hamilton, a copy of Gordon's letter, and at the same time invited his attention to accounts which had begun to appear in the newspapers of certain atrocities of vengeance which had been indulged in by Tewfik and his new Circassian Ministers at Alexandria on Nationalist prisoners made during the war. Torture had, it was related, been inflicted on Mahmud Fehmi, the engineer General, and the thumb-screw and kurbash were being used freely. I asked whether such was the state of things Mr. Gladstone had sent troops to Egypt to re-establish.

The letter brought a prompt and interesting answer, and one which proved of value to me a few days later when it came to my pleading that Arabi should not be done to death by the Khedive without fair trial.

"10, Downing Street, Whitehall,
"*September 8th*, 1882.
"I need hardly say that Mr. Gladstone has been much exercised in his mind at the rumours about these 'atrocities.' I can call them by no other name. Immediate instructions were sent out to inquire into the truth of them, and to remonstrate strongly if they were confirmed. I am glad to say that, as far as our information at present goes, the statements appear to be unfounded. The strictest orders have been given for the humane treatment of the prisoners. There seems to be some doubt as to whether thumb-screwing was not inflicted on a spy in one case; and searching inquiries are to be instituted with peremptory demands of explanation and guarantees against recurrence. You may be quite sure that Mr. Gladstone will denounce 'Egyptian atrocities' as strongly as 'Bulgarian atrocities.'

"I cannot help thinking that your and Chinese Gordon's opinion of Arabi would be somewhat modified if you had seen some of the documents I have read.

"Some months ago (this, please, is quite private) certain inquiries were made about Chinese Gordon. He had suggestions to make about Ireland, and the result of these inquiries were, to the best of my recollection, that he was not clothed in the rightest of minds."

The last paragraph is historically curious. The proof Gordon had given Mr. Gladstone's Government of his not being clothed in his right mind was that he had written, during a tour in western Ireland, to a member of the Government, Lord Northbrook, recommending a scheme of Land Purchase and, if I remember rightly, Home Rule as a cure for Irish evils.

I was thus once more in a position of semi-friendly intercourse with Downing Street and of some considerable influence in the country when the crowning glory of the war, the news of the great victory of Tel-el-Kebir, reached England, and soon after it of Arabi's being a prisoner in Drury Lowe's hands at Cairo. The completeness of the military success for the moment turned all English heads, and it was fortunate for me that I had had my say a fortnight before it came, for otherwise I should have been unable to make my voice heard, either with the public or at Downing Street, in the general shriek of triumph. It had the immediate result of confirming the Government in all its most violent views, and of once more turning

Mr. Gladstone's heart, which had been veering back a little to the Nationalists, to the hardness of a nether millstone. The danger now was that in order to justify to his own conscience the immense slaughter of half-armed peasants that had been made at Tel-el-Kebir, he would indulge in some conspicuous act of vengeance on Arabi, as the scapegoat of his own errors. His only excuse for all this military brutality was the fiction that he was dealing with a military desperado, a man outlawed by his crimes, and, as such, unentitled to any consideration either as a patriot or even the recognized General of a civilized army. I have reason to know that if Arabi had been captured on the field at Tel-el-Kebir, it was Wolseley's intention to give him the short benefit of a drum-head court martial, which means shooting on the spot, and that it was only the intervention of Sir John Adye, a General much older in years and in length of service than Wolseley, that prevented it later—Adye having represented to Wolseley the disgrace there would be to the British army if the regular commander of an armed force, whom it had needed 30,000 troops to subdue, should not receive the honourable treatment universally accorded to prisoners of war. At home, too, I equally know that Bright, in indignant protest, gave his mind on the same point personally to Gladstone. It must not, however, at all be supposed that anything but the overwhelming pressure of public opinion brought to bear, as I will presently describe, frustrated the determination of our Government, one way or other, to make Arabi pay forfeit for their own political crime with his life. Mr. Gladstone was as much resolved on this as was Lord Granville, or any of the Whig lords in his Cabinet. To explain how their hands were forced in the direction of humanity I must go into detail.

The capitulation of Cairo and Arabi's surrender to Drury Lowe were announced in the "Times" of the 16th, and with it a telegram from its Alexandria correspondent, Moberley Bell, who represented the Anglo-Khedivial official view, demanding "exemplary punishment" on eleven of the National leaders, whom he named, including Arabi. I knew that this could only mean mischief resolved on of the gravest kind, and I consequently telegraphed at once to Button, asking him what the position in official circles was. His first answer was reassuring. "I can't think there is the least danger of their shooting anybody. You should, however, take immediate steps to appeal for merciful treatment." Two hours later, however, a second message from him came. "I don't like official tone with regard to your friends. Write me privately such a letter as I can show to my chief." By his "chief" he, of course, meant Chenery, the "Times" editor, with whom, as I have said, he was on very intimate terms. I consequently wrote at once to Hamilton:

"I cannot think there should be any danger of death for the prisoners taken at Cairo, but should there be, I trust you will let me know in time, as I have certain suggestions to make regarding the extreme difficulty of obtaining them a fair trial just now, and other matters."

To this it is significant that I received no answer for two days, and then an off-hand one, to the effect that Hamilton was about to leave London for the country, "and so would be a bad person to depend upon for any intimation such as I wished." But I was not thus to be put off, and passing beyond Hamilton, I wrote once more direct to Mr. Gladstone. I did this after consultation with Button and with Broadley, whom I met at his house on the afternoon of the 19th. We decided that the latter would be the man for our purpose, and that the best chance of saving Arabi's and the other prisoners' lives would be for me to take Broadley out with me at once and produce him as their legal defender. Button, who knew the ins and outs of most affairs, was certain there was no time to lose, and we half engaged Broadley at a fee of £300, afterwards increased to £800 with refreshers. In the meantime Button rendered the cause a great service in the immediate crisis by managing that it should be announced next morning in the "Times" that Arabi and his companions were not to be executed without the consent of the English Government, and that they were to be defended by efficient counsel. Of course, we had not a shadow of authority to go upon for this statement, but the "Times" having announced it made it very difficult, later, for the Government to go back upon a humane decision so publicly attributed to them.

My letter to Mr. Gladstone, sent in the same evening, was as follows:

"Sept. 19, 1882.
"My Dear Sir,
"Now that the military resistance of the Egyptians is at an end, and Arabi and their chief leaders have surrendered to Her Majesty's forces, I venture once more to address you in the interests of justice no less than of those whom the fortune of war has thus suddenly thrown into your hands. It would seem to be contemplated that a Court Martial should assemble shortly to try and judge the military leaders for rebellion, and, in the case of some of these, and of civilians, a civil tribunal to inquire into their alleged connection with certain violent proceedings. If this should be the truth, I would earnestly beg your attention to certain circumstances of the case which seem to demand careful consideration.

"1. The members of the proposed Court Martial, if Egyptians and appointed by the Khedive, can hardly be free agents or uninfluenced in their feelings towards the prisoners. They would be chosen from among the few officers who espoused the Khedive's cause, and would of necessity be partisans.

"2. Even were this not the case, native false witness is so common in Egypt, and the falsification of Arabic documents so easy, that little reliance could be placed upon the testimony adduced. The latter would need to be submitted to experts before being accepted with any certainty.

"3. Native evidence, if favourable to the prisoners, will be given under fear. There will be a strong inducement to withhold it, and as strong an inducement in the desire of Court favour to offer evidence unfavourable. The experts charged with examining documents will, if natives, be equally subject to these influences.

"4. The evidence of Europeans settled in Egypt, though given without fear of consequences, may be expected to be strongly coloured by resentment. These Europeans are, it would seem, themselves in some measure parties to the suit. They will many of them have lost property or have been injured in their trade during the late troubles or have personal insults to avenge. The vindictive tone of the English in Egypt is every day apparent in their letters published by the English Press.

"5. It will be insufficient, if full justice for the prisoners is to be secured, that the ordinary form of Her Majesty's representative being present through a dragoman or otherwise, at the proceedings, should be the only one observed. Political feeling has probably run too high at Cairo during the last six months for quite impartial observation.

"6. Should English officers, as it may be hoped will be the case, be added to the native members of the Court Martial, they will be ignorant or nearly ignorant of the language spoken by the prisoners, and will be unable themselves to examine the documents or cross-examine the witnesses. They will necessarily be in the hands of their interpreters, who, if unchecked, may alter or distort the words used to the detriment of the prisoners. Nearly all the dragomans of the Consulates are Levantine Christians violently hostile to the Mussulman Arabs, while it may safely be affirmed that there are no Englishmen in Egypt both fully competent and quite unbiassed who could be secured in this capacity. Arabic is a language little known among our officials, and their connection with the late troubles is too recent to have left them politically calm.

"It would seem, therefore, that unless special steps are taken there is grave danger of a miscarriage of justice in the trial.

"To remedy this evil as far as possible I have decided, at my own charge and that of some of my friends, to secure the services of a competent English counsel for the principal prisoners, and to proceed with him to Cairo to collect evidence for the defence. I shall also take with me the Rev. Mr. Sabunji as interpreter, and watch the proceedings on behalf of the prisoners. My knowledge of Arabic is too imperfect for me to act alone, but Mr. Sabunji is a friend of the chief prisoners, and is eminently capable of speaking for them. He knows English, French, Turkish, and Italian well, and is probably the first Arabic scholar now living. The prisoners have full confidence in him, and I believe also that they have full confidence in me. Thus alone, perhaps, they will obtain, what I submit they are entitled to, a full, a fair, and—to some extent—even a friendly hearing.

"In conclusion, it may not be unnecessary that I should promise you that while thus engaged I, and those with me, would scrupulously avoid all interference with contemporary politics. I shall esteem it a favour if I can be informed at as early a date as possible what will be the exact nature of the trial and what the principal charges made. I hope, too, that every facility will be afforded me and those with me in Egypt to prosecute our task, and I cannot doubt that your personal sense of justice will approve it.

"I am, &c.,
"Wilfrid Scawen Blunt."

This letter, which I knew it would be difficult for Mr. Gladstone to answer with a refusal, especially after his recent assurances about "Egyptian atrocities" and "Bulgarian atrocities," I sent at once to Downing Street, having previously called there and seen Hamilton, to whom I explained my plan. He did not, however, give me much encouragement, as his answer to a further note I sent him next morning proves. My note was that I was writing to Arabi, and to ask him how the letter should be sent, and expressing a hope to have an answer from his Chief before Friday, the next mail day. Hamilton's answer suggests procrastination:

"Your letter, I am sorry to say, just missed the bag last night. It reached me about three minutes too late; but in any case I don't think you must count on a very immediate reply. Mr. Gladstone is moving about, and moreover will most likely have to consult some one before he gives an answer. I am absolutely ignorant myself as to questions which your intended proceedings may raise; and therefore I have no business to hazard an opinion. But is it not open to doubt whether according to international law or prescription a man can be defended by foreign counsel? I am equally ignorant about the delivery of letters to prisoners of war; but I should presume that no communication could reach Arabi except through and with the permission of the Khedive and our Commander-in-Chief. In any case Malet will probably be your best means of communication."

According to this suggestion I wrote a letter to Arabi telling him of our plans of legal defence and enclosed it, with a draft of the letter, to Malet, and for more precaution sent both by hand to the Foreign Office, to be forwarded, with a note to Lord Tenterden commending it to his care. By a singular accident, however, both note and letter were returned to me with the message that His Lordship had died suddenly that morning, and I was obliged, as the mail was starting, to send it by the same hand, Button's servant Mitchell, to Walmer Castle where Lord Granville was, and it was only just in time. In the sequel it will be seen that the packet, though despatched to Cairo, was not delivered farther than into Malet's hands and then with the instruction that my letter to Arabi should be returned to me. Malet's official letter to me performing this duty is sufficient evidence, if any were needed, to show how far the Government was from co-operating at all with me in my design of getting the prisoners a fair trial. It is very formal and unmistakable:

"Cairo, *Oct.* 4, 1882.
"Sir,
"Acting under instructions from Her Majesty's Principal Secretary of State I return you herewith the letter for Arabi Pasha which you sent to me to be forwarded in your letter of the 22nd ultimo.

"I am, etc.,
"Edward B. Malet."

My letter to Arabi had been as follows:

"To My Honourable Friend H. E. Ahmed Pasha Arabi.
"May God preserve you in adversity as in good fortune.
"As a soldier and a patriot you will have understood the reasons which have prevented me from writing to you or sending you any message during the late unhappy war. Now, however, that the war is over, I hope to show you that our friendship has not been one of words only. It seems probable that you will be brought to trial, either for rebellion or on some other charge, the nature of which I yet hardly know, and that, unless you are strongly and skilfully defended, you run much risk of being precipitately condemned. I have therefore resolved, with your approval, to come to Cairo to help you with such evidence as I can give, and to bring with me an honest and learned English advocate to conduct your defence; and I have informed the English Govern-

ment of my intention. I beg you, therefore, without delay, to authorize me to act for you in this matter—for your formal assent is necessary; and it would be well if you would at once send me a telegram, and also a written letter, to authorize me to engage counsel in your name. Several liberal-minded Englishmen of high position will join me in defraying all the expenses of your case. You may also count upon me, personally, to see, during your captivity, that your family is not left in want. And so may God give you courage to endure the evil with the good.

"Wilfrid Scawen Blunt.
Sep. 22, 1882.
"Crabbet Park, Threebridges, Sussex."

Gladstone's answer, which came sooner than I expected, shows as little disposition to favour any idea of a fair trial as was that of the Foreign Office. It came in this form from Hamilton:

"10 Downing Street,
"*Sept.* 22, 1882.

"Mr. Gladstone has read the letter which you have addressed to him about Arabi's trial and your proposal to employ English counsel. All that he can say at the present moment is that he will bring your request under the notice of Lord Granville with whom he will consult, but that he cannot hold out any assurance that it will admit of being complied with."

This was very plain discouragement, though short of a direct refusal, and a few words added by Hamilton in a separate note were even more so: "I confess," he says, "that the more I think of it the greater is the number of difficulties which present themselves to my mind involved by such a proposal as yours. You will, I presume, hear further on the subject in a day or two but not from me, because I am off as you know."

I was left, therefore, still in doubt while the situation was daily becoming more critical. I dared not leave for Egypt without having received a definite answer, for I knew that at Cairo I should be powerless, if unarmed with any Government authority, and should probably not even be allowed to see the prisoners, while Broadley, tired of waiting, had gone back to Tunis. The Parliamentary session was over and every one was leaving London, the work of the Ministers being left to Under-Secretaries, and all business practically at a standstill. Meanwhile the question of Arabi's death was being keenly debated in the Press, and all the Jingo papers were clamouring for his execution, only here and there a feeble voice being raised in protest. Sir Wilfrid Lawson's Egyptian Committee, which had done such good work during the summer, had become silent, and from Lawson himself I received just then a most desponding letter: "I greatly doubt," he said, "whether they will allow Arabi to have anything like a *fair* trial. They know well enough that if they do it will end in their own condemnation, and 'Statesmen' are too crafty to be led into anything of that sort. At any rate you are right in *trying* to get fair play for him." All I could do was to stay on in London and still worry Downing Street for an answer and go on prompting the "Times." Therefore, after waiting five more days, I wrote again to Gladstone for a definite answer, the situation having become to the last degree critical at Cairo.

"*Sept.* 27, 1882.

"I wrote to you about ten days ago, stating my intention of engaging competent English counsel for Arabi Pasha and the other chief Egyptian prisoners in case they should be brought to trial, and of going myself to Cairo to procure evidence for them and watch the proceedings; and I begged you to give me early notice of any decision that might be come to regarding them.

"Your reply, through Mr. Hamilton, though giving me no assurance that English counsel would be allowed, seemed to suggest that my proposal would be considered; and I accordingly retained, provisionally, a barrister of eminence to act for the prisoners, should it be decided they should be thus defended. In view also of the legal necessity of gaining the prisoners' consent to the arrangement, I wrote, under cover to Sir Edward Malet, to Arabi Pasha, begging his authorization of my thus defending him, a letter to which I have as yet received no answer; nor have I received any further communication from yourself or from Lord Granville, to whom you informed me the matter would be referred.

"Now, however, I see it reported in the 'Times,' from Cairo, that a Military Court to try all offenders will be named no later than to-morrow, the paragraph being as follows:

"'The Military Court to try all offenders will be named to-morrow. The Khedive, Sherif, and Riaz all insist strongly on the absolute necessity of the capital punishment of the prime offenders, an opinion from which there are few, if any, dissentients. Sherif, whose gentleness of character is well known, said to me to-day: "It is not because I have a feeling of spite against any of them, but because it is absolutely necessary for the security of all who wish to live in the country. An English expedition is an excellent thing, but neither you nor we want it repeated every twelve months.'"[2]

"If this statement is true it would seem to confirm my worst suspicions as to

---

2. Telegram from Moberly Bell.

the foregone decision of the Khedive's advisers to take the prisoners' lives, and to justify all my arguments as to the improbability of their obtaining a fair trial. I therefore venture once more to urge a proper legal defence being granted them, such as I have suggested; and, in any case, to beg that you will relieve me of further doubt and, if it must be so, responsibility in the matter, by stating clearly whether English counsel will be allowed or refused in the case of Arabi Pasha and the chief prisoners, and whether proper facilities can be promised me in Egypt of communicating with the prisoners, and obtaining them competent interpretation.

"In the present state of official feeling at Cairo, it would be manifestly impossible for me, and those I have proposed to take with me, to work effectually for the prisoners without special diplomatic protection and even assistance.

"The urgency of the case must be my excuse with you for begging an immediate answer."

This last letter, however, never reached its destination. Gladstone had left London, and Horace Seymour, his secretary in charge of his correspondence, under cover to whom I had sent it, handed it on, whether by order or not I do not know, to the Foreign Office. "Mr. Gladstone," he explained, "is out of Town, so upon receipt of your letter yesterday I sent the further communication with you addressed to him straight to the Foreign Office. . . . I did so because he had placed your former letter in Lord Granville's hands, as Hamilton informed you, and also because I gathered from your note that this would meet your wish and save time. I understand that you will shortly receive an official reply from Lord Granville conveying to you the view of the Government on the matters to which you refer." Gladstone, therefore, had shifted his responsibility of saying "yes" or "no" on to Granville, and Granville being of course also out of town it was left for the Foreign Office clerks to deal with according to their ways. In spite of Seymour's promise that the view of the Government would shortly be conveyed to me, all the answer I received was one signed "Julian Pauncefote," stating that Mr. Gladstone had referred my two letters of the 19th and 27th to Lord Granville, and that Lord Granville regretted that he did not feel justified in entering into correspondence with me on the subject. It was thus that Gladstone, who had made up his mind that Arabi should be executed no less than had the Foreign Office, finally evaded the responsibility with which I had sought to bind him. I give the incident in detail as an illustration of official craft no less than as one of historical importance.

This "Pauncefote" reply decided us to waste no more time. In consultation with Button and with Lord De la Warr, who had come to London and had been working to get an answer from Lord Granville on independent lines, and who now offered to share with me the costs of the trial if we could secure one (a promise which I may note Lord De la Warr failed to redeem), it was agreed that we should telegraph at once to Broadley at Tunis to hold himself in readiness to proceed to Egypt, and that in the meanwhile we should send out to Cairo by that very night's mail the first briefless barrister we could lay our hands on as Broadley's junior till his arrival, and be on the spot to act as circumstances should suggest. Lord Granville had not agreed, nor had he at that time the least intention of agreeing, to the appearance of English counsel on behalf of the prisoners. But the "Times," as we have seen, had already committed the Government to a statement that Arabi was not to be executed without its consent, and that he was to be defended by efficient counsel; and this they had not had the face publicly to disavow. And now Button's influence was so great with Chenery that he was confident he could again force Lord Granville's hand in the matter of English counsel through the insistence of the "Times" on a fair trial.

All that day, therefore, we searched the Inns of Court, which were almost empty, it being holiday time, and it was only at the last moment that we were fortunate enough to light upon the man we wanted. This was Mark Napier, than whom we could not have found a better agent for our purpose, a resourceful and determined fighter with a good knowledge of the law and one difficult to rebuff. He had the immense advantage, too, through his being the son of a former British Ambassador, of understanding the common usages and ways of diplomacy as also of speaking French fluently, a very necessary qualification at Cairo. Having agreed to go he received our short instructions, which were that he was to go straight to Malet and say that he had arrived as Arabi's counsel, and insist on seeing his client. This was all he could hope at present to achieve, and if he could do this he would do much. If Malet should refuse he was to protest and take advantage of every opening given him to emphasize the refusal. Above all he was to keep us constantly informed by telegram of what was going on, while we on our side would fight the battle no less energetically at the Foreign Office and in the Press. Mark, as I have said, had the great advantage of having had a diplomatic training and so could not be imposed upon by the prestige and mystery with which diplomacy is invested for outsiders, and which gives it so much of its strength. We could not possibly have lit upon a better man. He started, as proposed, that night by the Brindisi mail, taking with him a cipher code and two or three letters of introduction. That, with a hand-bag, was all his luggage.

As to myself, De la Warr, who knew the temper of the Foreign Office and their personal rage against me, was very insistent that I should not go to Cairo and to this I assented. At Cairo I should have been only watched by spies, possibly arrested and sent home, while here I could continue far more effectively the Press campaign which, of course, could only really win our battle. Button that very night managed a new master-stroke in the "Times." De la Warr had succeeded in getting from Granville an assurance that all reasonable opportunities would be given by the Khedive for the defence. This assurance was of course illusory as far as a really fair trial went, as the only legal assistance procurable at the time by the prisoners at Cairo was that of the various Levantine lawyers who practised in the international Courts, and these could be no better depended upon than were the terror-stricken native lawyers themselves to serve their clients honestly by telling the whole truth, though a defence of this perfunctory kind would be sufficient to serve our Government's purpose of being able, without risk of a conflict with English popular opinion, to ratify the intended sentences of death. It was intended to have the trial in the Egyptian Court over in a couple of days, and having proved "rebellion," to proceed at once to execution; and English counsel would, no doubt, have been ruled out of the proceedings as a preposterous intervention of foreigners with no legal status in the country.

Granville's words to De la Warr had been no more than this: "I have no reason to doubt that the Khedive, with whom the proper authority rests, will give all reasonable opportunities for Arabi's defence which may not involve any extraordinary or unnecessary delay, and it devolves on the prisoners and their friends to take such measures as they may think fit on their own responsibility." This Button cleverly reproduced next morning in the "Times" as follows: "Lord Granville has written that every reasonable facility will be afforded the prisoners in Egypt and their friends for obtaining counsel for their defence. Mr. Broadley has therefore been telegraphed to go at once to Cairo." It is clear from Lord Granville's angry expostulation with Lord De la Warr (see Blue Book) how little intention he had of having his words thus interpreted. But, once published in the "Times," he could not with any decency back out of the position; and thus by a very simple device we again forced his hand and this time on a point which, in the event, gained for us the whole battle.[3]

Nevertheless, we were very nearly being tricked out of our fair trial after all,

---

3. I have been recently asked to explain that the true reason why the "Times" so strongly supported us in our attempt at this critical juncture to obtain for Arabi a fair trial was the Macchiavellian one of forcing the British Government to undertake responsibilities which would entail their assumption of full authority in Egypt. I heard, however, nothing of this at the time, and I prefer still to believe that it was a generous impulse more worthy of the "Times's" better tradition and of Chenery's excellent heart.

and a singularly ugly circumstance of the position in our eyes was the sudden reappearance, just then at Cairo, of Colvin, the man of all others most interested, after the Khedive, in preventing publicity. The Foreign Office object clearly now was to hurry on the trial, so as to get it over before Broadley should have time to arrive, for Tunis was and still is without any direct communication with Egypt, and it was probable that ten days would elapse before he could be there. Of Napier's sending they had no knowledge. Orders, therefore, were at once given as a first step that Arabi should be transferred from the safe keeping of the British Army to the ill-custody of the Khedivial police, where communication with the outside world would be effectually barred for him without the English Government incurring thereby any odium. This was done on the 4th of October, two days before Napier's arrival; and the trial was fixed for the 14th, while Broadley did not succeed in reaching Cairo till the 18th. Nothing but Napier's unexpected appearance at the English Agency disarranged the concerted plan.

A further step taken to hasten the end and make an English defence difficult was to select the French criminal military code for use in the court martial, a form which under an unscrupulous government gives great advantages to the prosecution. According to it a full interrogatory of prisoner and witnesses is permitted before these have seen counsel and they are thus easily intimidated, if they take a courageous attitude, from repeating their evidence at the trial. Thus both Arabi and others of his fellow prisoners were during the interval between the interrogatory and the day fixed for trial secretly visited by a number of the Khedive's eunuchs, who brutally assaulted and ill-treated them in their cells with a view of "breaking their spirit." Lastly, the Egyptian Government were permitted to declare that no counsel should be allowed to plead except in Arabic, thus excluding those we were sending to the prisoners help. These particulars were telegraphed me by Napier soon after his arrival and made us anxious.

All that the English Government had done in some measure to protect the prisoners from the Khedive's unregulated violence was to appoint two Englishmen who had a knowledge of Arabic to be present at the proceedings. These by a great stroke of good fortune were both honest and humane men, and, as it happened, old friends of my own, Sir Charles Wilson, whom I had travelled with in 1881 from Aleppo to Smyrna (not to be confounded with Sir C. Rivers Wilson), and Ardern Beaman, whom I had known at Damascus, and who now was Malet's official interpreter at the Agency. Both these men had been favourably impressed by Arabi's dignified bearing during the days of his detention as English prisoner of war, and now willingly gave Napier what little private help they could.

With Malet himself Napier succeeded at least so far as to get his status and that of the solicitor Eve, whom he had fortunately found at Cairo, recognized as legal representatives of Arabi's friends, though he could not obtain from him any definite promise or more than a vague assurance that English counsel would be allowed to represent Arabi himself. His applications to see his client were constantly put off by Malet by referring him to Riaz Pasha, the Khedivial Minister of the Interior, who as constantly refused, and in the meanwhile the trial was being pushed forward with all haste, so that it was clear to Napier that he was being played with and that the trial would be over before the question of the admissibility of English counsel had been plainly decided.

Things were standing thus when on the 12th of October I received a sudden warning from De la Warr, who was still in communication with the Foreign Office: "From what I hear, unless vigorous steps are taken, Arabi's life is in great danger. You have probably received information from Mr. Napier." With this ill news I rushed off immediately to Button's rooms and there fortunately found him, and as all his information tallied with mine we agreed that a supreme appeal must be made to the public, and that the Foreign Office must be directly and strongly attacked and Gladstone compromised and forced into a declaration of policy. I consequently sat down and wrote a final letter to Gladstone, in which I spared nothing in my anger of accusation against Granville and was careful to insist on his own connection with the matter, and his early sympathies with the Nationalist leader, and, without troubling ourselves to ask for an answer in Downing Street, Button "plumped" it into next morning's "Times," Chenery generously giving it full prominence and directing attention to it in a leading article. He had ascertained that the intention of the Government was that the trial should commence on Saturday, that sentence should be pronounced on Monday, and that Arabi's execution should instantly follow. It was already Friday, so we only had three days (one of them a Sunday when no newspapers are published) in which to rouse English feeling against this *coup de Jarnac*. Fortunately it was enough. I believe it was on this occasion that Bright, learning from my letter how things stood, went down to Gladstone and told him personally and plainly that he would be disgraced through all history as a renegade from his humaner principles if he allowed the perpetration of so great a crime. Be this as it may, the Foreign Office capitulated to us there and then, and, admitting our plea of the necessity of a fair trial, gave instructions to Malet to withdraw his opposition and treat the counsel sent to Arabi favourably. The following telegram from Napier announces our success: "Granville has directed Malet to require that Arabi shall be defended by English counsel. Proceedings expected to be lengthy."

I have thought it necessary to go into very minute detail in narrating these early phases of Arabi's trial, because in this way only is it possible to refute the false and absurd legend that has sprung up in Egypt to the effect that there was from the first some secret understanding between Gladstone and Arabi that his life should be spared. I can vouch for it, and the documents I have quoted in large measure prove it, that so far from having any sentiment of pity for, or understanding with, the "arch rebel," Gladstone had joined with Granville in the design to secure his death, through the Khedive's willing agency, by a trial which should be one merely of form and should disturb no questions, as the surest and speediest method of securing silence and a justification for their own huge moral errors of the last six months in Egypt. It was no qualm of conscience that prevented Gladstone from carrying it through to the end, only the sudden voice of the English public that at the last moment frightened him and warned him that it was dangerous for his reputation to go on with the full plan. This is the plain truth of the matter, whatever glosses Mr. Gladstone's apologists may put on it to save his humane credit or whatever may be imagined about it by French political writers desirous of finding an explanation for a leniency shown to Arabi after the war, which has seemed to them inexplicable except on the supposition of some deep anterior intrigue between the English Prime Minister and the leader of the Egyptian rebellion.

This supreme point of danger past, it was not altogether difficult to foresee that the trial could hardly now end otherwise than negatively. A fair trial in open court with the Khedivial rubbish heap turned up with an English pitchfork and ransacked for forgotten crimes was a thought not to be contemplated by Tewfik without terror, while for the British Government as well there would be revelations destructive of the theory of past events constructed on the basis of official lies and their own necessity of finding excuses for their violence. The Sultan, too, had to be safeguarded from untimely revelations. The danger for the prisoners' lives was not over, but there seemed fair prospect of the thing ending in a compromise if we could not gain an acquittal. The changed state of things at Cairo is announced by Napier as early as the 16th October; and I will give the rest of my story of the trial mainly in the form of telegrams and letters.

Napier to Blunt, Oct. 16th:
"It is believed the Egyptian Government will try to quash the trial altogether, and that the chief prisoners will be directed to leave the country. I have not sufficient facts at my command to form a judgment on this point, but I think it not unlikely."

And again from Broadley, just arrived at Cairo:

Broadley to Blunt, Oct. 20th:

"Borelli Bey, the Government prosecutor, admitted frankly that the Egyptian Government had no law or procedure to go by, but suggested we should agree as to a procedure. He admitted the members of the Court were dummies and incompetent. He hoped I should smooth the Sultan and let down Tewfik as *doucement* as possible."

Napier to Blunt, Oct. 20th:

"I think now, we can guarantee a clean breast of the whole facts. It is as much as the Khedive's throne is worth to allow the trial to proceed."

The chief danger we had to face was a desire, not yet extinct at the Foreign Office, still by hook or crook, to establish some criminal charge against Arabi which should justify his death. Chenery writes to me 21st October: "Among important people there is a strong feeling against him [Arabi] on the alleged ground that he was concerned with, or connived at, the massacre in Alexandria. The matter will almost certainly come up at the trial." This danger, however, did not at Cairo seem a pressing one, and certainly it was one that the prosecution was least likely to touch, the Khedive himself being there the culprit. Nothing is more noticeable in the interrogatories than the pains taken by the members of the Court to avoid questions tending in that direction and the absence on that point of all evidence which could incriminate any one. It was one, however, of great political importance to our Government that it should be proved against Arabi, for on it they had based the whole of their wilful insistence in forcing on a conflict, and without it their *moral* excuse for intervention fell flatly to the ground. The same might be said in regard to another absurd plea, insisted upon personally by Gladstone, that there had been an abuse of the white flag during the evacuation of Alexandria, a supposition which he had caught hold of in one of his speeches and made a special crime of, though in truth withdrawal of troops while a white flag is flying is permitted according to all the usages of war. Otherwise the coast seemed clear enough of danger, for it was evident that the British public would no longer allow our Government to sanction Arabi's death for mere political reasons.

Meanwhile at Cairo things were going prosperously. On the 22nd Broadley and Napier were admitted to Arabi's cell and speedily found in what he could tell them the groundwork of a strong defence. Arabi's attitude in prison was a perfectly dignified one, for whatever may have been his lack of physical courage, he had moral courage to a high degree, and his demeanor contrasted favourably with that of the large majority of those who had been arrested with him and did not fail to impress all that saw him. Without the smallest hesitation he wrote down in the next few days a general history of the whole of the political affairs in which he had been mixed, and in a form which was frank and convincing. No less outspoken was he in denouncing the ill-treatment he had received since he had been transferred to his present prison from those scoundrels, the Khedive's eunuchs, who had been sent at night by their master to assault and insult him. Not a few of the prisoners had been thus shamefully treated; yet by a singular lack of moral courage the greater number dared not put into plain words a crime, personally implicating the cowardly tyrant who had been replaced as master over them. Nothing is more lamentable in the depositions than the slavish attitude assumed by nearly all the deponents towards the Khedive's person, hated as he had been by them and despised not a month before. A more important event still was the recovery from their concealment of Arabi's most important papers, which had been hidden in his house and which he now directed should be sought out and placed in Broadley's hand. It was with great difficulty that his son and wife in their terror could be brought to allow the search—for they, too, had been "visited" by the Khedive's servants—but at last the precious documents were secured and brought to Broadley by Arabi's servant already mentioned, Mohammed Sid Ahmed. They proved of supreme value—including as they did the letters written by order of the Sultan to Arabi and others of a like compromising kind. The news of the discovery struck panic into the Palace and there seemed every chance that the trial would be abandoned.

Napier writing to me October 30th says: "The fact is I believe we are masters now, and that the Khedive and his crew would be glad to sneak out of the trial with as little delay as possible. The fidelity of Arabi's servant and the constancy of his wife enabled us to recover all his papers but one. They are now in a safe deposited in Beaman's room at the Consulate.... The Government cannot face our defence. They will offer a compromise, banishment with all property reserved. What better could be got?... This question will probably soon have to be considered."

It will be understood that the changed aspect of affairs at Cairo found its echo, and more than its echo, in the London Press. Cairo was full of newspaper correspondents, and Broadley, who was a past master in the arts of journalism, soon had them mostly on his side. His hospitality (at my expense) was lavish, and the "chicken and champagne" were not spared. Malet and Colvin, supreme in old days were now quite unable to stem the torrent of news, and revelation followed revelation all destructive of the theory they had imposed on the Government, that Arabi and the army had been alone in opposing the English demands and that the National movement had been less than a universal one. Colvin was now become discredited at the Foreign Office as a false guide, and Malet's incapacity was at last fully recognized.

Lord Granville, furious at our success, and seeing the political situation in Egypt drifting into a hopeless muddle, did what was probably his wisest course in submitting the whole matter to Lord Dufferin for a settlement. I had early notice from Button of this new move and that Dufferin's first business on arriving at Cairo would be to bring about a compromise of the trial. My letter of instructions to Broadley in view of the new situation thus created is worth inserting here:

Blunt to Broadley, Nov. 2, 1882.
"I wish to state over again my ideas and hopes in undertaking Arabi's defence and that of his companions, which if they are realized will repay me for the cost even though larger than I had originally thought probable. Of course the main object was to save the prisoners' lives, and that I think we may consider already accomplished, for public opinion has declared itself in England, and, the preliminary investigation having so entirely failed in the matter of the June riots and the burning of Alexandria, no evidence that now could be produced, and no verdict given by the judges could any longer place them in jeopardy. Since your arrival, however, and through your skill and good fortune, a flush of trumps has come into our hands: Instead of Arabi's papers being locked up in the Foreign Office they are in our possession, and, as you tell me to-day, our defence is perfect while we hold such a commanding position over the enemy that we can fairly dictate them terms. We cannot, therefore, be content with anything less than an honourable acquittal or the abandonment of the trial. At present the latter seems the most probable. Lord Dufferin has been ordered to Egypt; the Premier yesterday threw out a feeler for a compromise, and from everything I hear proposals will shortly be made for some arrangement of the affair by which the scandal and discredit of an exposure will be avoided. It depends, therefore, entirely on us to save not only Arabi's life but his honour and his freedom, and also I believe the lives and freedom of all the political prisoners inculpated with him.

"I believe a strong attempt will be made by Lord Dufferin to get Arabi to agree to a detention in the Andaman Islands, or some part of the British Empire where he would remain a political prisoner treated with kindness but not suffered to be at large. I believe also he will endeavour to get from him a cession of his papers. Neither of these attempts must be allowed to succeed, and all proposals including them must be rejected. It is no business of ours to save the Sultan's or the Khedive's honour nor to save Lord Granville from embarrassment, and I shall consider our failure a great one if we do not get far more. I think Arabi should, in the first place, state that he demands a trial in order to clear his honour, and especially to demonstrate the innocence of those who acted with him during the war, viz., the whole nation, or, if not brought to trial, that the charges against them should be withdrawn as well as against himself. There should, in fact, be a general amnesty, also he should retain his papers, though probably he might give an understanding that they should not be published for a term of years. We cannot, under the circumstances, object absolutely to exile, because I suppose it would be argued the Khedive could exile him by decree, but even this I should make a matter of favour, because the Constitution of February, 1882 (which I hope you have closely studied, and which is a most valuable document from the fact of its having been confirmed by the Sultan as well as granted by the Khedive) forbids such exiling. Still the point would have to be conceded. We should, however, refuse anything like imprisonment. The Khedive might exile him from Egypt, and the Sultan from the Ottoman Empire, but neither would have a right to fix the place or nature of his abode beyond them.

"Nor could the English Government, having handed Arabi to the Khedive for trial, let him be taken back untried to be dealt with as a criminal by England. The English Government has recognized this by refusing so to take him back. Still less could it imprison him if so taken without trial. It is, therefore, clear that unless tried and convicted he must leave Egypt a free man. Nor can he legally be deprived in Egypt of his rank and pay. But I should suppose that he will agree to retiring with military rank only, and a small maintenance to save him from actual poverty and the necessity of working with his hands. I think these terms would be dignified, and they are terms we can insist upon. Otherwise I urge the necessity of a defence tooth and nail, and I sincerely trust that you will not listen to any proposal which may be made of a *pro formá* trial and letting the Khedive down *doucement*, as Borelli proposed. There should either be a real honest exposure of *all* the facts, or an honourable withdrawal of *all* the charges. I trust in you to cooperate with me fully in obtaining this result, without regard for the feelings of Consuls or Ambassadors or Viceroys. They are nothing to us, and our client's honour and cause are everything. Your diplomatic skill is, I have no doubt, a match for Lord Dufferin's, and it will be a great game to win. You have made Malet do what you wanted, and so you will make Dufferin do. If you achieve this we will not talk more about the fee. I enclose a letter of introduction to Lord Dufferin."

The following from Mr. Beaman, Malet's official interpreter, and a witness of unimpeachable authority, is of the highest historical importance. Beaman had been in charge of the Agency at Cairo during the last weeks before the bombardment, and being a good Arabic scholar knew more of the true state of affairs than any one employed there. He had been appointed a few days before the date of his letter to superintend, on Malet's part, the trial:

Beaman to Blunt, Cairo, Nov. 6, 1882.
" . . . This is our last day before the adjournment. . . . The Palace people here are in a great stew at the advent of Lord Dufferin, who arrives to-morrow. Broadley's arrival has been an agony to them, but this is the last blow. I believe Dufferin is a man who will quickly see through our friend Tewfik, and as I hear that his ears are open to everybody the temporary Embassy will be better informed, I expect, than the Agency has ever been. I had a great deal of intercourse with natives before the bombardment of all classes and parties, and knew the whole of the game from the four sides, English, Turkish, Arabi, and Tewfik. They were each quite distinct. As I could not have given my authorities, and as people would not have accepted my word for things I could have told, I kept my information for myself, but I have given some good hints to Sir Charles Wilson, who now has a fairer idea of the Egyptian question than any of our officials here. He is an extremely cautious man, with a great share of shrewdness and true judgment which he does not allow to be warped. Through him I have been able to get facts to Malet which I should never have told Malet himself. I think now that Malet has quite lost any respect he could ever have had for the Khedive. Throughout our proceedings he has acted with the greatest fairness to us, although dead against his own interests. . . . You know how deeply he was pledged to the Khedive, and it is quite bitter enough a cup to him to see his idol come down from the card house which is breaking up. . . . I think the Ibrahim Agha business alone is quite enough to show the Khedive in his true colours. I heard the whole story direct from the Palace, how the *titunji*, the Khedive's pipe bearer, had kissed the Khedive's hand, asked permission to spit in the faces of the prisoners, and it was on this that Sir Charles Wilson made inquiry and found it all true. Nevertheless, because it was evident that the Khedive had a very dirty piece of linen to be washed in the business, it was left alone. I suggested when all the witnesses swore falsely that the oath of triple divorce should be administered to them, and Sir Charles Wilson was in favour of it too, but it was hushed up. His Highness's own family now no longer pretend to deny it among themselves. And this is the man for whom we came to Egypt.[4]

---

4. The fact of Tewfik's having sent his eunuchs to insult the Nationalist leaders in prison is attested by Sheykh Mohammed Abdu, who was among the earliest arrested, and was himself one of its victims. He recorded his prison experience in a declaration submitted to Sir Charles Wilson 29th October, but which is absent from the Blue Books.

"If I was not bound by my position here not to advise Broadley, I could give him hints enough for his cross-examination to turn out the Khedive tomorrow. I hope it will come out nevertheless. The first man to be got rid of is Riaz. He is playing the very devil through Egypt. The other day he said: 'The Egyptians are serpents and the way to prevent serpents from propagating is to crush them under foot. So will I crush the Egyptians.' And he is doing it."

Matters stood thus in the first week of November, the date of Lord Dufferin's arrival at Cairo. It was a fortunate circumstance for us who were defending the cause of justice in England that Parliament that year happened to be holding an autumn session. It brought to our aid in the House of Commons several Members of first rate fighting value—Churchill, Wolff, Gorst, Lawson, Labouchere, besides Robert Bourke, Lord John Manners, W. J. Evelyn, and the present Lord Wemyss, of the regular Tory opposition, with two or three Irish Members. Percy Wyndham, to his credit, was the only Tory who had voted with the minority of twenty-one against the war.

SOURCE: Chapter 17 in *The Secret History of the English Occupation of Egypt* (London: T. F. Unwin, 1907).

Arabi and His Household.
LADY GREGORY

[Lady Gregory (1852–1932), a playwright and an associate of W. B. Yeats in the foundation of the Abbey Theater in Dublin, was a close friend of Wilfred Blunt and shared his interest in the story of Arabi's uprising and subsequent trial. Her essay was originally published in the *London Times* (1882).]

'Report me and my cause aright to the unsatisfied.' I wrote these last words of Hamlet on a photograph of Arabi which a friend asked me for at Cairo. But that friend had personal reason for supporting the rule of the English officials in Egypt, and had also doubt as to the possibility of a constitutional government succeeding in a country which could not boast a House of Peers. Other Englishmen have said to me, since I have come home: 'Arabi is a good man, and his aims are honest. I know it and you know it, but we dare not say it. A lady may say what she likes, but a man is called unpatriotic who ventures to say a word that is good of the man England is determined to crush; it may injure us if we speak as we think.' But I, like Master Shadow, present no mark to the enemy. I have spoken what I knew to be the truth all through the war, and I wrote down these recollections of Arabi and his family, which I knew

"The Sublime—'Super!'" In *Punch* 82 (16 September 1882): 127.

must make him appear less of an ogre than he was generally supposed to be some time ago, though not intending them for immediate publication. But now news has reached me from Cairo that Arabi's wife has had to find a refuge with a highminded princess, who has always been known as one who loved Egypt, and that that princess is consequently in danger of arrest; that Arabi's mother is hidden in a poor quarter of the town, afraid to face the vengeance of his enemies now in power; and it is hoping to interest Englishmen in this family—simple, honest, hospitable, as I found them, and who are now poor, hunted, in danger—that I publish them now.

In appearance Arabi is a tall, strongly-built man; his face is grave, almost stern, but his smile is very pleasant. His photographs reproduce the sternness, but not the smile, and are, I believe, partly responsible for the ready belief which the absurd tales of his ferocity and bloodthirstiness have gained. He always wears the blue Egyptian uniform, the red tarboosh pushed back on his head, and the sword, whose imaginary feats rival those of Excalibur, by his side. 'I make no more jokes,' said M. de Blignières, the sharp-tongued Controller, after Arabi had been made Minister of War; 'Arabi comes to the Council with his big sword on, and I think it better to be silent.' 'Arabi drew his sword, threatened the Notables, and told Sultan Pasha he would make his children fatherless and his wife a widow,' was the story sent to England when the Chamber demanded the right of voting the Budget. It was hardly necessary for the old and childless Sultan Pasha to deny this story altogether when brought to his ears. 'Arabi flourished his sword and broke several windows,' cries the hysterical correspondent of an English newspaper later on.

As a matter of fact, I believe him to be exceedingly gentle and humane. An English official, one of the fairest of his class, said to me: 'He has too much of the gentleness of the fellah, and too little of the brute in him to succeed. If he would take lessons in brutality at 100 francs a week, he would have a much better chance of getting on.' He was for months the almost absolute ruler of Egypt, and even from his enemies comes no story of cruelty or oppression, except that of the torture of the Circassian officers; and having searched the Blue-book laid before Parliament for proof of this, I can only find a despatch from our Minister saying a European gentleman has told him that two natives had told him that they had heard cries proceeding from the prison where the Circassians were confined, from which is inferred that they were being tortured.

I do not understand Arabic, the only language spoken by Arabi, so could not judge of his eloquence. It is said to be striking, and his words well chosen. His intimate knowledge of the Koran and all the literature of his religion, including our own Old Testament books, will account for this, just as a lifelong study of the English Bible is said to lend force and vigour to the language of one of our own great orators. He speaks very earnestly, looking you straight in the face with honest eyes. I have an entire belief in his truthfulness; partly from his manner; partly because from everyone, without exception, who had known him long or watched his career—some of them members of the Vice-regal family—I heard on this point the same report—'He is incapable of speaking untruth'; partly because it was many months ago—it was in November—that my husband first saw and spoke with him, and to every word he said then he has adhered ever since. The abhorrence of Ismail which he then expressed has been proved to be real, though long disbelieved, by the refusal to allow his emissaries to land at Alexandria in April, and the proposal to cut his name out of the Civil List when he was found to be spending his money in intrigues in Egypt. And his sentiments towards the Sultan seem to be the same now as when he said: 'We honour him as Caliph and as suzerain; we belong to him; his dominion is a great house, and Egypt is one of the rooms in that house; we acknowledge him as our lord, but we like to have our room to ourselves.' 'You may believe every word spoken by him,' said a Princess of the family of Mehemet Ali, 'because he is a man who fears God.' I believe it is the implicit faith in his honesty and truth which prevails that accounts for much of his immense influence, which undoubtedly exists. At Luxor, in January, we noticed the eager interest taken by the people in hearing of him; and European gentlemen, living as overseers on estates still higher up, told us that his was the name continually on men's lips. I have been told that when Sir Rivers Wilson first went to Egypt, and found the people groaning under the tyranny of Ismail, his name took possession of the people in the same way, and whenever a man suffered an injustice or a wrong, he said: 'The Wilson will be sure to set it right.' But later on the Control did not inspire enthusiasm, and Arabi became the centre of the people's desire. Of his childhood I know nothing, except that his old mother told me he was 'always a good son.' The first noteworthy action of his I can hear of was in the days of Said Pasha. Said devoted himself to his army, its drill and discipline. At one time he took it into his head that keeping the Fast of Ramadan was injurious to the troops, and he issued an order that the fast was not to be observed. After a few days he was told that some of the soldiers were neglecting his orders. Indignant at their disobedience, he himself went out, and, walking along the ranks, asked each man, 'Do you fast?' 'Do you?' A few confessed with fear and trembling—many denied. At last a young soldier stepped forward and said very respectfully, 'Oh, Effendina! I have read in the Commandment of God, given in the Koran, that we must fast. If I neglect the commands of my God, how shall I be faithful to those of an earthly ruler?' 'What is your name?' 'Ahmed

Arabi.' 'Take him from my sight!' No one expected ever to see him again, but next day he was not only sent back to his regiment, but with the increased rank of corporal. This is the man of whom we read in the despatches of last winter that the motive power of all his actions is cowardice.

I next hear of him in the disastrous Abyssinian War. His duty was to arrange for the transport of provisions and baggage—not much glory or fame to be gathered there, though no fault was found with his efficiency or discipline. But even then, I have been told by a European officer who went through the campaign, his influence was growing. Each night, when the day's work was done, it was round him that the soldiers gathered, and he preached, or spoke, or recited the Koran to them.

It was in February, last year, that the Egyptian authorities, having no ground of accusation against Arabi, but distrusting him as 'a man with ideas,' tried to put him out of the way quietly, but failed. He had a short time before, in conjunction with two other colonels, Abdullal, of the Black Regiment, and Ali Fehmy, presented a petition asking for an inquiry into the grievances of the army, which was accepted. In February, these three colonels received a summons from the Khedive to come to the Abdin Palace to receive orders for the arrangement of a procession which was to be formed next day on the occasion of the marriage of one of the Princesses. Their suspicions were aroused, and before going to the Palace they left a message with their regiments—'If we are not back at sunset, come for us.' As soon as they arrived at the Palace they were seized, thrown into a room, their swords taken from them, and the doors locked. Whether their friends would ever have seen them again is a matter for speculation; all Cairo to this day says 'No'; but at sunset the soldiers arrived, demanding their officers, and then it was too late to do anything but throw the doors open as quickly as might be and let the prisoners out. Those who saw the release say that the two other colonels seemed in a great hurry to be safe in their barracks again, but Arabi walked slowly out, calm and unmoved as usual. Those who take the trouble may read this story, plainly told in the Blue-books published in June. Why is it that one hears so often of Arabi's mutiny, but never of the first act in the piece which led to it?

I am not writing a history of Arabi, and need not go into the details of the September demonstration, when the soldiers who had learnt their way to the Palace to release the colonels appeared there again with a demand for a Constitution, which was promised them. In December the Khedive made him Under-Secretary of War, whether with the idea of strengthening the Government, or that Arabi's popularity would be lessened by his acceptance of office, I cannot tell.

In the Government of Mahmoud Samy, which came into office on the 3rd of February, he became Minister of War. His popularity was then at its height in Cairo. Many European officials paying the necessary formal visits to the new Ministers met him for the first time, and one and all came away with a more favourable impression of him than they had before. Men who a month earlier had spoken of him as beneath contempt now boasted of a few civil words from him. At the American public dinner, at which he was a guest and made a short speech in Arabic, those who were present, unable to judge of his eloquence, could talk of nothing but the charm of his smile.

It was just at this time that the Sacred Carpet was brought back from Mecca. It is a time of great rejoicing among the people, and all Cairo went out to meet it. When Arabi appeared in the procession the enthusiasm of the people knew no bounds. They threw themselves upon him, kissed his hands, his knees, his feet, tore his gloves into fragments to keep in memory of him. The soldiers tried in vain to beat them back, but he stopped them, and, lifting his hand, said quietly, 'Go back, my children,' and in an instant was obeyed. The Khedive's wife was looking on from a window ill-pleased. 'See,' she said, 'How this man is stealing the hearts of the people.' Her own husband had passed, receiving but little notice, just before.

I had already seen and spoken with Arabi, but it was not until the end of February that I went, with Lady Anne Blunt, to see his wife. They had moved some little time before to a new house, large and dilapidated looking, and which Arabi was represented as having fitted up in a luxurious style; in fact, at that time the crime most frequently alleged against him was that he had bought carpets to the amount of £120. I must confess that there were some pieces of new and not beautiful European carpets in the chief rooms, but I must add that if Arabi paid £120 for them he made a very bad bargain. I do not know how he has spent his official salary, but I have heard very lately, from one who has taken the trouble to investigate the truth of the stories of his avarice, that he has the same small amount of money to his credit now that he had before he was either Pasha or Minister, and that the foundation of the story of his having become a large landed proprietor is his having become trustee for the orphan child of an old friend of his who had been kind to him.

The sole furniture of the reception room of Arabi's wife consisted of small hard divans covered with brown linen and a tiny table with a crochet antimacassar thrown over it. On the whitewashed walls the only ornaments were photographs of him in black wooden frames, and one larger photograph of the Sacred Stone at Mecca. In the room where Arabi himself sat and received were a similar hard divan, two or three chairs, a table, and an inkstand covered with stains. His wife was ready to receive us, having heard an hour or two earlier of our intended visit. She greeted us warmly, speaking in Arabic, which Lady

Anne interpreted to me. She has a pleasant, intelligent expression; but, having five children living out of fourteen that have been born to her, looked rather overcome with the cares of maternity, her beauty dimmed since the time when the tall, grave soldier she had seen passing under her window every day looked up at last, and saw and loved her. She wore a long dress of green silk. 'My husband hates this long train,' she told us afterwards; 'he would like to take a knife and cut it off, but I say I must have a fashionable dress to wear when I visit the Khedive's wife and other ladies.' I think there are English husbands who, in this grievance at least, will sympathise with Arabi.

An old woman with white hair, dressed in the common country fashion—a woollen petticoat and blue cotton jacket—came into the room and occupied herself with the children. Presently we found that she was Arabi's mother. She spoke with great energy and vivacity, welcoming us and talking of her son with much affection and pride. 'I am only a fellah woman,' she said, 'but I am the mother of Ahmed Arabi.' She took me twice into another room to see an oleograph, of which she was very proud, representing him in staring colours. After a short time, a negro boy, the only visible attendant, brought in a tray, and we were invited to sit down and eat. The meal began with boiled chicken and broth, which were followed by forcemeat balls, rice, vegetables, sweet pastry, and other native dishes in abundance, though our hostess lamented the short notice she had been given of our visit. If she had known in time she would have had a cow killed. Two little girls, her daughters, waited on us, and brought water to wash our hands. She, herself, kept up an animated conversation, and gave us a vivid account of the imprisonment of the three colonels and their rescue. When they were in prison the others were frightened, but Arabi was not. He said: 'It is not the will of God that we should perish.' 'When I heard what had happened, though I was almost too ill to leave the house, I hired a carriage and drove up towards the palace to ask for news of them, but could hear nothing, and soon I had to come back, and that evening my baby was born. At the moment of her birth came the news that my husband had been released by the soldiers, so I called her "Bushra"' (good tidings). She was brought in for us to see, a tiny, thin, black-eyed creature, clinging to her grandmother. She is her father's favourite, they said—she and Saida, the eldest girl, who was with him when he was quartered at Alexandria, and Hassan, a bright-eyed little imp of four years. We had paid a long visit, and got away after many leave-takings and hopes for their wellbeing as well as that of 'El Bey.' 'Inshallah,' his wife, answered rather sadly. 'They say the Christian Powers want to do something to my husband. I don't understand it at all. We can't get on without the Christians, or they without us. Why can't we all live in peace together?'

In November I had been taken to see Madame Sherif Pasha, a voluble lady, full of importance, and telling us between the puffs of her cigarette how she had had a visit from Arabi's wife, and had spoken severely to her, and told her to go home and make her husband behave better and keep him from these *bêlises,* and the poor woman had cried and promised to do her best. Now, in February, Madame Sherif had retired to obscurity, and Madame Arabi was wife of the Minister of War.

Sherif himself I did not know, but those who knew him found him a pleasant companion, a plausible speaker, and a crack billiard-player. Arabi, terribly in earnest about some important question, calling at his house and finding him engrossed in a game of billiards, would retire in disgust. A clear-sighted foreign Consul said of him: 'Sherif is full of good intentions, but he has never any intention of carrying them out.' The most able of our English officials said of him, 'He is honest in intention, hazy in his ideas, indolent in action; but, as partisanship for his Ministry seems to be one of the chief causes that has led us into war, let us say the best of him now.'

Toward the end of March, before we left Cairo, Arabi came to say good-bye to us. A little worried and troubled by false accusations made against him in English newspapers, he was still confident that some day his character would be cleared. 'They must know some day that it is the good of the people that we seek.' A little time before their work was judged, that was all he asked. This has been denied him, and those who thought it well to 'bring things to a crisis and hasten intervention' by raising a quarrel between him and the Khedive have done their work. I spoke of my visit to his house, and he said: 'Our women have not been in the habit of receiving the visits of the ladies of Europe, so if in any way they failed in the courtesy and attention due to a guest, I hope you will understand it was not from want of goodwill, but from want of knowledge.' I showed him a picture of my little boy; he raised it to his lips and kissed it, hoping he would some day come to Egypt to be the friend of his children. Perhaps I have not been a fair judge in his cause since then.

A day or two before we left I went again to see his wife. She looked a little sadder, a little more anxious, than when I had last seen her, but was on hospitable cares intent, and soon went out of the room to see to the preparation of dinner. I had an Italian lady with me as interpreter, who spoke French and Arabic very well. They had expected me this time, and made more preparations, and when the meal was ready and I saw dish after dish coming in, I was in despair until I found that one of the children, my little bright-eyed friend Hassan, was quite ready to sit by me, and be fed from my plate, and so I disposed of my share to his great satisfaction. 'I like this better than having to wait downstairs till dinner is over,' he said; 'then they forget me and eat up all the good things.' By the time dessert arrived he said he liked me but hated other ladies, and would like to come and see me in England, but did not know how he could manage it, as his papa wanted the carriage every day. I advised him to learn English, and his mother said she would like to send him to one of the Christian schools in Cairo, 'But how can I send him where he would hear his father spoken ill of?' She seemed troubled, poor woman, because the Khedive's wife, who used to be good and kind to her, now says: 'How can we be friends when your husband is such a bad man?' The old mother sat in the corner attending to the children and counting over her beads. I said, 'Are you not proud now your son is a Pasha?' 'No,' she said, 'we were happier in the old days when we had him with us always and feared nothing. Now he gets up at daybreak and has only time to say his prayers before there are people waiting for him with petitions, and he has to attend to them and then go to his business, and often he is not back here until after midnight, and until he comes I cannot sleep, I cannot rest; I can do nothing but pray for him all the time. There are many who wish him evil and they will try to destroy him. A few days ago he came home suffering great pain, and I was sure then he had been poisoned; but I got him a hot bath and remedies and he grew better, and since then I keep even the water that he drinks locked up. But, say all I can, I cannot frighten him or make him take care of himself; he always says, "God will preserve me."'

'God will preserve me!' 'It is not the will of God that we should perish.' The words of a man who believes God has given him work to do and will support him while he does it—not the words of a coward. But those who wrote the published despatches say that cowardice is the mainspring of his character, and surely they know better than his old mother!

'The Khedive is unjust to him,' she went on; 'he will give him no help or support, and yet if anything goes wrong, or there is a disturbance ever so far away, Arabi is blamed for it.' She had a grievance against her son also. He had been already working hard towards the abolition of slavery, and I found that in this matter his foes were they of his own household. 'He ought not to do it,' the old woman said; 'he does not see the consequences as I do. All the slaves will leave as soon as they are freed, and European women will take their places, and they will seduce their masters, and their children will be stronger than ours, and we shall be driven out of the country.' Poor old soul! she must have had sore and anxious days since then. I often think of her, and of the poor wife, puzzled and troubled, 'Why should the Christian Powers want to harm my husband?'

SOURCE: Lady Gregory, *Arabi and His Household* (London: Kegan Paul, Trench, 1882). Pamphlet.

XIV
PILGRIMS, TRAVELLERS, AND TOURISTS

INTRODUCTION
Holy Lands and Secular Agendas
BARBARA HARLOW

WHILE THE SUEZ CANAL did facilitate, even speed, the "passage to India," abbreviating as it did the journey round the African continent and alleviating as well the travails of the overland route across Egypt, there were those other peregrinators who still preferred to stop on either side of the straits that the digging of the canal had created. Egypt might be, for Europe, the "key to India," but it was also, as Arabi reminded Gladstone, the "key of Mecca and Medina" (this volume, 708). And Jerusalem counted, too, in such itineraries for Christians, Muslims, and Jews alike. The oriental allure of Cairo no less than the barren attractions of the "empty quarter" figured just as prominently in the programs of European pilgrims, travelers, and tourists to the region. And there were as well the contradictions of nationalisms to be figured into the imperial designs.

E. M. Forster, to be sure, eventually arrived in India, but he would not altogether leave behind attachments formed in Alexandria. His *Alexandria: A History and Guide* (1922) provides both a history, "after the fashion of a pageant" (xviii), of the city and a meticulous guide to its artifactual possibilities. Whereas Alexandria, port of entry for visitors from Napoleon to Wolseley, connected Egypt with Europe across the Mediterranean, it was Cairo, at the juncture on the Nile between fertile delta and desert antiquities, that provided the congregating space for competing peoples and pilgrims. Pharaonic, Islamic, European and African—the city's historical palimpsest by the end of the nineteenth century had been otherwise divided between the European and Egyptian cities. Lady Duff Gordon, like so many others, went to Cairo for her health. Her *Letters from Egypt* (1875) detailed both her own physical recovery and the topographical deterioration of the city on the Nile.

The Suez Canal provided another access to the "holy places," and also enabled other, newer "crusades." From the Druses in Lebanon, whose belief in a coming Mahdi was as intimidating as the Mahdists in Sudan would come to be, to the ideals of Zion and the destinatory significance of Medina and Mecca, the terrain was coveted by European travelers and Arab dwellers alike. Richard Burton was well traveled throughout Africa and the Middle East as a diplomat and as reporter for the Royal Geographic Society. His *Personal Narrative of a Pilgrimage to Al-Madinah and Mecca* (1855) is a classic of the lengths to which European visitors would go to visit the holy places of the region. He was followed by others, most notably Charles Doughty, whose *Travels in Arabia Deserta* (1888) became a guidebook for the likes of T. E. Lawrence ("Lawrence of Arabia"). Lawrence wrote the introduction to Doughty's travelogue, in which he claimed that Doughty had "become history in the desert" (19). Doughty was followed, Lawrence goes on, by, among myriad others, Gertrude Bell—for neither were women averse to the difficulties of desert traversals. Bell was the second woman, after Lady Anne Blunt, to visit the Ha'il, and went on to provide important reconnaissance reports from the region for the British during the period between the Armistice of 1918 and the Iraq rebellion in 1921. There were, that is, political interests in these journeys. The East, as Benjamin Disraeli maintained, was a career. Nationalism was being consolidated in Europe and finding important expression in Europe's colonies. As George Eliot's *Daniel Deronda* (1876) put it: "Nations have revived. We may live to see a great outburst of force in the Arabs, who are being inspired with a new zeal" (525). And Thomas Cook Tours covered it all.

BIBLIOGRAPHY

Bell, Gertrude. *Syria: The Desert and the Sown.* London: W. Heinemann, 1907.
Blanch, Lesley. *The Wilder Shores of Love.* London: Murray, 1954.
Blunt, Lady Anne. *A Pilgrimage to Nejd.* London: J. Murray, 1881.
Disraeli, Benjamin. *Tancred: Of the New Crusade.* London: H. Colburn, 1847.
Eliot, George. *Daniel Deronda.* New York: Harper and Brothers, 1876.
Forster, E. M. *Alexandria: A History and Guide.* Woodstock, N.Y.: Overlook Press, 1961.
Kinglake, A. W. *Eothen.* 1830s. Lincoln: University of Nebraska Press, 1970.
Lawrence, T. E. *Seven Pillars of Wisdom.* New York: G. H. Doran, 1926.
Philby, H. St. J. B. *The Empty Quarter.* London: Constable and Co., Ltd., 1933.
Said, Edward. *The Question of Palestine.* New York: Times Books, 1979.
Stark, Freya. *The Southern Gates of Arabia: A Journey in the Hadhramaut.* New York: E. P. Dutton, 1936.
Thesiger, Wilfred. *Arabian Sands.* London: Longmans, 1959.
Trollope, Anthony. "A Ride Across Palestine." In *Tales of All Continents.* Vol. 2. London, 1863; reprint, London: Oxford University Press, 1931.
Watney, John. *Travels in Araby.* London: Gordon Dremonesi, 1975.

Cairo Is the Real Arabian Nights
LADY DUFF GORDON

[Lucie Duff Gordon's letters from Egypt cover the period from October 1862 until her death in July 1869, just months before the opening of the Suez Canal.]

Grand Cairo, November 11 1862.
Dearest Mother. I write to you out of the real Arabian Nights. Well may the Prophet (whose name be exalted) smile when he looks on Cairo. It is a golden existence, all sunshine and poetry, and, I must add, kindness and civility. I came up last Thursday by railway with the American Consul-General and had to stay at this horrid Shepheard's Hotel. But I do little but sleep here. Hekekian Bey, a learned old Armenian, takes care of me every day, and the American Vice-Consul is my sacrifice.

I went on Sunday to his child's christening, and heard Sakna, the 'Restorer of Hearts.' She is wonderfully like Rachel, and her singing is *hinreisend* [delightful] from expression and passion. Mr Wilkinson [the British Consul] is a Levantine, and his wife Armenian, so they had a grand fantasia; people feasted all over the house and in the street. Arab music clanged, women yelled the *zaghareet*, black servants served sweetmeats, pipes, and coffee, and behaved as if they belonged to the company, and I was strongly under the impression that I was at Nurreddin's wedding with the Vizier's daughter.

My servant Omar turns out a jewel. He has discovered an excellent boat for the Nile voyage, and I am to be mistress of a captain, a mate, eight men and a cabin boy for £25 a month. I went to Boulaq, the port of Cairo, and saw various boats, and admired the way in which the English travellers pay for their insolence and caprices. Similar boats cost people with dragomans £50 to £65. But, then, 'I shall lick the fellows,' etc., is what I hear all round. The dragoman, I conclude, pockets the difference.

The owner of the boat, Sid Ahmad el-Berberi, asked £30, whereupon I touched my breast, mouth and eyes, and stated through Omar that I was not, like other Ingeleez, made of money, but would give £20. He then showed another boat at £20, very much worse, and I departed (with fresh civilities) and looked at others, and saw two more for £20; but neither was clean, and neither had a little boat for landing. Meanwhile Sid Ahmad came after me and explained that, if I was not like other Ingeleez in money, I likewise differed in politeness, and had refrained from abuse, etc., etc., and I should have the boat for £25. It was so very excellent in all fittings, and so much larger, that I thought it would make a great difference in health, so I said if he would go before the American Vice-Consul (who is looked on as a sharp hand) and would promise all he said to me before him, it should be well.

It was pleasant to find that Hekekian Bey and the American Vice-Consul exactly confirmed all that Omar had told me about what I must take and what it would cost; they thought I might perfectly trust him. He put everything at just one-fourth of what the Alexandrian English told me, and even less. Moreover, he will cook on board; the kitchen, which is a hole in the bow where the cook must sit cross-legged, would be impossible for a woman to crouch down in. Besides, Omar will avoid everything unclean, and make the food such as he may lawfully eat. He is a pleasant, cheerful young fellow, and I think he rather likes the importance of taking care of me, and showing that he can do as well as a dragoman at £12 a month. It is characteristic that he turned his month's wages and the '£2 pounds for a coat' into a bracelet for his little wife before leaving home. That is the Arab savings-bank.

I dined at Hekekian Bey's after the excursion yesterday. He is a most kind, friendly man, and very pleasant and cultivated. He dresses like an Englishman, speaks English like ourselves, and is quite like an uncle to me already.

Mr Thayer, the American Consul-General, gives me letters to every consular agent depending on him; and two Coptic merchants whom I met at the fantasia have already begged me to 'honour their houses.' I rather think the poor agents, who are all Armenians and Copts, will think I am the republic in person. The weather has been all this time like a splendid English August, and I hope I shall get rid of my cough in time, but it has been very bad. There is no cold at night here as at the Cape, but it is nothing like so clear and bright.

Omar took Sally sightseeing all day while I was away, into several mosques; in one he begged her to wait a minute while he said a prayer. They compare notes about their respective countries and are great friends; but he is put out at my not having provided her with a husband long ago, as is one's duty toward a 'female servant,' which almost always here means a slave.

Of all the falsehoods I have heard about the East, that about women being old hags at thirty is the biggest. Among the poor fellah women it may be true enough, but not nearly as much as in Germany; and I have now seen a considerable number of Levantine ladies looking very handsome, or at least comely, till fifty. Sakna, the Arab Grisi, is fifty-five—an ugly face, I am told (she was veiled and one only saw the eyes and glimpses of her mouth when she drank water), but the figure of a leopard, all grace and beauty, and a splendid voice of its kind, harsh but thrilling like Malibran's. I guessed her about thirty, or perhaps thirty-five. When she improvised, the finesse and grace of her whole *Wesen* [manner] were ravishing. I was on the point of shouting out 'Wallah!' as heartily as the natives. The eight younger *Halmeh* (*i.e.*, learned women, which the English call *Almeh* and think is an improper word) were ugly and screeched. Sakna was treated with greater consideration and quite as a friend by the Armenian ladies with whom she talked between her songs. She is a Muslimeh and very rich and charitable; she gets £50 for a night's singing at least.

It would be very easy to learn colloquial Arabic, as they all speak with perfect distinctness that one can follow the sentences and catch the words one knows as they are repeated. I think I know forty or fifty words already.

The reverse of the brilliant side of the medal is sad enough: deserted palaces, and crowded hovels scarce good enough for pigstyes. 'One day man see his dinner, and one other day none at all,' as Omar observes; and the children are shocking to look at from bad food, dirt and overwork, but the little pot-bellied, blear-eyed wretches grow up into noble young men and women under all their difficulties. The faces are all sad and rather what the Scotch call 'dour' not *méchant* at all, but harsh, like their voices. All the melody is in walk and gesture; they are as graceful as cats, and the women have exactly the 'breasts like pomegranates' of their poetry.

A tall Beduin woman came up to us in the field yesterday to shake hands and look at us. She wore a white sackcloth shift and veil, and nothing else. She asked Mrs Hekekian a good many questions about me, looked at my face and hands, but took no notice of my rather smart gown which the village women admired so much, shook hands again with the air of a princess, wished me health and happiness, and strode off across the graveyard like a stately ghost. She was on a journey all alone, and somehow it looked very solemn and affecting to see her walking away towards the desert in the setting sun like Hagar. All is so Scriptural in the country here. Sally called out in the railroad, 'There is Boaz, sitting in the cornfield'; and so it was, and there he has sat for how many thousand years, and in one war-song Sakna sang as Miriam, the prophetess, may have done when she took a timbrel in her hand and went out to meet the host.

Wednesday.—My contract was drawn up and signed by the American Vice-Consul today, and my Reis kissed my hand in due form, after which I went to the bazaar to buy the needful pots and pans. The transaction lasted an hour. The copper is so much per oka, the workmanship so much; every article is weighed by a sworn weigher and a ticket sent with it. More Arabian Nights. The shopkeeper compares notes with me about numerals, and is as much amused as I. He treats me to coffee and a pipe from a neighbouring shop while Omar eloquently depreciates the goods and offers half the value. A waterseller offers a brass cup of water; I drink, and give the huge sum of twopence, and he distributes the contents of his skin to the crowd (there always is a crowd) in my honour. It seems I have done a pious action. Finally a boy is called to carry the *batterie de cuisine,* while Omar brandishes a gigantic kettle which he has picked up a little bruised for four shillings. The boy has a donkey which I mount astride *à l Arabe,* while the boy carries all the copper things on his head. We are rather a grand procession, and quite enjoy the fury of the dragomans and other leeches, who hang on the English, at such independent proceedings, and Omar gets reviled for spoiling the trade by being cook and dragoman all in one.

SOURCE: In *Letters from Egypt 1862–1869,* ed. Gordon Waterfield (New York: Praeger, 1969).

Suez.

RICHARD F. BURTON

[Richard Burton was a prominent explorer of England's Arabian and African imperial reaches. Like E. W. Lane, Burton translated *1001 Nights,* publishing a version that was both hailed and critiqued for its renditions of customary, sexual, and ethnic practices. His pilgrimage to the Muslim holy cities of Mecca and Medina took place in the early 1850s, and Burton's claim to have "passed" linguistically and ethnically as a visitor to the sacred sites is an important element in his narrative.]

Early on the morning after my arrival, I arose, and consulted my new acquaintances about the means of recovering the missing property. They unanimously advised a visit to the governor, whom, however, they described to be a "Kalb ibn kalb," (dog, son of a dog,) who never returned Moslems' salutations, and who thought all men dirt to be trodden under foot by the Turks. The boy Mohammed showed his *savoir faire* by extracting from his huge Sahará-box a fine embroidered cap, and a grand peach-coloured coat, with which I was instantly invested; he dressed himself with similar magnificence, and we then set out to the "palace."

Ja'afar Bey,—he has since been deposed,—then occupied the position of judge, officer commanding, collector of customs, and magistrate of Suez. He was a Mir-liwá, or brigadier-general, and had some reputation as a soldier, together with a slight tincture of European science and language. The large old Turk received me most superciliously, disdained all return of salam, and, fixing upon me two little eyes like gimlets, demanded my business. I stated that one Shaykh Nur, my Hindi servant, had played me false; therefore I required permission to break into the room supposed to contain my effects. He asked my profession. I replied the medical. This led him to inquire if I had any medicine for the eyes, and being answered in the affirmative, he sent a messenger with me to enforce obedience on the part of the porter. The obnoxious measure was, however, unnecessary. As we entered the Caravanserai, there appeared at the door the black face of Shaykh Nur, looking, though accompanied by sundry fellow-countrymen, uncommonly as if he merited and expected the bamboo. He had, by his own account, been seduced into the festivities of a coalhulk, manned by Lascars, and the vehemence of his self-accusation saved him from the chastisement which I had determined to administer.

I must now briefly describe the party of Meccah and Madinah men into which fate threw me: their names will so frequently appear in the following pages, that a few words about their natures will not be misplaced.

First of all comes Omar Effendi,—so called in honour,—a Dághistáni or East-Circassian, the grandson of a Hanafi Mufti at Al-Madinah, and the son of a Shaykh Rakb, an officer whose duty it is to lead dromedary-caravans. He sits upon his cot, a small, short, plump body, of yellow complexion and bilious temperament, grey-eyed, soft-featured, and utterly beardless,—which affects his feelings,—he looks fifteen, and he owns to twenty-eight. His manners are those of a student; he dresses respectably, prays regularly, hates the fair sex, like an Arab, whose affections and aversions are always in extremes; is "serious," has a mild demeanour, an humble gait, and a soft, slow voice. When roused he becomes furious as a Bengal tiger. His parents have urged him to marry, and he, like Kamar al-Zamán, has informed his father that he is "a person of great age, but little sense." Urged moreover by a melancholy turn of mind, and the want of leisure for study at Al-Madinah, he fled the paternal domicile, and entered himself a pauper Tálib 'ilm (student) in the Azhar Mosque. His disconsolate friends and afflicted relations sent a confidential man to fetch him home, by force should it be necessary; he has yielded, and is now awaiting the first opportunity of travelling gratis, if possible, to Al-Madinah.

That confidential man is a negro-servant, called Sa'ad, notorious in his native city as Al-Jinni, the Demon. Born and bred a slave in Omar Effendi's family, he obtained manumission, became a soldier in Al-Hijaz, was dissatisfied with pay perpetually in arrears, turned merchant, and wandered far and wide, to Russia, to Gibraltar, and to Baghdad. He is the pure African, noisily merry at one moment, at another silently sulky; affectionate and abusive, brave and boastful, reckless and crafty, exceedingly quarrelsome, and unscrupulous to the last degree. The bright side of his character is his love and respect for the young master, Omar Effendi; yet even him he will scold in a paroxysm of fury, and steal from him whatever he can lay his hands on. He is generous with his goods, but is ever borrowing and never paying money; he dresses like a beggar, with the dirtiest Tarbush upon his tufty poll, and only a cotton shirt over his sooty skin; whilst his two boxes are full of handsome apparel for himself and the three ladies, his wives, at Al-Madinah. He knows no fear but for those boxes. Frequently during our search for a vessel he forced himself into Ja'afar Bey's presence, and there he demeaned himself so impudently, that we expected to see him lamed by the bastinado; his forwardness, however, only amused the dignitary. He wanders all day about the bazar, talking about freight and passage, for he has resolved, cost what it will, to travel free, and, with doggedness like his, he must succeed.

Shaykh Hámid al-Sammán derives his cognomen, the "Clarified-Butter-Seller," from a celebrated saint and Sufi of the Kádiriyah order, who left a long line of holy descendants at Al-Madinah. This Shaykh squats upon a box full of presents for the "daughter of his paternal uncle" (his wife), a perfect specimen of the town Arab. His poll is crowned with a rough Shúshah or tuft of hair[1]; his face is of a dirty brown, his little *goatee* straggles untrimmed; his feet are bare, and his only garment is an exceedingly unclean ochre-coloured

---

1. When travelling, the Shushah is allowed to spread over the greatest portion of the scalp, to act as a protection against the sun; and the hair being shaved off about two inches all round the head, leaves a large circular patch. Nothing can be uglier than such tonsure, and it is contrary to the strict law of the Apostle, who ordered a clean shave, or a general growth of the hair. The Arab, however, knows by experience, that though habitual exposure of the scalp to a burning sun may harden the skull, it seldom fails to damage its precious contents. He, therefore, wears a Shushah during his wanderings, and removes it on his return home. Abu Hanifah, if I am rightly informed, wrote a treatise advocating the growth of a long lock of hair on the Násiyah, or crown of the head, lest the decapitated Moslem's mouth or beard be exposed to defilement by an impure hand. This would justify the comparing it to the "chivalry-lock," by which the American brave facilitates the removal of his own scalp. But I am at a loss to discover the origin of our old idea, that the "angel of death will, on the last day, bear all true believers, by this important tuft of hair on the crown, to Paradise." Probably this office has been attributed to the Shushah by the ignorance of the West.

blouse, tucked into a leathern girdle beneath it. He will not pray, because he is unwilling to take pure clothes out of his box; but he smokes when he can get other people's tobacco, and groans between the whiffs, conjugating the verb all day, for he is of active mind. He can pick out his letters, and he keeps in his bosom a little dog's-eared MS. full of serious romances and silly prayers, old and exceedingly ill written; this he will draw forth at times, peep into for a moment, devoutly kiss, and restore to its proper place with the veneration of the vulgar for a book. He can sing all manner of songs, slaughter a sheep with dexterity, deliver a grand call to prayer, shave, cook, fight; and he excels in the science of vituperation: like Sa'ad, he never performs his devotions, except when necessary to "keep up appearances," and though he has sworn to perish before he forgets his vow to the "daughter of his uncle," I shrewdly suspect he is no better than he should be. His brow crumples at the word wine, but there is quite another expression about the region of the mouth; Stambul, where he has lived some months, without learning ten words of Turkish, is a notable place for displacing prejudice. And finally, he has not more than a piastre or two in his pocket, for he has squandered the large presents given to him at Cairo and Constantinople by noble ladies, to whom he acted as master of the ceremonies at the tomb of the Apostle.

Stretched on a carpet, smoking a Persian Kaliun all day, lies Sálih Shakkar, a Turk on the father's, and an Arab on the mother's side, born at Al-Madinah. This lanky youth may be sixteen years old, but he has the ideas of forty-six; he is thoroughly greedy, selfish, and ungenerous; coldly supercilious as a Turk, and energetically avaricious as an Arab. He prays more often, and dresses more respectably, than the descendant of the Clarified-Butter-Seller; he affects the Constantinople style of toilette, and his light yellow complexion makes people consider him a "superior person." We were intimate enough on the road, when he borrowed from me a little money. But at Al-Madinah he cut me pitilessly, as a "town man" does a continental acquaintance accidentally met in Hyde Park; and of course he tried, though in vain, to evade repaying his debt. He had a tincture of letters, and appeared to have studied critically the subject of "largesse." "The Generous is Allah's friend, aye, though he be a Sinner, and the Miser is Allah's Foe, aye, though he be a Saint," was a venerable saying always in his mouth. He also informed me that Pharaoh, although the quintessence of impiety, is mentioned by name in the Koran, by reason of his liberality; whereas Nimrod, another monster of iniquity, is only alluded to, because he was a stingy tyrant. It is almost needless to declare that Salih Shakkar was, as the East-Indians say, a very "fly-sucker."[2]

2. "Makhi-chús," equivalent to our "skin-flint."

There were two other men of Al-Madinah in the Wakalah Jirgis; but I omit description, as we left them, they being penniless, at Suez. One of them, Mohammed Shiklibhá, I afterwards met at Meccah, and seldom have I seen a more honest and warm-hearted fellow. When we were embarking at Suez, he fell upon Hamid's bosom, and both of them wept bitterly, at the prospect of parting even for a few days.

All the individuals above mentioned lost no time in opening the question of a loan. It was a lesson in Oriental metaphysics to see their condition. They had a twelve days' voyage, and a four days' journey before them; boxes to carry, custom-houses to face, and stomachs to fill; yet the whole party could scarcely, I believe, muster two dollars of ready money. Their boxes were full of valuables, arms, clothes, pipes, slippers, sweetmeats, and other "notions"; but nothing short of starvation would have induced them to pledge the smallest article.

Foreseeing that their company would be an advantage, I hearkened favourably to the honeyed request for a few crowns. The boy Mohammed obtained six dollars; Hamid about five pounds, as I intended to make his house at Al-Madinah my home; Omar Effendi three dollars; Sa'ad the Demon two—I gave the money to him at Yambu',—and Salih Shakkar fifty piastres. But since in these lands, as a rule, no one ever lends coins, or, borrowing, ever returns them, I took care to exact service from the first, to take two rich coats from the second, a handsome pipe from the third, a "bálá" or yataghan from the fourth, and from the fifth an imitation Cashmere shawl. After which, we sat down and drew out the agreement. It was favourable to me: I lent them Egyptian money, and bargained for repayment in the currency of Al-Hijaz, thereby gaining the exchange, which is sometimes sixteen per cent. This was done, not so much for the sake of profit, as with the view of becoming a Hátim,[3] by a "never mind" on settling day. My companions having received these small sums, became affectionate and eloquent in my praise: they asked me to make one of their number at meals for the future, overwhelmed me with questions, insisted upon a present of sweetmeats, detected in me a great man under a cloud,—perhaps my claims to being a Darwaysh assisted them to this discovery,—and declared that I should perforce be their guest at Meccah and Al-Madinah. On all occasions precedence was forced upon me; my opinion was the first consulted, and no project was settled without my concurrence: briefly, Abdullah the Darwaysh suddenly found himself a person of consequence. This elevation led me into an imprudence which might have cost me dear; aroused the only suspicion about me ever expressed during the summer's tour.

---

3. A well-known Arab chieftain, whose name has come to stand for generosity itself.

My friends had looked at my clothes, overhauled my medicine chest, and criticised my pistols; they sneered at my copper-cased watch,[4] and remembered having seen a compass at Constantinople. Therefore I imagined they would think little about a sextant. This was a mistake. The boy Mohammed, I afterward learned,[5] waited only my leaving the room to declare that the would-be Haji was one of the Infidels from India, and a council sat to discuss the case. Fortunately for me, Omar Effendi had looked over a letter which I had written to Haji Wali that morning, and he had at various times received categorical replies to certain questions in high theology. He felt himself justified in declaring, *ex cathedrâ*, the boy Mohammed's position perfectly untenable. And Shaykh Hamid, who looked forward to being my host, guide, and debtor in general, and probably cared scantily for catechism or creed, swore that the light of Al-Islam was upon my countenance, and, consequently, that the boy Mohammed was a pauper, a "fakir," an owl, a cut-off one,[6] a stranger, and a Wahhabi (heretic), for daring to impugn the faith of a brother believer.[7] The scene ended with a general abuse of the acute youth, who was told on all sides that he had no shame, and was directed to "fear Allah." I was struck with the expression of my friends' countenances when they saw the sextant, and, determining with a sigh to leave it behind, I prayed five times a day for nearly a week.

We all agreed not to lose an hour in securing places on board some vessel bound for Yambu'; and my companions, hearing that my passport as a British Indian was scarcely *en règle*, earnestly advised me to have it signed by the

---

4. This being an indispensable instrument for measuring distances, I had it divested of gold case, and provided with a facing carefully stained and figured with Arabic numerals. In countries where few can judge of a watch by its works, it is as well to secure its safety by making the exterior look as mean as possible. The watches worn by respectable people in Al-Hijaz are almost always old silver pieces, of the turnip shape, with hunting cases and an outer *étui* of thick leather. Mostly they are of Swiss or German manufacture, and they find their way into Arabia *vid*. Constantinople and Cairo.

5. On my return to Cairo, Omar Effendi, whom I met accidentally in the streets, related the story to me. I never owned having played a part, to avoid shocking his prejudices; and though he must have suspected me,—for the general report was, that an Englishman, disguised as a Persian, had performed the pilgrimage, measured the country, and sketched the buildings,—he had the gentlemanly feeling never to allude to the past. We parted, when I went to India, on the best of terms.

6. Munkati'a—one cut off (from the pleasures and comforts of life). In Al-Hijaz, as in England, any allusion to poverty is highly offensive.

7. The Koran expressly forbids a Moslem to discredit the word of any man who professes his belief in the Saving Faith. The greatest offence of the Wahhabis is their habit of designating all Moslems that belong to any but their own sect by the opprobrious name of Kafirs or infidels. This, however, is only the Koranic precept; in practice a much less trustful spirit prevails.

governor without delay, whilst they occupied themselves about the harbour. They warned me that if I displayed the Turkish Tazkirah given me at the citadel of Cairo, I should infallibly be ordered to await the caravan, and lose their society and friendship. Pilgrims arriving at Alexandria, be it known to the reader, are divided into bodies, and distributed by means of passports to the three great roads, namely, Suez, Kusayr (Cosseir), and the Hajj route by land round the Gulf of al-'Akabah. After the division has once been made, government turns a deaf ear to the representations of individuals. The Bey of Suez has an order to obstruct pilgrims as much as possible till the end of the season, when they are hurried down that way, lest they should arrive at Meccah too late.[8] As most of the Egyptian high officials have boats, which sail up the Nile laden with pilgrims and return freighted with corn, the government naturally does its utmost to force the delays and discomforts of this line upon strangers.[9] And as those who travel by the Hajj route must spend money in the Egyptian territories at least fifteen days longer than they would if allowed to embark at once from Suez, the Bey very properly assists them in the former and obstructs them in the latter case. Knowing these facts, I felt that a difficulty was at hand. The first thing was to take Shaykh Nur's passport, which was *en règle*, and my own, which was not, to the Bey for signature. He turned the papers over and over, as if unable to read them, and raised false hopes high by referring me to his clerk. The under-official at once saw the irregularity of the document, asked me why it had not been visé at Cairo, swore that under such circumstances nothing would induce the Bey to let me proceed; and, when I tried persuasion, waxed insolent. I feared that it would be necessary to travel *vid* Cosseir, for which there was scarcely time, or to transfer myself on camel-back to the harbour of Tur, and there to await the chance of finding a place in some half-filled vessel to Al-Hijaz,—which would have been relying upon an accident. My last hope at Suez was to obtain assistance from Mr. West, then H.B.M.'s Vice-Consul, and since made Consul. I therefore took the boy Mohammed with me, choosing him on purpose, and excusing the step to my companions by concocting an artful fable about my having been, in Afghanistan, a benefactor to the British nation. We proceeded to the Consulate. Mr. West, who had been told by imprudent Augustus Bernal to expect me, saw through the disguise, despite jargon as-

---

8. Towards the end of the season, poor pilgrims are forwarded gratis, by order of government. But, to make such liberality as inexpensive as possible, the Pasha compels ship-owners to carry one pilgrim per 9 ardebs (about 5 bushels each), in small, and 1 per 11 in large vessels.

9. I was informed by a Prussian gentleman, holding an official appointment under His Highness the Pasha, at Cairo, that 300,000 ardebs of grain were annually exported from Kusayr to Jeddah. The rest is brought down the Nile for consumption in Lower Egypt, and export to Europe.

sumed to satisfy official scruples, and nothing could be kinder than the part he took. His clerk was directed to place himself in communication with the Bey's factotum; and, when objections to signing the Alexandrian Tazkirah were offered, the Vice-Consul said that he would, at his own risk, give me a fresh passport as a British subject from Suez to Arabia. His firmness prevailed: on the second day, the documents were returned to me in a satisfactory state. I take a pleasure in owning this obligation to Mr. West: in the course of my wanderings, I have often received from him open-hearted hospitality and the most friendly attentions.

Whilst these passport difficulties were being solved, the rest of the party was as busy in settling about passage and passage-money. The peculiar rules of the port of Suez require a few words of explanation.[10] "About thirty-five years ago" (*i.e.* about 1818 A.D.), "the shipowners proposed to the then government, with the view of keeping up freight, a Farzah, or system of rotation. It might be supposed that the Pasha, whose object notoriously was to retain all monopolies in his own hands, would have refused his sanction to such a measure. But it so happened in those days that all the court had ships at Suez: Ibrahim Pasha alone owned four or five. Consequently, they expected to share profits with the merchants, and thus to be compensated for the want of port-dues. From that time forward all the vessels in the harbour were registered, and ordered to sail in rotation. This arrangement benefits the owner of the craft 'en départ,' giving him in his turn a temporary monopoly, with the advantage of a full market; and freight is so high that a single trip often clears off the expense of building and the risk of losing the ship—a sensible *succedaneum* for insurance companies. On the contrary, the public must always be a loser by the 'Farzah.' Two of a trade do not agree elsewhere; but at Suez even the Christian and the Moslem shipowner are bound by a fraternal tie, in the shape of this rotation system. It injures the general merchant and the Red Sea trader, not only by perpetuating high freight,[11] but also by causing at one

---

10. The account here offered to the reader was kindly supplied to me by Henry Levick, Esq. (late Vice-Consul, and afterwards Postmaster at Suez), and it may be depended upon, as coming from a resident of 16 years' standing. All the passages marked with inverted commas are extracts from a letter with which that gentleman favoured me. The information is obsolete now, but it may be interesting as a specimen of the things that were.

11. The rate of freight is at present (1853) about forty shillings per ton—very near the same paid by the P. and O. Company for coals carried from Newcastle *vid* the Cape to Suez. Were the "Farzah" abolished, freight to Jeddah would speedily fall to 15 or 16 shillings per ton. Passengers from Suez to Jeddah are sometimes charged as much as 6 or even 8 dollars for standing room—personal baggage forming another pretext for extortion—and the higher orders of pilgrims, occupying a small portion of the cabin, pay about 12 dollars. These first and second class fares

period of the year a break in the routine of sales and in the supplies of goods for the great Jeddah market.[12] At this moment (Nov. 1853), the vessel to which the turn belongs happens to be a large one; there is a deficiency of export to Al-Hijaz,—her owner will of course wait any length of time for a full cargo; consequently no vessel with merchandise has left Suez for the last seventy-two days. Those who have bought goods for the Jeddah market at three months' credit will therefore have to meet their acceptances for merchandise still warehoused at the Egyptian port. This strange contrast to free-trade principle is another proof that protection benefits only one party, the protected, while it is detrimental to the interests of the other party, the public." To these remarks of Mr. Levick's, I have only to add that the government supports the Farzah with all the energy of protectionists. A letter from Mr. (now Sir) John Drummond Hay was insufficient to induce the Bey of Suez to break through the rule of rotation in favour of certain princes from Morocco. The recommendations of Lord Stratford de Redcliffe met with no better fate; and all Mr. West's good will could not procure me a vessel out of her turn.[13] We were forced to rely upon our own exertions, and the activity of Sa'ad the Demon. This worthy, after sundry delays and differences, mostly caused by his own determination to travel gratis, and to make us pay too much, finally closed with the owner of the "Golden Thread."[14] He took places for us upon the poop,—the most eligible part of the vessel at this season of the year; he premised that we should not be very comfortable, as we were to be crowded with Maghrabi pilgrims, but that "Allah makes all things easy!" Though not penetrated with the conviction that this would happen in our case, I paid for two deck passages eighteen Riyals[15] (dollars), and my companions seven each,

---

would speedily be reduced, by abolishing protection, to 3 and 6 dollars. Note to Second Edition.—The "Farzah," I may here observe, has been abolished by Sa'id Pasha since the publication of these lines: the effects of "free trade" are exactly what were predicted by Mr. Levick.

12. The principal trade from Suez is to Jeddah, Kusayr supplying Yambu'. The latter place, however, imports from Suez wheat, beans, cheese, biscuit, and other provisions for return pilgrims.

13. My friends were strenuous in their exertions for me to make interest with Mr. West. In the first place, we should have paid less for the whole of a privileged vessel, than we did for our wretched quarters on the deck of the pilgrim-ship; and, secondly, we might have touched at any port we pleased, so as to do a little business in the way of commerce.

14. Afterwards called by Sir R. F. Burton the "Golden Wire."

15. For the "Sath," or poop, the sum paid by each was seven Riyals. I was, therefore, notably cheated by Sa'ad the Demon. The unhappy women in the "Kamrah," or cabin, bought suffocation at the rate of 6 dollars each, as I was afterwards informed, and the third class in the "Taht," or amidships and forward, contributed from 3 to 5 Riyals. But, as usual on these occasions, there was no *prix fixe;* every man was either overcharged or undercharged, according to his means or

whilst Sa'ad secretly entered himself as an able seaman. Mohammed Shiklibha we were obliged to leave behind, as he could not, or might not afford the expense, and none of us might afford it for him. Had I known him to be the honest, true-hearted fellow he was—his kindness at Meccah quite won my heart—I should not have grudged the small charity.

Nothing more comfortless than our days and nights in the "George" Inn. The ragged walls of our rooms were clammy with dirt, the smoky rafters foul with cobwebs, and the floor, bestrewed with kit, in terrible confusion, was black with hosts of cockroaches, ants, and flies. Pigeons nestled on the shelf, cooing amatory ditties the live-long day, and cats like tigers crawled through a hole in the door, making night hideous with their caterwaulings. Now a curious goat, then an inquisitive jackass, would walk stealthily into the room, remark that it was tenanted, and retreat with dignified demeanour, and the mosquitos sang Io Pæans over our prostrate forms throughout the twenty-four hours. I spare the reader the enumeration of the other Egyptian plagues that infested the place. After the first day's trial, we determined to spend the hours of light in the passages, lying upon our boxes or rugs, smoking, wrangling, and inspecting one another's chests. The latter occupation was a fertile source of disputes, for nothing was more common than for a friend to seize an article belonging to another, and to swear by the Apostle's beard that he admired it, and, therefore, would not return it. The boy Mohammed and Shaykh Nur, who had been intimates the first day, differed in opinion on the second, and on the third came to pushing each other against the wall. Sometimes we went into the Bazar, a shady street flanked with poor little shops, or we sat in the coffee-house,[16] drinking hot saltish water tinged with burnt bean, or we prayed in one of three tumble-down old Mosques, or we squatted upon the pier, lamenting the want of Hammams, and bathing in the tepid sea.[17] I presently came to the conclusion that Suez as a "watering-place" is

---

his necessities. We had to purchase our own water, but the ship was to supply us with fuel for cooking. We paid nothing extra for luggage, and we carried an old Maghrabi woman gratis for good luck.

16. We were still at Suez, where we could do as we pleased. But respectable Arabs in their own country, unlike Egyptians, are seldom to be seen in the places of public resort. "Go to the coffee-house and sing there!" is a reproach sometimes addressed to those who have a habit of humming in decent society.

17. It was only my prestige as physician that persuaded my friend to join me in these bathings. As a general rule, the Western Arabs avoid cold water, from a belief that it causes fever. When Mr. C. Cole, H.B.M.'s Vice-Consul, arrived at Jeddah, the people of the place, seeing that he kept up his Indian habits, advised him strongly to drop them. He refused; but unhappily he soon caught a fever, which confirmed them all in their belief. When Arabs wish to cool the skin after a

duller even than Dover. The only society we found, excepting an occasional visitor, was that of a party of Egyptian women, who with their husbands and families occupied some rooms adjoining ours. At first they were fierce, and used bad language, when the boy Mohammed and I,—whilst Omar Effendi was engaged in prayer, and the rest were wandering about the town,—ventured to linger in the cool passage, where they congregated, or to address a facetious phrase to them. But hearing that I was a Hákim-bashi—for fame had promoted me to the rank of a "Physician General" at Suez—all discovered some ailments. They began prudently with requesting me to display the effects of my drugs by dosing myself, but they ended submissively by swallowing the nauseous compounds. To this succeeded a primitive form of flirtation, which mainly consisted of the demand direct. The most charming of the party was one Fattúmah,[18] a plump-personal dame, fast verging upon her thirtieth year, fond of a little flattery, and possessing, like all her people, a most voluble tongue. The refrain of every conversation was "Marry me, O Fattumah! O daughter! O female pilgrim!" In vain the lady would reply, with a coquettish movement of the sides, a toss of the head, and a flirting manipulation of her head-veil, "I am mated, O young man!"—it was agreed that she, being a person of polyandrous propensities, could support the weight of at least three matrimonial engagements. Sometimes the entrance of the male Fellahs[19] interrupted these little discussions, but people of our respectability and nation were not to be imposed upon by such husbands. In their presence we only varied the style of conversation—inquiring the amount of "Mahr," or marriage settlement, deriding the cheapness of womanhood in Egypt, and requiring to be furnished on the spot with brides at the rate of ten shillings a head.[20] More often the amiable Fattumah—the fair sex in this country, though passing frail, have the best tempers in the world—would laugh at our impertinences. Sometimes vexed by our imitating her Egyptian accent, mim-

---

journey, they wash with a kind of fuller's earth called "Tafl," or with a thin paste of henna, and then anoint the body with oil or butter.

18. An incrementative form of the name "Fátimah," very common in Egypt. Fatimah would mean a "weaner"—Fattúmah, a "great weaner." By the same barbarism Khadíjah becomes "Khaddúgah"; Aminah, "Ammúnah"; and Nafisah, "Naffúsah," on the banks of the Nile.

19. The palmy days of the Egyptian husband, when he might use the stick, the sword, or the sack with impunity, are, in civilised places at least, now gone by. The wife has only to complain to the Kazi, or to the governor, and she is certain of redress. This is right in the abstract, but in practice it acts badly. The fair sex is so unruly in this country, that strong measures are necessary to coerce it, and in the arts of deceit men have here little or no chance against women.

20. The amount of settlement being, among Moslems as among Christians, the test of a bride's value,—moral and physical,—it will readily be understood that our demand was more facetious than complimentary.

icking her gestures, and depreciating her country-women,[21] she would wax wroth, and order us to be gone, and stretch out her forefinger—a sign that she wished to put out our eyes, or adjure Allah to cut the hearts out of our bosoms. Then the "Marry me, O Fattumah, O daughter, O female pilgrim!" would give way to Y'al Ago-o-oz! (O old woman and decrepit!) "O daughter of sixty sires, and fit only to carry wood to market!"—whereupon would burst a storm of wrath, at the tail of which all of us, like children, starting upon our feet, rushed out of one another's way. But—*"qui se dispute, s'adore"*—when we again met all would be forgotten, and the old tale be told over *de novo*. This was the amusement of the day. At night we men, assembling upon the little terrace, drank tea, recited stories, read books, talked of our travels, and indulged in various pleasantries. The great joke was the boy Mohammed's abusing all his companions to their faces in Hindustani, which none but Shaykh Nur and I could understand; the others, however, guessed his intention, and revenged themselves by retorts of the style uncourteous in the purest Hijazi.

I proceed to offer a few more extracts from Mr. Levick's letter about Suez and the Suezians. "It appears that the number of pilgrims who pass through Suez to Meccah has of late been steadily on the decrease. When I first came here (in 1838) the pilgrims who annually embarked at this port amounted to between 10,000 and 12,000, the shipping was more numerous, and the merchants were more affluent.[22] I have ascertained from a special register kept in the government archives that in the Moslem year 1268 (A.D. 1851–52) the exact number that passed through was 4893."

"In 1269 A.H. (A.D. 1852–53) it had shrunk to 3136. The natives assign the falling off to various causes, which I attribute chiefly to the indirect effect of European civilisation upon the Moslem powers immediately in contact with it. The heterogeneous mass of pilgrims is composed of people of all classes, colours, and costumes. One sees among them, not only the natives of countries contiguous to Egypt, but also a large proportion of Central Asians from Bokhara, Persia, Circassia, Turkey, and the Crimea, who prefer this route by

---

21. The term Misriyah (an Egyptian woman) means in Al-Hijaz and the countries about it, a depraved character. Even the men own unwillingly to being Egyptians, for the free-born never forget that the banks of the Nile have for centuries been ruled by the slaves of slaves. "He shall be called an Egyptian," is a denunciation which has been strikingly fulfilled, though the country be no longer the "basest of kingdoms."

22. In those days merchants depended solely upon the native trade and the passage of pilgrims. The pecuniary advantage attending what is called the Overland transit benefits chiefly the lowest orders, camel-men, sailors, porters, and others of the same class. Sixteen years ago the hire of a boat from the harbour to the roadstead was a piastre and a half: now it is at least five.

way of Constantinople to the difficult, expensive and dangerous caravan-line through the Desert from Damascus and Baghdad. The West sends us Moors, Algerines, and Tunisians, and Inner Africa a mass of sable Takrouri,[23] and others from Bornou, the Sudán,[24] Ghadamah near the Niger, and Jabarti from the Habash."[25]

"The Suez ship-builders are an influential body of men, originally Candiots and Alexandrians. When Mohammed Ali fitted out his fleet for the Hijaz war, he transported a number of Greeks to Suez, and the children now exercise their fathers' craft. There are at present three great builders at this place. Their principal difficulty is the want of material. Teak comes from India[26] *vid* Jeddah, and Venetian boards, owing to the expense of camel-transport, are a hundred per cent dearer here than at Alexandria. Trieste and Turkey supply spars, and Jeddah canvas: the sail-makers are Suez men, and the crews a mongrel mixture of Arabs and Egyptians; the Rais, or captain, being almost invariably, if the vessel be a large one, a Yambu' man. There are two kinds of craft, distinguished from each other by tonnage, not by build. The Baghlah[27] (buggalow), is a vessel above fifty tons burden, the Sambúk (a classical term) from fifteen to fifty. The shipowner bribes the Amir al-Bahr, or port-captain, and the Nazir al-Safayn, or the captain commanding the government vessels, to rate his ship as high as possible; if he pay the price, he will be allowed nine ardebs to the ton.[28] The number of ships belonging to the port of Suez amounts to 92; they vary from 25 to 250 tons. The departures in

---

23. This word, says Mansfield Parkyns (Life in Abyssinia), is applied to the wandering *pilgrim* from Dárfúr, Dár Borghú, Bayárimah, Fellatah, and Western Africa. He mentions, however, a tribe called "Tokrouri," settled in Abyssinia near Nimr's country, but he does not appear to know that the ancient Arab settlement in Western Africa, "Al-Takrúr," (Sakatu?) which has handed down its name to a large posterity of small kingdoms, will be found in Al-Idrisi (I. climate, I. section,); but I do not agree with the learned translator in writing the word "Tokrour." Burckhardt often alludes in his benevolent way to the "respectable and industrious Tekrourys." I shall have occasion to mention them at a future time.
24. The Sudan (Blackland) in Arabia is applied to Upper Nubia, Senaar, Kordofan, and the parts adjacent.
25. Not only in Ghiz, but also in Arabic, the mother of Ghiz, the word "Habash," whence our "Abyssinians," means a rabble, a mixture of people. Abyssinian Moslems are called by the Arabs "Jabarti."
26. There is no such things as a tree, except the date, the tamarisk, and the mimosa on the western shores of the Red Sea.
27. This word, which in Arabic is the feminine form of "Baghl," a mule, is in Egypt, as in India, pronounced and written by foreigners "buggalow." Some worthy Anglo-Indians have further corrupted it to "bungalow."
28. "The ardeb, like most measures in this country of commercial confusion, varies greatly according to the grain for which it is used. As a general rule, it may be assumed at 300 lbs."

A.H. 1269 (1852 and 1853) were 38, so that each vessel, after returning from a trip, is laid up for about two years. Throughout the passage of the pilgrims,—that is to say, during four months,—the departures average twice a week; during the remainder of the year from six to ten vessels may leave the port. The homeward trade is carried on principally in Jeddah bottoms, which are allowed to convey goods to Suez, but not to take in return cargo there: they must not interfere with, nor may they partake in any way of the benefits of the rotation system."[29]

"During the present year the imports were contained in 41,395 packages, the exports in 15,988. Specie makes up in some manner for this preponderance of imports: a sum of from £30,000 to £40,000, in crown, or Maria Theresa, dollars annually leaves Egypt for Arabia, Abyssinia, and other parts of Africa. I value the imports at about £350,000; the export trade to Jeddah at £300,000 per annum. The former consists principally of coffee and gum-arabic; of these there were respectively 17,460 and 15,132 bales, the aggregate value of each article being from £75,000 to £80,000, and the total amount £160,000. In the previous year the imports were contained in 36,840 packages, the exports in 13,498: of the staple articles—coffee and gum-arabic—they were respectively 15,499 and 14,129 bales, each bale being valued at about £5. Next in importance comes wax from Al-Yaman and the Hijaz, mother-of-pearl[30] from the Red Sea, sent to England in rough, pepper from Malabar, cloves brought by Moslem pilgrims from Java, Borneo, and Singapore,[31] cherry pipe-sticks from Persia and Bussora, and Persian or Surat 'Timbak' (tobacco). These I value at £20,000 per annum. There were also (A.D. 1853) of cloves 708 packages, and of Malabar pepper 948: the cost of these two might be £7,000. Minor articles of exportation are,—general spiceries (ginger, cardamoms, &c.); Eastern perfumes, such as aloes-wood, attar of rose, attar of pink and others; tamarinds from India and Al-Yaman, Banca tin, hides supplied by the nomade Badawin, senna leaves from Al-Yaman and the Hijaz, and blue chequered cotton Malayahs (women's mantillas), manufactured in southern Arabia. The total value of these smaller imports may be £20,000 per annum."

29. Return Arab boats, at any but the pilgrim season, with little difficulty obtain permission to carry passengers, but not cargo. Two gentlemen, in whose pleasant society I once travelled from Cairo to Suez,—M. Charles Didier and the Abbé Hamilton,—paid the small sum of 1000 piastres, (say £10) for the whole of a moderate sized "Sambuk" returning to Jeddah.

30. Mother-of-pearl is taken to Jerusalem, and there made into chaplets, saints' figures, and crucifixes for Christian pilgrims. At Meccah it is worked into rosaries for the Hajis. In Europe, cabinet and ornamental work cause a considerable demand for it. Some good pearls are procurable in the Red Sea. I have seen a drop of fair size and colour sold for seven dollars.

31. I was told at Meccah that the pilgrimage is attended by about 2000 natives of Java and the adjoining islands.

"The exports chiefly consist of English and native 'grey domestics,' bleached Madipilams, Paisley lappets, and muslins for turbans; the remainder being Manchester prints, antimony, Syrian soap, iron in bars, and common ironmongery, Venetian or Trieste beads, used as ornaments in Arabia and Abyssinia, writing paper, Tarbushes, Papushes (slippers), and other minor articles of dress and ornament."

"The average annual temperature of the year at Suez is 67° Fahrenheit. The extremes of heat and cold are found in January and August; during the former month the thermometer ranges from a minimum of 38° to a maximum of 68°; during the latter the variation extends from 68° to 102°, or even to 104°, when the heat becomes oppressive. Departures from these extremes are rare. I never remember to have seen the thermometer rise above 108° during the severest Khamsin, or to have sunk below 34° in the rawest wintry wind. Violent storms come up from the south in March. Rain is very variable[32]: sometimes three years have passed without a shower, whereas in 1841 torrents poured for nine successive days, deluging the town, and causing many buildings to fall."

"The population of Suez now numbers about 4,800. As usual in Mohammedan countries no census is taken here. Some therefore estimate the population at 6,000. Sixteen years ago it was supposed to be under 3,000. After that time it rapidly increased till 1850, when a fatal attack of cholera reduced it to about half its previous number. The average mortality is about twelve a month.[33] The endemic diseases are fevers of typhoid and intermittent types in spring, when strong northerly winds cause the waters of the bay to recede,[34]

---

32. The following popular puerilities will serve to show how fond barbarians are of explaining the natural by the supernatural. The Moslems of Egypt thus account for the absence of St. Swithin from their drought-stricken lands. When Jacob lost his Benjamin, he cursed the land of Misraim, declaring that it should know no rain; Joseph on the other hand blessed it, asserting that it should never want water. So the Sind Hindus believe that Hiranyakasipu, the demon-tyrant of Multan, finding Magha-Raja (the Cloud King) troublesome in his dominions, bound him with chains, and only released him upon his oath not to trouble the Unhappy Valley with his presence. I would suggest to those Egyptian travellers who believe that the fall of rain has been materially increased at Cairo of late, by plantations of trees, to turn over the volumes of their predecessors; they will find almost every one complaining of the discomforts of rain. In Sind it appears certain that during the last few years there has been at times almost a monsoon; this novel phenomenon the natives attribute to the presence of their conquerors, concerning whom it cannot be said that they have wooded the country to any extent.

33. This may appear a large mortality; but at Alexandria it is said the population is renewed every fourteen years.

34. During these North winds the sandy bar is exposed, and allows men to cross, which may explain the passage of the Israelites, for those who do not believe the Legend to be a Myth. Similarly at Jeddah, the bars are covered during the South and bare during the North winds.

and leave a miasma-breeding swamp exposed to the rays of the sun. In the months of October and November febrile attacks are violent; ophthalmia more so. The eye-disease is not so general here as at Cairo, but the symptoms are more acute; in some years it becomes a virulent epidemic, which ends either in total blindness or in a partial opacity of the cornea, inducing dimness of vision, and a permanent weakness of the eyes. In one month three of my acquaintances lost their sight. Dysenteries are also common, and so are bad boils, or rather ulcers. The cold season is not unwholesome, and at this period the pure air of the Desert restores and invigorates the heat-wasted frame."

"The walls, gates, and defences of Suez are in a ruinous state, being no longer wanted to keep out the Sinaitic Badawin. The houses are about 500 in number, but many of the natives prefer occupying the upper stories of the Wakalahs, the rooms on the ground floor serving for stores to certain merchandise, wood, dates, cotton, &c. The Suezians live well, and their bazar is abundantly stocked with meat and clarified butter brought from Sinai, and fowls, corn, and vegetables from the Sharkiyah province; fruit is supplied by Cairo as well as by the Sharkiyah, and wheat conveyed down the Nile in flood to the capital is carried on camel-back across the Desert. At sunrise they eat the Fatur, or breakfast, which in summer consists of a 'fatirah,' a kind of muffin, or of bread and treacle. In winter it is more substantial, being generally a mixture of lentils and rice,[35] with clarified butter poured over it, and a 'kitchen' of pickled lime or stewed onions. At this season they greatly enjoy the 'fúl mudammas' (boiled horse-beans),[36] eaten with an abundance of linseed oil, into which they steep bits of bread. The beans form, with carbon-generating matter, a highly nutritive diet, which, if the stomach can digest it,—the pulse is never shelled,—gives great strength. About the middle of the day comes 'Al-Ghada,' a light dinner of wheaten bread, with dates, onions or cheese: in the hot season melons and cooling fruits are preferred, especially by those who have to face the sun. 'Al-Asha,' or supper, is served about half an hour after sunset; at this meal all but the poorest classes eat meat. Their favourite flesh, as usual in this part of the world, is mutton; beef and goat are little prized."[37]

---

35. This mixture, called in India Kichhri, has become common in Al-Hijaz as well as at Suez. "Al-Kajari" is the corruption, which denotes its foreign origin, and renders its name pronounceable to Arabs.

36. Beans, an abomination to the ancient Egyptians, who were forbidden even to sow them, may now be called the common "kitchen" of the country. The Badawin, who believe in nothing but flesh, milk, and dates, deride the bean-eaters, but they do not consider the food so disgusting as onions.

37. Here concludes Mr. Levick's letter. For the following observations, I alone am answerable.

768   Pilgrims, Travelers, and Tourists

The people of Suez are a finer and fairer race than the Cairenes. The former have more the appearance of Arabs: their dress is more picturesque, their eyes are carefully darkened with Kohl, and they wear sandals, not slippers. They are, according to all accounts, a turbulent and somewhat fanatic set, fond of quarrels, and slightly addicted to "pronunciamentos." The general programme of one of these latter diversions is said to be as follows. The boys will first be sent by their fathers about the town in a disorderly mob, and ordered to cry out "Long live the Sultan!" with its usual sequel, "Death to the Infidels!" The Infidels, Christians or others, must hear and may happen to resent this; or possibly the governor, foreseeing a disturbance, orders an ingenuous youth or two to be imprisoned, or to be caned by the police. Whereupon some person, rendered influential by wealth or religious reputation, publicly complains that the Christians are all in all, and that in these evil days Al-Islam is going to destruction. On this occasion the speaker conducts himself with such insolence, that the governor perforce consigns him to confinement, which exasperates the populace still more. Secret meetings are now convened, and in them the chiefs of corporations assume a prominent position. If the disturbance be intended by its main-spring to subside quietly, the conspirators are allowed to take their own way; they will drink copiously, become lions about midnight, and recover their hare-hearts before noon next day. But if mischief be intended, a case of bloodshed is brought about, and then nothing can arrest the torrent of popular rage.[38] The Egyptian, with all his good humour, merriment, and nonchalance, is notorious for doggedness, when, as the popular phrase is, his "blood is up." And this, indeed, is his chief merit as a soldier. He has a certain mechanical dexterity in the use of arms, and an Egyptian regiment will fire a volley as correctly as a battalion at Chobham. But when the head, and not the hands, is required, he notably fails. The reason of his superiority in the field is his peculiar stubborness, and this, together with his powers of digestion and of enduring hardship on the line of march, is the quality that makes him terrible to his old conqueror, the Turk.[39]

---

38. The government takes care to prevent bloodshed in the towns by disarming the country people, and by positively forbidding the carrying of weapons. Moreover, with a wise severity, it punishes all parties concerned in a quarrel, where blood is drawn, with a heavy fine and the bastinado *de rigueur*. Hence it is never safe, except as a European, to strike a man, and the Egyptians generally confine themselves to collaring and pushing each other against the walls. Even in the case of receiving gross abuse, you cannot notice it as you would elsewhere. You must take two witnesses,—respectable men,—and prove the offence before the Zabit, who alone can punish the offender.

39. Note to Third (1873) Edition.—I revisited Suez in September, 1869, and found it altered for the better. The population had risen from 6,000 to 20,000. The tumble-down gateway was still

SOURCE: Chapter 9 in *Personal Narrative of a Pilgrimage to Al-Madinah and Meccah* (London: Longman, Brown, Green, and Longmans, 1855–1856). This essay was written in 1855.

The Two Cities

STANLEY LANE-POOLE

[Stanley Lane-Poole was the son-in-law of Edward William Lane and a distinguished orientalist in his own right. In addition to *The Art of the Saracens in Egypt* (1888), he wrote and/or compiled historical studies of the Mughal Empire, Egypt in the Middle Ages, and of the *Arabian Nights* (which his father-in-law had translated).]

There are two Cairos, distinct in character, though but slenderly divided in site. There is a European Cairo, and there is an Egyptian Cairo. The last was once El-Káhira, "the Victorious," founded under the auspices of the planet Mars, but it is now so little conquering, indeed has become so subdued, that one hears it spoken of as "the native quarters," or even in Indian fashion as "the bazars." In truth European Cairo knows little of its mediæval sister. Thousands of tourists, mounted on thousands of donkeys, do indeed explore "the native quarters" every winter, but these do not belong to European Cairo; birds of passage they are, not inhabitants. The true resident, who has his cool shaded house and breezy balcony in the Isma'ilíya quarter, surrounded by hundreds of similar comfortable villas, does not by any chance

---

there, but of the old houses—including the "George Inn," whose front had been repaired—I recognised only four, and they looked mean by the side of the fine new buildings. In a few years ancient Suez will be no more. The bazars are not so full of filth and flies, now that pilgrims pass straight through and hardly even encamp. The sweet water Canal renders a Hammam possible; coffee is no longer hot saltish water, and presently irrigation will cover with fields and gardens the desert plain extending to the feet of Jabal Atakah. The noble works of the Canal Maritime, which should in justice be called the "Lesseps Canal," shall soon transform Clysma into a modern and civilised city. The railway station, close to the hotel, the new British hospital, the noisy Greek casino, the Frankish shops, the puffing steamers, and the ringing of morning bells, gave me a novel impression. Even the climate has been changed by filling up the Timsch Lakes. Briefly, the *hat* is now at home in Suez.

Note to Fourth (1879) Edition.—The forecast in the last paragraph has not been fulfilled. I again visited Suez in 1877–78, and found that it had been ruined by the Canal leaving it out of line. In fact, another Suez is growing up about the "New Docks," while the old town is falling to pieces. For this and other Egyptian matters, see "The Gold Mines of Midian" (by Sir Richard Burton).

ride donkeys, and is only dragged to "the bazars" rarely and with obvious reluctance by the importunity of some enthusiastic visitor. But even in European Cairo there are signs that another Cairo, an Oriental, Muslim Cairo, exists not far away. Let the English colony keep never so closely to itself and ignore "the native quarters," except as objects for just government and wise reforms, it cannot walk abroad, or even open its ears in its own chambers, without becoming conscious of the true Oriental world in which it lives but of which it is not. Go to the Post Office, a few minutes' walk from most of the hotels, and you are at once in a medley of East and West.

A German nursemaid, accompanied by the little daughter of the family, is asking for letters at the *arrivée* window, and an old sheykh in *kaftán* and turban is negotiating a money-order or a registered letter at the next bureau. Over the way a row of public letter-writers sit at their tables on the sideway, gravely imperturbable, awaiting illiterate correspondents. In the street, omnibuses and tram-cars rumble by, blowing strident horns; but the passengers who sit on the seats beneath the awning are not Europeans—they are Egyptians, efendis, clerks, shopkeepers, sheykhs, often simple fellahín come to town on business and driving in from Bulák or Kasr-en-Nil. On the footpaths—always uneven and often muddy, in curious contrast to the roads, which are kept clean by circular brushes and little girl scavengers—the European element, Greek, German, Italian, chiefly, is intimately blended with the Oriental: Sudány women closely veiled with the white *burko*, which sets off their swarthy brows and black eyes to advantage; Egyptian girls in blue gowns and black veils hanging loose and allowing the well-formed neck and line of cheek and chin to be seen, whilst concealing the only part a woman scrupulously hides in the East, her mouth; horrible blear-eyed old harridans, veiled with immaculate precision, squatting in rows against the house-fronts; Bedawis striding along in the roadway with the striped *kufiya* wound round their heads; strings of camels tied together, laden with *bersím*, the rich fodder of Egypt, and driven by the smallest of urchins; petty Government clerks, or efendis, clad in *stambúly* and *tarbúsh*, bunched up on donkey-back; all classes and ages and sexes mingled together in a jostling, perspiring, but goodtempered crowd; and everywhere the pungent pervasive odour of the East.

Even in the European quarters you still meet the veritable Eastern sights and sounds. As you look out of your hotel window you will see a native musician sauntering by, twanging the lute of the country; then a sound like the tinkling of baby cymbals informs you that the *sherbétly* is going his round, with his huge glass-jar slung at his side, from which he dispenses (to the unwary) sweet sticky drinks of liquorice juice or orange syrup in the brass saucers which he clinks unceasingly in his hand. Late at night sounds of

Eastern life invade your pillow: the "rumble of a distant drum" tells you that a wedding party is perambulating the streets, and if you have the curiosity to sally forth you will be rewarded by one of the characteristic sights of Cairo, in which old and new are oddly blended. Probably circumcision festival is combined with the wedding to save expense; and the procession will be headed by the barber's sign, a wooden frame raised aloft, followed by two or three gorgeously caparisoned camels—regular stage-properties hired out for such occasions—carrying drummers, and leading the way for a series of carriages crammed with little boys, each holding a neat white handkerchief to his mouth, to keep out the devil and the evil eye. Then comes a closed carriage covered all over with a big cashmere shawl, held down firmly at the sides by brothers and other relations of the imprisoned bride; then more carriages and a general crowd of sympathizers. More rarely the bride is borne in a cashmere-covered litter swung between two camels, fore and aft; the hind camel must tuck his head under the litter, and is probably quite as uncomfortable as the bride, who runs a fair chance of sea-sickness in her rolling palankin. In the old days the bride walked through the streets under a canopy carried by her friends, but this is now quite out of fashion, and European carriages are rapidly ousting even the camel-litters. But the cashmere shawl and the veil will not soon be abandoned. The Egyptian woman is, at least in public, generally modest. She detects a stranger's glance with magical rapidity, even when to all appearance looking the other way, and forthwith the veil is pulled closer over her mouth and nose. When she meets you face to face, she does not drop her big eyes in the absurd fashion of Western modesty; she slowly turns them away from you: it is annihilating.

As soon as you have turned your back on the European suburb and the hotel region, and escaped from the glass shop fronts and Greek dealers of the Musky, the real Eastern city begins to dominate you. It is quite easy to lose oneself in the quaint old streets of Muslim Cairo when only an occasional passer-by reminds one that Europe is at the gates. A large part of Cairo is very little spoilt: it is still in a great degree the city of the Arabian Nights.

In that stall round the corner who knows but that the immortal Barber is recounting the adventures of his luckless brothers to the impatient lover on the shaving stool? At this very moment the Three Royal Mendicants may be entertaining the fair Portress and her delightful sisters with the story of their calamities, and if you wait till night you may even see the "good" Harún er-Rashíd himself—though it is true he lived at Baghdád—coming on his stealthy midnight rambles with prudent Ga'far at his heels and black Mesrúr to clear the way. A few streets away from the European quarters it is easy to dream that we are acting a part in the moving histories of the Thousand and

One Nights, which do in fact describe Cairo and its people as they were in the Middle Ages, and as they are in a great measure still. In its very dilapidation the city assists the illusion. The typical Eastern houses falling to ruins, which no one thinks of repairing, are the natural homes of 'Efríts and mischievous Ginn, who keep away god-fearing tenants. But if in its ruined houses, far more in what remains of its glorious monuments does Cairo transport us to the golden age of Arabian art and culture. Among its mosques and colleges and the scanty remnants of its palaces are the purest examples of Saracenic architecture that can be seen in all the once wide empire of Islam. Damascus and Ispahan, Agra and Delhi, Cordova and Granada, Brusa and Constantinople, possess elements of beauty and features of style which Cairo has not, and they enlarge and complete our understanding of Arab art; but to view that art in its purity, uncorrupted by the mechanical detail of the Alhambra, unspoilt by the over-elaboration of Delhi, we must study the mosques and tombs of Cairo.

The blessed conservatism of the East has happily maintained much of the old city in its beautiful ruinous unprogressive disorder. There are of course new houses and rebuilt fronts and even glass window-sashes; the exquisite *meshrebíyas* with their intricate turned lattice work are nearly all gone to make way for Italian *persiennes*, and the stone benches in front of the shops have disappeared in deference to the modern exigencies of carriages. But the general aspect of the streets has not seriously altered in recent years, and the people who press through the crowded lanes, or sit in their little cells of shops at the receipt of custom, are unchanged. They dress as their ancestors dressed ages ago; their ideas and education are much what they always were, though the new schools are gradually infusing more modern notions; they are still as calm and easy-going and procrastinating as ever. The only conspicuous change is the dethronement of the time-honoured *shibúk*,—the long pipe of meditation and stately leisure and "asphodel and moly" and all that is implied in the ineffable dreamland of *keyf*,—in favour of the restless undignified cigarette; but *nargílas* and cocoa-nut pipes for hashish are still in full play among the lower classes. The tradespeople are the conservative element in Egypt, as everywhere else. The upper classes are becoming every year less Oriental in outward appearance and habits. They dance with "infidel" ladies, wear Frank clothes, and delight in the little French pieces played in the Ezbekíya garden. Even their national coffee cups are made in Europe, and save for the red tarbúsh, and certain mental and moral idiosyncracies difficult to eliminate and unnecessary to describe, the Egyptian gentleman might almost pass muster in a Parisian crowd. It is the tradesman who recalls the past, keeps up the old traditions, and walks in the old paths. The course of the world runs slowly in the working East, and the Cairene shopkeeper has placidly stood still whilst the Western world joined in the everlasting "move on" of modern civilization.

This is what one goes to Cairo to see, the real Eastern life in its Eastern setting. A scene like this repays one for many dreary calls, many tepid dances in the region of hotels. You may get hotel life, club life, polo and tennis, and even golf, excellently at Cairo—the European Cairo—but these things are common to all "winter resorts." In the "bazars," among the people, you get something that the Isma'ilíya quarter cannot give, that no other place can quite rival, something that painters love and that kindles the imagination. After all, the more interesting things are always the unfamiliar, and the first plunge into Egypt is a revelation of fresh ideas, new tones in colour, and the pungent odours of a strange native life.

It is in the "bazars" that one feels most the shock of contact with the unfamiliar; but, in a less intimate yet deeply impressive way, to drink in the full inspiration of the Muslim city one must climb to the ramparts of the Citadel about sunset and slowly absorb the wonderful panorama that spreads below and around. Unhappily, to get there one usually passes along the most terribly defaced street in all Cairo. The worst destruction took place, one is thankful to remember, before England took the reins of Egypt. It was Isma'íl, under French influence, who made that unspeakable atrocity, the "Boulevard Mohammad 'Aly," which cut through some of the most beautiful quarters, ruined palaces and gardens, and chopped off half of a noble mosque in order to preserve the tasteless accuracy of its straight line. Along its side are ranged mean and uneven offices and tenements, neither Europeanly regular nor Orientally picturesque. Old wine and new bottles are in close connexion. A Muslim school elbows a "Grog Shop for Army and Navy." Under the shadow of the stately mosque of Sultan Hasan an Arab barber is cutting hair with a modern clipping machine. A gaily painted harím carriage, guarded by eunuchs, stands at the door of the mosque: on the panel is a sham coat-of-arms, that last infirmity of Turkish minds—though for that matter heraldic bearings were used in Egypt at least seven hundred years ago. Solemn sheykhs pace slowly along without any sign of surprise at these strange sights. Overhead the guns boom out a salute, for it is the Great Festival, the *'Id el-kebír,* from Saladin's Citadel; but the garrison are not stalwart Turkmáns or wild Kurds, in picturesque garb and with clanking spear and mace, such as the great Soldan led against Richard of the Lion-heart, but British "tommies" unbecomingly attired in khaki. The Citadel itself is an arsenal of modern arms and stores, and English officers rule where once the Mamlúk Beys are massacred. Old and new are ever clashing in the mediæval fortress, and Private Ortheris mounts guard over the mosque of a Mamlúk Sultan.

But once we stand on the ramparts the flaring contrasts vanish and the jarring note is still. All in that wide range beneath the eye is of the East Eastern. The European touches are too small at such a distance to mar the purely Oriental tone. Countless domes and minarets, a glimpse of arched cloisters, a wilderness of flat-roofed houses, yellow and white and brown, with sloped pents to admit the cool breezes below; a patch of green here and there, with dark-leaved sycamores, revealing some of the many gardens of the old city, and beyond, a fringe of palms and a streak of silver where "the long bright river" rolls sleepily on between its brown banks; in the distance, against the ridge of the Libyan horizon, in the carmine glory of the sinking sun, stand the everlasting pyramids, "like the boundary marks of the mighty waste, the Egyptian land of shades." One after the other the tall forms of slender minarets separate themselves from the bewildering chaos of roofs and domes, and display their varied grace. Each has its story of victory or exile, of famine and invasion, of learning and piety, to tell. On the right, northwards, the fine towers of Muáyyad above the Zuweyla gate recall a hundred deeds and legends of that famous portal, once the main entrance of the caliphs' palace-city. Beyond them rise the minarets of the Nahhasín, a perfect gallery of Saracen art, and again beyond, the turrets of Hákim's great quadrangle. In front in the foreground stands Sultan Hasan, the largest and most imposing of Mamlúk mosques, and a little to the left one looks into the vast arcaded square of Ibn-Tulún, with its queer corkscrew tower overhanging the billowy mounds that reveal where Fustát lay a thousand years ago. Still more to the left a line of arches shows where the aqueduct that has brought water to the Citadel for five centuries stretches to the Nile, and behind we can look down upon the cluster of ruined domes and minarets of the southern Karáfa—the "Tombs of the Mamlúks"—and catch a glimpse of the old fortress of Egyptian Babylon and the mosque of the conqueror 'Amr. Looking over the Mamlúk minarets we can see the dim outlines of the cairns of Dahshúr and the conspicuous form of Sakkára's step-pyramid, separated from the Saracen domes by only fifteen miles of space but five millenniums of time; and as the glow of the sunset fades away the evening clouds gather in the west and the desert beyond takes up their shades of grey and blue like a vast mid-African ocean.

Here we realize Cairo for the first time as a city of the Middle Ages, and more than that, a city with an heritage from the dawn of history. It is true it has not the exquisite setting of the seven-hilled queen of the Bosporus; it is not even built about the Nile, which the silts of centuries have breasted away from the walls it once laved: but as one looks out from the battlements of the Castle one perceives that there are other oceans than those of water, and that the capital of Egypt can have no more fitting frame than the deserts which are her shield and the pyramids her title-deeds to her inheritance from the remote past. "He who hath not seen Cairo," said the Jewish hakím, "hath not seen the world. Her soil is gold; her Nile is a marvel; her women are as the bright-eyed houris of Paradise; her houses are palaces, and her air is soft with an odour above aloes, refreshing the heart: and how should Cairo be otherwise when she is the Mother of the World?"

SOURCE: Chapter 1 in *The Story of Cairo* (London: J. M. Dent, 1902).

Excerpt from *Travels in Arabia Deserta*
CHARLES M. DOUGHTY

[Charles Doughty was one of the classic travelers through "Arabia Deserta." Like Richard Burton before him, he sought to enjoy the privileges of disguise. The two-volume account of his passage has become a classic for such narratives, and the definitive third edition (1936) was introduced by T. E. Lawrence as a "bible of its kind."]

CHAPTER I. THE PERAEA; AMMON AND MOAB

The Haj, or Mecca pilgrimage, in Damascus. The pilgrim camp in the wilderness at Muzeyrib. The setting forth. Hermon. The first station. The pilgrimage way, or Derb el-Haj. Geraza. The Ageyl. Bashan. Umm Jemâl. Bosra. Jabbok, or the Zerka. Shebib ibn Tubbai. Ancient strong towers in the desert. Punishment of a caravan thief. Aspect of the Peraean plains. The Beduins. Beny Sókhr. Beny Seleyta. Wêlad Aly. Gilead. The Belka. Whether this fresh country were good for colonists? Rabbath Ammon. Heshbon. Umm Rosàs. The pilgrim-encampment raised by night. The brook Arnon. Lejûn. The high plains of Moab. Ruined sites. Dat Ras. Rabbath Moab. Kir Moab. "Heaps in the furrows of the field." The old giants. Agaba tribe. The land wasted by Israel. The ancient people were stone-builders. Kerak visited. Beny Hameydy tribe. Memorial heaped stones in the wilderness. Wady el-Hásy. The deep limestone valleys descending to the Dead Sea. Sheykh Hajellán.

A new voice hailed me of an old friend when, first returned from the Peninsula, I paced again in that long street of Damascus which is called Straight; and suddenly taking me wondering by the hand. "Tell me (said he), since thou art here again in the peace and assurance of Ullah, and whilst we walk, as in the former years, toward the new blossoming orchards, full of the sweet spring as the garden of God, what moved thee, or how couldst thou take such journeys into the fanatic Arabia?"

It was at the latest hour, when in the same day, and after troubled days of endeavours, I had supposed it impossible. At first I had asked of the *Wàly*, Governor of Syria, his license to accompany the *Haj* caravan to the distance of *Medáin Sâlih*. The Wàly then privately questioned the British Consulate, an office which is of much regard in these countries. The Consul answered, that his was no charge in any such matter; he had as much regard of me, would I take such dangerous ways, as of his old hat. This was a man that, in time past, had proffered to show me a good turn in my travels, who now told me it was his duty to take no cognisance of my Arabian journey, lest he might hear any word of blame, if I miscarried. Thus by the Turkish officers it was understood that my life, forsaken by mine own Consulate, would not be required of them in this adventure. There is a merry saying of Sir Henry Wotton, for which he nearly lost his credit with his sovereign, "An ambassador is a man who is sent to lie abroad for his country"; to this might be added, "A Consul is a man who is sent to play the Turk abroad, to his own countrymen."

That untimely Turkishness was the source to me of nearly all the mischiefs of these travels in Arabia. And what wonder, none fearing a reckoning, that I should many times come nigh to be foully murdered! whereas the informal benevolent word, in the beginning, of a Frankish Consulate might have procured me regard of the great Haj officers, and their letters of commendation, in departing from them, to the Emirs of Arabia. Thus rejected by the British Consulate, I dreaded to be turned back altogether if I should visit now certain great personages of Damascus, as the noble Algerian prince *Abd el-Kâder;* for whose only word's sake, which I am well assured he would have given, I had been welcome in all the Haj-road towers occupied by Moorish garrisons, and my life had not been well-nigh lost amongst them later at Medáin Sâlih.

I went only to the Kudish Pasha of the Haj, Mohammed Saîd, who two years before had known me a traveller in the Lands beyond Jordan, and took me for a well-affected man that did nothing covertly. It was a time of cholera and the Christians had fled from the city, when I visited him formerly in Damascus to prefer the same request, that I might go down with the Pilgrimage to Medáin Sâlih. He had recommended me then to bring a firman of the Sultan, saying, "The *hajjàj* (pilgrims) were a mixed multitude, and if aught befell me, the harm might be laid at his door, since I was the subject of a foreign government": but now, he said, "Well! would I needs go thither? it might be with the *Jurdy*": that is the flying provision-train which since ancient times is sent down from Syria to relieve the returning pilgrimage at Medáin Sâlih; but commonly lying there only three days, the time would not have sufficed me.

I thought the stars were so disposed that I should not go to Arabia; but, said my Moslem friends, "the Pasha himself could not forbid any taking this journey with the caravan; and though I were a *Nasrâny*, what hindered! when I went not down to the *Harameyn* (two sacred cities), but to Medáin Sâlih; how! I an honest person might not go, when there went down every year with the Haj all the desperate cutters of the town; nay the most dangerous ribalds of Damascus were already at Muzeyrîb, to kill and to spoil upon the skirts of the caravan journeying in the wilderness." Also they said "it was but a few years since Christian masons (there are no Moslems of the craft in Damascus) had been sent with the Haj to repair the water-tower or kella and cistern at the same Medáin Sâlih."

There is every year a new stirring of this goodly Oriental city in the days before the Haj; so many strangers are passing in the bazaars, of outlandish speech and clothing from far provinces. The more part are of Asia Minor, many of them bearing over-great white turbans that might weigh more than their heads; the most are poor folk of a solemn countenance, which wander in the streets seeking the bakers' stalls, and I saw that many of the Damascenes could answer them in their own language. The town is moved in the departure of the great Pilgrimage of the Religion and again at the home-coming, which is made a public spectacle; almost every Moslem household has some one of their kindred in the caravan. In the markets there is much taking up in haste of wares for the road. The tent-makers are most busy in their street, overlooking and renewing the old canvas of hundreds of tents, of tilts and the curtains for litters; the curriers in their bazaar are selling apace the water-skins and leathern buckets and saddle-bottles, *matara* or *zemzemîeh;* the carpenters' craft are labouring in all haste for the Haj, the most of them mending litter-frames. In the *Peraean* outlying quarter, *el-Medân*, is cheapening and delivery of grain, a provision by the way for the Haj cattle. Already there come by the streets, passing daily forth, the *akkâms* with the swagging litters mounted high upon the tall pilgrim-camels. They are the Haj caravan drivers, and upon the silent great shuffle-footed beasts, they hold insolently their path through the narrow bazaars; commonly ferocious young men, whose mouths are full of horrible cursings: and whoso is not of this stomach, him they think unmeet for the road. The *Mukowwems* or Haj camel-masters have called in their cattle (all are strong males) from the wilderness to the camel-yards in Damascus, where their serving-men are busy stuffing pillows under the pack-saddle frames, and lapping, first over all the camels' chines, thick blanket-felts of Aleppo, that they should not be galled; the gear is not lifted till their return after four months, if they may return alive, from so great a voyage. The mukowwems are sturdy, weathered men of the road, that can hold the mastery over their often mutinous crews; it is written in their hard faces that they are overcomers of the evil by the evil, and able to deal in the long desert way with the perfidy of the elvish Beduins. It is the custom in these caravan countries that all who are to set forth, meet together in some common place without the city. The assembling of the pilgrim multitude is always by the lake of Muzeyrîb in the high steppes beyond Jordan, two journeys from Damascus. Here the hajjies who have taken the field are encamped, and lie a week or ten days in the desert before their long voyage. The Haj Pasha, his affairs despatched with the government in Damascus, arrives the third day before their departure, to discharge all first payments to the Beduw and to agree with the water-carriers, (which are Beduins,) for the military service.

The open ways of Damascus upon that side, lately encumbered with the daily passage of hundreds of litters, and all that, to our eyes, strange and motley train, of the oriental pilgrimage, were again void and silent; the Haj had departed from among us. A little money is caught at as great gain in these lands long vexed by a criminal government: the hope of silver immediately brought me five or six poorer persons, saying all with great By-Gods they would set their seals to a paper to carry me safely to Medáin Sâlih, whether I would ride upon pack-horses, upon mules, asses, dromedaries, barely upon camel-back, or in a litter. I agreed with a Persian, mukowwem to those of his nation which come every year about from the East by Bagdad, Aleppo, Damascus, to "see the cities"; and there they join themselves with the great Ottoman Haj caravan. This poor rich man was well content, for a few pounds in his hand which helped him to reckon with his corn-chandler, to convey me to Medáin Sâlih. It was a last moment, the Pasha was departed two days since, and this man must make after with great journeys. I was presently clothed as a Syrian of simple fortune, and ready with store of caravan biscuit to ride along with him; mingled with the Persians in the Haj journey I should be the less noted whether by Persians or Arabs. This mukowwem's servants and his gear were already eight days at Muzeyrîb camp.

It was afternoon when a few Arab friends bade me God-speed, and mounted with my camel bags upon a mule I came riding through Damascus with the Persian, Mohammed Aga, and a small company. As we turned from the long city street, that which in Paul's days was called "The Straight," to go up through the Medân to the *Boábat-Ullah,* some of the bystanders at the corner, setting upon me their eyes, said to each other, "Who is this? Eigh!" Another answered him half jestingly, "It is some one belonging to the *Ajamy*" (Persian). From the Boábat (great gate of) Ullah, so named of the passing forth of the holy pilgrimage thereat, the high desert lies before us those hundreds of leagues to the Harameyn; at first a waste plain of gravel and loam upon limestone, for ten or twelve days, and always rising, to *Maan* in "the mountain of Edom" near to Petra. Twenty-six marches from Muzeyrîb is el-Medina, the prophet's city (*Medinat en-Néby,* in old time *Yathrib*); at forty marches is Mecca. There were none now in all the road, by which the last hajjies had passed five days before us. The sun setting, we came to the little outlying village *Kesmîh:* by the road was showed me a white cupola, the sleeping station of the commander of the pilgrimage, *Emir el-Haj,* in the evening of his solemn setting forth from Damascus. We came by a beaten way over the wilderness, paved of old at the crossing of winter stream-beds for the safe passage of the Haj camels, which have no foothold in sliding ground; by some other are seen ruinous bridges—as all is now ruinous in the Ottoman Empire. There is a block drift strewed over this wilderness; the like is found, much to our amazement, under all climates of the world.

SOURCE: Charles M. Doughty, *Travels in Arabia Deserta* (Cambridge: Cambridge University Press, 1888; 3d ed., London: J. Cape, 1936).

Itineraries from *Programme of Arrangements for Visiting Egypt, the Nile, Sudan, Palestine, and Syria*

DAILY ITINERARY OF THE TWENTY DAYS' VOYAGE—
CAIRO TO ASWAN AND BACK $340.75

[Thomas Cook was a significant innovator of the "conducted tour" in the nineteenth century. The first excursion that he offered was between Leicester and Longborough on a special train bound for a temperance meeting. Cook also ran outings to the Great Exhibition in 1851. He began his overseas service in the 1860s.]

Passengers are respectfully requested to read carefully the following Itineraries, from which they will gather information as to the approximate time of arrival at and departure from each of the stopping stations, and the arrange-

"Egyptian Native Types." In *The Story of the Cape to Cairo Railway and River Route*, vol. 2 (London: Pioneer Publishing House, n.d.).

ments for sightseeing. In order to avoid confusion and unnecessary trouble on the river banks, passengers must not leave the steamer until the dragoman or manager has announced that the donkeys are ready, intimation of which will be given by sounding the gong or ringing the bell.

First Day (Wednesday).—The steamer sails punctually at 10 a.m. from the landing stage of Thos. Cook & Son, Ltd., above the Kasr-el-Nil Bridge. The first impression of the Nile is a delightful one, for Cairo, viewed from a river steamer, is a very different place from the bustling town just left. Stately palaces on either bank, countless minarets of mosques, the noble Mokkattam hills and the Citadel at their foot form a fitting introduction to the beauties of the Nile, whilst the three great pyramids of Giza rise in stately dignity over the western plain.

The Tura quarries, whence the stone for the Pyramids was hewn, and Helwan, famous for its sulphur baths, are passed, the steamer arriving at Bedrechén soon after lunch. Here donkeys will be in readiness for the ride to the site of ancient Memphis.

It is difficult to imagine that one of the most famous capitals of antiquity once stood where now is but a picturesque grove of palm trees. Yet all that remains in view is a beautiful alabaster Sphinx and two colossal statues of Rameses II. An hour's ride further on, however, lies the vast Necropolis, in itself sufficient proof of the extent of the ancient city, which tells more of the life of its inhabitants than any ruin could do. The Step Pyramid of Sakkara, the tomb of King Zoser, is more ancient than the Pyramids of Giza. Early in 1925 a statue of Zoser was discovered bearing an inscription which confirms the view that this was his place of burial. Excavations now being made have revealed the proto-doric columns of Zoser's time shown in the illustration overleaf. The Serapeum is the Tomb of the Sacred Bulls, and the Tombs of Ti and Ptah-Hetep, wealthy citizens of ancient Memphis, offer in their mural decorations realistic representations of life in Egypt over 5,000 years ago.

Ample time is allowed for visiting, and after an hour's ride the steamer is reached about 5 p.m. The steamer will proceed south to the neighbourhood of Ayat (56 miles from Cairo).

Second Day (Thursday).—Leaving Ayat at daylight, the steamer passes Beni Suef, the first town of importance to be seen, and the "Gebel el-Teyr" or Bird Mountain, a precipitous cliff rising sheer out of the water. Tradition relates that all the birds of Egypt assemble here once a year, and, when departing, leave one solitary bird on guard until the following year. Upon the summit stands a Coptic convent. The boat will anchor for the night near Minia (157 miles from Cairo).

Third Day (Friday).—The steamer arrives at Beni Hassan in the morning, and an excursion is made to the grotto of Speos Artemedos and to the rock tombs, a ride of about forty minutes. Architecturally these tombs are of great interest, as are the scenes painted on the walls, representing carpenters, boat builders, bakers and others at work, and a company of merchants from the East bringing wares for sale in Egypt. The tombs of Ameni Amenamah and Khnum-Hotep will be visited.

Half an hour's ride brings the passengers to the steamer, which will proceed as far as Manfalut for the night (224 miles from Cairo).

Fourth Day (Saturday).—Asyut is reached during the morning, after passing through the Barrage lock. This Barrage is designed to hold up the river level during the spring and summer months and ensure delivery of water into the Ibrahimia Canal during low Nile. The Canal, commencing at Asyut, is nearly 200 miles long and supplies middle Egypt and the Falyum with water.

Donkeys will be in readiness for half an hour's ride through the town to the foot of the mountain to visit the tomb of Hapzefai, Prince of the Nome in the reign of Usertesen I., and the tomb of Kheti. It is well worth climbing to the top of the mountain, whence one of the finest views of the Nile valley is obtained.

The principal of the American college at Asyut extends a cordial invitation to passengers to visit the boys' college (a few minutes' walk or ride from the steamer) and the girls' school in the town (250 miles from Cairo).

Fifth Day (Sunday).—The steamer leaves Asyut at daybreak. Early risers should not miss the delightful views over the Nile valley after sunrise. For a couple of hours the delicate tints on the lofty sandstone cliffs, the broad fields of clover or corn at their feet, the clusters of mud hut and palm tree that form the native villages, and the broad bosom of the river itself, form an irresistible appeal to the lover of colour, whilst the first low rays of the sun strike the white sails of the picturesque "gyassas" or the whitewashed wall of some villa nestling on the river bank.

This will be a restful day as the steamer proceeds southward. The entire life of Egypt is found on or near the banks of the river, whilst picturesque sailing boats, laden with the produce of the land, are met at every bend. The steamer will anchor for the night near Girga (343 miles from Cairo).

Sixth Day (Monday).—Leaving early in the morning, Baliana, the starting point for visiting Abydos, is passed. The visit to this beautiful temple is postponed until the return journey, as the ruins are so grand and magnificent that they lose none of their charm and novelty even after Karnak has been seen. The steamer, therefore, continues the voyage, passing through the beautiful gorge of Abu Shusha, and the new Nag-Hamadi Barrage now in course of construction.

One item of interest illustrating the customs of Egyptian life occurs shortly after passing the Nag-Hamadi bridge. A small boat shoots out from the bank and slips alongside, and into this is dropped a bag of alms from the ship's crew. The occupants of the boat are the descendants of Sheikh Selim, who, it is said, sat stark naked on the bank at this spot for 53 years. He was believed to possess great powers in assisting navigation and every craft passing upstream gave alms for his support. He died in 1891, but his family still collects toll from every boat! His tomb will be seen on the bank.

The steamer will probably reach Dendera that evening (417 miles from Cairo).

Seventh Day (Tuesday).—It is but half an hour's ride from the steamer to the temple of Dendera. This wonderfully preserved temple is probably but little older than the beginning of the Christian era. It is dedicated to Hathor, the Egyptian Venus, and is closely associated with the beautiful Cleopatra. The famous portraits of Cleopatra and her son Cæsarion are on the end wall of the exterior. The famous Zodiac of Dendera, now in the Bibliothèque Nationale in Paris, was taken from the shrine of Osiris on the temple roof. A duplicate will be seen in the original position.

On returning from the temple, the voyage is continued; towards sunset the massive pylons of Karnak come into view, followed soon after by the colonnades of the Temple of Luxor, close to which the steamer is moored.

It is small wonder that the ancient Egyptians chose this site for their capital of Thebes. On both sides of the river the precipitous limestone cliffs retreat into the distance, leaving a broad and fertile plain, which no doubt then, as now, offered a pleasing prospect of prosperity. They could hardly have selected a more picturesque spot, and to this day the charm of Luxor is only rivalled by that pearl of Egypt, Aswan.

The steamer remains at Luxor for three days (460 miles from Cairo).

Eighth Day (Wednesday).—The morning is devoted to a visit to the great temples at Karnak, notably the Temple of Chonsu and the great Temple of Amen, justly considered one of the wonders of the world. The great Hypostyle Hall, although only a fragment of this colossal temple, covers an area equal to that of Notre Dame at Paris. It consists of 134 columns ranged in a space of 6,000 square yards, and for pure impressiveness is only equalled by the great Temple of Abu Simbel. The effect is particularly fine by moonlight.

The great Temple of Luxor is visited after tea.

Ninth Day (Thursday).—After an early breakfast the river is crossed in small boats to the western bank, where donkeys will be waiting for a ride of half an hour to the Temple of Kurna, and thence in about forty minutes to the Tombs of the Kings. The principal tombs are readily accessible, and are lighted by electricity. The walls are covered with exquisite paintings depicting the deceased king, accompanied by the sun-god, sailing through the underworld at night, finally rising with the sun to a new life in the next world. The tombs of Rameses IX., Rameses VI., and Seti I., in which the reliefs surpass all others in beauty of execution and even rival those of Abydos, are visited.

Passengers will then go over the Libyan Chain, commanding a glorious view over the Nile valley, descending near the "Chalet Hatasu," a rest house erected by Thos. Cook & Son, expressly for the use of travellers under their arrangements. Here lunch will be served. The terrace temple of Queen Hatasu is then visited, and on the way back to the river the Rameseum and the famous Colossi of Memnon are passed, the steamer being reached about 4.30 p.m.

Tenth Day (Friday).—After crossing the river again, it is half an hour's donkey ride to the Rameseum—the great Temple of Rameses the great—after visiting which another short ride brings us to the small temple of Deir-el-Medina (the judgment hall of Osiris), and to the temple of Medinet-Haboo, which was the palace and great temple of Rameses III., containing also a small temple of Thotmes III.

The tombs of Queen Nefertari, the beautiful wife of Rameses II., and Prince Amon-her-Khopshaf, the young son of Rameses III., will also be visited.

Lunch is taken on the return to the steamer.

Eleventh Day (Saturday).—The steamer leaves Luxor early in the morning and passes the Barrage of Isna by means of a lock. This Barrage was constructed in 1906-9 to regulate the irrigation of the province of Qena. Isna is reached about 10 a.m. and a visit is paid to the temple, which is only a short walk from the river side. This temple is of the Ptolemaic period, but so far only the vestibule has been excavated, the remainder being completely buried under the town.

The steamer leaves again about 11 a.m., proceeding as far as Edfu, where the Temple of Horus stands in almost perfect preservation. This temple is, in fact, practically complete, and, by comparison, enables one to visualize the wonderful monuments at Karnak and Thebes. An ascent to the summit of the pylon is recommended, the view being exceptionally attractive, not only over the temple itself but also over the whole countryside.

Ample time is allowed for inspection, after which the steamer may proceed further south.

Twelfth Day (Sunday).—The voyage is resumed early in the morning, passing through the gorge of Silsila, with its vast quarries, bearing the cartouches of Egyptian kings back for several thousand years. At Komombo a stay is made for about an hour to visit the temple, which stands in a commanding position on the bank of the river. This temple is duplex, and in that respect unique. One shrine is dedicated to Sebek, the evil deity, and the other to Amen, the representative of God as personified in the Sun. Many of the paintings are as brilliant now as when first produced. One item of interest which should not be missed amongst the mural decorations, is a representation of surgical instruments in use at the time. It is a surprising revelation that many of them can be recognized as identical with the instruments used at the present day. (See illustration on page opposite.)

As the steamer approaches Aswan the scenery undergoes a complete change. Vegetation ceases in places and the desert often extends down to the river banks. The sandstone cliffs have disappeared and huge granite rocks abound, even in the middle of the stream. As a rule the steamer arrives at Aswan after lunch.

There is no doubt that Aswan is the most delightful spot in Egypt. Situated at the foot of the First Cataract, where the Nile is dotted with innumerable islands and rocks, surrounded on all sides by the desert, equipped with excellent hotels and a centre for novel and interesting excursions, this picturesque little town offers all that can be desired by the traveller in search of health-giving pleasure.

Special mention must be made of the Cataract Hotel, which, like Aswan itself, has a charm and individuality differing from everything else in Egypt.

Aswan is 595 miles from Cairo by river.

Thirteenth Day (Monday).—After an early breakfast, donkeys will be taken for a twenty minutes' ride to the granite quarries, where lies an unfinished obelisk of colossal dimensions, still undetached from the living rock. Another forty minutes' ride and the Temple of of Philæ comes into view. Small boats are taken to visit this beautiful temple, but it should be pointed out that November and December are the best months for the visit, as afterwards the level of the water above the dam is raised and the temple thereby partly submerged.

The boats then sail down stream to the great Aswan dam, constructed in 1898–1902, the largest of its kind and one of the most impressive sights in Egypt. The dam will be crossed by trolley, and lunch is usually served in the picturesque chalet, overlooking the dam, with the reservoir above and the cataract below.

The dam is again crossed by trolley, and the donkeys are remounted for the ride back to the steamer by a different route.

Passengers for Abu Simbel and the Second Cataract sail from the Dam to the "Thebes" near Philæ.

Fourteenth Day (Tuesday).—Small boats will be taken to visit the Island of Elephantine, including the famous Nilometer and the museum. The town of Aswan and its bazaars will also prove of great interest, and the view from the terrace of the Cataract Hotel should not be missed.

All passengers who take any interest in Egyptian antiquities should visit the painted tombs of Mechu, Ben and Se-Renpu, situated on the western side of Aswan, which were opened out at the expense of Lord (then Sir Francis) Grenfell. They could be visited in the evening, but we strongly advise that they should be seen before breakfast in the morning, when the sun shines straight into the tombs, and shows out the colouring most distinctly.

Fifteenth Day (Wednesday).—The steamer leaves Aswan early in the morning and steams straight through to Luxor, which is usually reached the same evening.

Sixteenth Day (Thursday).—The morning is spent at Luxor in order to give those who wish an opportunity of revisiting any of the monuments.

The steamer leaves Luxor at 11 a.m. and will proceed as far as Nag-Hamadi.

Seventeenth Day (Friday).—Baliana is reached after breakfast, and donkeys are taken for a one and a half hours' ride to the magnificent ruins at Abydos. The wonderful temple of Seti I. is the apotheosis of ancient Egyptian art. It differs from all other temples in having seven sanctuaries instead of one, whilst the workmanship of the inscriptions and reliefs is incomparable. Here is the famous "Tablet of Abydos"—a list of seventy-six kings of Egypt, beginning with Mena, the first king of Egypt, the most wonderful genealogical record in the world.

Luncheon is taken in the temple itself, after which a visit is paid to the temple of Rameses II.

The steamer may proceed further north that evening.

Eighteenth Day (Saturday).—Asyut is usually reached about noon and after a short stay the steamer will pass through the lock and proceed north.

Nineteenth Day (Sunday).—The voyage is continued northwards, passing Minia, "Gebel-el-Teyr" and Beni Suef.

Twentieth Day (Monday).—Passing Wasta in the early morning, the Pyramid of Meidun, or the "false pyramid," comes into view, and Cairo is normally reached in the afternoon.

Passengers may remain on board the steamer until after breakfast on Tuesday morning, if they wish to do so.

Notes on the Return Voyage from Aswan

On the downward voyage the steamers stop for sightseeing at Luxor, Baliana (for Abydos), and Asyut. As the half-day stoppage at Luxor is simply to enable those who wish to see a second time any particular object they are interested in, no fixed programme will be announced, and passengers are requested to inform the dragoman or the Manager the night before what they specially wish to see, so that arrangements may be made for donkeys and guides.

Any passengers wishing to visit the western suburb of Thebes on the downward voyage must leave early in the morning to ensure being back in time for the steamer, which leaves at 11.0 a.m.

Should the steamer, through any unforeseen circumstances, not arrive at Luxor until the morning after leaving Aswan, it must nevertheless leave again at 11.0 a.m., to ensure the necessary time at Abydos.

REGULATIONS APPLYING TO COOK'S NILE STEAMER PASSAGES

Art. 1. Tickets.—Passages can be reserved at any of Cook's Offices on a deposit of half-fare per passenger.

The Tickets are personal and cannot be transferred without the consent of Thos. Cook & Son, Ltd., or their Manager in Cairo.

The Company reserve the right to substitute another steamer for any sailing.

In the event of any passenger not being able to leave Cairo by the steamer for which he or she may have been booked, and provided that notice is given at least a week before the departure of the steamer, the ticket will be available for the following steamer, providing there is room.

Passengers wishing to cancel their passage must give notice to that effect at least one month prior to the date of sailing from Cairo.

In the event of passengers failing to notify Thos. Cook & Son, Ltd., in accordance with the foregoing, half the passage money will be forfeited.

Art. 2. Baggage.—Personal baggage in any reasonable quantity may be conveyed on the steamers.

Baggage not required on the voyage should be stored with Thos. Cook & Son, Ltd., in Cairo, until the passenger's return.

Art. 3. Valuables.—Passengers having any valuable articles or coin are requested to deposit the same with the Manager of the steamer, who will give a receipt. Such articles should not, under any circumstances, be left about the cabins; the Company will not be responsible in case of loss.

"Time-Table of Steamer between Aswan and Halfa (Seven Days' Voyage)."

STEAMER	No. of voyage	Leave ASWAN (Shellal) Monday, 3.30 p.m.	Arrive ABU SIMBEL Wednesday, 6 p.m.	Leave ABU SIMBEL Thursday, 11 a.m.	Arrive HALFA Thursday, 5 p.m.	Leave HALFA Saturday, 8-30 a.m.	Visit ABU SIMBEL Saturday.	Visit KALABSHA Sunday.	Arrive ASWAN (Shellal) Sunday evening.
"THEBES"	2	1929 Dec. 9	1929 Dec. 11	1929 Dec. 12	1929 Dec. 12	1929 Dec. 14	1929 Dec. 14	1929 Dec. 15	1929 Dec. 15
"THEBES"	3	Dec. 16	Dec. 18	Dec. 19	Dec. 19	Dec. 21	Dec. 21	Dec. 22	Dec. 22
"THEBES"	4	Dec. 23	Dec. 25	Dec. 26	Dec. 26	Dec. 28	Dec. 28	Dec. 29	Dec. 29
"THEBES"	5	Dec. 30	1930 Jan. 1	1930 Jan. 2	1930 Jan. 2	1930 Jan. 4	1930 Jan. 4	1930 Jan. 5	1930 Jan. 5
"THEBES"	6	1930 Jan. 6	Jan. 8	Jan. 9	Jan. 9	Jan. 11	Jan. 11	Jan. 12	Jan. 12
"THEBES"	7	Jan. 13	Jan. 15	Jan. 16	Jan. 16	Jan. 18	Jan. 18	Jan. 19	Jan. 19
"THEBES"	8	Jan. 20	Jan. 22	Jan. 23	Jan. 23	Jan. 25	Jan. 25	Jan. 26	Jan. 26
"THEBES"	9	Jan. 27	Jan. 29	Jan. 30	Jan. 30	Feb. 1	Feb. 1	Feb. 2	Feb. 2
"THEBES"	10	Feb. 3	Feb. 5	Feb. 6	Feb. 6	Feb. 8	Feb. 8	Feb. 9	Feb. 9
"THEBES"	11	Feb. 10	Feb. 12	Feb. 13	Feb. 13	Feb. 15	Feb. 15	Feb. 16	Feb. 16
"THEBES"	12	Feb. 17	Feb. 19	Feb. 20	Feb. 20	Feb. 22	Feb. 22	Feb. 23	Feb. 23
"THEBES"	13	Feb. 24	Feb. 26	Feb. 27	Feb. 27	Mar. 1	Mar. 1	Mar. 2	Mar. 2
"THEBES"	14	Mar. 3	Mar. 5	Mar. 6	Mar. 6	Mar. 8	Mar. 8	Mar. 9	Mar. 9
"THEBES"	15	Mar. 10	Mar. 12	Mar. 13	Mar. 13	Mar. 15	Mar. 15	Mar. 16	Mar. 16

Art. 4. Dogs and other animals are not permitted on the Steamers.

Art. 5. Departures from Stopping Places.—Before leaving any station or stopping place, notice either by bell or whistle will be given three times before departure.

Art. 6. Breaks of Journey.—Any passenger leaving the steamer at an intermediate station will not be entitled to an allowance for the unused portions of the passage ticket.

Art. 7. Breaks of Journey at Aswan or Luxor.—Passengers desiring to break their journey at Aswan, or on the downward voyage at Luxor, can do so and resume their journey by a succeeding steamer providing they arrange through the Manager in Cairo, and also providing there are berths vacant on the steamer selected.

Art. 8. Medical Assistance.—A qualified doctor accompanies each steamer performing the 20 and 14 days' services, and is supplied with drugs and appliances considered necessary for the Nile Voyage. He is entitled to receive fees for his services not exceeding one guinea for a single consultation, or ten guineas for any individual patient for the whole of the twenty days' voyage, and six guineas for the fourteen days' voyage. Qualified doctors are stationed at Luxor and Aswan during the season.

Art. 9. Hours of Meals.—The meals consist of breakfast from 8.30 a.m., to 9.30 a.m., lunch à la carte from 12.30 p.m., to 1.30 p.m., afternoon tea at 4.30 p.m., and table d'hôte dinner at 7.30 p.m., but the Manager of the steamer will be at liberty to make any alteration when sightseeing and other circumstances require it, notice being given to the passengers.

Art. 10. Lights.—All lights will be extinguished in the saloons and on deck at 11.30 p.m.

Art. 11. Combustibles.—It is strictly forbidden to take guns, revolvers, cartridges, gunpowder, or fireworks on board without the special authority of the Manager of Thos. Cook & Son, Ltd., in Cairo. Should any accident arise through firearms or combustibles, the whole responsibility will rest with the owners of these.

Art. 12. Sightseeing.—The details of each excursion for sightseeing, with the hours of departure and arrival, will be announced to the passengers either verbally or by notice exhibited on the "Notice" board.

Arrangements in connection with Shore Excursions are made by Thos. Cook and Son, Ltd., in their capacity as Agents only, and they accept no responsibility for any injury, damage, loss, accident, delay or irregularity from whatsoever cause arising, sustained by the passenger and his, or her, personal belongings.

Art. 13. Interruptions or Delays.—In case of any delay or accident to the

Steamers through circumstances over which the Company have no control, it must be distinctly understood that the loss of time and extra expense (if any) will have to be borne by the passenger. Every exertion will be made to keep to time, but the Company will not be responsible for delays, and no claim will be admitted for any such loss of time or extra expense.

Art. 14. Control.—The full control and working of the steamer is entrusted entirely to the Manager of each steamer, and passengers having any suggestions or complaints of inattention on the part of the stewards or others are invited in the first instance to make them to the Manager of the steamer, and afterwards to address them in writing to Thos. Cook & Son, Ltd., Cairo.

Art. 15. Disputes.—Should any question arise in relation to the foregoing conditions the matter in dispute shall be settled in accordance with English law.

N.B.—All passengers are booked subject to the foregoing conditions and to any other conditions for the control of the steamer services which Thos. Cook and Son, Ltd., may find necessary to put into operation from time to time.

HINTS ON OUTFIT

Passengers' Mail, etc.

Our advice to travellers is: "Come out to Egypt and the Nile just as you would travel anywhere else in Spring or Autumn." Among the articles of *real* use are helmets, good wideawakes, "Terai," or other shady hats; these can be obtained in Cairo. For ladies, some suitable dress, such as the divided skirt, is also desirable for donkey riding. No one need be afraid of great heat during the Nile voyage on board a steamer; on the contrary, a warm rug, shawl, or a good overcoat should be taken, as the mornings and evenings are cool, and even during the day, when steaming against the wind, it is sometimes cold. Strong walking shoes are essential for sightseeing, and a seat stick is invaluable.

In Palestine, for gentlemen nothing can be superior to a warm Scotch tweed; for ladies a warm woollen dress; for both ladies and gentlemen good waterproofs are most essential as extras. Dress suits are not usually required in Palestine or Syria. Strong boots or shoes are the best, and goloshes may sometimes be used to advantage. A strong umbrella is frequently useful as a protection against sun or rain, and a puggaree round the helmet or hat is useful.

Letters and Telegrams.

The Cairo Postal Administrations have established an office on our premises for dealing with all mail matter addressed through Thos. Cook & Son, Ltd. Letters, etc., should be addressed: (Name), care of Thos. Cook, Ltd., Cairo. They will be re-forwarded by special mail-bag to the steamers up river. Telegrams to passengers should be addressed: (Name), care of Cook, Cairo. They can be retransmitted up river.

Letters for Europe and America may be posted at any station where the steamer stops, and they will be dispatched by first mail to destination.

Telegrams can be dispatched to any part of the world from all important places on the river.

Passports.

The traveller must hold a valid passport bearing visa(s) of a Consular representative in the United Kingdom for the country or countries to or through which he is proceeding. He must be careful to see that the endorsement and visas fully cover the period and route, as neglect of this may involve him in serious difficulties. Passports are obtainable through any of our Offices.

Money.

The Travellers' Cheques issued by us in denominations of £5, £10, £20, in sterling or dollars, will be found a convenient form in which to carry funds in the Orient and elsewhere. Besides being cashed at our Offices in Lower Egypt and in Palestine, payment of them can be obtained at Luxor, Aswan and Khartoum at current rate of exchange. They are also issued at the Cairo, Alexandria and Jerusalem Offices. We undertake the remittance of money by cheque and telegram between our principal Offices.

Guide Books.

Cook's Handbook for Egypt and the Sudan, by Sir E. A. Wallis Budge, M.A., Keeper of the Egyptian and Assyrian Antiquities in the British Museum. A new and revised edition (1925). Price 20/-

Cook's Handbook for Palestine and Syria, by Roy Elston, new edition (1929), revised by H. C. Luke, B.Litt., M.A., Late Assistant-Governor of Jerusalem, with an appendix on the historical interest of the Sites and Monuments of

Palestine by Professor J. Garstang, M.A., B.Litt., D.Sc. (Oxon.), Director of the British School of Archæology in Jerusalem, Director of the Department of Antiquities in Palestine. Price 10/6.

Cook's Handbook for Jerusalem and Judea (1924), Price 4/-.

Laundry.

Passengers on the Nile steamers may utilize the facilities afforded by the hotels at Luxor and Aswan for laundry purposes. The same facilities are afforded by the hotels in Palestine.

Hotels.

Hotel accommodation may be secured before leaving for Egypt through any of our Offices, at any class of hotel, from single bedrooms to suites of apartments on any floor, with whatever aspect may be desired. *En pension* terms are also arranged for an extended stay.

Baggage Insurance.

All travellers are strongly advised to make use of Cook's system of baggage insurance, particulars of which can be obtained at any Office.

Special Notice.

Thos. Cook & Son and/or Thos. Cook & Son, Ltd., give notice that the arrangements shown in this Programme, excepting such as apply strictly to their Steamers and Dahabeahs, are made by them in their capacity as Agents only. All tickets and coupons are issued by them, and all arrangements for transport or conveyance or for hotel accommodation, are made by them as Agents upon the express condition that they shall not be liable for any injury, damage, loss, accident, delay or irregularity which may be occasioned either by reason of any defect in any vehicle, or through the acts or default of any company or person engaged in conveying the passenger or in carrying out the arrangements of the tour(s), or otherwise in connection therewith, or of any hotel proprietor or servant. Such conveying, etc., is subject to the laws of the Country where the conveyance, etc., is provided.

Baggage is at "owner's risk" throughout the tour(s) unless insured. Small articles, coats, wraps, umbrellas and other hand baggage are entirely under the care of the passenger, who is cautioned against the risk attached to these being left in conveyances when sightseeing.

Thos. Cook & Son and/or Thos. Cook & Son, Ltd., accept no responsibility for losses or additional expense due to delays or changes in train, steamer or other services, sickness, weather, strikes, war, quarantine, or other causes. All such losses or expenses will have to be borne by the passenger.

HOW TO SEE MODERN PALESTINE

Visiting Jerusalem, Talpioth, Bethlehem, Hebron, Jericho, Dead Sea, River Jordan, Bethany, Tel Aviv, Petah-Tikva, Nablus, Tiberias, Dagania, Haifa, etc. (Occupying 8 days) Accompanied by a Private Dragoman

who is at the disposal of the traveller the whole of the time. The traveller is met at Jerusalem railway station and conveyed to the hotel. The itinerary has been carefully planned to include visits to places of historical interest, as well as to many of the modern settlements and other undertakings promoted by the Zionist movement.

Daily Itinerary

Note.—The order of sightseeing may be varied in any way more convenient, and the tour may be shortened or extended as required. The following itinerary has been drawn up on the assumption that the seventh day will be the Jewish Sabbath. If the Sabbath should fall on any other day in the tour, that other day will be observed as a day of rest, and the itinerary will be modified accordingly.

Day of Arrival in Jerusalem.—Morning: Visit the Wailing Wall, Zionist Information Bureau, Mosque of Omar, where once King Solomon's Temple stood, Golden Gate, Citadel of David, Jewish Quarter and Nissanback Synagogue, Hurvah and Ben Zakhay Synagogues.

Afternoon: Motor through Talpioth to Rachel's Tomb, Bethlehem, Solomon's Pools to Hebron and return to Jerusalem.

Second Day.—Morning: Visit the Museum of Antiquities, Tombs of the Kings, Excavations of the Third Wall, War Cemetery, Mount Scopus, Hebrew University and Jewish National Library, Mount of Olives with the Russian Tower on its summit, Head Office of Keren Hayesod.

Afternoon: Motor to the Dead Sea, River Jordan and Jericho, visiting

Elisha's Fountain and old Jericho, returning via Bethany, the Garden of Gethsemane and King Solomon's Quarries.

Third Day.—Morning: Visit the Zionist Agricultural Museum, Bezalel School of Arts and Crafts, Rechaviah, Head Office of the Jewish National Fund (to see Golden Book), Zionist Executive Headquarters, Hadassah Hospital and Jewish Blind Institution.

Afternoon: Free, affording an opportunity of visiting the various Zionist Institutions.

Fourth Day.—Morning: Motor to Tel Aviv, the modern Jewish town adjacent to ancient Jaffa, visiting *en route* Romema Aged Home, Diskin Orphanage, Motza Arsa, Dilb or Kiryath, Anavim, Ramleh, Bet-Dagon, Mikveh-Israel Agricultural School and Rishon-le-Zion, where a visit will be paid to the famous wine-cellars.

Afternoon: Sightseeing in Tel-Aviv and Jaffa, visiting the Hebrew Gymnasium, Zionist Agricultural Experimental Station, Tachkemoni School, Rutenberg Power Station, and some of the factories such as Lodzia Textile, Lieber Chocolate, Goralski and Krinitzi Furniture, and Silicate Factories.

Fifth Day.—Motor to Petah-Tikva and Nablus (Shechem). Visit the Home of the Samaritans, and in the afternoon continue *via* Jenin, Afuleh, Balfouria and Nazareth to Tiberias.

Sixth Day.—At Tiberias, on the Sea of Galilee. Motor to Migdal, Capernaum, Rosh Pina and Safed in the morning, and in the afternoon to the Tomb of Rambam (Maimonides), Tomb of Rabbi Akiva, Tomb of Rabbi Baahnes, Hot Springs, Kinnereth, and Dagania.

Seventh Day.—Day of rest (Sabbath). *See Note at head of Itinerary.*

Eighth Day.—Motor via Nazareth, Nahalal and the base of Mount Carmel to Haifa. In the afternoon visit Hadar Hacarmel, Acco, Technical College, Beth Sefer Reali, Mount Carmel, Bath Galim, the Flour Mills, "Shemen" Soap and Oil Factory.

Ninth Day.—Terminate with breakfast at Haifa.

Fares

1 person	2 persons.	3 persons.	4 persons.	5 persons.	6 persons.
$253.00	$316.50	$418.50	$506.25	$627.75	$705.75

Which include transfers between station and hotel; motor-cars during eight days; hotel accommodation including bedroom, lights and service, breakfast, table d'hote luncheon and table d'hote dinner (Kosher food if required), commencing with breakfast day of arrival and terminating with breakfast on the ninth day; Services of a Private Dragoman (Jewish if required); fees for sightseeing, drivers' fees and gratuities to hotel servants. The fares do not include rooms with private bath, afternoon tea, or fires in bedrooms. Baggage on the motor-cars is limited to suit cases.

SOURCE: Itineraries from *Programme of Arrangements for Visiting Egypt, the Nile, Sudan, Palestine and Syria* (New York: Thomas Cook and Son, 1929–30).

INDEX

Abbas Pasha, 681, 696
Act of Concession (Suez Canal), 619, 662
Adye, John, Sir, 718
Afghan Wars, xxii, 21, 173, 397, 528
Africa, xxi
Aida, 557–66, 570–71
Albert, Prince of Wales, 576
Alexander the Great, 57, 70, 222, 350, 593
Alexandria, 586–92, 747, 758; bombardment of, 604–7, 655, 658, 681; Forster on bombardment, 711–14; Gladstone on, 690; "Rioters at Alexandria" (ill.), 709. *See also* Egypt
Ali, Ameer, 286, 316–22
Ali, Haidar, 171, 173, 412
American Civil War, 21, 173
Amherst of Arracan, William Pitt Amherst, Earl, 357
Anglicism, 203, 227, 239
Anglo-Boer War, xxi, 638, 672
Anglo-Burmese War, 173, 397
Anglo-French Alliance (Suez Canal), 597–602
Anglo-Indians, 519–29
Anglo-Mysore Wars, 171
Anstruther, John, Sir, 355
Arabi (Ahmed), xxii, 655–61, 681–83, 696, 700–708; "Arabi's Appeal to Gladstone," 707–8, 714–36; Forster on, 712–14; Lady Gregory on, 736–44
Arabian Nights, 749, 769, 771
Arabi Trial, 714–36
Arabi Uprising, 7, 667–69, 683, 712–14, 747
Aryans, 204, 242, 520
Asiatic Society of Bengal, 203, 223, 261

Baboo (babu), 209–10, 382
Ball, Charles, 461–78
Baring, Sir Evelyn (Lord Cromer), 682–83; "The Mutiny of the Egyptian Army," 696–707
Baring Brothers, 603
Baroudi, Mohammed, Pasha, 698–700
Barwell, Richard, 33, 132, 355
Battle of Gwalior, 398, 400, 413
Battle of Plassey (1757), 1–2, 63–65, 74, 131, 391, 411
Battle of Tel al-Kebie, 681
Bell, Gertrude, 748
Bentinck, William Cavendish, 6, 71, 303, 334, 337–38, 369–74, 405, 417; "Minute on Indian Education," 227–38; "Minute on Sati," 350–61; "Sati Regulation XVII," 361–63
Beresford, Charles William De la Poer Beresford, Baron, 713
Berlin Conference (1885), xxi
Birdwood, George, xxvi
Black Hole of Calcutta, 64
Blunt, Anne, Lady, 714, 741–42
Blunt, Wilfred Scawen, 683, 736; "The Arabi Trial," 714–36
Bowring, John, Sir, 696
Brahma, 262
British East India Company, xxi, 1–85, 96, 101, 106, 107, 111, 118–19, 127, 277, 391–551; Court of Directors 33, 48–53, 135–36, 138; Marx on ("British Incomes in India"), 441–44
Broadley, A. M., 683
British South Africa Company, xxii
Burke, Edmund, 133; *Impeachment of Warren Hastings*, 143–62

Burmese Wars, 21
Burnell, A. C., 209–19
Burney, Fanny, 155–59
Burton, Richard, Sir, 748, 775; on Suez, 752–69
Busch, Hans, 555

Cameron, D. A., 611, 661–69
Campbell, Archibald, Sir, 412
Campbell, Colin, Sir, 397, 423, 480–84
Canning, Charles John ("Clemency"), Viscount, 392, 398, 444, 481, 482–83, 484–85, 486, 511, 537, 668
Canning, Charles John, Earl, 392
Canning, Charlotte, Countess Canning, 480, 481, 484
Catwall, 259–60
Cawnpore, 311–12, 327, 502–3, 505, 549–51
Cawnpore Massacre, 391, 481, 502
Cecil, Herbert Edward, Lord, 671–78
Charles II, 44
Charles XII, 70
Charter companies, xxii
"Charter of Concession" (Suez Canal), 612, 625–30
Chérif (Sherif) Pasha, 696, 724
China, 219–22; 496, Chinese War (1841), 210
Chomsky, Noam, 8
Chupattis, 451–57, 538–39
Clavering, John, Lieutenant-General, 33, 132
Cleopatra, 607, 783
Clive, Robert, xxiii, 7, 13, 21–24, 59–71, 127, 131, 185–86, 213, 251, 391, 411, 511, 530
Cobden, Richard, 597–98
Colebrooke, H. T., 241–42, 337; *Digest of Hindu Law*, 364–69
Collins, Wilkie, 172; *The Moonstone*, 195–200
Colvin, Auckland, Sir, 696–707, 716, 728, 732
Compagnie des Indes Orientales, 1
Compagnie Universelle du Canal Maritime de Suez, xxii, 7, 208, 612, 622, 629–30, 635–38, 642–55, 655–59, 671–78
"Confessions of a Thug," 308, 314–22, 421
Congo, xxi
Constitution of the East India Company, 2, 39–47
Cook, Thomas, and Sons, 748, 779–95
Cookson, Charles, Sir, 702, 704–5
Cornwallis, Charles Cornwallis, Marquis, 163, 171, 173, 176–79, 180
Crimean War, xxii, 210, 481, 532, 547, 576, 606, 612, 662
Cromer, Evelyn Baring, Earl of, 682–83;
"The Mutiny of the Egyptian Army," 696–707
Crusades, 232
Crystal Palace, xxiii, 576

Dalhousie, Fox Maule Ramsay, 11th earl of (Lord Panmure), 478–80
Dalhousie, James Andrew Broun Ramsay, 1st marquess of, 392, 397, 414, 415, 440, 445, 448–49, 531–32, 534, 547–48
De Kusel, Samuel Selig, Baron, 566–71
De Lesseps, Ferdinand, 7, 555–56, 568, 575–76, 578, 580–603, 605, 611–13, 616–17, 619–22, 769
Despotism, 15, 56, 58, 89–128, 150, 249, 252, 256–57, 260, 267, 588
Devi, 325–33
Dicey, Edward, 638–55, 687–90
Dickens, Charles, xxii, 338; "Death by Fire of Miss Havisham" (*Great Expectations*), 375–77
Disraeli, Benjamin (Lord Beaconsfield), xxiii, 391, 407, 436–40, 612–13, 652, 668, 670, 677, 687; *Sibyl*, 208–9
Doughty, Charles, 748, 775–79
Doveton, Major, 184, 190, 194
Drake, Francis, Sir, 13
Dravidians, 204
Dufferin and Ava, Frederick Temple Blackwood, Marquis of, 733–36
Duff Gordon, Lucie, Lady, 747, 749–52
Dufour, Arles, 598–99
Du Locle, Camille, 557–62
Dupleix, 71, 666
Dutch, 96, 100, 102–3, 119, 356
Dutch East India Company, 101, 119

East India Company Act (1773), 14, 31–39, 132; Marx on, 441–44
Edgeworth, Maria, 172
Egypt, xxi, 6, 228, 264; Arabi Uprising, 681–744; Cairo, 749–52, 758, 769–75; Suez Canal, 555–678; Tipu Sultan on, 182–90. *See also* Alexandria
Eliot, George, 748
Elizabeth I, 74, 89, 145
Ellenborough, Edward Law, Earl of, 444, 485
Empress of India (Queen Victoria), 7, 208
England's Great Mission to India, 509–29
English nationalism, 148–49, 546–47
Eugénie, Empress, 567–68
Eurasians, 519–29
Ewer, Walter, 355

Fehmi, Ali Bey (Colonel), 696–97
Fellahs, 612, 619–22, 681, 696, 762
Forster, E. M., 747; "The Bombardment of Alexandria," 711–14
Fort St. George, 2, 13, 139, 193
Fort William (Bengal), 31–39, 50, 68, 74, 131
France, and Egypt, 180–90
Francis, Philip, 33, 132
Free Trade Area of the Americas (FTAA), 8
Futtehgurh Mission, 489–509

General Agreement on Tariffs and Trade (GATT), 8
George II, 30, 33
George III, 30, 49, 132
Gilbert, Henry, 529–39
Gladstone, William Ewart, xxiii, 681–82, 668, 682, 715, 747; "Aggression on Egypt and Freedom in the East," 687–95, 707–8; and Arabi Uprising 714–31
Gordon, C. G. ("Gordon of Khartoum"; "Chinese Gordon"), xxii, 683, 715–17
Government of India Act (1833), 14, 49–53
Grand Trunk Road, 397, 501, 503, 548
Granville, Granville George Leveson-Gower, 2d Earl of, 436, 660, 718, 722–36
Greased cartridges, 449–51
Great Chain of Being, 204
Great Exhibition (1851), 779
Great Game, xxi
Gregory, Lady, "Arabi and His Household," 736–44
Gunga Din, 286
Gunpowder Plot, 272
Gwalior, 485

Haidar Ali (Hyder Ally; Hyder Naik), 75–76, 171, 173, 175, 412
Haj(j), 758, 775–79
Hamilton, 715–16, 718–19, 721–25
Hamlet, 317
Hardinge, Henry Hardinge, Viscount, 405
Hastings, Francis Rawdon-Hastings, Marquess of, 357–58
Hastings, Warren, 1–2, 7, 14–15, 33, 77–80, 90, 135–36, 163–67, 208, 216, 511, 701; *Memoirs Relative to the State of India*, 137–42
Havelock, Henry (General), 397–98, 399, 402, 448, 450–51, 454, 542–45, 548–51
Hegel, G. W. F.: on India, 219–22, 338; on Sati, 374–75
Help!, 286
Henty, G. A., xxii, 1; *The Tiger of Mysore*, 173–74; *With Clive in India*, 21–24

Hobhouse, Emily, xxii
Hobson-Jobson Dictionary, 209–19, 340–50
Hyder Saib, 179

Ibrahim Pasha, 681
Indian Law Commission, 280
Indian Penal Code, 268–81
Indian Railway, 125–27, 503
Indian Uprising (Sepoy Mutiny), xxi, 5–8, 210, 389–551, 606–7, 611–12; Marx on, 433–49; Queen Victoria on, 478–85
Infanticide, 375, 398, 496
"Inquiry into the Opinions of the Commercial Classes of Great Britain on the Suez Ship Canal," 580–603
An Inquiry into the Rights of the East India Company of Making War and Peace, 27–31
Ireland, 118
Ismail Pasha, 555, 567–71, 575, 612, 617–18, 646, 661, 663–69, 677, 681, 696, 700, 739

Jackson, Coverly, 392
"Jingoists," xxii, 613
"John Company" (British East India Company), 486, 510, 529
Johnson, Albert Osborne, 491–509
Johnson, Amanda Joanna, 491–509
Johnson, Samuel, 155
Jones, William ("Oriental"), 5, 203, 218, 223–27, 241–42, 249, 261–68, 341

Kalee (Kali), 291–92, 294, 317, 333, 507
Khartoum, xxi, 791
Khedive Tawfiq, 681, 699–701, 712–13, 719–36
Kidd, William (Captain), 2, 13
King of Oude, 392, 428–33, 446–49, 534
Kingsley, Mary, xxiii, 393
Kipling, Rudyard, "Grave of the Hundred Head," 539–42
Koran, 178, 323, 325, 471, 490, 491, 516, 707, 738, 740, 757

Lane, E. W., 752, 769
Lane-Poole, Stanley, 769–75
Lang, John, 399
Lawrence, D. H., 338
Lawrence, Henry, 398, 409–13, 481–82, 531–32, 534–35, 542, 701
Lawrence, John Laird Mair, 398, 532
Lawrence, T. E. ("Lawrence of Arabia"), 748, 775
Laws of Menu (Manu), 241, 249, 261–68, 366, 367–68
Lawson, Wilfred, Sir, 715, 723–24

Leopold, king of Belgium, xxii
Letters from Egypt, 747
Lindsay, John, Sir, 29
"Little Englanders," xxii
Loot, 210–13
Louis XVIII, 69
Lucas, Samuel, 2; *Dacoitee in Excelsis*, 72–80
Lucknow, 74–75, 164, 399, 409, 435, 449, 542–46
Lugard, Frederick, xxiii

Maastricht Treaty, 8
Macaulay, Thomas Babington, 5, 54–58, 59–71, 73–74, 133, 166–67, 203, 227–28, 239, 249–50, 268, 280; and Indian Law Commission, 268–81; Minute on Indian Education, 227–38
MacGee, Bob, 686–87
Machiavelli, Niccoló, 67, 663
Madras Council, 107, 127, 251
Mahabharata, 365
Maharaja Nandakumar (Raja Nand Kumar), 132
Mahmoud Pasha Baroudi, 698, 700
Mahratta (Maharattah) Wars, 77, 138
Marathas (Mahrattas), 58, 81, 83, 123, 150, 176, 533
Malcolm, John, Sir, 60, 67–69
Malet, Edward, Sir, 699–700, 705–6, 722, 724–36
Mariette, Auguste, 555–62, 564–66
Marx, Karl, 3, 14, 89, 117; *Capital*, 89, 433–49; on irrigation, 125; on Public Works, 119–20; on railway system, 125–26; on village system, 121–22, 126
Maspero Jingle, 379
Mecca and Medina (Al-Madinah), 188, 681, 708, 747–48, 752–69, 775–79
Meer Jaffier, 62–63, 65–66, 68
Mehemet (Mohammed) Ali Pasha, 587, 589, 594, 611–12, 647, 661–69, 677, 681, 764, 712–19, 739
Mercantilism, 3, 13, 89, 95, 147
Mill, James, 2, 47–48, 90; *Constitution of the East India Company*, 39–47
Mill, John Stuart, 3, 39, 48, 90; "Considerations on Representative Government" 113–17; on Jews, 115–16; *Principles of Political Economy*, 111–13; on slavery, 113–15
Milner, Alfred Milner, Viscount, 683
"Minute on Indian Education," 227–38
"Minute on Sati," 350–61
Missionaries, xxii; in India, 489–529
Moberly Bell, Charles Frederic, 604–7, 718

Mogul Empire, 58, 118, 124, 144, 392, 433
Mohammed Said Pasha, 575, 586–89, 593, 596, 599, 612, 619–20, 625, 646, 662–65, 681, 696, 776
Moluccas, 101, 103
Monopoly, 95–106, 149, 430–31, 759; French, on Suez Canal trade, 643–55
Monson, George, 33
Montesquieu, Charles de Secondat, Baron de, 3, 437; on oriental despotism, 92–95; *Persian Letters*, 92–95; *The Spirit of Laws*, 92
Moors, 107, 251–60
Mughals, 4
Müller, Max, 204, 205, 239–45

Nabobs, 7, 107–10, 132, 208, 213–17, 253, 257
Nana Saheb (Sahib; Dhoondu Punt), 392, 398, 399, 401–2, 423–24, 488–89, 507, 535, 537–38, 549–51
Napier, Charles, Sir, 485
Napier, Mark, 683, 726, 728–30
Napoleon Bonaparte, 16, 70, 81, 171, 402, 444, 563, 575, 593, 611, 662, 668, 747
Nasser, Abdel, 682
Nationality, 438
Nefertari, Queen, 784
Nelson, Horatio (Admiral), 69, 669
Nightingale, Florence, xxii
Nisbet, Hume, 419–28
Nizamat Adalat, 352, 355, 359–60, 363
North American Free Trade Agreement (NAFTA), 8
Nudjum-ul-Dowlah, Nabob, 25–27

Omichund, 61–63, 66–68
Opium, 2, 102, 132, 165
Opium Wars, 13
"Ordinances of Menu," 261–68
Oriental despotism, 59, 89–128, 133, 249
Orientalism, 203–45
Orme, Robert, 3, 90, 107, 249, 251; *Historical Fragments of the Mogul Empire*, 251–61; *Of the Government and People of India*, 107–10
Osman Pasha Rifki, 697–98
Ottoman Empire, 187–89, 594, 598, 611, 657, 682, 734
Oude, 72–80, 392, 435, 439; annexation of, 444–49, 533, 547–51; King of Oude's Manifesto, 428–33; Proclamation to the People of, 404–9
Oxford University, 223–24, 243–44

Palestine, 790, 792, 793–95
Palmerston, Henry John Temple, Viscount,

437, 446–47, 478–82, 527, 576, 605, 611–12, 640–41, 648, 661–68
Panama Canal, 576, 596–97
Parlby, Fanny Parks, 285; *Wanderings of a Pilgrim*, 307–14
Peel, Robert, Sir, 81, 399, 668
Peninsula Wars, 81, 435
Philology, 204
Pitt, Thomas ("Diamond"), 1, 13
Plassey, Battle of (1757), 1–2, 64, 74, 131, 391
Political economy, xxii
Portuguese, 96, 100–101, 118
Proclamation to the People of Oude, 404–9
Pundits, 217–19
Purdah, 375

Raffles, Stamford, Sir, 119
Ramaseeana, Vocabulary of the Thug Language, 285, 287–96
Ramayana, 73
Rameses II, 781
Rameses IX, 784
Rameses VI, 784
Rani of Jhansi (Lakshmi Bai), 5, 392, 399–400, 403, 413–19, 419–28
Renan, Ernest, 203, 611, 662; "On Suttee," 380–81
Rhodes, Cecil, xxi, xxiii
Riaz Pasha, 696–707, 724
Rilsey, Herbert, 204
Roman Empire, 58, 71, 106, 113, 276, 437, 593, 691
Rothschilds, 7, 208, 562, 603, 612
Roy, Ram Mohan, Raja, 337, 354; Petitions and Addresses on the Practice of Suttee, 369–74
Royal Geographic Society, 748
Royle, Charles, 655–61

Said, Edward, 203
Salvation Army, xxi
Sati (suttee), 57, 337–38, 340–87, 398; Petitions and Addresses on the Practice of Suttee (1818–31), 364–69; Sati Regulation XVII, 316–63
Sen, Sudipta, 4–5
Seringapatam, 173, 196–97
Seymour, Horace, 725
Shelley, Mary, 203; *Frankenstein*, 206–7
Shujah-ul-Dowla (Seraj-ood-Dowlah, Surajah Dowlah, Shoojah-Ood-Dowlah), Nabob, 25–27, 59–80, 131, 139, 140
Sikh Wars, 397–98
Singh, Kunwar, 401
Slavery, 113–18, 122, 744
Sleeman, William ("Thuggee"), 6, 285, 287–96, 297–307, 314–15, 322–34, 338, 414, 417–18, 449; *The Thugs or Phansigars of India*, 287–307
Smith, Adam, 3, 8, 89; on monopolies, 95–106
Smith, Spencer, 187–90
South Africa, xxii
Stanley, Henry M., xxiii
Steel, Flora Annie, xxii; "The Reformers Wife," 318–87
Stokes, John, Sir, 665
Sudan, xxii
Suez, 753–69
Suez Canal, xxi–xxii, 6, 555–607, 747; Gladstone on, 687–95; Suez Canal War (1956), 682
Suez Canal Company, xxii, 208, 612, 622, 629–30, 635–38, 642–55, 655–59, 671–78
Synge, M. B., 547–51

Tatya Tope (Tantia Topí), 399, 400, 403, 413, 423, 426
Taylor, Meadows, 285, 314–22, 421
Tennyson, Alfred, Lord, xxvi; "Defense of Lucknow," 543–46; "English War-Song," 546–47
Thousand and One Nights, 752, 771–72
Thuggee (Thagi), 6, 285–86, 287–334
The Thugs or Phansigars of India, 287–307
Tipu Sultan (Tippoo Sultan), xxii, 5, 75 n. 4, 81, 90, 171–200; and the French, 180–90
Treaty of Seringapatam (1792), 171, 181, 191–95
Tuker, Francis, Sir, 289; *The Yellow Scarf*, 322–34
Tula Ram, Rao, 400–401

Vedas, 262–65
Vellore Mutiny, 393, 409
Verdi, Giuseppe, 555–65, 570
Verne, Jules, xxii, 338; "Fogg Rescues a Sati" (*Around the World in Eighty Days*), 377–79
Victoria, Queen of England, xxi, 7, 74, 208, 287, 478–85, 537, 538, 547, 576; correspondence on Indian Uprising, 478–85
Vishnu, 196

Waterloo, 81, 173
Walsh, Rev. J. Johnston, 489–509
Ward, Andrew, 391
Wellesley, Arthur, Duke of Wellington, 64, 81, 172, 411, 484; "Memorandum on Mar-

quess Wellesley's Government of India," 81–85
Wellesley, Richard Colley, 1st Marquess Wellesley, 2d Earl of Mornington, 81–82, 85, 174, 180–83, 185–87
White Paper on the Nationalisation of the Suez Maritime Canal Company, 622–38
William IV, 446
Wilson, Charles, Sir, 728
Wilson, Horace, 353, 355–56
Wolseley, Garnet Wolseley, Viscount, 606, 667, 681, 714
World Trade Organization, 8

Yule, Henry (Colonel), 209–19

Zamindars (Zemindars), 4, 57, 110, 124, 258–59, 362, 409, 430

BARBARA HARLOW is the Louann and Larry Temple Centennial Professor of English at the University of Texas, Austin.
MIA CARTER is an associate professor of English at the University of Texas, Austin. They are coeditors of *Imperialism and Orientalism: A Documentary Sourcebook*.

Library of Congress Cataloging-in-Publication Data
Archives of Empire: volume I. from the East India company to the Suez canal / edited by Barbara Harlow and Mia Carter.
Includes bibliographical references and index.
ISBN 0-8223-3176-4 (cloth : alk. paper : v. 1)
ISBN 0-8223-3164-0 (pbk. : alk. paper : v. 1)
1. Great Britain—Colonies—History—Sources. I. Harlow, Barbara, 1948– II. Carter, Mia.
DA16.A73 2003   909′.0971241—dc21   2003010580

www.ingramcontent.com/pod-product-compliance
Lightning Source LLC
Chambersburg PA
CBHW050522300426

44113CB00012B/1918